"As I read Dr. Kendall on the Beatitudes from the Sermon on the Mount, I felt at times as if I were actually there—on that hill, sitting with the others—as the young teacher was speaking the most radical words our world has ever known."

ROB PARSONS, FOUNDER AND CHAIRMAN, CARE FOR THE FAMILY; AUTHOR, *BRINGING HOME THE PRODIGALS*

"R. T. Kendall's head, heart and hands are found woven through these pages, giving this volume credibility. The reader sees his amazing intellect and insight and feels his passionate heart. Those of us who have known and loved him through the years know also that these expositions from the Sermon on the Mount have actually been beaten out of the anvil of R. T.'s personal experience. These volumes will continue to bless generations to come long after those of us today are in the presence of Him who first preached this sermon."

O. S. HAWKINS, SENIOR PASTOR, FIRST BAPTIST CHURCH, DALLAS, TEXAS

"Once again R. T. Kendall has hit a home run with his monumental and magisterial work on the Sermon on the Mount. No stone is left unturned and no passages left without full comments and elucidation. Any pastor, student, teacher or Christian who studies the Sermon on the Mount would greatly benefit by utilizing this significant work."

DR. PHIL ROBERTS, PRESIDENT, MIDWESTERN BAPTIST THEOLOGICAL SEMINARY, KANSAS CITY, MISSOURI

"I had the privilege of being present while these sermons were preached. They appear as fresh and relevant today as they did then—full of theological insight, practical applications and God's heart for His children."

PAUL GARDINER, SOLICITOR, LONDON, ENGLAND; DEACON, WESTMINSTER CHAPEL

"Brilliant! Life as it is meant to be lived."

COLIN DYE, SENIOR PASTOR, KENSINGTON TEMPLE, LONDON, ENGLAND

THE SERMON ON THE MOUNT

R. T. KENDALL

Chosen

a division of Baker Publishing Group
Minneapolis, Minnesota

Published by Chosen Books
a division of Baker Publishing Group
11400 Hampshire Avenue South, Bloomington, MN 55438
www.chosenbooks.com

Printed in the United States of America

Library of Congress Cataloging-in-Publication Data is available for this title.

ISBN 978-0-8007-9472-9

Unless otherwise identified, Scripture quotations are from HOLY BIBLE, NEW INTERNATIONAL VERSION.® Copyright © 1973, 1978, 1984 Biblica. Used by permission of Zondervan. All rights reserved.

Scripture quotations identified ESV are from The Holy Bible, English Standard Version,® copyright © 2001 by Crossway, a publishing ministry of Good News Publishers. Used by permission. All rights reserved.

Scripture quotations identified GNT are from the Good News Translation in Today's English Version—Second Edition. Copyright © 1992 by American Bible Society. Used by permission.

Scripture quotations marked HCSB are taken from the Holman Christian Standard Bible®, Copyright © 1999, 2000, 2002, 2003 by Holman Bible Publishers. Used by permission. Holman Christian Standard Bible®, Holman CSB®, and HCSB® are federally registered trademarks of Holman Bible Publishers.

Scripture quotations identified NEB are from The New English Bible, © The Delegates of the Oxford University Press and The Syndics of the Cambridge University Press 1961, 1970. Reprinted by permission.

Scripture quotations identified NJB are from The New Jerusalem Bible. Text copyright © 1985 by Darton, Longman & Todd Ltd. and Doubleday, a division of Bantam Doubleday Dell Publishing Group, Inc. Used by permission.

Scripture quotations identified NLT are from the Holy Bible, New Living Translation, copyright © 1996, 2004. Used by permission of Tyndale House Publishers, Inc., Wheaton, Illinois 60189. All rights reserved.

Scripture quotations identified PHILLIPS are from The New Testament in Modern English, revised edition—J. B. Phillips, translator. © J. B. Phillips 1958, 1960, 1972. Used by permission of Macmillan Publishing Co., Inc.

Scripture quotations identified RSV are from the Revised Standard Version of the Bible. Copyright 1952 [2nd edition, 1971] by the Division of Christian Education of the National Council of Churches of Christ in the United States of America. Used by permission. All rights reserved.

Scripture quotations identified TLB are from The Living Bible © 1971 owned by assignment by Illinois Regional Bank N.A. (trustee). Used by permission of Tyndale House Publishers, Inc., Wheaton, IL 60189. All rights reserved.

Scripture quotations identified TNIV are from the HOLY BIBLE, TODAY'S NEW INTERNATIONAL VERSION.® TNIV.® Copyright © 2001, 2005 by Biblica. Used by permission of Biblica.® All rights reserved worldwide.

Scripture quotations identified KJV are from the King James Version of the Bible.

Cover design by Dan Pitts

Photography by Terry Pitts

13 14 15 16 17   7 6 5 4 3 2

In Memory of Dr. D. Martyn Lloyd-Jones

(1899–1981)

Contents

Foreword

In 2010, the world watched for a day and a half as 33 Chilean miners were brought to the surface of the earth having spent 69 days nearly one-half mile underground. The progress was accompanied by mini-biographies of each one and video of loved ones waiting topside to be reunited with these brave men. The buried men lived the first 17 days of their entombment ignorant of the fact that those charged with finding survivors did not know whether they were alive or dead under the 700 million tons of rock that had shifted.

Finally, the last man was lifted from the depths of the earth, and they had all been rescued! Each had been delivered from certain death and given a new chance at life.

The Bible uses the metaphor of rescue to depict how God has delivered His children from death to life. In Colossians 1:13–14, the apostle Paul writes, "He has rescued us from the domain of darkness and transferred us into the Kingdom of the Son He loves, in whom we have redemption, the forgiveness of sins" (HCSB). Two kingdoms are positioned against each other, with our eternal well-being hanging in the balance. We are born into the domain of darkness—separated from God. We are dead in the heart of the earth, as it were. But then God involved Himself and "rescued" us from death and "transferred" us to a new Kingdom. The word used for transferred is from *methistemi,* which originally meant deportation of a group of men or the removal of a group to form a colony. Paul indicates that we have been transferred into the Kingdom of God's Son, our Savior, Jesus Christ.

But too many followers of Christ seem to have lost the dynamic that we have been transferred into the living Kingdom ruled by the King of kings. This is in spite of Jesus' own ministry, which began with an emphasis on the Kingdom. "After John was arrested, Jesus went to Galilee,

preaching the good news of God: 'The time is fulfilled, and the kingdom of God has come near. Repent and believe in the good news!'" (Mark 1:14–15, HCSB). Jesus' public teaching was filled with references to God's Kingdom, a Kingdom that, according to His own words, had "come near." He said His ability to cast out demons was proof the Kingdom of God had "come to" His listeners (Matthew 12:28). He made the Kingdom the theme of His preaching both before His death (Luke 4:43) and after His resurrection (Acts 1:3), the focus of numerous parables (Mark 4:26, 30; Luke 8:10; 13:18–21), and commended it as the priority of our own lives (Matthew 6:33; Luke 12:31). Without doubt, the Kingdom was an important subject to the King.

He reminded His hearers that entrance into the Kingdom came about as people humbled themselves like little children, and that those who would not receive the Kingdom children had no other means of entry (Luke 18:17). He went on to say that entering into the Kingdom of God came through the new birth (John 3:3). The King also warned that rich people would find it very difficult to enter the Kingdom (Matthew 19:24), while the detested tax collectors and prostitutes would enter it sooner (Matthew 21:31).

Not only in the gospels, but in the Acts and the epistles, the Kingdom is given priority. The Kingdom of God is displayed in righteousness, peace, joy and power, but not in eating, drinking and talking (Romans 14:17; 1 Corinthians 4:20). The early Church preached and testified about the Kingdom (Acts 8:12; 20:25; 28:23). It is a subject that predates the Church and informs our understanding of the Church.

The New Testament proclamation of God's Kingdom was not the first Israel had heard of it. The coming Kingdom was the expected promise of the Old Testament. Immediately prior to Jesus' ascension, curious as to all that would take place next, the disciples asked whether He was about to "restore the Kingdom" to Israel. Thousands of years before, Moses sang of the reign of God, intoning, "The LORD will reign forever and ever!" The imperfect form of the Hebrew verb can carry the meaning that God, having once demonstrated His kingship, now reigns and will continue to reign forever. The Kingdom was the subject of the ancient prophets as well (Isaiah 9:7; Daniel 4:3).

We do well to remember that the Kingdom is both a reality for the here and now and a promise to be inherited (Luke 17:21; Galatians 5:21). It is a life to be lived and a future to be anticipated. It is the blessing of today and the hope of tomorrow. The Kingdom is not "dying and going to heaven." Instead it is "Your will be done on Earth as it is in heaven."

For many believers, the reality of the here and now too often gives way to the desire of the promise to be inherited. This is not to say that the coming Kingdom is unimportant; it is the end of the mission of God. But believers cannot forget the personal and corporate implications of Christ's current reign. We are the visible examples of the coming reign of Christ. Our obedience to the Scriptures, our life in community, the fruit of the Spirit and our love for the Savior all bear witness to the kingship of Jesus before billions who do not know Him. It is our responsibility to help others come to know King Jesus in His atoning death and resurrected glory.

Thankfully, R. T. Kendall has given believers a monumental blessing in the form of this book that explores the entirety of Jesus' Sermon on the Mount. Kendall's perspective that this is Jesus' seminal teaching on the work of the Holy Spirit is a fresh take on how this most famous message integrates the reality of God's Kingdom with the ministry of God's Spirit under the New Covenant.

As you read this book, evaluate the reality of God's Kingdom in your own life. Are the ethics of the Kingdom your ethics? Are the values of the Kingdom your values? Is the Kingdom of God the thing you are seeking first? If so, this is a great place to be encouraged; if not, this is a great place to start.

ED STETZER, PRESIDENT, LIFEWAY RESEARCH,
SOUTHERN BAPTIST CONVENTION; AUTHOR,
COMPELLED BY LOVE; WWW.EDSTETZER.COM

Special Recommendation

I did not know, when I became the pastor of the First Baptist Church of Hendersonville, Tennessee, in the summer of 2009, that I would at the same time become the pastor to R. T. and Louise Kendall. I had followed Dr. Kendall's ministry from afar for years. I had read some of his books. I had heard about his ministry at the great Westminster Chapel in London, England. I had no idea, until I began talking with the search committee, that he was a member of First Baptist.

One of the great honors of my life occurred a few months ago when R. T. asked if I might consider writing a special recommendation for his newest book on the Sermon on the Mount. I said I would be delighted to do so.

Dr. Kendall e-mailed me an unedited version of the book you now hold in your hands. I was mesmerized as I read again the words of Jesus in this incredible sermon. While it would be foolish to say that any human being brought new life to the words of our Lord, I believe it would be accurate to say that in this book R. T. Kendall has helped me understand the depth of the words that our Lord spoke. As you read this book you will be humbled at Jesus' words. You will be challenged. You will be energized.

Rather than focus on the commentary that Dr. Kendall has written, however, let me take a moment and focus on the man. R. T. and Louise Kendall are two of the finest people you will ever meet. Rarely do we know people with whom we agree on every subject; and I am certain there are areas in which R. T. and I would disagree. There is such a spirit and a kindness about him, however, that it draws you to want to know him better. He is gracious. He is joyful. He is wise. He is intelligent. Most of all, he walks with the Lord. To be in Dr. Kendall's presence is to be in the presence of greatness, which is true because R. T. has been in the presence of Greatness!

Dr. Kendall is one of the busiest retirees I know. This last year he has been in South Africa, the Middle East, Europe and all over North America. But on those occasions when he is home and sitting in a pew at the First Baptist Church of Hendersonville, it is rare that I do not get an e-mail or telephone call encouraging me on the sermon I preached that day. I am honored and thankful to call R. T. and Louise Kendall my friends.

You are about to be blessed as you read this book!

Dr. Bruce G. Chesser, senior pastor, First Baptist Church, Hendersonville, Tennessee

Special Recommendation

My first contact with Dr. R. T. Kendall, or "R. T." as he is affectionately known, was in October 1978 at the commencement of my pastoral training at the London Theological Seminary, founded by Dr. Martyn Lloyd-Jones in 1977. That first weekend in the capital, my wife and I headed straight to Westminster Chapel, London, which has always been a special place of pilgrimage for evangelicals from many parts of the world due to its reputation and influence as an outstanding preaching center. My wife and I were keen to hear their recently appointed minister, R. T. Kendall, an American already making quite a stir in the U.K. His striking style, freshness, courage and freedom, as well as his faithful biblical and prophetic voice on the greatest needs of the hour, were hitting home among discouraged Christians who needed to be rallied.

That first Friday evening in London, we attended R. T.'s weekly Bible study on Galatians, and were gripped by his authority and clarity as he unpacked with relevance and power Paul's "hottest" epistle on the issue of law and grace. The same effects occurred again at both Sunday services. We were captivated by the power of God's Spirit in such preaching.

This was very different from dull sermons we had often heard before. R. T. was loyal to the text, and forthright, therefore, in his challenge to wrongheaded thinking and legalism, while remaining utterly Gospel-centered and thundering out expansive views of our sovereign God. Weekends would never be the same! The grace of God was displayed so powerfully that conversions occurred regularly and God's people were increasingly liberated from any unhealthy introspection that had taken their eyes off Christ, then brought back to a renewed assurance of salvation and deeper joy in their Savior.

R. T.'s originality and stunning preaching salvos warned us against settling ever again for dull, irrelevant preaching. He was a great role model for aspiring preachers, and I have been indebted to him ever since for his example and provocation to prepare and preach well. One result was that we never followed our plan to visit as many London churches as possible during our time in London. Westminster Chapel became a magnet and our default position whenever I was not preaching myself.

I can honestly say that those two years changed our understanding of what preaching God's Word can and should be. It also transformed both of our lives. We joined "The Grace Revolution," embracing a new freedom from legalistic religion and celebrating our full justification in Christ. We rediscovered firsthand the necessity for the Holy Spirit's anointing on our lives and future ministry, along with a renewed conviction of the power of making Jesus Christ and His cross central to church life and to every sermon. Listeners should hear the Gospel regularly to meet Jesus again and again for the very first time, no matter what the Bible text or themes being addressed. Everything should lead to Christ.

Ever since those days, R. T. and his delightful wife, Louise, have held a special place in our hearts. In 1980 R. T. ordained me into my first pastorate in Winchester, and he was instrumental in initiating our eventual move 21 years later from Winchester Family Church to Westminster Chapel, at his own retirement on his 25th anniversary in London. His national and international ministry was a special gift of God—and from the U.S.A.—to our nation.

R. T.'s influence on British churches and movements is incalculable. He has spoken at nearly every major conference, convention or Bible Week in Britain. He is a major blessing wherever he goes. A prolific author of more than fifty outstanding books, including many major classics, R. T. has restored a love for God and the Bible to countless lives. I still recall the joy of reading his first book on Jonah. Now I have just finished this one on "the greatest sermon ever preached." In my view it is R. T.'s *magnum opus*.

This volume is a majestic treatment of the Sermon on the Mount. Packed with fascination and rich scriptural truth, it displays R. T.'s preaching skills to the full, in a style reminiscent of the sermons of Martyn Lloyd-Jones, in that he takes a microscopic and leisurely approach to the details of the text, then draws out profound teaching and messages from every word and sentence. These sermons are rich with insight, luminous thought and awesome power to touch hearts and consciences deeply. In them we meet Jesus.

Christ's condensed "Kingdom Manifesto" deserves such serious treatment by a master preacher. This is vintage R. T., a great work that joins the elite ranks of those who have taken Jesus' words seriously and been enabled to let them loose on a needy world so they are heard once more in surprise and awe. Christ Himself speaks in this fine book. Who wouldn't want to listen afresh to what He has to say?

GREG HASLAM, SENIOR PASTOR,
WESTMINSTER CHAPEL, LONDON

Preface

Not long ago I was asked to write an article on the book that had the greatest influence on me. I knew in an instant what that book was. It was Dr. D. Martyn Lloyd-Jones's *Sermon on the Mount.* The two volumes, based on his preaching of Matthew 5–7 at Westminster Chapel in London in the early 1950s, were given to me by the late Ernest Reisinger when I was a pastor in Ohio in 1963. I was 28 years old. Reading those sermons transformed both my thinking and preaching style. I was never to be the same again.

Dr. Lloyd-Jones's book helped me in two ways. First, it helped refine my theology, and second, it turned me into an expository preacher. I wrote opposite the title page, which Dr. Lloyd-Jones himself signed for me on July 30, 1963, "What I have read in this book has had a greater singular influence on me than any other book I can think of. . . . This book crossing my path has been one of the outstanding events of my life. It came to me when I needed it most."

Had you told me then that one day I, too, would be publishing my own sermons on Matthew 5–7, preached also at Westminster Chapel, I would have laughed you to scorn! And yet I remember the day I was unpacking my books and putting them on shelves in our new home in London, and came across the aforementioned two volumes. I immediately phoned the Doctor (as we all called him), read to him what I wrote opposite the title page and reminded him of the day he signed my book. "It is marvelous in our eyes," he responded, noting that neither of us could have predicted such a turn of events—that one day I would be in his pulpit.

Rightly or wrongly, I always felt it was his pulpit. I never felt worthy to follow him. He was clearly the greatest Bible expositor in the twentieth century and, for all I know, in Church history.

You will ask: Then why publish these sermons? Should not people merely read Dr. Lloyd-Jones's sermons? First, people in various parts of the world may not have easy access to them. Second, Dr. Lloyd-Jones's own view of the Mosaic Law and of Jesus' interpretation of it changed a few years after he preached the original sermons that were made into those two volumes. "There were things I said then I would not say now," he admitted to me. He added that a lot of what he said was aimed at attacking a particular kind of teaching that was popular at that time. I had the advantage of discussing with him his most mature views before he died. As a matter of fact, people said to me when I was teaching Galatians on Friday nights at Westminster Chapel, "You are teaching things Dr. Lloyd-Jones did not teach us." And this was when he was still alive! So I related to him what people said to me. He smiled. "Things are clearer to me now than they were then," he replied, referring to his understanding of the Law, especially Romans 7.

Dr. Martyn Lloyd-Jones was my mentor. He taught me so much, mostly how to think. There is not a word in my exposition of the Sermon on the Mount but what was a filling out of his own views. I am not saying that all I preached and all I did during my 25 years in London would have had Dr. Lloyd-Jones's approval. But I do say that my teaching of the Sermon on the Mount was consistent with what he believed about the Law and the Gospel at the end of his life. I always felt I was being true to the way he taught me to think.

I have dedicated this book in honor of my beloved friend and mentor, Dr. Martyn Lloyd-Jones. I look forward to seeing him again one day. Sometimes I can hardly wait.

I thank my former secretary, Mrs. Beryl Grogan, for typing up the sermons from a tape recorder. I have, however, edited them to make them easier to read. My greater debt, as always, is to my wife, Louise, who was my faithful, loving supporter and critic during those years at the Chapel. We miss the Chapel and our friends there so much. Most of all, I pray that what I have taught will be a blessing to you and bring glory to God.

R. T. KENDALL
HENDERSONVILLE, TENNESSEE

Introduction

"Jesus, yes. Paul, no." This phrase sums up the feeling and bias of quite a number of biblical scholars over quite a long time. The idea is this: We love the teachings of Jesus, but we certainly do not love the writings of Paul. Some go so far as to say, "If only Paul had never come along, Christianity would have been better off." It was Paul who messed things up, say these people. "If only we had merely the four gospels—Matthew, Mark, Luke and John." Some of these people are less happy with John. What about Acts? They aren't thrilled with Acts, either. But the worst thing to happen to the Church, it is alleged, was the conversion of Saul of Tarsus and the emergence of his subsequent teachings, when he was called the apostle Paul. We need to get "back to Jesus," say some of these people, and to understand Jesus as though Paul had never come along.

I reply: You cannot understand the Sermon on the Mount apart from the understanding of the Law that Paul gave the Church. Jesus' interpretation of the Law was made clearer to us by Paul's teaching on Galatians and Romans in particular.

There are those who want to build their theology totally, entirely and exclusively on the teachings of Jesus, as if there were no Paul. They are sometimes called "red letter" Christians, referring to Bibles that print the words of Jesus in red. It is as though the very words of Jesus are the only teachings we should trust and not the rest of the New Testament.

You might think, then, that my own book on the Sermon on the Mount would be acceptable to "red letter" Christians since it is an exposition of the words of Jesus in Matthew 5–7. I could wish for this, but the truth is, I regard the epistles of Paul as inspired as the words of Jesus. I do not believe you and I can understand the Sermon on the Mount apart from Paul's input. My interpretation of the Sermon on the Mount would not be possible without Paul's teaching.

There is more: The Sermon on the Mount would be impossible to understand apart from the Holy Spirit. All that Jesus taught was under the assumption that the Holy Spirit would fall on the Church after His death, resurrection and ascension—and that He, the Holy Spirit, would make sense out of Jesus' teachings.

I take the position that the Sermon on the Mount is in the main Jesus' doctrine of the Holy Spirit.

1. The Sermon on the Mount and the Holy Spirit

For I tell you that unless your righteousness surpasses that of the Pharisees and
the teachers of the law, you will certainly not enter the kingdom of heaven.

MATTHEW 5:20

It was Saint Augustine (354–430) who gave the name "Sermon on the Mount" to Jesus' teaching in Matthew 5–7. It is a title that stuck. John Stott reckons that this sermon is the best-known part of the teaching of Jesus but, arguably, the least understood—and, certainly, the least obeyed.

Dr. Martyn Lloyd-Jones stated that if you regard any particular injunction in this sermon as impossible, your interpretation and understanding of it must be wrong. "Our Lord taught these things," said Dr. Lloyd-Jones, "and He expects us to live them." He went on to say that Jesus lived and practiced what He preached, that the apostles also lived this sermon, "and if you take the trouble to read the lives of the saints down the centuries, and the men who have been most greatly used of God, you will find that, every time, they have been men who have taken the Sermon on the Mount not only seriously but literally."

A number of interpreters, however, have come up with a theological rationale that lets people off the hook by ignoring the teaching as relevant for us today. There are two extremes. At one end you have the liberal view, espoused by Albert Schweitzer, that this sermon was an "interim ethic." He argued that Jesus was making exceptional demands for an exceptional situation. Jesus, said Schweitzer, was expecting the end of history to arrive almost immediately, so He told His disciples to make total sacrifices, like leaving their possessions and loving their enemies—sacrifices appropriate only for that moment of crisis, as in an emergency.

At the other extreme, among those who reject the Sermon on the Mount as relevant teaching for our daily personal character and conduct, is a dispensationalist view. This perspective holds that the Sermon on the Mount is not relevant for us today, but rather is teaching that will be lived in the future Kingdom Age—the millennium after Christ comes again. This view, however, completely misses what Jesus meant by "the kingdom." It also allows for people to dismiss any responsibility to live by Jesus' teaching in this sermon. If one is convinced that the Sermon on the Mount isn't relevant for us today, you can be sure there will be no desire or effort to live as Jesus taught.

Jesus' Doctrine of the Holy Spirit

I take the view that you cannot understand the Sermon on the Mount and the Kingdom of heaven apart from Jesus' teaching of the Holy Spirit. Although Jesus' teaching on the Spirit is largely found in John 14–16, the Sermon on the Mount is a vital part of Jesus' doctrine of the Holy Spirit. And yet Jesus does not explicitly mention the Holy Spirit once! But that is exactly what Matthew 5–7 is. It is our Lord's teaching of the Kingdom: the way the Law has been fulfilled, how the Ten Commandments are applied by the Holy Spirit and what true godliness is. The book of Esther does not mention God once, but it is a very God-centered book. So, too, with the Sermon on the Mount. It is showing how the Christian life is to be lived, made possible only by the Holy Spirit.

As we will see in detail later on, the righteousness that Jesus envisaged for us—namely, a holiness that surpasses and outclasses the legalism of the Pharisees (Matthew 5:20)—could only be fulfilled in us by supernatural help of the Holy Spirit. The way Jesus interpreted the Law and the way He wants us to fulfill it cannot be carried out at the natural level. Such a righteousness—which includes blessing and loving our enemies—is possible, yes, but only by the Holy Spirit.

17

Not only that, the whole of the Sermon on the Mount is Jesus' way of unfolding the mission of the Holy Spirit in advance of His teaching in John 14–16. The Holy Spirit is our "Helper" (John 15:26; 16:7, ESV) and He enables us to manifest a level of holy living that the world rarely sees but longs to see. Such a glorious, even dazzling manner of life is described and explained to us in the Sermon on the Mount.

Matthew 5:1 says that when Jesus saw the crowds, He went up on a mountain and sat down. Matthew said several things about Jesus just before coming to the Sermon on the Mount: (1) that Jesus went throughout Galilee, teaching in their synagogues; (2) that He had already been teaching the Gospel of the Kingdom; (3) that He was a great healer of diseases and of those in severe pain; (4) that He healed demon-possessed people and those having seizures; (5) that news about Him spread all over Syria and that large crowds also came from Galilee, the Decapolis, Jerusalem, Judea and the region across the Jordan (Matthew 4:23–25). Therefore, when He saw the crowds, He went up on a mountainside. "His disciples came to him."

Some take the view that it was only the Twelve who heard the Sermon on the Mount—that Jesus' main purpose was to withdraw from the great crowds, that He had to escape and thus came to this mountain. But the word *disciple* means "follower" (Gr. *mathetes*), a word that could encompass more than the twelve disciples. Besides, at the end of the sermon, "the crowds were amazed at his teaching" (Matthew 7:28). Matthew clearly makes the connection with the crowds referred to in Matthew 4:25. Even if the Sermon on the Mount was primarily for the Twelve, the multitudes were privileged to hear the whole discourse.

Two Sermons or One?

The place was on the "mountainside." Michael Eaton has done considerable study on this matter and reckons that a correct translation could be "hilly countryside." In hot countries, one would want to go to a higher territory where it is somewhat cooler. It is thought this was where people both had a full vision of Jesus and were able to hear Him perfectly. There is an area like this in Galilee that you can still see today, just north of Capernaum, which provides great acoustics when making a speech. It is possibly where Jesus originally gave the teaching that became the basis for this famous sermon.

But in Luke 6:17, where Jesus taught many of the same things as contained in Matthew 5–7, the place of the teaching was on "a level place." Does this mean we are talking about two different sermons? Probably not. It is not incredulous to infer that it was on a level place in the hilly countryside to which I have referred. Luke's version is shorter: 30 verses, compared to Matthew's 107 verses. Each includes material absent from the other. Almost certainly we get only a part of it, even in Matthew. It doesn't take long to read the Sermon on the Mount. Dr. Eaton also suggests that the original teaching of Jesus may have taken several days and that someone, possibly Matthew, an ex-tax collector who would have been able to take notes, did so. John Calvin (1509–1564) observed that the design of both Matthew and Luke was to summarize the leading points of the doctrine of Christ and that, therefore, it is but a brief summary of what Jesus originally said.

When Jesus "sat down" to deliver the Sermon on the Mount (Matthew 5:1), He followed the rabbinic custom to sit when speaking with authority. In ancient times, sitting had an aura of authority more than standing. All rabbis sat when they taught. Today teachers and preachers tend to stand, but not so much then. This was true not only of rabbis but of those in secular authority as well. It was an ominous sign when Pontius Pilate made up his mind about having Jesus crucified and "sat down" on the judge's seat (John 19:13).

In the synagogue in Nazareth, Jesus "stood up to read," but when He rolled up the scroll and gave it back to the attendant, He "sat down." It was then that the eyes of everyone were "fastened on him," whereupon Jesus said, "Today this scripture is fulfilled in your hearing" (Luke 4:20–21). Sitting sent a signal to all those who witnessed that stunning moment. It almost certainly sent a signal of authority to those present on the mountainside.

Teaching or Preaching?

A sermon is usually thought of with reference to preaching. But Jesus "began to teach" (Gr.

didasko). Sometimes Jesus "taught," while sometimes He "preached" (*kerusso*—Luke 4:44). Is there a difference between teaching and preaching? Probably, but it is a technical point; the two words can overlap and be used interchangeably. In Luke 4:15 Jesus "taught in their synagogues," but in Luke 4:44 He "kept on preaching in the synagogues."

It would seem that the two words could easily and equally describe what Jesus did when He spoke. Teaching, generally, however, should be understood as the unfolding, revealing and passing on of knowledge. Preaching is essentially proclamation, exhortation and application of the truth. One can teach and preach simultaneously. Back in the hills of my home state, Kentucky, they thought the difference between teaching and preaching was that the latter was louder!

The Purpose of the Sermon on the Mount

The purpose of the Sermon on the Mount is to demonstrate the kind of teaching—and the kind of living with regard to character and conduct—that should govern the people of God through the power of the Holy Spirit. The Law could not produce this kind of living. What the Law could not do, "in that it was weakened by the sinful nature, *God did* by sending his own Son in the likeness of sinful man to be a sin offering . . . that the righteous requirements of the law might be fully met in us, who do not live according to the sinful nature but according to the Spirit" (Romans 8:3–4, emphasis mine).

The *general* theme of the Sermon on the Mount is "Kingdom of heaven." The *particular* theme is the way the Mosaic Law was to be fulfilled and hence applied by believers through the Holy Spirit.

The Structure of the Sermon on the Mount

The sermon begins with the Beatitudes—the "blessings" promised in Matthew 5:1–12. The Beatitudes form Jesus' "text" for His sermon. A preacher often takes a text, a verse in the Bible, then explains that verse and applies it. Jesus' text is the verses in Matthew 5:1–12. The rest of the Sermon on the Mount is, in varying degrees, His application of the Beatitudes. One cannot make this style, order or method too rigid. It is only Jesus' general approach as He unfolds the sermon.

2. The Kingdom of Heaven

Theirs is the kingdom of heaven.

MATTHEW 5:3, 10

As I have mentioned, the theme of Jesus' teachings generally and the Sermon on the Mount particularly is the Kingdom of heaven. The theme is also, speaking generally, as I have said, Jesus' doctrine of the Holy Spirit. So, is it possible to preach a sermon on the Holy Spirit and never mention the name "Holy Spirit"? Jesus does.

Jesus mentions "kingdom of heaven" as such six times in the Sermon on the Mount. He calls it "his kingdom"—meaning, "Kingdom of God"—in Matthew 6:33, and refers to the Kingdom in the Lord's Prayer: "Your kingdom come" (Matthew 6:10). Some think there is a distinction between the Kingdom of heaven and the Kingdom of God. Wrong. In Matthew 5:3 it is called "kingdom of heaven," while the exact statement in Luke 6:20 calls it "kingdom of God." They are the same. However, only in Matthew is it called "kingdom of heaven." In Mark, Luke and John it is called "kingdom of God."

Which word, then, did Jesus use? You must remember that Jesus spoke in Aramaic. It is open to dispute which term He used, "heaven" or "God." The Aramaic could almost certainly be translated either way. There is a Hebrew equivalent that means "God dwells" or "God is present." Since heaven was seen as God's dwelling place, it is likely that Matthew, speaking to Jews, chose the phrase "kingdom of heaven."

Jesus was not the first to use these terms. John the Baptist used them first: "Repent, for the kingdom of heaven is near" (Matthew 3:2). And yet neither was John the Baptist the first! This phrase was used during the Intertestamental Period (the era between Malachi and the New Testament). It was a "buzz word" and well known by the time John the Baptist and Jesus appeared. This does not mean that everyone understood it. People may have read in their own interpretation when they heard it, as the disciples themselves did all the time. For example, despite the many times Jesus referred to it, the disciples' question, "Lord, are you at this time going to restore the kingdom to Israel?" (Acts 1:6) showed they did not have a clue what Jesus had been talking about.

Definition of the Kingdom of Heaven

The Kingdom of heaven can have several true definitions. This is partly because the phrase is used more than one way in the Bible. Sometimes the definition is tied to eschatology, as when Paul said, "In the presence of God and of Christ Jesus, who will judge the living and the dead, and in view of his *appearing and his kingdom*" (2 Timothy 4:1, emphasis mine). But if I may come to the heart of the matter and give the definition that, in my opinion, best suits Jesus' teaching in the Sermon on the Mount, it is this: *the rule of the un-grieved Spirit in the believer.*

The Holy Spirit is a person—a very sensitive person—who can be grieved (Ephesians 4:30). When we grieve the Spirit, we forfeit His conscious presence. The Holy Spirit will never leave us (John 14:16), but only when He is un-grieved are we promised His conscious presence. This definition of the Kingdom, as found in the Sermon on the Mount, therefore presupposes the conscious and enabling presence of God—an equally valid definition of the Kingdom. It is the realm of the unhindered Spirit. It is what it is like when the Holy Spirit is at home in us—like being poor in spirit, meek, pure in heart, merciful or persecuted because of Christ. To inherit the Kingdom of heaven is therefore to enjoy the blessing and conscious indwelling presence of the Holy Spirit.

The Kingdom presupposes a monarch, and God Almighty was the sole monarch over ancient

Israel. The Prince of Wales refers to his mother, Queen Elizabeth, as "the monarch." In the Old Testament the monarch was God, for He alone was Israel's king (1 Samuel 12:12). Moses exclaimed, "The Lord will *reign* for ever and ever" (Exodus 15:18, emphasis mine). The prophet Isaiah said, "My eyes have seen the King, the Lord Almighty" (Isaiah 6:5). King David stated, "Your kingdom is an everlasting kingdom, and your dominion endures through all generations" (Psalm 145:13).

In the New Testament the monarch was Jesus. The Magi came from the east asking, "Where is the one who has been born king of the Jews?" (Matthew 2:2). The angel told the Virgin Mary that the child Jesus would "reign over the house of Jacob forever; his kingdom will never end" (Luke 1:33). Jesus said to Pontius Pilate, "My kingdom is not of this world . . . my kingdom is from another place" (John 18:36).

How Jesus Elsewhere Introduced and Explained the Kingdom

Jesus began His ministry by announcing that the Kingdom of heaven was "near" (Matthew 4:17)—close at hand—as if before their very eyes. He did not then fully explain what He meant by that. He spoke of the Kingdom in a manner that only made sense by the Holy Spirit.

The parables Jesus later gave were only truly understood in the light of Jesus' death, His resurrection, His ascension to heaven and the coming of the Spirit from heaven. For example, the statement "the kingdom of God is within you" (Luke 17:21) may seem perfectly clear to us now, but it was understood by the disciples only after the coming of the Spirit on the Day of Pentecost. Not long before His death on the cross, Jesus said, "I have much more to say to you, more than you can now bear" (John 16:12). This referred largely to the Spirit. There was simply no way the Kingdom of heaven could make sense to the disciples until the Holy Spirit came down.

Toward the end of His earthly ministry, Jesus explained that the Kingdom of heaven would be *invisible*. Everybody thought such a Kingdom would be visible. This is what the disciples wanted and hoped for—that King Jesus would overthrow Rome and put Israel on the map. When Jesus said

that the Kingdom of God does not come with one's "careful observation" (Luke 17:20), it was not what they wanted to hear. Everybody assumed the Kingdom of heaven would be observable and tangible.

And yet the Kingdom of heaven would be *inhabitable*! One could actually live in it. The promise to the poor in spirit was that the Kingdom of heaven was "theirs" (Matthew 5:3). Jesus talked about those who would "enter" the Kingdom of heaven and those who were "least" or "great" in it (Matthew 5:19–20).

The truth is, the Kingdom of heaven was *internal*. It would reside in the hearts of believers and be inherited only to the degree the un-grieved Spirit indwelt them. The apostle Paul summed it up: "The kingdom of God is not a matter of eating and drinking, but of righteousness, peace and joy in the Holy Spirit" (Romans 14:17). Not only that, but "the wicked will not inherit the kingdom of God" (1 Corinthians 6:9).

And so the Kingdom of God was to be *inherited*. An inheritance is what you receive from someone after that person has died. Nobody could inherit the Kingdom of God until Jesus died. "For this reason Christ is the mediator of a new covenant, that those who are called may receive the promised eternal inheritance—now that he has died as a ransom to set them free from the sins committed under the first covenant" (Hebrews 9:15). The inheritance of the Kingdom was given to those whose righteousness surpassed that of the Pharisees (Matthew 5:20)—but this was not possible apart from the Holy Spirit.

The Kingdom Means Salvation—from Sin

When Jesus came into Jerusalem on Palm Sunday, the crowds shouted, "Hosanna to the Son of David! . . . Hosanna in the highest!" (Matthew 21:9). Hosanna means "Save!" "He saves" or "salvation." But the kind of salvation the crowds had in mind was an earthly salvation—that is, that they would be saved from Rome and the tyranny of Caesar. For the disciples, therefore, to mentally make the transition from the level of nature (earthly salvation) to the level of the Spirit (eternal salvation) was no small adjustment.

The day would come when they realized that salvation meant deliverance from sin—that it was something that took place in the hearts of men and women through reliance upon the death of Jesus on the cross—that it was by grace through faith (Ephesians 2:8). The Sermon on the Mount, therefore, would make no sense until a person was "born again," a work of the Spirit that gave initial entrance into the Kingdom of God (John 3:3). Being born again opens one's eyes to see the Sin-bearer: "Just as Moses lifted up the snake in the desert, so the Son of Man must be lifted up, that everyone who believes in him may have eternal life" (John 3:14–15). This opens the way for inheriting the Kingdom of God while we live and guarantees eternal life in heaven when we die.

The Kingdom Presupposes Sovereignty

The Kingdom by definition presupposes a king. As we have seen, this means a monarch or a sovereign. The king or queen is a sovereign. The Kingdom of God, therefore, presupposes the sovereignty of God. Jesus Christ is our Sovereign.

Only a sovereign or monarch has the right to choose who comes into their presence. For example, those who go to Buckingham Palace are those—and only those—who have been invited. It is that way also with our Monarch, King Jesus. God said to Moses, "I will have mercy on whom I will have mercy, and I will have compassion on whom I will have compassion" (Exodus 33:19). In precisely this same way, as Jesus put it, "No one knows the Father except the Son and those to *whom the Son chooses* to reveal him" (Matthew 11:27, emphasis mine). "For just as the Father raises the dead and gives them life, even so the Son gives life *to whom he is pleased* to give it" (John 5:21, emphasis mine). In a word: Nobody enters the Kingdom by accident, but rather by God's sovereign invitation. And what a wonderful invitation it is!

"Congratulations!"

No wonder, then, that Jesus said, "Blessed" are the poor in spirit, "blessed" are those who mourn, "blessed" are the meek, etc. This is because the word "blessed" comes from the Greek *makarios*— "happy." Happy are you to be chosen—that you should be earmarked by God to be poor in spirit, hungering and thirsting after righteousness, merciful and persecuted.

"Blessed" means "approval." But there is more. Believe it or not, the word "happiness" comes from a word that means "lucky." I realize the word "lucky" has been largely off-limits for Christians, but it is a word definitely implied in Luke 10:31, when in Jesus' parable a priest "happened" (Gr. *sugkuria*—"by chance") to be going down the same road where a man had been attacked and hurt. This might be called "coincidence." But with God there are no coincidences. The person, therefore, who is called "blessed" would be called "lucky" by the world. But "blessed" describes *the person God approves,* because our Monarch has mercifully and sovereignly given that person grace to be poor in spirit, etc.

If God, therefore, has given you sovereign mercy, you are indeed "blessed." Consequently, the person who is blessed cannot boast in himself or herself, neither can they attribute things to "chance" but only to God's sheer grace. The word "blessed" can be summed up in one word: "Congratulations!" Not that we deserve it—quite the opposite! And yet when God bestows such grace on us, it is as though the angels say, "Congratulations!" We should say to every person born again, to every new believer: "Congratulations!" For not everyone enters into this happiness.

The Kingdom Is Inseparable from the Spirit

It is impossible to grasp the meaning of the Kingdom of heaven—and also to experience it—apart from the Holy Spirit. First, we are regenerated (born again) by the Holy Spirit. This is how we initially enter the Kingdom of heaven. It is the sovereign work of the Spirit. It is not what we do but what God does. "The wind blows wherever it pleases. You hear its sound, but you cannot tell where it comes from or where it is going. So it is with everyone born of the Spirit" (John 3:8).

Second, in order to enjoy an inheritance in the Kingdom we must enjoy the unhindered, unquenched and un-grieved Spirit in our lives. As the Dove was at home when alighting on Jesus (John 1:32–33), so He must be at home in us. It is the un-grieved Spirit who enables us to outclass the righteousness of the teachers of the Law and the Pharisees (Matthew 5:20).

I bring this chapter to a close with Dr. Lloyd-Jones's observation: "Here is the life to which we are called . . . I maintain again that if only every Christian in the Church today were living the Sermon on the Mount, the great revival for which we are praying and longing could already have started. Amazing and astounding things would happen; the world would be shocked, and men and women would be attracted to our Lord and Savior Jesus Christ."

3. Brokenness

Blessed are the poor in spirit, for theirs is the kingdom of heaven.

MATTHEW 5:3

The sacrifices of God are a broken spirit; a broken and
contrite heart, O God, you will not despise.

PSALM 51:17

"The way up is down" is a summary of so much of what Jesus taught. For example: "And whoever humbles himself will be exalted" (Matthew 23:12).

When invited to an important function, said Jesus, "Do not take the place of honor, for a person more distinguished than you may have been invited. If so, the host who invited both of you will come and say to you, 'Give this man your seat.' Then, humiliated, you will have to take the least important place. But when you are invited, take the lowest place, so that when your host comes, he will say to you, 'Friend, move up to a better place.' Then you will be honored in the presence of all your fellow guests. For everyone who exalts himself will be humbled, and he who humbles himself will be exalted" (Luke 14:8–11).

This principle coheres with several proverbs. "A man's pride brings him low, but a man of lowly spirit gains honor" (Proverbs 29:23). "Pride goes before destruction, a haughty spirit before a fall" (Proverbs 16:18). "Humility comes before honor" (Proverbs 15:33). Peter summed it up: "Humble yourselves, therefore, under God's mighty hand, that he may lift you up in due time" (1 Peter 5:6).

And yet I am still amazed at the opening line of this famous sermon: "Blessed are the poor in spirit." In one stroke, strange as it may seem, Jesus invites all who are feeling helpless, hopeless, in despair, unworthy and totally empty to feel good about it. But why? That they may see the true value of their condition. They are blessed but may not know it!

When one is feeling helpless and hopeless—and feeling devoid of value and worth—it is hard at first to see that this could be a good thing. But it is a good thing, says Jesus; be encouraged if this is the way you feel. It is precisely what primarily qualifies you for the Kingdom of heaven! It is the first thing you must show before you can move on. It is the equivalent of a credit card, a union card or entrance fee; it is the ticket that lets you in. Don't leave home without it! Lose this and you are disqualified for the Kingdom of heaven. Show this and you are ready to proceed to the most glorious invitation ever offered a human being: to have the Kingdom of heaven as your own.

Therefore, the opening statement of Jesus' sermon is not addressed to those who are "on top," or in control of themselves, or feeling good in themselves. No. It is a word to those who are feeling the opposite of that. Therefore, as you read these lines, if it happens that you yourself feel depleted of confidence, spirituality and goodness, and feel that you have no sense of worth, read on. There is hope for you. Indeed, God is at work on your case.

The Authority of Jesus' Word

As Jesus began the sermon, the King James Version gives us the translation of the original Greek: "And he opened his mouth, and taught them, saying" (Matthew 5:2). Modern versions tend to think it is redundant to translate this, and instead simply say, "He began to teach them, saying." So why does Matthew actually say that "he opened his mouth"? Answer: It was a Hebrew idiom indicating that something of great importance was about to be uttered.

Peter said, "If anyone speaks, he should do it as one speaking the very words of God" ("oracles of God," 1 Peter 4:11, KJV). Matthew is letting the reader know that the very words of God are coming. Although he was pointing out the obvious—that Jesus opened His mouth when He spoke—Matthew prepares the Jewish reader for a very significant moment. He therefore bothered to point out the obvious: that Jesus *opened His mouth* to speak! An authoritative word was at hand. And, indeed, when Jesus finished speaking, the crowds "were amazed at his teaching, because he taught as one who had authority, and not as their teachers of the law" (Matthew 7:28–29).

The Anointing of Being "Poor in Spirit"

As we saw earlier, "blessed" means "congratulations." It also means "approval." In this case, it refers to the approval of God. It comes down to one word: *anointing*. To be "blessed" in the way Jesus uses the term, then, means to be under the anointing of the Holy Spirit.

The Kingdom of heaven presupposes (1) the sovereignty of God—that you have been chosen; (2) the salvation of God—that you have been saved; and (3) the Spirit of God—who has performed an operation on you. Likewise, Jesus shows that the way the Kingdom of heaven is "ours" is via the route of our being broken. The Kingdom of heaven is the realm of the unhindered Spirit, but when the Spirit performs an operation on you it means a radical surgery on your own spirit. "Poor in spirit" refers to the human spirit; it is when you are spiritually impoverished. The divine surgery cuts away false illusions you had about yourself. It shatters your pride.

Our Lord is saying two things here: (1) If you are poor in spirit, God got to you, and (2) if you feel totally lost and without hope, God will find you. Indeed, He has found you. If, then, you feel you are the scum of the earth, that is a very good sign! If you are asking, "Will God ever notice somebody as lowly and unpromising as I?" I answer: He is on your case.

He is looking high and low over the planet for one kind of person—the weak, the rejected, the one who feels the most insignificant. He isn't looking for the strong—the one who has no need of anything. He is looking for the weak—those who know their true need very well indeed. So if you feel so utterly impoverished spiritually, God has been looking for such a person as you. Yes, He is already on your case! Indeed, He has found you!

The quickest way to get God's attention is not by shouting or by demonstrating a show of strength, but when you feel you are absolutely nothing. To quote from one of my favorite hymns:

Let not conscience make you linger,
  nor of fitness fondly dream;
All the fitness he requireth, is to feel
  your need of Him;
This He gives you; 'tis the Spirit's rising
  beam!

Joseph Hart (1712–1768)

The Beatitudes: A Ladder

There are important questions that I want to answer before moving on. First, why is this particular beatitude—of being "poor in spirit"—listed first? Answer: It demonstrates that the way up is down—that we must begin at the very bottom, taking the "lowest seat," humbling ourselves and being humbled, if we intend to enter and inherit the Kingdom of heaven. It is the foundation.

Subsequent beatitudes may be called the superstructure. Proceeding from brokenness to mourning to meekness, etc., is like climbing a ladder. We begin with brokenness, and we end up with being peacemakers and being persecuted for righteousness' sake. But we start with being poor in spirit. The foundation for inheritance in the Kingdom, then, is the opposite of pride, haughtiness, a lofty feeling of self-worth and arrogance. The way not to proceed is to say, "I am rich; I have acquired wealth and do not need a thing" (Revelation 3:17). If you are saying, "God, look at what I can do for You, with all my ability and good works," I say: God will ignore you.

The second question is, why is this beatitude stated differently in Luke 6:20? Instead of saying "poor in spirit," Luke's version states, simply, "Blessed are you who are poor, for yours is the kingdom of God." So, why did Jesus say "poor in spirit" in Matthew 5:3 and only "poor" in Luke 6:20? I don't know for sure, except to say that both are true. Those who are poor in spirit are blessed, that is for certain. But I also know that James would agree that the poor—those deprived of worldly goods—are primarily blessed. "The brother in humble circumstances ought to take pride in his high position. But the one who is rich should take pride in his low position, because he will pass away like a wild flower" (James 1:9). James believed that the poor man was in a "high position" and singularly blessed since God has chosen "those who are poor in the eyes of the world to be rich in faith and to inherit the kingdom he promised those who love him" (James 2:5).

I don't know if anybody has sought to document it, but I hear of stories of signs and wonders all the time—some of which I know to be true—that happen in Third World countries. I have friends who have personally witnessed miraculous healings among the poorest of the poor in Africa and India that, for some reason, do not seem to happen in the West. It certainly suggests that the poor are especially noticed by our heavenly Father. And I know that Luke's version mentions poor people. God cares about poor people. Mark Twain once commented that God must like poor people—He made so many of them! It also may be that in much the same way that Jews are first in the queue to be offered the Gospel (Romans 1:16), so the poor stand first in line to be offered the Kingdom of heaven.

The third question is, why does the promise "theirs is the kingdom of heaven" refer to both the "poor in spirit" (Matthew 5:3) and also those who are "persecuted because of righteousness" (Matthew 5:10)? In other words, why is the consequence of being poor in spirit the same as being persecuted for righteousness? The answer is partly because we must never outgrow being broken. One does not depart from brokenness in order to make room for mourning (the next beatitude). One *stays* broken all the way up the ladder.

Furthermore, brokenness is the foundation. The subsequent beatitudes form a superstructure over the foundation. Jesus shows that the height of the superstructure is to be persecuted for righteousness. The consequence of being persecuted for righteousness is the Kingdom of heaven—the same promise as when you are broken. Why?

Because to inherit the Kingdom of heaven is as good as it gets. The Kingdom is the realm of the un-grieved Spirit. That is what we enjoy when we inherit the Kingdom. It is what we enjoy when we are persecuted for righteousness.

The Presence of the Anointing

When Jesus says, "Blessed are the poor in spirit," He is stating God's opinion. It is what God says to the person who is broken. You may not see this at first as happiness or blessedness. But God says it is. It is God's affirmation of your spiritual state. He is giving you a report card. He says, "If you are broken, you are in good shape!" Furthermore, people may not see you as blessed or approved of God. It is the way God sees you. If you are poor in spirit, you are blessed—God says so. Can you live with God's point of view?

It is much the same as Paul's teaching of justification by faith. Our faith counts for righteousness (Romans 4:5). It is imputed; righteousness is put to our credit. It is what God says—He declares us righteous when we believe in His Son. You may not feel righteous. People may not see you as righteous. But God does.

So, too, with these beatitudes. God says, "Congratulations!" if you are broken. He calls you blessed. You have His approval, if no one else's. In fact, in this first beatitude Jesus is virtually saying, "You don't realize how happy you are!" For this is entering in at the narrow gate that leads to life, "and only a few find it" (Matthew 7:13–14).

Being poor in spirit is a state that defies a natural explanation. It is as supernatural as the dead being raised, the blind being healed or the deaf being able to hear. If you are poor in spirit, God has already worked on you as powerfully as raising a person from the dead. After all, says Paul, "You were dead in your transgressions and sins" but you have been "raised" and are seated "in the heavenly realms in Christ Jesus" (Ephesians 2:1, 6).

The Proof of the Anointing

If you are poor in spirit—broken—you are under the anointing. The anointing of the Holy Spirit is offered to everybody. It is not something only a preacher needs in the pulpit. "You have an anointing from the Holy One, and all of you know the truth" (1 John 2:20).

The anointing is offered to every believer. The first evidence: being poor in spirit. As for the poor, they, too, need to be poor in spirit to be saved. Being a poor man or woman does not in and by itself qualify you for salvation. It means that you get God's attention more quickly than anybody else.

Being poor in spirit is the way King David felt after being exposed and convicted of his sin of adultery with Bathsheba (2 Samuel 11:2–5). But David repented after being confronted by Nathan the prophet (2 Samuel 12:7–13). He prayed, "Have mercy on me, O God, according to your unfailing love; according to your great compassion blot out my transgressions. . . . for I know my transgressions, and my sin is always before me. . . . the sacrifices of God are a broken spirit; a broken and contrite heart, O God, you will not despise" (Psalm 51:1–2, 3, 17).

Brokenness is evident when you realize you have no bargaining power with God. You can do only one thing: ask for mercy. You ask for mercy when you have nothing to give in exchange, you have nothing to offer. You are spiritually bankrupt. That is when you know your real need—mercy. You can't broker a deal with God. You simply come empty before Him and beg Him for mercy. When you realize that God said, "I will have mercy on whom I will have mercy" (Exodus 33:19), you can also see why the meaning of blessedness is "congratulations!" For it is a wonderful thing when God bestows mercy. It is what you must ask for in seeking to get right with the God of the Bible. That is what David did. It is what every backslider must do. It is what anybody must do to enter the Kingdom of heaven.

> Nothing in my hand I bring, simply to
> Thy cross I cling;
> Naked, come to Thee for dress; help-
> less, look to Thee for grace;
> Foul, I to the fountain fly; wash me
> Saviour, or I die.
>
> Augustus Toplady (1740–1778)

The opposite of this is when you feel righteous in yourself, like the Pharisee. He prayed, "God, I thank you that I am not like other men—robbers, evildoers, adulterers. . . . I fast twice a week and give a tenth of all I get." Such a person was not justified before God, said Jesus—only the one who prays, "God, have mercy on me, a sinner" (Luke 18:11–14). Such a person has been softened by the Holy Spirit. It happens when God takes the hard, arrogant heart and the person sees his or her sinfulness before Him. It is when one is truly slain in the Spirit.

It means an absence of defensiveness. You are no longer explaining yourself, excusing yourself. It is the absence of being judgmental. There will be no pointing of the finger when you are broken. The one who points the finger needs to be broken!

The Paradox of the Anointing

Being poor in spirit is the way you get God's attention—and yet it shows in one stroke that God got *your* attention! When you are broken, you are needing and seeking God's attention. Yet it shows simultaneously He got what He wanted—you! The whole time He was seeking you.

Here is another paradox of the anointing of brokenness: It is the first step a person must take in becoming a Christian, but also the first step for a returning backslider, as we saw in the example of David. The person who comes to Christ in faith and the returning backslider have this in common: their need of mercy. And this is what they must ask for. Furthermore, not only must you never try to outgrow being poor in spirit, but you never—ever—outgrow the need of mercy. Every Christian, no matter how old, knowledgeable or godly, when praying to God asks first of all for "mercy" (Hebrews 4:16).

Brokenness is both the foundation and the superstructure. It is where you begin and it is where you end. The immediate consequence of brokenness is the Kingdom of heaven. But you remain broken all the way up the ladder—from mourning, meekness, hungering and thirsting after righteousness, being merciful, being pure in heart and a peacemaker, to persecution because of righteousness. The promise to those being persecuted for righteousness, then, is the same as the promise to the one poor in spirit: "theirs is the kingdom of heaven" (Matthew 5:3, 10). The brokenness that brings one into the Kingdom leads to the highest level of anointing—namely, the privilege of being persecuted because of righteousness.

The Kingdom of heaven is the greatest possession there is. It is the inheritance to which every believer is called. This is the paramount theme of the Sermon on the Mount: inheriting the Kingdom. The realm of the unhindered, ungrieved Spirit is the most sublime level of living on the planet. It is on offer to every believer. It begins with brokenness. And you must never try to move on without it, because you must never outgrow it.

4. Suffering

Blessed are those who mourn, for they will be comforted.

MATTHEW 5:4

Consider it pure joy, my brothers, whenever you face trials of many kinds.

JAMES 1:2

At first glance this particular beatitude—"Blessed are those who mourn"—must be one of the strangest verses in the Bible. John Stott said it could almost be translated, "Happy are the unhappy." You will recall that "blessed" means "happy," that "happiness" comes from a word that means "lucky." And if blessed in Matthew 5:3–11 may also be understood as "congratulations!" are we to understand that Jesus is saying, "Congratulations if you are unhappy"? Are you lucky if you are mourning?

Frank Sinatra died a few days before I preached from Matthew 5:4 at Westminster Chapel. I remember reading that there were five hundred mourners at his funeral, and that they all cried—"There was not a dry eye in the place." Am I to believe that these people are blessed because they mourned at Sinatra's passing?

Or take anyone who mourns at the loss of a loved one. Is Jesus referring to people who mourn because of a loved one dying?

Do not forget that "blessed" also means "approved of God." It is being chosen to be under a sovereign anointing of the Holy Spirit. The best possible thing that can happen to you is to be under a sovereign anointing of the Holy Spirit. But why would Jesus say you are blessed if you mourn?

The Greek word that is translated "mourn" is *pentheo*—meaning grief or sorrow of heart that is usually expressed by tears. In Luke's account of Jesus' similar teaching, we read, "Blessed are you who *weep* now, for you will laugh" (Luke 6:21, emphasis mine). Paul wished that the Corinthians had been filled with "grief" rather than being proud (1 Corinthians 5:2). James counseled, "Change your laughter to mourning" (James 4:9).

But if one weeps, is he or she anointed? I answer: Yes, if they are poor in spirit in the sense that Jesus means. You will recall that we must never outgrow asking for mercy. And when we move from beatitude to beatitude, we are not leaving one for another. One retains the same anointing while adding to it.

Mourning is an extension of brokenness. It is filling out the first beatitude—it is taking brokenness one step further. Jesus is also talking about a deeper sense of sin. It is not unlike what Isaiah experienced when he saw the glory of the LORD, then cried out, "Woe to me!" He became convicted of sin he had not known was there. "I am ruined! For I am a man of unclean lips, and I live among a people of unclean lips, and my eyes have seen the King, the Lord Almighty" (Isaiah 6:5). Isaiah was singularly blessed to have had this vision and the sense of his sinfulness. That is what Jesus is talking about, although that is not the whole story.

Two Kinds of Suffering

Jesus is talking about the result of effectual suffering. This means there are two kinds of suffering. There is a suffering that is not effectual—that is, the suffering did the person no good.

I fear I was that way for too long. I am ashamed to admit that for many, many years I grumbled and complained whenever a trial of any kind came my way. Whether it was losing my keys, blocked goals, interrupted plans or sudden disappointment, my reaction was not a pretty sight.

When any kind of trial or testing came, I did all I could to end it—to get it over with as soon as possible. And when it was over, it was over. I was no better off. I did not learn a thing. I did not grow or develop spiritually. I saw any trial as a nuisance. I might have dignified the trial, but no—I did anything but dignify it. I murmured the whole time.

It was not until the summer of 1979 that I came face-to-face with my folly. And it was only because I had to preach on James 1:2: "Count it all joy when ye fall into divers temptations" (Gr. *peirasmos*—trial, testing—James 1:2, KJV). It was the first Sunday my family and I were back in London from our vacation. I wanted a good sermon to begin the series on James, so that verse was on my mind a lot. It was during that time, while we were on vacation in Florida, I began seriously to prepare a sermon on James 1:2.

Strange as it may seem to you, my awakening came in the midst of a disappointment regarding a pizza in Kissimmee, Florida. I had looked forward to returning to a pizza place where, a year before, I had eaten the best pizza of my life. But when we came to the same place in 1979, everything went wrong.

First, the people at the restaurant lost our order—and we had to wait an hour. Second, sadly, I lost my temper with the manager for their error. Third, on our return to our hotel, a tropical rainstorm slowed down our driving, letting the pizza get cold. Fourth, when I opened the back door to retrieve my pizza, the hard rain on the brown paper bag caused my pizza to fall into a foot of water—the whole thing: the pepperoni, the mushrooms, the sausage, the green peppers and anchovies. I'm sorry, but I did not display the fruits of the Spirit. Louise and the children managed to retrieve their pizzas and were inside watching television and eating while I fumed. I headed back to the pizza restaurant, knowing I would have to face the manager.

But something extraordinary happened to me on the way back to the restaurant. God mercifully overruled. I said to myself, "Either James 1:2 is true, or it isn't." I had the presence of mind to dignify this trial. That is when the word *dignify* came to me. I repented of my selfishness and anger. I determined to dignify that episode to the hilt. I apologized to the manager. I promised myself that I would—from that day—welcome a trial, no matter how big or small. Believe it or not, I was never to be the same again. It was the greatest lesson I had learned in years.

That little trial in Kissimmee, then, turned out to be effectual. A trial that is ineffectual is when we moan through it all. Jesus did not say, "Blessed are they who moan." If only! I had been possibly the world's greatest complainer. I was determined that the episode regarding a pizza would make a difference. It did.

An ineffectual trial can be summed up this way: It is when you complain the whole time, get angry with God for letting it happen, blame everybody around you, neglect what God might be saying to you in it and try to get it over with as soon as possible. Ineffectual suffering is moaning instead of mourning.

But there is a suffering that is effectual. It is when you dignify the trial. This means you see the trial as being from God Himself. What God does is worth dignifying. You even thank Him for it—later if not now. The best thing you can do when in the midst of trial is to say, "God, I know You have allowed this trial for a reason. I pray for grace to take this with both hands, so that I will receive the maximum blessing You intend for me in this."

"Blessed are those who mourn" is a promise that is fulfilled to the full when suffering gets its intended result. That is effectual suffering: It takes place when the pain makes a positive difference in you. It is when the testing of our faith develops perseverance, patience or steadfastness. If this happens, then your trial can be regarded as effectual suffering. In other words, the trial worked! It was God's intent that the trial would make a positive difference, so that when it does, it is pleasing to God.

This is why mourning is called blessed. It creates an entry point in your heart through which God might get your attention. When you are happy-go-lucky, carefree and on top of the world, you are difficult to reach. God is not likely to get your attention when all is sweet and smooth for you, letting you have everything you want. We all mellow a bit when we get what we want, but that is not a real change of our ways. However, when

God allows that which produces mourning, just maybe, we will fall to our knees and seek His face. And learn from Him. That is the way it works. That is why mourning is a blessing.

As I said, I went for years and did not learn. I moaned. What about you? Are you in a trial right now? Could it be that God is giving you the tap on the shoulder through a very negative circumstance to get your attention? If so, would you not thank Him for this? The reason that James said we should regard testing as "pure joy" is because it could turn out to be the best thing that ever happened to us. I can testify that I have lived long enough to appreciate every single trial I have ever had. Not only that, but those trials I regarded as "the worst" at the time, I later thanked God as being the best thing that ever happened to me!

When James said "consider it" pure joy (James 1:2) ("count it," KJV), he uses the exact same word Paul uses in Romans 4:5—that our faith is "credited" ("counted," KJV; "reckoned," RSV) as righteousness. It is imputed—put to our credit as though we were actually righteous. As I said above, we may not feel righteous—and others may not see us as righteous—but God does.

So, too, with a trial. We count it pure joy; we impute pure joy to it. Why? Because (1) God tells us to, and (2) eventually we will see how true it was! I guarantee it. It does not mean that you feel joy. You only consider it joy. What you initially despise, you eventually treasure. So James says to us: Treasure it now! Count it joy—now.

This is the meaning of Jesus' words, "Blessed are those who mourn." They are under an anointing of the Spirit through which they will grow, develop patience, perseverance and steadfastness—and will look back on the trial with utter fondness. So, if we dignify it while it is going on, the angels say, "Yes!"

James says that when we persevere under trial, we have stood the test—and we will receive "the crown of life that God has promised to those who love him" (James 1:12). At the end of every trial, God pronounces a sentence in heaven: either "pass" or "fail." For years I failed. Passing is better! God wants you to pass if you are in a trial—whatever the magnitude—at the moment. You are "blessed" by having it, because it is the gateway to greater blessing.

The Result of Exposed Sin

There is, however, another reason you are blessed through mourning. Mourning is effectual when I see my own sin in the process. How many of the five hundred mourners at Frank Sinatra's funeral do you suppose saw their sin through their weeping? But this is mercifully what happened to me in Kissimmee. In the midst of my disappointment, I saw how foolish and selfish I had been. A trial is designed partly to make you see your sinfulness, which you would not see otherwise.

The purpose of God's allowing one to suffer is to see one's own sin—not another's sin. It does not take the Holy Spirit to see another's sin! But it takes a lot of grace to see your own. The fact is, if you can avoid mourning, you will. If you can avoid suffering, you will. If you can avoid seeing your sin—or that you are in the wrong—you will. If you can avoid saying, "Sorry, I got it wrong," you will. When, therefore, you are able truly to see your own sin, you rise above nature. You do that which has no natural explanation.

When Isaiah could say, "Woe is me—I am undone," it was the Holy Spirit directly working on him. The mourning that is blessed is mourning that enables you to see sin you had not seen in yourself before. It is when you can fully agree with the words of the old spiritual:

> It's not my brother nor my sister but
>   it's me, O Lord,
> Standing in the need of prayer.
> Not the preacher nor the deacon but
>   it's me, O Lord,
> Standing in the need of prayer.
>
> Anonymous

"The Lord disciplines those he loves" (Hebrews 12:6). The word translated "discipline" ("chastening," KJV) comes from a Greek word that means "enforced learning." It is when God teaches you a lesson. One of the greatest lessons to be learned in this world is to discover our sin. The unspiritual person thinks he or she has no sin. "If we say we have no sin, we deceive ourselves, and the truth is not in us" (1 John 1:8, ESV). It requires the Holy Spirit to expose our sin to us.

Mourning is one of God's most common ways to get our attention in order for us to see our sin.

If you ask, "Why is seeing our sin a good thing?" I answer: It will take you down a notch. It will humble you and help you to stop pointing the finger at others. Most of all, you begin to see yourself with objectivity and not with blinders—which is a very good thing, indeed.

The Power of the Spirit and the Power of Suffering

There are actually two ways of seeing our sin. First, by the direct power of the Holy Spirit—as in the case of Isaiah (Isaiah 6:1–5). It is when the Holy Spirit comes to our minds and hearts immediately and directly, not using suffering to achieve conviction of sin. This is what we would all prefer. I know it is what I prefer!

But the second way by which we see our sin is through the power of suffering. John Newton laid his heart bare when he wrote this hymn:

> I asked the Lord that I might grow in
> faith, and love, and every grace,
> Might more of His salvation know, and
> seek more earnestly His face.
>
> 'Twas He who taught me thus to pray,
> and He, I trust, has answered
> prayer;
> But it has been in such a way as almost
> drove me to despair.
>
> I hoped that in some favoured hour at
> once He'd answer my request;
> And by His love's constraining power,
> subdue my sins, and give me rest.
>
> Instead of this, He made me feel the
> hidden evils of my heart,
> And let the angry powers of hell assault
> my soul in every part.
>
> "Lord, why is this?" I trembling cried,
> "Wilt Thou pursue Thy worm to
> death?"
> "'Tis in this way," the Lord replied, "I
> answer prayer for grace and faith."
>
> John Newton (1725–1807)

God got Job's attention through suffering. Job had become self-righteous and defensive. Then one day God showed up out of the storm. Job said: "I am unworthy—how can I reply to you? I put my hand over my mouth" (Job 40:4). "My ears had heard of you but now my eyes have seen you. Therefore I despise myself and repent in dust and ashes" (Job 42:5–6).

There is, then, a difference between the direct power of the Spirit, which produces mourning and reveals our sin, and the power of suffering. God, if He chose, could reveal our sin and create growth in us through the direct and immediate witness of the Holy Spirit, without our suffering at all. But for reasons I will not try to explain, His normal pattern is to do that which creates mourning in us. "In this you greatly rejoice, though now for a little while you may have had to suffer grief in all kinds of trials. These have come so that your faith—of greater worth than gold, which perishes even though refined by fire—may be proved genuine and may result in praise, glory and honor when Jesus Christ is revealed" (1 Peter 1:6–7).

It is not that the Holy Spirit is absent when God chooses the indirect power of suffering. God uses suffering to get our attention. The purpose is to make us better men and women. One of the most mysterious truths of all is found in this verse about Jesus, the Son of God: "Although he was a son, he learned obedience from what he suffered" (Hebrews 5:8).

Two Causes of Suffering

We suffer for two reasons: when we are in the right, and when we are wrong. When we suffer for doing the right thing, it can be a real challenge. "If you are insulted because of the name of Christ, you are blessed, for the Spirit of glory and of God rests on you" (1 Peter 4:14). Joseph refused to go to bed with Potiphar's wife—and was put in prison for it (Genesis 39:7–20). Jesus was without sin, but was condemned to die on a cross. "It is commendable if a man bears up under the pain of unjust suffering because he is conscious of God" (1 Peter 2:19).

So, how does sin come into the picture when we suffer for doing the right thing? It is right then that we naturally feel indignant: "Why could this happen to me? I did the right thing and am no better off for it," one might say. Instead of being rewarded for doing what was right, we get falsely accused! But God lets this sort of thing happen—to test us. Here are relevant Scriptures:

> For it has been granted to you on behalf of Christ not only to believe on him, but also to suffer for him.
> PHILIPPIANS 1:29

> So that no one would be unsettled by these trials. You know quite well that we were destined for them.
> 1 THESSALONIANS 3:3

> I ask you, therefore, not to be discouraged because of my sufferings for you, which are your glory.
> EPHESIANS 3:13

> No discipline seems pleasant at the time, but painful. Later on, however, it produces a harvest of righteousness and peace for those who have been trained by it.
> HEBREWS 12:11

You can count on this: The greater the suffering, the greater the anointing. The more God puts you through, the more you will be used and blessed down the road. This is why Jesus could say, "Blessed are those who mourn." Are you in mourning? Congratulations!

Moreover, it is sometimes true that the greater the anointing, the greater the suffering. In other words, if you are under a great anointing of the Spirit, God ensures that such anointing will not go to your head. He puts you through more suffering. This was Paul's testimony about himself: "To keep me from becoming conceited," says Paul, " . . . there was given me a thorn in my flesh, a messenger of Satan, to torment me" (2 Corinthians 12:7). God uses the devil for His divine purposes in our lives. If God sees that we are likely to take ourselves too seriously, He will combine our anointing with a greater suffering.

But God equally lets us suffer for wrongdoing. I'm sorry, but this is the way it is. However, "It is better, if it is God's will, to suffer for doing good than for doing evil" (1 Peter 3:17). But some of us can expect a slap on the wrist from God—because we deserve it. "If you suffer, it should not be as a murderer or thief or any other kind of criminal, or even as a meddler" (1 Peter 4:15).

God may allow you to do something foolish—and let you pay dearly for it—in order to get your attention. And you will mourn. But it is worth all the pain when you see your sin, admit it, confess it to God and turn from it. When it changes your lifestyle, all that was required to get your attention was worth gold.

The Promise to Those Who Mourn

The mourning that God puts you through isn't for nothing. "They will be comforted." The Greek word is the verbal form of *parakletos*—Jesus' name for the Holy Spirit. It is impossible to translate this Greek word in merely one English word to make sense. Various translations include Comforter (KJV), Counselor (NIV), Helper (ESV), Advocate (NEB).

Parakletos means "one who comes alongside"—taking the place of Jesus. What Jesus was and is, so is also the Holy Spirit: He comes alongside to uphold us. When Jesus promised that mourners "will be comforted," the verb (future tense) of *parakletos* is used. Jesus did not say that they "are" comforted, but rather they "will be comforted." The comfort may come down the road.

But it also suggests the Holy Spirit *will* be present to give us comfort. You can count on this. God knows how much we can bear. "No temptation [trial] has seized you except what is common to man. And God is faithful; he will not let you be tempted beyond what you can bear. But when you are tempted [tested], he will also provide a way out so that you can stand up under it" (1 Corinthians 10:13).

Suffering is for a definite time and a real purpose. Every trial has its own built-in time span. *The trial will end.* While it lasts, we think it will go on forever. Wrong. It will end. God who started it will end it. This is why James said, "Let steadfastness have its full effect, that you may be perfect and complete, lacking in nothing" (James 1:4, ESV). In other words, don't try to rush it—don't try to end it. Let God end it. That way, you will derive the full benefit of the trial. But don't forget: Help is on the way.

The equivalent rendering by Luke says, "Blessed are you who weep now, for you will laugh" (Luke 6:21). Laugh? Yes. Sometimes the Holy Spirit can produce laughter! I've seen it a number of times.

My own wife, Louise, came out of a long depression through the ministry of Rodney Howard-Browne in 1995—through laughter. She reckons that on one occasion she laughed nonstop for 45 minutes. "For the kingdom of God is not a matter of eating and drinking, but of righteousness, peace and joy in the Holy Spirit" (Romans 14:17). "Whoever believes in me, as the Scripture has said, streams of living water will flow from within him" (John 7:38). The Holy Spirit bestows "the oil of gladness instead of mourning" (Isaiah 61:3).

But there is more. The mourning Jesus means in this second beatitude, if the suffering is effectual, leads to an increased anointing. This is why it is more precious than gold. It leads to a greater faith and a greater sense of the presence of God. It leads to intimacy with God. Paul called it being changed "from one degree of glory to another" (2 Corinthians 3:18, ESV).

The greater the anointing, the greater the suffering. The greater the suffering, the greater the anointing. That is why you are blessed when God brings mourning into your life. Don't despise it. Dignify it. It is more precious than gold.

5. Out of the Picture

Blessed are the meek, for they will inherit the earth.

MATTHEW 5:5

Many years ago, Louise and I would often eat in a cafeteria in Fort Lauderdale, Florida, where many of our Christian friends also dined. One day, I noticed a lady going from table to table, and then she came to us. I barely knew her. She wanted me to know that she had spent the previous week visiting people who were housebound, and what a blessing it had been to her.

I commended her for this good work. But she interrupted me to say, "The blessing you get from visiting people like this is in not telling it."

I wasn't sure I had heard her correctly. "Not telling it?" I asked.

"Yes," she replied.

"But you are telling me, aren't you?" I then queried.

"Well, yes," she admitted, "but you are the only one I'm telling."

Somehow I doubted this. The truth is, she was getting her blessing by telling everyone about her ministry to housebound people.

This lady was right to say that the blessing one gets in doing things for needy people is in "not telling it." This is the way one gets solid praise—when only God knows (John 5:44). But she chose to forfeit true joy. She got greater satisfaction in her boasting. She simply could not resist the temptation to talk about her endeavors. She wanted to be sure someone gave her credit for what she did.

But the credit she opted for was the empty praise from people—not God. This was hardly a demonstration of meekness, the subject of this chapter. The story simply shows what a real struggle it is for our human nature not to boast about our noble deeds.

Meekness, however, eschews making sure that people give us credit for our good deeds. There

is something about our fleshly nature that craves attention and praise from people. I used to ask my congregation in London, "How many of you could have tea with Her Majesty the Queen and keep quiet about it?" In truth, the honor of meeting the Queen assumes you get to tell it to your friends!

When I originally preached on this text at Westminster Chapel in May 1998, I remember saying that I felt like a fraud. I feel the same today in writing this chapter. I only promise that it is not entitled, "Humility and How I Attained It."

Meekness is easier described by what it is not rather than what it is. It is the opposite of self-righteousness, arrogance, haughtiness, smugness and defensiveness. Putting it positively, meekness is unpretentiousness, gentleness, sweetness and the grace to be utterly self-effacing. It is also the inner strength to accept criticism without sulking or arguing back. Meekness may be largely a reaction. It is the way we relate to unhappy circumstances and difficult people around us. It is both a verbal and nonverbal reaction to criticism. Verbal: by what we don't say. Nonverbal: by the way we speak physically, including our facial expressions. God hates a haughty look (Proverbs 21:4).

All of the Beatitudes are exemplified in us to the degree the Holy Spirit dwells in us un-grieved, unhindered. We inherit the Kingdom of heaven to the degree the un-grieved Spirit lives in us. For the Kingdom of heaven is the conscious presence of God. The degree to which we experience these Beatitudes will therefore be the degree to which we inherit the Kingdom. The degree to which we are poor in spirit, or fulfill God's purpose in mourning, will be the degree to which we reach meekness. As we have also seen, we must never outgrow these. We must climb the ladder of these excellent virtues—almost certainly in the general order in which Jesus gives them. We retain each virtue while moving on—and we must stay broken and dignify any trial God allows.

It is through dignifying God's trials for us, then, that we begin to edge toward meekness. When James urged that patience, or steadfastness, has its full effect, he meant that dignifying the trial will lead to greater maturity (James 1:4). The book of James is actually James's interpretation of the Sermon on the Mount. Dignifying the trial leads to the maturity God envisages for each of us.

There is, therefore, a logical sequence in these Beatitudes: One leads to the next. The result of seeing our sin, blushing because of it and then repenting, is to become meek. It makes us put our hands on our mouths, as Job experienced (Job 40:4). Seeing our sin leaves us stunned, and the consequence is seeing how unjust it is to be self-righteous and defensive.

Undoubted Achievement

One thing is for certain: Meekness is an achievement of considerable spiritual development. If one is truly meek, it is only because something very wonderful has happened—a sovereign operation of the Holy Spirit. Meekness is really unnatural—that is, it is not a fruit of one's natural temperament. It does not refer to one's natural disposition or tendency to be polite. Many are polite or kind only out of fear—they don't want people to bite their heads off! And yet meekness is not being weak or wishy-washy, nor is it being effeminate.

We are talking about an exceedingly rare quality. Jesus had it (Matthew 11:29). Moses was said to be the meekest man of his day (Numbers 12:3). As with all the virtues of the Beatitudes, there is no natural explanation for meekness. More than any grace we have yet examined, such is the awesome virtue of meekness: It is the polar opposite of what one is by nature. "But, Sir Winston, he is such a modest man," said a member of Parliament to Winston Churchill. "Yes," said Sir Winston, "and he has a lot to be modest about." But being modest is not necessarily meekness.

True meekness, as I said, means that something extraordinary has taken place: The person himself or herself does not realize it! God moved in at some stage and gave the person who began with being poor in spirit a quiet promotion. In such a case, perseverance has finished its work.

Although future beatitudes will demonstrate even more of the power of the Spirit, there is something about meekness that makes it the crown jewel of Christian virtues. Sadly, most of us never get there. Why? We abort the process before it is completed—by complaining, becoming bitter, being pretentious, self-righteous or self-conscious, seeking credit or pointing the finger. The result: Meekness eludes us.

Unconscious Anointing

Meekness is the opposite quality the world applauds. The world applauds the search for power, wealth, glory. Meekness is not the way political elections are won. Have you ever seen a meek politician? Elections are won by telling everyone why you should be elected and saying everything negative you can think of about your opponent. Polls consistently show that an election is won by your opponent having a 35 percent negative rating, not because you have a positive rating. You win by spreading fear regarding your opponent. Meekness would never do that, neither would it proudly boast of one's personal virtues. Meekness will not get you elected to office. Meekness in today's society achieves nothing.

The opposite of meekness is pulling strings to achieve what God already promised you. If you pull the strings, He gets off your case. Joseph got high marks for refusing to sleep with Potiphar's wife, but it was not his finest hour when he said to Pharaoh's cupbearer, "Remember me . . . mention me to Pharaoh and get me out of this prison" (Genesis 40:14). I reckon that God looked down from heaven and said, "Oh, Joseph, I wish you hadn't said that. You are going to need a couple of more years." Although meekness in today's society achieves nothing, with God it achieves everything. Meekness will not pull strings. Those who humble themselves will be exalted—in God's timing (Luke 14:11; 1 Peter 5:6).

And yet meekness is an unconscious anointing. If a person is truly meek, it is because God has brought such people to a higher spiritual level. They are not aware of it themselves. You may be aware of being broken, or of dignifying a trial by not complaining to people or to God. But you will never be aware of being meek.

In this particular beatitude, Jesus describes a virtue that one doesn't feel. And if you think you've got it, you just lost it. It is somewhat like an illustration the great C. H. Spurgeon used: "I looked to Christ and the dove flew in; I looked to the dove and he disappeared." The moment you become conscious of a virtue—or are looking over your shoulder to see what people think of you—any meekness that may have been present evaporates at once. Meekness is entirely an unconscious sense of God.

You may ask: What is the point of having it, then, if you can't feel it or enjoy it? I reply: It is like the eye of a slave that looks to the hand of his master (see Psalm 123). The ancient slave lived for it. He never—ever—took his eye off his master's hand. The slave lived for one thing: to be ready when his master snapped his finger. The slave was unconscious of anything around him. He only looked at his master's hand. We, too, are to do the same thing. "So our eyes look to the LORD our God, till he shows us his mercy" (Psalm 123:2).

In the exact same way, we are required to keep our eyes on Jesus (Hebrews 12:2). We don't want to miss His signal. We don't want to become deaf to His voice. We want to be ready when He beckons for us. The meekness Jesus is talking about will keep us ready for His call (Luke 12:35–36).

Moses

As we observed above, Moses was said to be the meekest man on the earth. The NIV says he was "more humble than anyone else on the face of the earth" (Numbers 12:3). But the word used in Numbers 12:3 in the Septuagint (the Greek translation of the Hebrew Old Testament) is the same Greek word—*praus*—as used in Matthew 5:5. Moses is said to be truly meek. What was it about Moses that earned him that kind of description?

The answer is partly this: Moses interceded in behalf of Israel when they turned against him. He went to God and pleaded in their behalf. God had even made a proposition with Moses: to destroy the Israelites and start all over again with a new nation. Moses said, "No!" In so many words he said, "Lord, You must not destroy them. Your great Name is at stake. What will they say about

You in Egypt? They will say You were not able to deliver Your people. So I say to You: Forgive them" (Numbers 14:12–19).

And God answered Moses' prayer. The psalmist picked up on this event. "So he [God] said he would destroy them—had not Moses, his chosen one, stood in the breach before him to keep his wrath from destroying them" (Psalm 106:23).

I can recall a moment when I was at Westminster Chapel that I might have welcomed God to say, "I will destroy those people who are against you!" It would have been a hard call for me had God offered this. But Moses on his own—without fanfare or calling attention to himself—pleaded for the survival and forgiveness of the very people who opposed him. That is meekness. Asking God to bless your enemy—when you really mean it—is meekness. It is what Jesus did (Luke 23:34).

On one occasion, Moses' face shone with a radiance everyone took notice of. Everybody knew about it but Moses himself. "He was not aware that his face was radiant because he had spoken with the LORD" (Exodus 34:29). When testifying before the Sanhedrin, Stephen's face shone like that of an angel (Acts 6:15). I doubt he himself was aware of it. I do know that, like Moses, he prayed for his enemies. The secret of Stephen's amazing anointing was revealed at the close of his life. While being stoned, he prayed, "Lord, do not hold this sin against them" (Acts 7:59–60). And then he died. What a way to die!

Abraham

Abraham showed meekness when he showed graciousness toward his nephew, Lot. He said to Lot, "Let's not have any quarrelling between you and me, or between your herdsmen and mine, for we are brothers. Is not the whole land before you? Let's part company. If you go to the left, I'll go to the right; if you go to the right, I'll go to the left" (Genesis 13:8–9).

King David

King David showed an amazing meekness at the lowest point in his life. First, he ordered Zadok the priest to return the ark of God back into Jerusalem. Said David: "If I find favor in the LORD's eyes, he will bring me back and let me see it and his dwelling place again. But if he says, 'I am not pleased with you,' then I am ready; let him do to me whatever seems good to him" (2 Samuel 15:25–26).

Second, during the time his son Absalom stole the kingship, and David was in exile, Shimei cursed David, pelting him with stones. Shimei said to David, "Get out, get out, you man of blood, you scoundrel! The LORD has repaid you for all the blood you shed in the household of Saul." David's response was that perhaps the Lord had indeed told Shimei to curse him. In any case, David's hope was that the Lord would see his distress and repay him "with good for the cursing I am receiving today" (2 Samuel 16:7, 12).

Unpretentious Attitude

Have you ever thought of trying to describe Jesus with one word? Other than using various divine attributes to describe Him, I would say the best word is *unpretentiousness*. One could even make a case that this was a major part of His glory. For part of His glory was that He intentionally concealed it. He refused to reveal His total identity to the crowds. He made Himself "nothing" (Philippians 2:7), of "no reputation" (KJV). His demeanor was the opposite of smugness, harshness, hardness, irritability, haughtiness. The last thing He tried to do was to impress people. It is what impresses me most about Jesus. This is why He could describe Himself as "meek" (Matthew 11:29, KJV). He could afford to say it, because that is exactly what He was.

Meekness was not, in fact, an impressive virtue. If anything, it was the opposite of what people would expect of their Messiah. He put out a huge hint when He said He was meek. It sent a signal that would suggest He was not going to be an assertive, charismatic, stunning or military figure who would cause people to be impressed. He was the opposite. He was like a "root out of dry ground," having no beauty or majesty to attract us to Him, nothing in His appearance "that we should desire him" (Isaiah 53:2). This is the characteristic of Jesus I myself find most challenging. When I think of being more and more like Jesus, I want to be more and more unpretentious—and approachable.

Yes. It was His approachability that was so amazing. What was it that would cause a leper—the most rejected kind of person in those days—to feel he could go right up to Jesus, then kneel before Him and expect to be accepted? That is what happened. Immediately after the Sermon on the Mount was over and the crowds went their way, a leper somehow knew that Jesus would not reject him. He said, "Lord, if you are willing, you can make me clean." Jesus replied, "I am willing," and cured him on the spot (Matthew 8:2–3).

I wish I could mediate the kind of impression Jesus gave—that anybody could approach me and feel accepted. "The common people heard him gladly" (Mark 12:37, KJV). The religious authorities and the learned rejected Him. But not so the ordinary people.

Jesus was given the unhindered, un-grieved Sprit without measure (John 4:34). He consequently had total control of His tongue (James 3:1–12), His temperament (James 3:13–18), even His thoughts (James 4:1–4). He enjoyed perfect liberty. The greatest liberty is having nothing to prove. Jesus felt no need to prove anything or prove Himself.

When the Holy Spirit controls my ego, it will mean that my ego is out of the picture. It is when my ego gets into the picture that I draw attention to myself. When the ego is out of the picture, there is not only no need to be intrusive—the opposite is the case. It is like a spy with the CIA or MI6: The spy is never seen. He not only stays out of the picture, he makes sure he is never photographed. It is like a ghostwriter for a famous person. The ghostwriter forfeits his own style to appear to write exactly as the famous author. When Ronald Reagan occupied the Oval Office, there was a plaque on his desk that read: "There is no limit to how far a person can go as long as he does not care who gets the credit for it."

Meekness will keep one's ego out of the picture, disdaining any credit. It is allowing other people to put the searchlight on me instead of doing it myself. Furthermore, we prefer to condemn ourselves rather than to allow someone else to condemn us. As John Stott put it, "I am quite happy to recite the Gospel Confession in church and call myself a miserable sinner," but "let somebody else come up to me after church and call me a miserable sinner, I want to punch him on the nose."

Ultimate Accomplishment

The meek shall "inherit the earth." How about that for an accomplishment? You get the whole world thrown in. What an inheritance! The whole Sermon on the Mount could be summed up: "Wow, we are to achieve an inheritance!"

This is what it means to have the Kingdom. To inherit the Kingdom is to inherit all that belongs to Jesus. His inheritance is the whole world. We are His brothers and sisters "in [Christ]" (Ephesians 1:4), "co-heirs" with Jesus (Romans 8:17). When we take His teachings seriously and apply them—which means to be meek—we inherit the earth. Everything. Not just inheriting wealth. Or a castle. Or becoming a billionaire, like Bill Gates. Or owning an island off Greece. Or to own property in London, like the Duke of Westminster. We get the whole world! It all belongs to God. He gives it all to us—because we are joint heirs with His Son. It is promised to the meek.

The word *inherit* is in the future tense. It means *reward*. "Great is your reward in heaven" (Matthew 5:12). This means two things: (1) an earnest of our inheritance here below—which is the anointing—and (2) enjoying our inheritance above, in heaven. I can't imagine what the latter will be like. Said Paul: "I consider that our present sufferings are not worth comparing with the glory that wil be revealed in us" (Romans 8:18). It will be worth it all when we see Jesus. Life's trials will seem so small when we behold Him.

Counterfeit Meekness

The Uriah Heeps of this world are the caricature of a counterfeit meekness. Those who say, "I am just a humble servant of God," try to impress others with their humility or lowliness. It is their ego in the picture that makes them talk that way. They are starving for recognition, but they get it by feigning humility.

An old song that came out of the South years ago says, "Lord, build me just a cabin in the corner of glory land"—as opposed to having a mansion! People who try to feign meekness do so as a defense mechanism. It is self-protection so people won't dislike them. Counterfeit meekness is motivated by a spirit of fear.

God promising the earth to the truly meek person is—if I may put it this way—God's style. You could call it His sense of humor. His own Son is a root out of dry ground. He appears first to shepherds rather than kings (Luke 2:8). And He ends up dying on a cross—the last place on earth sophisticated people would look in order to see God's power. Jesus was crucified in "weakness" (2 Corinthians 13:4).

Meekness results in the ultimate accomplishment: getting it all, having everything. It is what God can do so easily. He has "cattle on a thousand hills" (Psalm 50:10). It is what God wants to do for each of us. "Do not be afraid, little flock, for your Father has been pleased to give you the kingdom" (Luke 12:32).

It is, however, painful to be meek—to be tamed, controlled, utterly out of the picture. It is not natural to be like this. It is a sign that God somehow managed to get in.

Meekness is its own reward. Achieve this and you're there—you have arrived.

6. A Good Appetite

Blessed are those who hunger and thirst for righteousness, for they will be filled.

MATTHEW 5:6

I vividly recall an incident when I was eight or nine years old, when I spent the night with my Grandma Kendall. I dreaded a test I was going to have at school the next day—I was not prepared. I woke up with a feeling of sickness. I said, "Ma, I am sick—I won't be able to go to school."

"Okay, honey, just stay in bed."

But I protested that I wanted to eat breakfast first! She replied: "If you have a good appetite, there isn't much wrong with you. I'll prepare breakfast while you get dressed for school."

This is true at the spiritual level, too: If you have a hunger and thirst for righteousness, there isn't much wrong with you! Give me any Christian who has an appetite for righteousness, and there isn't much wrong with them. I used to long for a membership at Westminster Chapel who hungered and thirsted for righteousness. There isn't much wrong with a congregation like that!

"As the deer pants for streams of water, so my soul pants for you, O God. My soul thirsts for God, for the living God. When can I go and meet with God?" (Psalm 42:1–2). The psalmist had a good appetite. "My soul yearns, even faints, for the courts of the LORD; my heart and my flesh cry out for the living God" (Psalm 84:2). David prayed, "O God, you are my God, earnestly I seek you; my soul thirsts for you, my body longs for you, in a dry and weary land where there is no water" (Psalm 63:1). He longed for God. He wanted all of God he could get.

A. W. Tozer used to say you could have as much of God as you want. When I first heard that, I disagreed with him. But then I realized it is not merely feeling that way for a brief moment. It is when you feel this all the time—and are willing to do *anything* to have more of God.

What Jesus is talking about in this beatitude is that you are blessed if you have such an appetite that you can't live without what you are hungry for. The Greek word for *thirst* refers to what you can't live without. You've got to have it, or you can't live. He is not merely talking about being "peckish," as the Brits would say when they want a bite to eat. He is talking about desperation for food!

These words indicate what you feel at the natural level: starving. And what can be felt at the natural level can be felt by a longing of the soul. Imagine this: being hungry and thirsty for righteousness—not for roast beef and Yorkshire pudding or chicken tikka masala! Jesus puts before us the idea of having a craving for what defies a natural explanation. There is a natural explanation for wanting to eat when you are hungry: We are made that way. But when you have a consistent desire for the things that please God and honor Him, you have crossed over into the supernatural. There is no natural explanation for that.

The question is, whatever would bring a person to feel this way? When I turn on the television, I find that the natural appetite of people is for gourmet food, illicit sex and vain ambition. All the ads play into our natural desires. They put before us the most beautiful food, the most gorgeous people and the appeal to our greed, to get ahead and earn more money. But appealing to one's desire for godliness? Hardly.

Imagine someone taking a poll in New York's Times Square or London's Victoria. The question is put to passersby: "Do you have a hunger and a thirst for righteousness?" They would look at you and say, "Is this some sort of a joke?"

We are therefore talking about polar opposites: the desire for what comes naturally without any aid of the Holy Spirit, and what comes to us only by the entrance of the Holy Spirit in our lives. This is why the angels say, "Congratulations!" if one has an appetite for godly things.

A Great Awakening

What would cause a craving for true righteousness? Answer: a great awakening in the soul. It is the result of God getting one's attention.

It often requires something rather major for this to happen. It can be something negative or positive. Negative: when God shakes you to get your attention—as through sickness, accident, financial reverse, withholding of vindication or breakdown of friendships or even marriage. Positive: when through the Word and Holy Spirit one accepts what is taught from the Bible. It is good when the latter happens. Yet with most of us it takes something external to us—like the great fish that swallowed up Jonah—to bring us to seek God (Jonah 1 and 2).

The phrase "Great Awakening" is usually applied to the eighteenth-century move of the Holy Spirit in New England, from 1725 to 1750. During this time Jonathan Edwards observed that the whole town in which he preached was filled with talk about God. Can you imagine such a phenomenon? It boggles the mind. Imagine walking in Times Square and overhearing conversations about God. What would it be like if you walked down your town's main street and heard people talking about getting right with God and honoring Him? And yet—believe it or not—I predict this! Absolutely. It is coming. I believe soon. It is when the appetite for the world is replaced by a longing for God—and more of Him!

The high-water mark of the Great Awakening was probably in July 1741, when Jonathan Edwards (1703–1758) took his text from Deuteronomy 32:35 (KJV), "Their foot shall slide in due time." The Spirit of God came down in unexpected power during Edwards's sermon. It wasn't Edwards's oratory. He was a boring speaker who read his message. But when he finished speaking, strong men were seen holding on to church pews to keep from sliding into hell, and holding on to tree trunks outside the church to keep from sliding into hell. When the sermon went to print, it was given the title "Sinners in the Hands of an Angry God," a sermon that lives in infamy and glory. This sermon is what originally gave America its Bible Belt and shaped its conscience for decades. It was augmented by what church historians call America's "Second Great Awakening," namely, the Cane Ridge Revival in my own state of Kentucky in 1801.

What caused this great awakening in one's soul? Answer: Jesus' statement about meekness. You will recall that there is a logical sequence in the Beatitudes. One anointing triggers another. Brokenness leads to a mourning for sin. It leaves one with a stopped mouth. Meekness follows when one is stunned by the realization he or she has been defensive. Being defensive is when we say, "I'm not all that bad." If you want to know what you're really like, ask four or five people to give an assessment of how they perceive you. You will very possibly get somewhat of an index as to what you are really like. Therefore, a good test of whether you are meek is to ask people to criticize you—and really do it—and then take it all without the slightest defensiveness.

When you can accept criticism without being defensive, you are beginning to get free. Meekness is to admit, "I really am that bad!" If you say to me, "R. T., I think you have a problem with self-righteousness," and I reply, "I used to have a problem like that, but not anymore," it shows I am still self-righteous! So, too, with self-pity, jealousy and all the sins. When we deny having them, it shows how blind we are to ourselves. Meekness begins to emerge when we stop being so defensive.

But that isn't the end of the story. When I look more closely at what meekness really and truly is, I realize I'm not very meek at all—I am really quite the opposite. But one positive result emerged: When you realize that meekness is what you really and truly want and you long for it, it is a good sign. That is when hunger and thirst begins to show up. It all began with a great awakening in the soul.

A Godly Affection

Hungering and thirsting for righteousness is a godly affection. One thinks of Jonathan Edwards's book *Religious Affections*, which refers to spiritual manifestations and the desires of the heart.

Paul said, "Since, then, you have been raised with Christ, set your hearts on things above, where Christ is seated at the right hand of God. Set your minds on things above, not on earthly things" (Colossians 3:1–2).

The irony of godly desire is that it seems so natural. You want it so much that you can hardly tell it from true physical desire. It begins as something spiritual, yes—but when the desire persists and you keep praying for it, it is all you can think about. It begins to consume you. You think about it day and night. That is what the psalmist was feeling.

How about you? Have you known this kind of desire? I will never forget something Jackie Pullinger said to me: "To the spiritual person, the supernatural seems natural." That is profound. It is so true. One is not conscious of doing anything unusual—whether it be praying, exercising the gifts of the Spirit or doing what others marvel at. You will recall that Moses did not know there was a shine of the glory of God on his face. It reminds me of the saintly old lady back in Springfield, Illinois, who helped to mentor my own mother. At the age of ninety, she said, "I have been serving the Lord for so long now that I can hardly tell the difference between a blessing and a trial."

So, too, with hungering and thirsting after righteousness: It seems so natural after a while. It is not something you work up—it is simply there. But it is a glorious anointing, which means two things: (1) It is not only a sign you are a Christian, but (2) it also shows you are dwelling in the realm of the Holy Spirit.

Do not forget that the Kingdom of heaven is the realm of the unhindered, un-grieved Spirit of God. When the Spirit is not hindered, it follows that one lives for the things that please God. You love the will of God more than anything in the world. Jonathan Edwards commented that the devil cannot produce in us a love for the glory of God. He may counterfeit it, but he cannot produce it.

What This Righteousness Is Not

When Jesus talks about hungering and thirsting after righteousness, what exactly is He talking about? What is the kind of righteousness Jesus has

in mind when He says we are blessed to hunger and thirst after it?

First, it is not imputed righteousness He has in mind in Matthew 5:6. Jesus certainly believed in imputed righteousness. It is at the heart of the New Testament teaching of justification by faith alone. It is a wonderful teaching. It is the heart of orthodox Christian teaching. It means this: The moment you transfer the hope you had in your good works to the blood of Jesus, you are given a righteousness. It is a credited righteousness—imputed. That means it is put to your credit as though you really were as righteous as Jesus. It is the way God looks at you. It is forensic; it is legal. It is what assures that you have a home in heaven when you die. You are saved by His righteousness, not your own. This is a most important teaching. Jesus assumes it in the Sermon on the Mount.

But in this particular beatitude, Jesus is not talking about hungering and thirsting for justification by faith. If anything, imputed righteousness was implied in the first beatitude—when we are broken, being poor in spirit. The gift of imputed righteousness already took place in this pyramid of virtues, beginning with being broken. One assumes justification by faith in being poor in spirit, when we have nothing to give in exchange to God.

Neither is Jesus talking about moral justice when He says, "Blessed are those who hunger and thirst for righteousness." He is not saying blessed are those who seek after moral justice, although that would be true had He said it. God is pleased with those who seek after moral justice. Make no mistake about that. We should long to see social justices in our land put right. One longs for political justice. One longs for the eradication of racism, poverty, abortions, mistreatment of hurting people, unfair verdicts in the courts, laws that approve of unrighteousness. I have good friends who have made this their chief interest and calling. I do not criticize them—they must be true to their calling. But in Matthew 5:6, Jesus is not specifically referring to moral justice or social righteousness, however valid the cause may be.

Not only that, Jesus is not even talking about morality or outward righteousness. The righteousness Jesus has in mind is certainly not separated from an external righteousness. In some ways it borders on it. But He is not in the main talking about Christian duties, such as tithing (which I believe in). I am not sure that one would have a hunger for this kind of righteousness. You probably don't "yearn" for doing certain things that God requires you to do. It comes by an act of the will. You make a choice to tithe, to be faithful to your church or pastor's message, to visit the sick or to help the poor. These things, like social justice, are valid and highly important—and they certainly parallel what Jesus is putting to us. But it does not touch the heart of what Jesus means by righteousness in Matthew 5:6.

There is more: He is not talking about personal vindication. You may have been falsely accused. What has happened to you can only be called a gross injustice (if we knew your story). You long to have your name cleared. Your very body cries out for it. I understand this. I would know what you mean. But it is not what Jesus means when He says that we are to be congratulated if we long for vindication. I'm sorry, but that is not the meaning of Matthew 5:6.

What This Righteousness Is

What, then, is Jesus talking about? It is not an imputed righteousness but an *implanted* righteousness. James, whose brief epistle, as we have seen already, is his interpretation of the Sermon on the Mount, said: "Get rid of all moral filth and the evil that is so prevalent and humbly accept the word planted in you" (James 1:21). It is an internal righteousness. It is born in the heart.

Once this righteousness is implanted in us, the outward will inevitably follow. The implanted word creates this godly affection. It is seeing what you want, having seen what you lack—e.g., meekness. It is internal. It is infused and imparted by the Holy Spirit. When you see what you lack, it makes you yearn for a righteousness that exceeds that of the Moral Law.

It is an unseen righteousness. The righteousness of the Pharisees was not only seen, they made sure you saw it! Jesus warned, "Be careful not to do your 'acts of righteousness' before men, to be seen by them. If you do, you will have no reward from your Father in heaven" (Matthew 6:1). Indeed, Pharisees—hypocrites (Jesus called them)—announce their good deeds (as in giving to the poor) "with trumpets . . . in the synagogues

and on the streets, to be honored by men" (Matthew 6:2). "Everything they do is done for men to see," said Jesus (Matthew 23:5).

The righteousness that Jesus has in mind is an *unpretentious* righteousness. There is an absence of smugness, arrogance and haughtiness. As we saw earlier, unpretentiousness was a characteristic of Jesus. There is no putting on airs, no effort to impress, no looking over the shoulder to see who is noticing. It was a quality of Jesus that sent a signal to the leper that he would not be rejected. I wonder how many of us send this signal. When we are walking to church with our big Bibles, do we attract hurting people to us? It is a sobering question you and I need to face.

Moreover, Jesus is speaking of an *unconscious* righteousness. The righteousness of the legalist is always a conscious righteousness. "God, I thank you that I am not like other men—robbers, evildoers, adulterers . . . I fast twice a week and give a tenth of all I get" (Luke 18:11–12). The Pharisee made sure his left hand knew what his right hand was doing (Matthew 6:3). But there is an unconscious righteousness—when one feels utterly unworthy, even vile before God. The greatest saints have always seen themselves as the greatest sinners. But the world is not worthy of such, said the writer in Hebrews 11:38.

And yet it is also an *unappreciated* righteousness. It is not respected at the time. If anything, such a righteousness is disdained. It is seen in Jesus' word to the Pharisees (which revealed why the Jews completely missed their Messiah): "How can you believe if you accept praise from one another, yet make no effort to obtain the praise that comes from the only God?" (John 5:44). What kept the Pharisees blind to Jesus' glory was their insatiable need for one another's approval.

When you live utterly for the approval of God only, it is not likely to be appreciated by anybody. But that is the marvel of it! It is appreciated only by God. Jesus blesses those who are hungry for a righteousness that will be unappreciated in this life. Don't expect people to clap their hands for you. The most righteous person who ever lived was hated, with an incalculable hatred. "If the world hates you, keep in mind that it hated me first," said Jesus (John 15:18).

And yet one has a yearning, a longing for this righteousness. There is a fire in one's bones. It is when your heart is stirred, filled with an intense desire to please the Father. It is when your heart aches for the meekness and holiness of Jesus. It is when one simply wants to know Him. Said Paul: "I want to know Christ and the power of his resurrection and the fellowship of sharing in his sufferings, becoming like him in his death" (Philippians 3:10).

One of my heroes is Robert Murray M'Cheyne (1813–1843), the Scottish minister of Dundee, Scotland. He would pray again and again, "Make me a holy man." A touch of true revival broke out in his church while he was away. Instead of being jealous or threatened by what happened when he was not in his own pulpit, he affirmed it to the hilt. He died at the age of 29.

Six months later, a minister came to Dundee to find out all he could about Robert Murray M'Cheyne. "What was his secret?" he asked an elder in Dundee. "Oh, I can tell you," came the reply. "Come with me."

The elder took the minister to M'Chyene's desk. He then said, "Put your elbows on this desk, and your head in your hands, and let the tears flow." Then the two men went into M'Cheyne's pulpit. The elder repeated the same thing. "Put your elbows on the pulpit, and your head in your hands, and let the tears flow."

This is hungering and thirsting after righteousness. "Those who sow in tears will reap with songs of joy" (Psalm 126:5).

Guaranteed Achievement

Since God has promised that we will be "filled" if we hunger and thirst after this internal, unseen righteousness, we may reasonably assume that He did not create this yearning for nothing. He does not give us this hunger to mock us. He has put the desire there. "God cannot be mocked. A man reaps what he sows. The one who sows to please his sinful nature, from that nature will reap destruction; the one who sows to please the Spirit, from the Spirit will reap eternal life. Let us not become weary in doing good, for at the proper time we will reap a harvest if we do not give up" (Galatians 6:7–9).

God is gracious to give to the soul what that soul longs for. Another assumption is, you will eat when you are hungry! So when the food comes your way, take it by walking in all the light He gives you. Seek God with all your heart. "I have not departed from the commands of his lips; I have treasured the words of his mouth more than my daily bread" (Job 23:12).

This means you walk in all the light God gives you. God will test you. He did me. It means obeying the impulses of the Spirit. A lady once asked Arthur Blessitt: "How is it that God seems to speak to you but doesn't speak to me?" Arthur replied: "Have you ever had an impulse to talk to someone you don't know about Jesus?" She responded, "As a matter of fact, I have." Arthur looked at her and said, "Start obeying those impulses, and His voice will become clearer and clearer."

I remember many years ago feeling an impulse that I should get up at 5 A.M. to pray for two hours. I said, "Lord, if this is from You, please wake me up at 5 A.M." I forgot about it, but that night, after being in a deep sleep, lo and behold, I woke up with my mind as clear as a bell. I looked at the clock. It was dead-on at 5 A.M. So I got up to pray and prayed for two hours.

I felt I should do it again. So I said, "Lord, wake me up again at 5 A.M." The next morning I slept until 7:30 A.M. God did it once. But He expects us to follow through if we are truly seeking His face. "You will seek me and find me when you seek me with all your heart" (Jeremiah 29:13).

Question: How much do you read your Bible? How much do you pray? Are you walking in all the light God gives you? For me, this meant taking my friend Josif Tson's words seriously: "R. T., you must totally forgive them, for until you totally forgive them you will be in chains. Release them and you will be released."

There are questions you and I can think of about Matthew 5:6 that Jesus does not answer. He does not specifically say what we will be filled with. He does not say how we will be filled. Or where it will happen. Or when it will come. But we can assume that to some degree, we will be filled with the righteousness we are hungry for. What we were hungry for, we will be filled with.

But since it is an unseen and unconscious righteousness, you may not ever know if Jesus' words have been fulfilled in you. That is the paradox in this beatitude: It follows that we will not be aware that we have been filled. At the natural level, we know when we are full. But at the spiritual level, this anointing only triggers a further anointing. The more we eat, the hungrier we are. The more we drink, the thirstier we are. At the natural level, sadly, people do die of hunger and thirst. But we have a guarantee that we will be filled.

I have to say also that being filled with righteousness results in a further conviction of sin. "If we claim to be without sin, we deceive ourselves and the truth is not in us" (1 John 1:8). Being filled with Christ's righteousness will result in a greater sensitivity of the Holy Spirit, and also a greater awareness of how we may grieve the Holy Spirit. It is being changed from glory to glory by His Spirit (2 Corinthians 3:18).

Where are we likely to be filled? Answer: anywhere. D. L. Moody tells about walking in Brooklyn, New York, when the Spirit of God came on him. It was so powerful, said Moody, that "I asked God to stay His hand." He thought he would die!

When are you likely to be filled? Anytime.

However—and this is very important—we are not talking about an instantaneous, one-off experience with God. He may show up that way. But the filling is more likely to be an unconscious, unseen and unappreciated righteousness that results in a never-ending pursuit of God. We eat because we are hungry. We walk in the light because we see a new sense of duty. This can come anywhere—in church or when you are alone. And the quest for more of God may be keener when you are alone, for all I know.

Just know it is God's promise. You will be filled. It is the most God-honoring pursuit I can think of: to please Him. Enoch had this testimony before he was translated to heaven—that he pleased God (Hebrews 11:5). If we have an appetite like that—to please God—chances are that such a good appetite means there isn't too much wrong with us.

7. True Godliness

Blessed are the merciful, for they will be shown mercy.

MATTHEW 5:7

I have an inner conflict when it comes to the word *godly*. I am sure it is traceable to my own religious background, in which "godly" people were probably not so godly after all.

For one thing, godliness in my old church was inseparable from your external appearance—as in how you dress. Women did not wear makeup, were forbidden to cut their hair, could not wear any jewelry, and my mother did not even wear a wedding ring (the prohibition was wearing gold—1 Timothy 2:9). I was not allowed to go to the local cinema, could not go to a circus when it came to town, neither could I go to school dances. It was a big deal when my dad finally bought a television set. My understanding of godliness, then, was colored by this kind of Christianity as I grew up.

It wasn't all bad. My dad taught me to pray, as I reveal in my book *Did You Think to Pray?* My mother prayed for me every morning before I went to school, such being precious memories. They were faithful church members. My mother was the church organist; my dad was on the church board. We always had visiting preachers in our home. The conversations no doubt shaped my thinking to a large degree. I was in church virtually every time the door was opened. The truth is, I have no complaints. I do not feel impoverished when I consider the pluses and minuses. I turned out pretty well.

But the term *godly* still troubles me. This is partly because "godly" people have not always blessed me very much. I'm sorry, but my main enemies have been the "godly." They can be some of the meanest, hard, unloving and dull people on the face of the earth. Not all. But a lot.

So I have kept the word *godliness* in the title of this chapter, but I want to call it "True Godliness."

And I hope to be fair in doing so. For Matthew 5:7 describes true godliness—that is, being like God Himself: merciful.

I referred to A. W. Tozer in the previous chapter, that he said we can have as much of God as we want. I believe him. I think of Josif Tson's question to me, "How far are you prepared to go in your commitment to Christ?"

Matthew 5:7—"Blessed are the merciful"—actually presents us with the first major test in the Beatitudes. The previous verse brings us to the crossroads, for we must ask the question, "Are we truly hungering and thirsting after righteousness?" Jesus is telling us in the present verse that there is a way of finding out. Are you hungry for righteousness? How hungry? Are you thirsty for righteousness? How thirsty?

We have referred to the logical sequence of the Beatitudes. There is a reason that this particular beatitude is precisely here. Because if you are truly hungering and thirsting after righteousness, you will be tested. When you find yourself saying to God, "I will do anything You ask me to do," God says, "Really?" So He tests us. And the way He tests us is often when a person has hurt you, has let you down, has said unpleasant things about you and has been keen to blacken your reputation. What do you do when this happens?

You have two choices: to follow nature and seek revenge, or to cross over into the supernatural and show mercy.

So, dear reader, the next time you find yourself saying, "Have Your way with me, Lord," or "I will do anything You ask me to do because I am so eager to inherit the Kingdom," God will test you. Instead of rewarding you immediately with His presence, do not be surprised if He tests how earnest you are in your desire to inherit the Kingdom.

Guilt or Graciousness?

The question is, how do you make people feel who have let you down and hurt you deeply? Do you make them feel guilty—or do you show graciousness? This is the issue in the present chapter. When you show graciousness toward those who have been unkind or unfair, you show how much you want of God. If you seek to punish them or make them feel guilty, you show you don't want God as much as you thought you did.

We are not talking about having a stiff upper lip, as the Brits are so famous for. There is an old axiom that characterizes Special Air Forces of the military in Britain: "Never complain, never explain, never apologize." People who master this art are able to conceal their feelings to others. They overlook faults and never let on if they are hurt. They can show kindness and a smile that dazzles me.

I admire this quality, although I personally never achieved it during my 28 years of living in Britain. I'm afraid, sadly, that my emotions show all too transparently when I get my feelings hurt. But the ability to conceal your feelings is not the same thing as true godliness. True godliness is when you demonstrate graciousness even though it hurts. That is what Jesus means by being "merciful."

True graciousness—showing mercy—is letting people off the hook. It is doing what you can do to see they never get caught for what they did to you. You don't even tell people what they did to you. True graciousness is not reminding people of their faults, their failures or their past. It is not even letting on as if you know what they have done. It is letting them "save face," to use a familiar expression (covering for them, protecting their fragile egos). It is giving them every break, refusing to throw the book at them, refusing to point the finger at them—even at those who annoy you. Instead of giving them a guilt trip, then, for what they did, you set them free. That is being merciful because it is the way God is.

The Greek word for "mercy" is *eleos,* the opposite of *orgee* (wrath) or even *dikee* (justice, or righteousness). In Greek thought, *eleos* was seen as an emotion. The Stoics regarded *eleos* as a sickness, something unworthy of a sage. But in the New Testament, *eleos* is a gracious action, not merely an emotion. There is an equivalent word, *oiktirmones,* which means "pity" or heartfelt sympathy. It is used in Luke 6:36: "Be merciful, just as your Father is merciful."

In a word: Being godly is not giving justice (what they deserve) but mercy (what they don't deserve). And so grace is giving people what they don't deserve: favor. And mercy is not giving what they do deserve: justice. Paul could say, "I was shown mercy" (1 Timothy 1:13). Mercy triumphs over justice (James 2:13). So when you show mercy, you are being truly godly.

I don't mean to be unfair, but I fear this is a trait not seen often enough among the "godly." "Godly" people can sometimes seem so mean, legalistic, harsh—loving to play the game "Gotcha!"

Formidable Breakthrough

Recalling the logical sequence in the Beatitudes, we have already observed the reason Matthew 5:7 is listed next in the sequence: to test us in order to see how much of God we truly want. It comes as a surprise. None of us would be ready for this had Jesus put this beatitude first on the list. He reaches us where we are, leading us step by step, beginning with brokenness. He takes us through dignifying the trial, meekness and then hungering and thirsting after righteousness. But when you and I are enabled truly to show mercy, it means a formidable breakthrough in our Christian walk.

Take, for example, those who have been deeply hurt. Perhaps they were abused as a child. Let us say they were rejected by a parent or an authority figure. Perhaps they were lied about. They lost a job unfairly. They were betrayed. Maybe their spouse was unfaithful. Or possibly a close friend turned against them. People like this, following nature, long for the day when they get justice. I doubt not that Joseph dreamed of the day he could throw the book at those brothers who were so cruel. But when the day came that he might have thrown the book at them, he broke down and wept—and showed mercy to them. "Come close to me," he said to them, wanting to love on them (Genesis 45:4).

What a breakthrough it was for Joseph when he totally forgave his brothers. It defies a natural explanation. The most natural thing in the world is to want vengeance—and to see your enemy punished. The most unnatural—I would call it supernatural—thing in the world is when you show mercy and totally forgive the one who has hurt you.

An Act of the Will

Total forgiveness is a choice we have to make. When Josif Tson said to me, "R. T., you must totally forgive them" (a word that changed my life), it was up to me whether or not to do it. It is an act of the will. I made a choice, the wisest decision I made since my conversion.

So you, too, must make a choice. Instead of throwing the book at them, you let them off the hook and kiss vindication good-bye. You accept not only that they will not get caught, you welcome the knowledge that they will get away with what they did. Yes—welcome it! After all, is not that the way God was with you? You could have got caught, but you weren't! God was merciful to you. He now says: "Be that way if you want to inherit My Kingdom."

Like Joseph, you never tell people what you know about them. Joseph shielded them, protected them, made sure no Egyptian would ever find out what those brothers had done to him 22 years before. He would not let them feel nervous, although they were already scared to death. He wanted them to forgive themselves. "Do not be distressed and do not be angry with yourselves," he said to them. And as for letting them save face, Joseph said, "It was not you who sent me here, but God" (Genesis 45:4–8). He protected them from their darkest secret, not even allowing them to tell their father, Jacob, what they had done (Genesis 45:9–11).

This is why Joseph could be trusted with greatness. He was given a lofty position, being made the prime minister of Egypt. He could not have known that God earmarked this for him from the beginning. But God waited until Joseph forgave his brothers before he was exalted.

He will do that for you, too. There is something you can do that nobody else can do as well as you can. You may say, "But nobody knows about me." I reply: God will find you. He knows your address. He has been preparing you, too, for a special work. But you will almost certainly not know what He has in store for you until you, like Joseph, totally forgive those who have hurt you.

The greatest breakthrough you will ever have is to tear up that record of wrongs. Ronald Reagan said in Berlin years ago, "Mr. Gorbachev, tear down that wall." I say to you: Tear up that record of wrongs. Love keeps no record of wrongs (1 Corinthians 13:5).

The Father's Blessing

When you show mercy, the angels say, "Congratulations! You've been graduated to a higher spiritual level." When you show mercy, not anger or justice, you enter into a new kind of relationship with God. You enter into the Father's blessing. It is like hearing the words, "Come, you who are blessed by my Father; take your inheritance" (Matthew 25:34). It is when you know you are pleasing the Father. It is what brings a real fellowship with the Father (1 John 1:5, 7) and a new intimacy with the Holy Spirit.

The reason for this: You are being merciful like your Father is merciful (Luke 6:36). You are passing the Father's blessing to others. When He calls you "blessed" it is because He has given this to you. Your being merciful means you are passing this blessing to others. You treat others as He treated you. You know the feeling when God didn't throw the book at you!

We call it the Golden Rule: "Do to others as you would have them do to you" (Luke 6:31). We all know full well how we would prefer to be treated. Everyone you meet prefers to be treated with kindness. The beggar, the one who is struggling, the person hurt by racial prejudice, the person who has a low IQ, the person without a job—they all know the feeling when they have the finger pointed at them and when they are shown kindness. The Golden Rule means that we do not wait for others to treat us with kindness—we do it first. If you wait for others to treat you this way, you may wait a long time!

It is like the marital relationship. The husband is told to love his wife. The wife is told to submit to the husband (Ephesians 5:22–25). If the husband says, "I will love her when she submits," or the wife says, "I will submit when he loves me," the nightmare marriage emerges. But if each will do his or her duty—showing mercy, the Golden Rule—peace emerges. Don't wait for your spouse to get it right. You begin—now. This is true godliness.

Two Kinds of Mercy

When Jesus says, "Blessed are the merciful," there are two kinds of mercy—and both are relevant to Matthew 5:7.

First, there is affectionate mercy. It is when you feel affection toward the person. When Joseph said to his brothers, "Come close to me" (Genesis 45:4), he was feeling genuine affection toward them. When you feel affectionate toward people who had once been unkind to you, they will probably feel it when you are near them. That is one of the differences between the "stiff upper lip"—which may leave you cold—and the genuine love that emanates from someone.

There is, however, another kind of mercy: aggressive mercy. You go out of your way, possibly overruling your personal feelings. You do what is required. James talks about looking after orphans and widows in distress (James 1:27). You may not necessarily feel affectionate toward those you are being merciful to—but you do it because it is right to do. It is remembering the "poor man" (James 2:6, ESV). You are carrying out a Christian duty. "If anyone has material possessions and sees his brother in need but has no pity on him, how can the love of God be in him?" (1 John 3:17). The "pity," however, is not always an affectionate feeling but a following through with what God tells us to do. And yet you "get right into their situation," said Calvin, as in the case of the Good Samaritan (Luke 10:33). You must also do this with a person overtaken with a sin (Galatians 6:1). "Anyone, then, who knows the good he ought to do and doesn't do it, sins" (James 4:17).

The Promise to the Merciful

Why does Jesus add the words, "they will be shown mercy"? First, because it is true! The mercy you show will follow you.

It is an amazing thing to me, every time I think about it: how God appeals to our self-interest to get us to do the right thing! Jesus did not have to promise mercy to those who are merciful, but God does this all the time. "Give, and it will be given to you" (Luke 6:38). So, in this beatitude, Jesus motivates us to show mercy by the promise that we, too, will be shown mercy.

God remembers. He notices what we do. He makes a note in His book. It is like God waking up King Xerxes in the middle of the night and making him see the good things Mordecai had done for him (Esther 6). "God is not unjust; he will not forget your work and the love you have shown him as you have helped his people and continue to help them" (Hebrews 6:10).

A second reason, then, that Jesus adds this promise is indeed to motivate us to show mercy! God stoops to where we are, even appealing to our self-interest. He has always been like this, however. Does this surprise you? And yet God is like that, doing what it may take in order to motivate us to do the right thing.

In the equivalent sermon, Jesus says, "Love your enemies, do good to them, and lend to them without expecting to get anything back. Then your reward will be great, and you will be sons of the Most High, because he is kind to the ungrateful and wicked. Be merciful, just as your Father is merciful" (Luke 6:35–36). If you ask me, this is good enough reason to pray for those who hurt you, to turn the cheek, to give to those who ask, to let people take advantage of you—and, indeed, reason enough for being kind to those who are ungrateful.

True Godliness

The way Jesus is asking that we be is the way God Himself already is. Godliness is being like God. Godliness to some, sadly, is keeping outward morality or showing external appearances and also by what they don't do. True godliness, then, is manifesting the mercy to others that God shows to us. God sent His Son into the world. Why? To show mercy and to forgive us. Moreover, God is doing that all the time with all of us. Surely goodness and mercy shall follow us all the days of our lives (Psalm 23:6).

It is the hardest thing in the world to do. And yet the irony is, it is the fairest thing in the world to do. Not to show mercy is to be self-righteous and ungrateful. But God gives us a pragmatic reason for being merciful. It works! We will be shown mercy down the road. Count on it! God will see to it.

8. Seeing the Glory

Blessed are the pure in heart, for they will see God.

MATTHEW 5:8

When I was a teenager, I sang in the King David Quartet in Ashland, Kentucky. We were actually on the radio every Tuesday evening—on station WIRO in Ironton, Ohio, across the river from Ashland. My pastor would give a sermon and we would sing.

On one such occasion, he worked through the Beatitudes. But when he came to Matthew 5:8 he took a long time with it. He said that "a Nazarene preacher can spend a lot of time on this verse," because it was a key verse for their doctrine of entire sanctification. I have never forgotten this, and it has no doubt influenced my understanding of the words, "Blessed are the pure in heart, for they will see God."

I have therefore found this verse threatening. It is partly because I have never felt I truly understood it. But it is also because of my own theological background—to which I have just referred. You will also recall what I said in the previous chapter with regard to the word *godliness*. My old denomination made a big thing of Matthew 5:8, equating it with their view of sanctification. They regarded "heart purity" as synonymous with a heart devoid of any sin or presence of sin. Some (although not all) actually taught a theory of "eradication"—the claim that all "inbred sin" is completely gone when one is sanctified wholly. I will show that this is not what Matthew 5:8 is saying. But what *does* "pure in heart" mean?

Another reason why I find this verse threatening is because, as in previous beatitudes, it suggests something beyond my own experience—unless I am being too hard on myself. But looking at the verse on the surface, does it mean that the heart of a person can be truly pure—and without mixed motives?

"Pure" surely means *pure,* so taken literally it refers to a heart that has no debris—nothing impure, a heart that is without anything wrong or wicked. However, I cannot help but think of Jeremiah's observation, "The heart is deceitful above all things and beyond cure. Who can understand it?" (Jeremiah 17:9). Did Jeremiah merely mean his own heart, or that of all of us? I have thought the latter is the case, for it certainly describes me!

Or am I reading more into "heart purity" than Jesus meant? It reminds me of a commentary I read on the gospel of John. A well-known evangelical scholar admitted that after working through the gospel of John for years and years, he still felt he did not understand it. I feel this way about Matthew 5:8—and I have preached on it, referred to it and researched it for years.

Two questions obviously emerge, and both deserve answers: (1) What is purity of heart? (2) And what is seeing God?

The nearest biblical equivalent of Matthew 5:8 is Acts 15:9: "He [God] made no distinction between us [Jews] and them [Gentiles], for he purified their hearts by faith." This verse refers to the conversion of the Gentiles who had received the Holy Spirit without having been circumcised—which went right against the traditional understanding of the Jews in those days. But the plain truth was, Peter said, without their having been circumcised, God purified their hearts by faith.

But is the event described in Acts 15:9 the same thing Jesus is talking about in Matthew 5:8? Probably not. For the Beatitudes show a logical sequence—and what happened to the Gentiles seems to have taken place instantaneously, without their having experienced any prior development of such virtues as being meek or being merciful.

50

Is there any possibility that Matthew 5:8 can refer to eradication from inward sin, or sinless perfection? No. On this I can be unequivocal. For two reasons: (1) Jesus gave the Lord's Prayer for the Church to pray, and it includes the petition that we be forgiven of our sins, debts or trespasses (Matthew 6:12; Luke 11:4). Had Jesus envisaged a purity of life that ruled out the need of the Lord's Prayer, He would not have given it to us. But also (2) there is 1 John 1:8: "If we claim to be without sin, we deceive ourselves and the truth is not in us." That's a pretty strong verse, and it would make me most uncomfortable if I held to the view I could exist without any sin.

We may therefore conclude that "purity of heart" does not mean a heart that is without any sin. But what is the meaning of the phrase that says God "purified their hearts by faith"?

The Heart

The heart is the seat of personality. The personality is the sum total of mind, emotions, will. The mind refers to our intellect or understanding. The emotions refer to our feelings. The will refers to our making a decision or commitment. All three, summed up, mean our heart.

Jesus said one could commit adultery in his heart (Matthew 5:28). He also said that where one's treasure is, there is one's heart (Matthew 6:21). One could honor God with his or her lips, but the heart may be far from Him (Matthew 15:8). Out of the overflow of the heart the mouth speaks, Jesus also said (Matthew 12:34). He said that the greatest command is to love the Lord with all one's heart and soul and mind (Matthew 22:37). We can infer from these statements that the "heart" is the real you. "Guard your heart, for it is the wellspring of life" (Proverbs 4:23). What you believe in your heart is what you truly believe.

The heart is the decisive factor when it comes to salvation. The heart is also the seat of faith—our being convinced that Jesus died and rose—when it comes to assurance of faith. "If you confess with your mouth, 'Jesus is Lord,' and believe in your heart that God raised him from the dead, you will be saved. For it is with your heart that you believe and are justified, and it is with your mouth that you confess and are saved" (Romans 10:9–10).

We sometimes refer to what we believe in our "heart of hearts," that is, what we honestly feel to be true. That is what Paul means in these words: that we have been inwardly persuaded that Jesus Christ of Nazareth was really and truly literally raised from the dead after dying on the cross. It is not enough to say I believe in the Creed that says He was raised from the dead. Saving faith is not merely assenting to what the Church has asserted. One must believe for himself or herself that Jesus of Nazareth really did rise from the dead. That alone is the faith that saves.

The point here is: One believes with the heart. It is not head knowledge; it is heart knowledge. Such a persuasion in the heart is also what counts for righteousness. When God sees that we truly believe the Gospel of Jesus Christ in our hearts, He simultaneously declares us righteous and regards us that way for all time. This truth is the foundation of our being justified by faith.

However, the heart is also the seat of our problems! It is the seat of what is wrong with each of us. "Out of the heart come evil thoughts, murder, adultery, sexual immorality, theft, false testimony, slander," said Jesus. These evil thoughts and deeds make a person "unclean" (Matthew 15:17–20). The heart by which we believe, then, can be the fountain of evil as well as the seat of saving faith.

What determines which it will be? Answer: our response to the truth. If we are persuaded that Jesus died and rose from the dead, and we rely on this fact, our heart is purified. That is what happened to the Gentiles in Acts 15:9. It was not that sin suddenly disappeared. It was a case that the heart—the seat of faith—was washed, purified, by the blood of Jesus. This—the death of Christ applied by the Spirit—is what enables the heart to believe! The persuasion that Jesus died and rose from the dead, then, simultaneously purifies the heart, thus enabling the heart to believe.

It is the calling of every Christian, therefore, to maintain heart purity. The heart that is purified by faith when we first believe is required to stay pure. This is where our beatitude comes in. Matthew 5:8—"Blessed are the pure in heart"—is not a reference to our initial coming to Christ in faith. It is a description of one who has developed in these graces. Jesus promises a very special blessing to the person who has not only maintained a broken and contrite spirit and a continual awareness of sin, has become self-effacing, has maintained a good spiritual appetite and has been truly godly by being merciful—but also by having kept a pure heart. This is a wonderful, wonderful accomplishment by the grace of the Holy Spirit. It means that this person has been disciplined, focused and devoted to the honor and glory of God.

Indeed, when one is challenged by Jesus to be pure in heart, the indication is that a triumph of grace, if not graciousness, has set in. Grace is getting favor we don't deserve. Any accomplishment on the ladder of graces in the Kingdom of heaven is purely of grace. But why is this particular beatitude here? It indicates an absence of bitterness. The one who shows mercy suggests a heart that has overcome bitterness.

The Greek word translated "pure" is *katharoi*—free from stain or shame. It is the opposite of a divided heart, of being double-minded (James 1:8). Purity of heart means that the person is totally sold out to God. It means sincerity of motive.

Although we all have mixed motives when it comes to our rationale for doing what we do, it is still true that our motive can be sincere and narrowed down to one. "One thing I ask of the LORD, this is what I seek: that I may dwell in the house of the LORD all the days of my life, to gaze upon the beauty of the LORD and to seek him in his temple" (Psalm 27:4). There is no rival spirit within this person, as if he can't decide whom to follow. His mind is made up.

This person is virtually untouchable by the lure of money, sex or power. Such a person will not likely give in to being bribed, flattered or tempted into sinning. However, I suspect that the ego is the last to be conquered in that triplet—money, sex and power. Power is a reference to the ego. Joseph showed himself to be morally pure before he was able to forgive his brothers.

Temperamental Purity

You may recall that the Beatitudes form the "text" for Jesus' preaching this Sermon on the Mount. Each of the Beatitudes is applied or interpreted at some point during Matthew 5–7. Jesus certainly has purity of heart in mind when He comes to His exposition of the Ten Commandments.

For example, the sixth Commandment says, "You shall not murder" (Exodus 20:13). But Jesus interpreted this command with the heart in mind. "But I tell you that anyone who is angry with his brother will be subject to judgment" (Matthew 5:22). Jesus also calls this forgiving one "from your heart" (Matthew 18:35).

Purity of heart regarding one's temperament does not refer to one's natural disposition, but, rather, to controlling the temper. You cannot always help what you feel, but you can control what you say or do.

Sexual Purity

This is true also with sexual purity. We cannot always control what thoughts come to our minds. But if our hearts are pure, we will resist letting lustful thoughts control us. As we will see in more detail later on, Jesus warns that looking at a woman lustfully also means causing to lust (Matthew 5:28)—that is, you must not do or say what promotes lust. This includes avoiding any kind of pornography. It means staying away from people you know full well will mean temptation to you.

"Clothe yourselves with the Lord Jesus Christ, and do not think about how to gratify the desires of the sinful nature" (Romans 13:14). Sexual purity begins with heart control, not allowing your thoughts to lead you to say what may well ignite a flame. If one's heart regarding sexual relationships is pure—avoiding any thought, word or deed that is lustful—then giving in to sexual temptation becomes highly unlikely. Sexual sin is remote when there has been a careful maintenance of the heart regarding all our relationships.

Financial Purity

It could be plausibly argued that Jesus has more to say about money than any other subject, especially when you consider the parables. In the Sermon on the Mount, He mentions money when He speaks of laying up treasures in heaven, where moth and rust do not destroy. "For where your treasure is, there your heart will be also" (Matthew 6:21). Moreover, "You cannot serve both God and Money" (Matthew 6:24).

Financial integrity begins in the heart, and the safest beginning is to give to God here below—which is what Jesus means by laying up treasures in heaven. If one avoids the "love of money" (1 Timothy 6:10), financial purity is manifest. Not money, but the *love* of money is a matter of the heart.

Seeing God

And the promise is that such a person will see God—a reward that is incalculable. But what, exactly, does Jesus mean that the pure in heart will "see" God? And when exactly does this happen—in heaven or on earth? Furthermore, does it mean seeing God the Father in heaven—or the incarnate God, who is Jesus?

I do think seeing God partly means seeing God in heaven. Yes. But I have to say that we will not know the total answer to these questions until we get to heaven. The phrase "pure in heart," therefore, is not the only part of this verse that is difficult!

First of all, however, all people will see the incarnate God—whether or not their hearts were pure. It is only a matter of time when every single human being who ever lived—saved or lost—will see Jesus. "Look," said John, who was on the Isle of Patmos, "he [Jesus] is coming with the clouds, *and every eye will see him,* even those who pierced him; and all the peoples of the earth will mourn because of him. So shall it be! Amen" (Revelation 1:7, emphasis mine). There is coming a day—it is indeed a Day of days—when every knee shall bow and every tongue shall confess that Jesus Christ is Lord (Romans 14:11). And, yes, every eye shall see Him. Therefore, Matthew 5:8 does not refer to seeing Jesus "one day"—for the promise of seeing Him is not only to the pure in heart!

Or does Matthew 5:8 contain a promise that only the pure in heart will go to heaven—and see God in heaven? Jesus' words certainly seem to parallel Hebrews 12:14: "Make every effort to live in peace with all men and to be holy; without holiness no one will see the Lord." Many in the holiness movement have used this verse to prove that you cannot go to heaven if you are not first pure in heart—that is, sanctified wholly.

It is more likely that both Jesus and the writer to the Hebrews are referring to seeing God not only in heaven, but here below on our way to heaven. I believe Jesus and the writer to the Hebrews mainly mean seeing the transcendent glory of God. Although "no one has ever seen God, but God the One and Only," meaning Jesus (John 1:18), this would have to mean that no one has seen God face-to-face. Only Jesus has experienced this.

But there are occasions in Holy Writ in which one has seen something of the glory of God. Moses put a bold request to God: "Show me your glory." God replied, "I will cause all my goodness to pass in front of you, and I will proclaim my name, the LORD, in your presence. I will have mercy on whom I will have mercy, and I will have compassion on whom I will have compassion." But, God added, "You cannot see my face, for no one may see me and live." Then God commanded Moses to be in a cleft in a rock where Moses caught a glimpse of God's glory. "You will see my back; but my face must not be seen" (Exodus 33:18–23). What Moses experienced is the nearest thing to seeing God we can experience on our way to heaven.

Gideon feared he would die because he saw an angel of the Lord face-to-face (Judges 6:22–23). Samson's parents thought they would die as well. "We are doomed to die! . . . We have seen God!" But in fact they saw an angel—not God Himself directly (Judges 13:16–22). All occasions in which one thought that he or she saw God were not literally God Himself, but a glimpse of His transcendent glory—which is very powerful, indeed.

I believe that Jesus is promising that the pure in heart will see God in a very real and definite sense here below—so much so that it would not take faith to believe He is before your very eyes. Peter says, "Though you have not seen him, you love him." But it is nonetheless possible that God can be so real—our being filled with "inexpressible joy" (1 Peter 1:8)—that seeing Him with your naked eye would not make Him any more real to you.

Seeing God, then, is seeing a measure of His glory here on earth. It is what Moses experienced. It is what Jesus is promising to you and me if we maintain pure hearts. In a word: We will see God work so clearly, powerfully, obviously and magnificently that it would be true to say we have seen God.

Paul says we are being changed from "glory to glory" (2 Corinthians 3:18, KJV). When this happens, it is truly seeing God. It is what the priests in Solomon's Temple experienced when that temple was "filled with a cloud, and the priests could not perform their service because of the cloud, for the glory of the LORD filled the temple of God" (2 Chronicles 5:13–14). The glory of the Lord came into my old Nazarene church in Ashland, Kentucky, in April 1956. Eyewitnesses described a haze that filled the auditorium.

In a word: Jesus is promising to the disciplined person—the one who maintains purity of heart—a reward not merely in heaven but here below. It is when God is so real that it is the same as seeing Him. Seeing an angel is like seeing God. Seeing a vision is like seeing God. Hearing an audible voice is like seeing God. Witnessing a miraculous answer to prayer is like seeing God. Having Him step in when you need Him most is like seeing God. Having Him speak to you powerfully in His Word is like seeing God. Being filled with the Spirit is like seeing God.

That is what Jesus is promising. This experience is indescribable and the value incalculable. And it is so worth waiting for.

9. Making Friends

Blessed are the peacemakers, for they will be called sons of God.

MATTHEW 5:9

Shortly after our "retirement" from Westminster Chapel in 2002, and a few months after returning to America, I was invited by Canon Andrew White, the Archbishop of Canterbury's chief envoy to the Middle East, to meet with the late President Yasser Arafat. What was assumed would be a fifteen-minute session stretched to an hour and forty-five minutes.

To my surprise, Arafat and I got on extremely well. I think he was not prepared to believe that an American evangelical had been praying for him for over twenty years. I began praying for Yasser Arafat in 1982, never expecting that I would meet him. My first words to him were, "I'm your friend." He replied, "You're more than a friend." Tears filled his eyes more than once during that initial visit.

Our conversation was almost entirely theological—my stressing that Jesus died on the cross for our sins—but I was still invited back, and ended up visiting with him five times. I became a part of the Alexandria Peace Process, led by Lord Carey, former Archbishop of Canterbury. From this came a warm friendship with Rabbi David Rosen, Israel's most distinguished Orthodox Jewish rabbi. We published a book together, sharing our unedited correspondence with each other, entitled *The Christian and the Pharisee*.

I wish I could say that peace in Jerusalem came from our efforts. But we tried. It's not over yet, either. My relationship with David Rosen continues. I have also maintained a friendship with Dr. Saab Erekat, the Palestinians' chief negotiator with the Israelis. Although my own contribution remains theological, not political, the basic tension is, after all, religious. As long as I live, I shall pray for and try to work for the peace of Jerusalem (Psalm 122:6).

When Jesus pronounced peacemakers "blessed," could He mean any kind of peacemaking? Probably not. Herod and Pilate became friends because of a common enemy (Luke 23:12). Moreover, the kind of peacemaking Jesus had in mind may or may not have been what we tried to do in Jerusalem in recent years. The peacemaker, however, can be seen in many areas and in surprising places. What did Jesus specifically mean by "peacemaking" in Matthew 5:9?

We are moving toward the end of the Beatitudes. Keep in mind we are ascending a ladder of progressive virtues. Do not forget the logical sequence in these extraordinary verses. Jesus is showing the way of the un-grieved Spirit, that heavenly realm in which the Holy Spirit resides when He is welcomed and at home. Each successive beatitude shows a slightly higher level of maturity. Those who attain to purity of heart want one thing: more of God. The promise is, they will see God if their hearts stay pure—that is, they will see His glory and see Him work. Those with pure hearts may be best qualified to be peacemakers—bringing enemies together, healing marriages and families, getting people to speak to each other and, just maybe, bringing peace where no one dreamed.

The Purpose of This Beatitude

We always ask, "Why is this particular beatitude put here?" In this case, there are two questions: (1) Why bring in peacemakers at all? (2) And why is this beatitude precisely here, knowing they all show a logical sequence?

We can be sure of this: Jesus is showing what the Father deems important. He is also showing how the Christian life is to be lived. If godliness is showing mercy, so also is being a peacemaker a godly thing to do. God is the supreme

Peacemaker. He sent His Son into the world to die on a cross. "God was reconciling the world to himself in Christ, not counting men's sins against them. And he has committed to us the message of reconciliation" (2 Corinthians 5:19).

Why, then, is this beatitude here? The answer partly is this: A high level of maturity, such as purity of heart, means you will have some objectivity about yourself. You will be able to stand apart from yourself, to objectively judge yourself. You will not be especially biased for yourself, but will be biased for the truth. You are more likely to see yourself as others see you, and as God sees you. Peacemaking, therefore, follows purity in heart, giving you a wider perspective. You will be concerned for others—wanting to make peace. You will be concerned for God's people—the Church. You will be concerned for God's greater glory. Jonathan Edwards said that Satan cannot produce a love for the glory of God and concern for the wider reputation of the Church.

The reason, therefore, that this beatitude about peacemaking is put exactly on the ladder here is that the pure in heart delight in the peace and fellowship among God's people. The pure in heart rise above selfish concerns, staying above the "party line." They want peace, unfeigned unity and the genuine happiness of others.

As for the entrance of the subject of peacemaking, I ask: Who would have thought to bring this issue in? It is God's idea. But this statement also sent a signal about the nature of Christ's messiahship and kingship. "What a shock this must have been to the Jews," observed Dr. Lloyd-Jones, for they had envisaged a military overthrow of Rome—the opposite of peacemaking. They thought that the restoration of Israel's ancient glory was the chief purpose of Messiah.

This beatitude may have given the first possible hint regarding Jesus' messiahship. For here comes Jesus saying something different—talking about peace and peacemaking. This inevitably means love for enemies and getting opponents together. As it turned out, Jesus became the greatest peacemaker of all. By His death He reconciled God and humankind. By the Gospel being preached to all, the enmity between Jew and Gentile was over. "Now in Christ Jesus you who once were far away have been brought near through the blood of Christ" (Ephesians 2:13).

By one Spirit, all hostility—horizontally and vertically—was over. No longer should there be racial prejudice, Jew versus Gentile, Israel versus Rome. There would be no justification for divisions among God's Church or people trying to get even with one another. No wonder, then, "the crowds were amazed at his teaching, because he taught as one who had authority, and not as their teachers of the law" (Matthew 7:28–29).

An Unusual Privilege

It is an unusual anointing to have a role in peacemaking. It is one thing to have an anointing to teach, preach, preside, do your job well or have a talent of some kind. It is wonderful to see people healed, delivered and set free. But to have an anointing to engage in peacemaking—which also sets people free—is rare. It is therefore an unusual privilege to have a part in making friends, restoring a relationship or bringing enemies together.

Peacemaking is a God-approved anointing. Those who do it are "blessed." Yes, congratulations, if you are a peacemaker. The level of God's approval is shown by the promise to the peacemaker: They are called sons (or daughters) of God. If it is God's approval you want, here is a sure way to have it: Become a peacemaker.

There are other ways to become sons of God. "To all who received him, to those who believed in his name, he gave the right to become children of God—children born not of natural descent, nor of human decision or a husband's will, but born of God" (John 1:12–13). Furthermore, "Those who are led by the Spirit of God are sons of God" (Romans 8:14). But a certain dignity—a reputation in heaven—is given to those who are truly peacemakers. They have the privilege of being called sons of God. There is the expression "born to privilege"—often referring to the English gentry bred, or aristocracy. But the ultimate status is to be called a child of God by our heavenly Father.

An Unselfish Participation

Peacemaking is something you do—or allow to happen. This means getting involved, taking an active role. Or, you can be passive in being a peacemaker—by letting it happen. For example, what if you are the one needing to forgive or make friends? By your cooperation you become a peacemaker. In other words, in this case you are not the one who is getting others together. Rather, you are letting others persuade you to make peace with someone. It is a humbling but gracious thing to do. It is a passive way of qualifying as a peacemaker. I shall return to this below.

Being a peacemaker is, therefore, an unselfish role. It also means maintaining neutrality. Becoming a peacemaker is arguably the most unselfish thing you will ever do! It means you don't take sides. That is what a mediator is: You are in between—totally neutral and yet totally on both sides. That is what Jesus was and is. Jesus was and is equally God and man, and is fully trusted by the Father. We, too, can fully trust Him to represent us. "For there is one God and one mediator between God and men, the man Christ Jesus" (1 Timothy 2:5).

But perhaps the most stunning neutrality recorded in the Bible is when Joshua was put in his place shortly after arriving in the Promised Land. Joshua must have assumed God was biased for him. When the children of Israel approached Jericho, there stood a man—no doubt an angel—with a drawn sword in his hand. Joshua went up to him and asked, "Are you for us or for our enemies?" The surprising response was: "Neither . . . but as commander of the army of the Lord I have now come." Joshua fell facedown to the ground and was commanded to take off his shoes because he was on holy ground (Joshua 5:13–15).

When the one we thought was on our side is neutral, we can feel betrayed. We naturally expect that God should be prejudiced for us. But there is a higher level of issues going on—and it is in our interest that there be a peacemaker who is neutral, however disappointing at first this may seem.

There are two kinds of participation: active and passive. The active is trying to make peace happen. The passive is letting it happen. The active is when you take the initiative. The passive is responding positively if another takes the initiative.

Likewise, there are two kinds of initiatives: what you do directly in trying to turn your own enemy into a friend, and what you do for others when you try to make them friends. And yet there are also two kinds of passive participation: how you respond if someone tries to make friends with you, and how you respond if someone comes to you and tries to get you together with one with whom you have not been friendly.

In any case, we are talking about an unselfish participation. It is an enterprise in which the ego is put in suspension! You see, it is pride that delays reconciliation. It is no small step when we are willing to let our big, fat, fragile egos be put to one side in order for peace to come.

Four Scenarios of Peacemaking

Partly to summarize, partly to have a better perspective of the possibilities of peacemaking, consider four scenarios.

First, you are the active participant by taking the initiative toward a person with whom you have had a strained relationship. This takes lots of courage. Guts. It is sometimes the hardest thing in the world to do. Things could backfire in your face. And yet you are told to do it! "If you are offering your gift at the altar and there remember that your brother has something against you, leave your gift in front of the altar. First go and be reconciled to your brother; then come and offer your gift" (Matthew 5:23–24).

Jesus also said, "If your brother sins against you, go and show him his fault, just between the two of you. If he listens to you, you have won your brother over" (Matthew 18:15). Jesus offered a further word, suggesting a slightly different situation: "Settle matters quickly with your adversary who is taking you to court. Do it while you are still with him on the way, or he may hand you over to the judge, and the judge may hand you over to the officer, and you may be thrown into prison" (Matthew 5:25).

In any of these cases, you are taking the initiative and risking what the outcome might be. You could be rejected. But you will have done the right thing. I know what it is to do this and be spurned. But I have never been sorry for trying!

There are, however, obviously two possibilities: It could be their fault, or it could be your fault.

What if it is your own fault? If you are willing to admit it—and you should be—I urge you: Go on bended knee. Say, "I'm sorry. I was wrong. Please forgive me." Can you do this? I have had to do this more than I care to think about. But

I can tell you, it usually works! You feel so much better, too. And yet if the other person will not forgive you, you have the inner peace that you did your best. "If it is possible, as far as it depends on you, live at peace with everyone" (Romans 12:18).

The second scenario is when you are the passive participator. This is when someone comes to you to ask your cooperation. Let us say that you are in some difficulty regarding another person. It may be a "sworn" enemy. It may be a tense relationship. It may be you cannot get along with this person, no matter hard you have tried. Still, someone comes to you and says, "Please try." Or they say, "Please let me intercede, let me mediate."

The question is: Will you be a participator? Do you say, "Leave me alone—I don't want to have anything to do with that person"? If so, you have forfeited the privilege of being a peacemaker. But if you want the status of being a child of God you will say: "I am happy to make up with this person. I'll do anything I can."

If so, you have become a peacemaker in that moment! This is because you have allowed this other person to do the hard work. Your task is to want peace and say, if necessary, "I am so sorry I hurt you. I know I have been difficult. Let's be friends." Whatever the outcome, you are graced with the title "son or daughter of God"—for you show yourself to be a peacemaker. All that is required is to be willing to make peace when another takes the initiative in your behalf. By the way, thank God for that person!

The third scenario is when you are the active participant. You decide to take the lead in bringing two people together. There are at least two possible situations here. First, it could be you are going to try to bring people together who are not speaking to each other at the moment. This is one of the most challenging opportunities. You will need not only courage but a lot of wisdom, much love and a great measure of the Holy Spirit's power.

Furthermore, trying to bring enemies together can be highly dangerous. You make yourself a possible enemy of both! They may say to you, "Stay out of this!" Or, "This is none of your business!" But the reward is great. James ended his little epistle with these words: "Whoever turns a sinner from the error of his way will save him from death and cover over a multitude of sins" (James 5:20). And never forget Paul's caution when you do this sort of thing: "If someone is caught in a sin, you who are spiritual should restore him gently. But watch yourself, you also may be tempted" (Galatians 6:1).

The other possibility is when the two people you want to bring together don't know each other. My friend Lyndon Bowring does this all the time. He has done it with me, bringing me to meet people I would otherwise have not met. This possibility, then, is when you want two people to meet. They may have different backgrounds. They may have opposing theological views. There may be a vast cultural difference between the two you hope will like each other.

You may fail, and feel like a fool. But it is worth a try. Never forget that God esteems you for doing the valiant thing.

The fourth scenario is to enlarge on what I have mentioned already. It is when you are the passive participator—when one comes to you and says, "I'd like you to meet this person." Or, when there is already a strained relationship, they still plead, "I want you to become friends with this person."

Let us say you are a strong Protestant from Northern Ireland and they want you to make up with a Roman Catholic. Or, you are an Indian and they bring a Pakistani to you. The list is endless. You may be poles apart theologically, culturally, socially, financially, politically and even sexually (what if one of the persons is gay?).

The person who takes the initiative is being a peacemaker, but, I repeat: So are you also a peacemaker when you are willing to become friends with someone you had no thought of being friendly with. "Every person is worth understanding," says the psychologist Clyde Narramore, a statement that bears repeating throughout this book. To understand is often to forgive.

Being Seen As Vulnerable

We saw that peacemaking can be a vulnerable, even precarious, enterprise. In the first scenario above, you may go to a person and want to make up—and that person may reject you. In the second scenario, when one comes to you and wants you to make up with somebody, you may be embarrassed because it was that person's idea, not yours—and he or she gets the glory! In the third scenario, when you try to get others to reconcile, one or both may turn on you—and you may also be accused of taking sides. In the fourth scenario, you may be willing to make friends, but the other party refuses—and you feel rejected by the person you were willing to meet with.

You will recall how the ego must be put in suspension when it comes to being a peacemaker. You must be willing to get no glory whatever—or perhaps even to appear weak. You may fail in your efforts. You may be rejected. You may appear weak when you give in. But Jesus was crucified in weakness (2 Corinthians 13:4), and yet never was any person so strong as Jesus was. It takes tremendous ego strength to appear weak. That is what Jesus did. That is what the peacemaker must do.

Ultimate Prestige

When you decide to be a peacemaker, you forfeit earthly glory in exchange for the honor that comes from God alone (John 5:44). You make a choice: Which is more important, to be prestigious in the eyes of people here below, or be regarded as a son or daughter of God by your Father in heaven?

You must be willing to appear weak here below. You might even be seen as a compromiser. But God gives His opinion: "I am proud to call you My son," "I am pleased to call you My daughter." It is a wonderful feeling when God is unashamed of us.

There is no greater calling or reputation than being known in heaven as a peacemaker. This will also get you a reputation in hell! Jesus and Paul were known in hell. Apparently, not everybody on earth is known in hell, because few on earth give the devil much to worry about. One of the greatest sermons I ever heard was by the late Rolfe Barnard, who preached a sermon titled, "The Man Who Was Known in Hell." Jesus and Paul were such a threat to the devil's interest, but most people do not threaten Satan at all. Rolfe concluded: "I want to be known in hell because I am a threat to the devil" (Acts 19:15).

To be known in heaven as a peacemaker is to be known in hell as a threat to evil. To be a peacemaker is to give you a reputation where it matters most—in heaven.

What is your anointing? I would urge you to covet that unusual anointing of a peacemaker. Be willing to look weak. Make a choice to have the dignity of the Father's approval. When He looks at me and says, "I think you are okay," that's good enough for me.

10. As Good As It Gets

Blessed are those who are persecuted because of righteousness,
for theirs is the kingdom of heaven.

MATTHEW 5:10

We now examine the last of the Beatitudes. It is a small point whether there are eight or nine. Most interpreters say there are eight, this being the last. Verses 11 and 12—sometimes seen as a further beatitude because the word "blessed" is repeated—are probably an elaboration of this final beatitude.

In any case, Jesus saves the best for last. "Blessed are you when people insult you, persecute you and falsely say all kinds of evil against you because of me. Rejoice and be glad, because *great is your reward in haven*, for in the same way they persecuted the prophets who were before you" (Matthew 5:11–12, emphasis mine). What interests me further is that the reward to the poor in spirit—appearing in the first beatitude—and the reward of being persecuted for righteousness—here in the final beatitude—are exactly the same: "Theirs is the kingdom of heaven."

The Greek word for "persecuted" is from *dikoo,* which means "to follow." You are persecuted when your enemy follows you, won't stop pursuing you. It is like when the Pharisees went out and laid plans to trap Jesus in His words (Matthew 22:15). Certain Jews had been sent from Jerusalem to question John the Baptist (John 1:24). In this beatitude, Jesus is telling us we are blessed if people are so upset with our faith and message that they pursue us. Persecutors are like stalkers, always showing up to cause any annoyance they can. Paul's opponents—sometimes called Judaizers—followed the apostle wherever he went in order to undermine the message of grace.

Why is this chapter important? It is a reminder that having the Kingdom of heaven—the indwelling presence of the un-grieved Spirit—is as good as it gets. There is no greater worth—or joy—than having the Holy Spirit to be at home in you. It

is a taste of heaven below, having a little bit of heaven to go to heaven in.

Second, it is a reminder that we will never outgrow persecution—that is, to reach the place where people will applaud you rather than want to punish you. Did you ever think or wish that you will have so much of God on you that your enemies will look at you and say, "Wow, God is really with you. You are wonderful, how wrong I was about you"? Don't even think about it. It won't happen! Jesus had all of God that one can get, having been given the Spirit without any limit (John 4:34)—and think about what they did to Him! He said, "If the world hates you, keep in mind that it hated me first" (John 15:18).

I used to dream of this, however, wishing that my anointing would be self-authenticating and utterly convincing to those who doubted me. In 1956, I came back from Trevecca Nazarene College with a fresh experience with God and a new understanding of the Bible. I wanted my dad to see what I saw. He couldn't. My grandmother, too, was unable to appreciate what was so thrilling to me. It was my first taste of persecution—and I never dreamed it would come from the company of the "godly"! But it did. And, believe it or not, it has been this way ever since.

Apart from my family, my first persecution came when Louise and I lived in Carlisle, Ohio. A small church there rejected my ministry. The very ones who voted me in as pastor did their best to vote me out! Those were hard days.

Yet those were the same days in which I discovered Dr. Martyn Lloyd-Jones's *Sermon on the Mount.* I remember reading his exposition of these very verses that I am now sharing with you. What a tonic it was! Yes, they were simultaneously horrible and blessed days. And yet I was in the minor leagues then. Being in the major league would come later. Indeed, the best was yet to come! Just remember: You will never outgrow persecution. "In fact, everyone who wants to live a godly life in Christ Jesus will be persecuted" (2 Timothy 3:12).

Many years ago, I read about the martyrdom of Polycarp (circa A.D. 150), a convert of John the apostle. The account of Polycarp's death made a deep, lasting impression on me. The Roman authorities threatened to burn him at the stake. He was not intimidated, urging them to light the flame. They commanded him to praise Caesar and curse Christ. He refused, saying of his Lord, "Eighty and six years I have served him and He has done me no wrong; how can I deny my King now?" They started the fire, but as the fire increased a wind came into the stadium, and all the Christians witnessed it. The wind caused the flame to form a circle around Polycarp, and the fire did not touch him.

What amazed those looking on was that the miracle and apparent radiance of Polycarp did not faze the unbelievers. The division between the saved and the lost was distinct. The believers sided with Polycarp, this being part of the stigma they bore. Paul said, "Do not be ashamed to testify about our Lord, or ashamed of me his prisoner. But join with me in suffering for the gospel" (2 Timothy 1:8). As for Polycarp, the flames never touched him. But the persecutor threw a spear into his side to kill him. Blood and water gushed out and put out the fire. But Polycarp went to heaven. Wow—what a way to die!

The truth is, there is no spiritual victory, no state of grace, no level of vindication, no sphere of wealth or prosperity that will exempt you from the threat of persecution if you are a true follower of Jesus Christ. If it is an easy life you want, look elsewhere. If Christianity has been presented to you as the "good life" because of the promise of health and wealth, you have not been given the full picture of the Christian life. You may even discover you have not been converted at all because you accepted a "gospel" that is no gospel at all.

Experiencing the Beatitudes is as good as it gets. In a word: "In this world you will have trouble," said Jesus. "But take heart! I have overcome the world" (John 16:33). Said Paul: "I want to know Christ and the power of his resurrection *and*

the fellowship of sharing in his sufferings, becoming like him in his death" (Philippians 3:10, emphasis mine). Experiencing the power of Christ's resurrection is as good as it gets. But there can be no resurrection until there is a death. And the true follower of Jesus must be in a perpetual state of losing his or her life. We must die in order to bring forth more fruit. Moreover, "The man who loves his life will lose it, while the man who hates his life in this world will keep it for eternal life" (John 12:25).

So, don't look for utopia here below: Don't look for the Garden of Eden on earth today. The top of the spiritual ladder we have been looking at in these lines is "persecution because of righteousness."

How does this make you feel? Had you thought that one day you will have perfect happiness on this earth? Does this teaching go against your concept of Christianity? If what Jesus describes in the Beatitudes is as good as it gets, are you still ready to follow Him?

The Challenge of Persecution

A challenge means the testing of one's skill or strength. The strength that may be tested could mean strength of character or one's self-esteem. Persecution will present a challenge to your whole being, your entire personality and, of course, your faith. It therefore challenges you spiritually, emotionally and, in a worst-case scenario, physically. Persecution at any level never becomes fun. Why? It goes against our nature. It is sometimes embarrassing to our ego.

When we first began the Pilot Light ministry at Westminster Chapel, an evangelistic witnessing outreach, we had a tiny bit of persecution—from church members. There was a feeling among some of the traditional middle-class members that "this [witnessing on the streets in the shadow of Buckingham Palace] is not Westminster Chapel." There was a feeling that such a thing was "beneath" us. It would be okay for some churches to do this—as long as they stayed near Speaker's Corner near Hyde Park. But surely not in Buckingham Gate and in the streets of Victoria.

Those were not fun days. Some people would drive into central London just to see if I was really out on the streets! I could see some of them saying,

"There he is." It was, to be honest, a little bit embarrassing. I knew such an outreach hadn't been done by previous chapel ministers. Nobody could imagine Dr. G. Campbell Morgan or Dr. Martyn Lloyd-Jones stopping passersby to ask the question, "Do you know for sure if you were to die today would you go to heaven?" But it was what I had to do. And so, yes, it felt a bit strange. Perhaps it is unfair to call this persecution. But as the poet Steve Turner put it, persecution can take the form of being "put into perspective." I could certainly feel that. It was certainly challenging.

Persecution can be a challenge to our mental or emotional state when it tests our faith. The devil will come alongside and say, "You are a fool to do this." Satan plays into our fears and our pride. We wonder what people will think. But I think of places in the world where witnessing for Jesus Christ means physical torture. The little bit of persecution I have faced is hardly a drop in the bucket compared to suffering in many places in the world these days. I predict we will see it in the West before Jesus comes, not merely in Third World countries. One is never prepared for the new way persecution can come to us. The enemy switches tactics. It is always a challenge.

And yet you could say it is an inevitable challenge, partly because any peacemaker will almost certainly be persecuted sooner or later. This is why the verse about persecution is put here, following the promise of being a peacemaker. The person who tries to make peace will often be rejected. It will happen whether he tries to make peace with his own enemy or he tries to get two enemies to reconcile. He will be laughed at as weak and compromising. And he will be tempted to say, "What's the use?"

Yet Jesus calls us "blessed"—happy, anointed! The angels say, "Congratulations!" Really? Am I to believe that being laughed at, scorned or physically hurt is something good? Yes. This beatitude is an incongruous combination—"happy are the persecuted." It is almost talking about a hot snowball. And yet James said we should consider it "pure joy" when this happens to us (James 1:2).

How can happiness and persecution be put together? Surely they don't fit. Can one be happy in jail? "How can we sing the songs of the LORD while in a foreign land?" asked the psalmist (Psalm 137:4). And yet Paul and Silas were singing hymns to God in prison in the middle of the night (Acts 16:25)!

Jesus says that one can be simultaneously persecuted and blessed. It means a great anointing. It means you are approved of God. So we must take our Lord's word for it. On the contrary, says Jesus, "Woe to you when all men speak well of you, for that is how their fathers treated the false prophets" (Luke 6:26).

For one thing, being persecuted for righteousness is proof of godliness. As we saw above, all who would live godly in Christ Jesus will suffer persecution (2 Timothy 3:12). Did Paul overstate it when he said "all"? All I know is, that is what he said. So if you are living godly in Christ Jesus without persecution, get ready for it—it is coming to you! Not only that, it is proof of goodness. Peter said, "Live such good lives among the pagans that, though they accuse you of doing wrong, they may see your good deeds and glorify God on the day he visits us" (1 Peter 2:12).

There is more: Persecution is proof of great grace. In the early Church, the followers of Jesus were persecuted. They had a prayer meeting and brought their persecution to the Lord. When they finished praying, the place itself was shaken and they were all filled with the Holy Spirit. "Much grace was upon them all" (Acts 4:33).

One other thing: Persecution because of righteousness is proof of glory. "If you are insulted because of the name of Christ, you are blessed, for the Spirit of glory and of God rests on you" (1 Peter 4:14). No wonder, then, that Jesus would pronounce us blessed if we are persecuted for righteousness.

What if someone reading these lines is being persecuted now? You may say, "I am not happy." Jesus says, "You are." You are being pursued by those who hate the God of the Bible. You are categorized, "put in perspective," embarrassed, unvindicated and depressed. "I am still not happy," you say. But Jesus says that you are. You don't realize at the moment what this counts for. Wait and see! Don't listen to the devil. Resist him—keep your eyes on Jesus. It will be worth it all if you persevere under this kind of trial. I guarantee it.

I have to admit that in the days we began the Pilot Light ministry and did other things in Westminster Chapel that broke with tradition, it wasn't fun. It was hard. Christmas of 1984 was the hardest time I had ever known. But I have to say also that the sense of God in those days was very wonderful. The insights into Scripture that flowed were unprecedented. The messages that came were beyond my own ability to create. An anointing of one insight after another exceeded all I dreamed of. True, it wasn't fun—but it was worth it all. Peter said, "It is commendable if a man bears up under the pain of unjust suffering because he is conscious of God" (1 Peter 2:19).

Important Clarification

You should have noticed all along that Jesus did not say you are blessed if you are merely persecuted. He added a very important qualification: "because of righteousness."

As New Testament scholar Don Carson put it, Jesus did not say people are blessed "because they are objectionable, or because they rave like wild-eyed fanatics, or because they uphold some religio-political cause." Jesus, therefore, makes an important clarification. People can be persecuted for a wrong cause—because they are troublemakers, strange, weird or peculiar. One can be persecuted for spreading heretical views. After all, there are many cults and sects in the land today, and those who belong to them are persecuted.

Jesus, therefore, stipulates that the kind of persecution that is dignified with the title "blessed" is when you are persecuted "because of righteousness." *Righteousness* is the one word that undergirds all these beatitudes. And yet Jesus Himself further clarifies what He means by "righteousness," as we will see in the next chapter: "because of me" (Matthew 5:11). Righteousness is embodied in the person of Jesus, in what He did and what He taught. We are therefore not talking about moralism, legalistic righteousness or strict views about dress, diet or the length of one's hair.

The persecution that is crowned with the dignity of being anointed is when there is an upholding of the pure Gospel of Christ—who He was, what He taught and what He did. This book will show exactly what that Gospel is.

Inherited Crown

What intrigues me about this beatitude is that the first promise of these statements was that the poor in spirit—the broken person—inherits the Kingdom of heaven. And since we have seen a graduating scale of virtues from beatitude to beatitude, we might expect that the pinnacle beatitude would promise the highest possible blessing. It does: It is to inherit the Kingdom of heaven. It doesn't get better than that. The Kingdom of God is as good as it gets. God has made us kings and priests. The Kingdom of heaven is ours if these beatitudes describe us, and especially this one.

Wearing the crown is something to be given in the future but also, in a sense, in the present. It is for the future, in that at the Second Coming Jesus will establish His Kingdom (2 Timothy 4:1). Those who receive a reward will receive a crown, a prize (1 Corinthians 9:24–25). Not only that. Paul said at the end of his life, "The time has come for my departure. I have fought the good fight, I have finished the race, I have kept the faith. Now there is in store for me the crown of righteousness, which the Lord, the righteous Judge, will award to me on that day—and not only to me, but also to all who have longed for his appearing" (2 Timothy 4:6–8). To some, God will say, "Well done," at the Judgment Seat of Christ (2 Peter 1:11). That will be our inheritance in heaven.

But Paul also speaks of the earnest of our inheritance, which is the sealing of the Holy Spirit (Ephesians 1:13–14, KJV). God gives us a taste of what is to come. It is like being notified in advance that the crown, the prize, the reward is on the way. To those who are persecuted, this can be very real in the here and now; it is what keeps them going. Josif Tson has described what it was like to be interrogated day after day after day for months in Romania in the days of the Iron Curtain. At the end of the day, Josif would lift his eyes heavenward and say, "Father, are You pleased with me?" He would hear the reply, "Son, you have the victory."

I take the view that God may give us an inner witness of the Holy Spirit's approval of us right after a trial is completed, when we truly dignified the trial. This is part of the meaning of James 1:12: "Blessed is the man who perseveres under trial, because when he has stood the test, he will receive the crown of life that God has promised to those who love him."

This may come at death, at the Judgment Seat of Christ or at the end of a severe trial. If during a trial we honored God, didn't complain, trusted Him, didn't try to rush through it or get it over prematurely, the Holy Spirit sometimes testifies of His pleasure with us. I believe that is what happened after Jesus was tempted forty days in the wilderness and the angels came and ministered to Him (Matthew 4:11). God loves to do this sort of thing for those who have endured a terrible time of testing. He knows how much we can bear, and when the trial is over the devil is commanded to leave us for a season while the angels attend to us.

Those who undergo persecution are often given a very unusual sense of God and His presence. I recall hearing Jenny Eaton, the wife of my close friend Dr. Michael Eaton, lamenting that she had to be in London on one occasion when there was a great upheaval and surge of persecution back in Kenya where she lived. She literally wanted to be back there at that time.

"Why?" I asked. "Aren't you glad to be away from all that?" She explained that when things are horrible and almost unbearable in Kenya,

there is simultaneously an outpouring of the Sprit. Amazing things happen—great answers to prayer, healings, miracles. "People see angels," she added. She felt deprived that it was her lot to be in London at the precise time there was trouble back home in Kenya.

This explains in part why Jesus calls those "blessed" who are persecuted because of righteousness. The Kingdom of heaven is brought to us with an amazing sense of reality. Heaven comes down. God stoops down to touch those who are persecuted.

Reaching this plateau, then—being persecuted for righteousness—means you have graduated to the greatest realm to be known in this world. "My kingdom is not of this world," Jesus explained to Pilate (John 18:36). But it is in us! And when we have come to brokenness—and the suffering that we dignified (instead of grumbling)—we are given the honor of being like Jesus: persecuted. That is as good as it gets this side of heaven. For the greater the suffering, the greater the anointing. The greater the persecution, the greater the glory.

The only thing better than that is to hear from the lips of Jesus Himself, "Well done." That will be ecstasy that words even then will not be able to describe.

11. The Heart of Persecution

Blessed are you when people insult you, persecute you and
falsely say all kinds of evil against you because of me.

MATTHEW 5:11

This may or may not be a separate beatitude. It is more likely an extension of the eighth beatitude, which we examined in the previous chapter. Oftentimes in Hebrew literature, if something was very important, it was stated twice. So what Jesus does here is to state the same word in a slightly different way. In the ascending level of maturity in the Beatitudes, Jesus saves the best for last.

There is one subtle change when we compare the two verses. What is called "righteousness" in Matthew 5:10 becomes "because of me" in Matthew 5:11. The general term "righteousness" is narrowed to the real cause of another's anger: the offense that comes from your being associated with Jesus Christ. It is not merely *righteousness* that offends; the real stigma is Jesus.

Are you prepared to embrace the stigma of Jesus Christ?

The Honor of Persecution

We have seen that "blessed" means "approved." "Happy." "Chosen." "Anointed." The best summary of these comes down to one word: "Congratulations!"

We saw in Chapter 9 that being a peacemaker is to have an unusual anointing. But we are now seeing that the highest level of anointing of all is associated with persecution—if it is for Christ's righteousness. This is because once your righteousness brings persecution you have, more than ever, touched the heart of God.

All people—men and women—by nature hate God. Jonathan Edwards once described God as "man's natural enemy." So if your imitating God brings persecution, you touch His heart. You bring out man's hatred of Him. Persecution is when you feel His pain. Have you ever thought of experiencing God's pain? Persecution does

precisely this: You experience God's pain. You thought it was *your* pain. Wrong—it is what God feels.

Never forget this one thing: The most maligned person in the universe is God Himself. He remains unvindicated, hated, accused, scoffed at, degraded. And He Himself remains the excuse evil people use for not believing in Him. When people ask the question, "Why does God allow suffering?" they often only want to accuse God for being the reason they don't believe in Him. They reckon that they have trapped God. If God really existed, He would relieve people of suffering, and since people suffer, this proves there is no God. So it goes.

And do you suppose this doesn't bother God the slightest bit—that He is impassive? That He never feels? Wrong. He certainly does feel it. You cannot begin to know what He feels until people hate you because of Him. And if they hate you because of Jesus Christ, that is as far as you can go in feeling what God feels.

What an honor, what a privilege. Being persecuted for this reason is as good as it gets. It catapults your anointing to the level experienced only by the greatest saints in history. You suddenly enter the arena of Moses and Elijah, Isaiah and Daniel, Peter, Paul and Stephen. I cannot conceive of a greater glory.

Consider the anointing on Stephen. His persecutors were not able to resist the wisdom and Spirit by which Stephen spoke when he was subpoenaed to stand before the Sanhedrin. I would give anything in the world for that kind of anointing. I think of his countenance and radiance—although I doubt he was conscious of it when his face shone like that of an angel, reminding us of the glory on Moses' face (Acts

6:10–11; Exodus 34:29). Then consider how they killed him: He was stoned to death. The pain was horrible beyond description. And then remember his last words: "Lord, do not hold this sin against them" (Acts 7:60).

Jesus had prophesied this sort of thing. "They will put you out of the synagogue; in fact, a time is coming when anyone who kills you will think he is offering a service to God" (John 16:2). Peter summarized it: "If you are insulted because of the name of Christ, you are blessed, for the Spirit of glory and of God rests on you" (1 Peter 4:14).

If you are fortunate enough for this to happen to you, you exemplify the quintessence of the praise, honor and glory that comes from the true God. Being persecuted for righteousness is the nearest you get to feeling what God feels all the time. Is it fun? Probably not. But is it glorious? Yes. For the height of joy, the measure of anointing and sense of God Himself is as good as it gets. Stephen's last sight before he died was that of seeing Jesus standing at the right hand of God (Acts 7:56)—a sight I am sure he continued to behold without any interruption as he passed out of this life.

Earthly Honor

What do you suppose is the highest honor on earth? To be Her Majesty the Queen, who was born to privilege? To be the president of the United States or prime minister of Great Britain? To be knighted by the Queen—or seated in the House of Lords? To be a member of Parliament, a senator or governor? To know ten presidents personally, as Billy Graham has? I can remember thinking fifty years ago that Billy Graham was the most famous person in America. He has lived with that fame all his life.

Or is the greatest honor to win the Nobel Prize for Peace? To be the Archbishop of Canterbury? To win the Wimbledon tennis championship? To be the greatest golfer or baseball player of your time? To be the wealthiest person in the world, like Bill Gates? To win an Oscar, Emmy or Grammy?

I answer: The greatest honor of all is the secret realization that you please God. "Secret," you ask? Yes. It is an honor you have to keep to yourself. You must not announce to the world, "I have knowledge that I please God." You prove how

highly you prize it by not telling it. It is information between you and God. You should not violate this privileged information by sharing it. The secret of the Lord is with them that fear Him; He confides in them (Psalm 25:14).

I am sure that God would confide in us more often if we could keep quiet about it. The trouble is, someone who receives something unusual from the Lord (e.g., definite witness of the Spirit, a dream or vision) often blabs it to the world! God says, "Oh no, why did you have to tell it?" So He withdraws sharing things with so many of us.

But should He share with us the greatest knowledge there is—that we please Him—we are not to tell it but treasure it in our hearts, as Mary the mother of Jesus did (Luke 2:19).

I now refer again to the most challenging verse in the Bible (to me): "How can you believe if you accept praise from one another, yet make no effort to obtain the praise that comes from the only God?" (John 5:44). Our real reason for telling things like this is to get admiration. But if we are truly content with the knowledge of God's admiration of us, we prove it by not telling it. As for Mary, she kept the secret of Jesus' miraculous birth, the shepherds and other things for years and years until, finally, she shared this information with Luke and Matthew before she died.

In a word: Is there something grander than winning the Nobel Peace Prize or being president? Yes. It is knowing you please your heavenly Father. But if you ask, "What is the next best thing to knowing you please God?" I answer: to have the highest level of anointing of the Holy Spirit. But remember: The greater the suffering, the greater the anointing. Likewise, the greater the anointing, the greater the suffering. The anointing almost always comes with a great cost: suffering. It is for our good, says Paul. He needed a thorn in the flesh to keep him from being conceited (2 Corinthians 12:7). If he needed it, you and I need it.

You may say, "But I am not sure I truly please God—I would love this honor." I reply: If you are persecuted because of Jesus Christ, you've got it! Jesus says to you as you read these lines: "Blessed are you when people insult you, persecute you and falsely say all kinds of evil against you because of me." You are blessed with this sweet knowledge—that you please the Lord because you are suffering for Jesus! You are a singularly honored person. It is greater than being president or Her Majesty Queen Elizabeth II.

The Hallmark of Persecution

The distinguishing characteristic of persecution is of two kinds, generally speaking: verbal (what they say, as in insult) and nonverbal (what they do, like being in your face and, possibly, physically hurting you). This will come up again, later in the Sermon on the Mount. Here in Matthew 5:11, Jesus refers to the verbal persecution. It is when people insult you, lie about you and say evil things about you.

The instrument of persecution is people. "When people insult you." It is the devil who stirs people up. He plays into people's sinful nature—their jealousies, biases and fears. But it is not the devil himself physically leaping on you from out of the blue. Rather, he brings the worst out of people. It is they who are his instruments. Never forget that people—at best—are sinners, and want to think negatively in the first place. They are easy instruments for the devil already. They are waiting for an excuse to vent their hearts. People by nature want to think evil rather than good. So the devil comes along and vents their anger toward Jesus Christ by insulting the people who represent Him.

Satan brings out people's insolence. To insult means to speak in a way that hurts the feelings of one's pride. The purpose of this is to arouse anger. If people are insolent and you retort, they have won. Indeed, the devil has won! "Hurrah!" says the devil. "I made him mad."

Don't give the devil that pleasure. The issue is your own threshold: How much can you take? A threshold is understood two ways: (1) the lowest limit at which a stimulus becomes perceptible, as when persecution begins to "bug" you, and (2) the highest limit at which pain is bearable—when you can take no more. But remember: "No temptation [testing] has seized you except what is common to man. And God is faithful; he will not let you be tempted [tested] beyond what you can bear. But when you are tempted [tested], he will also provide a way out so that you can stand up under it" (1 Corinthians 10:13). God will step in, in the nick of time, to rescue you. But do your very

best not to retort—or to let the enemy know he is getting to you!

Some things bother you; some things don't. Some things may seem to get the best of you—for example, when people insult your intelligence. Or your culture, background, race, color of your skin or nationality. They hope to get others on their side. They may poke fun at your education—or lack of it. Your social standing. Your accent. Your personality, your mannerisms or eccentricity. There was a cartoon in a newspaper in George Whitefield's day that made fun of his being cross-eyed, his squint. The cartoon said you could come and hear Dr. Squintum at his "soul trap" in Tottenham Court Road. They may ridicule your doctrine, theology or point of view. Your job or quality of work. Your church. Your family. All these have varying degrees of effect on us. Whatever the hallmark of the persecution that comes to you, you are "blessed."

Then there is the intensity of the verbal persecution. It hurts when they don't represent you fairly. They not only insult you but "falsely say all kinds of evil against you." This is what Stephen faced. "They produced false witnesses, who testified, 'This fellow never stops speaking against this holy place and against the law. For we have heard him say that this Jesus of Nazareth will destroy this place and change the customs Moses handed down to us'" (Acts 6:13–14).

When people do this, it is not the truth they are after. Their minds are made up. They say things that would possibly legitimize their evil deed. Given the best interpretation, what they say is misleading. At worst, it is sheer lies. In this case, the person who is being persecuted is utterly helpless.

Jesus said, "Destroy this temple, and I will raise it again in three days." He might have said then and there that He was referring to His own body, but He didn't for some reason. However, these words were used against Him later—at His trial. "This fellow said, 'I am able to destroy the temple of God and rebuild it in three days'" (Matthew 26:61). But as I said, it is not the truth the enemy wants, in any case.

People tend to believe what they read in newspapers or magazines. And if a word appears in print that is negative about you, most people will believe it. "Throw enough mud on the wall and some of it will stick," as they say. "Where there's smoke, there's fire." So if they see it in print, the conclusion is, "It must be true."

What is their intention in lying about you? Why do they do it? What is the motive of those who persecute? The answer is, to hurt you and cause you pain. They want to punish you. To drive you to despair. They'd love it if you would retort. In the meantime, if they can undermine your credibility so that nobody will trust you, they are pleased. They would, of course, love to sideline you and put you out of operation.

The Heart of Persecution

These people unwittingly reveal who they are really angry with: It is the Lord Jesus Christ. It is "because of Me," says Jesus. In other words: "The buck stops with Me. I am the one they hate, I am the one they are angry with."

This means we must learn not to take persecution personally. In much the way that every leader must learn not to take rejection personally, as Samuel learned ("It is not you they have rejected, but they have rejected me," said the Lord [1 Samuel 8:7]), so with persecution. It is not you they are angry with—they are angry with God. Men hate God by nature—His holiness, His glory, His sovereignty. Jesus mirrors the Father, so they hate Jesus. That is why they crucified Him. So when we are truly persecuted because of our faithfulness to God, we mirror Jesus. And we must therefore never take persecution personally.

The heart of persecution is their hatred for God and His Son. That is the driving force, says Jesus.

The Holy Spirit also mirrors Jesus. He is called the Spirit of Christ in Romans 8:9 and Philippians 1:19. Therefore, whenever you follow the Spirit, walk in the Spirit or honor the Spirit, you make the devil angry. He will stir up people who will insult you, pursue you, lie about you. "It's all because of Me," says Jesus. Peter added, "Dear friends, do not be surprised at the painful trial you are suffering, as though something strange were happening to you. But rejoice that you participate in the sufferings of Christ, so that you may be overjoyed when his glory is revealed. If you are insulted because of the name of Christ, you are blessed, for the Spirit of glory and of God rests on you" (1 Peter 4:12–14).

Earlier, I made a distinction between the minor league and the big league. The greatest promotion you will get this side of heaven is to enter the big league of persecution—when you become a major threat to the devil. After being persecuted because of Christ, the next stop is heaven. Don't expect a Nobel Prize or a knighthood (although God could do that for you). The greatest honor is to enter God's hall of fame—when all suffering is because of Him. What an honor. And He doesn't forget it.

12. Graduating with Honors

Rejoice and be glad, because great is your reward in heaven, for in the same way they persecuted the prophets who were before you.

MATTHEW 5:12

This verse, which brings the section on the Beatitudes to an end, is essential to all I believe and live for. The New Testament teaching of reward at the Judgment Seat of Christ is a vital part of my doctrine of salvation. Some say, "I don't care about a reward in heaven—I am happy just to make it to heaven." I reply: You won't feel that way then—at the Judgment Seat of Christ.

Also, the apostle Paul took reward very seriously. Godly people do. "I beat my body and make it my slave so that after I have preached to others, I myself will not be disqualified for the prize" (1 Corinthians 9:27).

In Matthew 5:12, Jesus elaborates on what He has said about being blessed for being persecuted.

The Special Privilege of the Persecuted

Jesus has already said we are blessed if we are persecuted for righteousness and for suffering because of Him. He might have left it at that, saying no more. Indeed, we should believe it if only because He said it. God could do this all the time—whether regarding any obedience or sacrifice required—e.g., tithing, witnessing or praying. But He always stoops to our weakness and motivates us in terms of our own self-interest.

For example, regarding tithing, He says, "Bring the whole tithe into the storehouse . . . and see if I will not throw open the floodgates of heaven and pour out so much blessing that you will not have room enough for it" (Malachi 3:10). God did not have to promise blessing for doing what He required. But He did. That is merely an example of how God graciously appeals to our self-interest to secure our obedience.

And so now He does this regarding suffering for Christ's sake. "Great is your reward in heaven." Jesus tells us that those who are persecuted have

a right to rejoice. "Rejoice and be glad," He says to us if we are persecuted because of Him. After all, a great reward is in the making. We are now put into a special category, namely, that of the prophets. The big league.

Why would Jesus say this? To motivate us, to encourage us. Whoever said that being insulted is fun? It is the opposite. It is hard to take. Even Jesus despised the shame. "Let us fix our eyes on Jesus, the author and perfecter of our faith, who for the joy set before him endured the cross, scorning its shame, and sat down at the right hand of the throne of God" (Hebrews 12:2). Therefore, Jesus is helping us to have a different perspective if we are insulted or lied about.

This kind of rejoicing, however, is not likely to be spontaneous. It is not as though Jesus expects us to jump up and down and clap our hands because He tells us this. He gives a command to rejoice! A command comes because we aren't likely to do this otherwise. When Paul said, "Rejoice in the Lord always" (Philippians 4:4), we will only do it if we make the choice to rejoice. It is an act of the will. So, too, in these words, "rejoice and be glad." And yet we have every reason to rejoice and be glad! Why? Because it is true—great will our reward be in heaven. This is something very wonderful indeed.

And yet it seems that Peter and John rejoiced spontaneously when they were persecuted. They were reprimanded, flogged and ordered never again to speak in the name of Jesus. Their reaction to this: "The apostles left the Sanhedrin, rejoicing because they had been counted worthy of suffering disgrace for the Name" (Acts 5:41).

This moves me no end. I cannot be sure why they rejoiced. It may be because they were applying the teachings of Jesus. It could be because they, at least Peter, were given a second chance to get it right. You will recall how Peter had denied knowing the Lord, and felt so ashamed. But they were not going to blow this moment! They were thrilled to their fingertips that they were given this opportunity to suffer the shame of Jesus' name.

When Jesus tells us that persecution elevates us to the status of prophets, it is arguably the first explicit opinion God Himself gives regarding the Old Testament prophets. What an honor it must have been to be Moses, Samuel, Elijah, Elisha, Isaiah, Jeremiah or Daniel, et al.—wow. And yet we are not told that they knew they were blessed. It wasn't fun for them. I know of no similar message to prepare them. I do not recall that God ever said to any one of them, "You are special. You are set apart. Your reward will be great indeed." No.

So it is with any of us who may be called to a special task. We don't immediately get a big basket of flowers from the angels because we have obeyed. It is like the parable of Jesus in this regard: "Would [the man in charge] thank the servant because he did what he was told to do? So you also, when you have done everything you were told to do, should say, 'We are unworthy servants; we have only done our duty'" (Luke 17:9–10).

The prophets are like that. They went into the fire without any word that they would be honored. Even Shadrach, Meshach and Abednego went into the fiery furnace without any assurance whatever they would come out alive. But they did (Daniel 3). God does not give us a special commendation merely because we are doing the right thing. As far as I can tell, Martin Luther felt absolutely nothing positive—he actually felt deserted by God—the night before he testified to the church hierarchy. But it was his finest hour.

And so here God reveals His pleasure with the prophets. He tells *us* what, perhaps, they would like to have heard! Jesus implicitly affirms them to the hilt when He says, "Great is your reward in heaven, for in the same way they persecuted the prophets who were before you." That is pretty high praise for these prophets! But they never got it then. Their reward will be in heaven.

Can you live with that? Do you need to be rewarded now? Or can you continue knowing, like Hagar (who got her comfort from this), "You are the God who sees me" (Genesis 16:13). God does see us. He notices indeed. He notices now. But our reward is in heaven. So I ask again: Can you live with that?

Personally, I find this thrilling. Just knowing that God sees and understands. That will hold me until I get to heaven! Just know, dear reader, that God does see you and does understand what you are going through. You might like the affirmation now and a little reward now. But wait. It is coming. It is worth waiting for.

The truth is, God elevates us to a very special privilege—namely, that of the prophets. The only qualification for the privilege: that you have been insulted because of Jesus. Degraded. Treated as scum. God notices. You may not think He does, but He is fully aware of what you are going through. We are challenged to trace the rainbow through the rain and wait for the day to come when we get our reward.

In a word: If you are persecuted, insulted, lied about, "put into perspective" and marginalized behind your back, God gave you an unconscious elevation to a special category: the prophets. People who suffer for His Son like this are put in the class of a prophet—not a king or priest.

Jesus is telling you up front, "This is a supreme honor." It is the highest honor heaven recognizes—greater than being an angel, than being Gabriel or Michael, than being Solomon or Hezekiah. It is better than being aristocracy, royalty or gentry, prime minister or winner of a Nobel Prize. It is greater than being honored with land, houses or palaces. It is greater than being the Duke of Westminster, Bill Gates or the king of Saudi Arabia. The best list you can get onto in this life is to be in the category of the prophet. How do you get onto this list? When you are insulted for the Son of God.

You will say, "I am no prophet." I reply: If you have been insulted or degraded because of testifying for Jesus Christ, you are in the same elite class as if you were Isaiah himself! That is what Jesus is saying in this fitting conclusion to the Beatitudes: "Rejoice and be glad, because great is your reward in heaven, for in the same way they persecuted the prophets who were before you."

I don't recall reading anyplace in the Old Testament where God said, "The prophets are special in My eyes." He did not inform them as if to

say, "You have a very special place in heaven."
No. But He tells us that! Why? It is one of God's
peculiar ways. He loves to surprise us, to do the
unexpected. He conceals His feelings and then,
suddenly, He unveils what He had always thought.

So, the prophets were always special to Him.
They suffered more than anybody. They were always treated as second class. Nobody liked them.
God never came along to them and said, "You
poor souls, My heart aches for you, I am hurting
with you. I am going to reward you." No. But
He certainly rewards them in heaven. And now
He tells us that.

When we began the Pilot Light ministry at
Westminster Chapel, we all felt second class. This
is partly because so many of our older, middle-
class members were unhappy about this ministry.
But God was with us—I know it now more than
ever, although He did not tell us in those days,
"Wow! Well done, Pilot Lights. We in heaven are
so proud of you." Nothing like that came to us.

That is the way God often is with those who
please Him most.

The prophets were so unappreciated in their
time. Kings were extolled. Priests were honored.
The prophets were marginalized, categorized and
the object of contempt.

Why do I write this? So that you might see that
God does know what you are going through, too.
He is looking forward to the day—perhaps more
than you are—when He will unveil His thoughts.
The psalmist did tell us that His thoughts about us
"outnumber the grains of sand" (Psalm 139:18).

In a word: What God says He feels about the
prophets is what He also feels about you—if you
have been insulted for the name of Jesus Christ.
The way you get promoted to the rank of prophet
is not by claiming to be a prophet, but by being
insulted for your faith in Jesus.

Shadrach, Meshach and Abednego were
threatened with a fiery furnace if they did not
bow to the king's image. They did not have a
conference among themselves to say, "Let's stay
cool. We are suffering for God. He will reward
us." No. Nothing like that. They simply replied to
the king, "O Nebuchadnezzar, we do not need to
defend ourselves before you in this matter. If we
are thrown into the blazing furnace, the God we
serve is able to save us from it, and he will rescue

us from your hand, O king. But even if he does
not, we want you to know, O king, that we will
not serve your gods or worship the image of gold
you have set up" (Daniel 3:16–18). God brought
them through the fire.

And yet not all who suffer for God are delivered. Those warriors of faith in Hebrews 11
had different outcomes: Some "shut the mouths
of lions, quenched the fury of the flames, and
escaped the edge of the sword . . . others were
tortured and refused to be released . . . some faced
jeers and flogging, while still others were chained
and put in prison. They were stoned; they were
sawed in two [probably a reference to Isaiah's martyrdom]; they were put to death by the sword"
(Hebrews 11:33–37). These people were put in
the highest possible category in God's eyes.

So with you, too. When you are insulted for
the name of Christ, you are catapulted to the rank
of a prophet and those described in Hebrews 11.
It is a guarantee you will graduate with honors and
pass from this world with a dignity that exceeds
the rich and famous of this present age.

Little did the Old Testament prophets know
that one day God's one and only Son would cite
them as examples of what God's people should
rejoice in being. Jeremiah was seen as a traitor for
telling Israel to surrender to the Babylonians (Jeremiah 21:10; 38:6). Elijah was hated by Queen
Jezebel, who vowed to kill him because he eliminated false prophets (1 Kings 19:2).

Are you insulted because of your stand for
Jesus Christ? Congratulations! Do you know
the pain of being lied about? God calls you
"blessed"—happy. Consider what you have in
common with those who have suffered before
you: vilification in the same manner (insulted)
and the same treatment (lied about). Are you
happy to be in the succession of the prophets?
What a calling! What a privilege!

What is more, you are not required to have a
prophetic gift to get into this category. You don't
have to have the gift of a word of knowledge or any
other gift of the Spirit. The only requirement: to
be insulted and lied about because of the Gospel!

Sweet Promise

And what good is it to be vilified and treated like
a prophet? Answer: Great will your reward be in

heaven. Why rejoice and be glad? Because you have been put in the classification of the prophets. Not only that, you are promised a "great" reward.

This suggests two categories of reward. There is simple reward. "The man who plants and the man who waters have one purpose, and each will be rewarded according to his own labor" (1 Corinthians 3:8). Moreover, the person who builds a superstructure of gold, silver and precious stones [as opposed to wood, hay, straw] will receive a "reward" (1 Corinthians 3:14).

But in this closing beatitude, Jesus talks about a "great" reward in heaven. It shows what the prophets got in God's eyes then, and it shows what they will get at the Judgment Seat of Christ, still in the future. This shows what God will do for those who were insulted and lied about because of their obedience to the faith of Christ. They erected a superstructure of gold, silver and costly stones, which guarantees a reward. But in the case of the prophets, it is a "great" reward that they will receive because of the suffering they endured for Jesus Christ.

When and how do you receive this reward? Answer: in two ways. First, you've got it now, in the sense that you are privy to the greatest information there is: how much you please God. The only requirement: that you are persecuted because of Jesus. No other requirement is needed. You may be a waitress, a physician, a lawyer, one who works scrubbing floors, a truck driver, educated, uneducated, a teacher or a secretary. But in heaven you will be counted with the prophets, all because you were lied about or insulted due to your testimony concerning Jesus Christ. Isn't that wonderful?

So, in a sense you've got it now. Because God's Word tells you this. It's yours. The angels know. The sainted dead know. And you know how you are seen in heaven—as great. You are not seen with the wealthy or middle class, nor the famous or educated, nor the successful or popular. You are elevated to the category of prophet even though you do not have a prophetic gift. You simply suffered like true prophets do.

It is worth saying there will be prophets who get no reward at all—false prophets. Some are high-profile prophets. Jeremiah was outnumbered by the false prophets in his day. They had the

glory; he got the dungeon. Likewise, there are those who prophesy smooth things today. They get the glory, and those who are insulted for Christ are ignored.

Jesus says great "is" your reward. You've got it now! Believe it now. Enjoy it now. Don't blab it to the world—just enjoy it. It is what God says about you. Now.

But that is not the whole story. What is in heaven is being stored. It is now there on deposit. The immediate result below is an anointing, and knowing what God thinks about you. But there is coming a day when there will be a procession unlike anything you have ever seen or heard of. It is a procession greater than eight thousand people queuing up to the Queen's garden party. It is greater than being congratulated by the prime minister or president.

Picture this. Abel, called by Jesus a prophet (Luke 11:50–51), Moses, Samuel, Elijah, Isaiah, Jeremiah, Daniel, John the Baptist—all followed by a stream of unknown faces whose names will never appear in the *New York Times* or the *London Times*. They didn't have a funeral in Westminster Abbey. Their names were not known to the hierarchy of the Church. Some of them took in ironing to survive. Washed the clothes of the rich. Were insulted by family members, professing Christians and the world. The same God who will remember Moses and Elijah will remember you. Jesus Himself will look at you face-to-face—right into your eyes—and say, "Well done."

Listen to the way Jesus put it in the parallel account: "Blessed are you when men hate you, when they exclude you and insult you and reject your name as evil, because of the Son of man. Rejoice in that day and leap for joy, because great is your reward in heaven. For that is how their fathers treated the prophets" (Luke 6:22–23).

Note: He says "rejoice in that day." When is "that day"? Answer: on the same day when they exclude you. Rejoice right then! That is the earnest of your reward. Do you feel rejected, marginalized, categorized and put into perspective? Don't wait—rejoice now!

You will not need a command to rejoice when you are rewarded at the Judgment Seat of Christ. It will be a spontaneous moment of overflowing. You won't need a command then! But you perhaps need it now. Jesus is telling you to rejoice *now* if you have been marginalized for the Gospel.

Jesus went on to say the opposite of the way people naturally think. The natural way to think is to rejoice when everybody likes you, when you are popular. But Jesus says, "Woe to you when all men speak well of you, for that is how their fathers treated the false prophets" (Luke 6:26). But if, on the other hand, you are excluded? "Leap for joy"! About the only time I see people leap is when they score a goal or touchdown at a ball game. They leap!

Do it now, says Jesus. Do it when you are excluded. Rejoice at the moment you are insulted. Know that in the sight of the King of heaven—whose opinion is the only one that matters—you just graduated with honors. And one day you will get the official recognition from the lips of Jesus Himself. And everybody else will see it with you.

13. The Salt of the Earth

You are the salt of the earth. But if the salt loses its saltiness, how can it be made salty again? It is no longer good for anything, except to be thrown out and trampled by men.

It might be said that, in a sense, the "sermon" is about to begin with this verse, even though it is an introduction following the "text." The main course, therefore, is coming shortly.

Up to now we have had the "starters," the appetizers, namely, Jesus' "text"—the Beatitudes. The Sermon on the Mount in the main is the unfolding, exposition and application of the Beatitudes, although not in the chronological order in which they came in Matthew 5:1–12. Furthermore, verses 13–16 are not an exposition of the Beatitudes, but a link between the Beatitudes and Jesus' exposition. These verses about "salt and light" basically introduce the Sermon.

As you know, a little bit of salt can go a long way. The people of God are called "salt." We may wish we had been called "sand," "grass" or "trees," of which there is an abundance. This would have implied that our faith would become dominant and prominent in the world. But no. We are called "salt"—a pretty strong hint (if you ask me) that Christians with the anointing of the Beatitudes would be not only a minority in this present age but a small minority at that. Those who oppose the Christian faith sometimes say, "It if were so wonderful, why doesn't everybody go after it?" The reply may be: Jesus never said or thought that His followers would dominate the world in this present age. We are, simply, "salt."

I think I have become a bit of an authority on salt. In preparation for this chapter, I invited those who attended our School of Theology at Westminster Chapel to tell me what they knew about salt. I have learned at least forty things about salt, some of which I had not thought of. I think I could preach several sermons on the subject!

But let me remind you of a few things about salt plus some of its uses: (1) It is used for healing;

(2) it is a cleansing agent; (3) it helps to eliminate dye stains; (4) it helps get rid of tea stains on fine china; (5) it melts ice; (6) it keeps your feet from slipping on ice; (7) it is used as a gargle for a sore throat; (8) it is good for bathing tired feet; (9) it is good for bee stings; (10) it stops bleeding; (11) it kills unpleasant odors from garbage cans; (12) in washing, it keeps clothes sparkling white; (13) it helps lessen sour taste, as in a grapefruit; (14) on a dunghill or cesspit, it keeps disease away; (15) it is a seasoning, making food taste better; (16) it is a preservative, keeping things from spoiling; and (17) it is an antiseptic, killing germs. This is to name a few, and some of these I had not thought of.

Furthermore, in ancient times salt was used as a currency. Caesar's soldiers received payment in salt. In ancient China, salt was second to gold in value. Salt was sometimes fraudulently contaminated—for example, being mixed with a white dust but sold as salt.

Jesus said that "you are the salt of the earth" and then talked about people losing their saltiness. It is fairly well known today, however, that salt is always salt and does not lose its saltiness. But it certainly does lose it if it gets contaminated with other ingredients.

What, then, did Jesus mean by our being salt and losing "saltiness"? In answering this question we must begin with Jesus' own assumption. The statement "you are the salt of the earth" refers to those who have become what the Beatitudes describe and promise. This is important. Not anybody, just because he is a church member or calls himself a Christian, can apply this text out of context and say, "Oh, this describes me—I am the salt of the earth." Jesus is assuming we have taken the Beatitudes on board and that they describe us. We, therefore, are not going to be the salt of the earth if we are not exemplifying the Beatitudes.

It is true that the salt in this text is an implicit reference to the Church in the world and believers in society. It is also true that there is a type of "liberal Christianity" that seizes on this verse—often out of context—and pushes a social agenda that can sometimes be quite disconnected from the Gospel. Our being the "salt of the earth" is a valid description of the anointed child of God—not merely because we go to church, but because we have been exemplifying the spirit of the Beatitudes in the world.

As I noted above, salt losing saltiness happened often in ancient times through salt being contaminated by other ingredients. Losing saltiness is our Lord's way of describing a Christian who loses the anointing of the Spirit. A Christian never loses the Holy Spirit (John 14:16), but one can lose the anointing—that acute sharpness in us that the Spirit bestows. When we grieve the Spirit, then, we don't lose the Spirit but the anointing (Ephesians 4:30). The Beatitudes, as we saw earlier, refer to the anointing of the Holy Spirit. "Blessed" means you have the anointing. The Kingdom of heaven refers to the un-grieved Spirit in God's people.

Therefore, it is a huge assumption that lies behind our being called the "salt of the earth"— namely, that we *are* what the Beatitudes describe and promise. For example, the descriptions "poor in spirit," "hungering for righteousness" and "being a peacemaker" have corresponding consequences. There are promises: being comforted, being filled, being known as God's children. And don't forget the reference to persecution (Matthew 5:12). As "all roads lead to Rome," so all the Beatitudes lead to persecution. As Paul said, "Everyone who wants to live a godly life in Christ Jesus will be persecuted" (2 Timothy 3:12).

It is immediately following His reference to persecution that Jesus says, "You are the salt of the earth." But do not forget that the salt of the earth refers to those men and women who inhabit the realm of the un-grieved Spirit, who are under the anointing. I think this is so important if only because of the way Matthew 5:13 is sometimes used to uphold the "social gospel." It is hastily

assumed by some that all professing "Christians" are salt and therefore are admonished to get involved in social issues. But if the Holy Spirit in you is grieved, you still have the Spirit but will not have the promise of the anointing. You will not have power, you will not have clear thinking, you will not have insight—and therefore you will not truly be the salt of the earth or light to the world.

Just being a church member or professing to be a Christian does not make you the salt of the earth. It is when you are broken, pure in heart, hungering for righteousness, full of mercy and persecuted because of righteousness that you qualify to be the salt of the earth. That assumption lies behind Jesus' statement that we are the salt of the earth.

Salt Is an Antiseptic

Jesus thus gives an analogy between our anointing and being salt in the world. Analogy, as you may know, is a partial likeness between two things that are compared. So Jesus is comparing the anointing with salt in the world because of the condition of the world. Our anointing is like salt to the fallen world. The world is in decay; our anointing—like salt—is presented as an antiseptic.

Implicit in this verse, therefore, is our Lord's diagnosis of humankind—it shows Jesus' own view of the world and simultaneously reveals His doctrine of sin. His statement points to what humankind is like and what the world is like—that it is in decay. Jesus is therefore saying in this statement not only that we are salt, but that there is something seriously wrong with the world.

Salt also delays decay. Our anointing is to the world what salt is to food: It delays its being spoiled. In the ancient world, take salt away from food, and food rots overnight. There were no freezers or refrigerators, only salt. Our anointing is the only hope for lost people going to hell. But for the presence of the Gospel, many would have perished long ago.

Salt Makes One Thirsty

The world is uninterested in the Gospel, but salt makes one thirsty. How are we going to create a thirst for righteousness in those we see all the time? There is only one answer: the anointing in us.

John Wesley saw in the Moravians a peace and calmness as they were crossing through the storms in the Atlantic—a peace he knew he himself didn't have. It made Wesley thirsty for what they had. Consequently, he went to their Bible studies and was gloriously changed.

An Arab sheik kept watching Arthur Blessitt—taking note of the shining smile on his face—as Arthur sipped his Coca-Cola in a Holiday Inn in Amman, Jordan. The sheik said to Arthur, "I want what you've got." The result was that the Arab was converted, and Arthur was given an open door to many Muslims in that area within a few hours.

Salt Is a Preservative

There are some explanations why the world is not utterly and totally topsy-turvy. One explanation is God's common grace—His goodness to all humankind given commonly to all, saved or lost. This is why we have law, police, firemen, doctors, hospitals. It is God's goodness to all.

Another explanation is the presence of godly people in a nation. John Wesley's conversion led to a Great Awakening in the eighteenth century. Secular historians now concede that the Wesleyan revival in England is the single thing that kept the nation from the equivalent of the French Revolution and all its upheaval. Anointed people—even a minority—serve as a preservative in a nation, for a little bit of salt goes a long way.

Salt Is a Seasoning

Salt makes things taste better. The true Christian in today's society, though far from being appreciated, is nonetheless often the reason the world is a better place than it would have been without the presence of the anointing. In a state of hopelessness—in a time of political and financial corruption, with the media so biased against true righteousness and with so much that is wrong in the world—the presence of a true Christian often makes a noticeable difference to those in despair.

Salt makes sour things taste less sour and, if used rightly, can make sweet things taste sweeter. "Let your conversation be always full of grace, seasoned with salt, so that you may know how to answer everyone" (Colossians 4:6).

To me t'was not the truth you taught,
  to you so clear, to me so dim;
But when you came to me you brought
  a sense of Him.
Yes, from your eyes He beckoned me
  and from your heart His love was
  shared
And I lost sight of you and saw the
  Christ instead.

  Anonymous

The salt of the earth are those people who seek to be like Jesus—who have a burden for the lost, care for the hurting and make people believe there is a God. A saint is someone who convinces you there is a God and makes you want to believe in Him and be like Him.

Salt Is Painful to an Open Wound

The person who exemplifies the Beatitudes makes the world a better place, yes—but it does not follow that one is always appreciated. William Wilberforce spoke out against slavery and was hated by many for a long time. In a day when people uphold marriage between a man and a woman, oppose abortion, speak out against racial prejudice and fight pornography and sexual promiscuity, the message of true righteousness will be opposed and the Christian will be persecuted. The message is like salt on an open wound: It hurts. Salt is good but can be painful.

When the Pilot Lights of Westminster Chapel took to the streets near Victoria and Buckingham Palace, they were not always very welcomed. The Gospel is by nature offensive. The anointing clarifies the Gospel, which makes it the very opposite of what the world wants to hear. People do not like hearing that there is something wrong with them, that they are sinners and going to hell. The message-bearer is therefore hated. We should never be surprised that the first reaction to the Gospel is often fierce rejection. But those who come to know Christ come to love those who presented the Gospel to them.

Maintaining the Anointing

We all need to be warned: The Christian can lose the anointing. Billy Graham once said that his greatest fear was that God would take His hand off him. When Samson told his secret to Delilah, he did not know that the Lord had departed from him, a classic example of one temporarily losing the anointing (Judges 16:20).

Strictly speaking, as I said above, salt stays salt and does not lose saltiness. But it can be contaminated by mixture. If we bring in the methods of the world, are motivated by the approval of people and let ourselves be ensnared by the fear of man, we are in that moment on the verge of losing the anointing. We may justify our rationale at the time, but we lose the anointing in the end.

As I mentioned earlier, in the ancient world what was often sold as salt was sometimes highly adulterated—mixed with impure matter. What was then popularly called "salt" was a white powder, possibly from around the Dead Sea. While this white powder contained sodium chloride, it contained much that was impure. The sodium chloride was the most soluble component and could easily be washed out. The residue of white powder still looked like salt, and was called salt—but it neither tasted nor acted like salt, but was road dust.

The anointing as demonstrated in the Beatitudes was without mixture. We sometimes use the expression "worth its salt." Jesus said, "Salt is good, but if it loses its saltiness [as in being contaminated with a mixture], how can you make it salty again?" (Mark 9:50). James said, "You adulterous people, don't you know that friendship with the world is hatred toward God? Anyone who chooses to be a friend of the world becomes an enemy of God" (James 4:4). Your anointing is your most valuable possession. Lose it, and you are like road dust.

Our task is to maintain our anointing. We never outgrow the Beatitudes. Jesus' declaration that those who show the spirit and truth of the Beatitudes by their lives are the "salt of the earth" should be applied to all that you and I are called to be and do. But Matthew 5:13 refers primarily to the Gospel—the need to see people saved and to grow in grace, as the whole of the Sermon on the Mount demonstrates.

We should demonstrate social concerns, too—to help meet the needs of the poor, to fight racism, to help the homeless and to care for widows and the disabled in their distress. Again my concern is that some people—especially those espousing a liberal type of Christianity—borrow from the Sermon on the Mount the issues that happen to appeal to them, lifting certain verses out of their context (as is often done regarding Matthew 5:13–16). The greatest folly in any case is for a Christian to become an activist without the anointing as identified in the Beatitudes.

Matthew 5:13—"you are the salt of the earth"—is a word about a Christian's anointing in an uncaring, cold, godless world. When we live in the realm of the un-grieved Spirit, we are what Jesus says we are: the salt of the earth. It is God having His way with us. For this reason, a little goes a long way. That is why we are called "salt." The question then is: What is your salt worth?

It is not vogue nowadays to say that being the salt of the earth is Jesus' reference to soul-winning. But it is. The reference to persecution just before Jesus' statement about salt had to do with being insulted "because of Me." It is because of Jesus Christ—who He was and what He came to do—that people insult us. A social gospel, however valid in what it may aim to do, will not receive many insults. But become a soul-winner and you will find out what it means to be persecuted.

When I was seventeen years of age, just before entering Trevecca Nazarene College in Nashville, I worked in Washington, D.C. While there I was befriended by our Kentucky U.S. Senator John Sherman Cooper. For some reason he arranged for me to go where few were allowed: I was invited to sit at the desk of the vice president of the United States, just a few feet behind the Senate floor. As I sat there someone said to me, "All who sit in this chair get to make a wish." I had to think quickly. I bowed my head and prayed, "Make me a great soul-winner."

It was my wish then, and it is my wish now that I am 74. All my life I have tried to be salt. I cannot say I have seen all that many come to Christ. But I take comfort that a little bit of salt goes a long way.

14. Showing the Way

You are the light of the world. A city on a hill cannot be hidden.

MATTHEW 5:14

Jesus now switches metaphors. Having said that His followers are the "salt of the earth," He now says that they are the "light of the world." What is the difference? The first statement—that we are "salt"—shows us that as a passive people we make a difference to the world. It refers to what we are. By what we are we do make a difference in the world.

The second statement—that we are "light"—depicts us as both a passive people and an active people. It refers to what we are and what we do. A people of light cannot help but make a difference because we are so visible. Indeed, our being light is like a "city on a hill" that cannot be hidden.

There is to this day a little town in Galilee called Safed—very visible on the top of the mountain that is an extension of the same range from which the Sermon on the Mount was first preached. The city of Safed is visible day or night. Whether it is the same little city that Jesus had in mind, I don't know. But Safed is two thousand years old and certainly could have been the same city Jesus had in mind.

Both statements, whether referring to "salt" or "light," imply that something is definitely right about Jesus' followers and wrong with the world. The statements show the contrast between the anointing of the Holy Spirit and a world that is in trouble. The world is in decay; salt is a preservative. The world is in darkness; light shows the way.

Later on, in a different place, Jesus referred to Himself as light: "I am the light of the world. Whoever follows me will never walk in darkness, but will have the light of life" (John 8:12). He also said, "This is the verdict: Light has come into the world, but men loved darkness instead of light because their deeds were evil. Everyone who does evil hates the light, and will not come into the

light for fear that his deeds will be exposed. But whoever lives by the truth comes into the light, so that it may be seen plainly that what he has done has been done through God" (John 3:19–21).

It is our anointing that makes the difference. But there is a noteworthy contrast between Jesus' anointing and ours. Jesus had the Holy Spirit without any limit (John 3:34). His anointing was the ultimate filling of the Spirit, having all of God one can get. You and I only have a "measure" of faith (Romans 12:3), which means we have a limit on our faith. Even so, those who have been broken, are full of mercy, are pure in heart and are truly peacemakers do have a true anointing, being salt. But we can lose that anointing if it becomes contaminated with the world. Likewise, light can lose its effectiveness by being hidden. People do not light a lamp and then put it under a bowl, said Jesus.

There is something in the original Greek that the translation does not reveal. The word *you* has an emphasis in the Greek that really means "you and you alone." Jesus is not referring to the natural daylight, light provided by the sun. He uses a metaphor: What the sun is to darkness, the anointing is to people in darkness. The anointing does for lost people what the sun does for mankind: It shows what is there. It shows the way and leaves one without excuse.

I ask you: Does your testimony leave those around you without excuse? In other words, will they have to admit one day that you were faithful to your calling, that you did indeed show them the way by your clear witness? Are you a light—like a city on a hill that cannot be hidden?

It is said that John Fletcher, an early Methodist and contemporary of John Wesley, had a reputation of being a very godly person. One Sunday morning, a man walked down the road on his way to church. A friend shouted at him, "Where are you going?" The reply came, "I am going to see and hear John Fletcher preach today." A few hours later, on the return to his home, the same man was asked: "Well, did you see John Fletcher today?" There was a long pause. The man had trouble speaking. Finally, he replied: "No. I saw Jesus Christ and Him crucified."

Paul determined to know nothing among the Corinthians except Jesus Christ and Him crucified (1 Corinthians 2:2). I have been convinced for years that Paul was referring to the kind of person he intended to be among them, as much as referring to the objective message of the Gospel. By the way, Wesley's generation was also the generation of the French atheist Voltaire, an ardent opponent of Christianity. Voltaire was asked, "Did you ever meet anybody who you thought might be truly a Christian?" Voltaire replied, "I once met a man by the name of John Fletcher."

Those under this anointing as portrayed by the Beatitudes are unique. It is not science that shows the way. Scientists can't solve the problems of the world; they cannot figure out man. It is not learning; education is not the light of the world. Never in history have people been more educated, and never have people been more immoral.

Indeed, never has the world been a darker place and more unwilling to come to the true Light. It is not philosophy, psychology, psychiatry, religion, theology or even the Church generally that gives the answer today. The professing Church, generally speaking, is ashamed of the Bible. Ask a typical Church leader today, "Do you believe the Fall of man was a date in history and that the Garden of Eden was a place on the map?" and see what he will say. Not only that, theology can be orthodox without the anointing. To use Dr. Lloyd-Jones's expression: "Perfectly orthodox, perfectly useless."

The Kind of Light

What kind of light, then, is Jesus talking about when He says, "You are the light of the world"?

First of all, it is a regenerated light. This is what God has done in us. The "god of this world" (a nickname for the devil) has blinded the minds of those who do not believe. But the same God who said, "Let light shine out of darkness," has made "his light shine in our hearts to give us the light of the knowledge of the glory of God in the face of Christ" (2 Corinthians 4:4, 6).

Jesus said to Saul of Tarsus: "I am sending you to [Gentiles] to open their eyes and turn them from darkness to light, and from the power of Satan to God, so that they may receive forgiveness of sins and a place among those who are sanctified by faith in me" (Acts 26:17–18). Saul became the apostle Paul, who said, "You were once darkness, but now you are light in the Lord" (Ephesians 5:8). Said Peter: "You are a chosen people, a royal priesthood, a holy nation, a people belonging to God, that you may declare the praises of him who called you out of darkness into his wonderful light" (1 Peter 2:9). It all began with our being born again.

It is a reflected light. "We, who with unveiled faces all reflect the Lord's glory, are being transformed into his likeness with ever-increasing glory, which comes from the Lord, who is the Spirit" (2 Corinthians 3:18). Light could be referred to as the essence of God. "God is light; in him there is no darkness at all" (1 John 1:5). God lives in "unapproachable light" (1 Timothy 6:16). Jesus is God and is thus the "light of the world" (John 8:12; 9:5). Our light is but a reflection of that light. We are like the moon, which reflects the light of the sun.

Furthermore, the greater the anointing, the more brilliant the light. We see this in the way Shadrach, Meshach and Abednego replied to the king Nebuchadnezzar when he threatened them with a burning, fiery furnace if they did not bow to him: "We are not careful to answer thee" (Daniel 3:16, KJV), for "the God we serve is able to save us from it, and he will rescue us from your hand, O king. But even if he does not, we want you to know, O king, that we will not serve your gods or worship the image of gold you have set up" (Daniel 3:16–18). They were truly light in that dark place. They were dead to any proposition that would come from Satan. They didn't even have to pray about it.

It is a recognizable light. "A city on a hill cannot be hidden." The anointing, almost certainly, will be recognizable. I must be guarded here. Jesus had the ultimate anointing and was not recognized by His own people (John 1:11). Stephen's face shone like an angel, but it was not sufficient to stop the Jews from killing him (Acts 6:15; 7:57–60). But having said that, our witness in the world, though it may be rejected, will be visible. That is, we won't hide our light under a bowl.

It is a repugnant light. Indeed, "Everyone who does evil hates the light, and will not come into the light for fear that his deeds will be exposed. But whoever lives by the truth comes into the light, so that it may be seen plainly that what he has done has been done through God" (John 3:20–21). Those who are light in the world will be hated as Jesus Himself was. "If the world hates you, keep in mind that it hated me first" (John 15:18).

It is a responsible light. We are responsible not to hide our light under a bowl. We are responsible to keep the light unveiled. Whether you witness like a Pilot Light on the streets (giving out tracts and engaging in conversation), or you are a Christian witness at your place of work, you are responsible—sooner or later—to let it be known you are unashamed of Jesus Christ.

You need wisdom, of course, and I am aware of people imprudently witnessing for the Lord. But don't be like the lady in California whom Arthur Blessitt tells about. She felt she should never speak to people about Jesus, only witness "by her life." After several years, someone said to her, "You are different. What is it that is different about you? Oh, I know what it is—are you a vegetarian?" We are responsible not to hide our light under a bowl, but we are to be responsible in the way we manifest that light.

Consider this question: If a person you see all the time found out suddenly that you were a Christian, would they be surprised? The funny thing is, non-Christians have a pretty shrewd idea of what a Christian is supposed to be like. We are to keep the light unveiled, or we are like contaminated salt—good for nothing.

The light used in ancient times was a lamp that burned with oil. Behind any light is fire. The sun is a ball of fire. Jesus, said John the Baptist, would "baptize you with the Holy Spirit and with fire" (Matthew 3:11). No fire means no light. No fire means no anointing. Jesus cautioned, "Be dressed ready for service and keep your lamps burning,

like men waiting for their master to return from a wedding banquet, so that when he comes and knocks they can immediately open the door for him" (Luke 12:35–36).

The best way to wait for Jesus' knocking is to be near the door. Do you know what it is like to be away from the door when one knocks—and you miss the caller? Be near the door so you can open it immediately! "It will be good for those servants whose master finds them watching when he comes" (Luke 12:37).

Jesus said that the last days would be characterized by the Church being asleep. While the bridegroom was a long time in coming, "They all became drowsy and fell asleep" (Matthew 25:5).

There are certain characteristics of sleep.

First, you don't know you were asleep until you wake up. This is scary. You might be asleep right now! It is only after you wake up that you realize you were asleep. Could you be asleep now, spiritually speaking?

Second, you dream things you would not do if you were awake. So when we are spiritually asleep, we do things we absolutely would not do were we wide-awake! Question: What is it you are now doing you once said you'd never do? Are you doing things at this moment that you know in your heart of hearts you would not do if you were completely right with God?

Third, we hate the sound of an alarm when we are asleep. Could it be, you are unhappy with these lines? That they could serve to wake you up?

Jesus said that in the last days there would be a midnight cry—meaning that the awakening call came in the middle of the night when people were least expecting it. The result was, however, that the Church was awakened. Those who had taken oil in their vessels were ready and went to the wedding banquet. Those who had no oil were left out and cried, "Open the door for us!" The reply came, "I don't know you." "Therefore keep watch," said Jesus, "because you do not know the day or the hour" (Matthew 25:13).

Our being light to the world, then, is connected to the oil burning. Fire lies behind the light. And we are responsible to keep our light from being hidden. We are to be unashamed of our Lord and His servants. "If anyone is ashamed of me and my words in this adulterous and sinful generation, the Son of Man will be ashamed of him when he comes in the Father's glory with the holy angels" (Mark 8:38). Paul said to Timothy, "Do not be ashamed to testify about our Lord, or ashamed of me his prisoner. But join with me in suffering for the gospel" (2 Timothy 1:8).

As for the wake-up call in the middle of the night, I take comfort in these words from the Old Testament prophet: "Suddenly the Lord you are seeking will come to his temple. . . . But who can endure the day of his coming? Who can stand when he appears? For he will be like a refiner's fire or a launderer's soap" (Malachi 3:1–2). "Surely the day is coming; it will burn like a furnace. All the arrogant and every evildoer will be stubble, and that day that is coming will set them on fire" (Malachi 4:1).

My wisdom to every reader: Stay near the door with your lamp burning, so that you don't miss the moment when the Lord shows up. He could come at any time. Even this very day.

15. Good Works

Neither do people light a lamp and put it under a bowl. Instead they put it on its
stand, and it gives light to everyone in the house. In the same way, let your light shine
before men, that they may see your good deeds and praise your Father in heaven.

MATTHEW 5:15–16

This is one of the better known verses in the Sermon on the Mount. "Good deeds" are often translated "good works" (KJV, RSV, ESV, NJB), sometimes "good things you do" (PHILLIPS, GNT), and also "the good you do" (NEB). It is an elaboration of Jesus' point that we are "light"—which we are not to hide but to show to everybody.

Some people, however, misunderstand this verse and assume it means we are saved by good works. They think people get to heaven by their good works. Furthermore, if our works glorify the Father, it must mean this is the way we are saved. Wrong. This verse is not a reference to how we are saved. The Beatitudes—Jesus' "text" for the Sermon on the Mount—begin with our being broken. This shows the effectual work of the Holy Spirit.

Salvation is received by those who realize they are "poor in spirit," that they have no bargaining power with God. In other words, our being saved is an assumption when Jesus finished with the Beatitudes. We are saved by the sheer grace of God, and faith is the instrument by which our salvation is received. "For it is by grace you have been saved, through faith—and this not from yourselves, it is the gift of God—not by works, so that no one can boast" (Ephesians 2:8–9).

Jesus wants saved people to manifest good works by godly living. Saved people need to be encouraged, motivated and admonished to show good works. Paul exhorted Titus that "our people must learn to devote themselves to doing what is good" (Titus 3:14)—or, as the King James Version put it, be careful "to maintain good works." Why be careful? It is because we all need to be reminded to show good works.

Some people argue that our good works will necessarily and automatically flow if we are truly converted. Really? If so, why did Jesus remind us that this light is not to be put under a bowl but "put on a stand"? We all need to be reminded and cautioned. That is what Jesus is doing in these verses.

Indeed, having stated that we are saved by grace through faith, Paul added: "For we are God's workmanship, created in Christ Jesus to do good works, which God prepared in advance for us to do" (Ephesians 2:10).

Good works do not precede conversion but flow from having been created, regenerated and quickened. Don't put the cart before the horse!

The moment one puts the proposition that good works are a condition of whether we are saved, we will all—every one of us—focus immediately on good works, not the object of faith: our Lord Jesus Christ. The moment I am told that I must maintain good works in order to be saved or to have assurance of salvation, I will look to my works every time rather than Christ.

We are all made that way. We cannot help but look to what proves we are saved. Thank God, we look to Christ to prove that we are saved. As John Calvin put it, if we look to ourselves, that is "sure damnation." Or, to quote C. H. Spurgeon: "I looked to Christ and the Dove flew in; I looked to the Dove and he disappeared."

A Test—A Kind of Behavior

While showing good works is not presented as a test whether one is saved, it is indeed a test whether one has experienced the Beatitudes and is exemplifying them. We must remain teachable. It is an assumption that those who have experienced the Beatitudes must still be reminded to show good works. It is not merely living in the realm of the un-grieved Spirit or under the anointing. Those under the anointing still need to be told we must show good works. The anointing is to be manifested by a certain behavior, a certain manner of life.

What Jesus requires of us is, first, reasonable behavior. We are told, "In the same way"—that is, as you put a lamp on its stand so that it will give light to everyone in the house—so "let your light shine before men." As it would be unreasonable behavior to light a lamp then hide it from giving light, so would it be unreasonable behavior to have experienced the blessedness of the anointing and then conceal it. As a lamp is to illuminate the room, so your good deeds should not be in isolation, but rather out in the open for society and the world to see. Doing this glorifies God.

Jesus also requires of us radiant behavior. What does light do? It shows what is there. Light does not cause an item to be there—it shows it. Without light you cannot see the chairs, the tables, the pictures or the carpet. But when the light is on, you see these things. It causes you to see what was there already.

And yet light does not draw attention to itself. People don't stare at the sun or they will go blind. The sun rises every morning to show the landscape that was hidden overnight. When a light is turned on, you do not focus on the light but on what is illuminated. The light is taken for granted. We therefore show good works in a manner that does not cause people to focus on us. Our goal is not for people to say, "What a wonderful person you are," but rather to see what God has done in us—how He saved us and changed us, and how we give all the glory to God. Our light shows a radiant behavior.

What, then, does our light do? It shows the way. Jesus said, "A man who walks by day will not stumble, for he sees by this world's light" (John 11:9). Our light is to show people the Way—namely, that Jesus Christ is "the way and the truth and the life" (John 14:6). We cannot compromise on this principle. Jesus Christ is not "a" way to heaven—He is the only way. "You are all sons of light and sons of the day," said Paul (1 Thessalonians 5:5).

Our radiant light shows wisdom. "Blessed is the man who finds wisdom, the man who gains understanding" (Proverbs 3:13). "Wisdom is supreme; therefore get wisdom. Though it cost all you have, get understanding" (Proverbs 4:7). "The path of the righteous is like the first gleam of dawn, shining ever brighter till the full light of day. But the way of the wicked is like deep darkness; they do not know what makes them stumble" (Proverbs 4:18–19).

Our radiant light shows warmth. Our good works not only reflect the light for the way, but warmth as well. The sun gives light and warmth. That is why it gets cool when the sun goes down. Likewise, our anointing will not leave people cold and in shivers. Our light exudes warmth, not smugness. It will not give people an odd, weird feeling. It will not make them feel strange or kept away. The anointing beckons. It radiates a good, warm feeling. It makes people feel wanted and accepted.

"The wisdom that comes from heaven is first of all pure; then peace-loving, considerate, submissive, full of mercy and good fruit, impartial and sincere" (James 3:17). I love the King James expression, "easy to be intreated." The wisdom of the Holy Spirit is a warm beckoning that lets you know you will not be rejected. The leper knew his place in society, but he still felt in his heart that he could go to Jesus and be accepted. He was (Matthew 8:1).

Such Good Works Are to Be Seen

Note, too, that the wisdom that comes from above is "first of all pure." This is proof that sexual purity will characterize those with God's true anointing. In this day of immorality and promiscuity, our good works, which show wisdom, give undoubted contrast—beginning with sexual purity. The fruit of the Spirit is love but also "self-control" (Galatians 5:22–23).

Our behavior is a relevant behavior. It is "before men." It is not in solitude, not in privacy or in your home. It is out there to be seen by the world. It is not before angels, or even merely before God. "Let your light shine before men." It is before all people. The whole world is watching us.

It is a recognizable behavior. It is for all men to "see"—that they will "see your good deeds." You may well say, "I feel the presence of God when reading my Bible." Good. I certainly hope so. But that is not what Jesus means here. He commands us to live so that people can see what is true about us. And yet it does demonstrate that those who have a blessed anointing still need to be taught and led by good teaching. They need to be admonished and warned.

I have long been intrigued by Paul when he was in Athens waiting for Timothy to turn up. He might have said, "This is a good time to pray. I will fast and pray and wait on God until Timothy arrives." But no. When he saw such idolatry in Athens that his spirit was stirred within him, Paul made his way to the synagogue to speak to Jews and to the marketplace "day by day with those who happened to be there" (Acts 17:16–17). The result was that he was invited to address philosophers at the Areopagus, and some of them were converted.

The Result of Conversion

"Good deeds" mean righteous behavior. It is the result of conversion, of a changed life. "If anyone is in Christ, he is a new creation; the old has gone, the new has come!" (2 Corinthians 5:17). Saul of Tarsus was instantly and surprisingly converted. The next thing we learn is that he "began to preach in the synagogues that Jesus is the Son of God" (Acts 9:20).

Righteous behavior is the result of a returning backslider. Peter had embarrassingly let the Lord down when he denied knowing Jesus before a servant girl. But he was restored and left people astonished at his behavior. All the people observing Peter and John "were astonished and they took note that these men had been with Jesus" (Acts 4:13). Good deeds also mean a consistent holy living, no longer "tossed back and forth by the waves, and blown here and there by every wind of teaching" (Ephesians 4:14).

"Good deeds" will be what James says must be shown to the "poor man." When James said they had despised the "poor," the Greek literally says "poor man" (Gr. *protochon, accusative, masculine singular*—see ESV). And when James asks the question, "Can faith save *him* [accusative, masculine, singular]?" he had not changed the subject, but meant the same poor man of James 2:6. This is because the only thing that will have any good influence on such a poor man will be our works.

William Booth, founder of the Salvation Army, used to say it is hard to preach the Gospel to a man with an empty stomach.

I am indebted to Dr. Raymond Brown for this unforgettable story. A minister friend of his was in Calcutta, India, and rushed to get to his train on time. He was running late. If he missed the train, it meant he would have to wait for twelve hours in a crowded city with which he was unfamiliar and where he had no place to stay. As he made his way hurriedly to the station, he had to walk through a market. Doing so, walking swiftly with his suitcases, he accidentally knocked over a fruit and vegetable stand that was being run by a blind man. Fruit went in every direction—apples, bananas, mangoes, tomatoes and beans. But as this minister was late and so rushed, he hurried on.

He made it in time and was now sitting comfortably in his seat on the train. All he could think about, however, was that blind man and all the fruit that had fallen to the ground. Before the train began to move, the preacher got his suitcases, got off the train and made his way to the blind man's stand. The blind man was on his knees, reaching for his fruit and putting the fruit and vegetables in their boxes in order to be sold. The minister got down on his knees and began to help the blind man, and said to him: "I'm so sorry. I have ruined your day. The fruit are bruised. I will buy them all from you."

They filled the cart and the minister left. As he did so, the blind man shouted at him, "Sir, is you Jesus?" As soon as he heard those words, the minister knew that he had to do what he did. It was righteous behavior.

The Ultimate Purpose, Promise and Privilege

Best of all, such behavior brings glory to our heavenly Father. That is what should motivate us—to know that our good deeds bring praise to Him. We show good deeds not to be praised by men but to bring praise to God. The Pharisees did what they did for one reason, said Jesus: "Everything they do is done for men to see" (Matthew 23:5). Getting noticed by people is what mattered to them.

Jesus is telling us that there is a higher motivation: You do it to glorify God. I find it comforting to know that God is pleased when I show good works, whether talking to the lost, helping the poor and homeless, going out of my way to be nice, kind and helpful. Whatever we do, we should do it for the glory of God (1 Corinthians 10:31).

The ultimate purpose of showing good deeds is to glorify our Father. The ultimate promise is that such good deeds do indeed glorify and honor Him. It is the ultimate privilege. What an honor and privilege to do it—to bring honor and glory to God by letting people see our good deeds.

When William C. Burns was leaving Scotland for China, people said to him, "So you are going to China to convert the Chinese?"

"No," Burns replied. "I am going to China to glorify God."

It doesn't get better than that. Take this privilege with both hands.

16. The Law and the Prophets

Do not think that I have come to abolish the Law or the Prophets;
I have not come to abolish them but to fulfill them.

MATTHEW 5:17

We saw from the beginning of our treatment of the Sermon on the Mount that the Beatitudes formed Jesus' "text" for the sermon. But sometimes a minister takes more than one verse of Scripture for his text before his sermon.

You could say that Jesus does this, because Matthew 5:17–20, His introduction of the Law, could easily be seen as Jesus' second "text." Indeed, the rest of the entire Sermon on the Mount—from Matthew 5:21 to the very end—is an elaboration of both the Beatitudes and Jesus' way of applying the Mosaic Law.

I could make the case that Matthew 5:17 is the most important verse in the Sermon on the Mount. Dr. Martyn Lloyd-Jones said that the promise to fulfill the Law and the prophets was the most stupendous claim Jesus ever made. Think about this—that Jesus would Himself literally fulfill the Law during His lifetime. No person—ever—made such a promise, or accomplished what He did.

This verse and those that follow comprise an important key to Jesus' understanding of the Law. They serve as an entry point to the New Testament teaching generally about the Law. We need to understand this verse if we are to make sense not only of the rest of the Sermon on the Mount but also of the biblical doctrine of salvation, especially the apostle Paul's doctrine of justification by faith.

We now come to the "main course" of the Sermon on the Mount. We have had the "starters"—the Beatitudes (His "text"), followed by a further introduction (verses 13–16). But with Matthew 5:17 we have the entrée—the beginning of the sermon itself.

Jesus' First Reference to the Law of Moses

Jesus' explicit focus at this stage is the Law—the very Law that was given to Moses in approximately

1300 B.C. The Mosaic Law is perhaps better understood when you see that it is basically in three parts: (1) the Moral Law (the Ten Commandments), (2) the Ceremonial Law (the way God wanted His ancient people to worship) and (3) the Civil Law (the way the people of Israel were to be governed).

It was only a matter of time before Jesus would say something about the Law. Matthew tells us that Jesus went throughout Galilee "teaching in their synagogues, preaching the good news of the kingdom" (Matthew 4:23). But there was no mention of the Law. His opening verse in the Sermon on the Mount was, "Blessed are the poor in spirit" (Matthew 5:3). Is the preaching of the Law a prerequisite to being poor in spirit? No. But there would certainly be those listening to see what He would have to say about the Law.

The atmosphere in those days was charged with strong views and various opinions about the Law. We have a bit of this today in some Christian circles. F. F. Bruce once commented that there are two kinds of Scotsmen: those who go to church to hear the Gospel preached, and those who go to church to see *whether* the Gospel is preached! The latter would be that type of Jew who went to hear Jesus. They would listen carefully to see whether He agreed with their own interpretation of the revered Law of Moses.

Was the Law a new subject when Jesus comes to this part of the sermon? In other words, has Jesus actually changed the subject—or was not His understanding of the Law behind His teaching of the Beatitudes all along? Why does Jesus now explicitly mention the Law (and the prophets)? Does He say this—"Do not think I have come to abolish the Law"—because some of them were already thinking He would abolish the Law and prophets? Did they suspect that He *was* intending to abolish the Law? Were they wondering this in the light of what He had been saying?

Up to this point, Matthew has not related any controversy between Jesus and the Jews regarding the issue of the Law. There is no indication that Jesus said anything about the Law prior to His preaching the Sermon on the Mount. He certainly has not mentioned it, at least in Matthew, up to now. So why did Jesus say, "Do not think I have come to abolish the Law"?

Jesus certainly knew what His hearers were thinking, including those theologically minded, critical Jews who took their own interpretation of the Law very seriously. Was Jesus surmising that they anticipated some definitive statement from Him regarding the Law? Why did Jesus say, "Do not think . . ."?

Some of us, had we not been in the skin of certain Jews in Jesus' day, would say, "I hadn't thought You would change it." Some of us may say, "I wasn't thinking of the Law in the first place." It is Jesus who brings this up. Why explicitly bring in the Law here?

Why Did Jesus Say, "Do Not Think That I . . ."?

There are at least three possibilities.

First, some may have suspected that the Law wasn't needed in the light of Jesus' teaching. There was certainly no need for the Law at all for the Beatitudes to be experienced and exemplified. Look at each of them in their progressive order and you will see that what Jesus taught could have been said had there never been a Mosaic Law! No Law was needed in order to experience the Beatitudes.

We have already seen that the Sermon on the Mount is Jesus' doctrine of the Holy Spirit. We have further seen that the Kingdom of heaven is the realm of the un-grieved Spirit reigning in us. The Law was simply not needed in anything He taught so far. Some might have said, "If we take this Jesus of Nazareth seriously, we won't even need the Law of Moses." Some would be horrified at this. Some enemies of Jesus might have hoped to say, "I told you so." They may have thus concluded: "He is going to say sooner or later that He has come to abolish the Law."

But Jesus said: "Do not think I have come to abolish the Law." For that wasn't His purpose in coming into the world after all.

Second, Jesus may have said this—"Do not think I have come to abolish the Law"—because certain rumors were going around about Daniel's "Son of man" showing up. Jesus was perceived as a very unusual person, even an apocalyptic figure—one who appears suddenly as if from out of the blue. It could have meant discontinuity with the past, Jesus being revelation directly from God. There were indeed rumors of an apocalyptic figure—called the Son of man (from Daniel 7:13)—who would inaugurate a new era.

There were also rumors that this apocalyptic figure—when he came—would abolish the Law altogether and start all over again with something else. The Beatitudes certainly came close. Nobody had ever heard teaching like that.

So, what was different about the Beatitudes when compared to the Law? The answer partly is, a person was given an internal peace through brokenness, meekness, hungering after righteousness—without any Law whatever. Furthermore, Jesus' teaching promised a different kind of greatness, as inheriting the earth and seeing God. If one was poor in spirit, merciful and a peacemaker, they were seen as "blessed," happy, anointed.

Not only that—Jesus' teaching about the Kingdom of heaven was not so much about life here on earth but internal bliss—plus what lay beyond this sphere of life. In the Law the emphasis was entirely on the here and now. "You will be blessed in the city and blessed in the country. . . . The LORD will send a blessing on your barns" (Deuteronomy 28:3, 8). Jesus spoke of "reward in heaven."

No one had heard of talk like that before. Such teaching could have been seen as preempting the Law altogether. Remember, too, that the God of Israel was seen as Father (Matthew 5:16). With rumors abroad that an apocalyptic leader was going to do away with the Law, it would explain why Jesus said to them, "Do not think that I have come to abolish the Law."

Third, revolutionaries were around who would have relished such a possibility. They would have destroyed the Law in one stroke if things were left to them. As John Calvin said, any new form of teaching will find many common people at once jumping to it, hoping to overturn everything. Some people get tired of the status quo or tradition and welcome almost anything that comes along. (By the way, this is not a sign of spirituality. Some people who pray for revival would hope to destroy all existing structures—like Oliver Cromwell's followers, who destroyed beautiful buildings. Some of Martin Luther's followers were like this. There were people like that in Jesus' day—reading into words to overthrow anything and everything.)

But another reason Jesus brought in the Law in Matthew 5:17 was because He had just preached that our light should shine before others and show good works to glorify our Father. Could Jesus' way to produce good works have circumvented the Law? Yes.

Apart from further speculation as to what made Him say it, we only know that Jesus said: "Do not think I have come to abolish the Law or the prophets." Some Jews were thinking He would abolish the Law, but that was never His plan at all.

Not Only the Law but Also the Prophets

Why bring in the prophets? Were the prophets—like Samuel, Elijah, Jeremiah—a bone of contention? Yes. The prophets were seen as rivals to the priesthood.

The priesthood was an integral part of the Ceremonial Law. The priests were threatened by the prophets, who turned up years after Moses gave Israel the Law. The Sadducees in particular regarded themselves as the successors of the ancient priest Zadok. The Sadducees hated the idea of the prophets—indeed, they despised anything that smacked of the prophetic. They would not have wanted the Law to be abolished, but would have been thrilled if some apocalyptic figure would do away with the prophets. They would welcome almost any powerful figure who would render the prophets completely extinct, believing that the Elijahs and Elishas of this world were unnecessary in the first place.

But Jesus said that He had not come to abolish the Law *or* the prophets. "I have not come to abolish them but to fulfill them."

We need to be reminded from time to time that we probably do not have the whole of Jesus'

Sermon on the Mount. You can read the Sermon on the Mount, as we have it, in ten to twelve minutes. Yet Dr. Michael Eaton reckons Jesus preached it over three or four days! If so, what we have is but a very brief summary of the original sermon. Matthew, under the guidance of the Holy Spirit, has given us all that we need, however.

Jesus' First Reference to Himself

Matthew 5:17 also reveals when Jesus referred to Himself for the first time—"I," showing His self-conscious authority. "Do not think that I . . ." Some present might say, "Who does this man think He is, referring to Himself that way?"

But He knew all eyes were focused on Him. And they were wondering: "Who exactly is this man?" Never a man spoke like this man. Not only that—He referred to Himself twice: "Do not think that I have come to abolish the Law or the prophets; I have not come to abolish them but to fulfill them." This meant a conscious, personal, confident undertaking to fulfill the Law rather than nullify it.

But what an extraordinary thing to say! And yet what authority would He have to abolish the Law had He wanted to? He wasn't even a member of the Sanhedrin. The Law was 1,300 years old! And what authority would He have to abolish the prophets? The prophets go back to Samuel, not to mention Moses, the greatest of the prophets. Jesus later called Abel a prophet (Luke 11:50–51). What boldness! What presumption that He would even suggest He *could* abolish the Law and the prophets had He wanted to.

Behind this comment is a dignity and an unpretentious knowledge that unveils more authority than any mortal man had ever claimed or witnessed. His mere saying it suggests that He knew He had such authority—indeed, the power to do whatever He chose to do. He hadn't been on the scene long, perhaps only a few weeks or months. Here is a man talking about what He has come to do—or not to do! He exhibits an amazing purpose, but without any arrogance or impertinence. He was meekness and calmness personified, and yet He spoke as boldly as a lion!

These words—"I have come"—also show a self-conscious arrival, as if from elsewhere than Galilee. He knows He has appeared at such a time as this—and for a special purpose. He does not say what He might have said—that He was "sent" (e.g., John 3:17; 5:24; 7:28). He could have. But here He only says, "I have come."

A New Era Has Arrived

In speaking this, Jesus effectively announces a new era. Paul tells us that the Law was a temporary measure from the start—it was never intended to be permanent. It was only "added," and this was for a specific period of time (Romans 5:20; Galatians 3:19).

It turns out that the Law was a parenthesis in salvation history (a parenthesis that lasted 1,300 years). The Gospel was first announced to Abraham (Galatians 3:8; Genesis 15:6). This was around 1700 B.C., when Abraham was justified by his faith. The Law came 430 years later, which was when the parenthesis began (Galatians 3:17). The 1,300-year parenthesis ended when Jesus died on the cross.

And yet it was not presumptuous for Jesus to speak this way. He had already healed the sick, given relief to paralytics and cast out demons. He preached the Gospel of the Kingdom at a time when the atmosphere was charged with messianic expectancy.

Jesus' preaching was a personal, unobtrusive and non-imposing authority that came through as He spoke. He knew who He was, why He had come and that His appearance was pivotal on the world stage. He wore this unprecedented self-understanding with humility and grace. He had not yet been accused of breaking the Sabbath, and He had not been accused yet of blasphemy. That came later. The common people, in any case, heard Him gladly. He was developing an awe and appreciation from among grass roots.

Then came this straightforward assertion: "I have not come to abolish the Law but to fulfill it." Whatever reasoning among His critics there may have been, Jesus' teaching certainly didn't need the Law of Moses. Whatever the rumors, this apocalyptic figure could overthrow the Law and start all over again, had He chosen to do so. Whatever the hopes of certain revolutionaries—who would be glad if all tradition was smashed—Jesus sent a signal that would have thrilled some but disappointed others.

For it turns out that if Jesus' teaching gave hope to some that an abrogation of the Law was on offer, they would have to look elsewhere. If it was a radical discontinuity with Moses and the prophets they wanted, sorry. And if it was rejecting a righteous standard that would bless or exalt any nation (Proverbs 14:34), He made it clear He was not going to do away with such.

Continuity with the Law and Prophets

Far from there being any discord or break between His teaching and the Law, Jesus shows continuity between Himself and the Law and the prophets. The Greek word for "abolish" here is *katalusi*—which means to abrogate, to nullify. Jesus had not come to nullify the Law or to render it and the prophets irrelevant. Any such rumor is put to rest—any speculation about what He may do regarding the Law is now over.

It is interesting that Jesus puts the two together—Law and prophets. He would fulfill both of these. He might have said He would nullify the Law but affirm the prophets. That would have pleased some, no doubt. He might have said He would affirm the Law but reject the prophetic. That would have pleased the Sadducees. Had He said He was going to abrogate both the Law and the prophets, He would have pleased certain revolutionaries.

But in Matthew 5:17, Jesus says that both the Law and prophets have continuity and relevance for the new era He Himself was announcing at this moment. It is true there would be more application in the Sermon on the Mount regarding the Law than about the prophets (whom He does not mention again until Matthew 7:12). But Matthew himself would show how Jesus' ministry fulfilled Old Testament prophecy (see Matthew 8:17; 12:17; 13:14, 35; 21:4; 26:54, 56; 27:9). Most of the Sermon on the Mount is Jesus' interpretation of the Law—His doctrine of the Spirit.

The straightforward assertion was this: I will fulfill them, not abolish them.

And yet by saying He would fulfill the Law, He would be making a significant interpretation of it. In one stroke, Jesus asserts that the Law was always meant to be temporary, that it was never meant to be permanent in the first place. For fulfillment meant the Law would end.

Furthermore, Jesus is saying that the Law was not complete in itself—it represented unfinished business. This would upset a lot of Pharisees and Sadducees who would see the Law as the "be all" and "end all." For one thing, the whole sacrificial system—a part of the Law—pointed beyond itself. The Ceremonial Law—including the sacrifices of animals—needed to be fulfilled. The Moral Law also needed to be fulfilled—because no person had truly kept it. The Law then would be fulfilled by its being kept—which Jesus was promising to do.

The Law therefore required more work to be done. It had never been fulfilled. But Jesus announced that He Himself would do it.

The prophecies of the Old Testament also needed fulfillment. And yet they were being fulfilled as Jesus spoke. Messiah had been promised. It would be seen in days ahead that Jesus was that Messiah—God's promised anointed servant.

Thus came this most stunning affirmation from Jesus: "I will fulfill the Law and the prophets." He would do what had never been done. He would not only keep the Law but fulfill it—and be the fulfillment of the prophecies of the Old Testament. He would therefore be the fulfillment of the Law (including the Ceremonial Law) and the fulfillment of the prophecies of people like Isaiah, Jeremiah and Daniel.

The Law was actually pointing to Jesus from the first day it was announced by Moses, when it was accompanied with thunder and lightning at Sinai. The prophets of old, moreover—from Abel to Moses to Malachi—were talking about Jesus.

The Law and the prophets embody what we now call the Old Testament. Jesus could have said that He would fulfill "the Law of Moses, the Prophets and the Psalms," which was also His way of dividing the Old Testament (Luke 24:46). But it would suffice to say here that He would fulfill the Law and the prophets. Not end them, not nullify them, not abolish or abrogate them. He would fulfill them.

It was not only the most stunning and amazing statement Jesus ever made—it was the most stupendous claim any human being ever made.

He made this extraordinary prediction about Himself near the beginning of His ministry. As we will see in a further treatment of this verse in the next chapter, and in the exposition of the verses that follow—not to mention the event of the Cross—it was a promise Jesus kept. When He cried out, "It is finished" (John 19:30), He knew He had kept His word.

It was then that the unfinished business was completed. The parenthesis was closed. And Jesus became what Paul would call the end of the Law (Romans 10:4).

17. Mission Accomplished

Do not think that I have come to abolish the Law or the Prophets;
I have not come to abolish them but to fulfill them.

MATTHEW 5:17

This remarkable verse is pivotal in salvation history but also in the Sermon on the Mount itself, as we will see in succeeding chapters. Matthew 5:17 will therefore bear a further examination. In this chapter we will see further why this is such a profound verse.

The issue can be put this way: *continuity versus discontinuity.* It refers to whether the Law is to continue or whether it will be discontinued. Continuity in this case means the uninterrupted relevance of the Law. Discontinuity means the Law is completed and fulfilled.

What, then, did Jesus mean by His word that He had not come to abolish the Law but complete it? The Greek *plerosai* means "to fulfill," the opposite of "to destroy." It means that Jesus would bring about the event to which the Law and the prophets were pointing.

The Law pointed beyond itself; the prophets pointed beyond themselves. The Law had not been fulfilled because no one ever really kept it, not to mention the implications of the sacrificial system in the Ceremonial Law. The very content of the Law showed that it was incomplete in itself, which is the thesis of the epistle to the Hebrews. As for the prophets, they pointed to someone who was to come.

To fulfill the Law and the prophets, then, meant that some person and event would be the Omega Point toward which the Law and the prophets pointed. For at the time Jesus spoke these words, the Law had not been fulfilled. People then didn't even think about such a thing as its needing to be fulfilled. Such an idea was not on one's "radar screen"—that there would be a person who would fulfill the Law.

Matthew 5:17 is actually saying: "I am that person. I have come for that event." And yet

Matthew 5:17 is also prophetic, for Jesus hadn't done it yet! He had two or three years in which to do it. As we saw in the previous chapter, He had probably been on the public scene only for a few months. This statement is therefore a promise. It was a commitment that He would do what no other person had done: in His own person (His mind, heart and will), by His words and deeds. He Himself would be the very fulfillment of what the prophets foretold and what the Law pointed to.

It is simply another way of saying that Jesus was the fulfillment of the Old Testament. For the Law and the prophets are in one sense a summary of the Old Testament.

Mission Anticipated

When Jesus uses the words "I have come," He refers to the purpose of His being there and what He now undertook to do. As we saw above, Jesus might have used the word "sent"—as in the gospel of John. "My food," said Jesus, "is to do the will of him who sent me and to finish his work" (John 4:34). "As long as it is day, we must do the work of him who sent me" (John 9:4). "Now this is eternal life: that they may know you, the only true God, and Jesus Christ, whom you have sent" (John 17:3). The word *mission* means a work for which a person has been sent.

What mission, exactly, did Jesus anticipate He had to do if He kept His promise to fulfill the Law and the prophets? I have to say, if there ever was (humanly speaking) a "Mission: Impossible," this was it. This is what makes Matthew 5:17 so extraordinary. Do you know anybody who could make a statement like this with any credibility?

Consider the work cut out for Jesus if He kept this promise. To fulfill the Law meant perfectly obeying:

1. The statutes of the Law—all of its rules. Have a look at Leviticus.

2. The standard of the Law—the required level of quality of obedience.

3. The structures of the Law—Moral, Civil, Ceremonial.

4. The specifications of the Law—over 2,000 pieces of legislation as in Exodus, Leviticus, Numbers and Deuteronomy, in addition to the Ten Commandments.

5. The strictness of the Law—complete and total obedience without the slightest deviation.

6. The scrutiny of the Law—which meant a careful keeping of the minutest requirement. He would dot every "i" and cross every "t."

7. The servitude of the Law—which meant a curse on all who didn't fulfill all its demands. "Cursed is the man who does not uphold the words of this law by carrying them out" (Deuteronomy 27:26).

8. The shadow of the Law—since the Law was only a trace of what it pointed to. "The law is only a shadow of the good things that are coming—not the realities themselves" (Hebrews 10:1).

9. The sacrifices of the Law—since they were repeated year after year but never perfected those who drew near to worship (Hebrews 10:1–4).

You can see Jesus certainly had His work cut out for Him when He said He would fulfill the Law. He would fulfill all the Mosaic legislation. He would have to keep the festivals—going to Jerusalem three times a year. He would keep the Jewish Sabbath every week of His life. He would have to keep the "new moons," the "seventh year," the year of Jubilee, the Passover, the feasts of unleavened bread, of Pentecost, of tabernacles, of trumpets and the Day of Atonement.

Some of the above had already been accomplished by His parents (e.g., His circumcision—Luke 2:21). His role of being a priest after the order of Melchizedek (Psalm 110:4) would be carried on after His death, resurrection and ascension to the right hand of God (see Hebrews 7).

As for fulfilling the prophets, Jesus began to do this when He was born of a virgin (Isaiah 7:14). He had yet to become the prophet of whom Moses spoke: "The LORD your God will raise up for you a prophet like me from among your own brothers" (Deuteronomy 18:15). He would become the suffering servant of Isaiah:

> He was despised and rejected by men, a man of sorrows, and familiar with suffering. Like one from whom men hide their faces he was despised, and we esteemed him not . . . we considered him stricken by God, smitten by him, and afflicted. But he was pierced for our transgressions, he was crushed for our iniquities; the punishment that brought us peace was upon him, and by his wounds we are healed . . . and the Lord has laid on him the iniquity of us all. He was oppressed and afflicted, yet he did not open his mouth; he was led like a lamb to the slaughter, and as a sheep before her shearers is silent, so he did not open his mouth.
>
> ISAIAH 53:3–7

Jesus would be the Son of man of whom the prophet Daniel spoke (Daniel 7:13). He would be the one to dwell in a surprising place—in Galilee (Isaiah 9:1). He would be the one called "Wonderful Counselor, Mighty God, Everlasting Father, Prince of Peace" (Isaiah 9:6). There are countless other prophecies.

Mission anticipated: Jesus would fulfill the Law and prophets. Never before had anybody made such a claim, never before had people heard such a claim, and never before had anyone fulfilled such a promise.

Mission Accomplished

When Jesus uttered the words, "It is finished" (John 19:30), He was effectively saying, "Mission accomplished!" What had Jesus done?

First, He standardized the Law. Some thought (or feared) that He would abolish it and make it an irrelevant standard for righteous living. No. He had not come to abolish the standard of conduct by which the people of God were to live. The standard of moral righteousness would not change.

Second, Jesus accomplished His mission by submission. When Christ came into the world, He said: "Sacrifice and offering you did not desire, but a body you prepared for me; with burnt offerings and sin offerings you were not pleased.

Then I said, 'Here I am—it is written about me in the scroll—I have come to do your will, O God'" (Hebrews 10:5–7). This is that Word that was in the beginning with God, which was "with" God and became "flesh" (John 1:1–2,14).

By becoming flesh, Jesus became bone of our bone, flesh of our flesh. His submission consisted in His willingness to take on a body. The Word—the second Person of the Godhead—submitted to having a body. He took on Himself not the nature of angels but the seed of Abraham (Hebrews 2:16, KJV). Once the Word became flesh, moreover, it was submission to having a body forever and ever. That same body would be Jesus' body not only for some 33 years on earth but throughout eternity. The nail prints in Jesus' body will always be there (John 20:27).

Submission to the Law

His submission extended to being under the Law. He not only submitted to having a body, but in that body agreed He would be "under" the Law from the moment of His birth until He breathed His last breath. Therefore, Jesus did not put Himself above the Law but submitted to it. "But when the time had fully come, God sent his Son, born of a woman, born under Law, to redeem those under law" (Galatians 4:4–5).

He who was the eternal Word—*logos*—from eternity agreed with the Father on the timing, the form of earthly existence and His submission to the Law.

His mission was accomplished because of His sinlessness. He was the first and last man in world history to claim to fulfill the Law, and part of that was the promise never to sin. "There is no one who does not sin" (2 Chronicles 6:36). "There is not a righteous man on earth who does what is right and never sins" (Ecclesiastes 7:20). Pontius Pilate was constrained to say, "I find no fault in him" (John 19:4, 6, KJV). Jesus was tempted in every way, "just as we are—yet was without sin" (Hebrews 4:15). Said Peter, "He committed no sin, and no deceit was found in his mouth" (1 Peter 2:22). He was holy, "blameless, pure, set apart from sinners" (Hebrews 7:26). In Him is "no sin" (1 John 3:5).

Jesus perfectly kept the Ten Commandments. He worshiped only the Father. He came not to do His own will but the will of the Father. "I seek not to please myself but him who sent me" (John 5:30). He never abused the Father's name. He honored His parents. He never stole or lied. He never coveted or lusted. He never grieved the Holy Spirit. He never lost His temper or held a grudge, even praying for those who crucified Him: "Father, forgive them, for they do not know what they are doing" (Luke 23:34). He practiced what He preached.

His mission was accomplished by substitution. Everything He ever did was done as our substitute. His holy life became our sanctification (1 Corinthians 1:30). By His life, faith and obedience, He did what is required of us—because He did it not for Himself but for us. He believed for us—with a perfect faith (John 3:34; Hebrews 2:13; Galatians 2:20, KJV). He was baptized for us—to fulfill righteousness (Matthew 3:15). His holy life became a sacrifice for us. His keeping the Law was keeping it for us.

His perfection was our perfection, His righteousness was our righteousness, His obedience was our obedience. We are actually saved "through his life" (Romans 5:10). For His life was a constant, nonstop, perfect obedience from Day One. "For just as through the disobedience of the one man the many were made sinners, so also through the obedience of the one man the many will be made righteous" (Romans 5:19).

Suffering

His mission was accomplished by suffering. When Jesus was on the cross, He who knew no sin—and who had never sinned—was "made sin." There was a moment, at some time between noon and three o'clock on Good Friday, that Jesus was declared to be *sin* (2 Corinthians 5:21). Martin Luther said that on the cross Jesus was—legally—the world's greatest sinner. Why? Not because He ever sinned, but because the sins of the whole world were imputed to Him as though He were guilty of them all.

The Lord laid on Him "the iniquity of us all" (Isaiah 53:6). God charged Him with our sins, which is why Peter could say He "bore our sins in his body" (1 Peter 2:24). God punished Jesus. The wages of sin is death in any case (Genesis 2:17; Romans 6:23).

The penalty of presumptuous sin under the Law was death. Jesus took our punishment and died for us because all our sins—whether sins by a high hand or sins from weakness—were charged to Him. It was, therefore, another way He fulfilled the Law for us. The penalty of the Law for capital sins was death. Therefore, Jesus fulfilled the Law on our behalf by taking the blame for all our sins.

As our substitute for all our failures, imperfections and lusts, for our breaking all the Commandments, Jesus died. God punished Jesus instead of us. Jesus stepped in to take the blame for what we did.

During that moment on Good Friday, Jesus cried out, "My God, my God, why have you forsaken me?" (Matthew 27:46). Something happened. It was a transaction. That was when Jesus became sin for us. The most holy God could not look upon sin. Jesus felt utterly and totally deserted. Hard though it is for you and me to grasp, this was the height and worst of Jesus' suffering.

> We may not know, we cannot tell
> What pains He had to bear;
> But we believe it was for us
> He hung and suffered there.
>
> Cecil Frances Alexander
> (1818–1895)

Jesus fulfilled the Law by sacrifice. That means He who was the seed of the woman (Genesis 3:15) became our Passover Lamb. All the Old Testament sacrifices were "shadows" of things to come (Hebrews 10:1). Jesus was the fulfillment of what the animal sacrifices—bulls, goats, lambs, pigeons—pointed to. These sacrifices had to be repeated year after year after year. The fact that the sacrifices had to be repeated year after year after year ought to have been a pretty strong hint, suggests the writer to the Hebrews, that these sacrifices were not doing the job (Hebrews 10:1–4)! Every priest and worshiper ought to have suspected that there must be more to come than merely repeating the sacrificial offerings year after year.

And there was more. Having lived a sinless life for 33 years, including three years of public ministry, and after hours of flogging, unfair accusations and unspeakable humiliation, God's Lamb took away the sins of the world. That is when He became the fulfillment of the Ceremonial Law.

Mission accomplished! No sooner than Jesus uttered the words, "It is finished" (John 19:30), the veil of the Temple was torn from top to bottom. That sent a signal to every priest in the Temple that what happened on the cross of Jesus ended the sacrificial system. The Law was fulfilled. The 1,300-year parenthesis was over. The veil of the Temple being torn—plus bodies of the saints being raised from the dead in Jerusalem (Matthew 27:51–52)—was God's affirmation of the Cross: MISSION ACCOMPLISHED!

Satisfaction

Charles Spurgeon used to say that there are two words you need in your theological vocabulary: *substitution* and *satisfaction*. *Substitution* means that Jesus was our substitute. He took our place, living sinlessly and dying for us. *Satisfaction* means that the blood Jesus shed satisfied the divine justice. His death meant that our debt was paid in full.

The one thing that had not taken place since Adam fell in the Garden of Eden was the justice of God being satisfied. Indeed, the one thing that had not been achieved since the Law of Moses was given or had taken place throughout the history of Israel—even when God showed His wrath on His people for their sin—was His justice being satisfied.

Nothing achieved the satisfaction of God's justice, no matter how anyone tried. Adam's fig leaves didn't do it. The skins God prepared for Adam and Eve didn't do it. Enoch walking with God didn't do it. Noah building the ark didn't do it. The patriarchs didn't achieve it, whether by Abraham's sacrificing his son or Jacob's wrestling with God. The faith of Shadrach, Meshach and Abednego didn't satisfy God's justice. Daniel's faith and courage didn't do it. The loneliness and endurance of the prophets didn't do it. The head of John the Baptist didn't do it.

On the Isle of Patmos, John told how he wept when he saw that no one in heaven or on earth or under the earth was worthy to open the scroll. But one of the elders said to him, "Do not weep! See, the Lion of the tribe of Judah, the Root of David, has triumphed." Then, said John,

"I saw a Lamb, looking as if it had been slain," and they sang a new song: "You are worthy to take the scroll and to open its seals, because you were slain, and with your blood you purchased men for God" (Revelation 5:3–9). No human being—even the best (whoever that may be)—was worthy. No one was worthy, no one satisfied the justice of God—ever.

But there is one Person and one thing that did it: Jesus the Man and the blood that came from His body on the cross. His sinless life and blood on the cross did it. The blood of the God-man did it. Satisfaction. Mission accomplished!

> See, from His head, His hands, His
> feet,
> Sorrow and love flow mingled down;
> Did e'er such love and sorrow meet,
> Or thorns compose so rich a crown?
>
> Isaac Watts (1674–1748)

Isaiah saw it hundreds of years in advance: "He shall see of the travail of his soul, and shall be satisfied" (Isaiah 53:11, KJV).

Superiority

Jesus' mission was accomplished by His superiority. He not only fulfilled the Law, He exceeded the Law. His life and example went beyond anything anybody thought of. He not only fulfilled all the specifications of the Law, He lived in a manner that was not even suggested by the Law. No one lived as He lived, no one loved as He loved. His life exceeded the Law, indeed, exceeded the best of the holiest of men of old.

His example set a new standard of righteousness—a righteousness that surpassed that of the scribes and Pharisees. Far from abolishing the Law, then, Jesus' life would be called "the law of Christ" (1 Corinthians 9:21; Galatians 6:2), a standard beyond anything dreamed by the Law or the prophets.

Mission accomplished! Jesus made a promise: *I will fulfill the Law.* And He did it. The words "It is finished" come from the Greek *tetelestai*—a colloquial expression in the ancient marketplace that meant *paid in full.*

Our substitute became our satisfaction. We will sing His praises nonstop throughout eternity.

18. The Destiny of the Law

I tell you the truth, until heaven and earth disappear, not the smallest letter, not the least stroke of a pen, will by any means disappear from the Law until everything is accomplished.

MATTHEW 5:18

As we saw in the previous two chapters, Jesus' promise to fulfill the Law means He had His work cut out for Him over His next two to three years. The verse we deal with in this chapter shows that Jesus knew this very well and virtually acknowledged that He had a lot to do in order to make good His commitment. He did not have to do anything to make good His promise to fulfill the prophets; His ministry of teaching and healing would do that. But to fulfill the Law was something else. Indeed, "not the smallest letter, not the least stroke of a pen" would disappear from the Law until it was entirely accomplished.

Matthew 5:17 refers to the Law and prophets; verse 18 refers only to the Law. And from this point on until Matthew 7:12, it is the Law that gets the attention. Sometimes the Law can refer to the entire Old Testament, but here Jesus is only referring to the details of the Mosaic Law. He is not only referring to the Ten Commandments, but to 2,000 pieces of legislation that come out of Exodus, Leviticus, Numbers and Deuteronomy. Every single piece of the Mosaic Law must be fulfilled. In a word: The Law has a destiny. That destiny revolves around the Person of Jesus.

The NIV leaves out the word "for" (Gr. *gar*), which is not unimportant. In Matthew 5:18 Jesus elaborates on verse 17: "For I tell you the truth . . ." In light of His claim that He will fulfill the Law, Jesus admits not only that His work is cut out for Him. He also outlines—in detail—what has to be done before He dies on the cross.

It is a mistake some make to focus on Jesus' death without realizing that we are also saved by His life (Romans 5:10). All that Jesus did—His thoughts, attitude, words and deeds—was fulfilling the Law. Had Jesus not done this by His sinless life of 33 years, His death would not have atoned for our sins. In a word: It was not only His sacrificial death but His perfect life that fulfilled the Law.

Matthew 5:18 is telling us that everything pertaining to the Mosaic Law must be fulfilled. To stress this point, Jesus says, "Until heaven and earth pass away, not an iota, not a dot, will pass from the Law until all is accomplished" (ESV). He is not merely talking about His fulfilling the Ten Commandments. As mentioned, the Law even includes 2,000 pieces of legislation that will need to be fulfilled. Nothing could be put more strongly than that! The very end of the world will not transpire until the whole Law is fulfilled. In other words, the fulfillment of the Law has priority over the world coming to an end.

Heaven and Earth Will Pass Away

There are some "throwaway" comments that will bear our looking into. The first is that Jesus implicitly affirms that the world as we know it will end. It requires faith to believe that there was a beginning—namely, Creation—and that God created the world *ex nihilo*, "out of nothing" (Hebrews 11:3).

It also requires faith to believe that the present world will have an end. The world as we know it will not go on and on and on without God winding things up. No. The present age has an end. By "heaven" Jesus does not mean God's dwelling place—He is talking about the present universe. But John saw a "new heaven and a new earth," for the old order of things will pass away (Revelation 21:1, 4). Peter speaks of "the day of God" which will bring about "the destruction of the heavens with fire" (2 Peter 3:12). Some think this will come about, at least in part, by nuclear war. Perhaps. I can only say that it will take more than that to dissolve the whole universe.

Jesus may also be implicitly giving the first "sign of the times" in Matthew 5:18. We normally think of Matthew 24 as the chapter referring to the last days. Once the Law is fulfilled, however, we actually enter the "last days," a phrase used in Hebrews 1:2 (1 John 2:18). But Matthew 24 describes what I would call the very last days, the conditions one can expect in the same generation as the Second Coming of Jesus.

I would therefore make a distinction between the last days (which began 2,000 years ago) and the very last days—which I believe is described in Matthew 24 and, therefore, speaks of our own generation. I believe Jesus is coming very soon. It is the Second Coming that will mark the beginning of the end of the present age. But only the Father knows that predetermined date in history (Matthew 24:44). In any case, the one thing that would delay the end of the world: the Law remaining unfulfilled. But once the Law was fulfilled at the cross of Jesus, we entered the "last days"—which have gone on for 2,000 years.

We also have in Matthew 5:18 Jesus' view of the inspiration of Scriptures, especially the Law. When He speaks of every "jot" and "tittle" (KJV), "iota" or "dot" (ESV), He refers to the smallest letters in the alphabet. The Greek *iota* refers to the Hebrew *yod*—which is like a small comma. The "least stroke of a pen" (Gr. *keraia*) probably refers to the Hebrew *waw*. When you use the expression, "It doesn't make one iota of difference," you are referring to the Greek letter.

This is Jesus' way of saying there was not an idle comment coming from Moses at Sinai. As Don Carson put it, Jesus has the highest possible view of inspiration of the Old Testament. Nothing will be overlooked or left undone. "The Scripture cannot be broken" (John 10:35). "Heaven and earth will pass away, but my words will never pass away" (Matthew 24:35). God's Word is magnified above His name (Psalm 138:2, KJV).

A Solemn Declaration

"Verily I say to you" (KJV), "I tell you the truth" (NIV), "For truly, I say to you" (ESV) are translations of the Greek, "Amen, I say to you." The word *amen* is a Hebrew word, a Greek word, an English word and also Aramaic—the language Jesus spoke in. It means "certainly." We usually put it at the end of a prayer, but Jesus puts it at the beginning of this statement, as if He says, "I am telling you the truth."

God always tells the truth. It is impossible for Him to lie (Hebrews 6:18). But when our Lord takes a moment to say, "I am telling you the truth," it does not mean all else is to be taken with a grain of salt. He is rather saying something of gravest importance is about to follow. It is not only true, it is a word of immense weight. For He is about to elaborate on Matthew 5:17—that not one tiny letter of the alphabet will disappear until the whole Law is fulfilled. This important word is thus prefaced by "I tell you the truth." It means you had better believe it! Not only would Jesus not abolish the Law, but He has come to affirm it, to vindicate it to the hilt.

As far as we know, putting "Amen" at the beginning of a sentence is without parallel. It is not found in Jewish literature. It is a word that always comes at the end, as in a prayer. Saying "amen" means you underline with emphasis what you just said. When you say "amen" to another's prayer, you show your agreement with what they said. It was used in Hebrew with reference to a solemn formula, as in Deuteronomy 27. After each "curse," the people would shout in a loud voice, "Amen!" (Deuteronomy 27:14–26). It was used to affirm a curse or a blessing, and used without exception to answer the word of another. The ancient Israelite used it in connection with giving an oath.

Thus when Jesus uses "Amen" at the beginning of His application of Matthew 5:17, it was the equivalent of a prophet saying, "Thus says the Lord." The prophet said this to indicate it was not his word but the very Word of God. That is what Jesus intends here by putting "Amen" at the beginning, showing the force of an Elijah, Samuel or Moses himself speaking. After all, Jesus was the very prophet Moses said would come.

Scheduled Disappearance of the Law

Matthew 5:18 shows that two things will disappear: the present universe and the Law. Heaven and earth will disappear at some juncture after

Jesus' Second Coming. The specifications of the Law will disappear once Jesus finishes His own work. As for the disappearance of the heavens and the earth, there is a scheduled time—known only by the Father. "No one knows about that day or hour, not even the angels in heaven, nor the Son, but only the Father" (Matthew 14:36). It is a predestined date in history.

When it comes, there will be a great tumult. "The day of the Lord will come like a thief. The heavens will disappear with a roar; the elements will be destroyed by fire, and the earth and everything in it will be laid bare" (2 Peter 3:10). What a noise it will be! Not only that, "He is coming with the clouds, and every eye will see him, even those who pierced him; and all the peoples of the earth will mourn because of him" (Revelation 1:7). The KJV says all will "wail" because of Him. Have you ever heard the sound of someone wailing? It is a sound you won't ever forget: someone in deepest grief—the pathos, the hopelessness. That is the sound of countless people that will be heard when Jesus appears the second time!

But that day will also be a day of transformation. "I tell you a mystery," said Paul; "we will not all sleep, but we will all be changed—in a flash, in the twinkling of an eye, at the last trumpet" (1 Corinthians 15:51–52). "The Lord himself will come down from heaven, with a loud command, with the voice of the archangel and with the trumpet call of God, and the dead in Christ will rise first" (1 Thessalonians 4:16). It will be a day of triumph, too: "The seventh angel sounded his trumpet, and there were loud voices in heaven, which said: 'The kingdom of the world has become the kingdom of our Lord and of his Christ, and he will reign for ever and ever'" (Revelation 11:15). "Then the end will come, when he hands over the kingdom to God the Father after he has destroyed all dominion, authority and power" (1 Corinthians 15:24).

By the way, are you ready for that day? Can you say right now, "Come, Lord Jesus"? Would it thrill you for Him to come right now and end everything? There is a scheduled disappearance of heaven and earth. But we will survive. We will be given glorified bodies, to be like Jesus in His glorified body (1 John 3:3). We will be with the Lord forever and ever and ever. There will be no more sorrow, no more tears (Revelation 21:4).

But all this would be delayed if the Law were not fulfilled first. That is how strongly Jesus wants to affirm and vindicate the Law! However, Jesus accomplished the Law's fulfillment—hence its disappearance—some two to three years later when He uttered the words, "It is finished" (John 19:30), and died.

Therefore, when Jesus fulfilled the Law, it simultaneously disappeared! The Law became history once Jesus died. Notice that He uses the word "until" twice in Matthew 5:18: "until heaven and earth disappear" and "until everything is accomplished." When all is accomplished (fulfilled), something happens. No longer will it be required of you and me to fulfill the Law, because Jesus will have done it! Once we put our faith in Jesus and rely on His righteousness, God pronounces us to have fulfilled the Law. Christ's righteousness is put to our credit! Because Jesus fulfilled the Law—every jot, every iota of it—2,000 years ago, our trust in Him and not in our works counts for righteousness as though we did it ourselves.

This means that once we are in Christ, the specifications of the Law disappear. We are not obliged to uphold them. We are not obliged to keep the sacrifices of the Law. This is why we don't slaughter goats or lambs in our worship of God. Jesus has fulfilled all that for us. Neither are we under any of the restrictions of the Law.

Peter made a very interesting comment about this at the first Jerusalem council: "Why do you try to test God by putting on the necks of the disciples a yoke that neither we nor our fathers have been able to bear?" (Acts 15:10). Jesus did it all for us because He was our substitute, He took our place, He did it all in our behalf. That is why we are declared righteous when we rely on what He did. That is why you and I don't have to keep the Law. It has been done for us.

However, He is not referring to the morality of the Law, but rather the minutiae of it. Jesus is not talking about the standard of righteousness of the Moral Law, but the refinements of it, when He refers to every iota, the specifications of the Law as seen in Leviticus. Jesus fulfilled them in every detail. Consider these words: "Keep my decrees. . . . Do not plant your field with two kinds of seed. Do not wear clothing woven of two kinds of material. . . . Do not cut the hair at the sides of your head or clip the edges of your beard" (Leviticus 19:19, 27).

You can go to the Wailing Wall today and see Jews who look like this. But why don't you and I keep these laws? Because Jesus kept them all for us—all these minute specifications that are irrelevant for us today. I have broken the Law many times by wearing a wool suit with a silk tie. But when I am in Jerusalem on Shabbat and stay in a kosher hotel, I keep their laws whether I like it or not.

All these specific Levitical laws are no longer required of those who rely on Jesus' death. These laws have been kept for us by Him and have disappeared insofar as their needing to be kept any longer. The same is true of the feasts in Jerusalem three times a year, circumcision, day of atonement, holy days, slaughtering of animals—all the rites and ceremonies. They have been nailed to the cross (Colossians 2:14).

Jesus gave hints along the way that these laws would be disappearing. As for dietary laws, "nothing that enters a man from the outside can make him 'unclean,'" said Jesus. He thus pronounced all foods "clean" (Mark 7:18). Paul spoke against people who require one to "abstain from certain foods," since "everything God created is good, and nothing is to be rejected if it is received with thanksgiving"(1 Timothy 4:3–4). Paul also said, "Do not let anyone judge you by what you eat or drink, or with regard to a religious festival, a New Moon celebration or a Sabbath day"—which are a "shadow of the things that were to come." The reality is "found in Christ" (Colossians 2:16–17).

This is why Paul could say that the Law was "added" (Romans 5:20) and was temporary from the start (Galatians 3:19). The things in the Law would disappear. Furthermore, Jesus said to the Jews, "The kingdom of God will be taken away from you and given to a people who will produce its fruit" (Matthew 21:43)—such fruit being a righteousness that reflects Jesus' interpretation of the Law, as we will see later.

The strangest, if not funniest, thing just happened as I typed the previous sentence. I heard a *ping* on my computer, so I checked the e-mail. It was an invitation from a Christian organization: "You are invited to celebrate the High Holidays Erev Rosh Hashanah" (at a designated church).

They added, "Bring your shofars to blow with us." This organization is not doing this out of legalistic obligation (as far as I know), but is following a rather common practice nowadays to do "Jewish" things, as if this pleases God.

The Strategic Destiny of the Law

All will be required to fulfill this Law until "everything is accomplished." This means that at the time Jesus said this, the Law was still in force. Just because its disappearance was on the agenda down the road did not mean that those who listened to His words were off the hook.

Above all, Jesus Himself was not off the hook. He had a job to do. He was under a mandate—to keep the Law to perfection for the next two to three years until He could say, "It is finished." Until then, all were required to keep the Law. This is because that predestined parenthesis to which I referred earlier was still in force. (The 1,300-year parenthesis still had a couple of years to go.)

Therefore, all these things—the specifications of the Law—remained unaccomplished. The Jews were still slaughtering animals and sacrifices during this time. They were going on at the very moment Jesus was speaking. They were unfulfilled. Jesus still had His work cut out for Him.

But Jesus is saying nonetheless that the Law had a strategic destiny. It was "added" (Romans 5:20) to the covenant made 430 years earlier to Abraham. The Law had a strategic destiny from the beginning—but only added to the plan of salvation, a parenthesis that would end. During this 1,300-year era, the Law cried out to be fulfilled! But nobody could do it. No one. Peter said, "We can't do it, our fathers couldn't do it," as we saw earlier.

The strategic destiny meant a predestined purpose. That is, it needed to be fulfilled. The details and demands of the Law wanted satisfaction. The purpose was so definite that the end of the world would be delayed, if necessary, that the Law be satisfied. The universe would be sustained if for no other reason than the commitment of God Almighty that the Law be satisfied.

The strategic destiny also meant a predestined priority. There was something more important than any other consideration—namely, someone would come along and do what had never been done before: that is, satisfy the Law's demands. This would put an end to the sacrificial system and would show why the Law came in the first place. "I am that person," said Jesus. "You can mark it down. You can count on it. Between now and the moment I go to the cross, together with all that has gone on before [His parents' keeping of the Law, His circumcision, keeping the feasts], I will do it."

This shows that Jesus was the predestined person to do it. Moses gave the Law, but he couldn't fulfill it. Joshua perpetuated the Law, but couldn't fulfill it. King David loved the Law, but couldn't fulfill it. The prophets upheld the Law, but couldn't fulfill it. The Levites carried out the Law, but couldn't fulfill it. The Pharisees and Sadducees argued about the Law, but none of them could fulfill it. But Moses promised that God would raise up one like Himself (Deuteronomy 18:15). It was Jesus of Nazareth (Acts 3:22). He did it!

And yet a strategic destiny meant a predestined people. This people would not necessarily be those born of the seed of Abraham, Isaac and Jacob. After all, "Not all who are descended from Israel are Israel. Nor because they are his descendants are they all Abraham's children." Indeed, "It is not the natural children who are God's children, but it is the children of the promise who are regarded as Abraham's offspring" (Romans 9:6–8). "I revealed myself to those who did not ask for me; I was found by those who did not seek me" (Isaiah 65:1).

These people would include Jews, Gentiles and people from Jerusalem and Samaria. The people of God would be those on whom God had sovereign mercy. They would come from the east, west, north and south and constitute a multitude no one could count. Those people would believe God's promise as Abraham had done before the Law—before the parenthesis, before the specifications and structures and sacrifices of the Law came.

Their faith in Jesus fulfilled the Law. Long before there was the Law, long before there was Abraham, long before there were Adam and Eve, long before sin reared its ugly head in Eden's garden, long before there was a star, a planet, a sun, Jesus Christ was the Lamb slain from the foundation of the world—in eternity before Creation (Revelation 13:8; 1 Peter 1:19–20). After Creation came the Fall. After the Fall came Abraham. After Abraham came the Law. The Law had to be reckoned with. God's Son fulfilled it—He satisfied its demands.

> Not the labours of my hands can fulfill
> Thy law's demands;
> Could my zeal no respite know, could
> my tears for ever flow,
> All for sin could not atone: Thou must
> save, and Thou alone.
>
> Augustus Toplady (1740–1778)

Jesus promised to do this in Himself. "It will happen," He says. *It has to happen,* He adds. Today we can say: It happened.

19. Greatness in the Kingdom

Anyone who breaks one of the least of these commandments and teaches others to
do the same will be called least in the kingdom of heaven, but whoever practices
and teaches these commands will be called great in the kingdom of heaven.

MATTHEW 5:19

There is something that should stand out in bold relief when you examine our Lord's treatment of the Law of Moses. First, Jesus never, ever apologized for the God of the Old Testament. The God of the Old Testament is His own Father. He will not allow anybody to say (as we commonly hear), "I believe in the God of the New Testament, but not the God of the Old Testament." This does not please our Lord Jesus.

Secondly, you should see also that He does not apologize for the Mosaic Law. Even though it was temporary from the beginning, and even if it could be argued that there would never have been a Mosaic Law had not Israel sinned so grievously (Galatians 3:19), the fact is they did sin and the Law was imposed on them. A God of wisdom was behind the Mosaic Law. There has never been a more perfect standard of righteousness, neither could God's plan of redemption have been implied more beautifully than in the Ceremonial Law.

In this chapter, we deal with one of the more difficult verses in the Sermon on the Mount. The best of commentators are not in agreement, so far be it from me to argue for an infallible interpretation in this chapter. And yet it will not be very edifying if as we proceed we are not at peace as to the meaning of our Lord's words here.

The main issue is: To what extent, if any, is a Christian supposed to live under the Law of Moses? One realizes that the Law was not only temporary from the start but that Paul would later say, "If you are led by the Spirit, you are not under law" (Galatians 5:18). So, whatever did Jesus mean when He said that practicing and teaching these Commandments means we will be called "great" in the Kingdom of heaven? That is

not all. Whoever breaks these Commandments and teaches others to do so will be called "least" in the Kingdom of heaven.

Furthermore, is Jesus talking about the Ten Commandments, or is He including those aforementioned 2,000 pieces of Mosaic legislation? If Jesus fulfilled the Law, are we truly to keep the minutiae of the Law, such as Moses commanded?

Is Jesus saying that commands as these apply to us: "Three times a year you are to celebrate a festival to me" (Exodus 23:14)? What about the rules regarding touching a dead body (Numbers 19:11–13)? What about dietary laws, such as, "Do not cook a young goat in its mother's milk" (Deuteronomy 14:21)? Or agricultural laws, "Do not plant your field with two kinds of seed" (Leviticus 19:19)? Is a Christian not allowed to eat lobsters or shrimp (Leviticus 11:9–12)? Mind you, there are various religious sects and cults that stress Matthew 5:19 to the hilt, claiming we are indeed to live by all the Levitical Laws.

Don Carson has taken two different views on this verse. In one place (his little booklet on the Sermon on the Mount), he says Matthew 5:19 is referring to the commands that Jesus will shortly bring to His hearers, from Matthew 5:21 following. But in a later writing (his whole commentary on Matthew), Dr. Carson graciously changed his mind. It is a humble man who will admit to a change of mind in print. He said these Commandments refer to the Mosaic Laws as in verse 18—e.g., the "least stroke of the pen," etc. Michael Eaton says that the most "natural" way of taking Jesus' words is that they surely refer to what He just said in verse 18, which refers to the necessity of the Law being fulfilled before heaven and earth pass away.

But Dr. Eaton goes further. It would seem that Jesus Himself "relaxed" particular requirements of the Law and seemed to teach others to do so. For example, Jesus pronounced all foods "clean" in Mark 7:19. Jesus spoke against divorce, but the Law allowed divorce (Matthew 5:31–32; 19:7–9). Jesus prohibited taking of oaths, but the Law actually demanded them (Matthew 5:33–37). Jesus forbade revenge in personal relationships, although the Law did no more than restrain revenge from being too extreme (Matthew 5:38–39).

And now in Matthew 5:19, Jesus says: "Anyone who breaks one of the least of these Commandments and teaches others to do the same will be called least in the kingdom of heaven." How are these various verses and seemingly contradictory positions reconciled?

I think it is fair to conclude that Jesus' hearers almost certainly did not fully grasp His sermon at the time they heard it. We all surely know what it is like to hear a sermon—or read a book—and love it and then realize later we did not understand it very deeply at first. I am suggesting, therefore, that Jesus' words could not be very well understood until after Pentecost. His disciples may have been puzzled by a statement like this, who knows? And yet how could Jesus speak of not relaxing the Law, when He Himself seems to immediately bring changes in what obedience means in the Kingdom of heaven? Furthermore, how could there be a greater loyalty to the written Scriptures than what was shown by the scribes and the Pharisees, whom He upbraids later on?

Two Eras in the Kingdom of Heaven

We begin to answer the question by pointing out periods, or eras, of the Kingdom of heaven: the pre-Pentecostal period and the post-Pentecostal period.

The pre-Pentecostal period probably began with John the Baptist (Luke 16:16). Jesus preached the Gospel of the Kingdom (Matthew 4:23). Jesus' words in Matthew 5:19 were uttered at a time when the Law was still unfulfilled. In verse 17, Jesus promised to fulfill the Law. In verse 18, He showed how His work was clearly cut out for Him, not to mention the absolute certainty the Law will be fulfilled. In verse 19—the verse we are now dealing with—Jesus shows what

the responsibility of everyone was at that time. The Law was still unfulfilled. The parenthesis (as taught in Galatians 3:19) was not yet closed. Jesus had approximately two to three years left of keeping the Law in every detail.

The answer to the meaning of Matthew 5:19 is partly this: Since the Law was at that time unfulfilled, two things followed: (1) He Himself would keep it, and (2) His disciples must keep it as well. In other words, in this pre-Pentecostal period of two to three years, anyone who breaks "one of the least commands" (whatever those may be) would be regarded as "least" in the Kingdom. They would therefore be regarded as "least" if they broke them and taught others to do so.

Not practicing them nor teaching them would send the wrong signal to the revolutionaries who, as you may recall, relished any smashing of tradition for whatever reason. To break the least command would certainly have sent a wrong signal to Jesus' enemies. Jesus' words in Matthew 5:19 kept the Pharisees, for example, from having undue criticism of Him. His enemies would have been thrilled no end to get to charge Jesus with, say, "antinomianism" (breaking the Law), which would have justified their opposition to Him.

But Jesus did not give them a chance, not even a crumb to chew on. Indeed, anyone who breaks the least Commandment and teaches others to break the least Commandment would be called "least" in the Kingdom. He therefore affirmed the minutiae of the Law to the hilt. So He added that those who upheld the Law by practicing it and teaching it would be called "great" in the Kingdom. All possible criticisms of Jesus' teaching as being against the Law were rendered invalid in one stroke.

Jesus was therefore saying to all who heard Him that they are still under the Law and must keep all the commands—the Sabbaths, the feasts—and that there would be no relaxing of the Law. Jesus Himself would be obliged to keep the whole Law all the way to the cross, and not let any of His followers off the hook, either.

In other words, Jesus was still in the process of fulfilling the Law when He said what He did in Matthew 5:19. He would keep it, and His followers also must do the same—right to the end, up to the time He would say, "It is finished" (John

19:30). This is why Jesus still kept the Passover the night before the Crucifixion.

Therefore, the Mosaic Law was not nullified for those who wanted to be in the Kingdom of heaven during this pre-Crucifixion, pre-Easter, pre-Pentecost period. All the followers of Jesus must literally follow His example all the way.

Post-Pentecostal Period

After Jesus died and ascended to heaven, the Holy Spirit came down. Keep in mind, however, that at the time Jesus uttered these words in Matthew 5:19, His followers did not know there would be such a thing as a post-Pentecostal period. They still believed He would overthrow Rome. They still thought the Kingdom of God would be visible, that Jesus had come to restore Israel (see Acts 1:6). They, therefore, did not know at this stage what fulfilling the Law really meant—that Jesus would ultimately complete this by dying on the cross. This is why I pointed out above that it is not unlikely His disciples had not grasped what He said in these lines.

But in the post-Pentecostal period, it all came home! Jesus had indeed fulfilled the Law by His sinless life and sacrificial death. Moreover, we today continue to fulfill the Law by the Holy Spirit in us. The minutiae of the Law disappeared; the morality of the Law continued. Indeed, Christians are commanded to exceed the Law by the un-grieved Spirit in them—doing things that were never commanded by the Mosaic Law but only by the Law of Christ.

We today are in the post-Pentecostal period of the Kingdom. You and I recognize that Christ was our substitute; He kept the Law perfectly. Christ is our satisfaction (Isaiah 53:6; 2 Corinthians 5:21). Christ is our sanctification (1 Corinthians 1:30). Not only that—we demonstrate sanctification that is carried out by the un-grieved Spirit of God indwelling us.

Prestige in the Kingdom

Jesus also introduces a new concept: being called "least" or "great." But we must first ask: How did one get into the Kingdom of heaven at the time of Jesus—before He died on the cross and before Pentecost? Was it by keeping the minutiae of the Law? No. Were the Pharisees therefore already in the Kingdom? No.

The answer is: One was in the Kingdom by believing and following Jesus, then and there. He preached the Gospel of the Kingdom. Some believed Him, and by doing so entered it. Some rejected Him, and by rejecting Him didn't get in the Kingdom at all. Those who entered in did so by coming to Jesus. He said, "Come to me, all you who are weary and burdened, and I will give you rest" (Matthew 11:28). Those who were broken in spirit entered in (Matthew 5:3). Jesus had authority all His life. He was the God-man from conception. He was sinless and was the Lamb slain from the foundation of the world. He was the Lamb of God before He died on the cross (John 1:29). He forgave sins before He was raised from the dead.

And yet Jesus introduced a concept that may surprise you. There would be levels of prestige in the Kingdom. Some would be called "least" if they did not keep the Commandments and did not affirm them. Some would be called "great" if they did keep them and teach them to others. Note, too—which is very important—He did not say they were not "in" it. They obviously were, even if they were the "least" in it. Nor would they be ejected from it if they did not keep the Commandments. They were, at worst, the "least" in it. Jesus set a pattern here that would be relevant in the post-Pentecostal Kingdom.

Jesus, therefore, refers to rank in the Kingdom, which relates to righteousness in it and consequently reward in it. In this verse, it is also obvious that some commands are greater than others—some being "least of these Commandments," some apparently more important than others. But Jesus also shows that some followers in the Kingdom have varying degrees of greatness in it—and are affirmed accordingly.

Jesus appeals to one's self-esteem. God has always done this, appealing to one's self-interest. This should not surprise or offend you. It has always been that way. The first word God ever uttered to Abraham was, "Leave your country . . . and I will make you into a great nation and I will bless you; I will make your name great" (Genesis 12:1–2). Jesus shows a gradation of greatness and prestige. The rank: "least" or "great." Reputation: The same person "will be called" either "great" or "least." It is how God Himself will regard you, depending on whether you have sought for the honor that comes from Him only (John 5:44). But this verse implicitly refers to how others will regard you as well.

Do not be put off or offended by the idea of being rewarded. It is part of God's entire plan. Those who are persecuted for righteousness will be given a "great" reward in heaven (Matthew 5:12). Those who are saved by fire at the Judgment Seat of Christ will suffer loss—that is, they forfeit any reward (1 Corinthians 3:15).

Principles of Reward in the Kingdom

This teaching would have profound implications for those in the Kingdom in the post-Pentecostal era. Those who kept the "least" of these commands—who took them all seriously, doing their utmost to keep the minutiae of the Law—would be affirmed later, after the coming of the Spirit. For they would be the same kind of people who would take the greatest care not to grieve the Holy Spirit. Keeping the minutiae of the Law was training for the future, when the Holy Spirit would replace the Law.

There can be little doubt that faithful followers were earmarked—singled out—by God after the Spirit came down. When Jesus, who is the only one who kept the Law perfectly, cried out, "It is finished" (John 19:30), it must have been a wonderful feeling for Him. For He despised the shame and pain but looked forward to the joy set before Him (Hebrews 12:2). Those who followed Jesus and did not nullify the least of the commands—who did not disregard the refinements of the Ceremonial Law and respected the Civil Law, not to mention the Moral Law—were known by God in the post-Pentecostal period and were rewarded accordingly.

Why? Jesus said that those who were faithful in that which is least are also faithful in that which is much (Luke 16:10). Those who did not scoff at the details of the Law and followed Jesus would be the very ones who, after receiving the Spirit, would find greatest joy in keeping the internal commands that Jesus would teach in the Sermon on the Mount (Matthew 5:21–48). The same Lord who knows those who are His does not forget. "He who receives you receives me, and he who receives me receives the one who sent me . . .

and if anyone gives even a cup of cold water to one of these little ones because he is my disciple, I tell you the truth, he will certainly not lose his reward" (Matthew 10:40–42).

I reckon that the original disciples of Jesus, minus Judas Iscariot, would always be called "great" in the Kingdom of heaven. I believe this would have included people like Nicodemus and Joseph of Arimathea (see John 19:38–42). I think of those whose names are in the book of Acts. These are names that will live forever in glory.

But a question remains, which the reader no doubt will have on his or her mind: If Jesus relaxed some requirements, despite what He said, whatever is going on? Let me say two things.

First, He clearly relaxed certain requirements by declaring all foods kosher. But it does not follow that His followers immediately began eating bacon and eggs. Pronouncing all foods "clean" may only have been the gospel writer Mark making a post-Pentecostal comment about the event, which not all (if any) grasped at the time (Mark 7:19). So much of what Jesus taught was only understood after the Spirit came down at Pentecost. Jesus also prohibited the swearing of oaths, an entirely different perspective from Old Testament practice. He would not allow people to hold a grudge, although the Law did not require punishment if one did hold a grudge. So He did throw out hints along the way of what the commands of the Kingdom would be like after Pentecost.

Secondly, He intensified, embellished and outclassed the other commands, as we will see in more detail below. For example, lusting in the heart became adultery; hate became murder.

Here, then, is what was going on. Jesus was clearly moving in a direction by which the Law would be transcended. Not by being disregarded, but by being outclassed. Never forget that the Sermon on the Mount is Jesus' doctrine of the Holy Spirit. He would give out His own commands, "I tell you . . ." As we will see further, these commands outstrip and outclass the equivalent commands in the Mosaic Law.

Jesus rocked the boat more than any figure in human history. But at this time in His life, I repeat, He had some two to three years to go before His work was finished. So, in Matthew 5:19 you could say He didn't rock the boat, and He wouldn't let His followers rock the boat. He didn't give the Pharisees or Sadducees an inch by which they could discredit Him or justly accuse Him of letting the standards of the Law down. He kept the Sabbath (healing was not forbidden on the Sabbath). He simply refused to keep the traditions that were added to the Mosaic Law. He adhered strictly to the Word and insisted that His followers do the same. They would be rewarded by so doing.

Would there be "least" commands in the post-Pentecostal period of the Kingdom of heaven? Yes. "Whoever can be trusted with very little can also be trusted with much, and whoever is dishonest with very little will also be dishonest with much" (Luke 16:10). This is a general principle and can be aptly drawn from Matthew 5:19.

There would be "least" commands, and the more conscientious followers would develop a sensitivity to God's ways. David was conscience-stricken for cutting off a piece of Saul's robe (1 Samuel 24:5). This was developing a sensitivity to the ways of the Holy Spirit. It becomes what Jesus would call "surpassing" the righteousness of the scribes and Pharisees. It would also be what would make a person known as "great" in the Kingdom.

20. The Law Outclassed

For I tell you that unless your righteousness surpasses that of the Pharisees and
the teachers of the law, you will certainly not enter the kingdom of heaven.

MATTHEW 5:20

There are several definitions of the word *class*. It may refer to people or things that have the same characteristics in common. It could refer to people of the same social or economic level. It may refer to a division according to quality, like flying first-class or tourist class. It could refer to distinction, high quality, like a tennis player with class. Those who play at Wimbledon are "world class." President John F. Kennedy said of Richard Nixon, "He's got no class," which displays yet another kind of meaning.

I was once interviewed by Premier Christian Radio in London. When asked, "Whom would you love to have lunch with, living or dead?" I think they expected me to say John Calvin or Martin Luther. My answer: Joe DiMaggio. He was the center fielder for the New York Yankees. Apart from baseball records of his that will never be broken, DiMaggio did everything with class, whether swinging the bat at the plate, rounding the bases or catching a fly ball. He did everything with a touch of class that no other player matched.

DiMaggio became my hero when I was 10 years old. I met him when I was 32 and I swelled with pride like a child. He was immortalized by Simon and Garfunkel, was celebrated in print by Ernest Hemingway, was the greatest baseball player of his time—and possibly ever. President Kennedy said if he could give a knighthood, it would be to "Sir Joe DiMaggio." In a day of "checkbook journalism"—from which he could have made millions—DiMaggio never granted one interview. I call that class. He was, as they say, a "class act."

To outclass means to "surpass greatly," which is probably the best translation of the Greek *peris-seuse*—strengthened by *peleiov* ("more, greater") in Matthew 5:20. It means to have superabundance

of something. Therefore, Matthew 5:20 says that the righteousness of Jesus' followers must have a superabundance of righteousness—one that far surpasses even the highest achievements of those "masters of piety," the Pharisees and scribes, the teachers of the Law.

What a claim! Those who enter the realm of the un-grieved Spirit manifest a righteousness that exceeds the most self-righteous people who ever lived. What a challenge! But whoever could do this? If the original hearers grasped this statement, whatever must they have been thinking? Possibly they said to themselves, "Whoever *could* do this? Whoever could enter the Kingdom if the standard of righteousness is this high?" The famed piety of the Pharisees was one thing, but Jesus now poses a righteousness that outstrips, outdoes and outclasses even those who adhered strictly and rigidly to the Mosaic Law.

However can this be achieved? Verse 17 shows what Jesus promises to do. Verse 18, what He had to do to keep His promise. Verse 19, what His followers were to do until the Law was accomplished. But Matthew 5:20 shows the kind of righteousness that must characterize those who enter the Kingdom of heaven—namely, a righteousness that exceeds that of the supposedly most pious people around.

A Picture of Superficial Righteousness

Jesus lumps two groups together: the scribes (KJV), also known as teachers of the Law (NIV), and the Pharisees.

Who were the scribes, or teachers/doctors of the Law? Their Old Testament hero was Ezra (Ezra 7:6, 10). They became the elitist group, the professional interpreters of Scripture. They gathered and interpreted Israel's sacred literature. They were also copyists, those who had the tedious duty of writing out Scripture, not missing the slightest yod or iota, when putting it on a scroll. They were probably the ones who selected and fixed the Old Testament canon. They belonged to the Hassidim, whose name means "pious."

The Pharisees were an influential party in Jesus' day. You could almost call them a political party. Their hero was Ezra also, and they, too, centered on the Law. Their name derived from two things: (1) They were separatists, separate from the priestly interpretation of the Law and separate from the common people. And (2) they regarded themselves as being the superior interpreters of the Law. They were well-known for being legalistic and rigorous. Josephus said they were noted for strict accuracy in their interpretations and for being scrupulous in their adherence to them. They were also said to build a fence around the Law with their embellishments, the fence being their own interpretations and traditions (Mark 7:3–5).

Jesus lumps the two groups together as if they were not really different from each other. "The teachers of the law and the Pharisees sit in Moses' seat," Jesus said. "So you must obey them and do everything they tell you. But do not do what they do, for they do not practice what they preach. They tie up heavy loads and put them on men's shoulders, but they themselves are not willing to lift a finger to move them. Everything they do is done for men to see" (Matthew 23:2–5).

The teachers of the Law were indeed often Pharisees as well (Mark 2:16). They loved tradition (Matthew 15:3–4). As we have seen, they did not practice what they preached. They had no objectivity about themselves. They built the tombs of prophets and thought they were a cut above those who killed prophets (Matthew 23:29–30), claiming they would not have done such horrible things. They were strict tithers (Matthew 23:23; Luke 18:11–12). Their acts of righteousness were done only to be seen of men. They had no concept or sense of inward sin. Jesus called them "snakes" who were on their road to hell (Matthew 23:33). Jesus also held them responsible for the way the whole nation would be judged (Matthew 23:35–36).

The Pharisees in particular criticized Jesus for healing on the Sabbath (John 9:16). Some, however, even fasted with John's disciples (Mark 2:18). They loved to trap Jesus by His words (Matthew 22:15). They loved to play "Gotcha!" The teachers of the Law claimed that Jesus cast out devils by Beelzebub, the prince of devils (Mark 3:22).

The Influence of the Pharisees

Probably nobody ever dared to stand up to the Pharisees and doctors of the Law. These men felt the Law was theirs. They felt they had a monopoly, or franchise, on the truth about the Law. They were successors not only to Ezra but also to Moses. If God was going to do anything in Israel, they felt it would come through them. They fancied that they were the sole upholders of the Scriptures. But their righteousness was a superficial righteousness.

Jesus saw right through them. For one thing, they were not in the Kingdom of heaven. Not only were they not the "least" in the Kingdom, they weren't in it at all! Jesus even said they kept other people from entering it and that their "converts" were doubly sons of hell (Matthew 23:15).

I wrote in an early chapter that I have a friendship with Rabbi David Rosen, who is probably Israel's most decorated and respected Orthodox Jewish rabbi. David was given a papal knighthood by Pope Benedict. I also mentioned that we wrote a book together called *The Christian and the Pharisee* (his choice of title). I put forth the case that Jesus is Israel's Messiah, and David demonstrates why he disagrees with me. David and I have remained good friends. He sees himself as a Pharisee and is very happy indeed to be called that. He believes that the New Testament does not always give an accurate picture of what Pharisees were (and are) like—that perhaps some were as bad as they are depicted in the gospels, but not all. In writing this chapter, I could not help but think of David. He is a lovely, pious man and is certainly not like the showy type of Pharisee described in Matthew 6 and Matthew 23.

When Jesus stated that "unless one's righteousness went beyond that of the Pharisees and teachers of the Law," we must keep in mind that nobody had ever talked that way before. The common people took for granted that Pharisees were supremely righteous men. You dared not criticize them. The doctors of the Law, moreover, were off-the-charts righteous men, and if anybody got into the Kingdom by being righteous, they certainly did. It reminds me of an old southern-gospel song that stresses pious duties and acts: "If anyone makes it all the way home, Lord, surely I will." If righteous acts are what enable one to make it into the Kingdom, the most natural feeling in the world is, "I am good enough. If anyone gets in the Kingdom, Lord, surely I will."

The common people of Jesus' day never dreamed that they could equal, much less surpass, the righteousness of the Pharisees and scribes. Their standard of piety was beyond reproach. Their adherence to the Law was unquestioned. No ordinary Jew in Israel could even hope to be so pious. For one thing, the common people were outclassed by the culture and education of the Pharisees. The ordinary citizens of Israel were way behind the doctors of the Law from the start, even at a religious level. The Pharisees seemed to have a head start in piety!

Therefore, you can imagine the stunned silence—the sobered expressions on faces and the atmosphere of shock—when Jesus said, speaking to ordinary people, "I tell you that unless your righteousness surpasses that of the Pharisees and the teachers of the law, you will certainly not enter the Kingdom of heaven." Surpass? "We couldn't even come close," would be the typical feeling. However, can a person in Israel exceed the righteousness of the doctors of the Law and the Pharisees?

They could. The answer is quite simple. The Pharisees' righteousness was an external righteousness. The Pharisees and scribes were empty shells. Godliness to them was all about appearance, what people could see and be impressed with. "They make their phylacteries wide and the tassels on their garments long; they love the place of honor at banquets and the most important seats in the synagogues; they love to be greeted in the marketplaces and to have men call them 'Rabbi'" (Matthew 23:5–7).

When they gave a contribution, they wanted trumpets to sound. When they prayed, they wanted people to see them. When they fasted, they made sure it was obvious (Matthew 6:1–18). Their righteousness was an egocentric righteousness. It was all to bolster their own self-esteem by getting the praise of men (Luke 16:15). It was only an exhibitionist righteousness, all done for people to see (Matthew 23:5).

Jesus Was Fearless with the Scribes and Pharisees

Jesus was utterly unimpressed, unafraid and un-intimidated by them. The ordinary people, even some leaders, however, were intimidated by them. "Because of the Pharisees they would not confess their faith for fear they would be put out of the synagogue" (John 12:42). And now Jesus sends a signal to the most insignificant Jew in Israel—the most common worshiper, the frail Israelite who never thought he or she would amount to anything of note in this life—that they could have a personal righteousness that outclassed these professionals. The last would be first!

And yet such a surpassing righteousness was a possible thing. Jesus will explain how in the next section. It was also a *provided* thing, because Jesus would fulfill the Law. But the main thing, perhaps, is that it is promised to those who accept Jesus, His words and then believe.

How, then, is it possible that one could surpass the righteousness of the Pharisees?

Righteousness That Outclasses the Pharisees

First, it is surpassed by an *imputed* righteousness. Jesus fulfilled the Law as our substitute. Therefore, the moment you and I transfer the trust we once had in our good works—and abandon it (e.g., the thinking that "if anyone makes it all the way home, Lord, surely I will") to what Jesus has done on our behalf—the very righteousness of Jesus Christ is put to our credit.

In one stroke, the one who "does not work but trusts God who justifies the wicked, his faith is credited as righteousness" (Romans 4:5). The one who is "poor in spirit"—who comes to Jesus' beckoning (Matthew 11:28), and who realizes that his or her righteousness is like filthy rags (Isaiah 64:6)—God declares that person righteous. And it is an unimprovable, unchangeable and permanent righteousness that is put to our credit forever and ever.

And yet imputed righteousness is not entirely what Jesus means in Matthew 5:20. It is only partly what He means. Those who stop here, assuming that imputed righteousness is all Jesus has in mind, miss the main point, which is coming up in the next section of the Sermon on the Mount. Not only that, I fear that those who stop at the level of imputed righteousness (and never move on to what follows) could be needlessly vulnerable to being accused of antinomianism—something that Jesus will not allow for a moment.

Second, one surpasses the piety of the Pharisees by an *implanted* righteousness. This means that the Holy Spirit imparts the Word into our hearts. "Get rid of all moral filth and the evil that is so prevalent and humbly accept the word planted in you, which can save you" (James 1:21). This is something the Pharisees did not experience because, unlike such men as Nicodemus or Joseph of Arimathea, they rejected Jesus. But to those who would accept Jesus, there was the promise of the Holy Spirit who indwells us.

Third, one outstrips the righteousness of the doctors of the Law by an *internal* righteousness. The Pharisees only had an external righteousness. They thought you didn't commit adultery if you did not physically sleep with another man's wife. They thought you didn't commit murder if you did not take another person's life. But Jesus has an internal righteousness in mind. As we will see, lusting is committing adultery in the heart (Matthew 5:28), and hate is committing murder in the heart (Matthew 5:21). Such a standard of righteousness never crossed the minds of the scribes and Pharisees.

Fourth, one outclasses the Pharisees' piety by an *integrated* righteousness. It is something that affects the whole of a person's life—not just in public, but in private. Not only before men, but before God. It relates to one's body (Romans 12:1). It touches one's mind and one's spirit (Romans 12:2). It gives an ever-deepening sense of sin (1 John 1:8). The Pharisees had no concept or even consciousness of inward sin. This integrated righteousness gives an ever-increasing awareness of the Holy Spirit—an experience that was alien to a Pharisee.

Jesus, therefore, is promising a righteousness that is in superabundance, completely superior to the righteousness of the Pharisees. For the Kingdom of heaven is the realm of the un-grieved Spirit. One develops a sensitivity to the Holy Spirit, learning what grieves Him and allowing no bitterness or grudges. One develops an intimacy with the Father. One does not contribute to the church or to the poor in order to be seen of men. One prays for his or her enemies. All of this is done for the honor of God alone.

The Law never envisaged any of these things. Though the Law was a standard of righteousness that was as good as it gets, it was nevertheless external. It did not touch the heart. This is why God promised a New Covenant long before Jesus came (Jeremiah 31:31). Jesus became the mediator of the New Covenant and implanted a righteousness that rendered the Law outclassed.

It must bring glory to God and His Son when His people are self-effacing, seeking the honor that comes from Him and not people, forgiving those who have hurt them and loving their enemies, being lied about but holding no grudges. God loves a people who seek His face without telling the world they are doing so, who give in total secrecy and who honor Him by loving the truth.

What a contrast between the way our Lord wants His people to live and those self-righteous people who do "everything for people to see." The Pharisees described in the New Testament have "no class," to put the meaning on it that John F. Kennedy had in mind. But God wants to produce a people with real class—not necessarily being middle class, highly educated, of noble stock or culture. He looks high and low over the planet for those who want to hear from Him, who want to know Him intimately and who do heroic things for those hurting people nobody wants to have anything to do with—and keep quiet about it. That's class.

21. The Anger That Kills

You have heard that it was said to the people long ago, "Do not murder,
and anyone who murders will be subject to judgment." But I tell you that
anyone who is angry with his brother will be subject to judgment. Again,
anyone who says to his brother, "Raca," is answerable to the Sanhedrin.
But anyone who says, "You fool!" will be in danger of the fire of hell.

MATTHEW 5:21–22

You may recall that Jesus' introduction to the Mosaic Law in verses 17–20 form His second "text" for this immortal sermon. Indeed, along with verses 21–48, the rest of Matthew 5 is an application of Jesus' treatment of the Mosaic Law. And Matthew 6–7 are more of the same.

Jesus had just shocked His hearers when He said that one cannot enter the Kingdom of heaven unless his righteousness surpasses that of the Pharisees and teachers of the Law. Beginning with verse 21, Jesus explains precisely what He means by righteousness that outclasses the piety of the scribes and Pharisees.

We saw in the previous chapter that the Pharisees had but an external righteousness. These people were empty shells, their piety totally for outward appearance in order that they would be admired by people. The righteousness that surpasses that of the Pharisees is an internal righteousness—touching on the motives, intentions and condition of the heart.

The Sixth Commandment—"You Shall Not Murder"

We might have expected Jesus to go through the Ten Commandments in their chronological order. But He doesn't. Why? I don't know. Perhaps it is because He chooses a Commandment—the sixth—which probably relates more to how people grieve the Holy Spirit than any other. All I know is, He chooses first to refer to the sixth Commandment—"You shall not murder" (Exodus 20:13).

I do know that the first thing the apostle Paul said after having told us not to grieve the Holy Spirit was this: "Get rid of all bitterness, rage

and anger, brawling and slander, along with every form of malice. Be kind and compassionate to one another, forgiving each other, just as in Christ God for gave you" (Ephesians 4:31–32). Paul's words come very close to summarizing much of Matthew 5.

We need to remember that Jesus is speaking to Jews—a covenant people—when He says, "You have heard that it was said to the people long ago, 'Do not murder, and anyone who murders will be subject to judgment.'" He is talking to people who trace their ancestry to Moses and back to Abraham—"long ago."

When He says, "You have heard that it was said," He is referring to a consensus, common knowledge among the people. These people knew their Bibles fairly well, knew the Law and the traditions. He did not say, "You have read," but, "You have heard." The oral tradition was strong in those days. I doubt Jesus could come to the church today and speak this way. So many in church today don't know their Bibles. But Jesus' hearers then were acquainted with what we might call "the language of Zion." These were people who had a "head start," having been given the Law (Romans 3:1).

He begins with an act of extreme selfishness: murder. Murder is committed when a person removes another human being from this life, having no concern for that person's life or loved ones. Such selfishness is murder! When there is a threat and you are ruthless and selfish, you remove it—you just get that threat out of the way. So, whether that threat is an enemy or an unborn, unwanted baby, murder is sheer selfishness.

The origin of murder is the heart. Jesus later said, "Out of the heart come evil thoughts, murder, adultery, sexual immorality, theft, false testimony, slander" (Matthew 15:19). Murder comes from a selfish, evil heart. This is why modern Bible versions refer to "murder" not as the old KJV's "Thou shalt not kill." Murder exposes the intent of the heart. People murder because they become obsessed with hate—the opposite of love. Love is selfless concern; hate is selfish concern. Obsession is having one's thoughts occupied continually.

King Saul became obsessed with David, being more concerned with the threat of this young leader than he was with the Philistines, the enemy of Israel. Saul was driven to remove that threat. He never succeeded. But murder was in his heart and—though Saul did not succeed in killing David—in the sight of God, Saul was guilty of murder.

Murder is killing another human being on purpose. The sixth Commandment does not refer to plants or animals, as Albert Schweitzer might argue. This command refers to an offense—a homicide, killing another person. Note, too, that (in my opinion) this does not refer to war or capital punishment. In war, one is not angry with a soldier on the opposite side. Capital punishment is dealing with a crime; the punishment is not meted out by personal vendetta.

The sixth Commandment deals with a person wanting to remove another person who is a threat. Consequently, abortion is murder. When a newborn person is a threat—perhaps to one's plans or happiness, and the solution is abortion—it is murder. I am speaking generally and not with reference to mitigating circumstances, which could change the entire picture. I speak of killing an unborn child merely because one doesn't want the responsibility of that child. It is murder.

Gossip can be murder as well. The tongue can destroy another person forever. With one word, you can ruin another's life by rendering that person unreliable, unworthy, evil or not fit for whatever reason. This is why we must guard our language. This can be done without malice, no doubt. But when one intentionally wishes to kill another person's influence, or question their integrity or damage their reputation, it is tantamount to murder, says Jesus in these lines.

Murder is a self-centered act. Jesus' point: You don't need to kill a person physically for that act to be murder. If in your heart you want to eliminate another person's place in the world, you show hatred and hence violate the sixth Commandment in the sight of God.

But Jesus adds something that is not in Exodus 20:13 or Deuteronomy 5:17: "Anyone who murders will be subject to judgment." (The books of Moses—Exodus, Leviticus, Deuteronomy—nevertheless make this clear.) The one who murders will be held accountable for this external sin. After all, it is arguably the worst crime one can commit—taking another person's life. The consequence of this sin is that one is held accountable; one will face judgment.

The Mosaic Law makes it clear: If one murders, he will lose his own life. "Show no pity: life for life, eye or eye, tooth for tooth, hand for hand, foot for foot" (Deuteronomy 19:21). There was a provision for accidental killing (see Exodus 21:12–14). But when one kills deliberately, there would be a trial. Witnesses would be brought forward. "One witness is not enough to convict a man accused of any crime or offense he may have committed. A matter must be established by the testimony of two or three witnesses" (Deuteronomy 19:15).

Judgment

"Judgment" in this verse refers to more than one thing. It was certainly the way of dealing with murder in ancient times. There were legal proceedings. A court was set up in every town. There was a council of 23 persons set up to deal with criminal matters. However, Jesus has more than the ancient courts in mind, because He uses this phrase in a different way.

When He says that "anyone who murders will be subject to judgment," there was also the eye of God. God sees all that is happening. Sometimes people get away with murder. But God has a way of stepping in on His own. "Be sure that your sin will find you out" (Numbers 32:23). And yet this could also refer to the Final Judgment. One day every secret will be revealed. It will come out in the open—those who got away with murder, with abortion, with malicious gossip, with hurting someone's reputation.

Not only that, all men and all women will be summoned one day to give an account of their lives. I am accountable for all my acts. Indeed (and this is probably my least favorite verse in the Bible), "I tell you that men will have to give account on the day of judgment for every careless word they have spoken" (Matthew 12:36). How awful it will be when it is shown I have violated the sixth Commandment.

"But I Tell You"

We must pause for a moment and take note of a phrase Jesus will use all the time: "But I tell you." It shows His amazing, magnificent and fearless authority. It is Jesus' way of saying, "I have an interpretation of the Law that is superior to anyone else's. The Law says one thing, but here is what I say."

That is precisely what Jesus is saying again and again with these words, "But I tell you." Without any apology, Jesus sets Himself up as the supreme interpreter of the Law. "The Law says you shall not murder, but I say—you must not be angry." "The Law says if you murder you are subject to judgment, but I say—if you are angry, you are subject to judgment." No wonder the crowds were astonished at His teaching, how He spoke with authority and not like the teachers of the Law (Matthew 7:28–29).

Righteousness in the Kingdom of Heaven

What is going on here? Jesus is letting us know the standard of righteousness required for the Kingdom of heaven. It is a righteousness that exceeds that of the Pharisees. Jesus is giving His doctrine of the Holy Spirit. Indeed, He is anticipating the coming of the Spirit. The Pharisees were champions of the "letter" of the Law. Paul, however, pointed out, "The letter kills, but the Spirit gives life" (2 Corinthians 3:6).

Jesus said He was going to fulfill the Law. He would fulfill the letter of it, yes, but also the spirit of it. The letter of the Law must be fulfilled. But the keeping of the mere letter of the Law left it unfulfilled. Jesus practiced what He preached. On the other hand, Pharisees and Sadducees felt righteous because they didn't murder anybody with the sword. The irony is, they would end up killing

Jesus (John 16:1–4)! Another irony is that those who hold to the letter of the Law are sometimes the first to break it. They have a way of making themselves exceptions to the rule. So people with a "high view of the Law" will sometimes excuse their own sin until they get caught!

Jesus gave a different interpretation of the Law—showing the righteousness required in the heart—and He fulfilled it as well! He comes forward with an authority of exclusive superiority: "I." "But I tell you." No one else had this authority.

So the reason He chose to begin with the sixth Commandment, and not the seventh or the third, is probably because this command—when seen in terms of the motive of the heart—shows human sinfulness. And by showing we must not exhibit any hatred, He demonstrates the righteousness that surpasses that of the Pharisees. In a word: Jesus clearly displays how the external righteousness of the Law, the only kind the Pharisees could grasp, is outclassed.

Anger

But He brings in another word: *anger*. Whereas the Law says "murder," Jesus says "anger." No one until then had felt condemned because they were angry. Anger seems so natural, so reasonable, so just.

And what do you suppose the Mosaic Law had to say about anger? Nothing. It only restrained the expression of anger, namely, murder. There was no legislation against anger. The Law mentions the danger of God being angry. But it never has anything to say about anger among the Israelites. The Law was mainly concerned with external behavior. It was administered by magistrates and councils of elders and heads of families. The Law legislated anger only when it showed itself in some visible crime.

Jesus not only brings in the word *angry* but adds the phrase "angry with his brother." The King James Version adds "without a cause"—which occurs in some Greek manuscripts but apparently not the best. Some think the phrase "without a cause" was inserted by a copyist. Nevertheless, as John Stott put it, there is every reason to believe that the phrase "without a cause" correctly interprets what Jesus meant. Not all anger is evil.

Paul writes, "In your anger do not sin" (Ephesians 4:26). Jesus, moreover, exhibited righteous indignation when He was angry with the way things were going on in the Temple (John 2:15). I just wish all my anger was righteous anger!

Why did Jesus mention "brother"? Why not anger toward those in the world? I believe the answer is that most temptation to wrongful anger will be among those closest to you—your husband, wife, parents, not to mention siblings. And what about those in the church who disappoint you?

Jesus adds again: Those who are angry will be "subject to judgment." He now raises the bar. It is not only those who murder but those who are angry who will have to give an account.

But how would anybody know? Answer: God knows. The all-seeing eye of God knows the thoughts and intents of the heart. However, the main thing in these lines is this: *Anger grieves the Holy Spirit.* Because the Kingdom of heaven is the realm of the un-grieved Spirit, we are therefore called to a standard by which we do not grieve the Spirit by a bad attitude. You may not get caught by a court of law, but God knows.

To the person who has a care not to grieve the Holy Spirit, a teaching like this matters a lot. That person wants to be cautious in this area, so that our words—even our thoughts—do not cause the heavenly Dove to flutter away!

You see, the judgment Jesus now refers to is the verdict of the Holy Spirit Himself. Our anger grieves the Spirit. Others may not know what you are feeling and thinking. But the Holy Spirit knows. He is sensitive to any unrighteous anger, the anger of pride, getting our feelings hurt and remaining bitter, anger toward those who don't come up to our standard and any determination to get revenge.

With this language—"But I tell you"—Jesus shows further what sin is and how sins of the heart are prohibited in the Kingdom of heaven. He shows, indeed, a level of righteousness that was beyond the concept of the teachers of the Law. But it is a concept you and I must embrace if we are to be Jesus' true followers.

22. The Danger of Anger

Again, anyone who says to his brother, "Raca," is answerable to the Sanhedrin.
But anyone who says, "You fool!" will be in danger of the fire of hell.

MATTHEW 5:22

This verse used to terrify me when I was a little boy. I am not sure what precipitated the conversation, but my mother would say to me, "If you call somebody a fool, you will go to hell." It certainly had the effect of my making sure I did not call anybody a fool again!

I also feel that I am a bit of a fraud writing this chapter. I have had trouble controlling my temper all my life. It probably didn't help when, at the age of six, I burned my tongue on the porridge my mother had just made—and I shouted, "Why do you have to make things so hot?" She replied, "God can take that out of your heart when you get sanctified." I don't think I ever did get sanctified to that extent!

When we are angry, it always seems right at the time. The Lord said to Jonah, "Have you any right to be angry?" (Jonah 4:4). No, he didn't—but he thought he did. We all feel that way. When we are angry, it is just. When we are admonished not to let the sun go down on our wrath—"while you are still angry" (Ephesians 4:26)—it means we have a victory only if we don't wait until the next day. You see, we all cool off the next day, something that comes rather naturally. It is a victory only when we apologize immediately!

When Jesus fulfilled the Law on our behalf, He not only kept it outwardly but inwardly—which is the point of Jesus' application of the Ten Commandments. The Pharisees thought they kept the Law because they didn't kill anybody by the sword. But Jesus brings the Law down to the heart: He calls anger a sin.

Anger cannot be judged by a court of men—unless that anger leads to physical murder. But God sees our anger, and the judgment to which we are brought when we are angry is in the presence not of a court of men but of the Holy Spirit.

Four Uses of Our Being Subject to Judgment

When Jesus first says murder will be "subject to judgment," He's referring to the ancient courts of law. The second time He says "subject to judgment," He means that our anger makes us subject to the bar of God—the Holy Spirit. The third time, when He refers to calling our brother "Raca," He uses the words "answerable to the Sanhedrin," a body that parallels the ancient courts. The Greek word *sunedrio* means "council" (ESV). (Jesus may or may not have meant the Sanhedrin.) The fourth time—calling a person a fool—it parallels being subject to the bar of God, but He says "danger of the fire of hell." It parallels the second usage, meaning that God will judge us.

The Root of Anger

Where does anger begin? It is rooted in the heart. We are warned, "See to it that no one misses the grace of God and that no bitter root grows up to cause trouble and defile many" (Hebrews 12:15).

Anger is in the heart because we all inherit the sin of Adam. The early Methodists called it "inbred sin." Some also taught that sin can be dealt with like a dentist drilling on a cavity and ridding the tooth of all decay. We might wish the carnal nature were eradicated when we are converted or move closer to God, but, sadly, sin is there to be reckoned with as long as we live (1 John 1:8). Not that every person has a particular problem with anger as such. Your weakness might be in another area. To deny this is to set yourself up for a grievous fall and disillusionment. If you think you will never fall short in some way—or never lose your temper again—I'm sorry, but you will.

And yet there is another way to refer to this root. Damaged emotions from childhood must not be ignored. Some people are always angry and don't know why. There is, of course, the theological explanation—it is called "original sin"—but there are also psychological explanations. For example, one is brought up to be an achiever but doesn't always succeed. Such a person may be a textbook case of anger waiting to be triggered at any moment. Or take the person who had a perfectionist parent, so the offspring is always upset for coming short of perfection. There is also the person who received too little or too much attention at a certain age and seems to stay the same emotional age for the rest of his or her life. The list is endless. To quote again Clyde Narramore, "Every person is worth understanding."

There is repressed anger. It is when one denies that he or she is angry. We push anger down into the subconscious. A person like this may be smiling all the time, seemingly easygoing and in control, but may be angry the whole time. Are these forms of anger sin? Yes. Though there may be a psychological explanation, we are all still responsible for our own acts and attitudes. We will never get at the root if we explain it away.

Not only that, but the root of bitterness can cause a person to "miss the grace of God," which means forfeiting your inheritance. God just may pass you by. The wrath of man does not work the righteousness of God (James 1:20, KJV). In any case, repression is never good. It is far better to come to terms with our feelings, admit to the truth and confess it to God. One may never be free of anger, but he or she can improve by the genuine desire not to grieve the Holy Spirit. If I am totally honest, this has been the only way forward for me. I still struggle, but the wish not to grieve the Spirit has helped me a lot.

Degrees of Anger

And yet there is righteous anger. This does exist. When Paul says, "In your anger do not sin" (Ephesians 4:26), this is proof enough that one can be angry and not sin. Jesus demonstrated this.

Yet how can we know the difference? In other words, how can I know that the anger I am feeling is righteous anger—anger that is not sinful? It is not easy to answer this. "Fools rush in where angels fear to tread," said Alexander Pope. Can anger begin as righteous anger and then become

carnal anger? Yes. I think the answer may be: If you can be grieved by what you see without getting personally and emotionally involved, then just maybe it is righteous anger. Paul felt this in Athens (Acts 17:16).

My problem is, I can get upset (perhaps with some justification) when I watch certain TV preachers and—"having begun in the Spirit" as I critique their message—I end up in the flesh. It goes to show that beginning in the Spirit certainly does not mean you will be perfected by the flesh!

What, then, is righteous anger? It is when the Holy Spirit reveals His indignation with what you see. Your heart will ache, but you won't be agitated. When you feel agitated, you probably are disqualified to speak. Righteous anger is speaking the truth in love. You will be calm, even detached from personal feeling. You speak the truth objectively as if you weren't involved. The wisdom that comes from above is gentle, "easy to be entreated" (James 3:17, KJV). You will not be abrasive and, more often than not, the other person will accept what you say. It is when your personal ego is not involved. If it is, Jesus' words say you are disqualified from speaking.

Righteous anger is manifest because the sole honor of God is at stake. Martin Luther said there is an anger of love. It is when one wishes no person any evil, whereby you are friendly to the person but hostile to his sin. But once I feel agitated, I will invariably grieve the Spirit—and am disqualified from continuing—even if I began in the Spirit. If I am in the Spirit, I won't show agitation. But if I lose my temper—even if the point I wanted to make is right—I am wrong! You can be correct in the point you wish to make, but utterly wrong when you lose your temper.

But there is another level: jealous anger. There is nothing at all righteous here. This is when name-calling enters in. Jesus said if you call a brother "Raca," you are answerable to the council. The word Raca means "empty." It is the equivalent of calling someone stupid. It is insulting another person's intelligence, calling them "empty-headed," "nitwit," "blockhead," "numskull." When we are jealous of others, we love to make them appear stupid. We don't admit to being jealous. We go on the attack instead and say things to insult them. We make catty, spiteful remarks—whatever will put them down.

It is not easy to understand what Jesus means by being subject to the council. I suppose it applies to the fact that name-calling becomes obvious to others. The result is that a council of some sort is called to get involved in the situation. It is when your attitude becomes so horrible that you say things aloud, and it becomes so disruptive to the larger fellowship that a council of unbiased people needs to intervene and you get judged.

The worst-case scenario, according to Jesus, is a judgmental anger. "But anyone who says, 'You fool!' will be in danger of the fire of hell." This is when you judge another person's heart. The Greek word translated as "fool" is *moree,* from which we get the word "moron."

But in those days it referred to an outcast, an apostate or rebel. When you call someone empty-headed, you are trying to make that person look bad. Although there is no exact equivalent of the Greek word *moree,* it probably means that you are judging the person worthy of hell. "This person deserves to go to hell," you are saying, according to Jesus. In this case, you are not judging his or her intelligence—you are playing God. You have judged that person's heart, or spiritual state. You have decided that this person is no good.

Jesus puts this as the ultimate degree of anger. You have expressed contempt for someone's heart. In calling someone "Raca," you have shown contempt for this person's head, insulting him or her. But with *moree*—"fool"—you have decided this person is finished and deserves to go to hell.

According to this, if you tell another that he or she is doomed for hell, you are in danger of hell yourself. "Do not judge, or you too will be judged. For in the same way you judge others, you will be judged," Jesus will say later on in the Sermon on the Mount (Matthew 7:1).

Judgmental anger is a dangerous, dangerous domain in which to dwell, according to Jesus. Why? This belongs to God alone. A fool is someone for whom there is no hope. King Saul could say about himself, "I have played the fool" (1 Samuel 26:21, kjv), but David did not call Saul that. Never claim to know the person's heart so that you think you are qualified to pronounce sentence on them. That is God's prerogative. God doesn't like it if we try to do what He alone is able to do.

The Danger of Anger

We have seen that the Kingdom of heaven is the realm of the un-grieved Spirit. I might have defined it simply as the reign of the Holy Spirit in us, for so it is. But the proof He rules and reigns is that He is un-grieved. It is no small accomplishment for the Holy Spirit to be in us utterly un-grieved—which means He is at home in us, Himself in us. It means we are devoid of bitterness.

Yet when we grieve the Holy Spirit, it is not the end of the world. We've all done it. It doesn't mean you have lost your salvation. "Do not grieve the Holy Spirit of God, with whom you were sealed for the day of redemption" (Ephesians 4:30). Yes, I hold to the view: Once saved, always saved. So, what happens when we grieve the Spirit?

Basically, two things: (1) We lose presence of mind for the moment, so that we are not likely to think clearly and exercise sound judgment; and (2) we risk missing the grace of God, which means that things promised to us, such as our inheritance, could be forfeited (Hebrews 12:15). We should learn to value the presence of the un-grieved Spirit above everything else.

When we call someone "Raca"—"stupid"—Jesus suggests a collective consensus of men would decide our case. If He really did mean the Sanhedrin, it meant that the ancient council that dealt with murder was succeeded by the Sanhedrin, who sat in judgment on people's anger when it got out of control. Internal anger could not be dealt with, but once you break silence and openly insult a person's intelligence, you invite the Sanhedrin to judge your case.

Jesus may have sent a signal to both His hearers and the Sanhedrin: "Don't just deal with murder by the sword, but deal with vocalized anger as well." If Jesus did not mean the Sanhedrin but merely a "court," a body of responsible people, it could have meant church leaders who had to deal with church quarrels and had to referee.

The Fire of Hell

In any case, the ultimate danger of anger is the "fire of hell." The most common Greek word for hell—*gehenna*—is used here.

However, there is more than one way to look at the danger of the fire of hell. James speaks of how the unguarded comment—the failure to control the tongue—is like a spark that will set a forest on fire. "The tongue also is a fire, a world of evil among the parts of the body. It corrupts the whole person, sets the whole course of his life on fire, and is itself set on fire by hell"—*gehenna* (James 3:5–6).

Here is what happens: Once we give in to judgmental anger—judging the "whole person," including his or her motives and final destiny—all hell can break loose. We give the devil an authorization—a warrant—to ride on top of our anger. We open the door to Satan. He gets in and things get out of control. Once we play God and show contempt for another's heart, God walks away and the devil steps in.

But there are also eschatological implications as well. It may well refer to the fire in 1 Corinthians 3:15: "If it [the superstructure of wood, hay, straw] is burned up, he will suffer loss [of reward, or inheritance]; he himself will be saved [i.e., go to heaven], but only as one escaping through the flames." The same fire—*gehenna*, a supernatural fire that awaits those who are eternally lost—God will employ in that awesome day, the day of the Final Judgment.

Those whose superstructure is built of gold, silver and precious stones will survive the fire and receive a reward. The rest will suffer loss but will be saved. The fire of *gehenna* will burn up the faulty superstructure. A superstructure of gold, silver and costly stones is erected through overcoming bitterness and totally forgiving those who have hurt you. A superstructure of wood, hay and straw is erected by bitterness, anger and unforgiveness. Such a person's works are burned up, and they miss the grace of God and lose their inheritance. This is not the only way the fire of *gehenna* is to be grasped in the New Testament, but it is almost certainly one of the ways, as Joachim Jeremias says in the world's largest Greek theological dictionary (*Theological Dictionary of the New Testament,* vol. I, p. 658).

And yet if Jesus is referring to eternal punishment in Matthew 5:22—a person literally going to hell because they call someone a "fool"—it shows God's right to judge and punish as He pleases. After all, God will judge people by their works when they are not covered by the blood and righteousness of Jesus. "The evil man brings evil things out of the evil stored up in him. But I tell you that men will have to give account on the day of judgment for every careless word they have spoken. For by your words you will be acquitted, and by your words you will be condemned" (Matthew 12:35–37).

God may choose to vindicate His judgment on that day by reading back one's own words. I am not saying—and Jesus is not saying—that if one has been judgmental they will go to hell. After all, we've all failed here. Jesus merely said one is in "danger of the fire of hell"—a word that ought to make us to want to be more careful than ever when we speak.

No, I don't think Jesus is teaching that I will go to hell if I am judgmental. But if His frightening words can shake me rigid and cause me to be more guarded when I speak, this passage will have been applied in a way that honors His teaching.

23. The Danger of Anger—Part II

*Therefore, if you are offering your gift at the altar and there remember that your
brother has something against you, leave your gift there in front of the altar.
First go and be reconciled to your brother; then come and offer your gift.*

MATTHEW 5:23–24

We are not finished with Jesus' interpretation and application of the sixth Commandment, "You shall not murder." As mentioned, Jesus gives more attention to the implications of this Commandment than any of the others. His treatment is not only found in Matthew 5:21–26 but in verses 43–48. We therefore continue to look at this subject of anger.

Jesus' further treatment of the danger of anger can be summed up in two areas: (1) internal anger, including its direct connection to our relationship with God, and (2) external anger, how we hurt others through our anger. If we have totally forgiven those who have hurt us—which protects us against both external and internal anger—we will not tell others what "they" did to us. We will not let people be afraid of us or add to their sense of guilt. We will also let them save face, as opposed to "rubbing their noses in it." In other words, we refuse to play the game of "Gotcha!" We will protect them from their darkest secret (and we all have them), never revealing what we know.

On the other hand, when we have not totally forgiven others, it is only a matter of time until we will judge another person's heart—and play God. We also become the instrument of the devil, who is the great accuser (Revelation 12:10). We do his work for him. Never give the devil that privilege!

Internal Anger

There are certain pre-Pentecostal assumptions in these lines. They show that our edition of Matthew's gospel was written before A.D. 70, when the Temple was destroyed. There would be no point in recording this saying when there was no Temple. When Jesus talks about "offering our gift at the altar," He addresses people as they were at that time. In other words, they were still under the Law. This was part of the Ceremonial Law Jesus was referring to. He might have left out words like these in His sermon, since He would eventually be dying on a cross and putting an end to certain practices. But Matthew records what Jesus actually said to people who still worshiped in synagogues and respected the Temple patterns.

And yet it is surely easy for you and me to make the transition and see how such language can apply to us. We apply it to our intimacy with God; how we treat others has a direct bearing on our communion with Him. When you have hurt others and know it, and are aware things are not right with others, it affects your worship of God. In Matthew 5:23–24 Jesus is saying, as it were, "When you come to worship God and remember what you have done to that person, you have an obligation to put things right *first.*"

We are going to deal with something very delicate in this chapter. It could be painful for some to read. In a word: If you want more of God—more of the Holy Spirit—you must beware of any bitterness in your heart.

It would not matter what the reason is. We all feel a little bit justified when we are angry. As mentioned in the previous chapter, our anger so often seems right at the time. Bitterness—internal anger—is what can cause you to miss the grace of God, which means forfeiting your inheritance (Hebrews 12:15). You can be prayed for a thousand times, go on a forty-day fast and spend hours and hours singing praises to God—but if bitterness is not dealt with, your "worship" is far from what you may have thought it was. Like it or not, God will not bend the rules for anybody.

Internal anger—bitterness—results in murder in our heart, says Jesus.

"But you don't realize what they did to me," you may say. I accept that what has happened may have been very, very wrong—and it may have been very, very hard for you. We all have a story to tell. But if bitterness is not dealt with, our relationship with God will never be what it ought to be.

Total forgiveness means there will be no bitterness in one's heart. I don't say it will be easy. It is arguably the greatest challenge anybody ever—ever—faces. It is why we want to keep a record of wrongs. Why does anyone keep any kind of record? For one thing, to prove that a debt has been paid. You have a record to show it. But love "keeps no record of wrongs" (1 Corinthians 13:5). We must tear up the record of the wrong done to us. Why do we say, "I will remember that!" to someone who has hurt us? Answer: We want to use it against them down the road.

External Anger

"If you are offering your gift at the altar and there remember that your brother has something against you, leave your gift there in front of the altar. First go and be reconciled to your brother; then come and offer your gift."

Whereas internal anger is bitterness that is inside us, external anger is when it has affected others adversely. We must take positive steps to put things right with our brother or sister.

As we have seen, Jesus taught these things while the Law was yet unfulfilled. He was certainly going to keep it Himself and speaks to those listening in order that they may apply His teaching in this pre-Pentecostal era. The offering of a gift on the altar referred to an animal sacrifice. You brought a lamb, a dove or a pigeon. It could have been a peace offering, a grain offering, a sin offering or a fellowship offering. "Offering your gifts" did not refer to high holidays like the Day of Atonement. It referred to individual sacrifices you brought. Jesus was not allowing His followers to wait until after Pentecost to apply His teaching!

Having Objectivity about Oneself

There is a fringe benefit in all this, which I call *objectivity of self*. It is a wonderful thing to have objectivity about yourself. It is when you rise above yourself. You remember that "your brother has something against you." You don't justify it; you don't excuse yourself. You don't say, "That person gets their feelings hurt too easily. I am not responsible."

Why does this person have something against you? Perhaps you lost your temper with him or her. He or she may not feel forgiven, or may feel cheated, neglected, disillusioned, discouraged or defeated. And as you are worshiping God, you suddenly remember this!

It is likely to be the Holy Spirit who brings this to your mind. Be thankful when this happens. Not only that, but this person may be unable to worship God as they wish because of you. You have injured this person. But you now have objectivity about yourself, and you say, "I was wrong to say what I did." "I have hurt this person." "I have robbed them of blessing." "I must do something about this." This is what Jesus means.

So, what do we do next? "Leave your gift there in front of the altar." You stop worshiping for the moment. You refrain from carrying on in your worship. Indeed, there is no use to carry on. You have unfinished business with someone, and you need to put things right before you continue worshiping God. "First go," says Jesus. Leave that gift. Leave it there. "First go and be reconciled to your brother."

I'm sorry, but that is what Jesus says you and I have to do. If, when I am praying, I become aware that things are not right with someone, I refrain from further prayer until I have put things right. It may be your spouse, your parent, your son or daughter, your pastor, your parishioner, someone at work, a fellow student, a teacher, a boss.

Here is another way of saying it: Our vertical relationship with God will not be as it should be as long as our horizontal relationships with others are not as they should be. You and I can sweep the dirt under the carpet. We can live in denial. We can pretend. We can make excuses. But sooner or later we have got to put things right. It may mean phoning the other person, writing a letter or going to see him or her (if possible). But do not think you are going to have pure communion with God when either (1) you are holding a grudge against someone or (2) you realize you have hurt someone and you are that person's problem. "First go," says Jesus. You say to him or her, "I'm sorry. I have hurt you."

This is when you realize you are in the wrong. Only the Holy Spirit can bring you to this objectivity about yourself. This is because by nature we all feel we are in the right. Perhaps in your relationship with God you have developed such a sensitivity to the Holy Spirit and His ways that He can tell you, "Go now and be reconciled." This shows a remarkable maturity.

Or, you may say, "That person ought to be coming to me, not me to him." If this is the case—and sometimes it is—you are *not* to go to him. You must not go and say, "I forgive you for what you did," which is only a way of sticking the knife in. You must never do that! You forgive him instead in your heart, right where you are. It is something you can do. You really can!

By the way, it is often a fact that most people who have hurt you don't have a clue they have done you wrong—and that they have unfinished business with God. I reckon that 90 percent of the people who hurt us feel they have done nothing wrong at all. On the other hand, it does give a rather painful hint that we have probably hurt people and don't know it when they come to deal with us.

I am only saying that if we do know we have hurt others, we must do something about it at once. That is what Jesus is teaching in these lines. If you know you have hurt them, you must take the initiative to put things right with them. It may or may not thrill them to bits when you approach them in this manner. In any case, as Paul put it, "If it is possible, as far as it depends on you, live at peace with everyone" (Romans 12:18). There may be the difficult person who refuses to make up with you. But in this case you can return to the altar and worship with a good conscience. You certainly tried! Yes, when you have made every effort to make up with that person and they refuse, you are free.

"Then come and offer your gift." This is the meaning of the psalm, "You do not delight in sacrifice, or I would bring it; you do not take pleasure in burnt offerings. The sacrifices of God are a broken spirit; a broken and contrite heart, O God, you will not despise" (Psalm 51:16–17). A similar passage is, "If I had cherished sin in my heart, the Lord would not have listened" (Psalm 66:18).

Post-Pentecostal Period

It should now be rather obvious how all of us apply this passage today. Jesus has died, and the Law with all its demands has been nailed to the cross (Colossians 2:14). The Law has been totally fulfilled. There is no more Passover, no more animal sacrifices, no more feasts, no more Day of Atonement. The Spirit of God came to the Church at Pentecost. We today are therefore in this same post-Pentecostal era.

It is the task of all of us, then, not to grieve the Holy Spirit. The chief way we grieve Him is by bitterness (Ephesians 4:30). When the Spirit is un-grieved in us, we are set to worship in a way that pleases God.

The relevance of this worship is twofold: private worship and public worship. How do Jesus' words in Matthew 5:23–24 pertain to our private worship? We could begin with these words from Peter: "Husbands, in the same way [as Sarah obeyed Abraham] be considerate as you live with your wives, and treat them with respect as the weaker partner and as heirs with you of the gracious gift of life, so that nothing will hinder your prayers" (1 Peter 3:7). I speak now to married people: If you want effectual praying and worship, be sure there is no bitterness between you and your spouse. I could almost write a book on this. I know what it is to have a quarrel with my wife and then try to pray. I can't! That is the way it is.

One morning after I preached a sermon on "love your enemy," a minister approached me with this question: "Can your wife be your enemy?" I replied, "Yes." Hopefully when this happens, it is a very temporary situation. There are times when spouses have such rows with each other that an "enmity situation" emerges. The only solution: Love your enemy. Don't wait for them to become perfect! Love them in their worst state—that way you get a good internal victory. Why do you suppose Paul said, "Husbands, love your wives"? It is because it isn't always easy. All admonitions in Scripture are given because what God requires doesn't come "naturally" or easily.

Married or single, your relationship with people—especially those closest to you—is a major ingredient in your private communion with God. You may wish that being a recluse ameliorates your efforts to get closer to God. Not true!

You show your love for God by your willingness to be like Jesus when it comes to people.

"I don't have a problem with God. It is people who are my problem," is a common observation. The truth is, you cannot grow spiritually apart from overcoming bitterness. Retreating to isolation or reclusiveness is to run from the challenge that God wants us all to face. And bitterness will always relate to human relationships—not to animals or the beauty of God's creation.

Public Worship

Your worship at church—with the people of God—involves two things: your actual worship and your hearing from God. It will be difficult to worship when you are at odds with people you live with or work with.

Worship begins with praise. Praising God is basically an unselfish enterprise. You may feel nothing at first. It could be an effort. So you make a choice to offer praises to God. This is when you forget about yourself and concentrate on God—His glory, His Son, His creation, His love and His providence. Hopefully, your praise will also become worship, when you are enthralled with magnifying the goodness of God. You sense His presence, His pleasure.

My point is this. To experience the presence of God requires that we are at peace with one another.

The perfect situation when at church with God's people is that you hear from God. God may speak to you through the hymns and songs, through the reading of Scripture, through the sermon or in a manner you never thought possible, when He clearly witnesses to you in a manner that "you know that you know" you have heard from Him. However, this is not likely if you are at odds with those in your life or those around you in church. When the Holy Spirit is grieved, it is unlikely you will experience the presence of God or hear from Him.

This is particularly true regarding the Lord's Supper. Discerning the Lord's body is a requirement for partaking worthily at the Lord's Supper (1 Corinthians 11:29). When you are in serious conflict with fellow believers, it will affect your ability to discern the Lord's presence. In the ancient church at Corinth, sadly, some middle-class believers appeared to be very insensitive by walking all over those who were slaves. These slaves could not get to the meetinghouse as early as others. But nobody waited for them. By the time they arrived, the Lord's Supper had already taken place and the working-class people were left out. God did not like this one bit. It resulted in His stepping in with judgment (1 Corinthians 11:30).

When you know you have hurt someone who is also partaking of the Lord's Supper, you are only playing games if you proceed to worship. You may be sure that the Holy Spirit is grieved. You are to sort things out before you truly worship God.

Objectivity about yourself is when you "remember" that your brother or sister has something against you. You know that it is within your power to make that person feel better. If you don't do it, the Spirit will remain grieved, and you will not truly grow spiritually. Before you can truly worship, you must get in touch with that person and say: "I am sorry. I should not have said that. I am in the wrong." Soft words turn away wrath (Proverbs 15:1).

There is a rule of thumb. The person most in the wrong is the least gracious; the one in the right is the most gracious. My advice: Err on the side of love. Become vulnerable, be gracious and give no hint of pointing the finger.

Not only that, but be willing to accept the blame. Be willing to appear "weak." You can only do this when you are, in fact, strong. You are willing to be seen as weak. Our pride will make us want to look strong. But our humility will make us willing to be seen as weak, even though we may die a thousand deaths inside.

This was Paul's posture with the ancient Corinthians when they were accusing him of all sorts of things. He reminded them that Christ was crucified "in weakness" (2 Corinthians 13:4). He could have called down ten thousand angels but instead submitted to wicked men and let them crucify Him. The strong person can afford to appear weak. It is a humbling but wonderful way to live.

The bottom line is this: The danger of anger is that it militates against our worship and communion with God. I pray that your communion with Him is more important than your appearing to be right all the time.

24. The High Cost of Pride

Settle matters quickly with your adversary who is taking you to court. Do it while
you are still with him on the way, or he may hand you over to the judge, and
the judge may hand you over to the officer, and you may be thrown into prison.
I tell you the truth, you will not get out until you have paid the last penny.

MATTHEW 5:25–26

I have sometimes thought I must be the world's expert on not following through with the principles Jesus is teaching in this chapter. It is often said that anger is what makes us lose our temper and pride is what keeps us there. What we have in these verses is the worst-case scenario if anger is not nipped in the bud.

We have seen how worship is adversely affected by our anger. We have been told not to proceed with worshiping God if we know things aren't right with our brothers and sisters (verses 23–24). Jesus follows this up by showing what happens if we don't take His advice—namely, the price we pay if we don't get things sorted out immediately. "Settle matters quickly with your adversary" is further practical advice. What a kind favor Jesus does for us by this word.

In this chapter we will see two things: (1) what happens if we don't get reconciled with our brother or sister, and (2) what happens if we can't take criticism. If someone criticizes you, do you reject it out of hand? This verse also shows how your enemy will treat you if they are not pacified quickly. Not only should we become reconciled before we can unfeignedly worship God, we should do it to keep things from unnecessarily being blown out of proportion.

I need to insert at this point that, just maybe, there could be some exceptions to the way I interpret these verses. I certainly don't want to "water down" Jesus' teaching. But I also know there are difficult people with emotional problems who can make it almost impossible for us to keep carrying out Jesus' teaching.

I have come across people in over fifty years of ministry who will take advantage of you when

you attempt to be conscientious in following Jesus' principles. In a word: These principles will not always "work" with selfish, manipulative people. But I would also caution the reader not to use this "loophole"—if that is the right word—to avoid the plain words of Jesus, which we need to take seriously and apply to our lives.

What, then, do you do when your friends or enemies have something against you? Answer: Deal with it quickly. Never mind what they said. Never mind that they made you mad. Never mind that they are out of line, unfair, impertinent or grossly wrong. You had better swallow your pride immediately—or you will pay dearly down the road.

Jesus does not condone what your adversary will do. Jesus is stating a fact of life. He knows what people are like. Jesus was the greatest interpreter of the human psyche in the history of the world. Nobody—ever—understood people as He did. He graciously passes on some very prudent counsel—if we will take it. He is giving practical advice: Settle matters quickly, or things will get much, much worse—and you live to regret your stubbornness to no end.

This could apply to when you have made somebody angry or when you have a critic. It may apply when a person doesn't like you and is capable of doing you great harm. A typical scenario is when something begins very small. You get slightly irked. But if you are not very, very careful, that little spark will start a forest fire. This is what the present chapter is about.

The question is, are we prepared to listen to Jesus? We know anger is wrong. But what do we do when our anger has got us into trouble?

The Pride of Anger

All anger has its roots mostly in pride and self-righteousness. Our self-esteem—our self-righteous egos—are usually at the root of anger. It is sometimes said that anger is the result of blocked goals. But our pride is often what lies behind these blocked goals. When we don't get our own way, our feelings sometimes get hurt. We get annoyed and fear we are not being taken seriously.

This prideful anger must be nipped in the bud. Otherwise, before we know it, we will become judgmental and start pointing the finger. We "stick our foot in it" and things get out of control. If we aren't careful, we begin to degrade the other person. And then a fiercer problem emerges.

To put it another way, Jesus is demonstrating the folly of stubbornness. This characteristic surfaces because you refuse to listen—even to consider a different perspective—and cannot admit that the other person has a valid point. You may say, "There are a lot of people I can agree with, but I will never agree with him." Some say, "I'd rather go to hell than admit he got it right." It is as though Jesus says, "Really? Then that is, at least metaphorically, where you are going, because you asked for it." Being handed over to the judge and put in prison is somewhat like going to hell. Not eternal hell, but a most unpleasant judgment that could have been avoided.

In other words: Instead of settling matters quickly, we become defensive and stick to our guns. The result is that our enemy hands us over to a judge, the judge hands us over to the officer and we are thrown into prison.

This is what happened to President Bill Clinton a few years ago. I prayed for him as he went on television to make his case regarding Monica Lewinsky. I so wanted him to come clean and put things right. He was still proclaiming his innocence. I thought I discerned guilt all over his face. I turned to Louise and said, "He's blown it big-time." If only he had said, "I have been a fool, please forgive me." All he could do was to offer a mild apology and say, "I shouldn't have done this, but . . ."

The White House immediately issued statements of rejoicing, as if it were all over. Wrong. More information came out. Things got worse than ever. The eventual result was that Congress voted for his impeachment. The Senate narrowly let him off the hook or he would have been ejected from the White House. But all he needed to do was to admit from the start . . . the truth. The nation would have forgiven him.

The same was true with President Richard Nixon. Had he admitted to his compliance in the Watergate scandal from the start, he would have finished his terms of office with a measure of dignity. But no. His name will now always be under a cloud. The high cost of pride. There is "hell to pay" in the end.

Jesus is giving us good and kind advice: Settle matters quickly. Simple as that. "I tell you the truth," He says, "you will not get out until you have paid the last penny."

What Is an Adversary?

When you call somebody "Raca" (which means stupid) or "Fool" (when you judge and degrade the whole person), not only are you not speaking spiritual blessings to that person, but you have, like it or not, just created what Jesus calls an "adversary."

It didn't need to happen. In other words, you now have an enemy of your own making. What is more, you have a real problem on your hands. If your enemy's wrath is not defused at once, his or her animosity becomes deep resentment. Deep resentment leads to revenge. Your enemy's ire reaches the point that it cannot be stopped. As an example, perhaps you saw that your marriage was on the rocks but you waited too long. If only you had made peace when you had a chance to do it. The proverb comes to mind, "An offended brother is more unyielding than a fortified city" (Proverbs 18:19).

Never mind that he made you mad. You now have made him madder than you were! You have a tiger by the tail. Things have now gotten out of hand. You may well wish, "If only I hadn't said it," or, "If only I made peace when there was still time." The peril of animosity in this case is that this person's resentment knows no bounds. Your adversary is going to make you pay. You can't stop it—it is too late.

An adversary can sometimes be defined as "a brother offended." It is a person you have embittered by what you said or did. He is taking you to court because you got angry over his accusation. Perhaps you rejected his criticism out of hand. Instead of going to him and apologizing, you judged him and also went too far.

When first he criticized you, you might have said, "You are quite right." But no. Instead of saying, "I see exactly what you mean"—which is what meekness does—you let him lose face by dismissing his view out of hand. The result: You have a real adversary, a fierce enemy. He will now dig in his heels because he is deeply hurt. There will be hell to pay now.

Jesus' Practical Advice

Jesus is letting us know what people are like. Take a lesson on human nature from the God-man; this is your chance to learn from Him. In a word: If we demonstrate the meekness that Jesus mentioned in the Beatitudes, we could avoid needless adversaries in our lives.

"Settle matters quickly" means to settle out of court. The funny thing is, Richard Nixon used to say that the best way to deal with a crisis is to anticipate it and avoid it. If only he would have applied this to himself! "Starting a quarrel is like breaching a dam; so drop the matter before a dispute breaks out" (Proverbs 17:14). John Calvin said that we should settle "even at our own loss, rather than pursue our rights with unyielding energy."

So you have to make a choice: Stick to your guns and refuse to budge, or take Jesus' advice. Or, as Paul put it to the Corinthian Christians, who were taking each other to court before a pagan world with their family squabbles: "Why not rather be wronged? Why not rather be cheated?" Is that the worst thing in the world?

A person says, "I will not allow them to talk to me like that!" Jesus says: Settle. Calvin says: Settle even if you lose. Someone says, "I will not allow my spouse, my boss, my roommate, my employee, my son, my parent, that waitress, that person behind the ticket window, that jumped-up salesman to talk like that to me." According to Jesus, you will not only lose the battle—you will lose the war if you don't settle "quickly." It is such a pragmatic way to look at it. But why won't we look at it this way? Our pride.

Settling out of court means surrendering your rights. You may feel that your anger was a "righteous" anger. Whatever! You now have opened the floodgates of hell. What to do? Jesus tells us: Cut your losses and settle quickly. Demanding your rights is foolish. The truth is, you went too far. *Be glad for an opportunity to reconcile.*

Is it possible that you are reading this just in the nick of time? Thank God for this moment. Settle matters quickly! If you don't, says Jesus, you will lose and you will lose badly. Why? You are now in debt to this person—you owe them. You thought they owed you. Wrong. You now owe them and need to pay up—quickly.

Jesus was referring to an ancient system of justice. In ancient times, a person who defaulted on his debts could be thrown into a debtors' prison. He remained there until the amount was paid. An added problem was that while he was there in prison, he couldn't see anybody. Therefore, he could scarcely be expected to pay off his debt unless a friend came to the rescue. Jesus is not condoning this system, He is only pointing out the way people are and the way life is. You must not try to get people to adjust to you. Instead, you adjust to them.

So, what is the main practical advice Jesus is giving us? In a word: Accept criticism. If you agree with your adversary quickly, you have ended the matter. Soft words—a gentle answer—turn away wrath (Proverbs 15:1). Say to them: "I see what you mean, thank you." The person who gave the criticism will think you are great. You will even gain a friend in the process. If you are defensive, you will be more alienated and will unnecessarily push things too far in the wrong direction.

Reject criticism out of hand and the other person loses face—the last thing you want to do to someone. In Dale Carnegie's book *How to Win Friends and Influence People,* he says we should let the other person save face. He reckons you can win a friend for life by doing this. But if someone loses face, that person will be angrier than ever and hold it against you. You will be the one to pay.

Jesus is saying, "Let the other person feel he has told you off." Do so even if you don't totally agree! Let him vent his anger on you. Make him feel you have listened. If you are defensive, the worst-case scenario may suddenly be in your face. As it has been said, "For want of a horse a battle was lost, for want of a battle a war was lost, for want of a victory freedom was lost." "Consider what a great forest is set on fire by a small spark" (James 3:5).

Jesus says to agree with your adversary while you are still speaking to each other. Do it "quickly"—while there is still hope. "Do it while you are still with him on the way." If that person is allowed to brood, their anger will intensify and reach the point of no return.

"Life Is Not Fair"

The punishment that will be inflicted is so often out of proportion to the crime. This punishment—being thrown into prison—is unreasonable and unjust. Yes. But it is also predictable.

I repeat, this is the way people are. Life is that way. Or, as President John F. Kennedy used to say, "Life's not fair." William Congreve (1670–1729) said, "Hell hath no fury like that of a woman scorned." Or a man scorned! Men are just as bad.

John Kennedy also said, "Forgive them, yes, but don't forget their name and address." Don't expect the person whose advice or criticism you reject to have been immersed in the principles of "total forgiveness" or to have applied them! The natural reaction of the person who is not made perfect in love is to punish. And sometimes their way of punishing you in order to get even can be utterly ruthless. "There is no fear in love. But perfect love drives out fear, because fear has to do with punishment" (1 John 4:18).

By the way, have you ever been the person who does the punishing? We tend to see this issue in terms of the other person who punishes us. Yet have you been the person who is not pacified, but throws someone into prison (so to speak)? Have you ever made another pay to the full?

David would have, before he was king. Nabal rejected David's advice, namely, that Nabal show favor to David's men, who had been very trustworthy toward Nabal. But Nabal was churlish, arrogant and merciless. If it were not for Abigail, Nabal's wife, providentially stepping in, David would have destroyed Nabal's entire family and estate (1 Samuel 25:32). David was prepared to behave exactly like the person Jesus describes in Matthew 5:25–26.

A relevant question then is: Can you be gracious? What if someone calls you stupid or "fool"?

Have you ever been the person who casts another into prison? Have you ever made a person pay to the full because of what he or she did to you? David was stopped only moments before he would have taken vengeance into his own hands.

I remind you again: Jesus does not condone the ancient system. He certainly does not encourage a person to get vengeance. He is merely applying His interpretation of the sixth Commandment to everyday life.

What does Jesus mean by "the judge"? This is a metaphor, of course. Originally, it might have meant any court, if not the Sanhedrin (Israel's ruling court). I think for us it merely means a third person is involved. Here is what happens: A person criticizes you and you get angry. This person talks to another person. And because the offended person tells on you, he wins that other person over to his point of view. Now the two are against you and you look even worse.

The "officer" I take to refer to your wider reputation of looking pretty awful. By this time you are handcuffed (so to speak) and have lost all rights. Nobody believes in you, and you've got no chance of looking good. That is the way the process often works.

But if you defuse the person right away and become reconciled to him, it's all over. However, if you don't settle things immediately, you create an adversary and he will tell others all about you. Then you are in a no-win situation. He will make you look bad, and before you know it everyone is against you. The thing is, it doesn't compare with what made you angry in the first place. You have hell to pay because you would not settle out of court. The high cost of pride!

"Prison" is the worst scenario. This metaphorically could simply mean no chance of ever looking good. How could that happen today? Well, have you ever been stopped by a policeman, say, for speeding? If you argue very much—or start shouting at him—if he is not a smooth, gentle person he might put you in jail. It is far better just to be pliable. Or, let us say your marriage is in trouble and someone advises counseling. You say, "Not me." You refuse. The next thing is divorce. Now you would do anything to turn the clock back and go to counseling. Or, perhaps a situation has developed in the office where you work. You mess up with someone and would give a thousand worlds for a second chance.

Jesus' advice when any such situation comes up: Settle things quickly. This is practical advice that all of us can use. It is a most interesting aspect of Jesus' teaching. The person you would not settle out of court with will never forgive.

There is no possibility of appeal, says Jesus. "I tell you the truth" (here again is that "oath" level association), He says, "You will not get out until you have paid the last penny." There was a chance when you were walking with the person in the way. But not now. Jesus says that not only will you pay much, much more than you would have had you listened and negotiated earlier, you are going to pay the last penny. Your adversary is going to take all you have. As I just pointed out, it is like being put into debtors' prison: You can't get out because you can't earn any more to pay the debt that put you there! The high cost of pride—all because you were too proud to listen.

Everything we have seen in this chapter is analogous to our relationship with God. The principles seen in the Beatitudes represent serious, serious wisdom for us to take on board. Meekness, a rare virtue, will keep one from a lot of trouble. This is Jesus' wisdom. But because one has hated wisdom and the fear of the Lord, "then they will call to me but I will not answer; they will look for me but will not find me" (Proverbs 1:28).

Stay teachable. "Do not harden your hearts" (Psalm 95:8). Stay tender—even if you look like a wimp or weakling by doing so. You say, "I want a little respect shown to me." I reply, Jesus was crucified in weakness but was raised in power (2 Corinthians 13:4). Be willing to lose face and let another save face. Settle out of court, even if you lose—because you will win in the end.

25. Sexual Purity

You have heard that it was said, "Do not commit adultery." But I tell you that anyone
who looks at a woman lustfully has already committed adultery with her in his heart.
If your right eye causes you to sin, gouge it out and throw it away. It is better for
you to lose one part of your body than for your whole body to be thrown into hell.
And if your right hand causes you to sin, cut it off and throw it away. It is better
for you to lose one part of your body than for your whole body to go into hell.

MATTHEW 5:27–30

In his presidential campaign of 1976, Jimmy Carter admitted to committing adultery in his heart many times. This is because he said he "lusted in his heart," a very honest and vulnerable admission. And yet there is hardly a man on the planet who hasn't broken the seventh Commandment when you interpret it as Jesus did.

Jesus continues to show what He meant in Matthew 5:20: "Unless your righteousness surpasses that of the Pharisees and teachers of the law, you will certainly not enter the kingdom of heaven." To the Pharisees, righteousness was only external. But to Jesus, it was both external and internal. One could commit adultery without literally sleeping with a person besides their spouse.

Jesus interpreted the seventh Commandment—"You shall not commit adultery" (Exodus 20:14)—in the light of the tenth: "You shall not covet your neighbor's wife" (Exodus 20:17). Paul said that he thought he kept all the Commandments until he saw the implications of the tenth. It was then he realized he was a sinner: "Sin sprang to life and I died" (Romans 7:9). The Pharisees had no sense of inward sin. They felt that unless one committed the physical act, they were free from this sin. Wrong, says Jesus: "Anyone who looks at a woman lustfully has already committed adultery with her in his heart."

Adultery by definition in the *Oxford Dictionary* is the act of being unfaithful to one's wife or husband by voluntarily having sexual intercourse with someone else. That would be the strict definition. But there are those who look for loopholes. Some might argue that the seventh Commandment

refers to adultery (when one person is married) but does not refer to fornication. They would say it does not apply to premarital intercourse or sex between unmarried people. Some would also say this has to do with heterosexual sin, not homosexual sin.

But to argue like that, observed John Stott, is to be guilty of the very casuistry that Jesus condemned in the Pharisees. Casuistry is avoiding a principle by looking for loopholes. This perspective arose in the Middle Ages, when Jesuit priests and scholars dealt with various cases of conscience. The idea that "circumstances alter cases" seemed to have given them a right to look for loopholes, or exceptions. In the twentieth century, it became known to some as "situation ethics."

Jesus defines adultery as the mental act of lusting after one who is not your husband or wife. Inheriting the Kingdom of heaven presupposes sexual purity—which means both the outward and inward refraining from sexual activity outside of marriage.

The Sin of Adultery

Had not God given this command through Moses to ancient Israel, that nation would have collapsed. It came, however, in the nick of time—when Israel had risen up to play and indulge in sexual immorality in the wilderness (Exodus 32:6; 1 Corinthians 10:7).

Sexual promiscuity was sweeping the nation. Without the seventh Commandment, the disintegration of the family unit would have followed. There would be no need for genealogies;

such would have been rendered impossible. You could not have kept record of who the father of a child was. Sadly, we are living in a generation in which tens of thousands of children grow up not knowing who their father is. But God wanted to preserve the centrality of the nuclear family, and this was helped immeasurably by the seventh Commandment. The heart of the matter was fidelity in marriage.

On the other hand, you have to say that God made sex fun. Sex was not born in Hollywood but at the throne of grace. God gave sex to His creation—sexual desire being a natural, physical appetite. It is not merely a psychological desire, it is a physiological desire—like eating. There is no command that says, "Be sure to eat." If you don't have a good appetite, there is something wrong with you. We are created as sexual beings. But sexual activity is legitimized only by marriage. "For this reason a man will leave his father and mother and be united to his wife, and they will become one flesh. The man and his wife were both naked, and they felt no shame" (Genesis 2:24–25).

The chief reason for the seventh Commandment was to ensure the stability of the family. It is what would also provide security in the home and for the children. Children coming from homes where there has been infidelity are often emotionally damaged.

But another reason for the seventh Commandment was for the self-esteem of both the husband and wife. Sex outside of marriage not only violates you as a person when your partner commits it, but consider what infidelity does to your partner when you commit it. It is degrading and cuts right across one's self-esteem and worth, whenever a spouse is unfaithful to the other.

In a word: The seventh Commandment was for our good. But it was enforced by the fear of punishment, namely, death by stoning (Leviticus 20:10; Deuteronomy 22:22).

The Spirit of Adultery

Jesus was saying two things in this part of the Sermon on the Mount. First, He was interpreting the seventh Commandment in the light of the Tenth. But He was also applying the teaching of the Holy Spirit to this Commandment. Keep in mind throughout this book that the Sermon on the Mount is a way of applying Jesus' doctrine of the Holy Spirit.

In ancient Israel, the Law forbade a sexual relationship between a man and a married woman in the community of Israel. It did not originally refer to everything that a Christian today considers to be immorality, such as fornication. A sexual relationship with a single girl was not a crime like adultery. The penalty of committing adultery was death, whereas the penalty for sleeping with a single girl was that you had to marry her. Polygamy did not violate the Mosaic Law; neither was it a sin to have a concubine. Strictly speaking, adultery had to do with women married to an Israelite man. Both the man and the woman who committed adultery were executed by stoning. This way, a Pharisee in Jesus' day could feel he was without sin if he hadn't had intercourse with a married woman.

But Jesus is referring to the spirit of adultery in these verses. Paul said, "The letter kills, but the Spirit gives life" (2 Corinthians 3:6). Anyone who looks lustfully at a woman commits adultery in his heart. Jesus was concerned with the heart. As a man thinks in his heart, so is he (Proverbs 23:7, KJV).

Jesus' treatment of the sin of adultery goes to show that the Law of Christ (1 Corinthians 9:21; Galatians 6:2)—life in the Spirit—is a much higher standard than that of the Mosaic Law. If you evaluate the Ten Commandments through Old Testament eyes (before Jesus interpreted them)—as the ultimate standard of morality—you put the bar much lower than Jesus would do. Those who live by the Ten Commandments without the Holy Spirit could find loopholes that enabled them to feel they were above sin. Jesus' teaching is wider and deeper than that of the Mosaic Law. Lusting is committing adultery in the heart.

Jesus is also concerned about any woman—single or married, Jew or Gentile—unlike the seventh Commandment as originally understood. The seventh Commandment was only designed to protect a married Israelite woman. Jesus is concerned about the earlier stages of the sin in the signaling of the eyes. Ancient Law did not apply until the physical deed was done. Jesus starts further back, namely, with the intents of the heart.

Jesus' interpretation of the seventh Commandment should grip anyone who cares about God's opinion on this matter. If you want to live by the Ten Commandments without the Holy Spirit, you will find ways to sin without calling it sin! But if you care about God's opinion, you will be convicted of sin straightaway, accepting Jesus' way of interpreting the command, "You shall not commit adultery."

Otherwise, you can be like those who say, "If I don't get caught, it's okay." But you forget: God knows. This is what held Joseph back from committing adultery with Potiphar's wife. That came at a time, interestingly enough, before the Law came. Joseph gave this as his reason for not sleeping with Potiphar's wife: "How then could I do such a wicked thing and sin against God?" (Genesis 39:9). Joseph's verdict also goes to show that adultery was a sin before the Law came along. God hated adultery from the first day He made Adam and Eve.

Stages of Adultery

The physical act of adultery is not the beginning of the sin of adultery. It came along at a particular stage that preceded the physical act. The first stage is normal attraction—which is not sin. Normal attraction between a man and a woman is not sin, and it is not what Jesus was talking about. It is normal to notice a person of the opposite sex, especially if we think the woman is beautiful or the man is handsome.

The second stage is temptation. This, too, is not sin. There is a difference between temptation and sin. It is not a sin to be tempted (James 1:13). And yet it does mean that one has crossed over from the normal attraction to being tempted. It is not always easy to state at what point normal attraction becomes temptation. But temptation is not sin. Jesus was tempted in all points like we are, but without sin (Hebrews 4:15).

The third stage is obsession, when a persistent idea dominates a person's thoughts. This is when sin has entered—when carnal desire has moved in and taken over. The physical act has not been committed, but it is what Jesus meant by committing adultery in one's heart through lusting. Peter spoke of those who have "eyes full of adultery, they never stop sinning" (2 Peter 2:14). There are those

who are obsessed with sexual thoughts day and night. The seventh Commandment without the Spirit would not convict people like this. Jesus' view, like it or not, does so.

There is a possible fourth stage: causing a person to lust. Some scholars, like Don Carson and Michael Eaton, say (independently of each other) the Greek should be translated: "with the purpose of getting her to lust." In any case, the physical act may not have been committed in such a situation. You only *want* the other person to lust.

According to the Pharisees, no sin is committed in this situation. According to Jesus, the one who creates lust in the other—even if the other says "no"—sins. The attempt of a man to get a woman to be obsessed with him is committing adultery in his heart. Likewise, the attempt of a woman to get a man to be obsessed with her is committing adultery in her heart. Potiphar's wife committed adultery in her heart, but Joseph did not—he fled from her.

The fifth stage would be the physical act of adultery. This is the worst of all. Let no one conclude that "adultery in the heart by lusting" is just as bad as the overt act. Wrong. Even though adultery in the heart is sin in God's sight, the physical act is much, much worse. The act of adultery is what brings grief, loss of self-esteem, division and, possibly, divorce. Although lusting is sin, it does not compare with the consequences of overt adultery. So, dear reader, don't be a fool. Recognize the danger of lusting, but by all means resist the actual act. If you don't, you will regret it as long as you live.

A warning to both sexes is in order. The man who wants a woman—a woman he is not supposed to have—to be inflamed with lust toward him has grieved the Holy Spirit. And he has possibly made her vulnerable. He seduces her with words, with flattery, with a seemingly innocent touch. Such a person will grieve the Holy Spirit and, if it is not stopped, could forfeit his inheritance in the Kingdom of heaven.

In much the same way, a woman who wants a man to be inflamed with lust toward her will grieve the Spirit if she dresses and behaves in a way that causes the man to lust toward her. She knows how to look at him with her eyes and how to send a signal, and also how to say exactly what will excite him. According to the Pharisee, this is not sin. Jesus says it is sin.

There is, by the way, a huge difference between dressing to be attractive and dressing to be seductive. Women know the difference, and so do men.

Seriousness of Adultery

In the ancient Law, the penalty of the sin of adultery was carried out by stoning both the man and the woman to death. Jesus says: "If your right eye causes you to sin, gouge it out and throw it away. It is better for you to lose one part of your body than for your whole body to be thrown into hell."

The seriousness of adultery—in the heart and through the overt act—is seen in its effect in three areas. First, on others. If you have stirred up another to the point of mental seduction, you have hurt that person. If the person is married, you divided his or her affections from the spouse—to you. You, by your lusting and causing another to lust, have disrupted his or her life. It could lead to the total disintegration of the marriage. As for the physical act of adultery, you have changed that person's life forever. He or she will never be the same again.

Second, there is its effect on you. You have sinned against yourself. You will never completely get over it. It will haunt you as long as you live. You cannot remove the consequences of sin, even though God has forgiven you. And if the adultery in the heart has been your sin, you grieve the Spirit. And if you are married, it will interfere with your marriage. As long as you are obsessed with another person, you will not be the same or feel the same with your spouse.

Third, there is its effect on God. God's heart is grieved. The Holy Spirit is grieved. Do you want to cause the Father and the Spirit to grieve—to mourn—because of your sin? Whereas bitterness is the chief way to grieve the Spirit, it is not the

only way. After showing how bitterness and unforgiveness grieve the Spirit, Paul goes on to say: "But among you there must not be even a hint of sexual immorality, or of any kind of impurity" (Ephesians 5:3). This also shows how the Spirit can be grieved.

Fourth, there is God's punishment. "Marriage should be honored by all, and the marriage bed kept pure, for God will judge the adulterer and all the sexually immoral" (Hebrews 13:4). "It is God's will that you should be sanctified: that you should avoid sexual immorality . . . the Lord will punish men for all such sins [as immorality], as we have already told you and warned you" (1 Thessalonians 4:3, 6).

God has His own way of dealing with us. It could be severe judgment in advance of the Judgment Day, or it could wait until then. Payday, someday. Don't be a fool and think you are exempt. Be sure your sin will find you out. But if this word grips you, convicts you and brings you to repentance, fall on your knees and thank God for the warning. Just maybe you will be spared further judgment.

The Scandal of Adultery

You may say, "Well, I've already sinned—it's too late. I might as well continue." That would be the advice of the devil. Again, I say: Don't be a fool. If you are involved in an affair—or are on the brink of an affair—STOP IT! Break it off. Do it now. Furthermore, sexual sin brings incalculable sin on the Church and God's name. Billy Graham reckons that the devil brings down 75 percent of God's best people through sexual sin.

All of us have sinned. Furthermore, Jesus was gentle with the one who has sinned this way—to the grief of the Pharisees. He said it then, and He says it now: "Neither do I condemn you. . . . Go now and leave your life of sin" (John 8:11).

26. Sexual Sin

> If your right eye causes you to sin, gouge it out and throw it away. It is better for you to lose one part of your body than for your whole body to be thrown into hell. And if your right hand causes you to sin, cut it off and throw it away. It is better for you to lose one part of your body than for your whole body to go into hell.
>
> MATTHEW 5:29–30

These verses are full of metaphors, and I will try to explain the meaning in part here at the beginning of this chapter. First, the references to gouging out an eye and cutting off a hand are not to be taken literally. Origen, a Greek father in the early Church, took this passage literally and had himself castrated. (He was later sorry he did it.) Mrs. Martyn Lloyd-Jones told me a sad story of a sweet lady in Wales who cut off her hand to avoid going to hell. I know of a man in Tennessee who did the same thing, causing great turmoil in the community.

But Jesus is not saying that we should literally cut off a hand. John Calvin says Jesus uses hyperbole, a figure of speech that shows exaggeration. John Stott says Jesus is not referring to self-maiming but to ruthless moral self-denial—not to mutilation but to mortification (putting deeds of the body to death). I will deal with the "whole body going into hell" below.

You will recall from the previous chapter that the punishment for the sin of adultery in the Old Testament was being put to death through stoning. So, too, murder. In verses 22–23 Jesus shows how murder in the heart—anger—may be manifested: calling a person "Raca" or "fool." The implied punishment for such name-calling was being answerable to the Sanhedrin, if not in danger of the fire of hell. He gave illustrations how to deal with a grudge when praying (verses 23–24), then how to deal with an adversary to avoid the ultimate consequence of anger (verses 25–26). It is important to see a pattern: (1) sin in the heart, (2) how it can be manifested, (3) how we should respond and (4) how sins in the heart can be judged.

When it comes to adultery in the heart, Jesus says we are to avoid this sin by preventing it from emerging. This is done by dealing ruggedly with ourselves, doing what Jesus metaphorically calls "gouging out an eye or cutting off the hand" that causes one to sin. Just as we should agree with our adversary quickly as opposed to being put into prison, so it is better to "pluck out an eye than to be thrown into hell."

Jesus refers to the "fire of hell" as punishment for unbridled anger. So hell (*gehenna*—a place of fire) is the punishment for those lusting in the heart. We are, therefore, admonished to avoid the punishment for lusting by mortifying what offends rather having the whole body being put in hell. To summarize: Overt adultery was punished by death, where inward adultery (lusting) was punished by going to hell. Both murder and adultery were punished in ancient times by death. Jesus focuses on the heart and says that *gehenna* awaits anger and lust.

Questions We Must Ask

The immediate question follows: Is committing adultery in the heart going to be punished by our going to eternal hell? If so, we all are going to hell. Who among us has not sinned this way?

How literally are we to take this language? If "plucking out an eye" and "cutting off a hand" are metaphors, what about the reference to "hell"? Is Jesus speaking literally about what happens to angry people and lustful people when they die? If so, how can any of us be saved? Furthermore, do we lose our salvation if we have committed adultery in our hearts after being converted? And is escaping hell based upon sexual purity? I have agonized over these verses.

I want to say here that I believe in the classical Christian doctrine of hell—namely, that the unsaved will undergo conscious eternal punishment. I have preached this consistently for over 55 years, including every Sunday at Westminster Chapel for 25 years. The New Testament teaches this. As I show in my book *Outside our Comfort Zone,* I am not a universalist (the belief that all will be saved), and I am not an annihilationist (the belief that the unsaved will be obliterated as though they never existed). I believe in and preach—often—the truth of everlasting hell.

But I do not believe Jesus is talking about eternal punishment either in Matthew 5:22 ("in danger of the fire of hell") or in Matthew 5:29–30 ("your whole body to go into hell")—although I admit that the natural reading would suggest this. I believe the references to hell in these verses are partly metaphorical and partly eschatological. I believe these passages are fulfilled partly in the here and now and partly at the Judgment Seat of Christ.

In a word: I believe that "plucking an eye" and "cutting off a hand" are metaphors that refer to mortification. "Put to death," says Paul, "whatever belongs to your earthly nature: sexual immorality, impurity, lust, evil desires and greed, which is idolatry. Because of these, the wrath of God is coming" (Colossians 3:5). We will face our failure to mortify the deeds of the body at the Judgment Seat of Christ.

It is noteworthy, too, that Jesus does not propose to institute the ancient penalty of stoning the adulterer to death. Jesus places the whole matter between God and the individual who sins. This is further shown by the way Jesus dealt with the woman caught in adultery. He did not suggest that she be stoned but that she be forgiven and that she repent (John 8:1–11).

Jesus is requiring us to take an eternal perspective. Here is what matters most at the end of the day: What happens when you face God after you die? I asked one of Billy Graham's daughters what she reckoned was the secret to her father's success. She did not hesitate to answer. Her dad grew up being motivated by a chorus he sang in Sunday school:

> With eternity's values in view, with
> eternity's values in view,
> Let me do each day's work for Jesus
> with eternity's values in view.
>
> Anonymous

This is what Jesus is teaching in these lines. He is saying to us: Whatever is painful for us to do, whatever we may have to give up in this life, it is nothing compared to the way we will feel in the end when we realize we have lost forever what could have been ours.

There are profound implications in this verse. For one thing, the resurrection of the body is implied. Note the words: "whole body." Jesus might have merely said "the soul." But He mentioned the "whole body" going to hell. This presupposes the resurrection of the body first.

John said, "I saw the dead, great and small, standing before the throne [of judgment], and books were opened. Another book was opened, which is the book of life. The dead were judged according to what they had done as recorded in the books. The sea gave up the dead that were in it, and death and Hades gave up the dead that were in them, and each person was judged according to what he had done" (Revelation 20:12–13).

Before we face the outcome of our faithfulness in "plucking our eye," or our failure to mortify the deeds of the body, we will have been raised from the dead. In other words, the resurrection from the dead comes before the Final Judgment. This is where these verses are eschatological.

The Whole Body Means the Whole Person

You may recall that anger can bring on the "fire of hell" (*gehenna*) and that the tongue may corrupt the "whole person" (James 3:6). The phrase "whole person" is the translation of *olon to soma*—the exact same words found in Matthew 5:29–30, where it is translated "whole body." This goes to show that if "whole person" could be used in James 3:6, they are equally if not more appropriate for Matthew 5:29–30. Whereas our bodies will be resurrected in order to stand before the Judgment Seat of Christ, it will be our whole persons—our motives, hearts and minds, as well as how we disciplined our bodies—that will be judged.

This verse, therefore, points to the Judgment Seat of Christ and rewards. "For we must all appear before the judgment seat of Christ, that each one may receive what is due him for the things done while in the body [the whole person], whether good or bad" (2 Corinthians 5:10). Jesus is not speaking to the issue of saved or lost in Matthew 5:29–30. The Sermon on the Mount is about the Kingdom of heaven—the realm of the un-grieved Spirit. The assumption is that His followers are already saved and have entered the Kingdom of heaven.

And yet Jesus speaks as He does because of the assumption that there is a heaven and a hell. The way "hell" is used here in Matthew 5:29–30 is the same as in verse 22—not referring to the Christian going to eternal punishment, but rather the experiencing of supernatural fire that will be administered at the Judgment Seat of Christ. It was what Paul means in 1 Corinthians 3:15, being "saved . . . by fire" (KJV).

Therefore, Jesus is not saying that a Christian will go to everlasting hell because he has lusted. But He most certainly is saying we will suffer pain at the Final Judgment—if we have not repented in advance of that day. We will not be eternally lost, but we nonetheless will suffer loss, namely, the loss of our reward or inheritance. We will be saved as one escaping through the flames, as in 1 Corinthians 3:15.

Jesus' mention of the whole body going into hell is only partly reflecting His teaching elsewhere of eternal punishment for the unsaved. But, as I said, that is not what is meant in Matthew 5:29–30. The threat of eternal punishment is not the way Jesus wants the believer to see his or her own eternal state if they have trusted Him and His righteousness. He is warning His followers, rather, of the grave importance of demonstrating the righteousness that surpasses that of the Pharisees—and what happens if we don't. It is serious, serious business not to take His teaching to heart and apply it in our daily lives.

The believer's whole person going to *gehenna* means experiencing the fire—which could be the same as being "hurt" by the "second death" in Revelation 2:11. That comes with terminal chastening, a phrase I will explain below. It is when all of us will ultimately face the consequence of

our disobedience on earth. If eternal punishment is what Jesus is teaching in Matthew 5:29–30, He would be saying we are saved by works and self-denial, when in fact Paul states we are saved by grace through faith and not works (Ephesians 2:8–9).

Levels of Chastening

The Bible teaches three levels of chastening, or disciplining. God disciplines all His own children (Hebrews 12:6). To be without such chastening is to show one is not a true child of God (Hebrews 12:7–8). The word translated "disciplining," or "chastening" (KJV), comes from a Greek word that means "enforced learning." God has a way of teaching us a lesson.

The first level of chastening is *internal* chastening. This is Plan A. This is the best way to have your problems solved! It is through teaching, through preaching—when God speaks in a definite, sometimes severe, manner. Thank God for it. Take His sharp, two-edged sword with a willing heart, however painful. I would like to think that reading this very book will reach you at this level—the exposition of the Word achieving its goal and your responding to it. If I am doing my job well (assuming that the Holy Spirit applies it), the Word will cut—it will operate on your heart. May repentance be the outcome!

The second level is *external* chastening. This is Plan B. Whereas the first level is secret, inward and going on in your heart and mind, external chastening is not so secret. God may have to deal openly with you. It could be the need to be put flat on your back in a hospital. It could be financial reversal. It could be the withholding of vindication. And, yes, it could be getting caught—found out—when you have been involved in sexual sin. However painful this may be, thank God for it. It's better than hell—or the pain of the Final Judgment. "Why should any living man complain when punished for his sins?" (Lamentations 3:39).

Building a Superstructure over the Foundation

The worst scenario for the Christian is *terminal* chastening. In other books (as in *Are You Stone Deaf to the Spirit?* and *The Judgment Seat of Christ*), I have shown how terminal chastening is administered in the here and now. But I use the phrase in this section mainly to show what happens at the Judgment Seat of Christ to those who choose not to mortify the deeds of the body.

This will happen when we stand before the Judgment Seat of Christ. Jesus is therefore partly speaking of the Final Judgment in Matthew 5:29–30 to show what happens to the person who does not build his or her superstructure with gold, silver and precious stones, but instead erects it with wood, hay and straw (1 Corinthians 3:12).

Why does Jesus bring this in? He wants His teaching to make a difference in our lives *now*. The fire of *gehenna* is what will reveal the quality of our superstructure at the Judgment Seat of Christ. You and I have a choice of materials to be used to build a superstructure over the foundation. Christ is the foundation (1 Corinthians 3:11); all who are on it are saved. But we must "be careful" how we build (1 Corinthians 3:10).

It is only a matter of time before our work will be shown for what it is—e.g., whether we "gouged out our eye" or chose to commit adultery in our hearts. So over that foundation is a superstructure. The superstructure will indicate the kind of lives we led and the truth that was in our hearts. That superstructure will either be made up of materials such as gold, silver and precious stones (which cannot burn), or wood, hay and straw (which can burn).

A superstructure of gold, silver and precious stones is erected by our care to "pluck out the eye" or "cut off the hand." The superstructure will be tested by "fire" at the Judgment Seat of Christ, says Paul. The fire is *gehenna*. That day will bring the superstructure to light. "It will be revealed with fire, and the fire will test the quality of each man's work" (1 Corinthians 3:13).

If one has not resisted temptation but given in to lust, he or she erects a superstructure of wood, hay and straw. The fire of *gehenna* is what will burn up this kind of superstructure. I can't imagine how awful it will be for those of us who lusted and did not repent of it—or caused someone to lust—as opposed to mortifying the deeds of the body. It will be horrible. I want to do business with God now and take any caution, any external chastening that gets my attention, in order to avoid such terminal chastening. Jesus' teaching of the whole body—meaning the whole person—thrown into the fire is a reference to the Judgment Seat of Christ. It is the final stage of chastening—namely, terminal chastening.

Jesus wants His words to make a difference in our lives in the here and now. Notice His words "better for you." It is better for you and me to go through life with one eye or one foot than to have our unmortified, undisciplined bodies thrown into hell. It is to our advantage and in our interest for us to deal with things ruthlessly in our lives now that are not honoring to Him. Otherwise, we will have to face the unthinkable consequence on that Day of days.

We must regard plucking out an eye or cutting off a hand a priority. My advice: Make the Judgment Seat of Christ priority thinking in your life. I would have to say, speaking personally, that this teaching has shaped my thinking as much as anything I believe. I cannot exaggerate how much I have been motivated personally in life by the Judgment Seat of Christ that is coming.

Avoiding Temptation

Jesus' advice is summed up in Paul's words, "Do not offer the parts of your body to sin, as instruments of wickedness, but rather offer yourselves to God, as those who have been brought from death to life; and offer the parts of your body to him as instruments of righteousness" (Romans 6:13).

The key word here: "instruments"—e.g., instrument of lust, as the eye. "For everything in the world—the cravings of sinful man, *the lust of his eyes* and the boasting of what he has and does—comes not from the Father but from the world" (1 John 2:16, emphasis mine). The eye becomes a vehicle of lust which, if not dealt with, becomes an obsession. The eye can be an instrument of seduction—when you cause a person to lust after you. In a word: The eye is the instrument by which adultery is committed in the heart. The hand is also an instrument of lust. The hand is used to touch, to arouse sexual desire. Jesus could have added "foot" because your feet take you where you know you should not go.

The issue, then, is the possibilities of lust. Therefore, any "if"—"if your eye," "if your hand"—that causes you to sin must be removed from you, says Jesus. Not everyone reacts the same way to all objects. For some—let us say, especially for men—it may be mainly the eye. A man is aroused by sight. For some—let us say, especially women—it may be through touch.

Jesus did not say to "tear out your tongue," but He might have. Words can flatter and inflame lust—sometimes more than the eye or hand. Think of lust when you read James 3:5–6: "The tongue also is a fire, a world of evil among the parts of the body. It corrupts the whole person, sets the whole course of his life on fire, and is itself set on fire by hell."

At bottom, Jesus means for us to avoid temptation. Mortification is essentially having the power to avoid temptation. And the best way to avoid sin is to avoid the temptation. It is not strength to show how close you can get to sin, then resist it. The strength is knowing where the temptation will be found, and not to go there.

We must remove from our lives those things that tempt us—whether people, places, habits or things—including magazines and the Internet. It is claimed that pornography is the minister's greatest sin. At a recent church convention in a major city, when all the hotels were emptied of the businesspeople who were usually present and filled with ministers instead, it is reported that the pornographic movies were used as much if not more than usual. Paul said for us to make no provision for the flesh in order to fulfill one's lusts (Romans 13:14). Billy Sunday said the reason so many Christians fall into sin was because they treated temptation like strawberries and cream rather than a rattlesnake.

John Stott gives sane advice: Since temptation comes through your eyes, pluck out your eyes. That just means *don't look. Behave as if you had actually plucked out your eyes and flung them away and were now blind.* There could be readers who would almost rather be blind than to have the pain you now feel because you fell morally. You are the first to say, "It wasn't worth it." If your hand or foot means temptation will follow, don't go there! Don't visit places or people that will almost certainly mean having to confront temptation. I repeat: Your strength is not so much resisting temptation—it is avoiding it. That is mortification: putting temptation to death by avoiding it.

People vary in what is attractive to them. What may tempt you might not tempt me. Beauty is in the eye of the beholder. It will be certain television programs for some, a kind of music for another, a type of dress for still another person. Know yourself. Know your vulnerable area. It may mean giving up a relationship, avoiding a certain person. The pain can be very hard, indeed. Sanctification can be painful. The old-fashioned idea of "let go and let God" doesn't work here. We are talking about an act of the will. You resist. You have to resist temptation when it shows up, yes—but also resist going where you know temptation will show up.

The pain of resisting sexual temptation can be excruciating. Make no mistake about this. The sexual desire is physical as well as psychological. A person who is lonely is vulnerable. A person unhappily married is vulnerable. No one said it would be easy. Plucking out an eye could be unthinkably painful, and this is the way Jesus puts this matter before us. As Michael Eaton puts it, "Prayer alone is not enough."

I have counseled many people who fell—people who told me, "I prayed about it so many times, and I still fell." This is partly why Jesus said "watch and pray" (note the order) "so that you will not fall into temptation. The spirit is willing, but the body is weak" (Matthew 26:41).

Note, too, that Jesus did not say, "Watch and pray that you not fall into sin." He said to watch and pray not to fall into temptation. It is temptation that you need to be on the lookout for. You watch first! If you pray first, you will possibly take anything that comes along as having God's approval. There must be a prior commitment not to enter into temptation—then you pray. Not "pray and watch," but "watch and pray."

What will help, possibly more than anything else, is to envisage the day when you will stand before the Sovereign Judge. Believe me, you will stand before Him. Plan for it now. Paul said that if we judge ourselves, we won't come under judgment (1 Corinthians 11:31). He meant that if we deal with the malady that we know is there now, we set God free from having to judge us later. The pain of God's doing it—the whole person being thrown into hell—can be prevented by the pain of our dealing with our temptation now.

The Judgment Seat of Christ can be painful or joyous for us. John talked about having "boldness" or "confidence" on that day (1 John 4:17). One of the most neglected strains of the teaching of Jesus is His emphasis on reward. That is one of the things that propelled Paul. "I beat my body and make it my slave so that after I have preached to others, I myself will not be disqualified for the prize" (1 Corinthians 9:27). It is not a sign of spirituality to show contempt for reward. It is a salient New Testament teaching and a potent motive for holy living.

I want that "prize" Paul mentions. He also calls it a "crown" (1 Corinthians 9:24). It will come to those who remove from their lives that which is displeasing to God, lest they lose what will matter most on that great day.

27. Marriage and Divorce

It has been said, "Anyone who divorces his wife must give her a certificate of divorce." But I tell you that anyone who divorces his wife, except for marital unfaithfulness, causes her to become an adulteress, and anyone who marries the divorced woman commits adultery.

MATTHEW 5:31–32

These verses, alongside Jesus' other references to marriage and divorce, are among the most misunderstood of His statements. Some people build their whole case on divorce on these verses, often forgetting the context as well as the views of the apostle Paul. We must not forget that these verses—Matthew 5:31–32—are put in the Sermon on the Mount in the context of Jesus' teaching on adultery. It is how the seventh Commandment is interpreted that will show the way forward. It is important to realize that Jesus has not changed the subject.

The issue here can be summed up in one word: lust. Adultery is committed when one is divorcing to remarry because of lust. The issue of desertion (Paul's view in 1 Corinthians 7) is not covered here. Neither is covered here the issue of divorce when lust is not the real motivation. Jesus only uses marriage and divorce as illustrations of how people can commit adultery: when they divorce to remarry and when they divorce because of lust. Sadly, the NIV treats this as if it were a new subject, separate from adultery, and gives it a separate heading. It is not a new subject. Jesus has not changed the subject from adultery to marriage and divorce. He is using divorce as a further illustration of how some commit adultery—namely, by remarrying because they prefer another person (the reason being lust).

Many people have their minds made up on the divorce issue and don't want to delve into the matter very deeply. Some want to take a hard line, claiming categorically and inflexibly that there are no biblical grounds for divorce and remarriage. None, they say—end of story. Some take a hard line because they are afraid. Some because they are legalistic. Some because they want to be seen as spiritual.

I don't mean to be unfair, but some take a hard line because they have not had to face the problem very closely. This is often the way people with long marriages treat the subject. They have had to "battle it out" and want others to do the same! I actually heard one well-known minister say, "You people who are divorced and have re-married will go to hell unless you remarry your first husband or wife—or at least stop sleeping with each other—because you are in adultery." Some people, however, have softened on this issue if someone in their own family has had a divorce. Their theological views often change when they see a son or daughter mistreated. (I have no ax to grind. Louise and I have been married 51 years and there are no divorces in our family.)

But in this chapter, we will delve into the matter. Our motive is to get to the truth and, if possible, to the heart of Jesus. I want also to be governed by the spirit of love, not the letter of the Law. Nobody knows better than I what it means to be legalistic. I grew up where women were not to wear any pearls or gold because of 1 Timothy 2:9, which prohibits the wearing of gold or pearls. My own mother, therefore, never wore a wedding ring! She might have worn a silver ring, but the reply in those days: One must avoid the "appearance" of evil.

There is undoubtedly a pastoral issue here. What would Jesus say on these issues, knowing not only what He taught but how He treated people? Some might say: "He has already spoken, and His word is the final word." But how would Jesus view Paul's teaching? It is Paul, not

Jesus, who grants divorce for a reason other than infidelity.

We are dealing with a very delicate issue. One out of two marriages in America now ends up in divorce, and sadly the statistics are much the same in the Church. A lot of ministers are included in this—some with a very high profile. W. M. Tidwell, when he was eighty years old, was powerfully used in my life in Ashland, Kentucky, when I was fifteen. I have discussed this elsewhere. His sixty years of ministry were not accepted, however, by some in his denomination because his teenage marriage broke down. He remarried and went into the ministry.

Why did Jesus bring up the subject? Was He looking for an opportunity to speak on marriage and divorce? He brought up the subject because it followed what He had taught about adultery. Up to now, we may conclude He recognizes two ways of committing adultery: (1) overtly, by sleeping with another man's wife, and (2) inwardly, by lusting. But now He shows other ways one can commit adultery: (3) when you divorce your wife and marry another woman, and (4) when the divorced woman remarries. The latter two examples show they are living in adultery, says Jesus.

When you turn to a parallel passage in Matthew 19:8–9, you find the exact same thing. Jesus was not angling to speak on the issue. The Pharisees brought up the subject to Him. They asked: "Is it lawful for a man to divorce his wife for any and every reason?" We may ask: Why did the Pharisees want to divorce, and why did they bring up the subject? It was because of lust. The words "for any and every reason" reflect the situation Moses faced. Here is the Old Testament background:

> If a man marries a woman who becomes displeasing to him because he finds something indecent about her, and he writes her a certificate of divorce, gives it to her and sends her from his house, and if after she leaves his house she becomes the wife of another man, and her second husband dislikes her and writes her a certificate of divorce, gives it to her and sends her from his house, or if he dies, then her first husband, who divorced her, is not allowed to marry her again after she has been defiled. That would be detestable

> in the eyes of the LORD. Do not bring sin upon the land the LORD your God is giving you as an inheritance.
> DEUTERONOMY 24:1–4

Moses and Jesus

Moses wrote these words. Jesus never says whether Moses was right or wrong to do this, but He acknowledges it was a concession. Jesus appeals to Creation, not the Mosaic Law. God made us male and female, that a man should leave his father and mother and be united to his wife, "and the two will become one flesh." Therefore, "What God has joined together, let man not separate" (Matthew 19:4–6; Genesis 2:24).

But Moses gave them a right to divorce. And the right to divorce simultaneously implied the right to remarry. Not that Jesus was happy about this! Indeed, Moses "permitted you to divorce your wives because your hearts were hard. But it was not this way from the beginning. I tell you that anyone who divorces his wife, except for marital unfaithfulness, and marries another woman commits adultery" (Matthew 19:8–9).

Jesus knew the real reason people generally wanted to divorce: to marry someone else. It wasn't because one was treated cruelly, or deserted, or beaten, or because a cruel husband used paychecks on drink or drugs instead of feeding his family day after day. The issue was one thing: lust.

The Pharisees' way of applying Moses' concession missed the point. Jesus took them back to Genesis 2:24. He thus interposed a standard of marriage and divorce that was much, much higher than the Law and Moses' concession, which the Pharisees embraced.

The Institution of Marriage

Jesus directed the Pharisees back to Creation in Matthew 19. "Haven't you read," Jesus asked, "that at the beginning the Creator 'made them male and female' [so that their coming together made them one flesh?] So they are no longer two, but one. Therefore what God has joined together, let man not separate" (Matthew 19:4–6). In other words, Jesus took them back to the time long before the Law came in. Jesus bases His view of marriage not on the Mosaic Law but on Creation.

Two Schools of Thought

However, there were two rival rabbinic schools of thought at the time of Jesus, known as Shammai and Hillel. Rabbi Shammai took a rigorist line, namely, that Deuteronomy meant that the sole ground of divorce was some grave matrimonial offense—something "unseemly" or "indecent," but short of the physical act of adultery (since it was punishable by death). Whether this might have included desertion, mental or physical cruelty, who knows? Very possibly.

Rabbi Hillel, however, took a lax view, which meant a man could divorce his wife for any or every reason. This included the most trivial offenses—e.g., if she proved to be an incompetent cook or burned her husband's food, or if he lost interest in her because of her looks and became enamored of a beautiful woman. These things were seen as "unseemly" on her part, and justified a man divorcing her.

The Pharisees wanted to know which side Jesus endorsed. Their question revealed where they themselves stood—they clearly sided with Hillel: "Is it lawful for a man to divorce his wife for any and every reason?" (Matthew 19:3). This is why Jesus knew that lust lay behind their reason for wanting a divorce. They wanted to justify looking for anybody. They wanted to marry and to get rid of their wives for any reason. The real reason: lust.

And yet Jesus did not answer their question, but instead pointed to the institution of marriage. Marriage has been beautifully defined by John Stott: "Marriage is a divine institution between a man and woman by which God makes permanently one these two people who decisively and publicly leave their parents in order to form a new unit of society and then become one flesh." In a word: Marriage is God's idea. Marriage is heterosexual, monogamous and permanent. It is between a man and a woman. It is permanent and exclusive. They are no longer two but one flesh.

So the Pharisees asked: "Why . . . did Moses command that a man give his wife a certificate of divorce and send her away?" (Matthew 19:7). Jesus' reply was that it was a concession owing to the hardness of their hearts—and that the concession was not the way it was when God instituted marriage in the Garden of Eden.

Ideal Marriage

What Jesus described as marriage between the time of Creation and the entrance of the Mosaic Law was the ideal situation. It was permanent and exclusive—the two are "one flesh."

And yet even Moses' concession was to protect the wife. It gave her the right to remarry. Men in ancient times—and today, too—often treat women as second class. Moses' certificate of divorce protected her. She was allowed to marry. But she could never remarry her husband. He could never have her back again, either, even if he changed his mind. It makes one wonder what strict, legalistic preachers are thinking when they tell people they will go to hell if they don't remarry their former spouses.

Divorce always meant the right to remarry, a matter often forgotten. This does not mean that the divorced person *had* to remarry. It means they were free to do so if they chose to. The certificate of divorce meant the person was now free. Divorce then and now always meant that one is now legally free to remarry.

The idea that one can be divorced but has no right to marry is not the meaning of divorce. Divorce means freedom to marry again. But what Jesus does by His teaching is to put forward the ideal in marriage—not an impossible ideal, but ideal nonetheless. It is, however, an ideal from which many people have fallen. Now more than ever.

So, over against the Law of Moses, Jesus put His own view to the Pharisees: "I tell you that anyone who divorces his wife, except for marital unfaithfulness, and marries another woman commits adultery" (Matthew 19:9). This is what Jesus taught in our text in the Sermon on the Mount. So if you have been faithful in marriage but your spouse has been unfaithful to you, you are free to remarry. You are the innocent party. If your husband has been unfaithful to you, you are free. But if you divorce your wife because you have eyes for another person and then marry another, you are in adultery, says Jesus.

So Jesus puts His teaching in the Sermon on the Mount alongside that of Moses. "It has been said [referring to Deuteronomy 24:1], 'Anyone who divorces his wife must give her a certificate of divorce.'" But Jesus has His own opinion: "But I tell you that anyone who divorces his wife, except for marital unfaithfulness, causes her to become an adulteress, and anyone who marries the divorced woman commits adultery."

If, then, there is not infidelity and you divorce your wife, you make your wife vulnerable to adultery. Why? Because she has been one flesh with her husband—and if she marries another because you divorced her, she is having to break the bond of "one flesh." This is why Jesus says you have caused her to be an adulteress. Don Carson observed, "This arises out of the fact that divorced women, especially in first-century Palestine, would probably remarry. It was her only means of support." She was still "one flesh" with her husband.

Jesus retains the ideal view of marriage. He shows the Pharisees they were creating adulteresses when they followed Rabbi Hillel's interpretation of the Law. They also committed adultery when they married divorced women. Jesus' teaching upholds God's ideal: that marriage is monogamous and permanent.

Adultery in the heart grieves the Spirit. Jesus upholds the highest possible standard of marriage, a view that to this day honors God and the family. We must pray, "Restore, O Lord, the honor of Your name." We must always uphold the ideal. God hates divorce (Malachi 2:16).

Infidelity in Marriage

As we have seen, the penalty for committing adultery in Old Testament times was death by stoning. This meant that the person who committed adultery was as good as dead.

Yet it was a practice that ceased to be carried out. This is why the Pharisees put Jesus on the spot to see if He would call for an adulterous woman to be stoned (John 8:1–11). If an adulteress was put to death, the living spouse was free to marry. The one who has been sinned against is free to remarry *as if* his or her spouse were dead. For a person in this situation, to remarry does not grieve the Holy Spirit at all.

Irreparability of Marriage

Whereas Jesus only allows for unfaithfulness as a ground for divorce, the apostle Paul has a different perspective. Had Paul never written as he did, Jesus' statement would be the final word on divorce. There would be no other way forward for people who suffer with bad marriages that are not necessarily wrought with what Jesus calls "marital unfaithfulness." But because we believe that all of the New Testament is inspired, we accept the apostle Paul's view as well as that of Jesus.

Desertion

Paul allowed for divorce in the case of desertion. Paul stated this while still upholding the ideal of marriage. Here is the ideal: "If any brother has a wife who is not a believer and she is willing to live with him, he must not divorce her. And if a woman has a husband who is not a believer and he is willing to live with her, she must not divorce him" (1 Corinthians 7:12–13).

Nothing could be clearer than that. This means that a person can be "stuck" in an unhappy marriage, namely, being unhappily married to an unbeliever. "But if the unbeliever leaves, let him do so. A believing man or woman is not bound in such circumstances" (1 Corinthians 7:15). This means that infidelity is not the only grounds for divorce. Desertion was a valid reason for divorce, says Paul. When a husband or wife deserts their spouse, that spouse "is not bound"—meaning, he or she is free to remarry.

How could Paul do this? What made him think this way? He was totally cognizant of the Law. Paul would also have known Jesus' high view of marriage. But if Moses would grant a concession because of the hardness of their hearts, surely Paul could grant a concession when a person has been deserted. Jesus never blamed Moses—He blamed the hardness of the Israelites' hearts. And Paul was writing under infallible inspiration, which certainly meant he had Jesus' full approval for what he wrote in 1 Corinthians 7.

Paul was not granting a concession because of the hardness of believers' hearts, but rather because of the *brokenness* of their hearts. They were bruised reeds. It was said of Jesus, "a bruised reed he will not break" (Matthew 12:20). Paul came to their rescue.

There follows this question: In the light of Paul's allowance for divorce, are there not other grounds? Might there be other exceptions? What if a wife or husband suffers physical cruelty? What about mental cruelty, which can be tantamount to torture?

The "Letter" versus the "Spirit"

The issue is: Do we go by the "letter"—what is legalistic—or by the "spirit," which sometimes shows a less strict interpretation?

If you go by the letter, quoting a verse in Luke—"anyone who divorces his wife and marries another woman commits adultery, and the man who marries a divorced woman commits adultery" (Luke 16:18)—there is no way out. There are those who rest their case on this one verse. If this verse were all we had to go by—going by the "letter"—one cannot remarry without committing adultery.

But what was Jesus' purpose in making His statement in the first place? He who elsewhere said, "Go and learn what this means: 'I desire mercy, not sacrifice'" (Matthew 9:13), also brought up the subject of marriage and divorce in the Sermon on the Mount. The purpose of Jesus' bringing up this subject was to show that when lust governs a person's intent to divorce and remarry, he or she is guilty of adultery. Therefore, says Jesus, if a person is innocent when being mistreated this way—being faithful when his or her spouse isn't—then that person is free to remarry.

Between Jesus' view and Paul's view, there are two cases of mistreatment: (1) First, when your spouse is unfaithful. This is a painful thing for the innocent party. Jesus comes to the rescue: Such a person is free to remarry without grieving the Spirit. (2) Second, when your spouse has deserted you—which is a painful state for the person left behind. One is left helpless. Paul comes to the rescue and says that such a person is not "bound." This means he or she can remarry without grieving the Holy Spirit.

Let me address those who may be "hard-liners" on this subject. What about physical abuse? If you were a father or mother whose son or daughter was being battered by a spouse, how would you feel? Suppose a spouse abuses the child? What if he spends money on drink or drugs and will not provide? Would you sit back passively and say nothing? Would you say, "My son-in-law has abused my daughter and my grandson, my daughter-in-law has led my son to a nervous breakdown, but at least they haven't committed adultery"? I suspect you might even wish one did commit adultery, so your daughter or son would be free to divorce and remarry! I also know of cases where mental cruelty is so fierce that the agony of adultery would be a piece of cake by comparison. The person may not lust after another person, but the hell he or she causes would cause one to wish for adultery.

Am I to believe that our Lord Jesus would say, "Sorry about this, but you are stuck in this nightmare until your spouse commits adultery"?

Jesus' compassion on people, plus Paul's concession, convinces me that either would grant a further concession even while hating divorce and maintaining the supreme ideal of fidelity in marriage. In the kind of scenarios I have described above, I think I would say to my son or daughter without hesitation (thank God it has never even remotely happened): "I think you deserve a new start." This would not have to be because of just infidelity or lust, but because my loved one was treated like a nonperson, like an animal.

If I understand the spirit of Jesus, He would not sit idly by. I base that on the Sermon on the Mount, on the fact that Paul introduced another concession that had nothing to do with adultery at all. I think he introduced the issue of desertion because it came up as an issue. And had he been living in today's world—where physical abuse and child abuse are more and more common—I would fully expect him to provide yet another way forward. He would not be accommodating hardness but brokenness.

God hates divorce (Malachi 2:16). That will never change. God's ideal is that marriage is forever. One should never forget this.

I would also add: Most marriages can be saved—that is, if both partners would live by the principles of the Sermon on the Mount, which is about the Kingdom of heaven. The grass is not greener on the other side of the fence. Those who would enter the Kingdom of heaven can learn total forgiveness. Good counseling can also save a marriage on the rocks. I would have to add: Though your husband is not perfect, though your wife is not perfect, and they are faithful and not abusive—sorry, but you are stuck. You will in this case have to remain in an unhappy marriage. It is not a mere unhappy marriage that would allow for divorce. It is when one lives in hell, as I have sought to describe above.

The Pharisees were so legalistic. They wanted to get rid of their wives because they saw beautiful women who were more attractive than their wives, and they wanted to marry them. It was all about lust. Jesus will not compromise on this. When a person leaves his husband or wife in order to marry another, it is called adultery. But the Pharisees didn't see anything wrong with the loopholes Moses gave. By the way, those who marry because of lust will find that in a very short period of time they will be looking around again.

Divorce is never an ideal; it is always second best. Divorce followed by remarriage is a failure of God's ideal. But being remarried is not unforgivable. Otherwise, Paul would not have given his concession. Whatever is in your past, God is a gracious, forgiving God. He gives one a new start. Divorce is a sin, but God forgives sin.

Can a divorced person have another start? Yes. Jesus would not lower the standard, but His graciousness is amazing. All sorts of sinners have been given a fresh start, including those whose marriages have broken down.

One more thing: Adultery can be forgiven. David, the only person in Scripture called a man "after God's own heart," committed adultery. He should have been stoned to death. But he wasn't. He was, however, chastened severely—with that external chastening to which I referred in a previous chapter. God wasn't finished with David yet. Read Psalm 51, David's prayer after his adultery. He became a forgiven man, and God used him again.

My counsel to all who read these lines: Let's be Jesus to all those bruised reeds around us.

28. Name-Dropping

Again, you have heard that it was said to the people long ago, "Do not break your oath, but keep the oaths you have made to the Lord." But I tell you, Do not swear at all; either by heaven, for it is God's throne; or by the earth, for it is his footstool; or by Jerusalem, for it is the city of the Great King. And do not swear by your head, for you cannot make even one hair white or black. Simply let your "Yes" be "Yes," and your "No," "No"; anything beyond this comes from the evil one.

MATTHEW 5:33–37

One Sunday morning I playfully told my congregation, "Billy Graham phoned me today. Said he was praying for me, reading my books and listening to my sermons. Told me to give you his greetings." I could see they believed me! So I added, "When I put down the phone, it rang again—this time it was Prince Charles." They then understood—and laughed.

Why do we name-drop? To make the person look good whose name we bring into the conversation? Or to make ourselves look good? I think you know the answer.

Jesus now changes the subject. He has interpreted the sixth Commandment, then the seventh. Now He refers to the third Commandment: "You shall not misuse the name of the LORD your God, for the LORD will not hold anyone guiltless who misuses his name" (Exodus 20:7). He does not quote the third Commandment but summarizes it with a number of Old Testament passages:

> When a man makes a vow to the LORD or takes an oath to obligate himself by a pledge, he must not break his word but must do everything he said.
>
> NUMBERS 30:2

> Fear the LORD your God, serve him only and take your oaths in his name.
>
> DEUTERONOMY 6:13, CF. 10:20

Jesus might have quoted the ninth Commandment: "You shall not give false testimony against your neighbor" (Exodus 20:16). Yet He is not referring to the ninth but rather to the third.

This section is our Lord's treatment of the third Commandment, summed up: Do not take the name of the Lord your God in vain (KJV).

Why does Jesus take this approach? First, He is concerned about the honor of God's name. Second, He shows how easily we can grieve the Holy Spirit by our language—our everyday conversation, even so-called pious talk. Third, He shows how easily we can let the devil get in when we talk too much. "Simply let your 'Yes' be 'Yes,' and your 'No,' 'No'; anything beyond this comes from the evil one" (Matthew 5:37). Fourth, Jesus shows how easy it is to use God's name to make ourselves look good rather than make God look good. Fifth, He shows how we may further indeed surpass the righteousness of the Pharisees, who only used God's name to make themselves look good. They did not think in terms of extolling the honor of God's name, but focused only on themselves.

Background of Oaths and Vows

Why make a vow? Why swear an oath? The issue is one of credibility. How can you be sure one is telling the truth? How can I know I can trust you? Should I really believe you? Can I know for sure you will keep your word? Answer: If one swore an oath, you could be sure it was the truth. If one made a vow, you could count on its being fulfilled.

In a word: In ancient times, you could be sure one was telling the truth if one swore an oath. It put "an end to all argument" (Hebrews 6:16). If you made a promise, one may or may not believe it. But if you swore an oath or made a vow, one always believed it. One did not violate the oath.

Oath and *vow* were used interchangeably. An oath or vow was the guarantee that what was promised would be made good. A "promise" may or may not have been reliable, but the "oath"—when you say, "I swear"—was an absolute guarantee that the promise would be kept.

How was the oath carried out? An oath was executed by appealing to a greater authority—as to God Himself. A typical oath was: "I swear by God Almighty." Even those outside God's covenant might say, "I swear by the gods." The oath was regarded as totally reliable. Today, one may swear by laying a left hand on the Bible and raising the right hand, as when the president takes the oath of office at his inauguration. On a less solemn occasion, you might hear people say, "I swear on my mother's grave"—any language that will convince the other that one is telling the absolute truth. That is the purpose of the oath, then and now.

The Old Testament not only did not prohibit the swearing of an oath; it commanded and encouraged it. Indeed, "Take your oaths in his name" (Deuteronomy 6:13). There was, however, a warning: Be sure you tell the truth. "Do not swear falsely, and so profane the name of your God" (Leviticus 19:12). Not only that: "When a man makes a vow to the LORD or takes an oath to obligate himself by a pledge, he must not break his word but must do everything he said" (Numbers 30:2).

Therefore, we have this warning: "When you make a vow to God, do not delay in fulfilling it. He has no pleasure in fools; fulfill your vow. It is better not to vow than to make a vow and not fulfill it. Moreover, do not later protest and say, 'My vow was a mistake,' for, 'Why should God be angry at what you say?'" (Ecclesiastes 5:4–6).

It is therefore surprising that Jesus would say, "I tell you, Do not swear at all" (Matthew 5:34). We saw how Jesus' view of divorce could be contrasted with Moses' concession concerning it. Now He seems to be going right against Moses!

Jesus was more or less forced to take an oath before the high priest, who said to Him: "I charge you under oath by the living God: Tell us if you are the Christ, the Son of God." In order to show respect for the Law and the high priest, Jesus replied: "Yes, it is as you say. . . . But I say to all of you: In the future you will see the Son of Man sitting at the right hand of the Mighty One and coming on the clouds of heaven" (Matthew 26:63–64).

To keep the spirit of the third Commandment is not easy. It is one of the hardest Commandments of all to keep. Paul many times seems to have come close to transgressing in this area. I admit that I am puzzled by this. Paul more than once appeals to God in order to be believed! "God . . . is my witness" (Romans 1:9). "I call God as my witness that it was in order to spare you that I did not return to Corinth" (2 Corinthians 1:23). "I assure you before God that what I am writing is no lie" (Galatians 1:20). He says "God is our witness" that he did not wear a mask to cover up greed, that "you are witnesses, and so is God, of how holy, righteous and blameless we were among you" (1 Thessalonians 2:5, 10). Amazing!

And yet God Himself swears oaths. But because He could not swear by a greater—as there is no greater—He swore by Himself: "I swear by myself, declares the LORD, that because you have done this and have not withheld your son, your only son, I will surely bless you" (Genesis 22:16; Hebrews 6:13–14). God promised David "on oath" that one of his descendants would sit on his throne (Acts 2:30). God can swear an oath in mercy, as He did to Abraham, or in wrath, as He did to the children of ancient Israel: "I declared on oath in my anger, 'They shall never enter my rest'" (Hebrews 3:11).

One of the aims the writer of Hebrews sets before us is that God might swear an oath of mercy to us (Hebrews 6:9). Why would He do this? So that we might be fully assured of His Word. He might have put the onus on us merely to believe what He has written—and He certainly does that. But on some occasions He accommodates our weakness by giving us an inner testimony of His Spirit that is so powerful we can say, "We know that we know."

It is a wonderful thing when God swears an oath to you. It is when He lets you know unmistakably, unconditionally, irrevocably and infallibly what He thinks.

Popular Assumption—"You Have Heard . . ."

There was a respect for the Law, and it was well-known that one did not break an oath in ancient times. Once the name of the Lord (*Yahweh*) was mentioned, it meant you brought God in.

The ancient Jew had deepest respect for that name. Once His name was invoked, it became a debt to be paid to none other than *Yahweh* Himself. If a person owed money, he brought in God's name for assurance that his word would be kept. If a person owed money and his creditors wanted assurance the debt would be paid, he said, "I swear to you by the name of the Lord." The creditor felt good, knowing he would surely get his money. From that moment—for the debtor—it was like having to pay God Himself.

In a word: Bringing in the oath was perfectly just—it was absolutely right to do—as long as one told the truth and kept his word. So far, so good.

But people began to look for a loophole—something we have seen before, especially when it comes to legalistic matters. Was there a way of avoiding payment after all? Lawyers always look for a loophole—and the Pharisees did this. Here is how they did it: They used the rationale that "circumstances alter cases." There was an increasing feeling that perhaps you should not bring in the name of the Lord. So they began to swear by "heaven" instead, or by "earth" or by "Jerusalem." That was the loophole. This way, it was slightly less serious if you did not keep your word. So, by examining how closely the oath was tied to the name of the Lord determined whether or not it was absolutely binding after all.

In ancient times, there was a commentary called the *Mishnah*. A whole section was given to oaths, including which were binding and which were not. You would have thought that an oath was an oath! But this is the way legalistic people get around the Law—by looking for those loopholes. So if you swear "by" Jerusalem, you are not bound by your vow—but if you swear "toward" Jerusalem, you are bound.

Thus, the swearing of oaths degenerated into silly rules—showing when you can get away with lying and when you can't. Swearing evasively became a justification for lying. Later on, Jesus said to the Pharisees, "Woe to you, blind guides! You say, 'If anyone swears by the temple, it means nothing; but if anyone swears by the gold of the temple, he is bound by his oath.' You blind fools! Which is greater: the gold, or the temple that makes the gold sacred?" Jesus pointed out, "He who swears by heaven swears by God's throne and by the one who sits on it," showing the hypocrisy and inconsistency of their thinking (Matthew 23:16–22).

But the ancient Jews came up with categories, each one being removed slightly further from God's name. So they might swear by heaven—but this is not so binding. Or the earth, or Jerusalem. They would even swear by their "head"—which was a way of saying, "As far as I know," or, "I hope I will be able to do that."

In a word: Even oaths ceased to mean much.

Jesus' Application of the Third Commandment

"But I tell you," Jesus said, "Do not swear at all: either by heaven, for it is God's throne; or by the earth, for it is his footstool; or by Jerusalem, for it is the city of the Great King. And do not swear by your head, for you cannot make even one hair white or black" (Matthew 5:34–36).

This was obviously in a day before people dyed their hair! Jesus was once again going beyond the Law. The Law encouraged and required oaths. Jesus says, "Don't swear at all."

Here is a question we must cope with: Do we follow Jesus by the letter or by the spirit? When do we apply this literally? James said, "Above all, my brothers, do not swear—not by heaven or by earth or by anything else" (James 5:12). There are those who go by the letter, such as the Quakers. They take the words "do not swear" literally and will not take the oath in a court of law. They say it is a matter of conscience for them.

This Does Not Refer to Taking an Oath in a Court

There are several reasons Jesus' words (and James's) cannot possibly apply in a court of law. First, Jesus is talking about everyday conversation, not when you are commanded by the state to testify. Your reason for taking the oath in a court is to respect the law. It is not using an oath to vindicate yourself or make yourself look good, which is what Jesus is against. In a court of law, you have involuntarily been put into a situation you must respect.

Second, if we are never to take an oath at all, God Himself would not have required this in ancient times. God laid down legislation when oaths should be taken. This, moreover, was an Old Testament practice—e.g., when Abraham sent his servant to find a wife for Isaac. Abraham said, "Put your hand under my thigh. I want you to swear by the LORD, the God of heaven and the God of earth, that you will not get a wife for my son from the daughters of the Canaanites" (Genesis 24:2–3). Jacob asked Joseph to swear to him that he (Jacob) would be buried in Canaan (Genesis 47:29).

Third, when Jesus was required to swear whether He was the Christ, Son of the living God, He respectfully replied to the solemn charge of the high priest. Jesus had refused to vindicate Himself until the high priest said, "Are you not going to answer?" and commanded Jesus to say whether He was the Christ (Matthew 26:62–64).

Fourth, it was a custom practiced by the apostle Paul, as we saw above, who wrote by divine inspiration.

Finally, the marriage vows are under oath and are honoring to God, who wants total fidelity in marriage. The vows "for richer, for poorer, in sickness and in health" are part of the Christian marriage ceremony. We take them to ensure that we will be faithful.

Jesus is referring to everyday conversation. We are not to bring in God's name to make ourselves look more credible. We are to keep our word without having to swear oaths or make vows. Jesus says, "Do not swear at all"—keep God's name out of it! And don't swear by heaven because it is God's throne. Don't swear by earth because it is His footstool, His creation.

This would eliminate one from saying, "I swear by my mother's grave"—which would be swearing by creation, or earth. And don't swear by Jerusalem! In the Greek, you cannot tell whether it is "by" Jerusalem or "to" Jerusalem, but with Jesus it would not matter. He says, "Do not swear at all." As for Jerusalem, you should not use God's city in order to tell the truth. Tell the truth anyway, and without appealing to the city of the great King! As for swearing by one's "head," don't say,

"As far as I know, I will do it," "I will do my best," or, "If all goes well." You cannot make your hair white or black. God knows the future, and He will determine when you are gray-headed.

Practical Advice

Jesus says, "Simply let your 'Yes' be 'Yes,' and your 'No,' 'No'; anything beyond this comes from the evil one" (Matthew 5:37). Looking at this advice positively, Jesus is saying, "Let your word be your bond." Don't resort to God's name or any authority. Let every word you say be simple, straightforward and honest. Don't speak evasively but plainly, leaving people in no doubt what you really mean. Speak without it being complicated.

Looking at Jesus' advice negatively, what does it mean? Some think that the command not to misuse the Lord's name, or take it in vain, means swearing, cursing or using bad language. It would certainly include that, but that does not begin to touch what Jesus wants us to grasp.

"God Told Me"—Really?

First, it means don't vindicate yourself by appealing to—or "using"—God's name. People do this when they claim to be sure they are right—and they want others to know that God knows they are right! So they drag His name in.

It is dishonoring to Him when you use His name like this, and especially if you are dealing with an enemy. When we have an enemy, we are not allowed to say, "God is on my side." Leave God's name out when it comes to defending yourself! That is what Jesus is teaching in this section. God, behind the scenes, is saying, "I am on both sides—so, please, leave My name out!" Or, what if it is a situation like Joshua encountered, when he saw the angel with the drawn sword and asked, "Are you for us or for our enemies?" God replied: "Neither." This applies in family relationships, too, as well as in business or other personal relationships.

Moreover, this is extremely important when giving someone a prophetic word (if you are inclined to do this). Suppose you believe you have a valid word for someone. And what if it really is from the Lord? You want him or her to believe it is a solid and trustworthy word.

The huge mistake nearly every "prophetic" person under the sun makes is to say, "The Lord told me." I sometimes think God looks down from heaven and says, "Really?" It is the worst kind of name-dropping. I realize you are only wanting them to believe God has spoken. But the reason you are using God's name is so they will take your word seriously. You may not realize it, but chances are you are not doing this to make God look good—you are misusing His name, appealing to that name to make yourself look good. And credible.

That, dear reader, is one of the main ways we take the name of the Lord in vain. If you have a good word—and it may truly be from the Lord— you still don't need to "name-drop." I don't mean to be unfair, but it does not matter who you are or however "awesome" your prophetic gift is reputed to be. Simply say to people, if you believe you have a good word: "I have a word for you. You can think about it." If the word is truly from the Lord, they will see this without your having to pave the way by bringing that glorious name in. This way, you have protected God's name. Also, you won't have egg on your face if that word turns out to be not so accurate!

Second, don't casually talk about God to impress another with your piety. I want to cringe when I hear people say, "The Lord told me this," "The Lord told me that." This, again, is not making God look good. You only want to impress people with your piety. Don't! Or be careful when publicly using talk such as, "The Lord has been so real to me today." Go slow on this kind of talk, unless you are speaking to someone who already has your trust. But to go public with such language as, "Oh, I love the Lord so much," "His presence is so real," "God has been speaking wonderful things to me"—who are you trying to impress? You may think you are bringing glory to God when you talk like this. But I lovingly caution you: The heart is so deceitful (Jeremiah 17:9).

We need to be painfully honest with ourselves and realize that this pious talk almost always comes from people who are trying to impress. They have something to prove: that they are close to God. The truth is, the greatest freedom is having nothing to prove. By the way, if you really have been close to the Lord—and His presence

is real—let God cause others to see it. When you take it on yourself, you misuse His name.

Third, don't resort to the use of His name when you are under pressure or when being mistreated. This is the situation James addresses. There were workers in the field who had been mistreated by their Christian employers (James 5:1–6). Their employers had not paid them their wages—so they cried out to God! James assures them that God knows what is happening. But he nonetheless cautions those who have been abused, in so many words, "Don't bring God in and claim He is on your side!" He says to them, "Above all, my brothers, do not swear—not by heaven or by earth or by anything else. Let your 'Yes' be yes, and your 'No,' no, or you will be condemned" (James 5:12).

God is not a respecter of persons. James assures these unpaid workers that God is on their case, but cautions them that if they bring in God's holy name to bolster their case, God will actually turn on them as well.

In a word: Don't name-drop God.

One more thing: When you misuse God's name, Satan gets in. "Anything beyond this"— instead of speaking simply by letting your "Yes" be "Yes"—comes from the evil one. Do not take this closing phrase about the devil lightly.

Consider this: "Do not be quick with your mouth, do not be hasty in your heart to utter anything before God. God is in heaven and you are on earth, so let yours words be few" (Ecclesiastes 5:2). "When words are many, sin is not absent, but he who holds his tongue is wise" (Proverbs 10:19). The devil looks for an entry point. When we are falsely accused, we may be tempted, under pressure, to make ourselves look good and bring in God's name as though He were on our side. Don't do it. You will give occasion for the devil to move in—and you will regret it.

Jesus never defended Himself, even when He was blamed. "He did not open his mouth" (Isaiah 53:7). As we saw earlier, He was crucified in "weakness"—a chosen posture (2 Corinthians 13:4). He was in fact strong. It takes great strength to keep our mouths shut and appear as if we are very weak when we are under pressure.

Oath-taking could be protesting too much. Having to say, "The Lord told me," is not only name-dropping, it betrays our own insecurity. The question is: Will I be willing to be misunderstood? Will I allow vindication to be delayed in order for God to look good?

If we really want to please God, we will keep ourselves out of the picture by using (i.e., misusing) God's name when our big egos are involved. We should simply refrain from using God's name to make ourselves look good. Otherwise, if we are not careful, Satan will get in the picture: "Anything beyond this comes from the evil one."

29. Waiving Our Rights

You have heard that it was said, "Eye for eye, and tooth for tooth." But I tell you, Do not resist an evil person. If someone strikes you on the right cheek, turn to him the other also.

MATTHEW 5:38–39

We are now approaching what some would call the highest point of the Sermon on the Mount—Matthew 5:38–48, the section John Stott calls "the most admired and most resented." The material we look at in this chapter overlaps with Luke 6:27–31. It is a change of order, however. The Golden Rule is in Luke 6:31 and does not come in the Sermon on the Mount until Matthew 7:12. If Matthew and Luke are recording the same sermon, it shows that their rearranging was deemed appropriate.

This is the fifth time Jesus says, "You have heard . . . but I tell you." We have seen His handling of the sixth, seventh and third Commandments. Now we see a quotation from three different places in the Law. We have seen already how Jesus goes beyond the Law, demonstrating the righteousness that surpasses that of the Pharisees and scribes. We also have observed how Jesus goes way beyond the Law. The Old Testament gives guidelines regarding the swearing of an oath—but Jesus says, "Don't swear at all."

So in this chapter we see much the same thing. This leads to certain questions. Why did Moses give this word, "Eye for an eye and tooth for a tooth"? What did it mean in those days? This was part of what we have come to see as the Civil Law—how the people of Israel would govern themselves. But why would Jesus apparently go against it? How are we to apply Jesus' teaching today?

You will see that we are now entering a most difficult part of the Sermon on the Mount to grasp. It is the most radical teaching yet seen. For one thing, it puts us all to shame. It is most difficult to take this teaching on board. The question also comes to our minds: How literally are these words to be applied? Consider this: "Do not resist an evil person. If someone strikes you on the right cheek, turn to him the other also." Do we go by the "letter" or by the "spirit"?

Just as I needed to say that "plucking out an eye" or "cutting of a hand" in Matthew 5:29 was not to be taken literally, so here in this section: We go by the spirit of these words. For example, Jesus is not teaching that we don't need policemen—or that a policeman who is a Christian should not defend himself. Neither is He saying that we are not to defend ourselves against a violent attack—as when a woman is raped or someone breaks into your home. But there have been those who have applied it that way, just as there have been certain people who cut off their hands to avoid going to hell.

The Ancient Code

Jesus refers to the Law, but we need to see it in its context. The passage "eye for eye, tooth for tooth, hand for hand, foot for foot" refers to a pregnant woman who gets accidentally hit (see Exodus 21:22–24). This was the Law's way of dealing with accidental injury. The issue was this: What compensation should be paid when one person has injured another? The ruling was intended to control and limit revenge. The intent was not that the injured party was commanded to get compensation. It shows how far they could go if they wanted it.

The main point was that a person could go no further than the Law said. In other words, no more than the value of an eye should be taken for an injury to the eye. For example, the offending party should not be killed in revenge but only receive the true value of the injury. Therefore, such a penalty could be turned into a financial payment. There is no evidence that a literal mutilation

149

was the acceptable punishment in Old Testament times. Only in willful murder was it "life for life." Furthermore, "life for life" did not apply in a case of accidental killing—it was applied only in a case of murder. The Law allowed revenge, but in the payment of a fine. Again, the purpose was to limit the revenge. The Law made sure no compensation was excessive.

Another quotation was "fracture for fracture, eye for eye, tooth for tooth" (Leviticus 24:20). The context here dealt with any need for restitution. This dealt not only with murder but also with killing another person's animal. It shows the just rights of one who has been abused and what the injured party could justifiably demand. This, again, showed the limits so the person seeking payment does not go too far in their demands. The exception was in the case of murder.

This phrase appears also in Deuteronomy 19:21: "Show no pity: life for life, eye for eye, tooth for tooth, hand for hand, foot for foot." The context was when there is a malicious witness. Moses had ordered that "a matter must be established by the testimony of two or three witnesses" (Deuteronomy 19:15). But if one swore falsely—or if it was the result of a personal vendetta or getting someone to agree to swear falsely—God stepped in to ensure this was punished.

If the lie was uncovered, you now had a just right to appeal. One could do to the malicious witness the very thing he intended to do to you. If he was hoping to have you accused of murder, but you are innocent, you can now accuse him of murder and the sentence would be carried out. "The rest of the people will hear of this and be afraid, and never again will such an evil thing be done among you" (Deuteronomy 19:19–20).

Such were one's rights under Moses. We need to remember that these rules were under the civil code. The Ten Commandments was the moral code, whereas these three references above come from the Civil Law, with particular emphasis on damage to the person or to property.

All these references were instruction to the judges of Israel. They express what is *lex talionis*—law of retribution, or deserved punishment. It was the principle of exact retribution—"eye for eye and tooth for tooth." It had a double effect: It defined justice and restrained revenge. It

prohibited the taking of the law into one's own hands and going too far—like killing a person because he broke your tooth.

Apparent Contradictions

There are two apparent contradictions. The first is between Jesus and Moses. The second is between Jesus and other writers in the New Testament, viz. James and Peter.

So is Jesus contradicting the Law? Not one of Jesus' recommendations is to be precisely found in the Mosaic Law. They go far beyond the Law. They even change the Mosaic Law quite strongly.

And yet Jesus' teaching is not "new legislation." That is, He does not set aside the Law with His new law. The proof that it is not new legislation is that although He said, "Do not swear at all," He took the oath before the chief priest. Nor is Jesus setting aside the principle of retribution. He believed in the principle that you "reap what you sow." He would also say, "Do not judge, or you too will be judged" (Matthew 7:1). The New Testament quotes twice from Deuteronomy 32:35—"It is mine to avenge: I will repay"—in Romans 12:19 and in Hebrews 10:30. By the way, the cruelest thing you can do to your enemy is to do nothing. Because if you do nothing, God will step in—and He will get revenge better than you could have! And if you want to be nice to your enemy, then take vengeance into your own hands. You will mess up every time!

As Michael Eaton put it, Jesus is dealing with personal attitudes rather than hard and fast rules. Jesus did not speak against the idea of retribution. It was and is a good legal principle to this day. Legal retribution, however, must not be excessive. What Jesus does is to ensure that in personal relationships His disciples are invited to outstrip and outclass the Law.

In Matthew 5:38, "You" is plural—"You have heard that it was said." But in verses 39–42, "you" is singular. He is dealing with personal relationships and attitudes. So He says "you" in the singular four times: "Do not resist an evil person. If someone strikes *you* on the right cheek, turn to him the other also. And if someone wants to sue *you* and take your tunic, let him have your cloak as well. If someone forces *you* to go one mile, go with him two miles. Give to the one who asks *you*, and do not turn away from the one who wants to borrow from you" (emphasis mine).

We have an apparent contradiction between Jesus and James and Peter. Jesus says for us not to "resist" an evil person, but James says, "Resist the devil, and he will flee from you" (James 4:7). Peter says, regarding the devil who prowls around like a roaring lion, "Resist him, standing firm in the faith" (1 Peter 5:9). Therefore, why resist the devil but not an evil person? Do note that Jesus does not deny that an evil person is out there to injure you, that he or she will be malicious and lie about you and will be unfair and take advantage of you.

The devil is evil; a person out there may be evil. And yet we resist the devil but don't oppose the evil person. Why? First, the devil is supernatural. He does not qualify to have a relationship with people. Second, we are not required to get along with the devil, as if we should try to "win him over." No. Don't go there. The devil is forever unwinnable. The devil hates with an unchangeable, icy-cold hatred. God will deal with Satan at the end of the day. The next time the devil reminds you of your past, remind him of his future. In the meantime, we are to resist him and—it's a promise you can rely on—he will flee from you.

Why, then, are we told not to resist an individual who is evil and wants to harm us? The fact is, whereas we cannot compromise with Satan, we can sometimes win over that evil person. When we do win him over, he will look back on the time when he was so cruel and we were so gentle—and he will say to us, "You were great in those days."

Rule of thumb: Always treat enemies in such a manner that, should you win them over, they will salute you and applaud your Christlike behavior in those tense and difficult times. When they come to you and speak that way, it will be like hearing sweet music.

And what if you never win them? I reply: You should never enter into a lifestyle of total forgiveness expecting it to "work." Forget that. You "lose your life," doing what is absolutely right. We must not love our enemies only because we think we might win them over.

In a word: Whereas we cannot give in to sin or Satan, we can give in to an evil person whom God has allowed to test us. Retaliation belongs to God alone. Resist the devil and he will flee. Do not oppose evil people; leave them with God. Let God deal with them—He may change them. Showing contempt for the devil is healthy; showing contempt for others does not harm them—only yourself. Hate is always counterproductive. Hate always grieves the Holy Spirit. Let them hate you—that is out of your hands. Jesus will not allow us to hate them.

Hudson Taylor, the great missionary to China, went for years without conversions there. The Chinese hated him. For one thing, he always wore white (not very wise). But one day a person purposely rode a bicycle into a muddy puddle of water where Taylor was standing and splashed water on his white suit. Hudson Taylor fell to his knees and began to pray for that man on the bicycle. The Chinese saw this, and from that point his whole ministry changed. He began to win the Chinese and became a legend.

A Terrific Challenge

There is nothing more challenging than this: "If someone strikes you on the right cheek, turn to him the other also." In the light of the ancient civil code, the evil that can be done to us is either carried out nonverbally or verbally.

It is the verbal abuse that Jesus has in mind when He says to turn the cheek. Nonverbal abuse means physical violence. If you are literally slapped on the face, the immediate reaction is to defend ourselves by striking back or at least saying something. Jesus tells us to say nothing that is revengeful.

The only person to fulfill this totally was Jesus Himself. This also means Paul was less than perfect before the high priest. The high priest ordered someone to strike Paul on the mouth. Paul retorted: "God will strike you, you whitewashed wall! You sit there to judge me according to the law, yet you yourself violate the law by commanding that I be struck!" Those standing nearby said, "You dare to insult God's high priest?" Paul climbed down: "I did not realize that he was the high priest" (Acts 23:2–5). It was not Paul's finest hour.

Jesus, however, is not telling us not to protect ourselves against physical violence. A person being raped should defend herself. A policeman must defend himself. If someone attacks you, you should defend yourself. When Jesus tells us to turn the cheek, He means we should not return the attack verbally. For example, it refers to someone lying about you, attacking your integrity—when you are falsely accused, when you are made to look bad or stupid, or when it is a sheer personal attack. Jesus is saying: *Waive your rights.*

Yes, under the Law you have the right to fight back. You were protected by the Civil Law. You can make another person pay. If someone falsely accuses you, or maliciously testifies, you can seek proof of his dishonesty and you can throw the book at him. Jesus, however, won't let us do that. Jesus is saying: Don't even try to show they are false witnesses. Don't raise a finger to defend yourself or make yourself look good.

So there is a difference between the Old Testament era and our era. We have been instructed by our Redeemer. In ancient times, they were protected by Law. When Jesus says, "I tell you," it means we are protected by love.

In What Ways Do We "Waive Our Rights"?

First, in revenge or retaliation. We are not allowed to pay back for a verbal injury. We are not given permission to punish a person in return for what we may have suffered.

Second, when our reputation is attacked. We are not allowed to protect our name. We are not given the right to vindicate ourselves. We are not given permission to counterattack in order to protect our self-esteem. Don't rob God of doing what He loves to do so much—and what He does best—which is to vindicate you. He will do it in a manner you would have never dreamed.

Third, retribution—giving them a deserved punishment when you believe they have it coming. You could throw the book at them. You do nothing instead. You turn the cheek.

Fourth, resistance. When you could stop a line of verbal abuse or gossip from being successful to make you look good, what do you do? You don't stop it or oppose it. You let it carry on.

Fifth, repudiation—when you refuse to make your opponent or enemy look bad by repudiating them, by putting them down or calling them names, such as "liar."

Sixth, reproach. You willingly bear the shame for what you believe—like Peter and John, who rejoiced that they were counted worthy to suffer the shame of His name (Acts 5:41).

Seventh, rebuttal—when you refute or disprove evidence used to accuse you falsely. Leave things alone.

Eighth, retorting—quick, angry replying in kind.

Like it or not, this is what Jesus is teaching. Why does He do this? Because He wants us to inherit the Kingdom of heaven—the realm of the un-grieved Spirit. Defend yourself and the Spirit is grieved; refuse to defend yourself and the Holy Spirit is not grieved. When you retort or snap back—however "natural" it feels to do so—we grieve the Holy Spirit.

There is no fear in love. Perfect love casts out fear. Fear has to do with punishment (1 John 4:18). "Eye for an eye, tooth for a tooth" has to do with punishment. "I want my rights," we might well say. "I want them punished," we may honestly feel. But when I punish, it is because I am afraid. I am afraid that God won't deal with them, that the world will listen to them and believe them and hurt my reputation.

It is fear that lies behind my need to punish those who hurt me. When I retaliate, it is because I am afraid. When I want retribution, it is because I am afraid these people will get away with the way they will be. When I avoid reproach, I am afraid that my reputation will be damaged.

We are called to be like Jesus. All that is happening between our justification and glorification is a process called sanctification. We are in the process of being more and more like Jesus (Romans 8:29). Jesus set a high standard, a very high standard, indeed. He practiced what He preached. And the degree to which we practice what He preached and practiced will be the degree to which we inherit the blessing He has promised us.

It "ain't easy." Nobody said it would be easy.

The funny thing is, most commentaries water down so much of what Jesus said. They often spend time saying what this does not mean, what that could not mean. Granted, there will be times we may be forced to say, "It can't possibly mean this or that," during this section. But the greatest mistake we can make is to dilute and weaken the extraordinary teachings of Jesus Christ so that we end up never having to apply them to ourselves or feel guilty in the slightest.

Yes, we are now in the section that is "most admired and most resented." I don't claim to understand them fully. But as Mark Twain said, "It is not the verses in the Bible I don't understand that worry me; it is those I understand all too well that worry me."

30. A Time to Give In

If someone strikes you on the right cheek, turn to him the other also. And if someone wants to sue you and take your tunic, let him have your cloak as well. If someone forces you to go one mile, go with him two miles. Give to the one who asks you, and do not turn away from the one who wants to borrow from you.

MATTHEW 5:39–42

This passage is another that is difficult to grasp. I have always sought to take any statement in Scripture seriously. These are Jesus' words, which we must embrace. But some of these verses are like a pill that is hard to swallow. Also, I am always very uneasy having to say what a verse doesn't or cannot mean, but sometimes this seems necessary.

The obvious questions again are: Do we take these words literally? Tolstoy took these words as a rationale for having no military, no policemen. Mahatma Gandhi, who never became a Christian, was impressed with this language and is said to have applied them to some extent. The Quakers became pacifists because of this language—opposing any rationale for war.

So, did Jesus intend for us to take these words literally? He certainly did not mean for us to gouge out our eyes or cut off our hands; He was speaking metaphorically. His injunction "do not swear at all" could not have been an inflexible prohibition against an oath, or He would not have acquiesced with the high priest.

The last thing I want to do is to "water down" Jesus' teaching, but neither do I want anybody to be demoralized before they understand what He meant. Jesus often said things that were later interpreted differently from the original way His words could have been taken.

For example, when He said, "Destroy this temple, and I will raise it again in three days" (John 2:19), no one knew at the time He meant the temple of His body (verse 21). Neither did He bother to explain what He meant! His command that we should eat His flesh and drink His blood (John 6:53) obviously needed to be explained, but Jesus did not bother to do it.

I am an ambassador for Christ. An ambassador never apologizes for his government's position, even if he doesn't understand it. He simply gives the position. And yet John Stott, who is well-known to be a pacifist, observed, "Albeit to our great discomfort, there will be occasions when we cannot dodge this demand but obey it literally." But when? "There is a time for everything, and a season for every activity under heaven," including "a time for war and a time for peace" (Ecclesiastes 3:1, 8).

The context of Matthew 5:40–42 goes back to the quotations "an eye for an eye, a tooth for a tooth." Under the Mosaic Law, you had a right to defend yourself—that is, as long as you didn't go too far. You cannot get revenge by killing if they only broke your tooth. Jesus, however, told us to "turn the cheek" if we are slapped. We saw that this meant not to vindicate ourselves—let God do it. There comes a time when we waive our rights that might be upheld by the Mosaic Law. But it is the Kingdom of heaven we are wishing to inherit. This means living by a much higher standard than that entailed in the Law.

But our text today takes this further: "If someone wants to sue you and take your tunic, let him have your cloak as well. If someone forces you to go one mile, go with him two miles." I can live with the principle of not vindicating myself—and yet these lines are more challenging still. The Civil Law was to show how the people of God are to govern themselves. The principles of the Kingdom of heaven show how the family of God should live with each other.

Some of your greatest tests come from believers. Perhaps you know the little quip:

Living with the saints above—oh, that
will be glory;
Living with the saints below—well,
that's another story.

And yet Matthew 5:42 may refer to those out-side the family: "Give to the one who asks you, and do not turn away from the one who wants to borrow from you." Some commentators think this might refer partly to a Roman officer demanding a Jew to carry his luggage. Luke's account is even stronger: "Give to everyone who asks you, and if anyone takes what belongs to you, do not demand it back" (Luke 6:30).

People Who Offend
Putting this passage in context, we may assume the people we are going to meet up with are sometimes those who can only be called evil. Jesus actually said, "Do not resist an evil person" (Matthew 5:39).

We can assume there will be unreasonable people, those whose unkind behavior you will face all the time. These will not, therefore, always be people who have a care not to grieve the Holy Spirit. They will strike you on the face. They will take you to court for your clothes. They will command you to walk with them for a mile. They will ask for money, probably with a knack of making you feel guilty if you don't accommodate them.

This is a reminder that there are evil people about—Jesus says so. They will make insulting remarks to you or about you. They will make unreasonable demands. They will take advantage of you. They will be ruthless in their pursuits. So this reminder should help us not to be surprised that there are people like that in this world—and you will meet them. Don't be surprised when they show up, or where they show up. "There are people like that," says Jesus. They sometimes appear to be godly, believe it or not. They fool many people, but they are evil.

People like this will take the initiative—they are not passive. They are on the offense. The ones who will speak evil to you or of you will sue you if given a chance. They will take unfair advantage of you. They will put you on the spot and never blush for being that way.

The problem you and I face is, we are not to turn them away, says Jesus. Instead of demanding your rights, you waive them if it is the Kingdom of heaven you want to inherit. You turn the cheek and let them slap you again.

Prudence in Obedience
We need to be prudent in interpreting Jesus' words. Never forget that Origen in the third century foolishly had himself castrated because of Matthew 5:29. Tolstoy, as we saw, said we should not have a military—or policemen. And yet Paul said, "The authorities that exist have been established by God." "For he is God's servant to do you good. But if you do wrong, be afraid, for he does not bear the sword for nothing. He is God's servant, an agent of wrath to bring punishment on the wrongdoer" (Romans 13:1, 4). Even Jesus said to the high priest, "If I spoke the truth, why did you strike me?" (John 18:23). Against civil injustice, Paul appealed to his rights as a Roman citizen and demanded that the magistrates protect him and escort him from prison (Acts 16:37–40).

Therefore, when does Jesus' word not apply? I say this partly for the overly conscientious person who is so desirous of following Jesus to the hilt but could do something very unwise. Satan himself will take advantage of a person like this.

First of all, Jesus' words surely do not refer to sexual, seductive or sadistic abuse. I have heard of prophetic people who take advantage of others by claiming God told them that a person should submit to their desires. I wish it weren't so. But what if an unscrupulous person demands or forces a woman to submit to his unscrupulous wishes? Is she to submit? Not for a split second. But there are people like that—evil people.

Neither does Jesus mean for you to endure mental or physical cruelty, whether from a spouse or even a parent. Jesus is not talking about this. Nor is Jesus talking about motivation by guilt, as when one points the finger and makes you feel guilty. "God wants you to bless me financially, since you have the ability to do it," someone might say. A verse like this does not apply when your inner spirit testifies that God is not behind the appeal.

I was deeply impacted many years ago when reading *The Didache* (called the teaching of the

Twelve, circa A.D. 150). There is a section on how to recognize a true prophet, as there were so many traveling prophets in those days. There is one telling line: "If he asks for money, he is a false prophet." You need also to be true to yourself and your inner witness before giving to every person who comes along. You would sometimes do someone more harm than good by giving in to his or her demands, like supporting a habit of drink, drugs, prostitution and possibly laziness.

But there is a time when you give in. You show prudence by serving them. You turn the cheek—as opposed to retaliation—by loving them. When you know in your heart you will do them good, you must do it. Eschewing vindication of yourself is always right. It is never wrong to be gracious.

I can also envisage turning the cheek literally—when you are suffering for Christ, or when you are in ministry, witnessing or caring for the lost. This has happened thousands of times. It has not happened to me—yet. But it could. I would hope I would literally turn the cheek when physically accosted while in ministry and doing the work of the Lord.

When our Pilot Lights ministry first began witnessing in the streets of Buckingham Gate and Victoria in London, some of our newer people began giving money to beggars on the streets. The beggars in the area traced the source to us—at Westminster Chapel. They began coming to us in droves—expecting, if not demanding, that we give them money. I urged our Pilot Lights not to give money. And yet I counseled this reluctantly, remembering William Booth (founder of the Salvation Army), who would say it is hard to preach the Gospel to a man who has an empty stomach. But it was obvious we weren't called to do exactly what he did. We gave them what we had—not silver and gold, but the Gospel. I admit I broke my own rule at times and gave money to beggars. But I do not know of a single one who came to Christ as a result.

Principle of Ownership

Josif Tson says, "Nothing is given to us on the basis of ownership, only stewardship." This means that all we have is on loan from God. We are stewards. It is required of stewards that we be faithful (1 Corinthians 4:2, KJV).

The heart of what Jesus is talking about in the Sermon on the Mount is vindication, and the principle of nonvindication. The heart of the matter is one's ego, one's self-esteem. But He also brings up the issue of ownership—your possessions. Said Paul: "For who makes you different from anyone else? What do you have that you did not receive? And if you did receive it, why do you boast as though you did not?" (1 Corinthians 4:7).

So what you have—whether gifting or financial blessing—is yours on loan, what God has given you for the moment. You may say, "I have what I have because I have worked for it." I reply: Others have worked as hard as you but don't have what you have. You may say: "I am brilliant, I am clever." I ask: Who gave you that mind of yours? And is it not also true that there are people as brilliant as you but who don't have what you have?

What we have, then, is what God has given us. And what God gives He doesn't take away. If you lose it, it wasn't yours to keep in the first place. So we should always consider that what we have is not our own. "You are not your own; you were bought at a price" (1 Corinthians 6:19–20). These words come at the end of a chapter in which Paul upbraids his beloved Corinthians for suing each other. "I say this to shame you" (1 Corinthians 6:5).

Job said, "The LORD gave and the LORD has taken away; may the name of the LORD be praised" (Job 1:21). We all must learn to stay detached from whatever we own. When we try the hardest to hold on to something, we are in the greatest danger of losing it. According to Paul, Christians should never sue one another. If you are a Christian, never sue another Christian. If he or she sues you, settle out of court. "The very fact that you have lawsuits among you means you have been completely defeated already. Why not rather be wronged? Why not rather be cheated?" (1 Corinthians 6:7).

In a word: There is a time to give in.

According to the Old Testament, your cloak was an inalienable right. "If you take your neighbor's cloak as a pledge, return it to him by sunset, because his cloak is the only covering he has for his body. What else will he sleep in? When he cries out to me, I will hear, for I am compassionate" (Exodus 22:26–27). A tunic was like a suit or dress. The cloak was like an overcoat. Jesus says, "If anyone wants to sue you and take your tunic, let him have your coat as well" (Matthew 5:40).

Our time is not our own, either. Time is God's domain. When people interrupt us—want our time or circumstances during a day, or delay us when we have so much to get done—we must remember that time is God's domain. He lets things happen when we are so very, very busy. Perhaps to slow us down. Perhaps to get our attention. But we learn to accept that all interruptions—however they come—are within God's sovereign permission.

In Jesus' day, Roman soldiers who occupied the nation of Israel were allowed to demand that people they met on the road carry their military equipment. This shows how those outside the family can inconvenience us. Busy though we may be, Jesus said that "if someone forces you to go one mile, go with him two miles" (Matthew 5:41). He takes your time. It requires your energy. But do it, says Jesus—go the second mile.

And yet this is to say nothing about worthy people who don't demand from us but would appreciate a little help from us: to give them a lift to church or a store, to help them move, to give them food, time or money.

As for money, "What do you have that you did not receive?" (1 Corinthians 4:7). You received what you have from God. Our money is not our own. "Every good and perfect gift is from above, coming down from the Father of the heavenly lights, who does not change like shifting shadows" (James 1:17). God can take anything we have from us—anytime He may choose. And when we consider that our money is His, do not forget that the tithe is peculiarly His (Leviticus 27:30). John Wesley said that last part of a person to be converted is his wallet. And don't forget what we say in the hills of Kentucky: "When a fellow says, 'It ain't the money, it's the principle,' it's the money."

Whether it is tithing to the church or helping the poor, what we give is to the Lord Himself. On the Day of Judgment, the righteous will answer Jesus Himself: "Lord, when did we see you hungry and feed you, or thirsty and give you something to drink? When did we see you a stranger and invite you in, or needing clothes and clothe you? When did we see you sick or in prison and go to visit you?" He will reply: "I tell you the truth, whatever you did for one of the least of these brothers of mine, you did for me" (Matthew 25:37–40).

I knew of a minister who went to Calcutta to spend a few days working with Mother Teresa. It is said that poverty in Calcutta is the worst of any place in the world. At the end of his first day in the streets of Calcutta, Mother Teresa had one question for him: "Did you see Jesus today?"

"If anyone has material possessions and sees a brother in need but has no pity on him, how can the love of God be in him?" (1 John 3:17). Remember, too, that we should not forget to entertain strangers. By doing so, "some people have entertained angels without knowing it" (Hebrews 13:2).

Promise of Opportunity

What Jesus puts to us in these difficult verses should be seen as a promise of opportunity. For one thing, it is a test of where we are spiritually. When you are verbally abused, what is your reaction? When you retort with bitter words and defend yourself—sorry, you show you are not where God wants you to be in your spiritual pilgrimage. But when you can turn the cheek—keeping silent, as Jesus did before Herod and Pilate—you show that there is progress, and you're on your way toward inheriting the Kingdom of heaven.

When you are sued? Settle out of court. Don't give the world an opportunity to laugh. Sin on the side of being financially exploited, says Paul. It shows a detachment from worldly things. This pleases the Lord.

When you are inconvenienced by having to give your precious time, see it as an opportunity to show graciousness. Time is God's domain. He let that person interrupt you. He let that accident happen. He knows you are busy—of course He does. But He also wants you—and me—to be more like His Son. See the inconvenience as an unscheduled appointment from God, not to mention what you will do for another person. Our time is not our own.

When you are put on the spot—whether for a gift or a loan—chances are you will more likely regret turning a person away. I used to run into a professional beggar on the way to church all the time. He had a way of asking for money that made me feel guilty, and when I would refuse he would say something that wasn't very nice. One day I was impatient and said to him, "How dare you talk like that! I don't have to give to you every time." I walked away. But two minutes later, I felt awful. I went back to apologize. He wasn't there. I never saw him again. I wish I hadn't said it.

Applying the Principle of "The Second Mile"

How else might the "second mile" be applied? For one thing: forgiving again and again. And again. To the same person for the same offense. Has not God gone the second mile for you? Louise and I sometimes sing choruses together, and here is one of our favorites:

> Father, here I am again
> In need of mercy hurt from sin
> So by the blood and Jesus' love, let for-
> giveness flow.

The "second mile" means not only time with people, but people with the same old problems. Be careful about saying, "I can't help you." Try helping them one more time. And do it again next week. Jesus is there that way for you and me. And have not others helped you like that in the past?

You go the second mile by letting people use you—your talent, your help, your wisdom. It's time to give in.

You go the second mile by spending time with people who bore you. Allow people to annoy you without your saying a word or breathing a sigh. Show graciousness. Be willing to spend time with uninteresting people. Jesus did.

Go the second mile with eccentric people, egocentric people and those who can only talk about themselves. Maybe they are lonely. It's time to give in.

You go the second mile by letting people point the finger at you. You want to say, "Stop it!" Let them get away with it by your being completely and sweetly silent. Go the second mile.

Go the second mile with those who don't come up to your expectations. They disappointed you, let you down. Love them.

Go the second mile with those who are slow to learn, not quick or intelligent like you. Be patient with those who have an undeveloped theology. What good is your theology if you aren't showing the love of Jesus to people who haven't caught on, as you have?

Go the second mile with those who don't treat you with respect. When you know that a person's words are motivated by jealousy, don't ever reveal that you know what the real problem is. Go the second mile.

"[There's] a time to be born and a time to die, a time to plant and a time to uproot, a time to kill and a time to heal, a time to tear down and a time to build, a time to weep and a time to laugh" (Ecclesiastes 3:2–4). And . . . a time to give in. Give in. Let them use you.

The rule of thumb is: If you are not facing sexual or physical abuse, sin on the side of graciousness. You won't be sorry for being gracious. I don't think I can ever remember a time I had to ask the Lord to forgive me for being gracious. Ever. Pointing the finger? Oh yes. I have had to ask His forgiveness thousands of times for pointing the finger.

Writing this very chapter has reminded me what a failure I am. I feel like a fraud in giving all this advice and interpreting Jesus' words. But God is gracious. He keeps going the second mile with me. And with you, too!

31. Loving Your Enemy

*You have heard that it was said, "Love your neighbor and hate your enemy."
But I tell you: Love your enemies and pray for those who persecute you.*

MATTHEW 5:43–44

The Sermon on the Mount is the Swiss Alps of the Holy Scriptures. From start to finish, the sermon is breathtaking beauty. But we are now climbing the Matterhorn, the highest peak. Or, to use a different metaphor, if there is a high-water mark in this sermon, this is it. It doesn't get more stunning than this.

Best of all: It is within reach of all of us. You may not be able to climb the Matterhorn, but we are all invited to do that which defies a natural explanation: loving your enemy. You can do it; I can do it. This is also crossing over into the supernatural.

Perhaps you are like some who, almost cynically, say: "I've never seen a miracle. I hear people talking about the deaf hearing, the blind seeing. I have never seen that." I answer: Right under your nose is the potential of a genuine miracle. It shows the possibility of the supernatural: It is when you love your enemy. To do this matches any miracle in the Bible.

When you have been unjustly hurt by words or deeds, the most natural thing in the world is to want to see the person who hurt you punished. You naturally want to defend yourself; you naturally want the person who hurt you to get a just punishment. But when you reach the plateau where you love that same person, you have climbed the Matterhorn.

We've all got a story to tell—how somebody has hurt us. In some cases, the damage is extreme. Chances are that if I heard your story, I would blush that I ever thought I had been hurt by anybody. I do believe this: The greater the suffering, the greater the anointing. If you have been hurt more than any reader of this book, you therefore have a promise of greater blessing than any other reader.

This chapter is designed to give you the greatest breakthrough you have ever had. It will lead to the greatest blessing you have ever received: to come to love the person who has hurt you. I don't mean that you will have a deep affection for that person, that you will be close friends, that you will go on holiday together or that you will admire that person. But what Jesus means by love—which is an act of the will, not an emotional feeling—you can personally carry out and experience.

This theme was first introduced when Jesus chose to treat the sixth Commandment in Matthew 5:21–26. But for the last time in this sermon, He says, "You have heard . . . but I tell you." Whereas in previous times He quoted from the Moral Law and Civil Law, this time He quotes Leviticus 19:18—plus what people generally believed was implicitly taught in the Law. Leviticus 19:18 says, "Do not seek revenge or bear a grudge against one of your people, but love your neighbor as yourself. I am the Lord." But there is no Law that tells people to "hate your enemy." He says, "You have *heard* that it was said . . ."

There are two other passages that will bear mentioning. Jesus quotes from Deuteronomy 6:5: "Love the LORD your God with all your heart and with all your soul and with all your mind," which He calls "the first and greatest commandment." "And the second is like it: 'Love your neighbor as yourself.' All the Law and the Prophets hang on these two commandments" (Matthew 22:37–40).

Second, Paul says, "Let no debt remain outstanding, except the continuing debt to love one another, for he who loves his fellowman has fulfilled the law." The Law, says Paul, is summed up: "Love your neighbor as yourself." "Love does no harm to its neighbor. Therefore love is the fulfillment of the law" (Romans 13:8–10).

In other words: Exemplify these texts and you will not only fulfill the Law, but you will outclass the righteousness of the Pharisees.

Assumptions That Lie Behind Jesus' Words

Jesus acknowledges a consensus among Jewish thinking at that time: "You have heard that it was said, 'Love your neighbor and hate your enemy.'" There is an explicit reference to loving your neighbor in the Law, but no explicit reference to hating your enemy. So, why did Jesus say this?

Most scholars say the second part is only quoting a distortion of Old Testament understanding, since there is no such word as "hate your enemy." And yet this may well have been a first-century view, especially that of the Pharisees—this possibly being their party line. Jesus, therefore, was not quoting from the Law but the way the people interpreted the Law.

Dr. Lloyd-Jones reckoned that Jesus was quoting the teaching of the scribes and Pharisees. He adds that there does appear to be a certain amount to be said that "encouraged people to hate their enemies right out of the Law." For example, when the children of Israel were anticipating the Promised Land, they were told: "Make no treaty with them, and show them no mercy" (Deuteronomy 7:2). This certainly suggests they were encouraged to hate their Canaanite enemies.

King David must have felt justified in saying: "Do I not hate those who hate you, O Lord, and abhor those who rise up against you? I have nothing but hatred for them; I count them my enemies" (Psalm 139:21–22). He no doubt felt he was being loyal to the legislation concerning Israel's enemies: They were to be destroyed. "Let evil recoil on those who slander me; in your faithfulness destroy them" (Psalm 54:5).

Therefore, "hate your enemy" is a fair summary of what should be Israel's attitude to the Canaanites, as regarded by the Law. There was an assumption that the Law said "hate your enemies."

There is, however, another assumption that lies behind Jesus' words—namely, that all of us have neighbors we must love and that all of us have enemies. The ancient enemies of Israel were all other nations. But Jesus isn't merely talking about nations. He really means *love your personal enemy.* So the assumption is we all have an enemy. All who are Christians have angels encamping around us (Psalm 34:7)—but we have an enemy, too, almost certainly: someone who has hurt us and whom we have to forgive.

There are degrees of enemies on a scale of one to ten, as to how fierce our enemy might be. You may have a "ten"—the worst possible situation, where there is someone who lives to bring you down. You may have a "one"—someone you don't particularly like, who "needles" you and "gets your goat." They may not like your personality. Perhaps you are more intelligent than they are, and they resent this in you. Perhaps you are not so bright but are a greater success, and they don't like that. Perhaps you are self-effacing and they don't like that. The situation in any case is not so serious, but you are still required to love them.

Origin of an Enemy

Where does an enemy come from? Why do we have an enemy? There are three possible origins:

First, the flesh. Calvin calls "flesh" the "unregenerate part of the soul." It refers to fallen nature. It is what makes us all difficult to live with. The flesh is the explanation for when people cannot cope with your being just as you are. They will never, ever admit it, but enemies are more often than not those who are jealous of you. They also have their own guilt; they take it out on you. Why are they enemies? They may feel guilty that they regard you as they do. It could be repressed guilt (they would deny they feel guilty). They take it out on you.

But sometimes there is an ideological issue at the bottom of their feelings. You don't happen to be on the same page theologically, politically, geographically, culturally or socially. Perhaps you don't support the same party line. If you were on their side or supporting their party line, they would probably like you, agree with you. You just happen to be on the side of a different group they can't abide, and you get caught in the crossfire.

Sometimes these people are angry with God because He blesses you. You have friends they don't have, a good-paying job, a good reputation or education. They resent it that God would do this, although they may not consciously trace their animosity to Him. In a word: They don't always know it, but they are angry with God—and they take it out on you. They may convince themselves that what they feel is righteous indignation. They think they are therefore "speaking for God," especially if your enemy is a Christian. They sincerely feel they must warn others about you.

And yet a personality clash could be at the bottom of their being an enemy. They are simply irked that someone like you makes friends, influences people, achieves credibility and success and is given such a responsibility. In a word, the best explanation for their being an enemy: the flesh.

Second, the devil. The devil is sometimes the explanation for your having this particular enemy. At the Last Supper, the devil "prompted Judas Iscariot, son of Simon, to betray Jesus" (John 13:2). The devil often works through an enemy. Paul called his thorn in the flesh "a messenger of Satan" (2 Corinthians 12:7). We don't know exactly what Paul's thorn in the flesh was, but a strong possibility was that he had an enemy who would not leave him alone. Your enemy, therefore, could be precisely that—a messenger of the devil. Sometimes the devil blinds your enemy so that he or she will believe a lie.

How does Satan work on you through an enemy? He will get you to focus on or magnify what "they" say. He will make you think everyone will believe the person—that you will be ruined, buried or finished. He plants imaginary conversations in your mind so you will dwell on them hour by hour, day by day. Satan does this sort of thing. He will do this to divert your attention from God. The devil will cast you down and give you a feeling of "no hope."

Remember the Three Rs of spiritual warfare: recognize, refuse, resist. Recognize the devil's footprints, refuse to listen to his suggestions—and resist him and he will flee from you (James 4:7; 1 Peter 5:9). The best way to resist the devil is to love your enemy. Paul said that a further reason for forgiveness was to keep from being "outsmarted" by Satan (2 Corinthians 2:11, NLB).

When you do not totally forgive your enemy, you unwittingly beckon for Satan to enter—and he comes in like a flood. Don't give him that pleasure. When you love those who have mistreated you, you block Satan's way of bringing you down.

Could God Raise Up an Enemy?

Third, the origin of your enemy could be God Himself. Yes. "For the Scripture says to Pharaoh: 'I raised you up for this very purpose, that I might display my power in you and that my name might be proclaimed in all the earth'" (Romans 9:17). Pharaoh, the archenemy of Moses and the children of Israel, was literally raised up by God!

Would God do that to you and me? Yes. Why? It is what we need. To keep us humble. To keep us relying on Him. To test us to show where we are in our relationship to Him. It is said of Hezekiah that the Lord "left him to test him and to know everything that was in his heart" (2 Chronicles 32:31). God raises up an enemy to accomplish this! God also raises up an enemy in our lives to see if we really want to be like Jesus. If you say, "Lord, I really do want to be more like Jesus," you might hear God in heaven say, "Really?" He may well test that desire by raising up an enemy.

So don't be angry with your enemy. He or she may have been raised up by God! God knows exactly what we need. He is sovereign, and He will keep our enemies alive and well as long as we need them. Such enemies might be temporary. Or, they could be a "life sentence"; like a tablet prescribed by your physician, you have to take that pill the rest of your life. If God raises up any enemy like that for you, it is only because it is the only way He can get your attention and accomplish His purpose in you.

The Enemy's Objective or Purpose

What is on your enemy's mind? What is his or her objective? An enemy keeps you in your place, keeps you on your toes. It is good for us. Though it is not their intention, enemies might keep us, hopefully, from too many unguarded comments. There is a sense in which your enemy can keep you from being conceited. If God raised up your enemy, then do not forget that God knows what we need. He knows when we begin to take ourselves too seriously. We therefore need to be put in our place.

There are a number of ways God can bring us to a greater level of holiness. He could, should He choose to, achieve His purpose in us by the immediate and direct witness of the Holy Spirit. Isaiah experienced this when he saw the

Seraphim crying to one another, "Holy, holy, holy is the Lord Almighty; the whole earth is full of his glory." Isaiah cried out, "Woe to me! I am ruined! For I am a man of unclean lips . . . and my eyes have seen the King, the Lord Almighty" (Isaiah 6:2–5). Yes, God can make us more like Jesus in one stroke, faster than you can bat an eyelash, by the Holy Spirit's immediate and direct witness.

But for reasons known only to Him, He frequently chooses to work through our having an enemy. He raises up an enemy who may find us threatening, who may be jealous of us or who doesn't know why he or she feels that way. This person might say, "I am doing this to you for your own good." (Whenever someone claims to be doing something for our own good, remember he or she may be up to no good!)

What we know is such enemies want to punish us—for some reason. They want to make life miserable. They sincerely feel if they don't do it, it won't be done. They feel they are sometimes speaking for God. Funnily enough, they are right! Their motive might be jealousy; God's motive is for our sanctification. The bottom line: He raises up an enemy to punish us, to sort us out.

Overcoming the Enemy—How?

We now come to the greatest challenge that ever was. It is like climbing the Matterhorn. What we now examine is a greater challenge to the human spirit than science putting a man on the moon. It is the greatest challenge on earth! It is overcoming enemies with love. It is to overwhelm them.

How do you do this? By refuting your enemy. Through argument? No. By showing everyone how wrong your enemy is? No. By matching your enemy's hatred with your hatred? No. You overwhelm your enemy through love. "Love your enemy," says Jesus. You have heard that you should love your neighbor but hate your enemy, but "I tell you: Love your enemies and pray for those who persecute you."

My dear reader, when you did this, you crossed over into the supernatural. You have achieved the greatest challenge on the planet. And what is more: You have surpassed the righteousness of the Pharisees.

Act of the Will

It is true that love is an attitude, a way of thinking. But love is not merely a way of thinking, neither is it what you feel. Love is a choice. It is often said that you cannot help the way you feel. This is true. But you don't go by your feelings—you do what you know is right, and you do it with all your heart.

The question follows: Is love repression (denying what you feel)? Repression is never a good thing to do. Repression—living in denial—is involuntarily playing games with your mind and you don't know you are doing it. We repress when we find something so painful that without realizing it we push the pain down into our subconscious. But when we push it down into the cellar, it goes up into the attic. It will come out as irritability, high blood pressure, sleeplessness or a stomach ulcer.

Some people think they have totally forgiven people because they deny to themselves what really happened. Those who have been raped, been abused in childhood, witnessed a murder or been in a tragic accident will sometimes live in denial. They sincerely believe they have forgiven, when in fact they deny to themselves what happened. They say, "What they did to me could not have been that bad"—and they live as though nothing happened. That is not total forgiveness.

It is truly total forgiveness when you fully realize, accept and calculate what people did—*and then you forgive them*. That is what we are required to do. Not to live in denial but fully know what they did—and still let them off the hook. That is what Jesus means by love.

Love is keeping no record of wrongs (1 Corinthians 13:5). It is when we refuse to compute the wrong. We refuse to remember "what they did," or, which is often the case, hopefully we decide to tear up that record of wrongs. Instead of saying to your spouse, "I'll remember that"—and later quote what he or she said—you tear up that record. This way, the record of the wrong cannot be found.

The choice must be made in the heart. You choose either to forgive or not to forgive. Perhaps you say, "I can't help it—I cannot forget what they did. I cannot bear the thought they won't get caught or get what's coming to them." I reply: I do understand. What Jesus is talking about is what made His teachings so astonishing to the hearers. It may be astonishing to you.

Caution: Don't go to your enemy and say, "I have had a wonderful victory. I have got completely over what you did to me and I have totally forgiven you." Please don't ever, ever do that. Why? They will look at you with annoyance and say, "Whatever are you talking about? What have I done to you?"

I have said in a previous chapter: Nine out of ten people you ever have to forgive don't believe they have done anything wrong to you. You could put them under a lie detector and they would pass with flying colors by their testimony they have done nothing wrong. (By the way, could it be that you and I have hurt people and they are having to forgive us—but we have no idea what we did to them that was wrong?)

So often the reason we say, "I forgive you for what you did" is because we *haven't*—and we want to stick the knife in to let them know how hurt we are. We can't bear the thought they don't realize how gutted we have been. But you must consider that very likely possibility—that the person you have to forgive feels no conscience whatever for what he or she did.

The only time you ever say, "I forgive you," is when you know he or she wants to hear that from you more than anything in the world. Or, you can say, "I do forgive you," when people ask you to do this. Otherwise, your forgiveness must be in your heart without their ever knowing your pain. But God knows. He is glorified when you have forgiven in your heart.

Nelson Mandela spent 27 years in prison. I sat on a bench in Cape Town, South Africa, and gazed across the waters at Robben Island, where Mandela was imprisoned, even tortured. I was almost in tears. He came out of prison with no bitterness. He dazzled the world. People couldn't figure him out. "Why aren't you bitter?" they asked. He gave two reasons: First, he realized that bitterness was only hurting himself. Second, Mandela said that "if black people were in power, they would do the same thing that the white people did to us." He gave President Bill Clinton this advice: "If you hate, you give your enemy your heart and your mind. Don't give the enemy those two things."

The devil will come alongside and tell you that you should be upset and angry over what they did. The devil loves for us to be bitter. He relishes it in us. The devil will cause you to think that if you are sufficiently angry for a long time your enemy will eventually get what's coming. That's a lie. Satan loves for you to hope for vengeance. You won't get it as long as you are angry and bitter. All you do is to make Satan happy—that's all. Don't give the devil that pleasure.

Total forgiveness means that you will not tell people what they did to you. Isn't it interesting, the first thing we do when others hurt us is to get on the phone and tell what they did? Why? We can't bear the thought that the people who hurt us will be liked or admired anymore! So our weapon—the tongue—minimizes their credibility and respectability. By the way, how would you like it if God told all He knows about you?

Total forgiveness means we won't let people be afraid of us. You won't intimidate your wife or your husband. Any marriage could be healed in 24 hours if both husband and wife would absolutely stop pointing the finger. Pointing the finger engenders fear. Perfect love casts out fear (1 John 4:18). It means you won't make people feel guilty or increase their sense of shame. Moreover, instead of rubbing their noses in it, you let them save face. You also protect them from their darkest secret. (I repeat: We all have them, don't we?) Total forgiveness is something you do as long as you live—a life sentence. You choose to do this. The love Jesus speaks of in the Sermon on the Mount is a chosen way of life. We are, therefore, not talking about an emotional feeling. Jesus uses the word *agape*. This is selfless love, not an emotional feeling. Jesus did not use the Greek word *philia*, which means brotherly love, love for parent or family. And it is not *eros*—physical or sensual love. *Agape* love is an act of the will. It is a valiant, courageous and righteous decision to let them off the hook and even pray that God will bless them.

Jesus, therefore, not only said to love them but "pray for those who persecute you." Have you ever noticed that when Jesus prayed for His persecutors while hanging on the cross, He did not say, "I forgive you"? He said, "Father, forgive them" (Luke 23:34). You are boldly, consciously and honestly asking God to let them get away with what they did.

Some people say: "You don't have to forgive them unless they repent." Where did they get that? Not in the New Testament, I can tell you. Jesus prayed to the Father for Him to forgive them, since "they do not know what they were doing." Not only had they not repented—they didn't even know what they had done!

That goes to show how most people whom we have to forgive don't think they have done anything wrong. It really irritates us when they don't know how hurt we are. True—I do understand. But this is your moment to be brilliant—to be like Jesus, who prayed to the Father that the very people who nailed Him to the cross would be forgiven. G. Campbell Morgan, one of my predecessors at Westminster Chapel, observed that he expects to see in heaven the very men who nailed Jesus to the cross—in answer to Christ's prayer!

Your praying for them means not only that they will be forgiven, but that they will be blessed. That they will prosper. That they would be dealt with as you want God to deal with you. When you love your enemy as you love yourself, you pray that he will get off the hook as you would want to get off the hook. I ask, what do you pray for yourself? Is it not that you won't get caught or punished for what you did?

This kind of praying takes you into the supernatural realm. As I said, it is crossing over into the supernatural, where miracles happen. Indeed, it is as supernatural as Moses crossing the Red Sea, as Jesus raising Lazarus from the dead, as being baptized with the Holy Spirit. I don't mean to be unfair, but I say to you: Don't pray for miracles when you won't pray for your enemies. Don't pray for more of the Holy Spirit when you refuse to pray for your enemies. By praying, you don't merely say, "I commit them to You." You don't say, "Lord, them. Deal with them." You pray for two things: (1) that they will be forgiven—that they get away with what they did (as you yourself have gotten away with so much)—and (2) that God will bless them.

Love is a choice we make. By making that choice and staying with it, a rather amazing thing begins to emerge: It eventually seems natural. For to the spiritual person, the supernatural seems natural.

32. Praying for Your Enemy

But I tell you: Love your enemies and pray for those who persecute
you, that you may be sons of your Father in heaven.

One Sunday morning at Westminster Chapel, as I
led the singing of the great English hymn "Praise
My Soul the King Eternal," I noticed someone
in the congregation who has done irrevocable
emotional damage to one of our children. It upset
me deeply. I "lost it."

I struggled to keep singing. Then I had to read
the Scriptures, sing another hymn. I struggled.
This was followed by the pastoral prayer. I don't
know how I got through it—I could only think
of that person out there who had deeply hurt
one of our own. Never had I been so upset during a service.

What saved me was the taking of the offering, which gave me a few moments to collect my
thoughts. During that time, it was as though the
Lord Himself had a conversation with me. This
doesn't happen to me every day. I don't say what
I now report was verbatim, but it went something
like this:

"So, you are praying for revival in Westminster
Chapel?"

"Yes, Lord."

"Good. How badly do you want to see revival
in Westminster Chapel?"

"A lot."

"Really?"

"Yes, Lord."

"Which would you rather have, if you could
choose—for me to send revival to the Chapel, or
for me to send judgment on . . ."

After a moment or so, I said: "Revival."

"Good. Then pray for [that person]."

I said, "Lord, I pray for [that person]."

"That's not good enough. Ask Me to bless
[that person]."

"Lord, bless [that person]."

"Say it again."

"Bless him."

"Say it again."

"Bless him."

"Do you mean that?"

"Yes, Lord."

"And what if I really do bless that person?"

I said, "Lord, You wouldn't do that, would
You?" I was on the spot. I then had to pray, "Lord,
bless him, bless him, bless him." And to prove
I meant it, I had to put him on my prayer list
the next day—and pray every day for him from
then on.

The proof you love your enemies is not that
you are crazy about them or invite them to go on
vacation with you. It is that you pray for them—
and mean it sincerely. You don't merely "commit"
them to the Lord as so many of us might do. You
ask Him to do two things: (1) let them off the
hook—which means God won't judge them for
what they did—and (2) to bless them.

As you know, I use the phrase "total forgiveness." I have written earlier of my darkest hour
at Westminster Chapel, during which time Josif
Tson said to me: "R. T., you must totally forgive
them. Until you totally forgive them, you will be
in chains. Release them and you will be released."
Nobody had ever talked to me that way in my life.
It turned out to be my finest hour. I was never to
be the same again.

The proof that we love our enemies who have
severely hurt us is that we have totally forgiven
them. The proof that we totally forgive them is
therefore not that we want them to be our best
friend (highly unlikely), but that we sincerely pray
for them as I have just outlined above.

Total forgiveness is not approving of what they
did. If you say, "I can't forgive them; it would be
condoning what they did"—wrong. God forgives

165

our sins—but not because He approves of them. This is why His Son, Jesus Christ, shed His blood on the cross. Jesus refused to condemn the adulterous woman, not because He approved of what she did. But He then said to her, "Go now and leave your life of sin" (John 8:11).

Total forgiveness, moreover, is not necessarily reconciliation. You forgive them. It may or may not be right or practicable to have reconciliation as well. You forgive your best friend for sleeping with your spouse, but you don't go on vacation with him or her. You forgive the child molester, but you don't let him or her teach a children's Sunday school class.

The ultimate proof of total forgiveness is that you pray for them, as I have put above.

Matthew 5:44 (KJV) elaborates what enemies can be like. They curse you; they pray down God's wrath on you. They hate you; they long for your downfall. They despitefully use you, taking unfair advantage of you. They persecute you; they live to make your life miserable, keeping tabs on you, relentlessly trying to discredit you and destroy you. They are afraid people will admire you.

But Jesus says: Bless those who pray for God's judgment to come on you. Do good to those who want your demise. Pray for those who walk all over you, are obsessed with you and whose preoccupation in life is to bring ruin on you, whether it be your life or reputation.

Here is a succinct summary of how to know you have forgiven those who have been unkind and unjust to you: (1) You will not tell others what they did to you; (2) you will not let the person who hurt you be afraid of you; (3) you will not heap guilt on them, even helping them—if possible—to forgive themselves; (4) you let them save face; (5) you protect them from their darkest secret being disclosed; (6) you do it as long as you live—it is a "life sentence"; and (7) you bless them, including sincerely praying for them.

When you do these things, you cross over into the supernatural. I would have thought it is the highest level of spirituality there is—greater than Peter's preaching at Pentecost or his raising someone from the dead. Spirituality is seen in not in how much you do or pray, but how and for whom you pray.

In totally forgiving them, you have an opportunity to do something more spectacular than any public miracle—namely, quietly interceding in solitude for them. Nobody knows you are doing this but God and the angels. This is what showed Moses' greatness, when he "stood in the breach" in behalf of those who disregarded his leadership, to keep God's wrath from destroying them (Psalm 106:26; Numbers 14:19).

How do you pray for your enemies?

The Challenge

Praying for your enemies—and sincerely meaning for God to bless them—is arguably the greatest challenge in the world. Doing this is "exceedingly difficult," noted John Calvin. Chrysostom said it is the "very highest summit of self-control." After all, he who "ruleth his spirit" is greater than he "that taketh a city" (Proverbs 16:32, KJV).

Why is this such a challenge? First, it is because you go utterly against the flesh. The most natural thing in the world is to want to defend yourself and see your enemy punished. Therefore, when you pray for your enemy to be blessed, you indeed cross over into the supernatural because you do what defies a natural explanation.

Second, nobody will ever know you did it. You are not allowed to broadcast your intercession for your enemy. That would not only be a self-righteous thing to do, but it could mean you aren't very sincere if you need to tell people you are doing this. So be careful. If you pray for your enemy, this should be done in solitude. You can't go to your enemy and brag, "I hope you know I pray for you." Your motive would be wrong.

Third, it might break your heart if your prayer is answered! Keep in mind that when you pray for your enemy, you are actually setting God free to bless them. He will take you at your word—and bless them! Are you prepared for this? If not, you have not yet crossed over into the supernatural.

The Command

Jesus is not merely making a polite, pious and respectable suggestion. It is a command. "But I tell you: Love your enemies and pray for those who persecute you." It is a command so outrageous that you might dismiss it out of hand.

Some see this as a lofty but unrealistic goal. It is not. Stephen, as he was being stoned to death, must have been in great pain, and the temptation to strike back must have been terrific. The natural reaction would have been for him to retort, "God will get you for this!" But he said moments before he died, "Lord, do not hold this sin against them" (Acts 7:60). I would think this was the secret to his shining face and unusual anointing.

The command is straightforward. The request is not that we pray, "Deal with them, make them stumble, let them get caught, give them the punishment they deserve." Chances are, your enemy probably feels that way about you—not wanting to pray that you are blessed, but that you get your "comeuppance." By the way, how would you feel if you found out that your enemy has been praying for you—that you will be blessed as a result and let off the hook?

I reckon that the apostle Paul will want to thank Stephen for his dying prayer. Paul was one of those for whom Stephen prayed (Acts 7:60, 8:1).

Content of the Prayer

What, exactly, are you asking God to do? You are asking God to be good to them instead of giving them what they deserve. The Golden Rule, which comes up later in the Sermon on the Mount, is that we do to others what we wish they would do to us (Matthew 7:12). You, therefore, pray for them as you would want to be prayed for.

I ask again: What if, when you get to heaven, you discover that you were blessed as you were, precisely because your enemy had crossed over into the supernatural and prayed for you—and God heard this person? Do not underestimate this possibility! What if God were also to congratulate you—before this very person—for praying for them as you did? Yes, that is a very real possibility. What is more, you won't be enemies in heaven, either! We will all love each other in heaven. There will be no pointing of the finger in heaven.

A friend of mine was in deep agony over the way his son-in-law had been to his daughter. He said to me, "The most I can pray is, 'Lord, deal with him.'" I felt sad. It takes minimal grace to pray, "Lord, deal with them." It takes a lot of grace to pray, "Lord, bless them."

When you pray that they will be forgiven, you indeed set God free from punishing them. That is what Jesus did when He prayed for those who crucified Him (Luke 23:34). This means that the people for whom you pray get away with what they did! They don't get caught; they don't get found out. They are off the hook. (Would you like to be off the hook for what you have done?) They are given a fresh start.

Loving your neighbor as you love yourself would be doing this. So, too, with praying for enemies. The general blessing you pray for would almost certainly include their good health and prosperity.

You may ask: Do you not pray for their repentance? Yes. Do that. That is fair. But what if they don't repent? The answer is: You pray for those who persecute you "that you may be sons of your Father in heaven. He causes his sun to rise on the evil and the good, and sends rain on the righteous and the unrighteous" (Matthew 5:45).

Job was taunted unmercifully by his "friends." The expression, "With friends like that, who needs enemies?" probably comes from the book of Job. His so-called friends kept tantalizing him by pious platitudes—most of which were true! And Job had to hear from them again and again—principles he already knew. But never forget that "after Job had prayed for his friends, the LORD made him prosperous again and gave him twice as much as he had before" (Job 42:10).

I cannot promise that you will be blessed like Job if you pray for your enemies and so-called friends. But I can guarantee that you will have a greater blessing of the Holy Spirit than you dreamed possible. Is it a greater anointing you want? Entering the Kingdom of heaven, this is the way forward. After all, it is the Kingdom of heaven that Jesus focuses on throughout the Sermon on the Mount. He is showing us how to enter it.

I mentioned previously that when a minister asked me, "Can your wife be your enemy?" I answered, yes. Not only that, we will discover in heaven how many nightmare marriages were endured by many high-profile Christian leaders. Among them were John Wesley and George Whitefield.

Cause

Why would one pray for his or her enemy? What is the cause that lies behind it? Why do it? And how does one get motivated to pray for his or her enemy?

Keep in mind: We mean sincere praying. Don't play games with yourself or God. Praying that your enemy will be blessed is like signing your name to a document, having it witnessed and no turning back. There are five stages, each of them showing an ever-increasing degree of graciousness.

First, duty. We begin here. There is nothing wrong with praying out of duty. You don't ask God to bless your enemies because you "can't wait" to see them blessed. You do it at first out of sheer obedience. It is because the realm of the un-grieved Spirit is where you choose to reside. You want to be like Jesus.

Second, debt. You are a debtor, says Paul (Romans 1:14). A debtor to what? You have been given a guarantee by Jesus Himself: "Blessed are you when people insult you, persecute you." "Rejoice and be glad, because great is your reward in heaven" (Matthew 5:11–12).

You should be glad because of your enemy—photograph him or her, frame the picture! Your enemy is your ticket to a greater anointing and reward in heaven! Your great reward in heaven may well be traceable to your enemy. If you don't appreciate your enemy now, you will. You will one day see that your enemy was the best thing that could have happened to you. Enemies not only keep you on your toes—they also make you pray more. An enemy is a guarantee of blessing if you handle things as you should right away.

Why pray for your enemy? Because of your debt of gratitude to God for salvation. As far as the east is from the west, so far are your transgressions removed from you (Psalm 103:12). You got off the hook because Jesus died on the cross for you. You deserve hell, but you are going to heaven. Your sins deserve punishment, but Jesus took your punishment.

We, therefore, are debtors to pass on to others what Jesus has done for us—namely, by letting them off the hook. Remember also that your enemies may be bruised reeds like yourself. And what if your enemy has been excessively evil? Thank God that you have been restrained from being like that. We all are what we are because of the sovereign grace of God.

Third, dignity. We are given an enormous dignity when we forgive our enemies. We become sons and daughters of the Father, who sends sun and rain upon the just and unjust. Only when we love our enemies do we mirror the Father. This does not mean we have not become sons and daughters already; we are not adopted into the family by what we do but by what He does. But when we love our enemies, we dignify the Father's choice of us. He imputed righteousness to us by faith alone. And when we love our enemies, we fulfill that righteousness and exemplify it to the hilt. Sometimes we use the expression, "He is his father's son," "She's her mother's daughter," meaning that children mirror their parents. How wonderful, then, when we mirror the Father's love by loving our enemies.

By coincidence, as I wrote these lines just above, I turned to CNN to see unexpectedly an interview with Canon Andrew White, the Anglican Vicar of Baghdad. It was through Andrew, when he was the Archbishop of Canterbury's envoy to the Middle East, that I developed a relationship with Yasser Arafat and Rabbi David Rosen. Andrew was being featured on CNN because of what he does for the Iraqi people, whom he loves. The issue turned immediately to the very theme of loving one's enemies. His church has dentists and doctors who serve the community. Most of the people who get treatment are Muslims, he said. What a dignity imputed to Andrew for mirroring the love of the Father!

Fourth, desire. This is when you actually want to pray for your enemy—and do it. What began with duty ameliorates to praying for your enemies out of desire. You actually reach the place where you want to bless your enemies and pray for them. It becomes (almost) a natural thing. Or, to return to the insight of Jackie Pullinger: To the spiritual, the supernatural seems natural. You secretly intercede for your enemy—and you love doing it!

Fifth, durability. Praying for your enemy becomes a lifestyle. Take it on as a "life sentence," doing it forever—day and night. What Jesus did, you do. What Stephen did, you do. What Moses did, you do. You don't merely do it once. Or twice. You do it all the time—every day.

Consequence

What happens when you pray for your enemy? First, God may well answer your prayer, as I said. You may say, "Oh no!" But yes. Jesus' praying for those who crucified Him may have been partly responsible for 3,000 people converted on the Day of Pentecost. Moses' praying for his opposition resulted in a whole nation being spared.

At the time of this writing, President Barack Obama is not very popular with conservative Christians in the United States of America. For some he is the enemy. I wrote an article in a major Christian magazine—"Are You Praying for President Obama—If So, How?" Not all liked that article. I know a lot of people who pray for him—to fail. How sad. This is not right, and it is not what Jesus meant. If we oppose President Obama's views, that is fair enough. But we should pray for him—that God will bless him! If he is blessed we are all blessed. A whole nation is at stake. My responsibility is to pray for God to bless him. God can channel that prayer as He pleases. I do not have a warrant to pray any other way (1 Timothy 2:1).

Prediction: You will never regret praying that God will bless your enemy or those you disagree with. You can only regret not praying for them. God's Word is at stake.

The second consequence of praying for your enemy is that he or she might later become a friend. Yes. Today's enemy may turn out to be tomorrow's friend. That is what God did for the whole world: "God was reconciling the world to himself in Christ, not counting men's sins against them" (2 Corinthians 5:19).

On John Newton's tombstone is an epitaph he wrote himself: "John Newton, Clerk, once an infidel and libertine, a servant of slaves in Africa, was, by the rich mercy of our Lord and Saviour Jesus Christ, preserved, restored, pardoned, and appointed to preach the faith he had long laboured to destroy." No wonder he could write the enduring hymn: "Amazing grace, how sweet the sound that saved a wretch like me." He never got over it.

You can sometimes win over your enemies by loving them and praying for them. Even if you don't become the closest of friends, you may hear your enemy say to you down the road: "I was horrible, but you were brilliant"—because of your spirit during the time of testing.

In any case, by walking in the Spirit and praying for your enemy, you become "sons of your Father in heaven." The greatest feeling in the world is knowing you please God. Enoch had this testimony, that he pleased God (Hebrews 11:5). Wow. It doesn't get better than that. I can endure a thousand enemies when I know I am pleasing God. I can cope with the delay of blessing when I know I am pleasing God.

I have to admit that not all take Jesus' advice. I am so sorry about this. I have to say also that not all cross over into the supernatural. But some do. Why not you?

33. Uncommon Grace

He causes his sun to rise on the evil and the good, and sends rain on the righteous
and the unrighteous. If you love those who love you, what reward will you get?
Are not even the tax collectors doing that? And if you greet only your brothers,
what are you doing more than others? Do not even pagans do that?

MATTHEW 5:45–47

Many of us show grace only to our friends, people we know and like. How many of us are unusually kind to those we don't know—or those we don't like? Hence, it is *uncommon* grace when we show graciousness to those we haven't met or to those who haven't been very nice to us. But God is like that—He is good to the just and unjust.

Common Grace

These verses also call for a brief look at the teaching of "common grace." It arises partly from these very verses. *Common* grace is God's goodness to all men and women—the just and unjust, the evil and the good. Such grace is called "common" not because it is ordinary, but because it is given commonly to all—saved and lost.

In fact, common grace has nothing to do with salvation. It applies to everybody, whether or not they come to Christ. John Calvin called it "special grace in nature"—meaning, God's goodness to the sinful human race but without reference to salvation. God causes His sun to shine on the righteous and unrighteous. It is a reference to the good things God does for His entire creation.

A distinction, therefore, needs to be made between common grace and saving grace. Common grace refers to creation; saving grace refers to redemption. All that is required to be a recipient of common grace is to be created! There are certainly benefits to being created—heat, light, rain, food, natural abilities, talent, rule of law, policemen, firemen, doctors, nurses, hospitals, medicine, schools, government. No faith is needed to receive the benefits of common grace. Such goodness is given to all people, whether or not

they acknowledge it as being from a merciful God. Indeed, most, sadly, never do acknowledge it.

Saving grace, however, comes to those whom God has chosen from the foundation of the world (Acts 13:48). This grace is effectual to the people whom God foreknew, enabling them to trust Jesus' death on the cross for their salvation. To those who trust Jesus' blood, not their good works, there is given a promise of a home in heaven when they die. They know they will go to heaven—not because they deserve it. In a word: The Gospel has to do with saving grace, not common grace.

Common grace is also the explanation of your ability, your IQ, your job, your education, your talent. It is what lies behind great people excelling to unusual heights, whether in politics, music, science or industry. Yehudi Menuhin was arguably the greatest violinist of his day, but there is no indication (that I know of) that he was a saved man. Albert Einstein had an IQ of 212, but there is no evidence that he was converted. Einstein had what I can only call a maximum measure of common grace: one of the greatest intellects in human history. This was a gift of God.

I think, too, of great composers. I have on my iPod a lot of classical music. When I am on a plane, especially crossing the Atlantic, I often prefer listening to Rachmaninoff or Grieg rather than to "Shine Jesus Shine." I thank God for rich music that can cause my spirit to soar. But most of these great composers, as far as I can tell, were not Christians. And yet God is the only explanation for their talent.

Common grace is what keeps the world from going completely topsy-turvy. If you think things are bad in the world—with all the suffering, heartache, poverty and hunger—I can only say you have no idea how awful things would be were not God in charge. Things would be incalculably worse, I can assure you. So, thank God for common grace.

A problem, however, is sometimes the Church exists by common grace rather than the immediate and direct power of the Holy Spirit. This is why it is said that if the Holy Spirit were completely withdrawn from the Church today, speaking generally, 90 percent of the work of the Church would continue as if nothing had happened. Highly talented people in the Church can make things happen without the power of the Holy Spirit.

The thing is, those who have had a "double dose" of common grace—e.g., being mighty, noble, ingenious or powerful in this world—are seldom the recipients of saving grace, said Paul. "Brothers, think of what you were when you were called. Not many of you were wise by human standards; not many were influential; not many were of noble birth" (1 Corinthians 1:26).

Most of those of us who have been effectually called happen to be very, very ordinary people. Perhaps once in five hundred years God saves a Saul of Tarsus, a Saint Augustine, a Thomas Aquinas or a John Calvin.

Demonstrating God's Uncommon Grace

However, what I am calling uncommon grace is specifically what Jesus points to in Matthew 5:45–47. This is what those who inherit the Kingdom of heaven are called to demonstrate: showing grace to those we don't like. This is not common but uncommon. But it is the essence of godliness. It is when we mirror God's goodness to all people—showing graciousness indiscriminately to everybody.

We don't expect the unrighteous to do this. For one thing, they may not even believe in God! They are therefore not going to be thankful for God's lovely creation.

The question is, are we? How often do we thank God for the benefits of being created and sustained? We have been saved by sheer grace. We have been forgiven of all our sins. Are we thankful? Do we show it? Do any of us deserve to be saved? No, we certainly don't. But we should be therefore all the more thankful—that we have

been chosen, called and converted. Not only that, we should be thankful for God's general goodness to all people—His creation, its beauty, His faithful sustenance of things in the world we depend on: food, shelter, clothing, protection, health, government, law, traffic lights, hospitals.

You and I are called to mirror this same goodness to all people—just as God does. If God lets His rain fall on the just and the unjust, we, too, should be a blessing to everybody we meet. We don't deserve to be created—or to be saved. We are children of light.

It is surely a small thing to pass on His goodness. It is when we dignify our being adopted into the family. As we saw earlier, there is the phrase "like father, like son." A wise son makes a glad father. We, therefore, make God so happy when we are like Him—sharing the same love and goodness, His indiscriminate kindness and graciousness. In a word: It is showing uncommon grace to everybody—good and bad, friend and foe, saved or lost.

What, exactly, does God do? For one thing, He provides sun. Note the word "His" sun. It is God's sun. The next time you see the sun, remember that it is His. He can do with it what He pleases. But what He is pleased to do is that He "causes"—present tense—that sun to shine on the evil and good. This means that saved and lost have equal benefits. The sun basically provides three things: illumination, energy and heat. God does not channel these benefits to one group, one nation, one class, one tribe or Christians only. It shines on everybody.

So, too, with rain. The rain is poured out on the righteous and the unrighteous. The thing about rain is, we complain when it doesn't rain. And we complain when we get it! Think of how we are dependent upon rain for our food, crops, vegetables, fruit. This word would have had special relevance for Jesus' hearers. It was largely an agrarian society.

We need both sun and rain. The combination gives us our food. Flowers. Plants. Trees. It shows the beauty of God's creation. Louise and I used to walk at least once a week to St. James Park. We loved that time of the year when the tulips were out. Their beauty defies description. We should all be thankful for what God does. His rain falls and His sun shines on the just and unjust.

So, says Jesus, that is precisely what you and I are to be like: to love our enemies. Therefore, Jesus brings in this illustration of common grace and uncommon grace to demonstrate how we must love our enemies. God loves the lost. He gives sun and rain to those under His wrath. Evil people and unrighteous people are God's enemies, but He blesses them every day! He even provided a Savior: While we were yet sinners, Christ died for the ungodly (Romans 5:8).

And yet does God wait for His creation to show gratitude before He blesses them? No. Does He say to evil people, "Sorry, you have not been grateful, so I won't let my sun shine on you"? No.

Our Responsibility to Show Uncommon Grace

What God does, He also commands us to do. He "causes" His sun to shine on the just and the unjust.

We have the same responsibility. *We make it happen.* Showing forgiveness is an act of the will. You don't wait for years and years until you feel "led." You do it because it is right to do. To put it another way: Don't pray about it—do it! Love your enemy; pray for your enemy. "Causes" means that you take the initiative. You don't wait for the person to say, "Sorry." You may go to your grave before they apologize. Don't wait for people to do you a favor before you are nice to them.

In a word: We must make a choice. It is when we cross over into the supernatural. We can cross over into the supernatural by being like Jesus— that is, praying for our enemy. Praying for those who have hurt us is Christ-likeness. Doing good to those we don't like is God-likeness. That is true godliness.

To put it another way: You and I have a choice to make—whether to be common, ordinary, predictable. Being predictable means you wait for the other person to be nice first. Being predictable is to wait for the other person to do what is right. You say, "When they are grateful, when they treat me with respect, when they are good to me, then—and only then—will I be good to them." I answer: You are being most predictable. That is the way people are by nature. But when you take the initiative and "cause" your love to shine forth, you are being like your Father in heaven.

This works in the husband-wife relationship. If you wait for the other to take the initiative, chances are your marriage will soon be on the rocks or in perilous shape. I mentioned earlier Paul's admonition for husbands to love their wives and for wives to submit to their husbands (Ephesians 5:25, 22). A man may say, "I will love her when she submits to me, as Paul also said for her to do." A wife can choose to say, "I will submit to him when I feel loved."

But if both will be vulnerable, not waiting for the other to be responsible to the Lord and get it right, your marriage can be healed by sundown today. You "cause" it to happen. Don't wait for your spouse to initiate things—you do it. Do it for the honor and glory of God. It pleases Him. It mirrors His ways. That is godliness. You make a choice. It is what Jesus also meant by being a peacemaker (Matthew 5:9).

Rarity of Uncommon Grace

I wish it weren't so! But showing uncommon grace is rare. What is not rare: loving those who love you.

Some research suggests that 90 percent of human relationships are based on what we think the other feels about us. If we surmise that they like us, then we immediately like them. Indeed, if we sense they are pleased with us and love being with us, we reciprocate. However, when we sense they don't like us, we are so often immediately defensive. Rather than giving a relationship a chance to flourish, we sadly stop it because we are so sure they don't—or won't—like us. And we isolate ourselves.

This is why some people never seem to make friends. They try to figure out in advance whether this or that person will like them. If they don't think they will be liked or accepted, they dig in their heels. Someone has said that love is moving forward without any protection. This means you become vulnerable—and love that person regardless whether they show signs of loving you.

What also is not rare: greeting your "brother"—and those you know and like—but distancing yourself from the person you have not tried to know or perhaps don't like. "If you greet only your brothers, what are you doing more than others? Do not even pagans do that?" (Matthew

5:47). It takes no grace to be friendly with those you know and like already. It takes a lot of grace to "cause" your sun to shine on those you never met (or those you don't like).

Many churches get the reputation of being snobbish because they are unfriendly to visitors. As soon as the service is over, they head straight for their close friends. And we wonder why visitors don't come back! I always think of this striking verse: "Do not forget to entertain strangers, for by so doing some people have entertained angels without knowing it" (Hebrews 13:2).

This was Peter's foolish miscalculation. He had been willing to be friendly to Gentiles in Antioch, even eating with them—that is, as long as no Jew could see him. But when certain Jews from Jerusalem showed up, Peter distanced himself from the Gentiles, which exposed his hypocrisy. Peter suddenly but sadly felt he must adhere to the Jewish party line. "He was afraid of those who belonged to the circumcision group." It was hardly his finest hour (Galatians 2:11–13).

So many Christians can be like that. We are afraid to be associated with those outside our party line, especially if our peers would see us. What is thrilling about Jesus is that He was not bothered by those He mixed with—or who saw Him. He made Himself of "no reputation" (Philippians 2:7, KJV). He unashamedly sat with sinners—and even chose Matthew, a tax collector, as one of His disciples!

There is a background regarding the tax collector that is interesting. The Roman Empire used a tax-farming system. The government would specify the amount to be collected from a certain area and appoint a man to gather it. This man would in turn appoint men under him, who would appoint others under them. Each appointee had to obtain his quota, and whatever else he got he could keep. The potential for bribery and corruption was enormous. The Jewish tax collectors were loathed. But even these low, disgusting men had their friends.

The point, therefore, that Jesus is making is: How are we who follow Jesus in any way superior spiritually to the despised tax collectors, if they, too, only love their friends? "Do not even pagans do that?" Jesus asks.

Those who are alien to the Kingdom of heaven and its principles are good to their friends. Indeed, most evil people—liars, murderers and swindlers—are good to those they know. The "godfather" of the Mafia looks like a gentle, loving person when holding his grandson on his lap. He is good to his family and friends. The question therefore follows: Wherein are you and I different from "pagans" if we are only good to our family and those we like?

What is therefore not rare: people who accept those who accept them. People who like those who like them. People who mix with those of the same mold.

Are we truly different from the world? That is the question Jesus is asking. The exceedingly rare person is the one who accepts those who don't accept them. Who greets and mixes with those outside their comfort zone. Who crosses over party lines when greeting people. Who prays for his enemies. Who doesn't pay back "tit for tat." Who is good to the undeserving. The rare person is one who "causes" his sun to shine on those nobody else wants to be around.

The Reward of Uncommon Grace

Note carefully these words of Jesus: "If you love those who love you, what reward will you get?" Why do you suppose Jesus threw that word *reward* in? Does this surprise you? Luke's rendering of this teaching uses the word *credit*. "If you love those who love you, what credit is that to you? Even 'sinners' love those who love them" (Luke 6:32).

Why "reward"? Why "credit"? It is because there is an assumption in this teaching that God notices, blesses and rewards those who surpass the righteousness of the Pharisees. "Love your enemies, do good to them, and lend to them without expecting to get anything back. Then your reward will be great" (Luke 6:35). This language echoes what we saw in the Beatitudes: "Great is your reward in heaven" when you are persecuted because of Christ (Matthew 5:12).

There follows an opportunity of reward—if what you do defies a natural explanation. In other words, you don't get a reward for what comes easily or is natural—such as greeting your friends. The biblical principle here is always this: You get a reward for the unusual, the uncommon achievement.

In this connection, Paul asked the question if he even has a chance for a reward! The only thing he could come up with was that he preached to the Corinthians and refused any remuneration from them (1 Corinthians 9:18). Jesus is telling us clearly that a reward is in store for those who show uncommon grace—like "causing" the sun or rain to fall on the unworthy.

We should therefore seize upon any opportunity to show uncommon grace. When someone speaks against you, seize upon it—and love him or her! If someone distances himself or herself from you, seize upon it—and love that person! If someone is unkind to you, pray for that person! If someone is devoted to your downfall, take the opportunity with both hands and intercede in his or her behalf, as Moses did for Israel when they were against his leadership.

So, if someone is trying to discredit you, and you can be gracious to that person, God notices it. A reward is on offer. Take full advantage of a wonderful opportunity—not only to show uncommon grace, but to know God wants to motivate you by the promise of a reward. This is His idea. Take it with both hands.

And yet the "odds" of many people receiving such a reward is quite remote, I'm sorry to say. Putting it negatively, the odds are that if one speaks against you, you will defend yourself. If someone speaks against you, you will speak against that person. If someone is not nice to you, you will not be nice to him or her. If one does not greet you first, you won't bother to speak to him or her. The odds are, if someone else doesn't initiate reconciliation, there will be no reconciliation.

But you can beat the odds! How? By demonstrating uncommon grace. You do this when you *don't* protect your reputation. You do it when you move outside your comfort zone. You do it when you pray for those who despitefully use you. You

show uncommon grace when you demonstrate graciousness to the ungracious. What is more: You outclass the righteousness of the scribes and Pharisees.

The Purpose of Reward

Why reward? Simply this: to motivate us to go beyond the call of duty.

The self-righteous person says, "I don't need motivation like that." It is the self-righteous, "pious" type who claims to be above this sort of enticement to reward. But they are denying the truth about human nature. God stoops to our weakness—to motivate us to do what we will be so glad we did! He is that way, *so* gracious.

Paul did not want to be rejected for the reward. It was so important to him that he said, "I beat my body and make it my slave so that after I have preached to others, I myself will not be disqualified for the prize" (1 Corinthians 9:27). He was not talking about making it to heaven—he was already fully assured of going to heaven. What he was not so sure of was this prize.

Even Jesus was motivated by the joy set before Him. It was the joy from the Father He would receive later on that kept Him going. It is what helped Him to endure the cross and the shame (Hebrews 12:2).

Not all Christians will receive this reward. Not all will receive a "rich welcome into the eternal kingdom" (2 Peter 1:11). Such a reward comes to those whose righteousness exceeds the righteousness of the Pharisees. It is promised to those who love those who don't love them. It comes to those who "cause" their light to be shown to the ungracious. It comes to those who are full of mercy, "just as your Father is merciful" (Luke 6:36).

God did not have to imply a reward in such obedience. But He did. He always does.

And yet uncommon grace is so rare. What are we doing more than "pagans"?

34. Christian Perfection

Be perfect, therefore, as your heavenly Father is perfect.

MATTHEW 5:48

These words not only bring Matthew 5 to a completion, but summarize Jesus' six antitheses ("You have heard . . . but I tell you") regarding the Law and His interpretation of it. The word *therefore* indicates that Jesus is bringing this section of the sermon to a purposeful conclusion—namely, that we be "perfect" (Gr. *teleios*).

How does this make you feel? Are you perfect? I certainly am not! What does Jesus mean?

This is a difficult verse to understand. Some think Jesus is saying, "You will therefore be perfect"—meaning that we would be perfect if we took on board and practiced all He has said in this chapter. Indeed, one would be truly perfect if he never made an unguarded comment, never lusted, always turned the cheek when abused or was always gracious to those who have mistreated him.

However, Matthew 5:44 is probably a command—not a promise—that we should exceed the righteousness of the Pharisees by exhibiting the spirit and not the letter of the Law. This is what Jesus truly and realistically envisages for us in Matthew 5. That we become perfect—that is, trophies of grace, unfeigned examples of the kind of godliness that He knows is attainable. By this, He therefore means we will be complete in the life of the Spirit—that we will truly fulfill what He intends for us. In a word: that we will be *mature*, which is the meaning of *teleios* here.

This verse has given rise to several "perfectionist" movements over the centuries, one of which is the modern Holiness Movement. It arose out of John Wesley's teaching of "Christian perfection," although many who claimed to follow him took this concept beyond anything Wesley himself probably intended. I do know that not a few did teach "sinless perfection." Some said they actually lived without sinning and would make that claim with a straight face. I knew many of these people very well, indeed. I can safely tell you: Sincere though they were, they did not achieve what they claimed, not even my own dad, the godliest person I ever knew.

James said, "We all stumble in many ways, and if anyone does not stumble in what he says, he is a perfect man" (James 3:2, ESV). James's implication is clear: No one is perfect. We all sin. And he, the half brother of Jesus, indicates in his epistle how familiar he was with the Sermon on the Mount. I am so thankful that James said that.

The Greek *teleios* is probably the equivalent of the Hebrew *tamim*. It was used to refer to animals without defects (Exodus 12:5). It was used to describe those thoroughly committed to the Lord, such as Noah (Genesis 6:9). And yet Noah was far from perfect (Genesis 9:21). It was translated "blameless" in 2 Samuel 22:24, the words of David. And yet David was not perfect (2 Samuel 11:1–21). Ephesians 4:13 and Philippians 3:15 translate *teleios* as "mature."

There are several areas Jesus had in mind when He said, "Be perfect, therefore." First, one's temper, or rash words. When Jesus mentions anyone who is angry with his brother, or calls one "Raca" or "fool," He is referring to controlling your temper (Matthew 5:22.). This comes out in Matthew 5:39, turning the cheek when someone slaps you on the face. Clearly He is talking about controlling one's temper. Second, we are to resist any temptation to lust—or to do or say anything that would cause another to lust (Matthew 5:28). Third, we are never to bring God's name into our situation to make ourselves look good (Matthew 5:34.). Fourth, we are to pray for our enemies and bless them daily, just as the Father pours out His sun on the just and unjust (Matthew 5:45). "Be perfect, therefore."

175

A mild grammatical case can be made that Jesus is showing the consequence of following His teaching, putting it in the future tense. If so, it would be translated that if we follow the spirit and not the letter of the Law, we will be convicted in the area of tongue control—and will avoid name-calling. We will agree with our adversaries quickly and put things right with them immediately. We will, if we live in the realm of the un-grieved Spirit, avoid lusting or causing another to lust. We will not bring in God's name to make ourselves look good. We will not seek personal vengeance when we are hurt, but will intercede for those who have hurt us.

Comparison Between the Father and Us

"Be perfect, therefore, as your heavenly Father is perfect." This seems unfair, certainly if it were intended as an absolute command for Jesus' followers if they want to inherit the Kingdom. After all, God the Father is perfect absolutely in every conceivable way: in knowledge, wisdom and power, and in being present everywhere. And yet Jesus compares us to His Father—that we might imitate Him.

Like it or not, our children imitate us. It scares me to death when I think of my children completely imitating me! I remember how at my old church in Fort Lauderdale our three-year-old son, T. R., as soon as the service was over, would go up to the platform and sit in my chair. He would smile at the people. "Who do you think you are, T. R.?" people would say to him. "I'm my daddy," he would reply.

Jesus wants all of us to be like His Father. But His commands are not "burdensome," says John (1 John 5:3). This shows that Jesus did not mean we had to be absolutely sinless as God is sinless. First of all, hungering and thirsting after righteousness—a perpetual state for those who know what they lack—is put as a most desirable spiritual condition (Matthew 5:6). Not only that, but He would not have given us the Lord's Prayer, which includes the petition, "Forgive us our debts [sins, trespasses]" (Matthew 6:12). Moreover, we are told that if we claim to be without sin, "we deceive ourselves and the truth is not in us" (1 John 1:8).

Matthew 5:48 is not teaching that we should be sinlessly perfect or self-consciously perfect.

We are not encouraged to believe we can attain to a superior status whereby we can look down on others. Paul certainly did not feel he had "arrived," so to speak. Indeed, "Not that I have already obtained all this, or have already been made perfect, but I press on to take hold of that for which Christ Jesus took hold of me. Brothers, I do not consider myself yet to have taken hold of it. But one thing I do: Forgetting what is behind and straining toward what is ahead, I press on toward the goal to win the prize for which God has called me heavenward in Christ Jesus" (Philippians 3:12–14).

Dr. Martyn Lloyd-Jones observed that Jesus did not say that we are to be perfect as God is perfect, but rather "as your heavenly Father is perfect." He is referring to the way the Father treats us. Perhaps Paul summed it up best: "Aim for perfection" (2 Corinthians 13:11).

How We Are to Imitate the Father

God is, of course, the perfect Father. "Our fathers disciplined us for a little while as they thought best" (Hebrews 12:10). We all as parents do as we "think" best. That is the best any of us can do, as we try to get it right. But God is the perfect Father—He doesn't make mistakes. He has nothing to prove and deals with us with perfect wisdom.

Many of us correct our children to prove to others we are doing our job. We're constantly looking over our shoulders and thinking how we must appear to those watching, rather than doing what is best for our children. If our children misbehave in public, we will sometimes correct them publicly. But God has nothing to prove. He doesn't call the angels together and ask, "How do you think I did?" "God disciplines us for our good, that we may share in his holiness" (Hebrews 12:10). God never loses His temper when He disciplines us. But how many of us discipline our children when we have lost control?

We are to imitate our heavenly Father by controlling our temper. We will fail at this, says James. But with the words, "Be perfect," we are told to aim high—to keep working at it and not give up. God never loses His temper, being the perfect Father. But Hebrews 12:10 invites the comparison with earthly fathers, who are imperfect. Aiming for perfection is what Jesus means.

And not only controlling our temper, but our talk. God Himself never makes an idle comment. His Word is infallible, without error. If we control the tongue, we will be on our way to imitating the Father. But, thankfully, James, as I said, assures us that we all stumble in many ways with regard to tongue control. And yet if we walk in love—which is the same thing as walking in the un-grieved Spirit—"there is nothing in him to make him stumble" (1 John 2:10). You won't keep "sticking your foot in it."

We are to aim for perfection when it comes to sexual temptation. God Himself cannot be tempted (John 1:13). We must aim to reach the place that things don't tempt us as they once did. We will resist the temptation to lust, for example, so that our resistance becomes a habit or lifestyle. As for causing another person to lust—that is, intentionally stirring up his or her passions—this is unthinkable. God never tempts anybody. You and I are to be like Him. Never forget: The best way to avoid falling into sin is to avoid the temptation (Romans 13:14). It bears repeating: Strength in this area is not so much being tempted and resisting it as it is to anticipate where temptation will be and to avoid going there.

We are to imitate our Father by showing the aforementioned *uncommon* grace to those who have mistreated us. Being merciful to both the just and unjust is true godliness. Luke's rendering of the same principles shows Jesus saying, "Love your enemies, do good to them, and lend to them without expecting to get anything back." This is what makes us truly "sons of the Most High, because he is kind to the ungrateful and wicked. Be merciful, just as your Father is merciful" (Luke 6:35–36).

This is amazing. God does not even expect a thank-you from the unjust—but keeps on blessing them. This is an attainable perfection for us to seek after—to bless people, pray for them and do good to them "without expecting" any thanks for it! When Jesus prayed, "Father, forgive them, for they do not know what they are doing" (Luke 23:34), He did not expect them to thank Him. God doesn't even wait for the person to apologize—He just keeps on blessing!

There is a teaching in John Wesley's writings that will bear our examination, called "perfect love." "There is no fear in love. But perfect love drives out fear, because fear has to do with punishment. The one who fears is not made perfect in love" (1 John 4:18). When we are filled with fear, we want to punish those who have hurt us. But when we are made perfect in love, we back off from wanting to punish—and, instead, we pray for them.

This is the same love that will enable us to take the initiative—to move toward people to affirm them whether or not they will like us. If we wait for them to like us, we are no different from the world. When we love them regardless, we are showing love without any fear.

Attainable Perfection

Sinless perfection is unreachable and unattainable. But Matthew 5:44 is not talking about sinless perfection. It is Christian maturity. Here, then, are examples of reachable maturity:

Generosity. "Give to the one who asks you, and do not turn away from the one who wants to borrow from you" (Matthew 5:42). We can all do this.

In a previous chapter, we discussed how some people will take advantage of you—as they did with our Pilot Lights in London. But Jesus is saying to us: Let them take advantage of you. Give to them and do not expect to be paid back. In the same way that we do not expect a "thank you" from those we bless and pray for, so, too, here: Give, give and give—without expecting ever to be paid back.

As Jesus put it in another place, "Although they cannot repay you, you will be repaid at the resurrection of the righteous" (Luke 14:14). Not only that, "He who is kind to the poor lends to the LORD, and he will reward him for what he has done" (Proverbs 19:17). God loves a cheerful giver (2 Corinthians 9:7).

Gentleness. "The fruit of the Spirit is . . . gentleness" (Galatians 5:22–23). "Let your gentleness be evident to all" (Philippians 4:5). Perhaps the best single word to describe the Dove—the Holy Spirit—is gentleness. The wisdom that comes from "above" is "gentle" (James 3:17, KJV). This means that you are approachable, easy to talk with, not abrasive.

The easiest thing in the world to do is to grieve the Holy Spirit. The dove, at the natural level, is a very shy, sensitive bird. This is why the Holy Spirit is depicted as a dove. When you and I learn how not to grieve the Holy Spirit, the result will be that we will be gentle. Sweet.

Guilelessness. The opposite of guilelessness is being treacherous, or deceptive. The person who is imitating the love of the Father will be transparent. We will have no selfish agenda. One's behavior with the opposite sex will always be appropriate. There will be honesty in dealing with all.

Genuineness. In a word: The person is real. So many people we aspire to meet—admiring them from a distance—turn out to be less than genuine when you get up close to them. This is always so sad. The more you know about God, however, the more you love and admire Him and want to be like Him. It is a thrill, then, to meet someone you admire—and then, the closer you get to that person, the more "real" he or she is. We sometimes call it "the real deal." But people like that, I'm afraid, are rare.

Graciousness. This word, I think, is the sum total of all the Christian virtues. It is what puts people at ease. The Greek word *epeiekes* means "the opposite of judging." It is when you might have thrown the book at a person but let them off the hook instead. Graciousness is refusing to take a rigorous stand, although you might have done so with some justification. Being merciful as the Father is merciful sums up Jesus' teaching. What we call the Golden Rule comes up later (in Volume 2 of this book series)—doing to others as you wish they would do to you (Matthew 7:12).

Grace is getting what we don't deserve. Mercy is not getting what we do deserve, since we all deserve justice.

Would you like to throw the book at someone who has been manifestly unkind, who has sought to damage your reputation, who was cruel? Was it someone close to you? The natural reaction is to want justice—and to see that person get justice. Joseph hoped one day to say "Gotcha!" to his brothers. But he was gracious instead.

Perfect love casts out fear. Fear wants to throw the book. Perfect love is graciousness. That is Christian perfection.

35. No Reward in Heaven?

Be careful not to do your "acts of righteousness" before men, to be seen by them. If you do, you will have no reward from your Father in heaven.

MATTHEW 6:1

As we begin this next section of the greatest and most famous sermon ever preached, let me remind you that Matthew almost certainly has edited a lot of material and presented us with a distillation, or summary, of what Jesus taught on that mountain in Galilee. It was possibly preached over two or three days.

When Jesus gave us His sobering command, "Be perfect, therefore, as your heavenly Father is perfect" (Matthew 5:48), He was summarizing all He had taught regarding His interpretation and application of the Mosaic Law. But this command regarding perfection could equally be an introduction to what follows. I can tell you, keep the teaching that is coming up, and you will be perfect!

Jesus now returns to the subject of reward in heaven. He first mentioned this at the climax of the Beatitudes: "Great is your reward in heaven" when you are persecuted for His sake (Matthew 5:12). But for many Christians, the idea of reward is a new concept. I know some who actually find it offensive. You should not find this offensive at all. The truth is, the idea of reward is a very important strand in both Jesus' and Paul's teaching. It is a merciful motivation to get us to do, or not do, what we will later be so very thankful for.

Some might think Jesus is contradicting Himself. Having told us to let our good works shine before men (Matthew 5:16), He now warns us not to let our acts of righteousness be seen of men. But there is a big difference between these two commands. The first refers to our duty to let the world clearly see that our lives have been changed by grace—that we are unashamed to be the people of God. Such obedience therefore glorifies our Father in heaven. The teaching that Jesus now introduces in Matthew 6:1 warns us

against trying to be pious in order for people to admire us and stand in awe of us. Whereas the previous teaching was designed to glorify God, what Jesus now condemns is that which would glorify ourselves—not God—by our "show" of righteousness.

Jesus introduces this section with a negative—in fact, two negatives: "Be careful not to do . . . [or] you will have no reward." Except for the section on the Lord's Prayer, much of Matthew 6 is filled with negatives: how not to give, how not to pray, how not to fast, not laying up treasures on earth, not to worry. This is necessary teaching. We are all by nature self-righteous. If you don't see yourself this way, you have even a more serious problem!

An essential part of the Holy Spirit's convicting us of our sinful nature is for us to see our proneness to self-righteousness. As sparks fly upward, so do we yearn for people to admire us. We crave it. Dale Carnegie, author of *How to Win Friends and Influence People,* said the desire to feel important is the strongest urge in the world. Indeed, like a volcano waiting to erupt, there is that in us which starves for earthly approval and recognition. This is why Jesus began this section by saying, "Be careful."

This is very important teaching for another reason. It is very easy to lose a reward. John warned lest one lose what he has worked for, so "you may be rewarded fully" (2 John 8). One of the saddest things in the world is that a fellow Christian can cause another Christian to lose his or her reward. I have seen it happen. It makes one weep. Be sure that the advice you are getting from another Christian is solid and sound. What a pity if you lose your reward because you took bad counsel.

By the way, if you are opposed to the concept of "reward," I can give you a guarantee how you won't have to worry about receiving one in heaven: merely do your acts of righteousness for the purpose of being seen by people. That will take care of it. Those who say, "I don't need to be motivated by reward—I do it to glorify God," betray a very subtle self-righteousness creeping in. Jesus also warned about those who "justify yourselves in the eyes of men, but God knows your hearts. What is highly valued among men is detestable in God's sight" (Luke 16:15).

Not a Sinless Perfection

The perfection Jesus challenges us to reach is not a sinless perfection—but it is certainly a highly refined and yet attainable perfection. This perfection is an inward state that only God knows about—and we are to make sure that only God knows about it. It is unrewarded by people because they are unable to see it! We are cautioned by Jesus, therefore, to strive that only God sees when we do acts of righteousness. It pleases Him when we make sure He is the only one who knows.

So much of Jesus' teaching in Matthew 6 is summed up in that challenging verse, also directed to the Pharisees: "How can you believe if you accept praise from one another, yet make no effort to obtain the praise that comes from the only God?" (John 5:44). Living this way tests the human spirit to the hilt. It is a concept of righteousness that never entered the Pharisees' minds. And yet if we grasp this, I must ask: Are we up to this? Am I? It is not easy.

The Sermon on the Mount therefore gets more challenging with every sentence Jesus utters. This is arguably the most challenging section yet. But it is also the key to a greater anointing. This is the way to inherit the realm of the un-grieved Spirit of God.

When we compare the good works that Jesus mentioned in Matthew 5:16 to the acts of righteousness He espouses in Matthew 6, it is obviously a contrasted righteousness. As we saw, Matthew 5:16 says to let others see your good works, whereas Matthew 6:1 says to not let them see your good works. F. F. Bruce summed it up nicely: "Show what you are tempted to hide, hide what you are tempted to show." Matthew 5:16 suggests we must overcome a temptation to cowardice; Matthew 6:1 points to the temptation to vanity.

Two Kinds of Righteousness: Moral and Religious

There is another way to contrast the two kinds of righteousness: a moral righteousness and a religious righteousness. The moral righteousness is when you reflect the Ten Commandments. A religious righteousness is when you reflect an unsanctified ego.

The unsanctified ego wants to make sure people know how much you give, how much you pray and how often you fast. God wants these acts to be done in secret—absolutely privately—so that only He will know. That way, He alone gets the glory. Moral righteousness, however, is to be seen. This brings glory to God. Even though we are not under the Law, the outward lives of Jesus' followers will always reflect the outward righteousness of the Law. Always. But religious righteousness is to be inward and should not be seen.

You and I, therefore, have an opportunity to bring double glory to God: (1) outward morality—for people to see—and (2) inward obedience—for only God to see. I may be tempted to tell you of how much I give and pray because I want you to think more highly of me. But I make the decision not to tell you because I want only God to know. Our outward moral godliness leaves people without excuse. Our inward, concealed godliness gives God alone the glory.

We are therefore talking about a concealed righteousness in this section of the Sermon on the Mount. Notice how Jesus puts it: Be careful not to do your acts of righteousness before men "to be seen" by them. Doing this to be seen is what guarantees you no reward in heaven. But when you conceal your giving, praying and fasting, it glorifies God and guarantees a reward in heaven.

This cuts right across the Pharisees' religious spirit. Jesus said of them, "Everything they do is done for men to see" (Matthew 23:5). Their motivation to give, pray or fast is out the window if there is nobody there to watch! Their sole motivation was not the honor of God, but their pride. If there is nobody out there to see that they are righteous, they would not bother to be righteous at all.

Are you a Pharisee? Do you give so that people will know? Would you not give if you found out nobody would know? Would you lose heart to give if your giving were to be utterly concealed? Then you are like the ancient Pharisees. Worse still, however, is that you will receive no reward in heaven.

Awareness and Presence of God

Behind what Jesus is saying in this section is the realization of the presence of and awareness of God. "Nothing in all creation is hidden from God's sight. Everything is uncovered and laid bare before the eyes of him to whom we must give account" (Hebrews 4:13).

You may well wear a mask and keep people from getting to know you. But when it comes to approaching God, you may as well take the mask off—He sees right through you. Said David, "O LORD, you have searched me and you know me. You know when I sit and when I rise; you perceive my thoughts from afar. You discern my going out and my lying down; you are familiar with all my ways. Before a word is on my tongue you know it completely, O LORD" (Psalm 139:1–4).

The phrase "presence of God" is to be understood in more than one way. There is a time when God's presence is felt—which is wonderful. And there is a time when God's presence is not felt—but He is equally there. This is because He sees all, knows all, and nothing whatever escapes His notice. Nothing. We love it, of course, when God makes His presence felt. It is what we long for and pray for. But never forget that He is with you whether or not you feel Him. Therefore, be aware that He is aware—60 seconds a minute, 60 minutes an hour, 24 hours a day.

When I was a boy I used to hear this old spiritual:

> He sees all you do, he hears all you say,
> my Lord's a-writin' all the time.
>
> Anonymous

It reminds one of Malachi 3:16: "Then those who feared the LORD talked with each other, and the LORD listened and heard. A scroll of remembrance was written in his presence concerning those who feared the LORD and honored his name." God sees all, hears all, knows all. When we realize this, then you and I should learn to get our joy totally from knowing He knows and sees. He equally sees our hearts and knows our motives, whether we do what we do to be seen by people or not.

Here is a word that I have called my most un-favorite verse in the Bible: "But I tell you," said Jesus, "that men will have to give account on the day of judgment for every careless word they have spoken" (Matthew 12:36). I hope no reader of this book will be standing near me when I am made to give an account of every idle word I have spoken!

Concealed righteousness means that we will not let it compete with what is for God's eyes or ears alone. If I don't conceal it, then it means I did what I did for people to see. But if I conceal it and nobody knows, it is only for God—and that makes all the difference!

> Two roads diverged in a wood, and I,
> I took the road less traveled by,
> And that has made all the difference.
>
> Robert Frost (1874–1963)

A Chosen Righteousness

We must make a choice. We are therefore talking about a chosen righteousness. I choose to be careful or not to be careful. I choose to conceal my "righteous acts" or reveal them. I choose to seek the honor that comes from God only, or pursue the honor and praise that comes from telling people. It is not an easy choice to make. This does not merely refer to the examples Jesus will use—giving, praying, fasting. It affects every area of your life and mine. For example, do I angle to receive a compliment? Do I make people notice whether I am a man of prayer, am misunderstood or have sacrificed for the Lord?

The question is: Whose "well done" is more important to you—from people or from God? I remember preaching at an Easter People conference in southern England. It was a rather important conference with a lot of people present, and I really wanted to do a good job. When I finished, not a single soul said a word! The organizers merely said, "Thank you for coming." I hoped for a crumb at least. Nothing. I was tempted to say, "I trust I was a blessing tonight," but I knew that would be fishing! I worried as I drove all the way back to London—did I do okay, or not?

Every public speaker and every preacher under the sun knows exactly what I am talking about. But I see this sort of challenge as a test of whether or not the praise from God means more than what people say.

If they compliment you without your hinting for it, you don't lose your reward. But when they compliment you after you reminded them, then—sorry—you lose your reward. "Let another praise you, and not your own mouth; someone else, and not your own lips" (Proverbs 27:2). If I conceal my "acts of righteousness," God will say, "Well done." If I reveal my thoughts and righteous deeds, God says, "That's all the reward you get." Remember the old spiritual, "Nobody knows the troubles I've seen, nobody knows but Jesus"? That's the way God likes it. He wants to be the only one "in the know" about you!

We must not forget that this is an inner righteousness that Jesus has commanded. It is a command not to unveil any piety you may have before people. God is a jealous God. He wants you all to Himself. He wants to know whether His "well done" means more to you than man's "well done." We are commanded to outdo the righteousness of the Pharisees and teachers of the Law. The difference is that they tell it—making sure all see what they have done—and we cannot do that. That way, by not telling it, says Jesus, we surpass their righteousness—in God's sight. They made "no effort," said Jesus, to obtain the honor and praise that comes only from God (John 5:44).

But we all forget, and sometimes we don't realize we are tooting our own horns when we let something slip out. I like to think that lady back in Fort Lauderdale who visited housebound people all week didn't realize what she was revealing when she told a group of us what she did, then added, "The joy is in not telling it." The principle is the same—whether we can go through a trial without complaining, sacrificing without telling it or giving up a lot for God and keeping quiet about it. A man in England known for his cynicism surprised his friends by accepting a knighthood from the Queen. When asked why he accepted it he said, "Nobody should reject a knighthood unless they

can keep quiet about it. I knew I couldn't, so I accepted it." Honest man!

What Jesus does in these lines is to promise us a crowned righteousness. God will crown our success in seeking the honor that comes from Him alone, with His own reward. It is a reward worth seeking and waiting for. I would have thought it is the greatest single thing that can come to a child of God—to receive that honor from Him. What is more, it is within the reach of everyone—whether you are a high- or low-profile Christian, whether or not you are educated, whether you are the "eye or the hand" in the body (see 1 Corinthians 12:14–26). God knows who concealed their piety and who gave in to the temptation to blab their righteous deeds to people around them.

Note this: Jesus refers to a reward "in" heaven not a reward "of" heaven. Had He said "reward of heaven," it would imply salvation by works—that our giving, praying and fasting without telling it gets us to heaven. No. Salvation is by grace through faith—not of works, lest anyone should boast (Ephesians 2:8–9). But it is a reward "in" heaven. It is what *will* be given to us. God may give an earnest of that reward here below, as in a greater anointing—that is not unlikely indeed. But Jesus is anticipating what Paul would teach: that at the Judgment Seat of Christ, one gives an account of the things done in the body (2 Corinthians 5:10).

There are Greek words that are relevant: *misthos*—"reward," used 29 times in the New Testament, 5 times in the Sermon on the Mount; *brabrion*—"prize," as in 1 Corinthians 9:24 and Philippians 3:14; *stephanos*—"crown," as in 2 Timothy 4:8 and James 1:12; *charis*—translated "credit" ("if you love those who love you, what credit is that to you?") in Luke 6:32; *doxa*—"glory," "praise," "honor" as in John 5:44.

It will not be a pretty sight when Christians who have shown contempt for this teaching on rewards themselves receive no reward. They will watch others hear our Lord say, "Well done," and look on. They will be saved by fire (1 Corinthians 3:15) but have no crown to cast before King Jesus. Never forget: The greater our reward, the greater His glory. Our crowned righteousness will be recognized by Him before all. God will not be jealous of our receiving glory then—it was His idea. His jealousy will be shown toward those who could not wait for praise but had to have it here below.

"No reward in heaven" is a threatening promise. Jesus gives a clear guarantee: Those who can't wait but feel the need to get glory and praise now, who complain about their trials and tribulations and who boast how much they do for God, will receive no reward. That is a guarantee, says Jesus.

Martin Luther said he expects three surprises in heaven: (1) There will be those in heaven he did not expect to be there; (2) there will be those absent he thought would be there; but the greatest prize will be (3) that he is there himself! If I may paraphrase Luther, I expect three surprises: (1) There will be those who receive a reward I thought wouldn't get one, (2) there will be those who didn't receive a reward I thought would surely receive one, but the greatest surprise will be (3) that I myself will hear Jesus' "Well done."

I want that more than anything in the world.

36. Whose Admiration Matters?

*So when you give to the needy, do not announce it with trumpets, as
the hypocrites do in the synagogues and on the streets, to be honored by
men. I tell you the truth, they have received their reward in full.*

We are seeing in this section of the Sermon on the Mount a deeper and more subtle kind of perfection. Much of Matthew 5 pertains to moral righteousness—outward, what people see—but Jesus now turns to religious righteousness—inward, what they are not supposed to see. The Pharisees wanted their righteousness to be seen in order to have the praise of people. Jesus is telling His followers to be different—to keep this righteousness hidden. Why? Because a reward in heaven is at stake.

Religious righteousness refers sometimes to spirituality—that is, how spiritual or godly you really are. How much communion with God do you have? How well do you really know God? How much do you love Him? Do you truly hear from Him? How much do you pray or read your Bible?

The difference between Jesus and the Pharisees can be summed up: Jesus wants spirituality to be before God alone, for our piety to be absolutely in secret. The Pharisees wanted their righteous acts to be seen. After all, said Jesus, "Everything they do is done for men to see" (Matthew 23:5).

This deeper or subtler perfection Jesus is now requiring is a further example of how Christians are not only to outclass the Law but to surpass the righteousness of the Pharisees and teachers of the Law.

Four Assumptions

As we look at Matthew 6:2 we see four assumptions. First, that you and I will be financial givers—which includes giving to the poor.

Jesus says "when," not "if," in giving to the needy. Behind this teaching are Moses' words: "Give generously to him [the needy] and do so without a grudging heart; then because of this the LORD your God will bless you in all your work and in everything you put your hand to. There will always be poor people in the land. Therefore I command you to be openhanded toward your brothers and toward the poor and needy in your land" (Deuteronomy 15:10–11). Jesus also said this: "You will always have the poor among you" (John 12:8). Moreover, if you need a further motivation to give to needy people, remember this: "He who is kind to the poor lends to the Lord, and he will reward him for what he has done" (Proverbs 19:17).

I sometimes wonder about churches that are almost entirely middle-class—and want to keep it that way. We all know by now the evil of ethnic cleansing in certain parts of the world. But when we try to control the type of people who come to our churches, it is a greater evil. The poor we have with us always, but when we try to erect a church devoid of the poor, we not only go against Jesus' own assumption but also avoid a solemn responsibility to the poor. We should welcome our share of poor people into our ranks, lest we grieve the Holy Spirit.

The second assumption is that a reward for giving is inevitable. There is a reward that comes from God, and there is a reward that comes from people. If you give to be seen by men, then you forfeit any reward from our Father in heaven. If you give to be seen by men moreover, you will be rewarded, yes—but that will be the sum total of your reward.

Receiving the reward "in full" means that the pleasure you received from people knowing is the only reward there is. There is none to come from God. But the notion of reward is assumed one way or the other. This means it is not a question whether you will be rewarded for giving. The question is, who rewards? God or men?

The third assumption in these lines is that God sees everything we do. This is a reference to the unconscious presence of God. You may not feel Him. But you are in His presence, and He is right there looking at all you do.

Like it or not, you can't run from God. "Where can I go from your Spirit?" asked the psalmist. "Where can I flee from your presence? If I go up to the heavens, you are there; if I make my bed in the depths, you are there. If I rise on the wings of the dawn, if I settle on the far side of the sea, even there your hand will guide me, your right hand will hold me fast" (Psalm 139:7–10). So, if you give without fanfare, doing so quietly and secretly, "your Father, who sees what is done in secret, will reward you" (Matthew 6:4).

There is a fourth assumption in these verses that underlies this entire section: Whose admiration matters? We must make a choice between the admiration of people and God's honor, as in John 5:44: "How can you believe if you accept praise from one another, yet make no effort to obtain the praise that comes from the only God?" "They loved praise from men more than praise from God" (John 12:43).

I used to feel so sad when a person would hand me a check for Westminster Chapel and ask me to give it to the treasurer. They wanted to make sure I saw it first! Such a person simply chose to get their reward from my knowing rather than God knowing.

The issue is whether we demand getting the credit for the good that was accomplished. Are you willing to forfeit the credit? Or is it too much to allow another to get the credit? As we saw above, the desire to feel important is the most urgent desire we have. And so the question is, are we willing to get the feeling of significance from God Himself—alone? Or must we instead have the praise of people?

We Are Created with a Need for Significance

We all want to be affirmed. We all want to have significance. God made us that way. But must that significance come from God—or men?

Psychologists refer to one's "self-image"—how you see yourself. Whether you have high or low self-esteem. Whether you have a sense of self-worth or you have a feeling of being inadequate all the time. We tend to develop this from childhood, from parents, authority figures and peer relationships. God made us with a need of feeling significant, but do we get that significance from God—or from people's affirmation?

If affirmation from people comes despite your sincere effort to receive the praise that comes from God, this is legitimate and may even be one of the ways God reveals His pleasure with you. But if you deliberately choose to put the praise of people first, then the only reward you get is their praise.

I can tell you, there is tremendous help that is being offered to you in these lines. There is not only spiritual help implied, but also psychological help, emotional help. If you and I were to develop an appetite for the praise that comes from God, the satisfaction is enormous when God gives it. It can come in more than one way: It may come immediately and directly from the Holy Spirit, or God may have someone affirm you to encourage you. When you were seeking first His Kingdom (Matthew 6:33) and someone encourages you without your manipulating things to make it happen, it is a strong hint that God is pleased with you!

When you live for one thing—the praise of God—He looks down and says, "Good!" And He has a way of communicating to you His pleasure. It is a wonderful, wonderful feeling to sense that "God says I'm okay."

Jesus Draws a Caricature

Jesus portrays a caricature of vain people who give to be seen. They hire a band to play when they give! "So when you give to the needy, do not announce it with trumpets, as the hypocrites do in the synagogues and on the streets, to be honored by men." He describes those who could not give and keep quiet about it. Indeed, they made sure the world knew when they gave to the poor! If they could not get credit, they took no delight in giving.

The question is, can you give—whether to the poor, to charity or the church—and keep quiet about it? Some people only give if there are strings attached, if they can control how the money is spent, or especially if some sort of recognition is promised. I recall a delicate situation at the Chapel. A man left a sizeable sum of money to the Chapel after his death—but with one stipulation, that a plaque was put somewhere for everybody to see.

What were we going to do? The decision was eventually made by the deacons to reject the money. What disappointed me, however, was that the man who died had sat a good while under my own ministry! I would have thought he would know better. It goes to show that people can hear teaching week after week and never apply it to themselves as they should.

It is unsettling to see how vain people can be. It is unsettling to see how vain religious people can be. There are probably those around you whom you admire, their apparent devotion and godliness. But it is often true that if you got very close to them you might be disillusioned.

I had two such disillusioning experiences. I recall an old veteran of the faith—a legend in his movement as I grew up. People almost "whispered" his name, he was so revered. Then one day I saw him for myself. I was barely ten years old, hardly old enough to have a lot of discernment. But even as a ten-year-old boy I noticed this man's arrogance. He wore a white suit, guaranteeing that people noticed him. Nobody else had a white suit! But he did. It was obviously to draw attention to himself.

My second disillusioning experience was when I asked a man to pray for me, to lay his hands on me that I might have a greater blessing of God on my life. Just before we prayed, I (for some reason) asked him how old he was. Perhaps I shouldn't have, but I did. As soon as he finished praying for me—I mean, immediately after he said, "Amen"—he asked, "Don't tell anybody my age." I don't remember a single thing he prayed—I only remember him saying, "Don't tell anybody my age." It was such a letdown moment for a young Christian.

My point is this. There are those we admire—perhaps a little bit too much—until we get close to them. I have lived long enough to report to anybody that every single person I have ever found myself admiring a little bit too much sooner or later disappointed me.

Everybody admired the Pharisees in Jesus' day. Jesus takes off their masks and points out that their piety was entirely external and synthetic. They were not genuine people. They wanted to be seen.

There is no evidence that almsgivers literally blew trumpets on their way to the Temple. But public fasts were sometimes proclaimed by the sounding of trumpets. At such times, prayers for rain were recited in the streets. Some thought that the giving of alms insured the efficacy of the fast. Whatever, the idea of "tooting your own horn" comes from this caricature Jesus paints to describe Pharisees.

Three Kinds of Hypocrites

The word *hypocrites* is a pure Greek word: *hypokrites*. In the ancient Greek, a *hypokrite* was an actor. By the first century, the term came to be used for those who play roles and see the world as their stage.

There were apparently three kinds of hypocrites: (1) one who feigns goodness but is actually evil and knows he is being deceptive, (2) one who is carried away by his own acting and deceives himself, being unaware of his own deceit but not fooling most onlookers, and (3) one who deceives himself into thinking he is acting for God's best interests—and also deceives onlookers. In Matthew 6:2, we are told their method: They announce their giving with trumpets. They do it in synagogues and in the streets. But their motive is narrowed down to one thing: to be seen of men. The love of the admiration of men. Everything they do is for men to see. If nobody sees, they will not give. It is not the needy they care about—their focus was on themselves. They make sure they get credit—from below, not from above—for what they do.

Whose admiration matters? The people's admiration. The admiration of people meant everything to them. It is what they lived for. Their piety was a charade—all for the glory of man. Take that away, and their motivation evaporates like water under a hot sun.

There is an unmistakable irony in all this. The irony is, instead of Jesus saying that the Pharisees would lose their reward, He said they got it—in full! "I tell you the truth, they have received their reward in full." So, do people like this really get a reward? Yes. They are rewarded in full, namely, the praise and admiration of men who saw them give. The honor of men is what they wanted—the honor of men is what they got. What they aimed for they got, in full. But that is all they will get.

"I Tell You the Truth": The Force of an Oath

You may recall that the phrase "I tell you the truth" is tantamount to the oath. It had the force of an oath. It is not that Jesus hadn't been telling the truth all along; it merely shows the absolute sense of dismay God Himself registers in heaven when people give with motives like that.

Jesus wants to demonstrate that God sees through people like this and rolls up His sleeves as if to swear an oath in wrath: "People like that will never get a reward beyond the praise of men in this life." I would hate to think God said this about me. It stirs me to want to give in a way that guarantees only God knows. The phrase "I tell you the truth" has a double force. It is Jesus' way of saying, "Mark it down. Count on it."

God swears an oath in two ways: in mercy and in wrath. He swore in mercy with regard to Abraham, who became willing to sacrifice his son Isaac. God was so pleased with Abraham's obedience! "I swear by myself, declares the LORD, that because you have done this and have not withheld your son, your only son, I will surely bless you and make your descendants as the stars in the sky and as the sand on the seashore" (Genesis 22:16–17).

When God swore this oath, the content of the promise was no different from what God had said to Abraham previously (Genesis 15:5). But by swearing an "oath," it put "an end to all argument" (Hebrews 6:16). It meant that nothing—ever—would stop his seed from being like the stars in the heaven or the sand on the seashore. There were two unchangeable things—the promise and the oath (Hebrews 6:18)—but the oath gave an infallible assurance. So when Jesus says, "I tell you the truth," He is intensifying the promise, as if to send a solemn signal to take this word very seriously indeed.

When God swears in wrath, it means that nothing, ever, will change it. He swore in His wrath that the ancient people of Israel would not enter into His rest (Hebrews 3:11). They tried to enter after God swore the oath, but they never made it. The oath finalizes the promise and guarantees its fulfillment regardless of circumstances once the oath has been sworn.

Therefore, when we made a choice for people to know that we have given, instead of only God knowing—mark it down, says Jesus: They have already got their reward in full. I don't want that to happen to me. Ever. God sees right through us when we angle for the praise of men and put the admiration of people prior to God's approval. When the praise of people is what we aim for—bull's-eye! And that sadly becomes our only reward.

Receiving the praise that comes from God is worth waiting for. "Since ancient times no one has heard, no ear has perceived, no eye has seen any God besides you, who acts on behalf of those who wait for him" (Isaiah 64:4). I will admit this to you: Waiting for God's honor and denying man's praise is not easy. Our egos don't die easily. But if we will somehow overcome the need to get our joy from the admiration of frail people, and seek God's praise, it is an honor worth waiting for indeed.

37. Who Gets the Credit?

But when you give to the needy, do not let your left hand know what
your right hand is doing, so that your giving may be in secret. Then
your Father, who sees what is done in secret, will reward you.

MATTHEW 6:3–4

This is one of the most important chapters in this section. It touches the heart of that verse we have seen again and again: "How can you believe if you accept praise from one another, yet make no effort to obtain the praise that comes from the only God?" (John 5:44).

Jesus' teaching on this matter is arguably the most challenging to the human ego of any I know. We all instinctively want to be thanked, to be noticed and to get recognition for something good we accomplished. The thought of being utterly anonymous is easy to admire but extremely difficult to apply and consistently carry out.

Although this chapter is mainly about giving to the poor, a fundamental principle lies behind the thinking of Jesus in these lines. It is: Who gets the credit for the good thing that is done? Whether in politics, medicine or the church, you find that people everywhere have huge egos. We cannot bear doing something worthwhile and people not noticing it.

I remember meeting a doctor in Florida who claimed to have had major input in John F. Kennedy's life before he became president. The doctor gave certain details, and I sensed the man wasn't making it up. The problem was, this doctor was bitter. He claimed to have made a significant difference in Kennedy's health, but Kennedy never gave him credit for it. So he ended up telling everybody his story.

I have seen something similar in the Church. When a great move of the Spirit breaks out, a person with a prophetic gift says, "Didn't I tell you this would happen?" When a person is healed, someone comes out of the woodwork to say, "I have been praying for this person for years." I know of at least two people who claim they were

the visiting evangelist when Billy Graham was converted. I know of a man who preached a great sermon—except that it was someone else's. (The one who wrote the original sermon could not bear not getting the credit, and the man who preached it acted as if it was his own.) Former President Ronald Reagan wanted to ensure he got the credit for ending the Cold War. Yet, as I have mentioned, he had a plaque on his desk that read: "There is no limit to how far a person can go as long as he doesn't care who gets the credit for it."

When we do what is right, will it be noticed? When we do what is commanded in Scripture, will people see it that way? When we do what is honorable, will it be appreciated?

Joseph did the honorable thing when he refused to sleep with Potiphar's wife (Genesis 39:7–20), but there is no hint he was ever vindicated in his own time. His vindication apparently came posthumously when Moses wrote up what actually happened. This alone suggests to me that it might sometimes be a good thing to be falsely accused and keep quiet about it—to see what God will do with you! In Joseph's case, he was an accused foreigner—an alleged Hebrew rapist—who was made prime minister of Egypt without being cleared of the crime that put him in prison in the first place. God can do anything.

Jesus' teaching about not letting our left hand know what our right hand is doing shows how easily we tend to take ourselves too seriously. I hope to show in this chapter some steps how we might not take ourselves so seriously. This word applies to those who fear that due recognition or appreciation won't come soon enough. Most of all, it shows God's timing and manner of giving us a recognition that is worth waiting for.

Healthy Giving

There is a pattern in Jesus' words that's worth noting: four pairs. The first pair is in His assumptions "when," in verse 2 and verse 3: "When you give to the needy." The second pair is "do not," in verse 2 and verse 3: "Do not announce it . . . do not let your left hand know."

Note the order: If we don't adhere to the first "do not," we certainly won't attain to the graceful habit of not letting our left hand know what our right hand is doing. Jesus said he who is faithful in that which is least is faithful also in much (Luke 16:10). The "least" is not to let anybody know we give. This builds up a habit whereby we don't even tell ourselves that we gave!

The third pair shows two purpose clauses: "to be honored by men" (verse 2) and "so that your giving may be in secret"(verse 4). The fourth pair shows the reward that follows each: "they have received their reward in full"—this being earthly praise (verse 2) and "your Father, who sees what is done in secret, will reward you" (verse 4)—when God shows what He will do if He gets all the glory.

There are two questions we might ask: Who gets the credit, and who gives the credit? Do you want people to give you the credit, or for God to give the credit? If you choose for God to give the credit, you will be rewarded in the way Jesus is urging for us to experience.

Healthy giving is refusing even to allow ourselves to think, *I've done well.* We should build up a discipline of not congratulating ourselves for something that is right. We must not only conceal our giving from people, we must refuse to gloat inwardly that we have done something big by our giving.

Logical Impossibility

And yet we are talking about a logical impossibility. Not letting your right hand know what your left hand is doing not only seems impossible but seems way out of reach. To achieve this lofty goal means we begin by hiding our giving from other people who might praise us. As long as you tell others what you did that was good and right, you are not going to be able to keep this knowledge from yourself!

The logical impossibility, then, is to overcome the obvious fact that you most certainly do know what you have given—to whom, when and how much.

But this line of thinking crosses over into other disciplines. We know how much we pray and fast—and how often. We do know the wrong that people have done to us. We also know whether we have totally forgiven them. We know when we have experienced deep and severe trials—and whether we tried to dignify those trials.

What about compliments given to us? We do remember the compliments—and also the complaints and the criticisms. When you witness to a lost person—a wonderful thing to do—you know what you did. You know whether you helped someone get to church with ease, whether you helped in doing menial things at church, whether you welcomed strangers.

In other words, we all have a fairly shrewd idea if we have done what is right and good and whether we did a job well. It is, therefore, a logical impossibility not to let your left hand know what your right hand did. So, how do we do it?

This means we refuse to congratulate ourselves for something that was absolutely right to do. This does not mean you live in denial or repress knowledge of what happened. To quote Michael Eaton, this is Jesus' playful and humorous way of speaking of our deliberately not focusing on ourselves or what we are doing.

In a word: We do it as unto God—and then forget it. As John Stott put it, not only are we not to tell other people—there is also a sense in which we do not even tell ourselves. Why? It is because self-consciousness can quickly become self-righteousness. When you are self-conscious in doing what is right, you are in danger of becoming smug—if not also obnoxious. Our aim, said John Calvin, must be that God is our sole witness.

It is like coming to Christ in the first place. As the hymn writer Toplady put it, "In my hand no price I bring, simply to Thy cross I cling." You aren't gloating about your need; you are focusing on Christ. In the same way, when you have done what is right you focus on God. You should no more want credit for what you did than you want credit for being a sinner. We come on bended knee for mercy in need of grace. It is much the same when we have done what is right: We are all unprofitable servants, only doing our duty (Luke 17:10).

An Honorable Motive

Our motive, said Jesus, is to give "in secret." What we gave, when, why, where, how, to whom and how much is "secret." Likewise, our praying and fasting is "secret"—known only to God.

Not only that, the wrong done to us is "secret." Total forgiveness begins with not telling anybody what "they" did to us. But there is more: When we have totally forgiven them, we must not boast of this to the world. Nor do we say to the person, "I forgive you for what you did to me" (almost always counterproductive). It must happen in the heart. (Tell them you forgive them only when they want to hear this.) Furthermore, don't gloat that you have forgiven them. After all, total forgiveness is your duty before God.

As for the great trial you are in, pour your complaint out only to God—a legitimate and edifying thing to do (Psalm 142:2). It might be a good thing if you kept your compliments to yourself, too—that it is a sweet secret you share only with God (and it also helps keep others from being jealous). How you cope in dignifying the trial should also be for God's ears only. God loves being the sole witness. When we can sing with the slaves in the Deep South of generations ago, "Nobody knows the troubles I've seen but Jesus," remember that He likes it that way—being the only One in the know.

What if the day came when God said to you in an unmistakable manner, "Now I know you really love Me?" He did that with Abraham!

To do what is put in this chapter requires internal willpower. We begin by refusing to think about it—the good we've done or the evil done to us; the compliment or the criticism. There is a story about the beloved "Uncle Buddy Robinson" in my old denomination. Someone came up to him after a sermon, "Uncle Buddy, that is the greatest sermon I ever heard." Uncle Buddy prayed, "O Lord, don't let me get puffed up." Seconds later someone said to him, "That is the worst sermon I ever heard." He then prayed, "O Lord, don't let me get puffed down!" We must constantly reject thoughts that make us feel self-righteous so that it becomes a graceful habit.

It is wrong to keep a record of wrongs (1 Corinthians 13:5)—which means throwing up the other's past mistakes. It is equally wrong to keep a record of rights—that is, registering when you have done a good thing. And never, ever say, "I told you so" (which shows you kept a record of wrongs).

A Lofty Goal

We all sin when it comes to carrying out Jesus' words perfectly. None of us is perfect. But if we aspire to receive the honor that comes from God only, this "road less traveled" is the choice we must all make. We are talking about a lofty goal—one we can aim at. God could do it for us in one stroke—if He chose to. He did this for Moses, whose face shone but Moses did not know it (Exodus 34:29). Apart from God doing it for us, Jesus is telling us what you and I can do. If we were to carry out Jesus' recommendation consistently, we would reach the place we become almost impervious to criticism and praise. If we keep this up, we won't take ourselves so seriously.

The problem is, we all want to impress each other. We are all desperate for approval.

Jesus knows this. He is giving us a way forward. His words are a lesson how to fight against self-conscious valor, virtue and value. This apparently will be achieved by some. "The righteous will answer him, 'Lord, when did we see you hungry and feed you, or thirsty and give you something to drink? When did we see you a stranger and invite you in, or needing clothes and clothe you? When did we see you sick or in prison and go to visit you?' The King will reply, 'I tell you the truth, whatever you did for one of the least of these brothers of mine, you did for me'" (Matthew 25:37–40).

Living like this is a lifelong pursuit. Call it a "life sentence," if you will—you must do it as long as you live. We are not talking about a self-conscious, once-for-all achievement. (In such a moment, we just lost it.) In the instant we think to ourselves, *Ah, I have managed not to let my left hand know what my right hand did,* it shows we did let our left hand know what our right hand did!

It is a lifelong interaction of keeping your eyes on Jesus. You pursue this, work at it and keep at it until you are unaware you do it. It makes me think of Arthur Blessitt, who has probably witnessed to more lost people on a one-to-one basis than anybody I know. And yet Arthur told me in all honesty that his greatest failure is that he does not witness to enough people. He comes pretty close to not letting his left hand know what his right hand does.

The best fishing guide on the planet is Harry Spear. He works harder than any guide I have fished with, poling the boat with enormous energy and rigor. I once asked him, "Harry, how do you do that?" His reply: "Once you think about it you've lost it, so one doesn't think about it."

Hidden Graciousness

All of our "acts of righteousness" are to be concealed, says Jesus. Giving is a gracious thing to do, but it should be a hidden graciousness. Forgiving evil that is done to us is a gracious thing to do, but we are not to broadcast to the world what noble thing we did. When tempted to say "I told you so," we are to say nothing. The closest Jesus came to this was merely looking straight at Peter when the rooster crowed (Luke 22:61). That look—without anything being said by Jesus that would add insult to injury—caused Peter to sob his heart out.

The moment we advertise how we got it right, we forfeit the greatest joy of heaven and earth—the Father's own reward. I fear that few enjoy this. Our goal, therefore, is to do our best to keep any graciousness hidden. If I say "I am being gracious to you," I haven't made you feel better. I am only calling attention to my deed, thus focusing on myself. And even if I but think I have shown valor and courage, I will begin to feel self-righteous. That self-righteousness will stand out like a hideous, running sore, not to mention my forfeiting the greatest honor that anybody can receive: the Father's praise.

I appreciate that what I have written in this chapter goes against our grain. We do not find this easy to do. This is why I said at the beginning of this book that it is arguable whether the "perfection" Jesus commanded in Matthew 5:48 referred to what He had already taught or what He was getting ready to teach. We are all self-righteous by nature. Its twin—self-pity—is always lurking by our side as well. Aim nonetheless for utter secrecy when it comes to doing what is good, right and noble.

Guaranteed Honor

Even if few experience this, the promise is not in vain: "Then"—*then*—"your Father, who sees what is done in secret, will reward you." Note the two words, "when" and "then." When we do our good deeds in secret, then our Father will reward us openly. When we have dignified the trial—which is done in part by keeping quiet about it—then the Father will reward us. When we are gracious, then the Father will show His pleasure.

"When" refers to God's timing. It may be in the here and now; it may be in the then and there! Don Carson says that the locale and nature of the reward is in time and eternity. God may reward us below (2 Corinthians 9:6–8). He may vindicate us below (Revelation 3:9). But the inexpressible and incalculable joy will be on that Day of days when we hear from the lips of Jesus Himself, "Well done." When the Righteous Judge of the universe begins the roll call, you will hear names nobody has heard of. One by one they will reply, "Me? Me? What did I ever do to receive such a smile from God?"

It is because God sees. Hagar learned this a long time ago: "You are the God who sees me" (Genesis 16:13). God knew her every hurt and her every move.

The devil loves to flatter. He will put thoughts in your mind that are geared to make you take yourself too seriously. He comes as an angel of light (2 Corinthians 11:14). The best word I ever read from the great William Perkins was, "Don't believe the devil even when he tells the truth." When you meet someone who knows his or her "worth," it is a complete turnoff.

Who gets the credit? Who said it first? Who gave the money? Who had that idea? Who prayed for the healing? Who brought enemies together? Who was the mover or shaker that made this or that happen? Do you insist on getting the credit? Or can you wait until God's "then"? "Then your Father, who sees what is done in secret, will reward you."

I will say it again. It is a reward worth waiting for.

38. Why Not Pray?

And when you pray, do not be like the hypocrites, for they love to pray
standing in the synagogues and on the street corners to be seen by men.
I tell you the truth, they have received their reward in full.

MATTHEW 6:5

Jesus now introduces the subject of prayer, but in doing so He applies His current theme. He gives the same lesson on prayer as He had just given regarding giving. This is not, in fact, the first reference to prayer in the Sermon on the Mount. He previously talked about loving our enemies and praying for them (Matthew 5:44). But He is now prepared to treat this matter of prayer in more detail, ending up with what the Church calls the "Lord's Prayer" (Matthew 6:9–13).

The way He treats prayer in these verses is in two sets of negatives and positives: The first negative tells us how not to pray (6:5), while the first positive tells us how to pray (6:6). The second negative tells us further how not to pray (6:7–8), while the second positive tells us how to pray by introducing the Lord's Prayer.

What a privilege to learn from our Lord, the greatest man of prayer who ever was. He shares with us why one should not pray: to be seen by men. He then amazingly shares with us why one should pray: to be rewarded. Does this surprise you? So we are going to be spoon-fed by Jesus Himself on this glorious subject of prayer.

How often do you thank God for the privilege of prayer? It is a privilege that no amount of words can calculate.

In this chapter, we will focus on how not to pray. Why not pray? There is a good reason not to pray—if your motive is to be seen of men.

As in the case of giving, Jesus begins with an assumption: that His followers will pray. The people of God are a people of prayer. "When you pray," not "if" you pray. This also assumes there is a time when we pray.

Question: Is there a time when *you* pray? Do you have a set time in your daily life for prayer? I

was deeply influenced when I was young by hearing Mrs. E. Howard Cadle singing each morning over the radio, "'Ere you left your room this morning, did you think to pray?" From this I wrote what could turn out to be my most important book, *Did You Think to Pray?*

So my question: Is there a time when you pray? Is it in your schedule? If it is not in your schedule, chances are you won't do it—at least very often. Do you remember to get to work each day on time? Do you manage to read a paper or catch the news? Jesus assumes there is also a time when we pray. This also means there is a time when we are not praying. Remember, there will be no praying in heaven. What praying that is done will be carried out here on earth.

Giving is an effort, and so is prayer. We must take the time to do it. Paul says "pray continually," yes (1 Thessalonians 5:17). But there is also prayer that is specific, timed, planned, looked forward to, enjoyed and experienced. This is rather different from being in a constant attitude of prayer, or praying when you are in trouble or when things aren't going well. Jesus is talking about a time to pray when everything else for the moment is put to one side. It requires concentration, undivided attention and care.

Sometimes, although not necessarily always, prayer can be work. Try it when praying with others. You will find it is easier to talk with each other than to stop talking and do nothing but to pray. John Wesley once reckoned every Christian should spend twice as much time in prayer as they do talking with each other. When I met the famed Romanian pastor Richard Wurmbrand (1909–2001) years ago, he said to me, "Young man, spend more time talking to God about men than you do talking to men about God." It is easier to talk to one another than to pray. But Jesus assumes there will be a time "when you pray."

How much do you pray? Children spell love T-I-M-E. What if God measured your love for Him by the amount of time you spend in prayer?

It is no small thing to pray, to take the time to do it and realize what you are doing. It is therefore not only a privilege to learn from Jesus, it is such a privilege to pray. And yet Jesus said of the hypocrites, "They love to pray." That phrase gives me pause. Hypocrites love to pray. It is enough to put you off prayer! One wants to be the very opposite of people like that, but we must not let that sort of thing deter us. Neither must we allow their self-righteous example push us to another extreme and make us falsely modest about praying.

Listen to Paul: "I kneel before the Father" (Ephesians 3:14). "We pray for you" (Colossians 1:3). "I constantly remember you in my prayers" (2 Timothy 1:3).

He was not trying to impress the Ephesians, the Colossians or Timothy—he wanted to encourage them. We can therefore encourage people when we let them know we pray for them. Josif Tson, another Romanian pastor, broke down in tears when Dr. Lloyd-Jones told him he had prayed for Josif every night for several years.

Some Lessons for Us

There are some lessons for us in this section of the Sermon on the Mount. First, there is a kind of praying that does not please God. Does this surprise you? One might have thought that any kind of praying is surely a good thing. Wrong. There is a praying that profanes God's name and is contrary to His nature.

Wrong praying is when you abuse His name and show contempt for what He is like. For example, "I am the LORD; that is my name! I will not give my glory to another or my praise to idols" (Isaiah 42:8). The God of the Bible is a God of glory. This means He is a jealous God and that He wants all the glory for everything! You might not like this, but it is the God of the Bible—the Father of Jesus Christ—to whom we are praying. Therefore, it requires us to know something of His ways—and respect them—if we are to be heard from on high.

Second, there is a kind of praying that does more harm than good. The harm is when the prayer shows contempt for God's glory and perpetuates what is pretentious. Such a prayer could encourage people to imitate this, as when the Pharisees prayed only to be seen of men. The harm is further to be feared when you recognize that such praying could bring down God's wrathful oath and judgment. Not only would this mean no reward but God's actual judgment.

Third, there is a kind of praying that doesn't get God's attention. Prayer is talking to God and asking Him to act. After all, the purpose of prayer is to be heard by Him. When God hears it means He will honor our requests. It is when He takes our requests on board. But there is a kind of praying that is not talking to God at all—it is mainly for people to hear, not Him. Therefore, when we pray to be seen and heard by people, it most certainly will not persuade God to do anything except to guarantee your reward is but the pitiful praise of men and women.

You must never lose sight that the theme of Matthew 6, generally, is the principle inherent in Jesus' question: "How can you believe if you accept praise from one another, yet make no effort to obtain the praise that comes from the only God?" (John 5:44). I have sought to be governed by this verse for over fifty years. I pray it will grip you to the core of your being.

When Prayer Is a Performance

You will recall that the Greek word *hypokrites* meant acting, like in a play. An actor or actress puts on a performance. Personally, I love to see a great actor perform, whether Lord Olivier, Charlton Heston, Sir Alec Guinness or Dame Judi Dench. I know what it is to stand and applaud a performance with tears in my eyes. I admire great acting on the screen or the stage.

The problem, says Jesus, is that the Pharisees did this when they prayed. They are hypocrites, play-acting, says Jesus. There was no thought whether the One to whom they were praying was listening, nor did the matter of His name or honor enter their minds. Their praying was all for show—it was a performance. "They love to pray."

And yet it must be added that praying to be seen—or heard—was not always wrong. Daniel unashamedly prayed to the Lord his God knowing fully he was being watched. He was warned not to do so. That made him want to do it all the more, so he did: "He went home to his upstairs room where the windows opened toward Jerusalem. Three times a day he got down on his knees and prayed, giving thanks to his God, just as he had done before" (Daniel 6:10). This was done not to bring praise to himself but to God.

Jesus was not forbidding public praying. "If two of you on earth agree about anything you ask for, it will be done for you by my Father in heaven. For where two or three come together in my name, there am I with them" (Matthew 18:19–20). Jesus' last command just prior to His ascension to heaven was for the disciples not to leave Jerusalem but to wait for the coming of the Spirit. Consequently, "They all joined together constantly in prayer" (Acts 1:4, 14). The early Church had set times of prayer (Acts 3:1) and prayed collectively with great effectiveness (Acts 4:24–31).

When I was the minister of Westminster Chapel, I prayed publicly every Sunday. I was conscious of being heard by the people but hoped—always—that it was preeminently before God that I prayed. Dr. Lloyd-Jones used to caution against "beautiful prayers," and I know exactly what he meant by that. However, I have to say that some written prayers by some of the Church's greatest saints are timeless, edifying and—though not necessarily intended to be so—beautiful. My wife, Louise, has produced a book—*Great Christian Prayers*—which contains some of the most magnificent prayers of all time. It is not always easy to know when you have crossed over the line from being conscious of people listening and wanting to focus solely on God. The issue is whether the glory of God is the aim. With the Pharisees it was all a show—a performance.

"They love to pray." As I said, this worries me a bit—I, too, love to pray. But in their case, it was praying "standing in the synagogues and on the street corners to be seen by men." There is certainly nothing wrong with loving to pray. I would that every reader of this book would develop an unfeigned love of praying. But with the Pharisees, it was not only play-acting. It was like playing—being sheer fun. It was playing a game.

When you play a game you hope you win. They were playing a game to win approval of people. Their pleasure was carnal to the core.

Posture

Their posture was "standing." There is nothing wrong with this. It is possibly the most common posture in Israel today. Go to the Western Wall ("Wailing Wall") and you will see Jews standing to pray. With the ancient Pharisees, their posture was not only in synagogues but "on the street corners." In one of His parables, Jesus referred to the Pharisee who stood and prayed about himself: "God, I thank you that I am not like other men" (Luke 18:11).

Posture is not the important thing. David sat before the Lord. Moses was sometimes prostrate before God. Perhaps the most common New Testament example of posture is kneeling (Acts 7:60; 9:40; 20:36; 21:5). My dad always knelt when he prayed. Our "family altar" (as he called it) was when we as a family knelt to pray every night before I went to bed. In my old church in Ashland, Kentucky, we often knelt to pray as a whole congregation. Kneeling shows a certain reverence. But there is nothing wrong with standing or sitting. The point Jesus made is that they stood to be "seen."

In synagogue services in ancient Israel, public prayer was customarily led by a male member of the congregation. He stood in front of the scroll of the Law and discharged his responsibility. Don Carson noted that man could easily succumb to the temptation of praying—or playing up—to the audience. The acceptable clichés, a sonorous sound, a well-pitched fervency easily became tools to win approval, perhaps to compete with the one who prayed previously.

Place of Prayer

At times of public fasts—possibly at the time of the daily afternoon Temple sacrifice—the trumpets would blow as a sign that prayer should be offered. Right where he was—in the street—a man would turn and face the Temple to offer his prayer. Dr. Lloyd-Jones reckoned that the meaning here also implied that a man on his way to the Temple to pray is anxious to give the impression that he cannot even wait until he gets to the Temple—so he stands and prays at the street corner.

The place where one prays does not ultimately matter. Jesus made this point to the Samaritan woman: "A time is coming when you will worship the Father neither on this mountain nor in Jerusalem . . . the true worshipers will worship the Father in spirit and truth, for they are the kind of worshipers the Father seeks. God is spirit, and his worshipers must worship in spirit and in truth" (John 4:21–24). The French monk known as Brother Lawrence, in the classic devotional *The Practice of the Presence of God* (which I highly recommend), told how the presence of God was so real to him that the clutter of the kitchen where he worked did not keep him from sensing God. Indeed, God was as real in his menial tasks as worshiping "before the blessed sacrament."

And yet collective praying with the people can be a most wonderful thing. When the disciples finished praying on one occasion, the place where they assembled "was shaken," and they were all filled with the Holy Spirit and spoke the Word of God boldly (Acts 4:31).

The Purpose of Prayer

The purpose of these hypocrites was to be seen by men. This is why they did it. This is why prayer to them was but a performance—even a carnal pleasure. The reason "they love to pray" is because of what it did for their pride. If people weren't watching, the praying stopped. If no one was watching, there would be no praying.

Jesus inserted the real reason we should pray: to be seen in secret so the Father will "reward you." There is therefore a reward for praying, if it is done to the glory of God. He is pleased to see us praying when no one but Himself knows you are praying. He loves to see His child—whether kneeling, sitting, standing or facedown on the floor—calling on His name. He "sees what is done in secret." It is communion between the Father and you. Nobody else is involved. God likes that.

We must keep Jesus' cautions in mind when we meet together to pray. Prayer meetings can be most wonderful occasions. But if people go only to be seen, it is wrong. On the other hand, numbers are an encouragement. If you go not to be seen but to encourage, this is different. This can be edifying and pleasing to God. Isaiah, however, foretold of a people who "honor me with their lips, but their hearts are far from me. They worship me in vain" (Mark 7:6–7). Jesus said that the teachers of the Law strut about in their flowing robes, devouring widows' houses and "for a show make lengthy prayers. Such men will be punished most severely" (Mark 12:40).

People can go to church for the wrong reasons. Some like to get a reputation for being religious. But how can we pretend we are worshiping God or praising Him when we are chiefly concerned that people will notice us, admire us and praise us?

The people who pray in order to be praised by men and women here below are rewarded, yes. But what a reward! The mere admiration of people. What kind of reward is that? And yet it is precisely what entices some people to go to church, to give, to pray and to do religious acts: to be seen. They sought the praise of people, and that is exactly what they get—the praise of men. Paid in full, says Jesus.

Is there for them a further reward in heaven? Not a chance. Choosing the approval of others is the silliest and most regrettable choice people can make. They forfeit the most important reward of all: God's reward. They are stuck with the lowest possible payment: people's admiration. The Pharisees made a choice—and they lived with that choice. The Pharisees and hypocrites of our day make the same choice—and they also have to live with it.

Why not pray? Jesus tells us why we shouldn't. If we choose to be like the ancient Pharisees, we will do more harm than good.

39. Behind Closed Doors

But when you pray, go into your room, close the door and pray to your Father, who
is unseen. Then your Father, who sees what is done in secret, will reward you.

MATTHEW 6:6

The predominant theme in Jesus' teaching on prayer is that it should be done for God's glory—not ours. We make a choice: Whose approval do we want? This does not mean we cannot receive compliments or man's approval. Sometimes God blesses us with the encouragement of people. The issue is whether we manipulate situations in order to get people's admiration.

Contrast

As we examine Matthew 6:6, we see a contrast between the right way to pray and the way the Pharisees prayed. The right way, says Jesus, is to enter into your room and "close the door." Praying to be received and heard in heaven must be behind closed doors. This way no human being can see or hear what is going on. But the Pharisees stood in synagogues and in streets for everybody to see. The motive of these hypocrites was to be seen by men—whereas the motive for right praying is to be seen by the Father alone.

The contrast is further seen in the merit that follows each kind of praying. Those who do their praying behind closed doors will receive a reward from the Father. Note: The Father *"will"* reward you"—thus putting it in the future. The reward comes later. But with the Pharisees, the reward comes immediately—they are "paid in full" by the people they wanted to impress.

Jesus' words would be a big turnoff for the Pharisees. They would say "no thanks" for the opportunity to pray behind closed doors. That had no appeal to them. After all, what they did was done for everyone to see, said Jesus (Matthew 23:5). They could not get interested in any praying that was not observed by people.

Jesus thus gives a recipe for the kind of praying that reaches heaven and gets a reward. Behind closed doors means no one knows that you are going to pray. No one knows what goes on behind closed doors, nor will one ever know what went on.

This is the genius of real praying. It was the genius of Mordecai, who did a heroic deed that saved the king's life—and kept quiet about it. God overruled, kept the king awake one night and led him to look at certain record books. The king noticed that Mordecai had done something stupendous, saving the king's own life. He then inquired as to what reward had been given to Mordecai. None. But the king stepped in, Mordecai was vindicated and beautifully rewarded and nothing for the Jews was ever the same again. Who knows, then, what you can accomplish when you are willing to let God do the work for you behind the scenes?

The Main Principle to Be Grasped

Jesus' words are not always to be taken literally. Jesus Himself couldn't apply it literally. He had no home or private room! "Foxes have holes and birds of the air have nests, but the Son of Man has no place to lay his head" (Matthew 8:20).

As Michael Eaton put it, the vast majority of the human race do not have a private room. Most people in the world live two to three to a room at least. In Hong Kong, it is common that seven or eight people live in a room. It was said a few years ago that students in preparation for exams would go to the airport or other public places just to study, as it was impossible to do so at home. Therefore, Jesus' words must not be taken literally here. He Himself went to lonely places or into hills to pray. Sometimes He prayed in the mornings (Mark 1:35), sometimes at night when all were asleep (Luke 6:12).

When I was twelve years old, I was deeply moved by a minister who prayed a lot. For some reason, I was gripped to do this, too—even at that age. I read in my King James Version that one was to enter into his "closet" and shut the door. I was blessed to have my own bedroom. In it was a closet. I took Jesus' words literally and went into the closet to pray. This meant it was dark and I had all my clothes on hangers around me. Not too inspirational. But I only wanted to get it right. I thank God that a desire to pray was instilled in me when I was young. I later understood that Jesus only meant to do your praying in private and not tell people you prayed.

The principle Jesus imparts in these lines is that we must deny ourselves, kissing any recognition good-bye other than God Himself seeing us. We are, therefore, required not only to take time to pray but to do so with God being the sole witness.

Privacy in Prayer

The Greek word for *you*—"when *you* pray"—is in the second person singular here. It is speaking to each person, one by one, to have for himself or herself a private, personal, secret prayer life.

We have seen that the New Testament embraces public praying and praying in meetings. We all need public praying and gatherings for prayer, by the way. We are to assemble together (Hebrews 10:25). But all those who meet publicly should have their own quiet times of prayer in solitude. Privacy means no disturbance, no distraction and having the ability to concentrate. You must shut the world out. My heart goes out to those who do not enjoy this privacy because of their situation in life. It should convict all of us who have places where we can go and be alone to pray.

From the beginning of my ministry at Westminster Chapel, I recommended that each member should pray thirty minutes a day. I have no idea how many did, but I believe a good number did. Nobody was ever sorry they prayed that much. You will have no regrets at the Judgment Seat of Christ about time you spent in prayer. Rob Parsons reckons that nobody ever was quoted as saying on their deathbed, "I wish I had spent more time in the office." But you may wish you had spent more private time in prayer. You should see your private quiet time as "God's time."

What does privacy allow? First, personal identity. When "you" pray, "go into your room, close the door." God affirms and authenticates you as a person when you come to Him like this. You get His undivided attention. You have a personal audience with God.

Once when in Rome, a man staying at our hotel was keen to tell about his audience that morning with the Pope. He was filled to overflowing with joy. I asked: "How do you get to have an audience with the pope?" He replied, "How many cardinals do you know?" (I could only think of getting Stan Musial's autograph.)

But think of this: a personal, private audience with the Most High God! You have a personal invitation from Jesus Himself to have private, quality time with your Creator, Redeemer and heavenly Father. It is so wonderful. When you pray in a group, it shows a measure of sacrifice. The "you" in such a case would be second person plural, as when Jesus introduces the Lord's Prayer: "This is how you [meaning 'you all'] should pray." But in these lines in Matthew 6:6, Jesus speaks to you—just you. And this is behind closed doors. God wants to esteem you, give you significance and treat you as a very important person—which you are.

Immediacy

This means personal immediacy. There is a difference between the indirect and direct, the mediate and the immediate. God may speak to you indirectly, as when someone gives you a word that encourages you. That word is mediated and purported to be from God. In such a case, you have to weigh that word and discern whether or not you believe it rings true. God can indeed speak to you, mediating a word indirectly from Him. And if He does, take it with both hands.

But behind closed doors, be prepared for God to speak to you immediately and directly—from the throne of grace to your heart of hearts. It may happen as you read the Bible, read a hymn or ancient prayer, sing a chorus or just pour out your heart to Him. He may overwhelm you. With His presence. With clear insight. With joy unspeakable. *Do not underestimate this possibility.*

Be willing, however, to accept the go-between in your life—generally, a person who mediates a word. He or she may intervene or intercede and give you a word perfectly timed and fitly spoken. Never be closed to this. Don't despise prophesying. Prove all things (1 Thessalonians 5:20–21). Therefore, God may choose to mediate a word to you—through a go-between. And yet if God were to speak to you immediately or directly, it could be a word for someone else. He may give you a word for yourself. But prayer should not be only about yourself. It should include praising and thanking God and intercession.

Therefore, behind closed doors you have a private audience with God. Lay your heart before Him and say: *Lord, I lay myself before You. Enable me to praise and worship You and be thankful. Use me to intercede for others. Speak to me as I need to be spoken to.* Just be open, willing and ready. When we look at the Lord's Prayer line by line, we will learn more about the content of solid praying.

Intimacy

The Greek word translated "room" is *tameion* and is used in different ways in the New Testament. It is translated "inner rooms" (Luke 12:3) and "storeroom" (Luke 12:24).

R. V. G. Tasker said that the storeroom is where treasures might be kept. Think about that. Your room in which you pray becomes a storeroom of treasure, because it is there you meet God regularly. It is when you get to know God intimately, like Moses did when God spoke to him face-to-face (Exodus 33:11). When you meet with God regularly, you get to know Him and know His ways.

It means the possibility of personal insight. Has it occurred to you that God may show you something that He kept from the high and mighty scholars of the world? If you can keep quiet about it, God might confide in you (Psalm 25:14). He may reveal to you something He has shown to no one else. It may be a word just for you.

I know what it is for God to show me something after I preached a sermon but which had been kept from me. And I wasn't allowed to preach it—it was just for me! He will do that with you, too. I once thought I heard God say to me, "Love the Word more than preaching it." I may have heard that before from someone else, true. But it was fresh to me, and I choose to believe it was He who gave it to me. I know it wasn't the devil!

Praying for Others

Do not forget this matter of intercession. I challenge you to become a personal intercessor. I know of a few who have interceded for me over the years. People like this are more precious than gold.

I was struck some fifty years ago by a pamphlet entitled *Where Are the Intercessors?* Interceding—standing in on one's behalf—is a lost enterprise, one of the most unselfish things you can do. "I looked for a man among them who would build up the wall and stand before me in the gap on behalf of the land so I would not have to destroy it, but I found none" (Ezekiel 22:30).

Moses was a great intercessor. Part of his greatness was that he did not farm out the ministry of intercession to everyone else but was himself a powerful intercessor. "So [God] said he would destroy them—had not Moses, his chosen one, stood in the breach before him to keep his wrath from destroying them" (Psalm 106:23).

But I do ask: Can you be an intercessor and keep quiet about it? It is a grand thing when one can be a faithful intercessor without telling the world that he or she does this. Even rarer is to intercede for someone without meddling in his or her affairs. People will say to high-profile leaders, "How can I pray for you?" That sounds so good. But next they want their phone number and address and regular feedback on how their prayers are doing. The last thing the Billy Grahams of this world need is people who pray for them as long as they can be in touch with them.

But to be a low-maintenance intercessor, requiring nothing of the person you pray for, is a magnanimous ministry. This honors God and the person you pray for. Let your reward be in heaven, let it come from God, who sees you in secret. A great fringe benefit of being an intercessor is that you get to know God and His ways better than ever. I urge you: Have a prayer list and pray through it regularly.

Praying behind closed doors is, therefore, one of the best ways to experience the presence of God, manifesting Himself as He will in your little unpretentious place of prayer. After all, God is already there "in that secret place" (NJB). He waits for us there, welcomes us, watches us and witnesses to us. He "sees what is done in secret" and "will welcome you."

Surprising Presence

The presence of God is the only presence in the universe that is utterly satisfying in itself. For example, what is the advantage, reason or wish to meet with a famous person? Is it not to tell it? If you could never tell it, would you still want to meet that person? What would his or her presence really do for your soul?

But in the presence of God is inexpressible joy (Psalm 16:11). For in this secret place, you have His sole presence with no other witnesses. There you have His secret presence (hidden from the world and unrecognizable by the world), His sensed presence (you can feel Him), His silent presence (no one outside the door would hear a sound), His special presence (He has any number of ways by which He makes Himself known), His surprising presence (we are never prepared for the manner He often chooses to show up), His spectacular presence (God often keeps the public at bay when He does His most notable acts), as when He raises someone from the dead (Luke 8:54–56; 4:32–37).

Why Pray behind Closed Doors?

What is the purpose of praying behind closed doors? Mainly this, that nobody knows but God that you are praying. You show by praying in this manner that He means more to you than anybody—and you prove it by not telling anybody. He therefore sees that you really do love . . . just Him. The Father knows He has you all to Himself. He also knows that He might confide in you, to share with you His secrets (Psalm 25:14), knowing you won't be blabbing it to the world.

The purpose of praying behind closed doors is further seen by revealing your motive—namely, that what is done is for His eyes and ears only. I fear there are not many people who love God that much. God delights to show how much He loves those who do love Him that much. And yet the very fact that we love Him is traced entirely to the truth that He loved us first (1 John 4:19).

There is a slight problem—you might like to call it an impediment—when praying behind

closed doors. God is "unseen." God is invisible (John 1:18; 4:24). Jesus is letting us know that when you shut the door behind you, nobody is there. God doesn't show up visibly to compensate for there being nobody else in the room with you. So when you are behind closed doors, you might find yourself staring at the floor, the walls, the ceiling, the furniture. You begin talking to one you cannot see. So you carry on in faith—the assurance of what we hope for and certainty of what "we do not see" (Hebrews 11:1). What makes faith *faith* is that you cannot see God and that you keep on praying.

A verse I have found helpful is David's word: "I have set the Lord always before me. Because he is at my right hand, I will not be shaken" (Psalm 16:8). If David could do it, so can I. I "set" the Lord before me—that is, I picture Him there before me. I can do this because He is already there—at my right hand, says David. Because He is at my right hand, my "setting" Him before me doesn't make Him show up. He is there already! But by picturing Him there, I sometimes find it easier to talk with Him. I do this a lot.

The promise follows: The Father who sees and hears me in secret will reward me. How? For one thing, He answers. I may not always be conscious of His answer, but He always answers. I can even pray "according to his will"—which means I have been heard (1 John 5:14), but I do not know I have been heard. Never forget that Zachariah prayed for a son and was "heard"—but was not notified that he had been heard for many years (Luke 1:13).

If I am not "heard," it does not mean God is not listening. It means He overrules my request because He has a better idea than mine. That is always the case. When God seems to say, "No," it is because He has a better idea than I had. Jesus said no to healing Lazarus, but decided that raising him from the dead was a better idea (John 11).

Whereas the hypocrites have already received their reward when they opt for people knowing they pray, there is no end to what God will do. The promise is open-ended, being in the future. "No eye has seen, no ear has heard, no mind has conceived what God has prepared for those who love him"—which also means that we "wait" for Him (1 Corinthians 2:9; Isaiah 64:4). The reward may begin here below. It may happen as you pray. The reward may come tomorrow. It will certainly culminate in heaven. Being unrewarded for praying in secret is a categorical impossibility.

Praying behind closed doors is the greatest privilege in the world. It is a privilege that (I'm sorry to say) few take advantage of. The question is: Will you?

40. Why Pray?

And when you pray, do not keep on babbling like pagans, for they
think they will be heard because of their many words. Do not be like
them, for your Father knows what you need before you ask him.

MATTHEW 6:7–8

Having told us there is a wrong way to pray, Jesus elaborates on this in the present chapter. He tells us how not to pray. Note again the assumption, however: "when" you pray. He assumes almost everybody prays! Even pagans, as we will see. It lets us know that prayer is a universal thing. Every religion under the sun emphasizes prayer—Muslims, Hindus—even atheists! General Douglas MacArthur used to say that there are no atheists in foxholes. As I write these lines, millions are praying.

When Louise first went to the streets of Westminster as a Pilot Light, a young man with a Che Guevara T-shirt approached her. She offered him my tract *What Is Christianity?* To her amazement, tears filled his eyes. He looked at her and said, "I am an atheist, a Marxist. But five minutes ago, I was in a church and said, 'God, if You are really there, let me run into someone who believes in You.'" He had to catch a train, and we will not know until we get to heaven what happened to him. In any case, here was an atheist who was praying!

But when Jesus says "when you pray" He is referring to one who follows Him. The "you" is in contrast to millions out there. The question is, is your prayer any different from all the rest? Jesus wants those who follow Him to break the mold—to be different. Why does He say "when you pray"? It is to show we are truly following Him, that we are listening to Him. For what matters is that our prayer will be heard in heaven if we follow certain principles.

Ignorant Praying

Jesus wants to show us basically two things in Matthew 6:7–8: (1) how not to pray and (2)

why pray at all? He shows false assumptions that some, such as pagans, have regarding prayer. "For they think they will be heard because of their many words." "Think" is the translation of *dokousin*—which means to imagine or to assume. People who don't understand prayer imagine things. In the case of the pagans, they thought they would be heard by their many words, that a lot of speaking and repetition helped them to be heard. The pagans would sometimes name all their gods and repeat them. The worshipers of Baal shouted louder and louder in order to be heard (1 Kings 18:28).

In a word: This is ignorant praying. The word translated "babbling" is found nowhere else in the New Testament, nor is it found in ancient Hellenistic literature or in the Septuagint (the Greek translation of the Old Testament). Nobody knows how to translate it. William Tyndale in the early sixteenth century translated it "babbling"—a word that stuck. If I said "gobbledygook," you would see that we are talking about rubbish, utter nonsense.

And yet we need to be clear on what this verse does not mean. Jesus does not condemn praying for someone or something more than once. He Himself prayed a second and third time in the Garden of Gethsemane that He might avoid the cross (Matthew 26:42). The apostle Paul prayed three times to be delivered from his thorn in the flesh (2 Corinthians 12:7).

Neither is this babbling a reference to speaking in tongues (1 Corinthians 14:2). Speaking in tongues is not babbling. It does not necessarily mean raising your voice in prayer, either. The early disciples raised their voices when they prayed (Acts 4:24). Jesus is condemning ignorant

201

praying—when you keep on saying the same thing over and over again. I know that many sincere Christians come close to this when they will say, for example, "O Lord God, I come to You. Lord God, have mercy, Lord God. Lord God, we love You, Lord God, we pray, Lord God," etc. If you were talking to a person in a room with you, it would be odd if you kept repeating his or her name over and over like that. But sometimes people do this when they pray. Some people think they must work themselves up to reach God. Some people pray themselves into a state that makes them think they can get God's attention—as if to wake Him up! That is what Elijah's opponents were doing. He taunted them: "Maybe he is sleeping and must be awakened" (1 Kings 18:27). All this is ignorant praying.

Sometimes people will imitate each other when they pray. Christians can make this mistake, trying to sound like someone they have heard. Some even change their tone when they pray and repeat phrases they have heard. They do not show the anointing of the Spirit but their particular culture. It is sometimes comical. Sincere though they may be, they "think" they will be heard if they sound like someone they have admired.

Some are locked into their comfort zones when they pray and never realize how silly they sound. But they convince themselves they are being heard. They apparently are not conscious they are talking to a personal God—the Father. They may mean well, but sometimes they are doing little more than talking to themselves. We all would do well to heed this ancient advice: "Do not be quick with your mouth, do not be hasty in your heart to utter anything before God. God is in heaven and you are on earth, so let your words be few" (Ecclesiastes 5:2).

What Is Required in Being Heard

The fundamental purpose of praying is to be heard. The Hebrew word *shemar* may be translated "to hear" or "to obey." When God chooses to "hear" us, it means He has taken our request on board and will *obey* our request. Pagans—and some ignorant Christians—keep thinking they will be heard by the amount of words. But if we ask anything in God's will, as we saw earlier, we are "heard" (1 John 5:14). The ancient Jews wanted

to be "heard on high" (Isaiah 58:4). The goal of prayer is therefore to be heard, and Jesus informs us that a lot of words won't make it happen.

Two things are required to be heard: God's will and our need. Subjectively, it is called "need." "Your Father knows what you need before you ask Him." Objectively, the way to be heard is to pray in God's will. So if we ask anything according to His will, we will be heard (1 John 5:14).

God's will is essentially two things: (1) His revealed will—His Word, or the Bible—and (2) His secret will—His own pleasure. Regarding the latter, God only wants what is best for us and He keeps this a secret sometimes. It is this secret will of God you must tap in to if you want prayer to be answered. "For I know the plans I have for you," declares the Lord (Jeremiah 29:11). His plans are better than ours. If we will submit to Him, we will never be sorry, even if it means waiting. No good thing will He withhold from those who love Him (Psalm 84:11). Paul referred to God's secret will when he said that we have been chosen "according to the plan of him who works out everything in conformity with the purpose of his will" (Ephesians 1:11).

There are two ways to know God's secret will. First, it is when you know the revealed will of God so well that you have a fairly good idea what is just and right when you ask for things—as opposed to asking what is wrong (James 4:3). This comes from knowing the Bible well. It comes from spending a lot of time reading the Word of God. Second, the immediate and direct witness of the Holy Spirit can reveal God's will. John meant exactly this when he said, "If we know that he hears us—whatever we ask—we know that we have what we asked of him" (1 John 5:15). That is a big "if"—knowing we have been heard. I have had this happen, but not often. I wish it happened more often. But God may be pleased to convey to you His will by His Spirit. Failing this, then, you and I are required to know God's Word so well that we will be less likely to pray outside His will.

But there is yet one other way by which you may know you have been heard on high: your need. God knows your need. He knows what we need even before we ask Him! And God promised to supply all our needs (Philippians 4:19).

Indeed, God has dedicated Himself to supply our needs. He didn't have to. But He did. Jesus will later say in the Sermon on the Mount, "Look at the birds of the air; they do not sow or reap or store away in barns, and yet your heavenly Father feeds them. Are you not much more valuable than they? . . . So do not worry, saying, 'What shall we eat?' or 'What shall we drink?' . . . your heavenly Father knows that you need them" (Matthew 6:26, 31–32).

By the way, don't persist in praying beyond your need! God may give it to you, and you will eventually be very, very sorry. Israel persisted in asking for a king, and God gave in to their request. "So he gave them what they asked for, but sent a wasting disease upon them" (Psalm 106:15).

The fundamental purpose of praying, then, is to be heard. Not by ignorant, shouting prayers or repeating pious phrases you may have heard people use. We must learn to pray simply—in God's will and in accordance with our true need. If you are wise, you will let Him decide what your need is. He already knows! You will live long enough to thank God for unanswered prayer. When He doesn't answer, you can be absolutely sure it is because He has a better idea for you than you yourself have.

Foreknown Providence Regarding Prayer

The big contrast between pagans and believers is that we have what they don't: a heavenly Father who knows the future as well as the past and present. First, you have a Father who chose you in the first place. "For he chose us in him [Christ] before the creation of the world" (Ephesians 1:4). Jesus announced that all whom the Father chose would come to Him (John 6:37). He said that nobody knows the Father but the Son "and those to whom the Son chooses to reveal him" (Matthew 11:27). Jesus could say to Nathaniel, "I saw you while you were still under the fig tree" (John 1:48), showing how the Lord has His eye on us before He reveals Himself to us.

Yes, we are chosen by a gracious God who reveals Himself as Father. The Father became our Father through His Son, Jesus Christ. God had only one "natural" Son, Jesus Christ—and yet you and I are children of God! How? By being adopted into the family (Romans 8:15; Ephesians 1:5). As many as received Jesus were given the right to be called sons of God (John 1:12).

Note Jesus' words: "*your* Father." God is His Father and our Father. Furthermore, your Father knows exactly what you have need of—before you ask Him! Before you ask Him, He is there waiting to be asked. He is a Father who knows everything. It therefore follows what we don't have need of does not apply. We may think we need this or that, but God may say, "You don't need that." This is why He withholds certain requests. It is for us.

But the question follows: If God is Father and knows our need and promises to supply that need, why pray?

Five Reasons to Pray Although God Already Knows Our Need

First, we pray because He invites us and commands us to pray. Jesus gave a parable encouraging us to pray and to never give up (Luke 18:1). Martin Luther said that we are instructing ourselves, not Him, when we pray. Calvin said that we do not pray with the view of informing God, but in order that we may arouse ourselves to seek Him. In a word: that we may declare that from Him alone we hope and expect, both for ourselves and others, all good things. John Wesley said that God does nothing but in answer to prayer. By the way, don't worry about asking God for small things; with God all things are small. As Michael Eaton put it, "It is we who need to pray, not God."

Second, God who ordained the end ordained the means to the end. That means is prayer. "Ask of me, and I will make the nations your inheritance, the ends of the earth your possession" (Psalm 2:8). "Ask and it will be given to you; seek and you will find; knock and the door will be opened to you" (Matthew 7:7). Granted, prayer is an unfathomable mystery. God chose prayer to keep us humbled; it puts us on our knees, reminding us who God is. For prayer reveals the nature of God—His omniscience, power and sovereignty. The sovereignty of God refers to what He is pleased to do.

Third, God chooses to honor our obedience. You can be governed by logic and conclude that since He knows our need and promised to supply it, there is no need to pray. I'm sorry, God doesn't honor logic but our obedience. "You do not have, because you do not ask God," said James (James 4:2). You may wish to be cynical and say, "Answered prayer is only a coincidence." Charles Spurgeon said, "When I don't pray, coincidences don't happen; when I pray, coincidences happen." God may even use suffering to drive us to Himself. Being swallowed by a big fish got Jonah's attention—and then he prayed (Jonah 2:1, ESV). When Peter was imprisoned, the Church interceded "earnestly" for him (Acts 12:5). God honored their obedience.

Fourth, God knows our need but dignifies us by letting our prayer make a difference. It is a truism: Prayer changes things. Prayer gives us the privilege of changing things. We can have a hand in diverting a disaster. We can have a hand in moving God's hand. The angel said to Jacob, "You have struggled with God and with men and have overcome" (Genesis 32:28; you have "power with God" Genesis 32:28, KJV).

Fifth, God promises to answer prayer. Not when we stay on the sidelines, but when we actually pray. This means He will act when we pray. It also means He may not act *until* we pray. It may be God getting our attention by things getting worse and worse because we are too proud or busy to pray. Never forget it: It is we who need prayer, not God.

Everybody prays. But not everybody is heard. Jesus thus gives a little tip to His loved ones and not the world. That tip will make the difference in whether our prayer is heard.

41. The Lord's Prayer

Our Father in heaven, hallowed be your name, your kingdom come,
your will be done on earth as it is in heaven. Give us today our daily
bread. Forgive us our debts, as we also have forgiven our debtors. And
lead us not into temptation, but deliver us from the evil one.

MATTHEW 6:9–13

This, then, is how you should pray.

MATTHEW 6:9, TNIV

I grew up in Kentucky, where it was actually required to recite the Lord's Prayer in the classroom every morning. I now know more than ever how blessed I was as a child. It seems a little strange to say that I learned it not at home or even church but in school. How fortunate that I got in on this before the law in America prohibited saying the Lord's Prayer in public schools. I cannot recall praying the Lord's Prayer at our church services—I suppose they felt doing so was too liturgical, nor did it seem to occur to us as a family to pray it, although we had devotions together daily.

Why do I say that learning the Lord's Prayer as a child was such a blessing? First, anyone who gets a head start in learning what God ordains is singularly blessed. This is why Israel was so blessed. Jews were given a head start in the things of God. This is why they are said to have an advantage—because they, before all others, have been entrusted with "the very words of God" (Romans 3:2). Second, when we are required to repeat something again and again we naturally memorize it. This is why I myself memorized the Lord's Prayer a long time ago. I am so thankful for this. If you don't know it by heart, perhaps you should consider doing so because you never know when you may need to recall this prayer.

The next dozen chapters—42 through 53—focus on the Lord's Prayer. It is the greatest prayer ever uttered, devised or imagined. It was originally uttered, authored and verbally conceived by Jesus Christ Himself—which is why we call it the Lord's Prayer. I regard it as a high privilege and great honor to write on this section, with the intent of examining the Lord's Prayer line by line. I pray it will change your life.

Not every prayer in this world is inspired by the Holy Spirit, including too many of my own prayers. It is possible to ask "amiss" (James 4:3, KJV), or ask "wrongly" when you pray (ESV). Praying wrongly is when we don't pray in God's will, either from wrong motives or ignorance. A prayer prayed outside the will of God may or may not be answered, but the only guarantee of answered prayer is to pray in God's will. We know this because God promises to hear us when we pray in His will. "This is the confidence we have in approaching God: that if we ask anything according to his will, he hears us" (1 John 5:14, TNIV).

The difficulty is, we don't always know we are praying perfectly in the will of God. Sometimes God lets us know we are praying in His will: "If we know that he hears us—whatever we ask—we know that we have what we asked of him" (1 John 5:15). But this does not happen all the time. However, when you pray the Lord's Prayer you pray in His will. And yet it does not follow that the prayer will be answered immediately, as in the case of Jesus' high priestly prayer for the unity of the Body of Christ (John 17:22).

But is it not a wonderful feeling to know you are praying exactly in God's will? Come with me now as we begin to examine this magnificent prayer.

42. The Perfect Prayer

When you pray, say.

LUKE 11:2

The Lord's Prayer is verbally inspired by the Holy Spirit and therefore perfectly worded. It is a revelation of how we should pray because it mirrors God's will for His people. It cannot be stressed too much that Jesus Himself is the formulator of it—every single word—and if you want to know at least once that you prayed in God's will, the Lord's Prayer is for you.

I would hope that God would certainly not answer my prayer when I ask for things outside His will. I cherish the knowledge that Jesus my High Priest and intercessor is seated at God's right hand, putting through to the Father only what is His will. I always want the Lord Jesus to filter my praying and not let wrong requests be passed on to the Father. I therefore want Jesus not only to intercede for me but also to intercept my ill-posed requests. Jesus knows what is best for us.

The worst thing that could happen to us is for a wrong request to be put through to the Father and then be answered. Getting all you want would bring incalculable damage and grief to you. Be thankful for unanswered prayer. It may be a sign of God's favor.

One of the most frightful verses in the Bible is this: "So he gave them what they asked for, but sent a wasting disease upon them" (Psalm 106:15; "sent leanness into their soul," KJV). Such happens when God's people persist in asking for what God has clearly shown to be out of His will—and God finally acquiesces, to their sorrow.

There are some lessons for us as we approach the Lord's Prayer. First, there is a kind of praying that does not please God. It is praying that profanes His name and His nature. Second, there is a kind of praying that does more harm than good. This happens when a prayer shows contempt for God's glory and encourages people to do the same

thing. Third, there is a kind of praying that doesn't get God's attention: for example, when praying is done to impress others.

We therefore should never want what God is against. After all, as the late Cardinal Basil Hume put it, "God only wants what is best for us." God did not want Israel to have a king, for example. "I am the LORD, your Holy One, Israel's Creator, your King" (Isaiah 43:15). God Himself was already Israel's king. Samuel warned the people against their having a king as other nations had, but they persisted. God said to Samuel, "Listen to them and give them a king" (1 Samuel 8:22). God thus granted their request but sent leanness to their soul. It was a pivotal and bad moment for Israel. The day would come that a prophet would say, "So in my anger I gave you a king, and in my wrath I took him away" (Hosea 13:11).

We should always aim to pray in God's will. Praying the Lord's Prayer is to pray perfectly in His will.

Misusing the Lord's Prayer

We could, however, pray the Lord's Prayer with a wrong motive. The NIV translates the Greek word *kakos* (often translated as "sick" or "evil") in James 4:3 as asking with "wrong motives." The truth is, although praying the Lord's Prayer is certainly praying in the will of God, one could use the prayer wrongly. How? By believing that the very praying of the Lord's Prayer is a worthy act in itself that makes you righteous before God merely because you pray the prayer. If we repeatedly pray the Lord's Prayer over and over and over again—thinking that merely praying it counts for righteousness before God and scores points in heaven—I would regard this as praying it with a wrong motive. That is hardly the point of the Lord's Prayer.

You could also misuse this prayer by praying it from the head and not the heart. In other words, repeating the Lord's Prayer from memory and not praying it from your heart of hearts could be much the same as the vain repetition for which Jesus rebuked the Pharisees (Matthew 6:7). The Lord's Prayer should be prayed in faith from the heart. In short, you should mean what you say when you utter these words.

To be fair, I suspect that we've all used the Lord's Prayer inappropriately at times. I would not have wanted you to read my mind every time I led Westminster Chapel in praying the Lord's Prayer every Sunday morning. I tried to pray it from my heart each time, but I know that I didn't always do this. There were times my mind was on the sermon to be preached later on, or I would be distracted by someone in the congregation. When you know the Lord's Prayer so well from memory it is easy to repeat the words without faith or feeling.

Two New Testament Accounts

The Lord's Prayer is mentioned twice in the New Testament. In the Sermon on the Mount (Matthew 5–7) the Lord's Prayer comes in the context of Jesus' telling His disciples how not to pray, as well as how to pray (Matthew 6:9–13). He spoonfeeds them, giving them a prayer to pray—line for line, word for word. The other place the Lord's Prayer is mentioned is when one of His disciples asked Him, "Lord, teach us to pray, just as John taught his disciples." Jesus then gave them virtually the same prayer as before (Luke 11:2–4).

As I said, we call it the "Lord's" prayer because Jesus Himself was the author of it and also because it was He who told us to pray it. Some think it should be called "the disciples' prayer" since the Lord Jesus Himself would not need to pray it; we do. Some would point out furthermore that Jesus' high priestly prayer in John 17 deserves the title "the Lord's Prayer." But we will not be pedantic; the Lord's Prayer is the common title to this magnificent prayer we are given by Jesus, and we should be very, very thankful indeed for it.

Whereas Luke's account of the Lord's Prayer came as a result of Jesus' disciples' request—"Lord, teach us to pray, just as John taught his disciples" (Luke 11:1)—Matthew's account came in the context of Jesus' observations of the way Pharisees prayed.

This examination is not a scholarly treatise, so I will not highlight the small differences between Luke's account and that which comes in the Sermon on the Mount. The interesting point is, Luke reveals that John the Baptist had taught his disciples to pray. Two of Jesus' own disciples had been followers of John (John 1:35–37). We have no idea what John's prayer was like or where he got it. We do know that Jesus was not threatened by the disciples' request. He merely complied and said, "When you pray, say," and gave virtually the same prayer as we have in the Sermon on the Mount.

When to Pray the Lord's Prayer

It is good to pray the Lord's Prayer both publicly and privately. I certainly recommend it publicly. Even if it is sometimes used inappropriately, it still finds its way into one's memory. You never know when you will be glad you have it memorized. Some churches regularly make it a liturgical part of their services. Why not? After all, it was originally addressed to the corporate Body of Christ.

I realize there are churches that react negatively to anything that smacks of liturgy. Dr. Martyn Lloyd-Jones went so far as to suggest that it is spiritual pride, if not arrogance, to refuse to pray the Lord's Prayer with others. Like it or not, all churches have their own form of liturgy, in any case. I would personally urge every church leader to find a place in a service once a week to insert the Lord's Prayer. It will do no harm and only good.

However, there is a fairly strong hint in Matthew's account that Jesus could have meant for the prayer to be prayed privately and behind closed doors. The context of Jesus' inserting this prayer in the Sermon on the Mount was His caution we should not be like those who "love to pray standing in the synagogues and on the street corners to be seen by men" (Matthew 6:5). He said that when you pray, "Go into your room, close the door and pray to your Father, who is unseen. Then your Father, who sees what is done in secret, will reward you" (verse 6). He concluded this section by introducing the Lord's Prayer.

I would therefore urge that the Lord's Prayer be prayed with other believers and also that you pray this alone in your quiet times. Include it in your family devotions. Pray it with your roommate. Pray it on your way to work. Pray it at work. Pray it with friends. Pray it at Bible studies. Pray it in small groups. Pray it as often as you feel like it—but do so from your heart.

The Purpose of the Lord's Prayer

Jesus showed us how not to pray (like the hypocrites who want to be seen by everybody) and how to pray (with believers and behind closed doors). Then He indicated the very reason for praying—namely, to be "heard" and "rewarded" by the Father. Does this surprise you? The purpose of praying is that the Father "will reward you" (Matthew 6:6). God Himself loves to appeal to our self-interest. Hence He encourages us to pray in order to be heard and rewarded, on these conditions: (1) We pray to be seen only by Him and (2) to put forth requests that are in His will.

To put it another way: The aim of prayer is to be heard by the Father. This is Hebraic thinking that goes back to the Hebrew word *shema*. Every Jew knows about the Shema: "Hear, O Israel: The LORD our God, the LORD is one" (Deuteronomy 6:4). *Shema* means both to hear and also to obey. You may have said to your child, "Did you hear me?" implying they must not have heard because they did not obey. That is the idea with *shema*. When God hears us in the *shema* sense, it means He will obey our request. "Your prayer has been heard," the angel said to Zechariah (Luke 1:13). "If we ask anything according to his will, he hears us" (1 John 5:14). Some thought they were "heard because of their many words" (Matthew 6:7). The aim of prayer, then, is to be heard by the Father.

When we pray the Lord's Prayer we are assured of being heard by our heavenly Father. I have been struck by a statement that Dr. Martyn Lloyd-Jones made in this connection. He said, "I have always been comforted by this thought, that whatever I may forget in my own private prayers, as long as I pray the Lord's Prayer I have at any rate covered all the principles, the condition, of course, that I am not merely mechanically repeating the words, but am really praying from my heart and with my mind and with my whole being."

Why Pray?

Just before introducing this prayer, Jesus added a word: "Your Father knows what you need before you ask him" (Matthew 6:8). It should not surprise us that God knows what we need before we ask Him because He knows everything. Essential to His very character is His omniscience (He is all-wise, all-knowing). "Before a word is on my tongue you know it completely, O LORD" (Psalm 139:4). It may be surprising to some that Jesus would say God knows what we need before we ask Him—and then urge us to pray! But it is thrilling that God would remind us of this just before we pray. Why does He do this? Would not this be a deterrent to praying if God already knows what we have need of and always wants what is best for us? Then why pray?

First, because He invites us—even commands us—to pray. The same God who knows in advance who will be saved equally tells us to preach the Gospel to every creature (Mark 16:15). We merely obey Him.

When I was at Westminster Chapel we had our Pilot Light ministry. Twenty or thirty of us were out on the streets of Victoria every Saturday morning within the shadow of Buckingham Palace doing one thing: presenting the Gospel to passersby. I urged the Pilot Lights not only to present the Gospel but to do all they could to convert them. "Treat each person as though their destiny were in your hands," I urged. And yet all this was done with a theological underpinning, namely, that God knew in advance who would receive the Gospel. This made no sense to some people. "If God already knows who will be converted, why try to convert them?" Answer: Because God told us to present the Gospel to every creature and commands everyone to repent (Acts 17:30). As a matter of fact, Paul stated that God even determined where each person should be born and live in order that they should seek God (Acts 17:26–27). It is our job to make sure they hear the Gospel.

So in a similar way, the same God who knows the end from the beginning (Isaiah 46:10) invites us to pray even though He knows what we need before we ask Him. We are instructing ourselves, not God, when we pray, said Martin Luther. And I remind you of John Calvin's observation: We do not pray with the view of informing God, but in order that we may arouse ourselves to seek Him. By the way, don't worry about asking God for small things—with God, everything is small. It is we who need to pray, not God, said Michael Eaton.

Second, God, who ordained the end, ordained the means to the end. That means: prayer. "Ask of me, and I will make the nations your inheritance, the ends of the earth your possession" (Psalm 2:8). "So I say to you: Ask and it will be given to you; seek and you will find; knock and the door will be opened to you. For everyone who asks receives; he who seeks finds; and to him who knocks, the door will be opened" (Luke 11:9–10). Jesus told His disciples a parable "to show them that they should always pray and not give up" (Luke 18:1). Granted that prayer is an unfathomable mystery, only a fool will refuse to pray. It drives pride away; it brings us to our knees, remembering who God is. For prayer reveals the nature of God—not only His unsearchable wisdom but His sovereignty, what He is pleased to do and not to do.

Third, God chooses to honor our obedience. He wants us to obey without having to figure everything out first. It is not unlike Moses, who wanted to see why the burning bush was not consumed. Moses had been looking at this extraordinary sight, a bush that was on fire but did not burn up. Moses said to himself, "I will go over and see this strange sight—why the bush does not burn up" (Exodus 3:3). God told Moses to stop: "Do not come any closer . . . the place where you are standing is holy ground" (verse 5). So with us. Logic would dictate that since God knows our need and promised to supply it, there is no need to pray. Yet God does not honor our logic but our childlike obedience. "You do not have, because you do not ask God" (James 4:2). Charles H. Spurgeon used to say, "When I don't pray, coincidences don't happen; when I pray, coincidences happen."

Fourth, God knows our need but dignifies us by letting our praying make a difference. It is an old truism: Prayer changes things. Some Christians may object to the idea that prayer has power. I can understand that. Prayer in itself has no power; it is the person whose prayer is applied by the Spirit who makes the difference. And yet God stoops to our weakness, making us feel affirmed. Like a wise, loving parent, God could do a thousand things in our behalf without letting us lift a little finger; but He lets us participate in the divine scheme of things, giving us dignity, joy and a feeling of being needed. He gives us the privilege of changing things through prayer. We can have a hand in diverting disaster. We can have a hand in moving God's heart, following Jacob's example: "I will not let you go unless you bless me" (Genesis 32:26).

Fifth, God promises to answer prayer. That is good enough reason for me. If God promises to answer prayer, I am going to pray! I cannot guarantee that John Wesley was absolutely right when he said that God "does nothing" but in answer to prayer—but God does not promise to act unless we seek Him first. He wants us involved in all He does. For that reason, to be candid, I pray about everything. *Everything.* "In all your ways acknowledge him, and he will make your paths straight" (Proverbs 3:6; or "he shall direct thy paths," KJV).

"All your ways" means everything. I would say this covers a lot! I pray about a grocery list before I go into town. Louise and I prayed for our cat, Gizmo, when we feared she was dying. I started praying for Billy Graham every day in 1981. I ask God to help me know when to say yes and when to say no, in all that pertains to us. You may be sure I pray about every sentence I write in this book. I take Proverbs 3:6 seriously and literally. This verse means He will act when we pray. It probably also means He won't act until we pray. Why? I reckon it is because God gets our attention this way. As we observed above, it is we who need prayer, not God. Prayer is for us, not Him. He promises to answer prayer that we might spend more time with Him. What is more, He likes our company, as I wrote in *Did You Think to Pray?*

Having said that our heavenly Father knows our need before we ask Him, Jesus proceeded to tell us what to pray. Hence, the Lord's Prayer.

A Pattern Prayer

What, then, is the point of the Lord's Prayer? Although it is a prayer to be prayed by all of us, it is a pattern prayer. For example, it begins with acknowledging God, worshiping Him and focusing on His interests. Then come the petitions that pertain to us. This pattern is designed to show that we are not to rush into the presence of God, snap our fingers toward heaven and expect the angels to jump! We begin with proper worship.

All good praying should, in some way, be consistent with the pattern, order, content and intent of the Lord's Prayer. It is a prayer to be prayed, but the words of the Lord's Prayer serve also as an outline of appropriate praying. We should see each line of the Lord's Prayer—that is, each petition—as the solid foundation for truly worshipful and selfless praying. Thus, everything we say should be an extension, or filling out, to some degree, of every line in the Lord's Prayer. Our praying should build on the Lord's Prayer. How we enlarge on each petition, filling out each one in a way that faithfully reflects what Jesus meant, becomes a superstructure on that foundation.

The Lord's Prayer, therefore, is the foundation; our own praying is the superstructure. The foundation is not intended to be the way we are to pray verbatim all the time. I repeat: It is certainly good to pray it, even daily, privately or publicly. But it is not the way we should always pray or what we should recite every time we turn to God. Don Carson noted how ironic it is that the context of the Lord's Prayer in the Sermon on the Mount forbids meaningless repetition in prayer, and yet no prayer has been repeated more than this, too often without understanding. Even the Didache—known as the "teaching of the Twelve," from the second century—prescribes that Christians should repeat this prayer three times a day. This is surely unnecessary. There are several prayers in the New Testament and in the book of Acts. The Lord's Prayer is not mentioned. Jesus did not say that this is the "only" way to pray. He Himself prayed several other times, and it was not this prayer.

There are, of course, many times a day we will turn to God without remembering the order of the Lord's Prayer. In the perfect world we keep our Lord's order in mind: who God is, where He is, what His interests are, etc. But there are times when in desperation we simply cry out, "GOD!" "JESUS!" "LORD, HELP ME!" And He hears us. So do not take this book to imply that all praying must be a literal filling out of the order and content of the Lord's Prayer.

Jesus is teaching us how to pray. He sets before us the model prayer, the perfect prayer. We should learn from it and hopefully make it the way we pray when we seek God's face. And we should do so as much as possible.

How you and I pray, then, should as much as possible be an extension or filling out of the Lord's Prayer; it should be a superstructure on top of the foundation that builds on what Jesus gave us. All good praying will be consistent with the original words of the Lord's Prayer. Throughout Church history, people have marveled at this prayer. Men such as Saint Augustine and Martin Luther have observed that there is nothing more wonderful in the entire Bible than the Lord's Prayer. John Calvin stated that the petitions include everything that we may rightly wish from God.

Do not forget that it is a commanded prayer. When you pray, Jesus said, "Say" (Luke 11:2). This is stated in the imperative mood; it is how we should pray. "This, then, is how you should pray" (Matthew 6:9, TNIV). It is also a corporate prayer. "You" is second person plural in the Greek. Not only that, when Jesus said to pray, "Our Father," it reflects all of God's people, not one person, praying. It is the Church's prayer—how "you" should pray—not how Jesus prays. After all, He did not need to pray for forgiveness. It is a perfectly worded and correct prayer; we are told exactly what to say. It is a complete prayer. There are six petitions (some would say seven, depending on how you count "And lead us not into temptation, but deliver us from the evil one"), which include everything we may rightly wish from God. As the Law was in two tables—the first part with reference to God, the second to humankind—so the first three petitions here focus on God's glory; the second part, to our benefits.

Interpreting the Will of God

Since to pray the Lord's Prayer is to be sure you are praying perfectly in the will of God, so, too, may we be confident we are praying in the will of God as long as what we utter reflects this prayer faithfully. If we can remember that the unembellished Lord's Prayer is the foundation, our own praying being the superstructure, we should want to know our praying is in the will of God.

In 1 Corinthians 3, Paul talks about a superstructure being comprised of gold, silver and precious stones, but also wood, hay and straw, referring to our lives in anticipation of the Judgment Seat of Christ (1 Corinthians 3:12–15). The point here is that the superstructure that will stand the test at the Final Judgment is one comprised of gold, silver and precious stones. Such will not burn up when the fire is revealed. The wood, hay and straw will be consumed.

I would borrow this analogy and apply it to our praying. I would therefore urge that we pray in a manner that demonstrates gold, silver and precious stones. This would be praying in the will of God; it would reflect the beauty and honor of God. Asking amiss—praying wrongly and contrary to the will of God—would be using wood, hay and straw in erecting a superstructure that will not stand the test.

Our purpose is not only to examine each line of the Lord's Prayer but to learn how to interpret the will of God. If you understand the Lord's Prayer, you will be more able to pray in His will. You will develop a spiritual aptitude that equips you to pray rightly and not wrongly. You will develop a spiritual sense that sets off an inner warning, "Do not go here," when you begin to ask amiss. This comes by knowing what each petition means. As long as your praying is a faithful and true extension of each of the petitions, you will sense a Voice that says, "This is the way; walk in it" (Isaiah 30:21). I am not saying you will always know that what you ask for is what God wants for you. Even Paul admitted he did not always know how to pray (Romans 8:26–27). But it does mean that you will be spared of continually asking for what is displeasing to God.

As we will see, if we can develop a sensitivity to the Holy Spirit, it will greatly enable us to pray in the will of God. As you know, the context of the Lord's Prayer in Matthew is the Sermon on the Mount and the focus of that sermon is the Kingdom of heaven. The Kingdom of heaven is best defined as *the conscious presence and enabling grace of God*. When you learn to recognize the conscious presence of God, which comes partly from developing a sensitivity to the Holy Spirit, you will find yourself praying more and more in the will of God and in sync with the Lord's Prayer. This is because when you begin to wander outside what God wants, you will sense a lack of peace and a lack of the consciousness of God's presence. That is a warning to stop, to not pray in that direction any longer. It comes because you have developed an intimacy with the Holy Spirit. This issue will come up again.

The way to know you are praying in the will of God, then, is to keep the Lord's Prayer in mind. Remember the pattern, the content and purpose of it. My study here is designed not only to give an exposition of the Lord's Prayer but also to help you to know if you are praying in the will of God. You cannot make the God of the Bible do what you want. But if you delight yourself in the Lord, He will give you the desires of your heart (Psalm 37:4). That is His promise; it is a guarantee.

If you can find yourself delighting in the Lord's Prayer, then, it is a good sign—a very good sign—that you are delighting in God Himself. This means that the desires of your heart will be yours, sooner or later. The test, however, is whether you will affirm the foundation—the Lord's Prayer itself—and build on it with materials that magnificently show you want to pray in God's will. If you do, congratulations! This means you are pleasing the Lord and your praying is being heard in heaven.

43. The Fatherhood of God

Our Father in heaven.

MATTHEW 6:9

In his invocation at the Inauguration of President Barack Obama, Pastor Rick Warren closed his prayer with the Lord's Prayer. Although he referred to the Jewish *Shema* ("Hear, O Israel: The LORD our God, the LORD is one") and endeavored to show appropriate respect to all cultural backgrounds, Warren received criticism from some people who felt that the Lord's Prayer made the occasion completely "Christian." And yet there have been Christians who have criticized the Lord's Prayer generally on the basis that it is not a Christian prayer! Some have opined that since the prayer does not end in the words, "in Jesus' name," it is not a prayer Christians should pray.

However, Rick Warren did something very intriguing and bold. He ended his own prayer by introducing the Lord's Prayer in a manner that left no doubt his inaugural prayer would be prayed explicitly in Jesus' name. Having prayed that President Obama and his family would be committed to God's loving care, Pastor Warren concluded: "I humbly ask this in the name of the One who changed my life: *Yeshua* [Hebrew for Jesus], *Essa* [Arabic for Jesus], *Jesus* [Spanish for Jesus], Jesus [English], who taught us to pray: 'Our Father who art in heaven.'"

What if Pastor Warren had merely ended his inaugural prayer with the Lord's Prayer? Would it have been a Christian prayer? Yes. This is because "praying in Christ's name is implicit," said Dr. Martyn Lloyd-Jones. "No man can truly say 'Our Father which art in heaven,' save one who knows the Lord Jesus Christ and who is in Christ." He went on to say, "It is only those who are true believers in the Lord Jesus Christ who can say, 'Our Father.'" In other words, only the Christian—and the Lord Jesus Himself—has the right to call God *Father*.

Why is this? First, the Lord's Prayer was given to believers—Jesus' disciples—who are told to pray this prayer. Whether you take it from the Sermon on the Mount (Matthew 6:9–13) or Luke's account, which shows Jesus responding to their request, "Lord, teach us to pray" (Luke 11:1–4), the prayer was designed for believers. The assumption in the Sermon on the Mount was that His followers have taken on board what Jesus has stated in this discourse up to that point—for example, the Beatitudes (Matthew 5:3–12), His teaching about the Law and His promise to fulfill it (vv. 17–20), the way He applied the Law (vv. 21–42), His teaching on blessing your enemies (vv. 43–48) and what He said about praying not to be seen of men (6:1–8). He would not have brought in the Lord's Prayer to those who did not believe what He had taught already.

Second, it can never be stressed too often that Jesus is the eternal Son of God, the Father's one and only Son. Jesus has a unique relationship with the Father. We are children of God, yes, but this relationship is made possible only through Jesus. He came unto His own (the Jews), but "his own did not receive him. Yet to *all who received him, to those who believed in his name*, he gave the right to become children of God—children born not of natural descent, nor of human decision or a husband's will, but born of God" (John 1:11–13, emphasis mine). In a word: Only those who receive Him and believe in His name have the right to be children of God and, therefore, to pray the Lord's Prayer.

Nobody Needs to Feel Left Out

If you feel left out because you are not a believer, would you like to have the right to pray the Lord's Prayer? This right is offered to you—right now.

You don't need to feel deprived, rejected or left out. All you have to do is receive Jesus—right now. He is being offered to you—right now.

First recognize that you need a Savior. You cannot save yourself. If you could, there would have been no need for God to send His Son into the world. The angel said to the shepherds, "Today in the town of David a Savior has been born to you; he is Christ the Lord" (Luke 2:11). A major part of His being Savior was that Jesus never sinned—ever. He fulfilled the holy, perfect Law of Moses (Matthew 5:17). Therefore, when He died on the cross at the age of 33, He said, "It is finished" (John 19:30).

In these words, Jesus acknowledged that He had kept the Law and fulfilled His mission on earth. Not only that, the words "It is finished" are a translation of the Greek word *tetelestai,* which was a colloquial expression in the ancient marketplace that meant "paid in full." Jesus paid the entire debt you owe to God by dying for you. If you can accept this, which is what is meant by "receiving Jesus and believing in His name," you qualify to pray the Lord's Prayer. But I would suggest nonetheless, so that your relationship with God is clear in your mind, you pray the following right now:

> Lord Jesus Christ, I need You. I want You. I am sorry for my sins. I know I cannot save myself. Thank You for dying on the cross for my sins. Wash my sins away by Your blood. I welcome Your Holy Spirit into my heart. As best as I know how, I give You my life. Amen.

Now you are qualified to pray the Lord's Prayer.

Congratulations! Welcome to the family of God. You have just become a member. You have been born again. You are now a Christian. There are various other words for what has just happened to you, such as *converted, saved, regenerated, justified.*

However, there could be an exception to what I have been saying. It is possible that people can actually become Christians by praying the Lord's Prayer—if they understand what they are saying and mean what they are saying. In other words, praying the Lord's Prayer could be the very way a person is brought into a true relationship with God—if the person realizes what he or she is praying and does so from his or her heart.

This is why it is a good thing for the Lord's Prayer to be prayed publicly, with unbelievers present. The Lord's Prayer could become an evangelistic tool. God can use the Lord's Prayer to awaken a person's soul and bring him or her to God, even if it does not happen the first time it is prayed. Would you be surprised if someone was actually converted when Pastor Rick Warren led countless millions to pray the Lord's Prayer, especially if they had heard the prayer before?

We must not forget that although it can be prayed by individual believers, the Lord's Prayer is a corporate prayer. You know that Jesus told the disciples to pray this. "When you [second person plural in the Greek] pray," He said to them. Therefore, it follows that we pray, "Our Father," not "my Father." That is humbling, and it puts all of us in equal standing before God. No person can claim to be God's "favorite" or to be special. No one can claim to be more accepted by God because he or she has been a Christian for a longer period of time, or because he or she has done some pious duty more than others. Neither should anyone think he or she is at the "head of the queue" because he or she has suffered a lot, has a handicap, has been neglected or has been mistreated. God is my Father, yes; but He is your Father, too. And when we address Him as we are told to do in the Lord's Prayer, we simultaneously affirm our standing both with God and with the rest of the Body of Christ as well.

When we pray the Lord's Prayer, then, we join a multitude "no one could count, from every nation, tribe, people and language" (Revelation 7:9). Each of us is one out of many. I pray the Lord's Prayer and get the Father's full attention while knowing full well that He equally and simultaneously listens to others—tens of millions and millions all at once, with equal concern for each of them. One aspect of prayer that makes it miraculous is that God not only loves every person as if there were no one else to love, as Saint Augustine put it, but listens to every person as if there were no one else praying. I must not forget that when I address God as Jesus has taught us, I pray, "*Our* Father."

There Are Other Names by Which We Address God

Jesus is not trying to tell us that addressing God as "Father" is the only way to call on Him. There are other prayers in the New Testament that do not address Him as Father. The first recorded prayer after Jesus ascended to heaven shows the disciples addressing God (they may have meant Jesus) as Lord: "Lord, you know everyone's heart. Show us which of these two you have chosen to take over this apostolic ministry" (Acts 1:24–25).

The next corporate prayer by the Church that is recorded shows they "raised their voices together in prayer to God," saying: "Sovereign Lord . . . you made the heaven and the earth and the sea, and everything in them" (Acts 4:24). They may have assumed God the Father when they said "Sovereign Lord," but they could have meant Jesus. This shows that we are not required necessarily to address God as "Father" each time we pray. Stephen prayed just before he went to heaven, "Lord Jesus, receive my spirit" (Acts 7:59). The apostle Paul certainly meant Jesus when he said, "Who are you, Lord?" (Acts 9:5). Peter was apparently talking to Jesus when he said, "Surely not, Lord!" (Acts 10:14).

This brings up another interesting question: Can we pray directly to the Holy Spirit? Yes. *Because He is God.* The three Persons of the Trinity are equally divine: God the Father, God the Son and God the Holy Spirit. Although there are no recorded prayers in the Bible showing that someone addressed the Holy Spirit directly, there are countless examples in our hymnody: "Come, Holy Ghost, all-quickening fire" (Charles Wesley), "Holy Spirit, truth divine, dawn upon this soul of mine" (Samuel Longfellow), "Lord God the Holy Ghost, in this accepted hour, as on the day of Pentecost, descend in all Thy power" (James Montgomery), "Spirit of God, descend upon my heart" (George Croly), "Breathe on me, Breath of God" (Edwin Hatch) and many more. If it is appropriate to sing to the Holy Spirit, it is surely right to pray to Him.

My point is this: Although the Lord's Prayer is a pattern prayer, it is not meant to be the only way we pray but rather to be seen as a skeleton that we have to clothe. The apostle Paul offered many prayers in behalf of Christians and repeatedly showed he prayed to the Father (see Ephesians 1:17; 3:14; 5:20; Colossians 1:3, 12; 3:17; 1 Thessalonians 1:3; 3:11).

The Term "Fatherhood of God" Can Be Abused

The phrase "Fatherhood of God" is a lovely phrase, but it has been taken over by many unbelieving people who deny that Jesus is the only way to God and the only way to heaven. Some would add to these words and say they believe in the Fatherhood of God and the brotherhood of man. The idea is expressed by these people that God is the Father of everybody, saved or lost. They would add that everyone is our brother or sister, whether or not they are believers. Some would say that people don't need to be converted in the first place to have God as their Father, that He already is the Father of all. They would say it is not necessary to pray in the name of Jesus, because all people are equally God's children whether they come to faith in Christ or not. This teaching is alien to the New Testament and is an utter denial of the true Christian faith.

And yet the term "Fatherhood of God" is a good and proper phrase, rightly understood. Therefore, the Fatherhood of God needs to be defined and explained. So, too, the phrase "brotherhood of man," a good term, rightly understood.

John Stott observed that the essential difference between pharisaical, pagan and Christian praying lies in the kind of God we pray to. In telling us to address God as "Our Father in heaven," Jesus' concern is not with protocol but with the consciousness that we might come to God in the right frame of mind. We need to know at least some elementary truths about the God of the Bible. It is a wonderful privilege to talk to Him. But the very reason for this skeleton prayer is that we might know something of the true God. It is always wise, before we pray, to meditate by recalling who He is.

The idea of God being our Father is almost entirely a New Testament teaching. The term *father* with respect to God does occur in the Old Testament, but not with reference to addressing God. He is called "a father to the fatherless, a defender of widows, is God in his holy dwelling" (Psalm 68:5). "As a father has compassion on his children, so the LORD has compassion on those who fear him" (Psalm 103:13). Isaiah comes close to addressing God as Father, but not quite: "But you are our Father, though Abraham does not know us . . . you, O LORD, are our Father, our Redeemer from of old is your name" (Isaiah 63:16). "Yet, O LORD, you are our Father. We are the clay, you are the potter; we are all the work of your hand" (Isaiah 64:8).

It was Jesus who explicitly addressed God as Father. He was the unique Son of God. He was and is God's only "natural" Son. God is uniquely His Father. We are made children of God by adoption. We have been adopted into the same family (Romans 8:15; Ephesians 1:5). Not only does Jesus address God as Father, He also commands us to address God in the same way. There is no sibling rivalry, no jealousy whatever, between Jesus and the children of God. Let me share one of the most dazzling truths I know: God loves you as much as He loves Jesus! That's right—we are joint heirs, co-heirs, with Jesus. Jesus even prayed that the world would see that the Father loved His family "even as you have loved me" (John 17:23).

There are many people, perhaps some who read these lines, who know what it is to have both an adopted child as well as a natural offspring. They love both equally. They will tell you that they can tell no difference in the love they feel for each. I have talked with a number of parents who testify to this. That is the way the Father is with Jesus and that countless multitude! He loves us as much as He loves His own Son. Not only that, but we are as secure in the family of God as Jesus Himself is in the Godhead. What do you suppose the chances are that Jesus could be dislodged, or disenfranchised, from the Trinity? None—absolutely none. So are we kept secure, eternally secure, in the family of God. We are loved with an "everlasting love" (Jeremiah 31:3). "Both the one who makes men holy and those who are made holy are of the same family. So Jesus is not ashamed to call them brothers" (Hebrews 2:11).

It is true that all men and all women everywhere are God's children in a sense—and each of them are brothers and sisters in a sense. This is because we have been created in the image of God (Genesis 1:27). Human beings all have in common that they are made in God's image, unlike plant life or animals. When Paul addressed the philosophers of Athens at the Areopagus he quoted one of the Greek poets, "We are his offspring," showing that all of us are God's offspring (Acts 17:28–29). God made every single human being who ever lived, and He is upholding each of them as Creator and Sustainer.

But this is not the same thing as being God's adopted children. The Bible makes a sharp distinction between those who belong to God and those who do not. This is the major point John wanted to make: "How great is the love the Father has lavished on us, that we should be called children of God!" (1 John 3:1). He immediately contrasts this with the world: "The reason the world does not know us is that it did not know him" (1 John 3:1). Jesus clearly said in His high priestly prayer, "I am not praying for the world, but for those you have given me, for they are yours" (John 17:9). This is an unmistakable contrast between those who are God's children and those who are not. Jesus even said of certain Jews, "You belong to your father, the devil" (John 8:44). In a word: The Fatherhood of God is a good and valid term, but only when it refers to the fact of our being adopted into the family by God's grace. And when Jesus told us to address God as Father, He was speaking to believers.

Understanding God as Father

How do we understand God as Father? He is personal. Theologian Paul Tillich wanted to define God as the ground of all being, which is panentheism. This is simply not compatible with the notion of God's divine Fatherhood. God is just as personal as we are, only more so. Theologian Joachim Jeremias has shown how exceptional and stunning Jesus' use of addressing God as Father must have been at first to His Jewish disciples. Jews in ancient times preferred only exalted titles for God. They would address Him as Sovereign Lord or King of the Universe. Jesus even used the Aramaic *abba*, the word used by children to address their father, "daddy." Our adoption into the family makes us joint heirs with Jesus; hence, "we cry, '*Abba*, Father'" (Romans 8:15).

He is the perfect Father, a being "than whom no greater can be conceived," as Anselm (c.1033–1109), Archbishop of Canterbury, put it. For those who have not had a good relationship with their parent, there is difficulty in calling him "Father." I can sympathize with this. I love and honor my dad, and feel I have been exceptionally blessed to have the parents I had. But I always felt I did not come up to my father's standard. "As" and "Bs" weren't good enough on my report card; my dad wanted all "As"—and no "A minuses"! And yet this is to say nothing of those who grew up being abused. People like this have extreme difficulty—some never get over it—calling God "Father."

If you have trouble calling God "Father," try to remember that Jesus said, "Anyone who has seen me has seen the Father" (John 14:9). Get your image of God from Jesus, not from your earthly parent. Picture Jesus, of whom it was absolutely true, "A bruised reed he will not break" (Matthew 12:20). Picture Jesus, who could not bear to see somebody deeply hurt. "Don't cry," He pleaded with the widow who was burying her only son (Luke 7:13). Picture Jesus, who is able to sympathize with all of us to the hilt (Hebrews 4:15). Picture Jesus, who accepts us as we are, who never moralizes and never shames us when we slip and fall. He is the perfect Father. When our parents discipline us, said the writer to the Hebrews, they do so "as they thought best." So often, that is not good enough. But when the perfect Father disciplines us, He never loses His temper or punishes us to impress anybody; He does what is absolutely for our good (Hebrews 12:10).

Remember this: When God chastens us—and we all need it from time to time—He does not do it to "get even." He does not play "tit for tat." God got even at the cross! "As far as the east is from the west, so far has he removed our transgressions from us" (Psalm 103:12). God never disciplines us to prove anything. The greatest freedom is having nothing to prove, and God has nothing to prove. He disciplines us for one reason: He loves us (Hebrews 12:6). He wants us to be partakers of His holiness (Hebrews 12:11).

Our heavenly Father is, furthermore, always present. "God is our refuge and strength, an ever-present help in trouble" (Psalm 46:1). "Where can I go from your Spirit? Where can I flee from your presence? If I go up to the heavens, you are there; if I make my bed in the depths, you are there. If I rise on the wings of the dawn, if I settle on the far side of the sea, even there your hand will guide me, your right hand will hold me fast" (Psalm 139:7–10). The best of parents cannot always be present. It may be that they are busy, preoccupied or have to be elsewhere. They cannot be in two places at once. But God is always present with us. As He listens to each of us as though no one else were addressing Him, so also He is with each of us as though He were nowhere else.

Some grow up with an absentee parent, especially a father who is never around. I fear that I myself have been this way with our children more than I care to admit. In *Totally Forgiving Ourselves,* I lament that I put my church first, thinking I was putting God first, as our precious son and daughter grew up in London. I now believe that if I had put my family first I would have preached just as well, but I cannot get those years back. I have had to forgive myself—which I have done. But it cannot erase the deprivation that our children did not deserve. In any case, God is the perfect Father—always there, always present, always available, always listening. He is in heaven, yes; but He is equally here with us. He is closer than our hands or feet, closer than the air we breathe. He is but a cry away. We don't have to remember the skeleton outline of the Lord's Prayer. As I have said, we can just cry "GOD!" "JESUS!" and He is there.

The Fatherhood of God implies the existence of a family, especially when we realize the implications of saying "our" Father. In his prayer for the Ephesians, Paul said he knelt before the Father, "from whom his whole family in heaven and on earth derives its name" (Ephesians 3:15). It is another reminder I am one out of many (Revelation 7:9). The multitude that no one is able to count is made up of those God predestined to be the "firstborn among many brothers" (Romans 8:29).

The Fatherhood of God points to equity in the family. Said Peter, "You call on a Father who judges each man's work impartially" (1 Peter 1:17). God treats every member of the family with absolute equity. He is another person's Father as well as yours. It is a sober reminder that should your enemy be a Christian, the Father loves that brother or sister as much as He does you. Our

Father does not want quarreling in the family. How do you feel when your children quarrel? This is partly why we have the petition, which I will deal with in considerable detail in a subsequent chapter, "Forgive us our trespasses, as we forgive those who trespass against us."

I must come back to the point this chapter began with: This teaching also indicates the exclusiveness of God's family. I'm sorry, but God is not the Father of all people indiscriminately. Although Jesus died for all people indiscriminately (John 3:16; Hebrews 2:9), not all for whom Christ died receive Him as their Savior. You may be interested to know that the early Church prohibited non-Christians from reciting this prayer as vigorously as they forbade them from joining with believers at the Lord's table. While I myself think they may have gone too far by keeping certain people from praying this prayer, this practice does indicate that the Lord's Prayer implies the exclusiveness of God's family.

The only time Jesus addressed the Father as "God"—not as "Father"—was when He cried out on the cross, "My God, my God, why have you forsaken me?" (Matthew 27:46). That was the precise moment that the righteous Son who knew no sin was made sin for us (2 Corinthians 5:21). This was the moment Isaiah saw hundreds of years in advance, when "the LORD has laid on him the iniquity of us all" (Isaiah 53:6).

It is a reminder that when we say "Our Father," we approach a Father whose justice has been satisfied, once for all. He therefore has no swings of mood; He holds no grudges. He is never diverted from listening to us because He is preoccupied with someone else's problem or a problem of His own. He is happy with Himself and is content to listen to each of us. He knows our frame, remembers that we are dust (Psalm 103:14). The perfect Father calls us to pray—and He gives us the perfect prayer. It leaves nothing out that we need.

44. Being Put in Our Place

Our Father in heaven.

MATTHEW 6:9

Do you know what it is like to be put in your place? As I was preparing this chapter, for some reason an embarrassing memory came into my mind which I thought I would share. It goes back to 1953, when I was an eighteen-year-old freshman at Trevecca Nazarene College.

I had enrolled in a New Testament course. Claude Galloway was the professor. We went through the New Testament that semester from Matthew to Revelation. On the week before we got to the book of Revelation, Professor Galloway said, "Next week we come to the book of Revelation. Frankly, I am not sure I understand this book. Does anybody here understand it?" My immodest hand went up. "Oh, Brother Kendall, would you like to teach the course next week?" "I certainly will," I replied with absolutely no shame. The day came. I had looked forward to what I imagined as my finest hour. I expected the anointing to come down on these poor, ignorant students and the deprived professor with such power that all would need to be carried to their next classes.

I taught the book of Revelation that day (as I understood it then). I thought I was at my best. Nothing was so clear to me. I spoke with stunning authority. On a scale of one to ten regarding confidence, I was twelve. But when my lecture was over, it was over. The members of the class, about thirty, filed out quietly. Not a soul spoke to me. Except one student, who said, "Do you always let your lower jaw fall to one side like that when you speak?" Then he left. Only the professor hung around. I expected his accolades. He simply said, "Well, Brother Kendall, you may be right. That is the view I used to take, but I'm not so sure now. Thanks for doing this. Nice try."

I was devastated. Humiliated. I got what I deserved. I was put in my place.

The words "in heaven" are meant to put us in our place—but without the kind of embarrassment I just described. That our Father is "in heaven" should give us a feeling of awe, true reverence, an awareness that we are but one among many and should keep us from rushing thoughtlessly into God's presence. If we understand why Jesus put these words there, it will help us to know Him better. It will help us know ourselves better. Merely repeating these words may not reveal why these words are there. I am sure you could pray the Lord's Prayer many times without grasping the reason for these carefully chosen words.

If you are used to praying, "Our Father, which art in heaven," keep in mind that is the King James translation, which most of us are used to using. I happen to love it—and I still pray this as in the KJV. However, for this book I am using the New International Version, which uses modern language.

So have you ever wondered what the Lord's Prayer would be like had Jesus not added these words, "in heaven"? Did you think this was an incidental, if not redundant, phrase merely to explain that the Father dwells in heaven? Jesus is doing far more than merely telling us where God the Father lives. The two words "in heaven" are at the beginning of the Lord's Prayer in order to help us see our place—to humble us—and give us some objectivity about ourselves. It is not that God rebukes us or slaps us on the wrist by these two words. It is rather that our Lord intended to give us a perspective that should help us see our place before the Father.

Has it occurred to you that your Father in heaven—along with Jesus at His right hand—is already being worshiped there, whether or not we pray to Him? There are billions and billions of angels that praise and worship Him sixty seconds a minute, sixty minutes an hour, twenty-four hours a day, seven days a week, every day of the year. The seraphs worship, saying, "Holy, holy, holy is the LORD Almighty; the whole earth is full of his glory" (Isaiah 6:3). The four living creatures never stop praising God day and night: "Holy, holy, holy is the Lord God Almighty, who was, and is, and is to come" (Revelation 4:8). All of those now with the Lord—Abraham, Isaac, Jacob, Isaiah, Daniel, the apostles, our departed loved ones who were in Christ—are worshiping Him day and night.

We also are to worship God day and night here on earth. But it is not physically possible for us to do this as we will in heaven. We can, however, continually offer to God our spiritual worship, as Paul puts it in Romans 12:1. So much worship here below is vain worship, as Jesus said to the Pharisees (Mark 7:6–7). When we get to heaven we will worship without any constraints because we will have glorified bodies without sin (Romans 8:30).

You may ask, "Does God really need our worship? What can you and I add to Him by praying the Lord's Prayer?"

This is what is so amazing. He still wants you and me to talk to Him. He wants our attention. He likes our company. He listens to each of us as if there were no one else, though He is hearing countless cries and praises to Him all the time. Jesus simply wants us to be aware of this when we talk to God. He is in heaven where He is extolled, adored and honored continually by praise and worship.

Two Old Testament passages are relevant here:

Guard your steps when you go to the house of God. Go near to listen rather than to offer the sacrifice of fools, who do not know that they do wrong. Do not be quick with your mouth, do not be hasty in your heart to utter anything before God. God is in heaven and you are on earth, so let your words be few. As a dream comes when there are many cares, so the speech of a fool when there are many words.

ECCLESIASTES 5:1–3

Our God is in heaven; he does whatever pleases him.

PSALM 115:3

God is in heaven and we are on earth. That is a simple, but very profound, fact.

Taking Ourselves Too Seriously

To put it another way, the purpose of the phrase "Father in heaven" is to keep us from taking ourselves too seriously—and our heavenly Father not seriously enough. Jesus is the first ever to pray to the Father, that is, to call Him "Father" and to teach us to call Him that. As we saw earlier, Jesus also would refer to *abba* Father, Aramaic for our equivalent of "daddy." And we are not discouraged from feeling or doing the same. Far from it! Being adopted into the family of God, we are loved with the same love that the Father has for Jesus, and we also have the same security He has. That security and intimacy are part of our being in the family.

However, by adding these words "in heaven" Jesus reminds us how big and how great God is. This is partly to ensure also that we will never become overly familiar with Him.

A few years ago, someone who was said to have a prophetic gift had a "word" for me, namely, that I should start calling God "daddy" from now on in my private quiet time. Since Paul admonished us not to despise prophesying, to prove all things and hold on to the good (1 Thessalonians 5:20–21), I tried it for a while. I would not want to criticize you if you do this—or if you call God "papa," as a friend of mine does. But for me it was contrived and unnatural. Not everyone needs to use the word "daddy" in addressing God to experience intimacy. But there is nothing wrong with this, and I am sure God Himself does not mind.

In this chapter, we are to see that "Our Father in heaven" encompasses two perspectives in approaching God. "Our Father" invites intimacy with God; "in heaven" points to His supreme majesty. Therefore, "Our Father in heaven" simultaneously embraces both approaches to God. And although they may seem contradictory, we are to approach God with a feeling of awe and intimacy at the same time.

There is implied in this discussion a conviction I have taught all over the world—namely, that there has been a silent divorce in the Church, speaking generally, between the Word and the Spirit. When there is a divorce, sometimes the children stay with the mother, sometimes with the father. In this divorce, you have those on the "Word" side and those on the "Spirit" side. Those on the Word side stress God's sovereignty and majesty—the need to uphold the faith once delivered to the saints, a return to the God of Martin Luther and Jonathan Edwards, an emphasis upon expository preaching. These people tend also to sing the old hymns, especially such as those of Isaac Watts and Charles Wesley. Those on the Spirit side emphasize signs, wonders and miracles—spiritual power as we see in the book of Acts, where prayer meetings resulted in small earthquakes; where getting in Peter's shadow meant supernatural healing; where lying to the Holy Spirit brought instant death. These people also tend to sing new songs and choruses.

It is my view that both sides are essentially right but that one emphasis without the other creates an imbalance, plus a very inadequate presentation of the Gospel. It will not result in a restoration of the honor of God's name so desperately needed at the present time.

Consider for a moment how some "Word" people may at times address God—and do so in a hushed, holy and respectful tone: "Almighty and most holy God, our sovereign Savior and gracious Lord, we come humbly into your presence." For people who are introduced to the Christian faith in this kind of atmosphere, two reactions sometimes follow: (1) a feeling that this is the only way to approach the true God; (2) a feeling that this God is remote and unknowable. Those who have the latter reaction are often ready to listen to an approach to God that does not make Him appear so remote, if not harsh.

The Contrast between Our Heavenly Father and Our Earthly Father

Jesus identified our Father *in heaven* also that we might see the immediate contrast between our heavenly Father and our human father. God the Father is in heaven; our human fathers are on earth. The writer to the Hebrews contrasted human fathers with the perfect Father (Hebrews 12:9–10). Therefore, when you pray the Lord's Prayer, you should remember that you are not talking to your own dad. Neither is God like your own father. Jesus' giving us the Lord's Prayer is

an immediate, implicit command to make the switch from the way we look at our human father. We may have to switch off how we see our human father. As I said in the previous chapter, many of us have difficulty calling God "Father" because of the subconscious perception we have of our own fathers; we prefer to call him "Lord," "Jesus," "Dear Lord," "Lord God," "Sovereign Lord." Our frame of reference for the term "Father" is often loaded with baggage which we project onto God; we see Him as being like our own father, who may have been abusive, unloving, aloof or never there.

When Jesus told us to address our Father "in heaven," it was a command to look beyond the present realm. This Father is different; He is in heaven. No one has ever known a father like our Father in heaven. You may have to put to one side an earthly frame of reference, especially if you had an undesirable father; you are moving beyond the realm of nature and above the level of nature. This is not a human father you are addressing; this is your heavenly Father. Your human father has limited ability; he can't do everything. Your human father has limited authority; he can't control everything. Your human father has limited availability; he can't always be there.

Your Father *in heaven,* however, has unlimited ability. One of Job's greatest discoveries at the end of his ordeal was this: "I know that you can do all things; no plan of yours can be thwarted" (Job 42:2). God has unlimited authority. "I make known the end from the beginning, from ancient times, what is still to come. I say: My purpose will stand, and I will do all that I please" (Isaiah 46:10). God has unlimited availability. "Where can I flee from your presence? If I go up to the heavens, you are there; if I make my bed in the depths, you are there. . . . If I say, 'Surely the darkness will hide me and the light become night around me,' even the darkness will not be dark to you; the night will shine like the day, for darkness is as light to you" (Psalm 139:7–8, 11–12).

And yet with our heavenly Father we have it both ways! He is in heaven, yes, but also close at hand. He is in heaven, but a very present help in time of trouble. He is in heaven, but we can feel His presence.

Characteristics of Our Heavenly Father: Invisibility

When Jesus refers to our Father in heaven He also means the Father's invisibility. He is out of sight.

> Immortal, invisible, God only wise,
> In light inaccessible hid from our eyes,
> Most blessed, most glorious, the Ancient of Days,
> Almighty, victorious, Thy great name we praise.
>
> Walter Chalmers Smith
> (1824–1908)

God is Spirit (John 4:24). That is why faith is required. What makes faith *faith* is that we cannot see God with our natural eye. "No one has ever seen God, but God the One and Only, who is at the Father's side, has made him known" (John 1:18). "Though you have not seen him, you love him; and even though you do not see him now, you believe in him and are filled with an inexpressible and glorious joy" (1 Peter 1:8). One of the chief reasons for the second Commandment ("You shall not make for yourself an idol in the form of anything in heaven above or on the earth beneath or in the waters below" [Exodus 20:4]) is to make room for faith. An idol is visible and shows no need for faith to see it; it plays into our fleshly nature to want to see before we believe. Faith, however, "is being sure of what we hope for and certain of what *we do not see*" (Hebrews 11:1, emphasis mine). When you see the person you are talking to, you don't need to exercise faith that you are talking to them. You do, however, with your heavenly Father.

God's Independence

Jesus even wants to show the Father's independence. God is in heaven, and when He is as high as the heavens are above the earth, you know you can't snap your fingers and expect service. When I was in Kenya I saw an aristocratic man snap his fingers at a servant—and that servant came running in a split second. I was startled to watch this. I didn't think this sort of thing went on nowadays. And yet there are those who have an attitude toward God that they can snap their fingers and expect God to jump! The truth is, it should be the other way around: If God would snap His fingers, we are the ones to jump. This was the main point of one of the psalms of ascent: "As the eyes of slaves look to the hand of their master, as the eyes of a maid look to the hand of her mistress, so our eyes look to the LORD our God, till he shows us his mercy" (Psalm 123:2). The picture is that of a slave whose eyes are focused on their master's hands, so that they are ready to obey in a split second. Therefore, we should look to God and want to be ready when He calls for us. We are fortunate whenever He beckons for our attention. The truth is, God can give or withhold mercy and still be just. He does not need us; He is not tied to us; He is not dependent on us.

However, it is extraordinary to think that God confides in us (Psalm 25:14). He called Abraham His friend (Isaiah 41:8; James 2:23). Abraham is a type of the Christian believer (Genesis 15:6; Romans 4:1–5). We should follow Abraham in our faith and also in seeking to be God's friend.

God's independence is a missing note in much Christian thinking today. We all need to see that God is not controlled by us and that He certainly doesn't want us to try to control Him. He does not need our wisdom. He does not consult the highest archangel, or any of us, to know what to do next. "The God who made the world and everything in it is the Lord of heaven and earth and does not live in temples built by hands. And he is not served by human hands, as if he needed anything, because he himself gives all men life and breath and everything else" (Acts 17:24–25). Our Father in heaven is not dependent upon His creation but remains independent. He has not turned over the reins to His mortal, finite creatures. When we therefore pray, "Our Father in heaven," we affirm two things: (1) His independence and (2) our dependence and need of Him.

God's Inscrutability

There is more: "Our Father in heaven" refers to God's inscrutability. This means He is impossible to understand except in measure. This means you can never fully, ultimately figure Him out. If you think you know Him and know what He is up to, you will probably realize very soon how little you knew! You think you understand Him, then shortly you realize you have hardly begun to understand Him! "My thoughts are not your thoughts. . . . As the heavens are higher than the earth, so are my ways higher than your ways and my thoughts than your thoughts" (Isaiah 55:8–9). And again: "Our God is in heaven; he does whatever pleases him" (Psalm 115:3).

You cannot predict what He will do; you cannot even completely fathom what He has done already. "Oh, the depth of the riches of the wisdom and knowledge of God! How unsearchable his judgments, and his paths beyond tracing out! Who has known the mind of the Lord? Or who has been his counselor? Who has ever given to God, that God should repay him? For from him and through him and to him are all things. To him be the glory forever! Amen" (Romans 11:33–36). God is in heaven; you are on earth. He is in control; you are not in control of Him.

Be careful if you say that you know for sure what God is going to do. As Rob Parsons sometimes says, "If you want to make God smile, tell Him your plans." When Moses saw the burning bush that was not consumed, he reckoned he would get to the bottom of it. God said, STOP! "Do not come any closer. . . . Take off your sandals, for the place where you are standing is holy ground" (Exodus 3:5). Moses was not allowed to figure out what was going on. Nobody knew why Jesus of Nazareth was dying on a cross, until after it happened and the Holy Spirit came to explain. And all of us are still trying to take this in. God is in heaven and is inscrutable. Don't try to figure Him out.

Being Overly Familiar with God

Is being overly familiar with God a bad thing? Yes. Why is it wrong, and what is the consequence of an overfamiliarity with God? Familiarity means assuming a greater degree of informality or friendship than is proper. It is when you know a person almost too well and begin to presume. It is when you cross over from respect and awesome reverence to impertinence. It is when you begin to control a relationship and forget another's personhood. When that happens in a human relationship, something is lost; one feels used. Any lasting relationship is based upon mutual respect, when neither person becomes manipulative, manipulated or used.

Overfamiliarity sometimes happens in one's relationship with God. It is when you think you know God so well. It is when you begin to think you have a claim on God—that He is indebted to you, that He owes you something. It is also when you think you have fully understood Him and are closer to Him than anybody else is. You begin to feel too special. You begin to feel He needs you. You begin to feel He has told you so much that you have a relationship with Him like no one else has.

This kind of thing can begin innocently; no harm by us is intended. For example, it may begin when God draws very near to you; you feel His presence, His power. You feel a definite sense of guidance. You are able to pray with liberty. But before you know it, you imagine He has communicated more than He Himself actually told you! You begin to presume; you think you know so much. It is not unlike when Joseph and Mary thought Jesus was in their company and proceeded without Him (Luke 2:43–44). I have done this more times than I would want you to know.

What happens then? Usually a huge disappointment. God may hide His face and withdraw Himself, and you feel suddenly alone and betrayed. You wonder if you really knew God at all. You feel angry. Joseph and Mary actually felt angry with Jesus: "Why have you treated us like this?" Mary said to Him (Luke 2:48).

When God Hides His Face

What, then, is truly going on? The answer is: God hides Himself for our good. This hiding is like a cleansing process; it rids us of thoughts we put there and that God didn't put there at all.

Nobody took himself more seriously than Elijah. He regarded himself as the only prophet on earth. "I am the only one of the LORD's prophets left" (1 Kings 18:22). Not only was Elijah completely wrong to say this; the boldness he exhibited on Mount Carmel (1 Kings 18:24–40) was followed by his being scared to death the next day, when Jezebel was trying to find him (1 Kings 19:1–3). Elijah was gently and lovingly put in his place (1 Kings 19:15–18). The psalmist, in a depressed frame of mind, said, "Darkness is my closest friend" (Psalm 88:18). At such times

God seems to betray us, having previously been so real to us.

It is not that God really does betray us; He only seems to do so. It is sometimes His way of saving us from ourselves. He must be true to Himself; after all, the buck stops with Him. He does us no favor to let us manipulate Him, to let us think we know Him better than we actually do, or to let us see Him as though He needed us. We all, unless we are stopped, are in danger of taking ourselves too seriously. I am ashamed to think how often I have done this.

What Jesus has done for us at the beginning of the Lord's Prayer is to remind us that we have a Father in heaven, but that He is very different from our human father. It is to remind us to let God be God, that God is wholly "other." He is in heaven; we are on earth. This shows us in one stroke how big He is, how small we are; how much He knows, how little we know.

But the words "in heaven" are not intended to limit God to one area or sphere. God isn't limited to a place called heaven. Solomon said it best: "The heavens, even the highest heaven, cannot contain you" (1 Kings 8:27). Not only that, God can come alongside us by the Holy Spirit in a hundredth of a second, to console us and make us feel special.

By inserting these two words, "in heaven," then, Jesus reminds us of the tenderness of God yet also His greatness. He reminds us not only of the love of God but His loftiness; not only of the sweetness of God but His sovereignty. We certainly do have an *abba* Father relationship with Him. But we must never outgrow our reverence for Him.

With some relationships, the more you get to know a person the less you truly respect them. I sometimes have people say to me, "I enjoy your preaching. I would love to get to know you better." I then hear myself say in my heart, *Don't spoil it.* But with our heavenly Father, the more you get to know Him the more you respect Him. If, then, you can understand more and more what you are saying when you pray the Lord's Prayer, the more you will respect your heavenly Father. You will come to love, respect and worship Him for being exactly the way He is.

45. Pausing to Worship

Hallowed be your name.

MATTHEW 6:9

This is the first petition of the Lord's Prayer: "Hallowed be your name," a petition designed that God will be put in His rightful place by our worship. You could equally conclude that Jesus is keeping us from rushing into God's presence. The most natural tendency in the world when we pray is to turn to God for our wants and wishes—putting our requests without any regard for the Father Himself—or what may be His agenda.

Another way of putting it: The Lord's Prayer is given to teach us primarily to seek God's face, not His hand. Seeking His hand is to ask Him to "do this" or "do that" for us. Seeking His face is to honor His personhood, His character, His heart and His own agenda. Most of us think of our own agenda when we pray; it usually does not occur to us that God has an agenda, too.

But Jesus knows this. He has given us that greatest prayer ever conceived, and it protects the throne of grace from abuse by our using prayer as a way of getting only what *we* want. Jesus knows that His Father has plans for Himself and a purpose for each of us. Our Lord Jesus therefore has worded this prayer in a manner that focuses on God before we get to our personal wants. It is a God-centered prayer.

Two Halves

Perhaps the best way to understand the Lord's Prayer is to divide it into two halves: God's Prayer List and Our Prayer List. God sets the agenda in both. Does God really have a prayer list? Yes. And the first thing He does is to put His prayer list first. He has three requests, that we pray for (1) His name to be hallowed, (2) His Kingdom to come and (3) His will to be done on earth as it is in heaven.

In a word: The Lord's Prayer gives an immediate invitation to pause and worship before we get

224

to anything else. God wants only what is best for us, and it is best that we learn to focus on God Himself before we focus on our personal needs.

However, keep in mind that Jesus is giving us a pattern for *ideal* praying. As I have said previously, there will be moments when you won't think to recall the pattern of the Lord's Prayer but instead will cry out for help! David apparently did this when he was in exile and felt so helpless with a bleak future. He was low and desperate. He simply prayed, "O LORD, turn Ahithophel's counsel into foolishness" (2 Samuel 15:31). And God answered (2 Samuel 17:14). Stephen was being stoned and in great pain just before he died. He simply cried out, "Lord, do not hold this sin against them" (Acts 7:60). God understands this. Our heavenly Father is not imposing the Lord's Prayer on us as an inflexible standard in order to get His attention. It is a guide, a pattern, a skeleton to help us to pray and to know Him.

In a Good Place

If saying "Our Father in heaven" is given to put us in our place, saying "Hallowed be your name," if we pray it from our hearts, demonstrates we are truly in our place when we approach God. It means we are in a good place, a very good place indeed. Keep in mind that this prayer is perfectly worded, that the order of the petitions sets a pattern for all praying.

Consider Hebrews 4:16, one of the great verses in the Bible to motivate us to pray: "Let us then approach the throne of grace with confidence, so that we may receive mercy and find grace to help us in our time of need." This verse is also carefully worded and designed to keep us from rushing into God's presence and enumerating our needs before we recognize who God is. It tells us that the first thing we do is to receive mercy when we approach God. Does this surprise you? This verse is addressing Christians, not the lost. And yet every Christian, when he or she prays, according to Hebrews 4:16 is to seek God for mercy before we do anything else. Mercy is what the lost sinner requests in order to be accepted by God. The person who is justified before God is the one who prays, "God, have mercy on me, a sinner" (Luke 18:13). And yet Christians are equally told to ask God for mercy when we approach the throne of grace. Why? We never outgrow the need of mercy. Hebrews 4:16 therefore makes us focus on God and His character before anything else.

Jesus' Loyalty to the Father

That is the purpose of this first petition, "Hallowed be your name." We are asked to pause to acknowledge the Father's name. "Don't move on in praying," says Jesus, "until you acknowledge My Father's name." Jesus was eternally loyal to the Father. "The Son can do nothing by himself; he can do only what he sees his Father doing" (John 5:19). His priority was always the Father's name. And now, teaching us how to pray, the first thing He does is to teach us also to be loyal to the Father. All that Jesus ever did was with the Father's name in mind. "I have come in my Father's name, and you do not accept me" (John 5:43). "'My food,' said Jesus, 'is to do the will of him who sent me and to finish his work'" (John 4:34). He could say near the close of His earthly ministry, "I have revealed you to those whom you gave me out of the world" (John 17:6).

Talk about loyalty! It is a rare commodity, a rare jewel. You have no way of knowing when you meet a new person whether he or she will be loyal. When you interview someone for a job, or you are looking for someone to work with you, it is virtually impossible to tell whether this person will be loyal. Loyalty is what you want in your spouse. It is what parents want in their children. It is what a manager wants in his office. It is what any leader or head of state wants of his or her people. It is what a pastor wants in his church. Jesus was unflinchingly loyal to the Father. Everything Jesus did was to uphold the name of His Father.

Now when Jesus tells us how to pray, He says, as it were, "Before you ask for anything else, say 'Hallowed be your name.'" The Greek word is from the verb *hagiazo,* "to be holy." The word is used in the imperative passive: "Let Your name be hallowed"—or, "treated as holy," as John Stott put it. Jesus is not saying, "Holy is Your name"; rather, it is a plea that the Father's name will be regarded everywhere as holy. Mind you, His name is holy anyway. "Holy and awesome is his name" (Psalm 111:9). "Praise his holy name" (Psalm 103:1). "Whose name is holy" (Isaiah 57:15). This petition, therefore, is not a plea that His name becomes holy, but that His name will be seen as holy.

We must ask ourselves a question: Do we regard the Father's name as holy? In this petition, we are made to pause, to acknowledge that name which, according to Paul, is "above every name" (Philippians 2:9). How can we ask that this name be hallowed if we ourselves do not treat His name as holy? We therefore are to be still, to think, to ponder this name. We are not merely approaching the Father; we are to acknowledge His name.

What's in a Name?

There are two essential things in a name: identity and reputation. "Moses said to God, 'Suppose I go to the Israelites and say to them, "The God of your fathers has sent me to you," and they ask me, "What is his name?" Then what shall I tell them?' God said to Moses, 'I AM WHO I AM. This is what you are to say to the Israelites: "I AM has sent me to you"'" (Exodus 3:13–14). The name *Yahweh* means "I am who I am," or, "I will be who I will be." That is God's name, which identifies the God of Israel.

In ancient times a person's name was closely related to what he or she was. The name was often explanatory and revelatory. The name Abraham, for example, means "father of many" (Genesis 17:5). The name Israel means "he struggles with God" (see Genesis 32:28). Shakespeare asked, "What's in a name?" but certainly he did not take biblical names seriously when he said, "A rose by any other name would smell as sweet." For God's name could only be *Yahweh.*

A name also is tied to one's reputation. "A good name is more desirable than great riches; to be esteemed is better than silver or gold" (Proverbs 22:1). Moses appealed to God's name and reputation when he interceded for Israel. The Lord told Moses He was going to destroy the people of Israel for their unbelief and start all over with Moses to build a new nation. But Moses said, "No!" "Then the Egyptians will hear about it! By your power you brought these people up from among them. . . . If you put these people to death all at one time, the nations who have heard this report about you will say, 'The LORD [*Yahweh*] was not able to bring these people into the land he promised them on oath'" (Numbers 14:13, 15–16). Moses thus appealed to God's great name—both His identity and reputation—and asked that God forgive the people instead. God did (Numbers 14:20).

Joshua interceded in the same way, fearing what enemy nations would think if God did not show mercy and intervene. Joshua asked, "What then will you do for your own great name?" (Joshua 7:9). The name of God was of paramount importance in ancient Israel. "Ascribe to the LORD the glory due his name" (1 Chronicles 16:29). David's chief motive in wanting to build the temple was for "the Name of the LORD my God" (1 Kings 5:5). God said, "I have chosen Jerusalem for my Name to be there" (2 Chronicles 6:6). What an honor for a city! What a reputation to maintain!

The Lord's Prayer should be prayed with earnest and tearful zeal that the name of the Lord be hallowed, that it be treated as holy. Both the identity and the reputation of God's name are meant when we pray this petition. I appeal to all who read these lines: Learn to respect the Father's name; pray that you will have a deep conviction and jealousy with regard to the name of the Lord. Pray that you will be grieved when His name is desecrated.

Participating in the Father's Name

To pray this first petition means to participate in the mystique and glory of the Father's name: the LORD, *Yahweh*. It is such a privilege to do so. God might have even kept us from knowing it. You could suggest that it is because Moses put God on the spot, as it were, that we even know His name (see again Exodus 3:13). God actually went for centuries without revealing His name to the patriarchs. He told Moses, "I appeared to Abraham, to Isaac and to Jacob as God Almighty,

but by my name the LORD [*Yahweh*] I did not make myself known to them" (Exodus 6:3).

Why is the name of the Lord awesome? It is because nobody else could have that name: *I am that I am.* Only God had no beginning. "From everlasting to everlasting you are God" (Psalm 90:2). Every child asks, "Where did God come from? Who made God?" The answer is ever the same: *God always was and is.* There is no more staggering thought. He always was; He never had a beginning. No brilliant intellect can fathom this. All we can do is to take off our shoes, for we are on holy ground. We have been given the privilege of participating in the divine nature (2 Peter 1:4). How do we participate in the glory and mystique of the Father's name? For one thing, by carefully pausing to acknowledge His name. By being guarded when we speak (Psalm 141:3). By admitting we are out of our depth. By realizing it is such a privilege. By praise and adoration. And now, with some knowledge of God's identity—and concern for His reputation—we can pray the Lord's Prayer with more care.

We must learn to praise and adore the name of our Father and Jesus' Father by our lips. "Not to us, O LORD, not to us but to your name be the glory, because of your love and faithfulness" (Psalm 115:1). "Glorify the LORD with me; let us exalt his name together" (Psalm 34:3). We do this when speaking, witnessing, in times of public prayer, as when those who feared the Lord "talked with each other, and the LORD listened and heard" (Malachi 3:16). Not only that, "A scroll of remembrance was written in his presence concerning those who feared the LORD and honored his name" (Malachi 3:16). We do it when singing, "Sing to the LORD a new song; sing to the LORD, all the earth. Sing to the LORD, praise his name" (Psalm 96:1–2). We do this when we pray, as did the Israelites in Nehemiah's day when they said, "Blessed be your glorious name, and may it be exalted above all blessing and praise" (Nehemiah 9:5).

We show deference to God's name by our conversation. I have said that my most "un-favorite" verse in the Bible is when Jesus said, "But I tell you that men will have to give account on the day of judgment for every careless word they have spoken" (Matthew 12:36). If that is true—and it is—the continual awareness of the honor of God's name will help me to be more guarded when I speak. We honor God's name by speaking blessings, as when Paul said, "Let your conversation be always full of grace, seasoned with salt, so that you may know how to answer everyone" (Colossians 4:6). What would our conversation be like if Jesus were physically present with us? Well, He certainly is present by the person of the Holy Spirit!

We honor our Father's name by our loyalty. That is the point I made above. Jesus was utterly loyal to the Father. Were we to become jealous for the honor of God's name, we would be mirroring the person and likeness of Jesus to a very great measure. There is a godly jealousy that extols God's name (2 Corinthians 11:2).

We Make a Pledge

When we pray "Hallowed be your name," it is a pledge to be accountable to that name. Accountability is when you are obliged to give a reckoning or explanation for your actions. If I pray for God's name to be treated as holy, yet have no regard for manifesting holiness in my own life, I am a hypocrite. I therefore regard my prayer for God's name to be hallowed as a commitment to be the kind of person who brings glory to God's name. We all are accountable to the Father for our actions. My prayer that His name be treated as holy will be applied by my sincere effort to honor His name by my personal life.

I must be careful never to abuse or misuse the name of God. The third Commandment, "You shall not misuse the name of the LORD your God" (Exodus 20:7), is vast and far more profound than many suppose. It certainly means I must not use profanity, that I never say things like, "Oh God," in anger. But that is the bare beginning of understanding the third Commandment. Jesus taught the fuller meaning of this in the Sermon on the Mount (Matthew 5:33–37). This includes dragging God's name into our personal interests—as in a pet doctrine or project—and claim to have God's backing for what we stand for. We all want to believe that God is on "our" side. When we use His name as we would a respected person to support our point of view, we misuse that precious name. It is not right to pray that God's name will

be treated as holy and then I turn around and use His name to endorse my enterprise in order to make others endorse it, too. Not only that, when I say, "The Lord told me this," chances are I am not trying to make Him look good but to make me look good. That is misusing His name. To pray "Hallowed be your name" is to embrace and live the meaning of the prophet's word, "I am the LORD; that is my name! I will not give my glory to another" (Isaiah 42:8).

Therefore, when I pray "Hallowed be your name" it is not something I utter with my mouth only; it is like a pledge—a solemn promise—to put this into practice. Praying the Lord's Prayer is not something you are called to do by praying it and then forgetting about it; praying it is a reminder to put it into practice, as we shall see with all the petitions. Praying the third petition is a pledge to treat God's name as holy since you are His child; you represent Him in the world and you are the nearest some people will ever come to seeing the Father's face.

But there is more. To pray "Hallowed be your name" is to pray for the advancement of the reputation of the Father's name. You are thus praying that the Father's name will be held in the honor that name deserves, in order that people may never think of Him without highest reverence. It is our prayer that the whole world will bow before God.

You can certainly apply this prayer to your own church. Would you not like God to put His name in your church as He did Jerusalem? What greater honor can there be? Pray then that God will esteem your church to the degree He is pleased to put His name there. Why? Because His reputation is at stake—and He knows that your church upholds His name, which is why He would not be ashamed to put His name there.

Does God Need Prayer?

This first petition of the Lord's Prayer is therefore like a prayer request from God that He Himself will grant that His name be hallowed. You might overlook what is obvious: This is God's own request! It is God's request that we pray for the honor of His name to be evident on the earth.

It may seem ironic. Should you pray for God? Does He need prayer? Not quite. But in this case He wants us to participate in the advancement of

His glory. He could in one second cause the whole world to hallow His name. But He has chosen instead to ask us to participate in a huge process. We therefore pray to Him that He will see to it that His name will be treated as holy. It is not unlike praying that He will manifest His glory, for God's glory and His name are inseparable. It is summed up well by the prophet Ezekiel: "I will show the holiness of my great name, which has been profaned among the nations, the name you have profaned among them. Then the nations will know that I am the LORD, declares the Sovereign LORD, when I show myself holy through you before their eyes" (Ezekiel 36:23).

Finally, if God does not seem to respond to our prayer, "Hallowed be your name," we continue to pray anyway, "Hallowed be your name." It is one thing to worship when He is pleasing us and coming through every day by answering our requests; it is another to worship when He isn't doing exactly what we want. The Lord can give or take away; "May the name of the LORD be praised" (Job 1:21). Or, as the three Hebrews put it when they were threatened with the possibility of a burning fiery furnace: "If we are thrown into the blazing furnace, the God we serve is able to save us from it. . . . But *even if he does not,* we want you to know, O king, that we will not serve your gods or worship the image of gold you have set up" (Daniel 3:17–18, emphasis mine).

Do not forget that the Father's name is holy already. He is holy in Himself. His name is all that is true of God, for God's name is what He is. But we pray that this will be demonstrated in *our* lives, whether all of those around us bow to God or not. The first petition of the Lord's Prayer, therefore, is a call to worship—to worship God for being just as He is.

46. Focusing on God's Interest

Your kingdom come.

MATTHEW 6:10

Jonathan Edwards (1703–1758), the greatest theologian in American history, taught us that one of the things the devil cannot do is to produce in us a love for God's interest and glory. Satan is a great counterfeiter. But he cannot put in your heart an unfeigned concern for what concerns God.

Why is this important? For one thing, if you have a love for God's glory, it shows you have been genuinely converted. I take the view that the primary basis of assurance of salvation is to look to Jesus Christ, who died on the cross for our sins. If you trust Him—not your works—you are saved. But there are some who feel they have done this and yet worry whether they have been saved. If so, Edwards's teaching provides a secondary ground of assurance. If you love God's glory and what interests Him, you can be sure you have crossed over from death into life; Satan did not put that love there. He is indeed a great counterfeiter, but he is simply unable to make you focus freely on God's concerns.

In giving us the second petition of the Lord's Prayer—"Your kingdom come"—Jesus further turns our attention to what interests God. Most of us care about what interests us—our needs, our wants, our wishes. We are living in the Me Generation—"What's in it for me?" So much preaching, teaching and theologizing today is man-centered. Much praying is man-centered. It wasn't always like that, but I'm afraid it is now. And getting worse.

Jesus makes us focus on God. He does it at the beginning of the prayer, not the end. It is the opposite of the way too many of us pray. We turn to God and start enumerating our requests, then at the end, just maybe, we say, "And we will give You all the praise for what You do"—and that

is about as much focus as God gets. When you realize that God wants only what is best for us, you should know also it is best for us to learn to focus on God before we focus on ourselves. Doing things His way is always best.

We have seen that God has a prayer list of His own, and He puts His requests right at the beginning of this remarkable prayer. First on God's prayer list is that we will pray that His name will be treated as holy on the planet He has made. His second request is that we pray for the coming of His Kingdom. God did not have to unveil His wish how we should pray. I have long been amazed at what He communicated through the psalmist. Having said that He has cattle on a thousand hills, He added, "If I were hungry *I would not tell you,* for the world is mine, and all that is in it" (Psalm 50:12, emphasis mine). And yet here He asks us to pray for the honor of His name and for the coming of His Kingdom.

Focusing on God Is in Our Best Interest

Why does Jesus reveal the Father's heart in this candid way? *It is for us.* He would do us no favor to let us carry on with a preoccupation of self-interest. When we become full of ourselves and keep putting our personal requests to God all the time, we set ourselves up for more selfishness and self-pity—which gets us nowhere. The best thing our Father could do for us is to require us to meditate on Him.

Are you depressed at the moment? Are you worried? Has everything suddenly gone wrong for you? What if you were thrown into prison like Paul and Silas, for doing the right thing? In the middle of the night they began singing praises and hymns to God. I for one would love to see a DVD replay of that scene when we get to heaven! While they were singing, a violent earthquake shook the foundations of the prison. The result was that the jailer and his family were converted (Acts 16:25–34).

We had a Sunday afternoon prayer meeting each week at Westminster Chapel prior to the evening service. I decided one day to get the group to postpone putting a request to God, but only to thank Him for things. It was slow getting started. We are in such a habit of putting forth our requests, even valid ones. But I kept the people from asking for anything for fifteen minutes each week—and then we could ask for things. Never forget Paul's exhortation: "Do not be anxious about anything, but in everything, by prayer and petition, *with thanksgiving,* present your requests to God" (Philippians 4:6, emphasis mine).

Thanksgiving takes discipline on our part. It takes effort. This is why the writer of Hebrews refers to "a sacrifice of praise" (Hebrews 13:15). In much the same way, our prayer of "Hallowed be your name, your kingdom come, your will be done on earth as it is in heaven" lifts us out of ourselves in order to participate in God's concerns. It not only honors Him but it is good for us, to get our eyes off ourselves. Not only that, it will lift your spirit. Try singing hymns when all hell is breaking out. God may send an earthquake and turn you into a soul winner!

When Paul had some time on his hands in Athens, he decided to go to the marketplace to witness to those who "happened to be there" (Acts 17:17). This led to what was arguably the most prestigious invitation Paul ever got—to address the philosophers at the Areopagus. It would be like giving a talk to the faculty at Oxford or Cambridge. Paul did not engineer the invitation; it fell in his lap. And all because Paul used his time to focus on God's interest.

In the Lord's Prayer, God lets us share in His own heartbeat. It is such a privilege. You and I are invited to partake in the greatest enterprise in all creation: the reason God sent His Son into the world in the first place. Talk about getting significance! There is no higher calling, no greater goal, no greater mission. You are I are given a mandate to pray for that which is greater than politics, greater than economic success, greater than national security: that God's Kingdom may come. It doesn't get better than that.

The Message of Jesus

The first message of Jesus was "Repent, for the kingdom of heaven is near" (Matthew 4:17; Mark 1:15). The opening sentence in the Sermon on the Mount is, "Blessed are the poor in spirit, for theirs is the kingdom of heaven" (Matthew 5:3). When Jesus told us to pray, "Your kingdom come," this is asking God to actualize—that is, to let us experience—what Jesus has been talking about up to then in the Sermon on the Mount. In other words, what Jesus had said was "near," or at hand, was now to be made real, actual.

However, the Kingdom of heaven that Jesus had in mind was vastly different from what the disciples hoped it would be. It is unlikely they grasped the meaning Jesus intended. Even after His resurrection they could not get out of their mind-set that Jesus had come to set up His Kingdom (Acts 1:6). They thought it would be visible, victorious and exalting Israel over all other nations, especially Rome. Wrong. The Kingdom does not come with "your careful observation," Jesus would later say, because the "kingdom of God is within you" (Luke 17:21). This coheres with all Jesus said about the Kingdom in the Sermon on the Mount, and further shows what Jesus meant by our praying, "Your kingdom come." Although the Kingdom of God can also be described in eschatological terms—meaning the Second Coming—Jesus clearly meant what is invisible, not what is visible. The Kingdom of God takes place in the heart.

The highest privilege and the greatest joy on earth is consciously being in God's Kingdom. Jesus said it comes through brokenness (Matthew 5:3), persecution (vv. 11–12) and exceeding the righteousness of the Pharisees (v. 20). And yet we are told in the Lord's Prayer to pray for it to come.

Question: Do you want the Kingdom of God to come? If so, would you believe that God the Father wants it to come more than you do? What should be most important to us—the wish for the Kingdom to come—is most important to God. God was grieved when ancient Israel asked for a king, to be like other nations. "I am . . . your king," God would say to them (Isaiah 43:15). But God gave in to their request and ordered Samuel to let them have their own way: "Listen to all that the people are saying to you; it is not you they have rejected, but they have rejected me as their king" (1 Samuel 8:7). I think of that scary verse in Psalm 106:15: God gave them their request "but sent leanness into their soul" (kjv). Never forget, too, that the prophet would say later on: "In my anger I gave you a king, and in my wrath I took him away" (Hosea 13:11). God Himself was their king, but God being their king was not enough for them; they wanted to be like other nations.

What God wanted was that He Himself would dwell in the hearts of the people of Israel, to reign over them and rule in them. This is exactly what Jesus came to bring: the Most High God, who inhabits eternity, would live in the hearts of His people. But for the disciples to grasp this perspective meant a paradigm shift, a changing of gears, a radical readjustment in their perception. They were looking for the nation of Israel to be put back on the map.

Grasping the Meaning of the Kingdom of God

What exactly did Jesus mean by "the kingdom"? There are several definitions that could be basically right. First, the fundamental meaning of the phrase "Kingdom of God" is simply the realm of God's domain. This realm is called a Kingdom because God alone is sovereign in it. His realm is in heaven and He reigns there. There is no rebellion to His will in heaven; He has no competition there, no rival. Heaven was emptied of all revolt a long time ago (2 Peter 2:4; Jude 6). God is worshiped there by all the angelic creation as well as all the believers who have died.

But His Kingdom extends to the earth as well. His presence inhabits the whole of His creation, although "we do not see everything subject to him" here below (Hebrews 2:8). But one day that will change; every knee will bow before Jesus Christ and every tongue confess Him as Lord and King (Romans 14:11; Philippians 2:9–11). This will be the ultimate manifestation of God's Kingdom. This is partly what Jesus means when we pray, "Your kingdom come."

However, the chief meaning of "kingdom" in the Lord's Prayer is what Jesus meant by it in His teaching, as revealed in the Sermon on the Mount. The Kingdom is the immediate, direct and conscious witness of the Holy Spirit. It is

God's conscious presence and enabling grace. Jesus primarily meant the rule of the un-grieved, unquenched Spirit in our hearts. The plea "Your kingdom come" was actually meant in Matthew 7:7: "Ask and it will be given to you; seek and you will find; knock and the door will be opened to you." Jesus said this in the Sermon on the Mount when, had His hearers been grasping what He was teaching, they would be hungry for God Himself. The Sermon on the Mount should make one thirsty for God. Jesus said if we are hungry and thirsty for righteousness, we would be filled (Matthew 5:6). If His hearers (or readers, in our case), took in what Jesus had been saying up to that point, then Matthew 7:7 would appeal to those who are hungry and thirsty for God. Whereas Matthew 7:11 promises "good gifts" to those who ask, the parallel account in Luke 11:13, also following the Lord's Prayer (Luke 11:2–4), inserts "Holy Spirit." Read the two accounts alongside each other (Matthew 7:7–11 and Luke 11:9–13) and you will see this.

The Kingdom Jesus describes simply comes to this: the Holy Spirit. After Jesus died, rose again and ascended to the right hand of God, a broader meaning of the Kingdom emerged: the Second Coming. The two men in white said to the disciples as they looked at the clouds into which the ascending Jesus disappeared, "This same Jesus, who has been taken from you into heaven, will come back in the same way you have seen him go into heaven" (Acts 1:11).

Paul also referred to the Kingdom as meaning the Second Coming when he said Jesus will judge the living and the dead "in view of his appearing and his kingdom" (2 Timothy 4:1). The point being, when Jesus comes again He will come in great power and glory, and the Kingdom of God will mean the defeat of all evil (1 Corinthians 15:24–28). This is understanding the Kingdom in an eschatological sense. Not only that, we have a perfect right to interpret "Your kingdom come" in the Lord's Prayer to mean the Second Coming. We say with John, "Come, Lord Jesus" (Revelation 22:20). It is perfectly right to pray for the Second Coming when you pray the Lord's Prayer.

However, I do not think this is what Jesus primarily meant at the time He was presenting the Lord's Prayer to His followers. Yes, we certainly can wish for the Second Coming when we pray the Lord's Prayer. But both in the Sermon on the Mount and Luke 11:3–13, the Kingdom is to be understood in terms of the Spirit, and we do well to apply it in that manner. If we think of the Kingdom as being only eschatological and futuristic, we will miss a great deal of what Jesus meant then—and what God wants to do now in all of us.

To interpret the Kingdom of God to mean only the future is to make the Sermon on the Mount basically irrelevant at the present time. It lets us off the hook and makes such righteousness unnecessary. I believe that the Sermon on the Mount is to be lived in the here and now. The Kingdom was taught by Jesus as being the kind of experience God wants for His people—now—before Jesus comes again. This means experiencing an internal righteousness that exceeds the righteousness of the Pharisees (which was only an external righteousness). What Jesus was teaching was utterly alien to the Pharisees. For example: having no hatred in the heart but rather blessing your enemy (Matthew 5:21–22, 43–48), no lusting (5:27–30), giving and praying to be seen only by God (6:1–8).

Therefore, when Jesus told us to pray, "Your kingdom come," He meant inviting the Holy Spirit so to dwell in us that we demonstrate the very righteousness Jesus has preached. We also simultaneously pray for the Second Coming of Jesus when we say, "Your kingdom come." Yes, we have it both ways.

The Paradox Regarding God's Kingdom

And yet there is a paradox in understanding the Kingdom of God. The Kingdom of God has been established by Jesus, and yet we nonetheless pray for it to come. God is sovereign and in complete control. So we do not pray for Him to be our sovereign, our monarch, our king. He already is. Jesus now reigns at the right hand of God. And yet we pray for His Kingdom to come, that it will become apparent in our hearts—and in the world, that all will know that Jesus Christ is Lord. This is a recurring theme in Ezekiel: "And so I will show my greatness and my holiness, and I will make myself known in the sight of many nations. Then they will know that I am the LORD"

(Ezekiel 38:23). And yet when we pray for the Second Coming, this is what we are hoping for.

There is a second paradox: the open declaration that we all see Jesus Christ is coming anyway, and yet we pray for it. This will happen on a date already set by God the Father (Matthew 24:36). Nothing can stop this. But why pray for it? I can give two reasons. First, if John Wesley is basically right, that God does nothing but in answer to prayer, we should pray for the Second Coming. Secondly, there is a sense in which we may speed the day of His coming (2 Peter 3:11–12). God is sovereign in all His timing. But—and don't try to figure it out—prayer makes things happen.

There is actually a third paradox. Praying for the Kingdom to come is an unselfish request—it focuses on God's interest—yet it is in our own interest to pray this. It is unselfish in that we rise above our personal requests and pray for God's greater glory. We see sin and rebellion in society; poverty and hunger; corruption in politics and business; millions of abortions; evil and suffering; a world that does not know God; a world that hates God. We long for God to be glorified and recognized. And yet to pray, "Your kingdom come," becomes almost selfish. The Holy Spirit will give us a love for God's interest and glory, and we might even get carried away with wanting God's honor. It becomes a part of you—you can't tell whether it is a natural or spiritual desire, whether it is what God wants or what you want—because you want it so much. "Come, Lord Jesus."

What is the purpose in praying for God's Kingdom to come? Why focus on God's interest? The answer is, partly, that we will get our eyes off ourselves. As we have said, before bringing our personal requests, we focus on God and what is His burden. God is the most maligned Person in the universe, the most unvindicated Person who ever was or is. I want to be around when God clears His own name. He looks forward to it, too. So let us make every effort to get our eyes off ourselves and our personal vindication and seek God's.

There are two things further I want to mention in this chapter: First, the un-grieved Spirit. This is what I mean: The Holy Spirit is a very sensitive person and can be grieved (Ephesians 4:30). When He is grieved, it is as if the dove (a

New Testament symbol of the Spirit) gets frightened and flies away. Not that the Holy Spirit utterly leaves us—no, that is not the case. But we temporarily lose the blessing of the Spirit—the anointing. When the Holy Spirit is grieved, the anointing lifts from us; when the Holy Spirit is not grieved—and the Spirit is Himself—the anointing enables us to do what had been utterly impossible. This is why I said earlier that the Kingdom is the rule of the un-grieved Spirit, and that is precisely what we pray for when we say, "Your kingdom come."

Second, there is the silent divorce between the Word and the Spirit. I believe that the Word and Spirit will be remarried—and that the simultaneous combination will result in spontaneous combustion. This will bring the Kingdom of God in power like our generation has not seen. Therefore, when you pray, "Your kingdom come," it is most fitting to pray that the Kingdom will come in this apostolic power—as in the book of Acts. I urge you to pray for this. I believe this will happen before the Second Coming, resulting in power to the Church that is unprecedented since the days of the early Church. I believe the blindness on Israel will be lifted, resulting in countless thousands of Jews coming to see Jesus as their Messiah. I believe Islam will be penetrated by the Gospel and millions of Arabs will be converted to Jesus Christ. All this will come as a result of the Word and Spirit coming together as in the earliest Church.

To pray, "Your kingdom come," is to pray for the success of the Gospel. It is to be raised above our own personal needs for a moment. Focus on God—His prayer requests. What God wants is always what is best for us. What began as an effort, a discipline and a sacrifice—putting our needs to one side—ends up as a blessing: being filled with the Holy Spirit and an experience of the Kingdom of God that Jesus had in mind all along.

47. Wanting What God Wants

Your will be done on earth as it is in heaven.

MATTHEW 6:10

This is the third petition of the Lord's Prayer—you could say God's third "prayer request"—but it is all for us. In any case, before we are allowed to turn to our personal situation in the Lord's Prayer we are particularly blessed with an invitation to pray for God's will.

I am so glad this petition is there. The sweetest place in the world to be is in the will of God. I would rather have this than anything; I would rather pray for this than anything. What a privilege to pray like this. How wonderful that God wants this for us.

The most thrilling thing to me is that (1) God has a will of His own and (2) He wants us to participate in it. This petition militates against a theological perspective that has been vogue for a few years called "open theism." It is deadly. But it has caught on with a surprising number of people. The idea is that God has no definite will of His own but cooperates with us; we and God are in it together; He gets input from us to know what to do next. Not only that, there is no guarantee that God will be victorious at the end of the day if you take this perspective seriously. He could lose in the end. Wrong. God losing is not possible.

Not only does God have a will of His own— our Lord instructs us to acknowledge His will before we move on. The fact that Jesus said to pray, "Your will be done," shows that God has a will, an opinion.

There is an inseparable connection between the will of God and the glory of God. The root word of the Greek *doxa* (glory), from which we get "doxology," means *opinion*. The heart of the glory of God is God's opinion. I once wrote a catechism for a church of which I was pastor in Oxfordshire before coming to London, and in it I defined the glory of God as the "dignity of His will." There

is nothing greater, nothing wiser, nothing safer, nothing nobler, nothing better than the will of God. For the will of God reveals His glory.

Has it occurred to you that God has an opinion on the matter confronting you at the moment? Do you realize that God has an opinion as to what is going on in the world today? Do you not know that God has an opinion on what you should do next?

I, for one, want His opinion. Don't you? Of course you do.

You honor a person by asking for their opinion, their wisdom. I ask for people's opinions all the time. I will have a number of friends read the manuscript of this book before it is published. Why? Because in a multitude of advisors there is safety (Proverbs 11:14). I want to get it right. My greatest fear is that I would accept and teach error.

Therefore, when Jesus tells us to pray, "Your will be done," the assumption is that the Father already has an opinion. His opinion is what lies behind His will. Jesus takes this for granted. This is really no great revelation, that God has a will. It is merely that I have learned to appreciate this fact the older I get.

So what Jesus requests of us is that we acknowledge that God has a will. We don't inform Him what His will ought to be. We only want Him to have His way. "Your will be done." We don't want anything to stop His will from being perfectly carried out. We respect His opinion; we want it carried out.

By mentioning the Father's will, then, Jesus shows that (1) God is independent from us; He has a will of His own without our input; and (2) God thinks for Himself; He has a mind of His own. In a word: God has a plan. It is an architectural blueprint drawn up from the foundation of the world. Long before we were born, long before our parents were born, long before their parents were born, long before Adam and Eve were created in the Garden of Eden, long before there was ever a tree, a blade of grass or a star, God had a plan. "I make known the end from the beginning, from ancient times, what is still to come. I say: My purpose will stand, and I will do all that I please" (Isaiah 46:10). "When I was woven together in the depths of the earth, your eyes saw my unformed body. All the days ordained for me were written in your book before one of them came to be" (Psalm 139:15–16).

The Revealed Will of God

One of the main things I learned from studying the Puritan William Perkins (1558–1602) at Oxford was that the will of God is to be understood in two ways: (1) His revealed will and (2) His secret will. The revealed will of God is, simply, the Bible. The Bible includes 66 books, 39 in the Old Testament, 27 in the New Testament. The Old Testament is generally comprised of the Law (the first five books), the Psalms and the Prophets. But there are also books of poetry and historical books. The New Testament is generally comprised of the teachings of Jesus and letters, mostly from the apostle Paul.

Do you want to know the will of God? Read the Bible! That is the best, most God-honoring way to know His will. It is caring enough about Him to read what He has said. As the hymn put it, "What more can he say than to you he hath said?" I don't mean to be unfair, but you probably get to know God's will largely in proportion to how much you actually love God—that is, love His revealed will, His written Word.

Sadly, most people want a shortcut to God's will. Reading the Bible takes too long! They want to know right now what they should do. But the truth is, the more you know the Bible the more you know His will. You get to know God basically one way: by spending time with Him. And this is done basically two ways: reading the Bible and praying. When you spend time each day praying and reading your Bible, you are going to get to know God more and more! That's a guarantee.

A friend of mine who is known for his prophetic gift told me how he gets tired of dozens of people coming up to him every five minutes, asking, "Do you have a word for me?" He was weary of this, but one evening in church a lady asked him again, "Do you have a word for me?" He was angry (although, fortunately, the lady didn't know it), and he handed her his own Bible and said, "Yes, I have a word for you—read this!" She took it as a word from God. When the same man with the prophetic gift returned to the same church two years later, everyone said this lady knew the Bible more than anybody in the town! She had taken his word as a "rhema" word, which I now will describe.

There are at least two Greek words translated "word": *logos* and *rhema*. Although you cannot push the distinctions too far (because sometimes they overlap), there has been a craze in recent years for a "rhema" word—known as a prophetic word, a word of knowledge, a direct word from God what to do next. You hear it on "Christian television" all the time: "Don't change the channel! Stay turned and receive a 'rhema' word!" This is what so many people want. In the day of fast foods—McDonald's and Kentucky Fried Chicken (which I confess I enjoy!)—too many of us want a quick word from God because we are too busy to read the Bible. I don't think He likes that very much. You esteem God's glory more by seeking His will in His Word than by focusing on a "rhema" word. I do believe God gives an immediate word on occasion; I have had that happen, for which I am most grateful. But by and large, the best way to know God's will is to know His Word so well that you hardly need to want anything more than this.

The Secret Will of God

This refers to the details of His plans that He conceived before creation. This aspect of God's will is vast and profound. It refers to His infinite wisdom, His unrevealed plans for us, where we will be five years from now, who will be saved, the exact date of the Second Coming, whom one should marry, what your career should be, where you should live, when the Holy Spirit will come in unprecedented power.

The secret will of God is meant when the prophet said, "My thoughts are not your thoughts, neither are your ways my ways" (Isaiah 55:8). Paul was referring largely to God's secret will when he said, "In him we were also chosen, having been predestined according to the plan of him who works out everything in conformity with the purpose of his will" (Ephesians 1:11). Mind you, it is the *revealed* will here (Paul's word) that shows there is a *secret* will. The trouble is, we tend to seek out what God's secret will is before we get to know His revealed will.

A "rhema" word usually refers to God's secret will. In June 1970 God gave me a "rhema" word, showing Louise and me in a second—clearly, absolutely and unmistakably—that we were to resign our church in Fort Lauderdale and complete my theological education, which eventually led us to England. There was never a doubt in my mind from that moment. However, that sort of thing (at least for me) does not come every day.

The secret will of God is linked to predestination. For example, "This man [Jesus] was handed over to you by God's set purpose and foreknowledge" (Acts 2:23). "They [Pontius Pilate and those who crucified Jesus] did what your [God's] power and will had decided beforehand should happen" (Acts 4:28). "All who were appointed for eternal life believed" (Acts 13:48). It is God's revealed will that tells us that God has a secret will.

Sometimes the two overlap. When Ananias informed Paul, "The God of our fathers has chosen you to know his will" (Acts 22:14), it was a reference to God's secret will for Paul. But knowing what God's will was in Acts 22:24 meant God's revealed will. Ananias actually meant that the Holy Spirit was going to reveal the truth of God's Word to Paul, which he had not grasped before. I can think of no greater gift than for God to reveal the knowledge of His will—the Bible—to me. My greatest aspiration is to understand the Bible.

I suppose the secret will of God is more interesting, more compelling, more exciting and sometimes more sensational than the revealed will. Getting an undoubted word of knowledge is easier than hours and hours of wrestling with God in reading the Bible and praying. But the latter should be our immediate and fundamental search; the secret will of God will be clear to you when you need to know it. Seek to know the secret will of God as a primary focus, and it will

elude you; aspire to know the revealed will of God and you will gain the general knowledge of His will—and receive a "rhema" word when you aren't expecting it.

The more you seek to know God's revealed will, the more you will see His secret will unfolded. Paul was determined to go to Asia because he was obeying God's revealed will (to preach the Gospel to every person). But to his surprise, he was kept by the Holy Spirit from preaching the word in the province of Asia (Acts 16:7). The revealed will would mean, "Go to Asia." But the secret will said, "Stop—don't go to Asia." This could only mean that God would have someone else go to Asia—or that Paul would do it later on. But not then.

The Will of God in the Lord's Prayer

When Jesus told us to pray, "Your will be done," did He mean God's revealed will or His secret will? Answer: both. We pray that the truth of God as revealed in Scripture will be carried out on this earth. We equally pray that all that God has planned for us will be carried out, in His time. It is a prayer for both the success of what God has promised in His Word and the execution of all His purposes in the world.

When you pray, "Your will be done," it also means you accept His will. When you say, "Your will be done," you affirm His revealed will (Scripture); also you accept what He has willed (the unfolding of His plans). When Paul could not be persuaded to avoid going to Jerusalem, everyone acquiesced, saying, "The Lord's will be done," although they were not very happy about it (Acts 21:14). Job said, "The LORD gave and the LORD has taken away; may the name of the LORD be praised" (Job 1:21).

Accepting God's will means that you approve of it, you honor it. Not that you are always thrilled to your fingertips, but you dignify His will. Why? You want what God wants. We all must follow Jesus to Gethsemane. There Jesus prayed, "Father, if you are willing, take this cup from me; yet not my will, but yours be done" (Luke 22:42). If we know what God wants, we say, "Yes." If we don't know what God wants, we sign a blank check. I write my name at the appropriate place and say to God, "You fill it out."

Dignifying God's will is to show our love for His glory. The glory of God is the dignity of His will; we show we love His glory by dignifying His will—approving it, wanting what God wants.

And yet when we pray, "Your will be done," we are appealing for God to carry out His will. Whatever God has in mind, we say, "Do it." The sooner the better, "Your will be done." It means surrendering to His will, surrendering our so-called rights (which we thought were ours). It means surrendering to His plan and wishes. It is like the hymn put it, "My ambitions, plans and wishes at His feet in ashes lay."

It is not always easy to know the next step forward in knowing the secret will of God. In the Old Testament, people would cast lots. This is how the tribes of Israel knew where to settle (Joshua 18:10). Gideon put forward his fleece to know for sure he was hearing God (Judges 6:39–40). The urim and thumim (when the priest would reach into his pouch and pull up a white stone or black stone) were used to know the will of God. A white stone meant "yes," a black stone "no"—or something like this let the priest know what to do.

In the New Testament, the way forward to know the will of God was to know the Word of God so well and be filled with the Spirit that you had clear guidance. Dr. Martyn Lloyd-Jones used to say that the Bible was not given to replace the miraculous; it was given to correct abuses. Therefore, we may have the kind of relationship with God that we know His Word backward and forward, but also know the Holy Spirit in a manner that we can sense His "yes" and "no." We read that the Holy Spirit said to Philip, "Go to that chariot and stay near it" (Acts 8:29). This intimacy and obedience led to the conversion of the Ethiopian eunuch. God can do that today, too.

The Accomplishment of God's Will on Earth

What we want to see, then, is the accomplishment of God's will. "Your will be done on earth as it is in heaven." We pray that God's will shall be accomplished on earth without any resistance. *The will of God is being done perfectly in heaven.* There is no rebellion in heaven. There will be no more revolts in heaven (Jude 6; 2 Peter 2:4). All the angels that remain are elect angels (1 Timothy 5:21).

The Lord's Prayer therefore gives us a mandate to pray that God's will on earth will be carried out as perfectly as it is in heaven. All the inhabitants of heaven worship God without any constraint or reluctance. The angels, the cherubim, the seraphim, those with the Lord (Hebrews 12:23) are all worshiping God with total freedom.

Our prayer, then, is that God's will in heaven will be mirrored on earth, without any interference, reluctance or rebellion. But should we pray for what will never be accomplished until the end of the world? Yes. Jesus' high priestly prayer is not fully answered yet: "My prayer is not for them alone. I pray also for those who will believe in me through their message, that all of them may be one, Father, just as you are in me and I am in you. May they also be in us so that the world may believe that you have sent me" (John 17:20–21). So, yes, we keep praying for that which is not answered yet.

But what can we fully wish for now? I should pray that, as far as we are concerned, there will be no revolt left in us, no rebellion in us, no stubbornness in us, no reluctance in us. I can't answer for the world; I can't answer for you. I can answer for myself. I want God's will to be carried out in me as perfectly as it is being carried out in heaven.

Some people take the view that this prayer is a mandate for people's healing. The view is there is no sickness in heaven; therefore, we should ask God to heal people and expect them to be as it is in heaven. Nice thought. But I don't think that is the meaning. There is no evil in heaven, either. Evil will remain until Jesus comes. So, too, with sickness and suffering; they will be around until Jesus comes. God can heal and sometimes does heal. But not because it is His secret will that everybody be healed. We all have to die sometime. I think it is quite right to pray for people's healing and to do so with the Lord's Prayer in mind, as long as you submit to the possibility that He may choose not to heal. Then is the time to say, "The will of the Lord be done." It shows that you dignify His will.

The basic meaning of this third petition, "Your will be done," is that we plead with God to have His way below, as revealed in Scripture. That righteousness will prevail. That the Church will flourish. That the Gospel will succeed. We keep praying—on and on and on—whether or not we see our prayers answered. Why keep praying? Because we are commanded to do so.

It is a prayer we must mean with all our hearts. As John Stott said, it is folly to resist God's will. It is wisdom to discern it, to desire it and to do it. Our prayer, therefore, is that God will get what He wants in *us,* at least. I cannot speak for anybody else. I am responsible to mean it when I say, "Lord, in *me,* Your will be done as You have wanted it accomplished in heaven." I pray that what God envisages for me will be carried out without a whimper or a whine, but only with complete submission. It means dignifying His will. That is what God is after.

48. Daily Dependence

Give us today our daily bread.

MATTHEW 6:11

This is the fourth petition of the Lord's Prayer, the first on God's prayer list for us. The prayer changes from "your" to "us" and "our": "Give us this day our daily bread" (KJV). This suggests we are a part of a wider body of believers—a part of the family of God. We are all in this together. We think of ourselves, yes, but also of others who are praying this prayer.

God not only wants what is best for us by asking us to focus first on Him; He shows He cares about our daily struggles by focusing on our daily needs. We are now given the green light to give attention to ourselves when we pray.

But He sets the agenda! Yes, He now ordains that we pray for ourselves. But He knows what is best for us and in what order the needs should be mentioned. The remaining petitions pertain to what we need. God has promised to supply all our needs according to His riches in glory (Philippians 4:19). Jesus will say later on in the Sermon on the Mount, "So do not worry, saying, 'What shall we eat?' or 'What shall we drink?' or 'What shall we wear?' . . . Your heavenly Father knows that you need them" (Matthew 6:31–32). So here we are invited to pray for our needs.

It may seem an incongruity: to pray for what God has already promised to supply anyway! But that is the way it is. He invites us to participate in His care for us. There are times when we wonder if God has forgotten. It is comforting to know that He knows this, too; hence we pray daily for these essentials to life. The grandeur and glory of God now condescend to our own personal situation. I also think of John Wesley's principle, that God does nothing but in answer to prayer.

Imagine this! The great Creator and sovereign God of heaven and earth stoops to where we are. "For this is what the high and lofty One says—he

who lives forever, whose name is holy: 'I live in a high and holy place, but also with him who is contrite and lowly in spirit, to revive the spirit of the lowly and to revive the heart of the contrite'" (Isaiah 57:15). The Most High God invites us to pray about the smallest of things. But don't worry about praying over small things; with God everything is small.

And yet to pray for daily bread is no small thing. When we live in a land of plenty, this may seem small. But when you live in a place where you don't know where your next meal is coming from, this request is far from small.

As I was writing this book, the economy throughout the world is on the brink of collapse. Many are saying it is the worst financial crisis since the Great Depression of 1929. My dad lived during that time. He used to talk about it. He used to describe how he once watched five hundred men stand in line for employment when there was only one job to be given out. The sight was so traumatic that my dad would weep as he recalled it. It is possible that we are entering into another era like that of 1929. If so, the petition we now deal with—"Give us today our daily bread"—is very relevant indeed.

Physical Bread Is Our Lord's Priority for Us

Jesus begins with the undoubted priority: our daily bread.

But this surprises some. For this reason, many suppose that "daily bread" refers to spiritual bread, since Jesus called Himself the "bread of life" (John 6:35). Could this petition therefore refer to spiritual food? I reply: It might have referred to spiritual food and drink, but not in this case. You may think that God would put our spiritual needs first—as praying for forgiveness, to be led away from temptation, etc.

But no. He Himself tells us what to pray for first. He begins with the body. The Lord's Prayer deals with the whole man: body, soul, spirit. God chose to give us bodies. God gave Jesus a body. "A body you prepared for me" (Hebrews 10:5), our Lord envisaged, before the Word became flesh (John 1:14). God dignified our bodies by preparing a body for the Second Person of the Godhead when He came to the earth. So in this magnificent prayer, God begins the unfolding of His prayer list for us with a reference to our body. "For he knows how we are formed, he remembers that we are dust" (Psalm 103:14).

But why would God begin with the body and not the soul?

The truth is, it is extremely difficult to cope spiritually when we are unwell—hungry, thirsty, tired, deep in debt, going without sleep and having no money. I think that is why Jesus put this request first, prior to spiritual needs. General William Booth, founder of the Salvation Army, used to say it is hard to preach the Gospel to someone with an empty stomach. Likewise, it is hard to pray when we are overwhelmed with daily physical, emotional and material problems.

I think also that Jesus begins with this particular petition in order to let us know that God knows our situation and remembers what we are like—"dust," as the psalmist put it. God knows we have to eat to live. God made this a priority.

I believe, too, that God put this petition here to remind us that there are starving people all over the world. When we sit down to eat, we should pray for those who have no food. I fear that most of us take for granted that we will eat today and tomorrow. It does not worry us. But it should at least make us grateful that we have bread on the table. This petition is designed, therefore, also to make us grateful, and to pray for those in deep need.

Not only that, when we pray, "Give us today our daily bread," we should be conscious of the entire Body of Christ. If, for example, I have a pain in my toe or hand, I might say, "My toe hurts," or, "My hand hurts," but it is also right to say that "I hurt." In other words, my whole body feels the pain. Likewise, if there are those around us who suffer, we should feel their pain. And if there are those who are in fear of not having food for today,

we should feel for those in the Body—wherever they may be in the world—when we pray, "Give us today our daily bread." If there is one person suffering who is a part of the Body of Christ, I should feel it—and should pray for anyone who is suffering at the present time. That is partly what is meant by this petition, "Give us today our daily bread"—not just my daily bread, but yours, too.

The Lord's Prayer ought to make us aware of that multitude no one can count and make us feel what all believers are feeling. We are told to rejoice with those who rejoice and weep with those who weep (Romans 12:15). Praying this particular petition, then, ought to serve to make us share in the sufferings of fellow believers in our immediate community yet also throughout the world. We are a part of a vast Body. It is huge. It includes all those who have been chosen from the foundation of the world. We must feel we are indeed our "brother's keeper" (Genesis 4:9). We should, therefore, think of others—those in need—when we pray, "Give us today our daily bread." It is a way—even if it is a small way—that we can intercede for those who do not have what we have. And it certainly ought to make us very grateful indeed that we are so blessed.

"Daily Bread" Means Essential Needs

"Daily bread" refers not only to food on our tables but to life's essential needs. This petition does not refer to literal bread only. "Bread" in Hebrew meant all kinds of nutrition. But it is even more than that. "Daily bread" refers to everything nonspiritual that we must have in order to live and cope. It refers to physical needs, emotional needs, material needs—every need not specifically mentioned in the petitions of the Lord's Prayer.

Therefore, when you pray, "Give us today our daily bread," you are asking God to step in to give you not only food but also shelter and clothing; to supply your financial needs; to give emotional strength and clarity of mind; to give you friends and fellowship; to grant transportation as needed; to equip you for your job, career and future; to help you get done what you need to get done this very day; to be at your best; to help you in your preparation and to provide providences that further God's plan for your life. "Our daily bread," then, covers everything that is essential to our well-being in life.

The psychologist Abraham Maslow (1908–1970) argued that people everywhere are subject to what he called a "hierarchy of needs." At the bottom are things such as food, shelter and sleep, these being elementary physiological needs. Next come the basic needs for safety and security. As you move up Maslow's "pyramid" you come to what he called "belonging needs" (love, acceptance, affiliation). Then come "esteem needs" (self-respect, social status, the approval of others). At the top of the pyramid is "self-actualization" (a musician must make music, an artist must paint, a poet must write, etc., if they are going to be at peace with themselves). It is not farfetched to apply this petition, "Give us today our daily bread," to these kinds of needs. We all have these needs. Our Lord graciously leads us to pray for such. What a wonderful God we have!

What Maslow calls self-actualization is what I call one's anointing, or gifting. It is what you are born to do—and what comes easily. We all need to discover our gifts, our calling. Praying the Lord's Prayer, therefore, includes the petition that you will discover your own particular calling. If, then, you feel you have not yet discovered your calling—what your own anointing is—you have a perfect right to pray this petition with precisely that in mind!

This petition is also a reference to nature. Contrary to many of the Church fathers, "our daily bread" is not a reference to our spirituality. The Church fathers missed this point entirely—including Tertullian, Cyprian and Augustine, who said this request referred to spiritual food. They allegorized this petition, claiming that it referred to invisible bread, the Lord's Supper. "Absurd," said John Calvin, who normally affirmed the Church fathers. The reformers were down-to-earth in their treatment of this petition. Calvin said this petition refers to whatever God knows to be essential. Martin Luther said it meant everything necessary for the preservation of this life: food, a healthy body, good weather, house, home, children, good government—even peace.

John Stott observed that to decline to mention our needs on the ground that we should not bother God with such trivialities is as great an error as to allow trivialities to dominate our prayers.

This petition is therefore a reference to essential nourishment of the whole man—body, spirit, soul, mind. There can be no doubt that this petition also reflects the Old Testament account of the daily manna that God provided supernaturally from heaven. The children of Israel were given "manna" every day—enough for everyone, and twice the amount on Friday, so that they would not have to go looking for manna on the Sabbath (Exodus 16:13–30). Although the manna itself was supernatural, the purpose was to keep the Israelites alive.

While some of us, sadly, live to eat, Jesus assumes we must eat in order to live. Furthermore, unless we are fasting on purpose, the assumption is that we must nourish our bodies every day; we should be thankful for food to eat every day. Keep in mind, too, that Jesus originally addressed an agrarian society. One crop failure spelled disaster. Not only that, laborers were paid daily for the work they achieved. The pay was so low that it was almost impossible to save anything. The day's pay purchased the day's food.

This petition, then, was no empty rhetoric for Jesus' original hearers. Food nowadays, however, comes to countries like the United States and the United Kingdom from all over the world. When I grew up we got to eat strawberries, for example, only once a year. But now you can eat strawberries every day! This is true with most fruits and vegetables.

God Himself is the ultimate source of every good thing. "Every good and perfect gift is from above, coming down from the Father of the heavenly lights, who does not change like shifting shadows" (James 1:17). This refers also to having a job. The prayer does not mean, "Do not work—just ask God to feed you," however. We are all under the curse of the Fall. Like it or not, the decree in the Garden of Eden—"By the sweat of your brow you will eat your food until you return to the ground" (Genesis 3:19)—is still in play. Said Paul to his converts: "For even when we were with you, we gave you this rule: 'If a man will not work, he shall not eat'" (2 Thessalonians 3:10).

Thank God for your job. Thank Him for income. But do not take the Lord's Prayer as a way of avoiding your responsibilities!

Sleep is a physical need. "He grants sleep to those he loves" (Psalm 127:2). There are times I feel the Lord does not love me—as when I can't sleep! I know what it is to fear not sleeping when I have to get up early in the morning. It is a neurotic problem I have had most of my life. When I do not have to get up early, I can usually sleep well. When I know I have to get up early to meet a schedule, I know what it is to stay awake a whole night! I have learned to be thankful for every good night's sleep. When I have not slept well, I cannot think as clearly. I have difficulty reading my Bible and praying—not to mention writing. The Lord's Prayer, therefore, is a request to get the sleep we need. And I am very thankful indeed for a good night's sleep.

Your daily bread includes the ability to work. We should be thankful we can work, and we should keep in mind those who cannot because of disability or being bedridden. Thank God that you have a job; thank Him that you have an ability to do your job. Thank Him for strength, health, intelligence, peace. My own calling is teaching and preaching. I live for insight. If Maslow's concept of self-actualization is correct, I am at the peak of my anointing when I am seeing things in Scripture I had not read before or thought of before. I pray all the time for insight. It is my daily bread, so to speak. We all need encouragement, approval, appreciation and acceptance in order to perform at our best. When I receive insight, it makes me feel more accepted by my heavenly Father than anything! And yet when I also have the encouragement and acceptance of those around me, it spurs me on to work better.

This petition, therefore, refers to emotional needs. You need attention, to be noticed, to be recognized, to be affirmed. It is a natural need. Be thankful every day that such needs are met. Think of those who are suffering in this area at the moment. They are all around you. Pray for them, "Give us this day *our* daily bread," for those in the Body of Christ who suffer emotional deprivation. And be thankful that your needs are being met. Be thankful every single day.

We can all do with a compliment now and then! I will never forget two letters I received the same day. The first I opened was regarding my book *The Anointing*. A man tore it to shreds, really

putting the book down in his letter. I was quite devastated. I then opened the second letter. It, too, would you believe, was about my book *The Anointing*. The person wrote to thank me and to tell me how much it encouraged them!

This petition is a reference to *now*. "Give us *today* our daily bread." It is easier to pray about the distant future than to pray, "Give us today our daily bread." Most of us in the affluent West have enough for today and tomorrow, with food in freezers. Why should you and I pray for daily bread "today"? Because we must stay conscious of daily dependence, whether for strength, energy, sleep, health—all that will challenge us today.

This word "daily" comes from a Greek word that is found nowhere else except in Matthew 6:11 and Luke 11:3, the two references to the Lord's Prayer in the New Testament. It is a word not found in Hellenistic literature nor in the Septuagint (the Greek translation of the Old Testament). Most scholars believe that the Lord has coined a word. What does "daily" bread mean? Don Carson believes the best translation is "coming day." If prayed in the morning, it means *today*. If prayed in the evening, it means *tomorrow*.

But what about Matthew 6:34, "Do not worry about tomorrow, for tomorrow will worry about itself"? Michael Eaton says praying about tomorrow is the means by which we are free from anxiety about tomorrow. If I pray the Lord's Prayer in the evening, I pray for the needs of the coming day, so I can go to sleep. After all, Paul said, "Do not be anxious about anything, but in everything, by prayer and petition, with thanksgiving, present your requests to God" (Philippians 4:6).

The Purpose of This Petition

The purpose of the petition, "Give us today our daily bread," is to warn us against greed. Why? Because it refers to what is immediate—"today" (or tomorrow, if prayed at night). Not next week or next month or next year. It pertains only to what you and I need. It is not a prayer to win the lottery. In economics there are essentially three levels: needs, comforts, luxuries. This prayer embraces only *needs*. Necessities. What I have to have to survive day by day. Most of us in the affluent West have more than enough.

I return to this matter of being thankful. The purpose of this petition is to teach us gratitude. God loves gratitude; God hates ingratitude. The psalmist learned gratitude. "Give thanks to the LORD, for he is good" (Psalm 106:1). "Give thanks to the LORD, for he is good" (Psalm 107:1). "Since we are receiving a kingdom that cannot be shaken, *let us be thankful*" (Hebrews 12:28, emphasis mine). Learn to be thankful for the smallest thing. And then . . . tell Him! When ten lepers were miraculously healed by Jesus, only one came back to Him to say, "Thank You." Jesus' immediate comment was, "Were not all ten cleansed? Where are the other nine?" (Luke 17:17). God notices when we are thankful, and when we are not (or forget to tell Him).

We should also take the time to thank God for our food before we eat. This should be done when you are alone and when you are in public. Do not be ashamed to pray out loud if this is appropriate. And you don't need to bow your head (and close your eyes) and give thanks to be seen of people (that would be a wrong motive), but to be unashamed and thankful to God. We should realize our debt to God every single day. God does not owe us these things. The irony of today's generation is that our wealth has made us more thankless than ever. It is an outrage, a disgrace. God have mercy on us! May we fill in the gap whenever we have a chance—to be thankful to God and tell Him so.

The further purpose of this petition is to show our daily dependence on God. We referred above to the manna. God provided every day, never in advance (except for the Sabbath), so there would be a daily sense of debt and dependence on our Father. The Israelites were totally and absolutely dependent on God, one day at a time. They were in the desert, where there was no food. How would you like that kind of existence? And yet that is the way God wants us to trust Him. One of the most startling verses in the Old Testament is this: "The manna stopped the day after they ate this food from the land"—that is, after they entered the land of Canaan (Joshua 5:12).

Never, never, never take for granted all the good things God provides us. Where would we be without food, shelter, clothing, job, friends, emotional support, health, sleep, gifting to do our job? We are dependent every day.

A farmer in Kansas was worried about his wheat crop. There had not been rain in weeks. To keep his crops from being totally lost, he took buckets of water from his well and poured water on the crops. This meant hour after hour after hour of pouring water on the soil so that he would not lose everything. But the well also began to go dry, until the farmer realized he had to stop using this water. He was seemingly at the end of hope. He merely said, "Lord, unless You send rain immediately, all I have is gone." The next day he saw clouds that began to form rain. The rain came and soaked the area thoroughly in just a few moments. The farmer took a chair out to the wheat field and sat in the chair as the rain came down on his face. His wife said, "Have you lost your mind?" "No," he replied, "I am just enjoying seeing God do so easily what was so hard for me to do."

In 1962–1963, Louise and I lived in Ohio, where I was a pastor of a small church. We went through a very difficult time. The treasurer had to cut back on our salary, which was never very adequate in the first place. We had no money in the bank. We wondered how we would make it through the day. That very day a gift came in the mail from someone we had not seen in years. An old friend wrote to say, "My wife woke up thinking of you, and felt we should send you this check." This is something that only God could make happen.

God is never too late, never too early, but always just on time.

49. A Plea and a Declaration

Forgive us our debts, as we also have forgiven our debtors.

MATTHEW 6:12

It is my view that the greatest need of the Church today is to heed the petition now before us. I have prayed that this part of my book will make a definite difference in your own personal life. I don't want this chapter to give you any pseudo-guilt, neither do I want what follows to be threatening to you. But I do suspect that there will be many who read this book who will feel that this is the most important section of the Lord's Prayer. If so, our Lord Himself would agree with you. Because at the close of the Lord's Prayer Jesus added a P.S., this being His only and immediate comment on what He just said: "For if you forgive men when they sin against you, your heavenly Father will also forgive you. But if you do not forgive men their sins, your Father will not forgive your sins" (Matthew 6:14–15). Of all the six (or seven) petitions He gave, this is the only one He referred to.

This fifth petition of the Lord's Prayer is the first that deals with our spiritual needs. Many of us are familiar with the wording, "Forgive us our trespasses, as we forgive those who trespass against us." The similar account in Luke 11:4 reads, "Forgive us our sins, for *we also forgive everyone who sins against us*" (emphasis mine).

My best-known sermon is probably the one called "Total Forgiveness." Wherever I preach it all over the world, the response is quite tremendous. I preached this once to 5,000 people. I would estimate that 4,500 stood and came forward when I gave the appeal. Frequently, the overwhelming majority of all my congregations will respond by publicly admitting they have not forgiven but promise to do so at once. I sometimes believe I could preach the same exact sermon three weeks later and get a similar response from the same people. Why? Forgiving those who have been unjust, wicked, evil and vile is the hardest thing

in the world to do. Not only that, you have to keep doing it—days later, weeks later, years later. I know what I am talking about. I struggle in this area; I have to keep forgiving all the time. It is easy to slip and repeat the same sin. This is why the Lord's Prayer needs to be prayed all the time.

I suppose this petition has made liars out of more people than any document in human history! But don't blame Jesus for this. Just be sure you mean what you say when you make a plea—"Forgive us our trespasses"—and then make a declaration, or promise, in the same breath, "as we forgive those who have trespassed against us."

This petition is a plea and a declaration, or promise. The plea is for forgiveness. "Forgive us our sins." So far, so good. But the declaration is that we also have indeed forgiven those who have sinned against us. If "declaration" is too strong a word (stating that we *have* forgiven others), it is at least a promise that we *will* do so. If I feel convicted of an untruth as I pray this petition, I immediately want to promise God that, from now on, I will forgive those who have sinned against me.

However, my insertion of making a promise to God is my own idea. It is not what Jesus said. Taking Jesus' word literally, I am either telling the truth—or I am not—when I say to Him that I have forgiven those who have trespassed against me. But if, when I pray this petition, I fear that I may not have forgiven those who have sinned against me, I want to promise Him at once that I certainly will forgive them—and do so immediately.

Do we realize what we are saying when we pray this heart-searching petition? First we are asking God to forgive us our sins—our "debts." The Greek *opheilemata* means "what is owed." It is used interchangeably with *hamartias*—"falling short" or "sins," as in Luke 11:4 and Matthew 6:14–15. We owe a great debt to God: pure obedience. Anything that comes short of His glory is sin. This is why all have sinned and come short of the glory of God (Romans 3:23). We are all sinners. There is no one who does not sin (2 Chronicles 6:36). We owe God lives of transparent obedience. But we all fail.

We therefore ask God to let us off the hook. The Greek word means to "let be" or "send away." We therefore pray that God will overlook our debt. Instead of our having to pay, we pray He will leave it as it is without our having to pay, that He will let it be without His holding us responsible. We simply ask God to wipe away our debt.

Aren't you glad that Jesus gave us this petition? God knows our frame and remembers that we are dust (Psalm 103:14). The same God who requires us to be holy (Leviticus 11:44; 1 Peter 1:16) simultaneously gives the green light to pray for forgiveness because He knows we will fall. This is so wonderful. He is so gracious and understanding.

I was brought up in a church that taught not only that we must not sin but that we can indeed live above sin. The impact of this teaching went so deep that I still feel the effects of it to this day. I will not attempt to explain their rationale for how we could live without ever sinning, only to say that I wondered in those days why we have the Lord's Prayer if indeed it is possible to live without sin. Why would Jesus even give us this prayer if there was a possibility that Christians could live without ever sinning? The Lord's Prayer sets us free from the sinless perfectionist syndrome of those who fancy they can live without sin. Some manage this kind of sanctification (1) by refusing to call some sins *sin* by substituting the word "mistake," "error" or "shortcoming," so they can claim to have lived without "sin"; or (2) because they see sin only as external—e.g., the physical acts of murder or adultery (not apparently realizing that Jesus regarded hate or lust as sin). The point is Jesus knew we would sin and would need to pray this prayer He gave us, which He worded perfectly for our benefit.

But, as we have seen, the Lord's Prayer goes a step further. We might wish Jesus had not added this. But with the plea for forgiveness, He adds a declaration we make when we pray—that we have already forgiven others as God has forgiven us. Oh dear. What a declaration! We claim that we have forgiven others as God has forgiven us. We are put on the spot to forgive everyone—or forfeit praying the prayer altogether.

Why would Jesus put this petition this way? It is bringing His teaching home to us in a very personal way. You might feel this is unfair. If so, you would not have liked His teaching in the Sermon on the Mount, as when He said, "Love your enemies and pray for those who persecute you" (Matthew 5:44). If, then, we are going to be followers of Jesus, we do get a wonderful fringe benefit—to be able to pray the Lord's Prayer—but we are trapped! We have to promise to forgive. We cannot pick and choose which of these petitions suit us. We are brought face-to-face with the heart of Jesus' teaching on the Kingdom of heaven, and are forced to apply His words—or not pray this prayer at all.

So this petition is a plea and virtually a promise: a plea for forgiveness and a declaration that we have forgiven. And I would have thought that if we pray the prayer, and realize we have lied when we profess to have forgiven those who sinned against us, that we would turn that declaration into a promise to forgive—at once.

What the Prayer for Forgiveness Is Not

The plea "Forgive us our trespasses" is not a prayer for salvation. It is not a prayer to be saved, born again or justified before God. It is not a "sinner's prayer," as in the parable of the two men in the temple. The publican prayed, "God, have mercy on me, a sinner" (Luke 18:13). But this petition is not that at all.

The proof that this petition is not a prayer for salvation is that we are saved by faith—plus nothing! "For it is by grace you have been saved, through faith—and this not from yourselves, it is the gift of God—not by works, so that no one can boast" (Ephesians 2:8–9). If we pleaded for forgiveness on the basis of what we have done ("as we have forgiven those who trespassed against us"), salvation would be conditional. It would mean that we are saved on the condition that we have forgiven already, as if this qualifies us to be saved. That would also mean salvation by works. Forgiving others is a work—and a very noble work indeed. We could never claim we are saved by the sheer grace of God if our salvation depended upon forgiving others. If that were the case, who would be saved?

Nobody could be saved if we had to forgive before we could be justified. Forgiving others is a grace of the Holy Spirit. When you bless your enemies, you have crossed over into the supernatural. You could only do this by the Holy Spirit, and you do not have the Holy Spirit until you have been converted. Therefore, you—and no one else—are required to forgive those who have sinned against you *before* you can be a part of the family of God. And even if you take the view that you promise to forgive if you realize you haven't, this, too, is not a condition for being saved; it would mean that you are saved by works. It would also imply you are kept by works. Wrong. We are saved by grace and kept saved by grace. In a word: We are not saved by forgiving others; we are not kept saved by forgiving others.

Why, then, this petition? It is a necessary prayer for a child of God who has already been saved in order to *enjoy fellowship with the Father* and also to *inherit fully His Kingdom.* "But," someone will ask, "is not salvation the same as forgiveness of our sins? And is not this what we are commanded to pray for?" Yes. But it is also the kind of prayer every Christian continues to pray. We are brought to salvation by praying for the forgiveness of all our sins, yes; but we continue to pray this way after we are saved. The wonderful verse, "If we confess our sins, he is faithful and just and will forgive us our sins and purify us from all unrighteousness" (1 John 1:9), is actually a prayer for the Christian to pray, although it has been used countless times to lead a person to Christ. John also said, "If we claim to be without sin, we deceive ourselves and the truth is not in us" (1 John 1:8), a verse that flies in the face of sinless perfection teaching. "Who can say, 'I have kept my heart pure; I am clean and without sin'?" (Proverbs 20:9). "There is not a righteous man on earth who does what is right and never sins" (Ecclesiastes 7:20). The closer we are to God, the more aware we are of our sin; and the more we inherit the Kingdom and enjoy fellowship with

the Father, the greater will we feel the need to pray the Lord's Prayer (see Isaiah 6:1–5, where the prophet Isaiah felt convicted of sin when he saw the glory of God).

What the Prayer for Forgiveness Is

The Lord's Prayer is a believer's prayer. First, we pray "our Father," which (as we saw earlier) presupposes we are in the family of God. Second, the petition, "May Your name be treated as holy," would only be uttered by a converted man or woman. Third, to pray, "Your kingdom come," is to be uttered by one already in the Kingdom but who is wanting to inherit all that God has for him or her. All Christians have the Holy Spirit, and yet Paul urged us to "be filled with the Spirit" (Ephesians 5:18). That is arguably the main point of the Lord's Prayer. Fourth, praying for the forgiveness of sins is not a green light to sin on and on, but a consciousness that we have fallen short. We want to keep short accounts with God and confess our sins immediately, to enjoy His presence and fellowship.

A further purpose of this petition, then, is not only to enjoy fellowship with the Father in ever-increasing measure, but also to keep us from a feeling of self-righteousness. Self-righteousness is deadly. It is the easiest sin to commit and the hardest to see in ourselves. Only a profound grasp of Scripture and a great sense of God's holy presence will keep one alerted to his sinfulness; otherwise, self-righteousness creeps in painlessly like a cancer and will be our downfall if not detected. Strange as it may seem, Christians who grievously fall are often the most self-righteous, before and after their sin. Only the Holy Spirit will make us aware of our sin.

The truth is, we need the daily forgiveness of our sins as much as we do our daily bread. Keep in mind that this is the first spiritual petition in the Lord's Prayer. It is a prayer to be cleansed. As Calvin put it, our sins are like a dividing wall, which prevents God from coming close, and like a cloud, which stops His eyes from seeing us. "You have covered yourself with a cloud so that no prayer can get through" (Lamentations 3:44). Therefore, when we want to get close to God, we start not by telling Him how faithful we have been, or how righteous we are, but by praying for the remission of our sins. This way, we are sure our prayers reach God. This is why, when we come boldly to the throne of grace, our first request is to ask for mercy in order to find grace to help us in our time of need (Hebrews 4:16). Mercy is what we ask for in the "sinner's prayer," as we saw above; it is what we ask for first when we approach the throne of grace. Let no one think that he or she ever—*ever*—outgrows the need of mercy!

Basic Assumptions

There are two assumptions in this petition. First, that we need to be forgiven. Let us not take this for granted. Jesus knows we will need to be forgiven. Let me say emphatically that He is not talking about sin with a high hand, as deliberately breaking the sixth or seventh Commandment. Not that committing murder or adultery cannot be forgiven (it can; see Psalm 51, the prayer of David after his adultery and murder). Some Christians have fallen grievously and bring shame upon God's name. Jesus is not talking about sin that we intend to commit as soon as we get the chance; that would be mockery. The prayer of 1 John 1:9 means that you are truly sorry. Praying the petition, "Forgive us our debts," is a prayer of contrition, that you are truly sorry for your debts, trespasses, sins, failures.

The first assumption, then, is that we are not perfect. Jesus wants us to be aware of the fact that we are not perfect but have come short of His glory—and do so all the time. Anyone with a degree of conscientiousness and awareness of God's holiness knows this. This is why we pray: because we are weak.

The second assumption is that people have hurt us. We know that we ourselves have come short of God's glory. Other people, too, have come short of God's glory and have hurt us. Have you ever considered the possibility that when an acquaintance of yours prays this petition, it is actually you they are having to forgive? Does this surprise you? We have all been hurt. We have all hurt others. The cliché "hurt people hurt people" is so true. We all have failed.

We all have a story to tell about how hurt we have been. Some have been hurt more than others. I know what it is to be hurt, but when I hear of another's suffering, I blush that I could have even thought of being hurt. Some of you reading these lines have been sinned against terribly. There are those who have been raped. Abused as a child. Lied about. Walked over by an authority figure. Let down by a Christian leader. Had an unfaithful spouse.

Or, let us say it is a "lesser evil." Someone hurt your feelings. You did not get invited to a party. Someone did not speak to you as they passed you (maybe they didn't see you!). You did not get the credit when you did a good deed. You thought someone would be nicer than they were. You thought they would say yes to your request, but they turned you down.

Sometimes we have to forgive a person who did no wrong at all! I had to forgive a famous theologian for not recommending one of my books when I thought he should. He did no wrong, but I had to forgive him! (I didn't tell him of course; it happened in my heart.) By the way, don't walk up to someone and say, "I forgive you." He or she will ask, "For what?" And you will incur a greater misunderstanding and tension than ever. The only time you say, "I forgive you," is when another is asking for forgiveness. The real reason we usually say, "I forgive you," without someone asking for it is that we want to be sure he or she knows how hurt we are! Saying you forgive him or her will always backfire and be counterproductive.

It is a sobering fact that most of the people we have to forgive don't even think they have done anything wrong. I can safely guarantee that if I told you of my deepest hurts and won you over to my point of view, and you went to my offenders, they would say with a straight face they did nothing wrong at all. They would pass a lie detector test with flying colors! It is absolutely true that most people who have hurt us don't think we should be hurt at all. But we feel the same way toward those who are having to forgive us. I believe there are many people who have had to forgive me. For exactly what I do not know, but I am sure their hurt is utterly real to them.

The truth is, we have all sinned and we have all been sinned against. Jesus gives us this petition in order that we will be forgiven of our own sin and failure—and that we in turn will show our gratitude for being forgiven, by forgiving everyone who has hurt us.

Jesus shows that He knows what we know: *We have been hurt.* It is so kind of Him. We may have been discredited, dishonored, disappointed. We are, therefore, hurt. We have been lied about, taken advantage of, people haven't shown appreciation. Some have been disloyal to us.

Thus, two assumptions lie behind this petition: We need to be forgiven; we need to forgive.

However, this petition is an admission that we need forgiveness. Don't pray the Lord's Prayer if you feel no need of forgiveness or feel that you are so perfect in yourself. This petition is an implicit admission: "It is forgiveness I need."

But, as I said above, it is an admission—a declaration—that you have already forgiven those who have sinned against you. I don't meant to be unfair, but have you? Have you forgiven those who have hurt you, let you down, disappointed you? Have you? You need to decide whether you will stop praying the Lord's Prayer or truly let others off the hook as God has let you off the hook. You must decide whether to pray this petition and pray for their not having the book thrown at them, as you want God not to throw the book at you? Or do you want God to throw the book at you? Are you prepared to say that you have done nothing wrong—that you are willing for all that is knowable about you, your thoughts and deeds, to be laid bare before all who know you?

This Petition Is a Covenant

This petition is actually an agreement, indeed, a covenant with God. A covenant is a contract between two parties. In this petition, you put yourself under a covenant with God—and implicitly with those who have sinned against you, even though the party who has offended you will have no idea you are making this agreement. The agreement is this: You agree to forgive them as you pray for your own forgiveness. Implied in this covenant is that you agree to be forgiven *in proportion* to the way you forgive. Yes. How does that make you feel? You agree for God to forgive *you* in proportion to the way you have let *others* off the hook. In other words, the degree to which you have let others off the hook will be the degree to which you ask God to let you off the hook. Are

you okay with this? I can tell you, that is what this petition really means.

Some take the view that you don't have to forgive them unless they are sorry. Really? Where did you get that? I suspect that people adopt this view to keep from having to let people off the hook. Caution: If you wait until they are sorry, I predict you will go to your grave in bitterness. This is the devil keeping you from being like Jesus. Who was sorry at the cross of Jesus? Who was repenting that they nailed in the nails? Instead of waiting for them to be sorry, Jesus prayed, "Father, forgive them, for they do not know what they are doing" (Luke 23:34). It may get our goat that they don't know what they have done to us. But they did not know what they did to Jesus, and He forgave them.

There are no conditions accompanying the Lord's Prayer that give even a loophole not to forgive until they are sorry. We don't have that luxury. It takes minimal grace to forgive when another is sorry; it takes maximum grace to forgive when they are not sorry or don't know what they have done. This petition is an invitation to explore maximum grace! To cross over into the supernatural—to do what defies a natural explanation!

Paul asked the Ephesians to forgive each other "just as in Christ God forgave you" (Ephesians 4:32). When you pray this petition in the Lord's Prayer, you are declaring yourself to forgive others as you ask for your own forgiveness. You are implicitly agreeing to this, that you yourself will be forgiven by God in the same measure as you have forgiven them.

To put it another way: If you want to be forgiven, you agree to be forgiven to the extent you yourself forgive. This is the covenant implicit in this prayer. In a word: To be forgiven, you agree to forgive; if you don't forgive, you forfeit your own forgiveness. As Don Carson put it, there is no forgiveness to the one who does not forgive. But, thankfully, this is not a prayer for justification before God. Thank God, it is not a prayer for salvation. It is a prayer for continued fellowship with God. "If we walk in the light, as he is in the light, we have fellowship with one another [that is, primarily with the Father, secondarily with each other], and the blood of Jesus, his Son, purifies us from all sin" (1 John 1:7).

Do you like the Lord's Prayer? Perhaps you need to decide whether to stop praying it, or to mean it from the heart. I urge you to pray it; I plead with you to pray it. Paul said that a further reason for forgiveness is to keep us from being outsmarted by Satan (2 Corinthians 2:11, NLT). When you hold a grudge, you beckon Satan to walk right in. Don't do that; don't give him that pleasure. Not only that, holding a grudge can be damaging to your health. It can lead to arthritis, high blood pressure, heart disease and kidney disease. Not forgiving can also damage you emotionally and cripple you with guilt. Total forgiveness is what will lead you to discover what you have been born to do. You will find your true anointing; you will enjoy self-actualization.

Total forgiveness means you get freedom in return. Great liberty indeed: a sense of God you may have lost years ago. Do you want that great nearness of God back again? Set others free. Let them off the hook. Ask God to bless them. What is more, you will be praying the Lord's Prayer from your heart.

50. The Unnecessary Pitfall

And lead us not into temptation.

MATTHEW 6:13

We now deal with this sixth petition, "And lead us not into temptation, but deliver us from the evil one." Some say we have two petitions here. In any case, I choose to deal with them one at a time.

The petition, "Give us today our daily bread," deals with our physical, natural needs. But when Jesus introduced forgiveness, He brought in the spiritual dimension. This petition, "And lead us not into temptation," continues with our spiritual state. If we meant what we said when we prayed, "Forgive us our debts, as we also have forgiven our debtors," a wonderful fellowship with the Father is in existence. It means the Holy Spirit in us is un-grieved.

But there is more than one way to grieve the Holy Spirit. When Paul said, "And do not *grieve* the Holy Spirit of God, with whom you were sealed for the day of redemption" (Ephesians 4:30, emphasis mine), he used a Greek word that means to get one's feelings hurt. We hurt the Holy Spirit's feelings chiefly by bitterness. This is why Paul followed this admonition with, "Get rid of all bitterness, rage and anger, brawling and slander, along with every form of malice. Be kind and compassionate to one another, forgiving each other, just as in Christ God forgave you" (Ephesians 4:31–32). When we grieve the Holy Spirit He does not desert us, but we do lose an anointing of peace, clear thinking and a sense of His presence and fellowship.

Whereas bitterness and unforgiveness grieve the Spirit, so does one succumbing to sexual temptation. Paul continues in Ephesians 5:3: "But among you there must not be even a hint of sexual immorality, or any kind of impurity, or of greed, because these are improper for God's holy people." Therefore, the spiritual dimension of the Lord's Prayer embraces three areas: (1) forgiving one another by keeping a sweet spirit with no bitterness; (2) living a holy life and not falling into shame and unbelief; and (3) being spared of Satan succeeding with us (which I will deal with in the next chapter).

The Most Difficult of the Petitions

The petition we now unpack is the most difficult to understand: "Lead us not into temptation." Many volumes have been written on this petition. New Testament scholar C. F. D. Moule has even written a probing monograph, "An Unsolved Problem in the Temptation Clause in the Lord's Prayer." So, can I get to the meaning of this petition in one chapter?

We are dealing with the mystery of an unusual petition. This mystery turns generally on two matters: (1) the translation of the Greek *peirasmon*, which means either temptation, testing or trial, or all three; and (2) the strange request that God should not lead us into temptation or trial, which implies He may well so lead us. This is strange, considering also this verse: "When tempted, no one should say, 'God is tempting me.' For God cannot be tempted by evil, nor does he tempt anyone; but each one is tempted when, by his own evil desire, he is dragged away and enticed" (James 1:13–14). So, if God cannot tempt us, is not Jesus implying otherwise in this petition?

But if *peirasmon* means "testing" or "trial," James also said, "Consider it pure joy, my brothers, when you face trials of many kinds, because you know that the testing of your faith develops perseverance" (James 1:2–3). This verse sounds like it is a good thing when you face trials of many kinds! If this is "pure joy," why pray to avoid it? As John Stott said, if trials are beneficial, why should we pray not to get led into them?

Before the New Testament came along, the Greek word *peirasmon* rarely ever meant temptation in the sense of "enticement" to sin, as in temptation to sexual sin. Basically, it meant "testing." But James clearly takes this word partly to refer to lust. *Peirasmon* is thus used two ways by James: (1) signifying testing or trial (James 1:2 and also James 1:12: "Blessed is the man who perseveres under trial, because when he has stood the test, he will receive the crown of life that God has promised to those who love him"); and (2) signifying lust, almost certainly sexual lust (James 1:13: "When tempted, no one should say, 'God is tempting me'"). Only the context helps us know the exact meaning. First Corinthians 10:13, possibly the first verse a new Christian should memorize, can be taken either way, too: "No temptation has seized you except what is common to man. And God is faithful; he will not let you be tempted beyond what you can bear. But when you are tempted, he will also provide a way out so that you can stand up under it."

The problem is further complicated by two more verses: "Things that cause people to sin are bound to come, but woe to that person through whom they come" (Luke 17:1). "I have told you these things, so that in me you may have peace. In this world you will have trouble. But take heart! I have overcome the world" (John 16:33). This means that testing and temptation will always be around; they are unavoidable. Why, then, would Jesus have us pray, "Lead us not into temptation"? The implication is that God could keep us away from temptation, or bring us out of temptation, trial or testing.

The buck stops with the Father. He has the power to keep us from a condition conducive to testing. Jesus said, "Watch and pray so that you will not fall into temptation. The spirit is willing, but the body is weak" (Matthew 26:41). But in the Lord's Prayer we are told to ask that the Father will not lead us, which, as I said, implies He might do so. That, then, is where we begin: We are dealing with the mystery of an unusual petition. How do we make sense of it?

This petition points to the misery of what may be an unnecessary pitfall. A pitfall is unsuspected danger or difficulty. We must keep Luke 17:1 and John 16:33 in mind, along with these verses: "There is something else meaningless that occurs on earth: righteous men who get what the wicked deserve, and wicked men who get what the righteous deserve" (Ecclesiastes 8:14). "I have seen something else under the sun: The race is not to the swift or the battle to the strong, nor does food come to the wise or wealth to the brilliant or favor to the learned; but time and chance happen to them all" (Ecclesiastes 9:11).

The Father's Heart

The heart of the Father is revealed in the Lord's Prayer. And this petition shows that He does not want us to suffer. He also knows the pain we will feel if we fall into sin. This is the essential reason for this petition. Our heavenly Father does not want us to suffer as a result of falling into sexual sin or falling into unbelief. Falling into sexual sin brings pain, sooner or later; falling into unbelief leads to grumbling, which grieves the Holy Spirit. Our Father is looking out for us in this petition.

It is a wicked world we live in. The Father knows this; Jesus knows this. Our gracious God wants His own people to avoid the misery of a needless pitfall. Therefore, He shares with His family what is on His heart, namely, that we might avoid temptation. You don't sin without temptation preceding it. The best way to avoid sin is to avoid temptation. That is, I believe, our Lord's rationale in giving us this petition.

Temptation and Testing

There is an essential difference between temptation and testing. Temptation is what God *allows* to test us; and yet it comes immediately from within. We read that "God tested Abraham" (Genesis 22:1). It was a major test to see whether Abraham would obey when God put to him what appeared to be an unreasonable proposition: to offer his son, Isaac. Sometimes God leads us in a manner that makes no sense at the time. This is the essence of testing. And yet we also read that "Jesus was led by the Spirit into the desert *to be tempted by the devil*" (Matthew 4:1, emphasis mine). This temptation was a testing. It was necessary that Jesus should become like us in every way, and part of this was to be made "perfect through suffering" (Hebrews 2:10). This was so He, having learned what temptation is, would be "able to help those who are being tempted" (Hebrews 2:18). In other words, there was a good reason the Spirit would lead Jesus into the wilderness to be tempted by Satan.

It is a reminder that there is a good reason for every way God leads us, including what He allows to happen. It is all for a purpose. It turns out that Abraham was ready for his testing; he came through with flying colors. He fully intended to offer Isaac but, at the last moment, was prevented. An angel stepped in and stopped Abraham. And God said, "Now I know that you fear God, because you have not withheld from me your son, your only son" (Genesis 22:12). The result was that God swore an oath to Abraham—arguably the highest privilege God ever bestows on His children here on earth (Genesis 22:16–17; Hebrews 6:13).

Jesus, too, was ready for His testing. He resisted every overture Satan made to Him. After overcoming Satan in the desert, the "devil left him, and angels came and attended him" (Matthew 4:11). Mind you, this was not the first nor the last time Jesus would be tested. The whole of His life was one of continual pleasing the Father and resisting the devil. The desert experience was no doubt one of the most difficult ordeals for Him. But He had to resist temptation and fulfill the Law throughout His entire lifetime, all the way to the cross. When He uttered, "It is finished" (John 19:30), it not only meant that our debt to God was paid in full but that Jesus' ordeal of testing was over. After His life was over, having sat down at the right hand of God (Hebrews 12:2), it could be said that Jesus was tempted at all points as you and I are, but "without sin" (Hebrews 4:15). Had Jesus sinned—even once—He would have been disqualified to be our Savior. But He passed the test, and having been "made perfect, he became the source of eternal salvation for all who obey him" (Hebrews 5:9).

Temptation, particularly sexual temptation, comes from within (as we saw from James 1:13). We cannot blame God for our temptation. Temptation does not come from God but from inside ourselves. We are responsible for our own temptation. Indeed, temptation is our own responsibility. The immediate thought we often have when we are tempted is to imagine that it is a "setup" from God—that God is behind it and will overlook it if we give in. It is true that God allowed it, but it is not true that He is responsible for it. When God allows sexual temptation, it is a test, to see whether we will pass or fail.

Joseph, son of Jacob, could not have known he was being earmarked as a future prime minister of Egypt. When he worked for Potiphar, an Egyptian officer, he faced sexual temptation. Potiphar's wife was attracted to Joseph and pleaded with him day after day, "Come to bed with me!" Joseph refused (Genesis 39:7). He may have felt nothing but pointlessness in refusing her. Still, the angels said "Yes!" Joseph passed the test with flying colors.

All of us must pass the test of sexual temptation. If we fail, God may give us a second chance. Billy Graham said that it seems the devil gets 75 percent of God's best servants through sexual sin. Sexual temptation is natural and normal; it is not a sin to be tempted. We are all tempted. Jesus was tempted. It is sin when we give in to temptation.

It is, therefore, true that God may test us by allowing us to be tempted. If you ask me, "To what extent is it God's purposeful will to cause something to happen? And to what extent does He merely allow things to happen?" I reply: I don't know. Nobody does. We all, like Moses, want to get close to the burning bush to see why it doesn't burn up, but God says to all of us: "Stay back, and worship" (see Exodus 3:5). Don't try to figure everything out. It is impossible in this life to know the difference between what God purposes and what He allows. He wants us to worship Him and affirm Him without knowing everything first. If we knew all the answers we would no longer need faith. But when we don't know the answer, yet trust Him nonetheless, that is true faith—and it pleases God (Hebrews 11:1, 6).

The Importance of the Word "Into"

If testing is for our good—if overcoming temptation is a necessary victory in our development—why would Jesus have us pray, "Lead us not into temptation"? We are to pray that we shall not be brought "into" temptation. Michael Eaton reckons that the prayer makes sense if we emphasize the word *into*. We are not praying that we shall not be tempted; we know that we will be tempted, sooner or later. We are not praying that we shall not be tested; we know that we will be tested, sooner or later. We are praying that we shall not be *prematurely tested* by being brought into something that is beyond our strength. We pray that nothing will bring us into temptation and testing prematurely and unnecessarily.

Dr. Martyn Lloyd-Jones used to say to me that the worst thing that can happen to someone is to succeed before they are ready. This is because success often goes to one's head, and we are better off to have success delayed until we are mature. In much the same way, we pray that we will not be thrown into the deep end of testing until we are ready for it. This is what Michael Eaton means, and I believe this is a brilliant insight of his. We should pray that God will spare us of testing that we are not ready for, because we would possibly fail the test if such testing came too soon. Even Jesus' temptation in the desert came at the age of thirty, and He was the Son of God! This is surely the basic meaning of this petition.

There is such a thing as an unnecessary pitfall. We have all seen people who succeed before they are ready. And I have also seen people fall at an early age. I think of teenagers who face temptations far fiercer and greater than when I was a teenager. What is out there in the world at the present time is unimaginable evil and wickedness. The Lord's Prayer needs to be reintroduced to churches and Christians everywhere and prayed with utter earnestness. I commend churches that pray the Lord's Prayer regularly. And I feel that the churches that never think of praying it do their members no favor by neglecting this extraordinary prayer.

King Saul is an example of a man who succeeded before he was ready. The temptation to pride seemed to have overcome him. He took himself too seriously, fancied that he could offer the burnt offerings even though he was not called to do this (1 Samuel 13:9). He became yesterday's man at the age of forty.

Our prayer to God, therefore, is that He will not let us fall into a situation greater than we can cope with—that is, sooner than we are able to cope with it. The truth is, we never know how strong we will be. I remember a conversation I had with Francis Schaeffer years ago, when I contemplated a certain academic course. He cautioned me that intellectual temptation is like sexual temptation; we never know how strong we will be. We must admit to our weakness. God knows what it is. We are, therefore, to be on bended knee, that our Father will not allow us to be in an unnecessary situation.

You may ask, "What about 1 Corinthians 10:13?" This is the verse I believe every new Christian should memorize as soon as possible: "No temptation [in Greek, *peirasmon*—testing, trial, temptation] has seized you except what is common to man. And God is faithful; he will not let you be tempted beyond what you can bear. But when you are tempted, he will also provide a way out so that you can stand up under it." You may understandably argue that God will honor this word, regardless whether or not a person is being tested prematurely. True. We are all responsible, and God has made it clear that if we succumb to temptation or fail in the testing, we are going against grace that was promised to us. But I would hope that my new grandson—Tobias Robert Stephen Kendall, born during the writing of the present book—would be spared a heavy testing and trial for a long, long time. It is any father's or grandfather's concern. And, likewise, it is our heavenly Father's concern for us. He is telling us to pray to be spared of falling *into* temptation, trial or testing. My heart would ache to see my loved ones going through severe testing. I would not want it for them; you would not want it for your children and grandchildren. That is God's fatherly love for each of us, too.

Two Possible Attitudes When Praying This Petition

There are two ways you can pray this petition, "Lead us not into temptation." The first is, quite foolishly, to challenge God by demanding that He do it all for us—demanding He give us grace so that we won't feel so tempted. Take, for example, a person who is willing to fall. It may be that potential temptation is at hand. Perhaps they know they will meet someone this very day who will provide a very luring temptation. They know they should not give in. They also know they should avoid the temptation. But they say, "Okay, God, give me grace today not to give in. If I give in, it is because You did not give me sufficient grace."

That is blaming God. It is also what Jesus called tempting God. When Satan told Jesus to jump off the pinnacle of the Temple, since it was promised that the angels would deliver Him and keep Him from hurting Himself, Jesus replied: "It is also written: 'Do not put the Lord your God to the test'" (Matthew 4:7).

When I willfully walk into a situation I know beforehand will mean fierce temptation, and I put the onus on God to uphold me, I am tempting Him. Therefore, to pray the petition, "Lead us not into temptation," when I am challenging God by walking deliberately into temptation, I am mocking Him. If I say, "But I prayed the Lord's Prayer, and the temptation still came," I am shifting the blame from myself to God. It is what the flesh will always try to do. This is precisely why James said, "When tempted, no one should say, 'God is tempting me.' For God cannot be tempted by evil, nor does he tempt anyone; but each one is tempted when, by his own evil desire, he is dragged away and enticed. Then, after desire has conceived, it gives birth to sin; and sin, when it is full-grown, gives birth to death. Don't be deceived, my dear brothers" (James 1:13–16).

But there is a second way to pray this petition, "Lead us not into temptation." It is to pray with the fear that God may well allow one to fall. This is scary. When you pray, "Lead us not into temptation," being so mindful of your own weakness, as well as the possibility that God thinks you are equal to it, you are very sobered, indeed. You, therefore, plead this petition on bended knee, as if to say, "O God, please help me, please, please do not let me come *into* temptation."

This second way of praying is the right spirit. It honors God. It takes into account that you know how weak you are. You know how easily you could fall. You don't want to fall, you don't want to displease God, you don't want to grieve the Spirit. So, when you utter this plea, "Lead us not into temptation," you do so with gravity and earnestness, and pray that God will indeed answer your prayer and not let you enter into temptation. This second way of praying is a heart-cry to the Father, and this is the way Jesus means for us to pray this petition.

Question: How do you, the reader, pray this petition?

The proof that you mean this prayer is that you will do all you can in your own power to avoid a temptation situation. You may recall that Jesus said in the Garden of Gethsemane, "Watch and pray so that you will not fall into temptation. The spirit is willing, but the body is weak" (Matthew 26:41). Note the order: "Watch and pray." He did not say: "Pray and watch." When you watch before you pray, you are already looking out for the danger. If you pray before you watch, you might want to shift the blame to God. "I prayed about it," you may say, "but the temptation still came. So, God certainly let it happen." This is the devil talking. Jesus wisely asked the disciples to "watch and pray," which shows that you are assuming certain mature responsibilities as you pray. This is what pleases God.

Paul said, "Clothe yourselves with the Lord Jesus Christ, and do not think about how to gratify the desires of the sinful nature" (Romans 13:14). Hearing Saint Ambrose preach on this text led to Saint Augustine's conversion. Augustine was a man who led a profligate lifestyle. The best way to avoid falling into sin is to avoid the temptation you know is out there. Evangelist Billy Sunday used to say that the reason so many Christians fall into sin is that they treat temptation like strawberry shortcake rather than a rattlesnake!

You prove how strong you are not by how you cope when being tempted, but by seeing how far you can get from temptation.

Remember also that falling into sin can happen to anybody. This is why Paul cautioned us, "Brothers, if someone is caught in a sin, you who are spiritual should restore him gently. But watch yourself, or you also may be tempted" (Galatians 6:1). Never approach the fallen Christian with a "pointing the finger" attitude. This will be counterproductive in your efforts; your self-righteousness will disqualify you from being a blessing. You can count on being rejected. Always go to the person who has fallen with this attitude: "This could have happened to me as easily as it happened to you. I am not better than you. It could be me next time, but by the grace of God." The fallen person will more likely listen to you and get the help you have to offer when you approach him or her in that spirit.

The temptation, or testing, is mainly: (1) sexual temptation and (2) unbelief, which are essentially testing. The two can come together simultaneously. You may find yourself asking, "Why did God let this happen to me? How could this happen, since I have prayed for it not to happen?" This is where unbelief will try to set in.

One of the main purposes of testing is to increase our faith. Testing has to come, sooner or later. You pray it comes not one hour sooner than you are ready for it. But you may never feel you are ready. I think of some of the trials we had at Westminster Chapel. My 25 years in London were both the best years and worst years of my life. I had the greatest trials I ever knew, yet also the greatest thrills. I thank God that Josif Tson reached me with his warning, "R. T., you must totally forgive them," precisely when it came. The trial I was experiencing at that particular time was a picnic compared to what would come later. God graciously taught me to forgive—in the nick of time, I would say. It is what equipped me for greater testing. I am admitting that God was extremely gracious to me. He did not let me be tested to the extreme until I was ready. What is more, my faith was increased. What I once thought was the worst thing that ever happened to me proved to be the best thing that ever happened to me. That's the truth!

Why Unanswered Prayer?

The mystery of this unusual petition is compounded by trying to grasp the meaning of unanswered prayer. The issue is this: What if, after you prayed this petition, "Lead us not into temptation," from your heart—and after avoiding every possible pitfall—you still fall into a severe testing? I reply: God knows you are up to it. You are ready for it. Not only that, take it with both hands!

Here is why. When James said, "Consider it pure joy, my brothers, whenever you face trials of many kinds" (James 1:2), the Greek literally reads (as in the King James Version) to count it all joy when you "fall" into temptation. You fell into it. You didn't go out looking for it. It came to you—you passively fell into the trial. James did not say you fell morally—you merely fell into the trial. In a word: It came to you. The reason James said to consider it pure joy is because you can take that kind of trial as a gift from God.

The word "consider" in James 1:2 (NIV), or "count" (KJV), is the same exact word that Paul uses in Romans 4:5, where it is translated "credited": "To the man who does not work but trusts God who justifies the wicked, his faith is *credited* as righteousness." We are justified by faith alone, not works. But we may not *feel* righteous. We take God's word for it; He credits us with righteousness. We are counted righteous as though we really were; and we *are* righteous—in His sight. We take His word for it that we are righteous. Feelings are one thing, faith another.

So, too, with James 1:2. We "count" or "consider" it pure joy when we fall into trials. We don't feel joy. Far from it; it may be the worst day of our life! But James said that we should count, or impute, to the trial pure joy. Why? Because if we knew the results of the trial, we would believe God's reason for counting it joy. As I said above, the worst trial of my life became the best thing that ever happened to me. I must admit to you, sadly, that I did not consider it pure joy at the time. It was horrible. I should have, though. I did try to dignify that trial, and I even believe I did. But did I consider it "pure joy"? Probably not.

The point is this: We will later see what God had in mind for us when He allows us to "fall" into temptation, in His perfect timing. It is only a matter of time that we will see something of His rationale and strategy for letting it happen when it did.

So, to answer the question: "Why did God not answer our prayer when we prayed not to enter into temptation, but did enter into it despite our prayer?" It means we were equal to the trial. God knew we could take it. He dignified us! We did not have to face it prematurely. We were ready for it. And we should pass the trial with flying colors! You were handed on a silver platter the means of sanctification: to refine your faith and character. "We also rejoice in our sufferings, because we know that suffering produces perseverance; perseverance, character; and character, hope" (Romans 5:3–4).

I hope this helps to clarify the mystery of an unusual petition. We do, indeed, pray to avoid testing, even knowing that falling into trial is beneficial. We rejoice when persecuted (Matthew 5:11–12), but we don't go looking for it. God knows we will be equal to it if we wait for His timing. And when the sudden trial comes, accept it as from His hands. As the hymn put it,

> Every joy or trial falleth from above,
> Traced upon our dial by the Sun of
>   Love;
> We may trust him fully, all for us to do;
> They who trust Him wholly find Him
>   wholly true.
>
> Frances Ridley Havergal
> (1836–1879)

Perhaps Matt Redman said it best: "Every blessing you pour out I'll turn back to praise; when the darkness closes in, Lord, still I will say, 'Blessed be the name of the Lord.'"

In a word: Don't go looking for testing, but welcome it when it comes. Just realize that a sovereign God permitted it. The heart of the Father is that we will be happy and holy. This is why we have this petition. He wants us to be spared of the misery of unnecessary pitfalls. But should He allow them after we have avoided them and prayed to avoid them, "Consider it pure joy" (James 1:2).

You will eventually treasure the trial you are now in. Consider it pure joy—now.

51. Daily Deliverance

But deliver us from the evil one.

MATTHEW 6:13

This is the final petition in the Lord's Prayer. Whether it is part of the sixth or considered a seventh petition does not matter. But I do feel nonetheless these words deserve special attention: "But deliver us from the evil one." For some reason, the traditional ending—"For yours is the kingdom and the power and the glory forever. Amen"—does not seem to be in the older manuscripts. I do, however, intend to treat that phrase in this book. Furthermore, there is certainly nothing wrong with saying it!

Keep in mind that this final petition, "But deliver us from the evil one," is a part of the plea to be spared an unnecessary pitfall. Although temptation is inevitable, we must not go out looking for such. Although trials are beneficial, it is still wise to avoid such if we can. Persecution is a blessing, yes; and yet Jesus instructed the disciples, "When you are persecuted in one place, flee to another" (Matthew 10:23). If, however, prayer to avoid falling into temptation is not answered, it means we are up to facing it. "Your strength will equal your days" (Deuteronomy 33:25). This explains James 1:2: "Consider it pure joy, my brothers, whenever you face trials of many kinds." You will treasure what you went through eventually; start considering it pure joy right now. God knows you are equal to the testing. It shows you are strong.

And yet in this extended phrase, "But deliver us from the evil one," we see another reason why Jesus puts this after, "Lead us not into temptation." Why? It is because the devil is obviously behind the pitfall of testing, trial and temptation. Anything the devil is in we should want to avoid. It is the devil who tempts people to sin. It is the devil who brings trouble. When you know that his evil hand is behind what is going on, you want

to avoid it with all your might. Do not give him any room—not an inch.

It might be argued that this second clause, "But deliver us from the evil one," is redundant, unnecessary. After all, if we are not led into temptation, we are therefore spared of the evil one. Why did Jesus add this?

The Existence of Evil

By telling us to pray, "Deliver us from the evil one," Jesus has acknowledged that evil is already here. God never explains the origin of evil. We may well wish He had. But had He done so, there would be no need for faith. Nearly every non-Christian I have ever witnessed to for any length of time, especially if he or she is a bit cerebral, asks, "If God exists, why doesn't He stop all the suffering and evil and injustice that is in the world?" It is as if they are saying, "I would believe in God if there were no evil."

I reply: If you knew the answer to that question, there would be no need for faith by any of us. What makes faith *faith* is that we do not know why God allows suffering. Why did God create man and woman knowing they would suffer? I don't know. Thank God I don't know; for not knowing is what makes room for faith. It is only by faith that I can be justified (Romans 4:5), and it is only by faith that I can please God (Hebrews 11:6). If the privilege of faith were taken away from me, I would not have any opportunity to be made righteous before God, nor would I have the incalculable joy of pleasing Him.

God sent His Son into the world because evil exists. "The reason the Son of God appeared was to destroy the devil's work" (1 John 3:8). God in His infinite wisdom has chosen to deal with evil in two stages: (1) by sending His one and only Son, Jesus Christ, to die on the cross for our sins;

and (2) by the Second Coming of Jesus, when He appears "from heaven in blazing fire with his powerful angels. He will punish those who do not know God and do not obey the gospel of our Lord Jesus. They will be punished with everlasting destruction and shut out from the presence of the Lord and from the majesty of his power on the day he comes to be glorified in his holy people and to be marveled at among all those who have believed" (2 Thessalonians 1:7–10). This will also result in the ultimate defeat of Satan, who will be thrown into the lake of fire to be tormented day and night forever and ever (Revelation 20:10).

The petition, "But deliver us from the evil one," acknowledges that evil is present; we face it every day. As we pray for daily bread, forgiveness and not to be led into temptation—essential praying for our spiritual lives—so, too, must we pray for daily deliverance, until the day comes we are finally delivered by witnessing Satan's total and absolute defeat.

This petition shows that the Christian is in a war. It is called spiritual warfare. "Be strong in the Lord and in his mighty power. Put on the full armor of God so that you can take your stand against the devil's schemes. For our struggle is not against flesh and blood, but against the rulers, against the authorities, against the powers of this dark world and against the spiritual forces of evil in the heavenly realms. Therefore put on the full armor of God, so that when the day of evil comes, you may be able to stand your ground, and after you have done everything, to stand" (Ephesians 6:10–13). But do note carefully: These lines show that spiritual warfare is almost entirely defensive. You take your "stand." This means you don't go on the attack; you don't go out looking for a chance to pick a fight with Satan. Beware of this. You will get in over your head. Never—ever—initiate a quarrel with the devil. You will fall. But if he attacks you, you will win, when you remember Paul's words.

When you were converted, an enemy you did not know you had was awakened. Prior to your conversion you were spiritually blind, for the "god of this age has blinded the minds of unbelievers, so that they cannot see the light of the gospel of the glory of Christ, who is the image of God" (2 Corinthians 4:4). Every Christian should be reminded: You now have a new enemy—the devil. We must not have a naïve view of life but be wise as serpents, harmless as doves (Matthew 10:16). A solid, sound doctrine of evil is essential both to a good theological foundation and also to practical Christian living.

The Evil One Is the Explanation for All Troubles

Jesus simply stated, "In this world you will have trouble" (John 16:33). We might wish He had not said that. I myself wish He had not said that. I wish He had said, "Because I have appeared on the scene, you will have no more trouble in this world." I wish He had said, "All who follow Me and receive My word will be rewarded by having no problems in this life." I wish Paul had said, "All Christians are exempt from suffering, ill-health and financial adversity." Mind you, there are preachers abroad who imply this! They mislead people right, left and center; it is an outrage. Some teach that all people can prosper, all people can be healthy. One popular television preacher even said that if the apostle Paul had had his faith, Paul would not even have had a thorn in the flesh! Wrong. All of us have thorns in the flesh to some degree. Why? Because in this world there is evil. The devil has not been totally defeated yet. Like it or not, this is the way it is. Why is there trouble in this world? Because of the devil's existence. Why is there temptation? Because there is an evil enemy out there, walking about, seeking whom he may devour (1 Peter 5:8).

This is why in the Lord's Prayer Jesus did not end with, "Lead us not into temptation," but added, "But deliver us from the evil one." This implicitly shows that Satan is the reason for temptation and trouble in this world. God did not put evil on this earth. God did not put tears in babies' eyes. God did not bring death to His creation. God did not bring suffering and pain.

This is why we want to avoid temptation; we don't want to get near anything Satan is behind. Satan—not God—is the reason for suffering. Satan—not God—is the reason for evil. Satan—not God—is the reason for injustices. Satan—not God—is the explanation for earthquakes, famine, poverty, hatred, racial prejudice, war, corruption in politics, injustice in the banking system, immoral teaching in our schools.

There is, therefore, a connection between temptation and the devil. The devil is called "the tempter" (1 Thessalonians 3:5). We saw in the previous chapter that the devil tempted Jesus (Matthew 4:1). He hoped to defeat Jesus before Jesus barely got started in His ministry. He knew who Jesus was: his true enemy. Never forget this: The devil is your enemy and Jesus' enemy. Do not dignify anything the devil puts before you. Stay utterly on the side of Jesus; never—ever—give in to anything that gives pleasure to Satan. Only when God allows you to fall into trials can such trouble be welcomed (James 1:2).

The Essence of Evil

Many of us are used to praying the Lord's Prayer, "Lead us not into temptation, but deliver us from evil"—not "the evil one." But the probable translation is "evil one." The Greek word is *ponerou*—"evil." This word by itself could be masculine or neuter gender. The neuter gender would appear in these verses (all emphases mine): "The evil man brings *evil things* out of the *evil* stored up in his heart" (Luke 6:45). "Hate what is *evil*; cling to what is good" (Romans 12:9). "Avoid every kind of *evil*" (1 Thessalonians 5:22). These are examples of a neuter gender.

The masculine gender, however, appears in the following verses: "When anyone hears the message about the kingdom and does not understand it, *the evil one* comes and snatches away what was sown in his heart" (Matthew 13:19). "The weeds are the sons of *the evil one,* and the enemy who sows them is the devil" (Matthew 13:38–39). Continuing with the aforementioned passage on spiritual warfare, "In addition to all this, take up the shield of faith, with which you can extinguish all the flaming arrows of *the evil one*" (Ephesians 6:16). "Do not be like Cain, who belonged to *the evil one* and murdered his brother" (1 John 3:12). "We know that we are children of God, and that the whole world is under the control of *the evil one*" (1 John 5:19). Also, in this petition in Matthew 6:13 the Greek *tou poverou* shows the definite article—"*the* evil one." Not only that, the word *apo*—"from"—in, "Deliver us *from* evil," almost always refers to a person, not things. I am satisfied that the correct translation is "the evil one," not merely evil.

And yet this phrase in the Lord's Prayer certainly refers to evil generally as well. Evil is in society, the media, government, business, science, medicine, law, the educational systems. Evil refers to how wickedness is compounded when people who hate God and people who hate righteousness unite. King Herod and Pontius Pilate compounded the evil when they approved of the crucifixion of Jesus without a just trial.

There is also a wickedness that would get utterly out of control were it not for common grace. We have addressed common grace. It is God's special grace in nature and is the reason the world is not topsy-turvy. When you consider how wicked and unjust the world is, have you ever wondered why it isn't worse than it is? Answer: God's common grace, His goodness to all men. It has nothing to do directly with salvation; it is God's general goodness to everybody. The reason we have hospitals, doctors, nurses, laws, traffic lights and government is due to common grace. The reason people have talents, intelligence, abilities and motivation to do good is owing to common grace. You could have a "high level" of common grace and compose a Grieg's Concerto in A Minor, be an Albert Einstein with an IQ of 212 or play the piano like Arthur Rubinstein and not be a Christian or even moral. Common grace explains how God rules the world generally: showing His goodness to everybody, whether or not they are believers. All who are converted had common grace before they came to faith; but not all who have common grace—even a high level of ability—come to faith. This common grace maintains a certain control in the world lest things get totally out of hand. Common grace even keeps a lid on wickedness to a high degree, or things would be infinitely worse than they are.

What, then, does Jesus tell us about the devil? Four things: (1) that he is there—he exists, (2) that he is evil—totally wicked, (3) that he is active—alive and well, and (4) that he is still under God's control. Satan is not all-powerful—God is. Otherwise, Jesus would not have given this petition. The reason we can pray for daily deliverance from the evil one is because God is greater than the devil. God even allows the devil to promote His purposes in the world.

Examples of Evil

Let us examine ways we face the evil one every day. I said he is active. What does he do? First, he loves to terrorize. That is his specialty. It is what he does. All of us at times fear. He is the author of fear. He implants fear. He wants to make you fear and live in utter anxiety. Are you afraid? Do you live in fear? Are you motivated all the time by a spirit of fear? If so, the devil has succeeded with you to some extent. Being afraid is exactly what the devil wants of you. Satan works through fear. One of his nicknames is "accuser of our brothers" (Revelation 12:10). He works by fear and through fear, so Paul assured us that God has not given us a spirit of fear (2 Timothy 1:7). The more you are set free from fear, the greater your strength when Satan attempts to terrorize you.

Know this about the devil: He is a liar. "When he lies, he speaks his native language, for he is a liar and the father of lies," said Jesus (John 8:44). When he accuses you, it is often to make you think you are evil, unworthy and certainly not justified in calling yourself a Christian. He will also point out things about you that are true—to bring you down, reminding you of your faults and failures. This is why the great William Perkins said not to believe the devil, "even when he tells the truth"!

Second, the devil's job is to tempt. As we saw already in this chapter, he is called the tempter; he tempted Jesus in the desert. But his style is to work through our weaknesses. The devil knows us better than we know ourselves. He is shrewd, clever, canny, crafty. He has a computer printout on your nature, habits, past and lifestyle, and knows exactly how to bring you down by exploiting your weakness. He works through our natural weakness to achieve his end: our downfall.

There are basically three ways he seeks to defeat us: (1) *through pride*. Pride is at the bottom of all hate and unforgiveness. Do not forget 2 Corinthians 2:11: a good reason to forgive is to keep from being outsmarted by the devil. Furthermore, it may be anger that makes us lose our temper; our pride *keeps* us angry. We hate to admit we are wrong. It is what makes us jealous; we cannot bear

another's success. He appeals to your ambition and self-esteem in order to make you stumble. "Pride goes before destruction, a haughty spirit before a fall" (Proverbs 16:18). Our fall through pride is the devil's work.

(2) He seeks to defeat us *through sexual temptation*. We dealt with this in the previous chapter. But let me add that Satan loves to achieve success by getting a Christian, especially a leader, to fall; it brings disgrace upon the name of Christ and gives the world a chance to mock the Church. Pride is also at the bottom of sexual temptation; we are flattered by compliments, we need our esteem to be empowered. Satan knows this. My loving and earnest counsel to you, dear reader: Have such an esteem for God's glory and a care for another's life that you would not want to bring shame upon God's name or pain to another person. Sexual sin will lead to the greatest possible regret. Don't let it happen to you. And if, as you read these lines, you are at the moment in an affair, STOP IT! Or are considering an affair: STOP IT! *And stop it now.* Don't give the devil an opportunity; make no provision that he can work through your sexual desires (Romans 13:14).

(3) He seeks to defeat us *through unbelief.* Satan began to tempt Jesus by saying, "If you are the Son of God," trying to impart a doubt that maybe He isn't (Matthew 4:3). He did this with Eve in the Garden of Eden: "Did God really say, 'You must not eat from any tree in the garden'?" (Genesis 3:1). The first thing the devil did was to implant doubt in Eve's mind that God did not say what He said—and also to twist God's word. For God never said for her not to eat of "any" tree but only the Tree of Knowledge of Good and Evil (Genesis 2:17). The devil wants to make you doubt—your salvation, the Bible, God's love for you, His plans for you. Resist the devil and he will flee from you (James 4:7).

Third, the devil wants to test us. He is the great counterfeiter. "Satan himself masquerades as an angel of light" (2 Corinthians 11:14). The devil plays into our lack of discernment, even into our desire to be godly. He will set up false prophets and unscrupulous ministers to divert us from the truth. He hates truth. He hates good teaching. He hates the Gospel of Christ. He hates a true exposition of the Bible. When Christians are not knowledgeable in the Scriptures, they are easy targets for the devil to bring down. "My people are destroyed from lack of knowledge" (Hosea 4:6).

The more we develop a sense of discernment, the more we will be able to recognize the true presence of God, and the more we will be able to recognize the counterfeit. Don't try to be an expert in what is counterfeit. Don't read up on all the cults and false doctrines; get to know the Bible so well and the presence of God so well that you can instantly tell when the false lifts up its ugly head.

These are examples you and I will face to some degree every day. If we can anticipate the devil's setup in these three areas—terrorizing, tempting, testing—we will not likely be taken by surprise. We, therefore, pray daily that we will be spared. Remember: The devil never sleeps. He works day and night—in your dreams when you sleep (if he can), and in broad daylight through all I have just said. I also think of something my father used to say to me over and over again: "The devil is very crafty, second only to God in power and wisdom."

Deliverance from Evil

There are degrees of the need for deliverance. The most serious level is to be demonized or even demon-possessed. It is when one comes under the devil's domain and seems helpless. Such a person may desire to be out of such misery but is powerless. How many readers will need to think along this line when praying, "Lead us not into temptation, but deliver us from the evil one," I do not know; but I do not feel I can ignore this possibility.

There are two extremes when it comes to the study of the devil. One is to ignore him entirely—to deny that he exists (which he loves). The other is to be preoccupied with him and see a demon on every bush (which he also loves). I worry about those who have a preoccupation with spiritual warfare and seem to want to become "experts" in this area. I sometimes think they have more fear of Satan than they have trust in the power of God. Is it not interesting, too, that Jesus waited until the end of the Lord's Prayer to mention the devil?

There is, however, a most neglected kind of exorcism—and do you know what it is? It is called total forgiveness. You can look high and low across the continent for the person who is supposedly filled with the most power to cast out devils and be disappointed. But if you were to forgive—totally—I can promise you that the devil will make his exodus as you bless your enemy and refuse to seek any vengeance. I don't rule out those who have a ministry of deliverance, but if you are filled with bitterness and expect the demon to exit under another's gifting, you are going to be disappointed.

I recommend: Truly forgive that person who mistreated you—forgive them where you are right now. You may need a wise person to counsel you as well (this could be very important), but there is a deep well to be explored that is right under your nose. Defeat the devil by total forgiveness. I will have more to say about this a bit later.

The Three Rs of Spiritual Warfare

I have mentioned the "three Rs" of spiritual warfare: recognize, refuse, resist. Let us review them here, in context of this important subject.

First, *recognize* that it is the evil one at work. This is not always easy to do. Spiritual discernment is a gift of the Holy Spirit (1 Corinthians 12:10). But it does not follow that you need this particular gift to recognize the devil. When you are terrorized by fear, when the temptation is vehement, when the testing is overpowering—count on it: This is the devil. That is the first step in spiritual warfare: Recognize the devil when he molests you, diverts you from godly thoughts, makes you lose concentration when you pray or read the Bible.

Second, *refuse*. This may not be easy. But do your best to refuse to think about the thoughts he puts in your mind. For example, when you get a strong urge to doubt God's love, it is the devil; refuse to dignify these thoughts. In a word: Refuse to think about anything that is not wholesome. "Whatever is true, whatever is noble, whatever is right, whatever is pure, whatever is lovely, whatever is admirable—if anything is excellent or praiseworthy—think about such things" (Philippians 4:8). When the devil puts a negative thought in your head, refuse to think about it.

Third, *resist*. This means to persevere in refusing to listen to him. Resist. Resist. Resist. When the devil sees you are not going to give in to his cunning ways, he will leave you. That is the teaching of the New Testament. "Submit yourselves, then, to God. Resist the devil, and he will flee from you" (James 4:7). "Be self-controlled and alert. Your enemy the devil prowls around like a roaring lion looking for someone to devour. Resist him, standing firm in the faith, because you know that your brothers throughout the world are undergoing the same kind of sufferings" (1 Peter 5:8–9). Remember, too, that a characteristic of a lion is to roar. This is so his prey will suppose they are defeated before the lion even starts! The devil is like this. He roars, to make you think you don't have a chance, that you may as well give in. Wrong. Resist him. He will flee. As Martin Luther put it, "One word will quickly fell him." The lion's roar is to scare you, to make you dread today, tomorrow, your future. He is a liar; recognize, refuse, resist.

What I have said in this chapter should hopefully bring some coherence to this petition, "Lead us not into temptation, but deliver us from the evil one." It means a daily deliverance. You need it today. You will need it again tomorrow. This is not the same thing as demon possession; deliverance regarding being demonized may be a one-off matter. But apart from that, you will need a victory over the devil every day—over fear, over sexual temptation and testing of your faith. It is a daily matter. Expect it. Don't be surprised that you need to pray this petition often—and do all you can to act upon it, as we saw in the previous chapter. "Watch and pray" (Matthew 26:41).

The End of Evil

The Lord's Prayer will eventually be answered in full. You will ultimately be totally delivered from the devil. When Jesus comes the second time, it will spell Satan's final end. Until then, it will mean a daily deliverance.

The devil knows his end. The demons shouted at Jesus, "What do you want with us, Son of God? . . . Have you come here to torture us before the appointed time?" (Matthew 8:29). The "appointed time" signaled an eschatological event—in the future—when Satan and all his fallen angels will be punished. They know this is coming. The Lord Jesus will destroy the devil "with the breath of his mouth and destroy [the devil] by the splendor of his coming" (2 Thessalonians 2:8). When Satan was overcome by the blood of the Lamb, the admonition came: "Therefore rejoice, you heavens and you who dwell in them! But woe to the earth and the sea, because the devil has gone down to you! He is filled with fury, because he knows that his time is short" (Revelation 12:12). Yes. His time is short. He will not always be around. As has been said, "The next time the devil reminds you of your past, remind him of his future!"

We never outgrow praying the Lord's Prayer this side of going to heaven. We don't outgrow one single petition, as if to say, "Well, I won't need to pray that again." Sorry, but you will need to pray this as long as you live. Yet one day God will say to His angel to sound the trumpet. "For the Lord himself will come down from heaven, with a loud command, with the voice of the archangel and with the trumpet call of God, and the dead in Christ will rise first" (1 Thessalonians 4:16). "In a flash, in the twinkling of an eye, at the last trumpet. For the trumpet will sound, the dead will be raised imperishable, and we will be changed" (1 Corinthians 15:52). When that day comes, you can count on it: "So we will be with the Lord forever" (1 Thessalonians 4:17).

We won't be praying the Lord's Prayer in heaven! This prayer will have been completely answered by then. So pray it now!

52. The Kingdom, the Power and the Glory

For yours is the kingdom and the power and the glory forever. Amen.

MATTHEW 6:13

There is some doubt whether this final phrase at the end of the Lord's Prayer was in the original Greek New Testament—and for that matter in Jesus' teaching (He spoke in Aramaic). It is thought that some people in the Church chose and added this benediction (blessing) to close the prayer and that the words were incorporated in later manuscripts. But also keep in mind that it is very possible, indeed, that these were the actual words of Jesus.

One thing is quite certain: Many of us have prayed these beautiful words—and I myself shall continue to do so. After all, the words are absolutely true, even if Jesus did not say them. And if we repeat these words when we pray the Lord's Prayer, it certainly would be good to know what we are saying!

The origin of this phrase goes back to King David. When David praised the Lord in the presence of the whole assembly, he said:

> "Praise be to you, O LORD, God of our father Israel, from everlasting to everlasting. Yours, O LORD, is the greatness and the power and the glory and the majesty and the splendor, for everything in heaven and earth is yours. Yours, O LORD, is the kingdom; you are exalted as head over all. Wealth and honor come from you; you are the ruler of all things. In your hands are strength and power to exalt and give strength to all. Now, our God, we give you thanks, and praise your glorious name."
>
> 1 CHRONICLES 29:10–13

This is a wonderful statement of praise. A summary of King David's words of adoration bring the Lord's Prayer to a magnificent benediction: "Yours is the kingdom and the power and the glory forever. Amen." Many people say, "Forever and ever. Amen."

The Kingdom

When David said, "Yours, O LORD, is the kingdom; you are exalted as head over all" (1 Chronicles 29:11), this was Israel's king acknowledging the kingship of God. King David humbly and rightly acknowledged that he himself was under God, Israel's true King. Every existing monarch in the world should do this. "I am your King," God wanted Israel to know and never forget (Isaiah 43:15). Therefore, King David makes up for Israel's failure. They demanded their own king, to be like other nations (1 Samuel 8:19–20). God acquiesced and told Samuel to let them have their way (1 Samuel 8:7, 9, 22). God granted their request but sent leanness to their soul (Psalm 106:15, KJV).

What Israel failed to affirm, then—that God was their true King—King David made up for. He was careful never to forget that God was his and Israel's King. He refused to take himself seriously as did King Saul. Saul became "yesterday's man" (as I have described elsewhere). We, too, will become yesterday's men or women if we take ourselves too seriously, promoting ourselves to the level of a calling that did not come from God. We can know we are today's men and women to the degree the Holy Spirit rules in us un-grieved. Therefore, before all Israel David proclaimed, "Yours, O LORD, is the kingdom; you are exalted as head over all" (1 Chronicles 29:11). When we repeat the words, "Yours is the kingdom," we affirm not only that God our heavenly Father is our King, but also that the Kingdom belongs to Him. It is His, not ours; He shares it with us as He is pleased to do. Jesus said of those who are poor in spirit, "Theirs is the kingdom of heaven"

(Matthew 5:3). He also said it of those who are persecuted for the cause of Jesus Christ: "Theirs is the kingdom of heaven" (Matthew 5:10). This did not mean that they owned it, or that they were in charge, as if they were the head. No. But it did mean that they inherited the Kingdom by God's sovereign pleasure, and were given a special consciousness of the very real presence of God. Jesus said, "Do not be afraid, little flock, for your Father has been pleased to give you the kingdom" (Luke 12:32).

When Jesus said, "Ask and it will be given to you; seek and you will find; knock and the door will be opened to you" (Matthew 7:7), He primarily was referring to our receiving the Kingdom. To inherit and enjoy the Kingdom is what Jesus is emphasizing in the Sermon on the Mount. Many people take Matthew 7:7 out of context and apply it to almost everything they have a wish for; and God may even accommodate them. But the context of Matthew 7:7 is that we will be hungry for God and thirsting after the righteousness Jesus has described. To those who want this, Jesus simply says, "Ask for it, and you will receive it." Yes, it is the Father's good pleasure to give us the Kingdom.

However, we must also remember that the Kingdom of God is to be understood in more than one way. When you and I pray, "Yours is the kingdom," we, too, need to incorporate more than one meaning simultaneously.

The saintly Scottish preacher Robert Murray M'Cheyne (1813–1843) reckoned that our Lord Jesus Christ wears two crowns: one pertaining to the state, one pertaining to the Church. This was M'Cheyne's way of saying that God is both ruler over the nations and is the head of the Church. He is Lord over the political realm, of government and all those issues we saw earlier regarding "common grace." God is sovereign over all—everybody and everything. This means He is in charge of all elections; He puts people in office. "The authorities that exist have been established by God" (Romans 13:1).

We can pray for our personal choices and vote according to our consciences, but at the end of the day God decides. However, a nation that does not acknowledge that God is supreme over the nation, and does not believe that the nation is

blessed whose God is the Lord (Psalm 33:12), may inherit evil rulers who will bring calamity and misery to a country. This is why the Church should pray that God will overrule and give us not what we deserve but what is best for us.

So, too, is our Lord Jesus the head of the Church. "He is the head of the body, the church" (Colossians 1:18). The buck stops with Him. All church hierarchy, church politics, church officers, pastoral leadership and members are under the headship of Jesus Christ. But if a church strays from the Gospel and the revealed will of God—the Bible—that church will lose its right to exist. It will be like Paul foretold long ago, as having a form of godliness but denying its power (2 Timothy 3:5).

That is when the church becomes an empty shell. King Jesus has the right to remove a church's lampstand from its place, as He warned (Revelation 2:5). This means that a church will lose its anointing or, the worst possible scenario, become apostate (fallen, in utter powerlessness and disgrace). It does not necessarily mean that a church is wiped off the map, although this can happen, too; it mainly means that a church can have a name that it lives but is in fact "dead" (Revelation 3:1). Someone has said that if the Holy Spirit were taken completely from the Church today (speaking generally), 90 percent of the work of the Church would carry on as if nothing had happened.

The Church is God's visible vehicle for expressing Kingdom power. "His intent was that now, through the church, the manifold wisdom of God should be made known . . . according to his eternal purpose which he accomplished in Christ Jesus our Lord" (Ephesians 3:10–11). You and I are a part of this visible instrument. Therefore, when you and I utter the words, "Yours is the kingdom," we represent the Church. But in these words we also affirm God's jurisdiction over the whole world. We acknowledge that Jesus Christ is our Supreme Head, but are at the same time following David in acknowledging the sovereign rule of God over all the earth. And as the Lord's Prayer is addressed to the Father, we are therefore honoring Him as being the absolute Lord of heaven and earth—and over our own lives. We bow to Him. He is our Sovereign, our

Monarch. He is the Great King "than whom no greater can be conceived."

This benediction, therefore, acknowledges that God is the One who rules the world, nations and the Church—and can replace rulers, heads of state and ecclesiastical leaders. "No one from the east or the west or from the desert can exalt a man. But it is God who judges: He brings one down, he exalts another" (Psalm 75:6–7). As Hosea said later, referring to the generation that demanded a king, "So in my anger I gave you a king, and in my wrath I took him away" (Hosea 13:11).

Finally, to utter the words, "Yours is the kingdom," is to honor and accept His verdict regarding our own inheritance in the Kingdom. God said to Moses, "I will have mercy on whom I will have mercy, and I will have compassion on whom I will have compassion" (Exodus 33:19). We cannot twist God's arm and make Him immediately give us this great sense of His presence. It is His good pleasure to give it to us—but in His timing and on His terms. To say, "Yours is the kingdom," is to stop snapping our fingers at God and expect Him to act at our command.

When Jesus told Peter how the apostle would die, Peter wanted to know God's will for John as well. But in so many words Jesus said, "That's none of your business—you just follow Me and don't worry about John" (see John 21:18–22). God has a particular, special and individual will for each of us. "He chose our inheritance for us" (Psalm 47:4). We may wish to look over our shoulders curiously to see what God has decided for others around us. But He says, "Stop looking at others and follow Me." We have enough to do merely to walk in the light God has given to *us*, not others. When we say, "Yours is the kingdom," we are agreeing to do just that!

The Power

"Yours is the kingdom and the power." The power in these words refers to the Holy Spirit. There are at least two Greek words that can be translated "power": *dunamis* (enabling) and *exousia* (authority). The word here is *dunamis*—the enabling energy or power that makes things happen. Jesus might have used either or both words, but He used *dunamis,* from which we get the word *dynamite.* Therefore, when we say, "Yours is the power," we

refer to the Holy Spirit's power. It is the word Jesus used when He said to the disciples before His ascension, "Stay in the city until you have been clothed with power from on high" (Luke 24:49). "You will receive power when the Holy Spirit comes on you; and you will be my witnesses in Jerusalem, and in all Judea and Samaria, and to the ends of the earth" (Acts 1:8).

The point here is that only the enabling power of the Spirit can make the Kingdom real to us. To say, "Yours is the power," is to confess our helplessness without that power. This power can sometimes be used interchangeably with anointing. It is what opens our eyes, dispels the blindness and enables us to understand truth. It is what gives us insight into Holy Scripture. It is what helps us overcome fear. It is what gives us confidence when we talk to others about Jesus Christ. It was the power of the Holy Spirit that enabled the disciples to witness in Jerusalem, Judea, et al. Peter did not believe Jesus when he was told he would deny Christ (Mark 14:29–31). But he was an utter coward hours later before a servant girl, and, indeed, denied even knowing Jesus (Mark 14:66–72). How could Peter do this and be so weak? It was because he was left to himself and filled with fear; he was empty of strength and confidence within himself. In a word: He was devoid of the Spirit's power. He was so sure he would be strong within himself and sincerely thought he would never deny Jesus. But he did.

However, on the Day of Pentecost, Peter was as bold as a lion, preaching with power, liberty, confidence and authority before thousands of fellow Jews—and he startled them all. Instead of mocking and laughing at Peter, his hearers were "cut to the heart" and pleaded, "What shall we do?" (Acts 2:37). It was power that the person had in mind when he said that if the Holy Spirit were completely taken from the Church today, 90 percent of the work of the Church would continue as if nothing had happened. This is the meaning of those words, "Having a form of godliness but denying its power" (2 Timothy 3:5). Paul also said to Timothy that God has not given us a spirit of fear but "of power, of love and of self-discipline" (2 Timothy 1:7).

Many Christians today seem to be afraid of the Holy Spirit. There are denominations whose doctrine of the Trinity could be summed up, "God the Father, God the Son and God the Holy Bible." They have the Bible but not the Spirit's power. They are sound in many ways but are so cold, formal and seemingly lifeless, demonstrating a 10 percent reliance on the Holy Spirit.

I was born and raised in Kentucky. A century before I was born, a phenomenon known as "camp meetings" emerged in Bourbon County, Kentucky, just over a hundred miles from my Nazarene church in my hometown of Ashland. Thousands came to a place called Cane Ridge in Bourbon County in their covered wagons from several states, representing various denominations. On a Sunday morning at Cane Ridge in July 1801, a Methodist lay preacher stood on a fallen tree, taking his text from 2 Corinthians 5:10: "For we must all appear before the judgment seat of Christ; that every one may receive the things done in his body, according to that he hath done, whether it be good or bad" (KJV).

An estimated fifteen thousand people had gathered to hear him preach. When he finished, there were hundreds of people prostrate on the ground, seemingly unconscious. For the next several days, there was never a time but that at least five hundred people were flat out on the ground. A bit of panic set in, and some thought they were dead. But after a few hours, these same people would revive with loud shouts of assurance of salvation. It was like "the sound of Niagara," someone said, referring to the noise of the people, which could be heard a mile away. Some cynical, mocking people would make their way to scoff at the happenings, only to be smitten and converted when they reached Cane Ridge. Now known as the Cane Ridge Revival, it is regarded as America's Second Great Awakening.

There is no valid natural explanation for this— only the power of the Spirit. That is what it must have been like immediately after Peter preached. It is when thousands are converted in hours. It is when people who are opinionated, blind, cold and hard—and apparently unreachable—become soft, tender, open and eager to do whatever God prompts them to do. Dr. and Mrs. Martyn Lloyd-Jones used to talk to me about the Welsh revival and stories that came from it. Mrs. Lloyd-Jones was actually present in Wales for a while to see

it. Her father took her out of school in London and put her on a train at Paddington Station in order for her to go to Wales in 1904. He was criticized for taking her out of school. He replied: "She can always go to school, but she may never see revival again."

Dr. Lloyd-Jones told me of a coal miner who was thoroughly annoyed with his wife for not cooking his meal when he got home from work. She was at the local church instead, enthralled with the Welsh Revival. He could take it no more. Determined to make a scene and end the revival meetings, he went straight to the church. But he could not get in because of the crowds of people around the door. But he pushed his way through those at the door and made his way to the back pew of the church. The next thing he remembers was finding himself on his knees in front of the pulpit crying out to God to save him. Those present said what happened was that he stood on the back pew, then stepped on the back of each pew, one at a time, toward the pulpit until he fell at the front of the church—in submission to God. That is the kind of power that was present in Wales during that time.

You cannot manufacture that kind of power. You cannot work it up. You cannot legislate it. You cannot make it happen. It belongs to God. "Yours is the power." And yet I fear it is what is missing in the Church, speaking generally, at the present time. The absence of this power is the explanation for long "altar calls," trying to plead people into moving. It is the explanation for the absence of Gospel preaching, appealing to people's self-interest instead. It is the reason the Church's influence is minimal in so many countries at the present time and why people don't take the Church seriously. It is why there is little fear of God in the world today. That is why people blaspheme God and godliness right, left and center, with no worry that there is a God in heaven who sees and hears.

You cannot force God to open your own eyes or anyone else's. You may open your Bible to read it and pray for guidance and insight. But unless the Spirit comes on you, you will read and read with no spiritual understanding. The Bible is a spiritual book. It is not like reading a book on architecture, psychology, philosophy, history, literature or even theology. You can read these disciplines and understand what you read. But not the Bible. The greatest intellect cannot grasp the true meaning of Scripture at the natural level. He or she may say, "It makes no sense to me," thinking it is their great brain that dismisses the truth of God's Word. But should the Spirit come upon a person, whether that man or woman is educated or simple, God's Word will be clear, brilliant and full of insight.

Jesus told the disciples to tarry—to wait for this power to come. We need to do this today. We must not settle for anything less. God is sovereign and has a will of His own. But He has also encouraged us to pray for this power. We should go to Him on bended knee. Yes, pray the Lord's Prayer on bended knee. And remember that it is the Holy Spirit who is meant when we say, "Yours is the power."

The Glory

"Yours is the kingdom and the power and the glory." This mainly means that we must not forget to give God the credit for what He does, should He answer any of the petitions in the Lord's Prayer. We must always give Him the credit if He answers any of our prayers. We never have a right to pat ourselves on the back and think that any success or answer to our prayers is due to our perseverance or faithfulness, although God wants us never to give up. God gets all the glory—the credit—for what is done.

As the phrase "Kingdom of God" can be explained accurately in several ways, so, too, this word *glory*. This to me is an exciting study. I have been enthralled with this word for over fifty years and am still trying to understand it.

In the Old Testament, the Hebrew word is *kabodh*. It means "heaviness." We may say of someone today, "He or she is a heavyweight," meaning they are not common or ordinary but have a lot of importance—as a senator, member of parliament or bishop. We will use the expression that someone "throws their weight around"—like an officer in the military, or a political or even an ecclesiastical figure. That is the idea of the *kabodh*. The God of the Bible is a God of glory. But this heaviness can also be almost physical, even visible. When the Ark of the Covenant was

brought into the Temple for the first time, the Temple was "filled with a cloud, and the priests could not perform their service because of the cloud, for the *glory of the LORD* filled the temple of God" (2 Chronicles 5:13–14, emphasis mine).

One should wish that the glory of God would come into a church so that the entire proceedings were disrupted and that all plans had to be suspended. I used to see this at times when I was a boy growing up in my old church in Ashland. I have seen the presence and power of God build up over a time, such that conviction would set in so powerfully that people stood up and ran to the front to pray before the preacher could finish his sermon—and he would stop preaching. I have sometimes thought that, perhaps, a touch of the Cane Ridge Revival was still around in Ashland in my earliest days. I do know that they called us Nazarenes "Noisy-renes"!

The New Testament word for glory is *doxa*, from which we get "doxology." It means "praise." But it comes from a root word that actually means "opinion." This is very important. God has an opinion. As a matter of fact, He has an opinion on everything! Furthermore, He wants to share His opinion—and for us to take it seriously. This is because He wants praise and glory for every idea He has, every opinion He shares.

The verse that I have sought to be governed by is John 5:44, for me the most important verse in the Bible, which I read every day to myself: "How can you believe if you accept praise from one another, yet make no effort to obtain the praise that comes from the only God?" I was introduced to this verse in the King James Version: "How can ye believe, which receive honour one of another, and seek not the honour that cometh from God only?" This is the way I learned the verse. I am glad that it reads as it does, hinting that it is God's praise alone—"God only"—that matters. That is the way I understood the verse from the beginning. I grew to want only His honor—not that which comes from people—and that I should be motivated by this alone.

This verse uncovers the reason the Jews missed their Messiah. They were locked into wanting one another's praise so much that when their own promised Messiah showed up under their noses, they missed Him entirely. Surprise, surprise, said

Jesus. "How *can* you believe?" Jesus was implying, "You can't." It would be impossible to believe when they are preoccupied with praise for one another without making any effort to seek the praise that comes from the true and only God.

That is how they missed what God was doing in their day. It is why we can miss what God is doing in our day, too. Jonathan Edwards taught us that the task of every generation is to discover in which direction the Sovereign Redeemer is moving, then move in that direction. But if we are consumed with the wish to have praise from one another—making no effort to seek God's praise—we, too, will miss what God is up to in our day, as the Jews missed it two thousand years ago.

God is a jealous God. His name is Jealous (Exodus 34:14). As a consequence of this, He resents it when He does not get all the glory for what He does. Like it or not, that is the way He is. And when we pray the Lord's Prayer, concluding with, "Yours is the kingdom and the power and the glory," we are promising not to forget to give Him all the glory!

Do you? Do you give Him all the glory for what He does? The worst mistake you and I could make is to underestimate how much God wants all the credit for what He does. Don't even come close—not even an inch—to elbowing in on His glory. It is a scary thing to do. And yet we must all be taught this. That is precisely what Jesus was doing when He gave us the Lord's Prayer. And whether it was Jesus or the Church that gave us these words, "Yours is the kingdom and the power and the glory," they are absolutely true. And we are impoverished if we neglect them—and wonderfully blessed if we take them very seriously indeed.

"Forever. Amen."

The intent here is that God wants us to remember that the Kingdom is eternally and irrevocably His, that the power always comes from Him (and not from within us) and that the glory must always go to Him. This is an unchangeable, eternal truth and principle. "I the LORD do not change" (Malachi 3:6). "Jesus Christ is the same yesterday and today and forever" (Hebrews 13:8).

Amen is an Aramaic word that means "so be it." We use "Amen" to endorse another's prayer; we say it at the end of our own prayer, as if to confirm we mean what we just said.

With these brief closing comments, my exposition on the Lord's Prayer is finished. But our Lord isn't quite finished yet, so neither am I. We turn now to His final observation regarding this prayer.

53. Jesus' P.S. to the Lord's Prayer

For if you forgive men when they sin against you, your heavenly Father will also forgive
you. But if you do not forgive men their sins, your Father will not forgive your sins.

MATTHEW 6:14–15

Because of these glaring two words—"for if" (Gr. *ean gar*)—immediately following the prayer Jesus gave to us, we instantly see that He has purposefully not changed the subject yet. Although He did not apparently add this P.S. when He gave the prayer to the disciples in Luke 11:2–4, He certainly reveals He is not finished with this prayer in the Sermon on the Mount. He clearly has more to say about the Lord's Prayer before He moves on in the Sermon on the Mount.

When Jesus included the petition, "Forgive us our debts [sins], as we also have forgiven our debtors [those who have sinned against us]," in the Lord's Prayer, it was not the first time He taught this in the Sermon on the Mount. The first indication was in Matthew 5:7: "Blessed are the merciful, for they will be shown mercy." It was further implied in His stunning teaching that hate was the same as murder in Matthew 5:21–22, but in Matthew 5:44 He clearly said: "Love your enemies and pray for those who persecute you." He added, "Be perfect, therefore, as your heavenly Father is perfect" (Matthew 5:48). He wants us to forgive like God forgives.

From this general context it might be argued that Jesus' chief reason for giving the Lord's Prayer in the first place was to teach love and forgiveness again. If so, this is why He stated at the end of the prayer, "For if you forgive men when they sin against you, your heavenly Father will also forgive you" (Matthew 6:14). However, I am sure that there were many reasons—not merely forgiveness—He gave us the Lord's Prayer. The immediate context is about prayer—showing what prayer ought not to be and what it should be (Matthew 6:5–8), whereupon He gave us the Lord's Prayer. You may recall that the context in Luke 11 was in response to the disciples' request, "Lord, teach us to pray" (v. 1).

In any case, Jesus could have moved on to another subject in the Sermon on the Mount as soon as He finished giving the prayer itself. But He didn't. He had more to say on the matter and referred to only one of the petitions, namely, that petition that said, "Forgive us our debts, as we also have forgiven our debtors" (Matthew 6:12).

He apparently considers this the most important of the petitions, and the one that needed the most attention.

Does this surprise you? The truth is, the teaching of forgiveness is the greatest need of the Church today. Until fairly recently, nearly all books on forgiveness related to God forgiving us, and almost none on the subject pertaining to our forgiving others. Jesus' teaching on this is plain as day, but we all have a way of sweeping it under the carpet. I myself did—for years and years. Until one day, in my darkest hour, Josif Tson had the courage to say to me: "R. T., you must totally forgive them; until you totally forgive them, you will be in chains. Release them, and you will be released." Nobody had ever talked to me that way in my life. "Faithful are the wounds of a friend" (Proverbs 27:6, KJV). How I thank God for Josif Tson.

All I know is, Jesus returns to the subject. He will not let us off the hook. Someone has said, "The truth which makes us free is for the most part the truth which we prefer not to hear." How true. Is there anything more painful than being told we must let those who have hurt us totally off the hook and even pray God's blessing upon them? Can anything be harder than that? Probably not. But it is certainly the most emancipating teaching there is.

If Jesus did not change the subject, I felt I, too, must not close my book on the Lord's Prayer just yet either. I therefore feel I have a duty to deal with Matthew 6:13–14, even briefly, before the book is complete.

I will say it again. As for the teaching on total forgiveness, you and I can never get enough of it. I need it as much as ever. As a matter of fact, almost twenty years ago I took upon myself a discipline to read Luke 6:37 every day: "Do not judge, and you will not be judged. Do not condemn, and you will not be condemned. Forgive, and you will be forgiven." Why do I read this regularly? Because I need it so much. My weakness is to judge. I need to be reminded all the time to be gentle and button my lip when the temptation is to criticize or find fault.

We point the finger because we do not totally forgive. If we totally forgive, the need to judge evaporates like water in the tropical sun. Reading this verse regularly has been very, very helpful to me personally. The heart is deceitful (Jeremiah 17:9); we think we have mastered the art of totally forgiving, only to discover we failed yet again.

I am convinced this is why Jesus did not change the subject when He finished the Lord's Prayer. He knew that the disciples needed it, that the Church would need it. The truth is, we all need it.

The Foundation for a Greater Anointing

How many of us have realized that when Jesus said, "Whatever you ask for in prayer, believe that you *have received it*, and it will be yours," He didn't stop there? He added: "And when you stand praying, if you hold anything against anyone, forgive him, so that your Father in heaven may forgive you your sins" (Mark 11:24–25, emphasis mine).

Believing that you have received what you pray for is a very high level of faith indeed. As a matter of fact, it is God's faith—the faith of God. Jesus actually introduced this by saying, "Have faith in God," but the Greek reads *ei echete pistin theou*—literally, "If you have faith of God" (Mark 11:22, as in the margin of some editions of the KJV). I will only observe that saying to a mountain, "Go, throw yourself into the sea," and not doubting it will happen (Mark 11:23), is given only to those who have a supernatural level of

faith. Whether the scholars translate *pistin theou* as faith "in" God or faith "of" God is for them to decide. I will only ask: When is the last time you heard of someone speaking to a mountain to have it cast into the sea? Only God can do that. And yet Jesus encouraged us to have this kind of faith.

My point is this. This section is concluded by Jesus' word about forgiveness: "If you hold anything against anyone [when you stand praying], forgive him, so that your Father in heaven may forgive you your sins" (v. 25). Whether anyone has ever caused a mountain to fall into the sea, one thing is for certain: Jesus is showing we should not even expect to have faith like that unless we have totally forgiven all those who have sinned against us.

The prerequisite for having the kind of faith as described in Mark 11:22–25 is total forgiveness. It is the only way forward for a greater anointing. It is probably the most neglected teaching when it comes to the need for power and seeing the miraculous. Giving millions to the Church will not do it. Giving to the poor won't do it. Giving your body to be burned won't do it (1 Corinthians 13:30). A forty-day fast will not do it. Total forgiveness is what is required. It is God's faith we should pray for: to forgive "just as in Christ *God forgave you*" (Ephesians 4:32, emphasis mine).

I have long admired and wanted to be like Stephen, a truly great hero portrayed in the New Testament. His opponents could not resist the wisdom or the Spirit by whom he spoke. What an anointing he had! His face shone like that of an angel (Acts 6:10, 15). What do you suppose was the key—the explanation for such an anointing? I answer: He was devoid of all bitterness. When he was dying from being stoned by his persecutors, he prayed—these being his last words, "Do not hold this sin against them" (Acts 7:60). What a way to die!

We all have hurts. We all have a story to tell. Jesus knows that. This is why He says "when" in Matthew 6:14. "If you forgive men *when* [not *if*] they sin against you" (emphasis mine). It is only a matter of time until someone will hurt us, lie about us, falsely accuse us, be jealous of us, neglect us, sometimes physically hurt us, not keep his or her word to us, possibly be unfaithful to us, embarrass us, take advantage of us, totally let us down and disappoint us, shock us, walk all over us and, if possible, abuse us. Jesus' teaching is so practical—and possible to apply. We may like to think it is not possible, but it is. We simply have to keep doing it when we fail.

Totally forgiving those who have been unjust is to let them completely, utterly and totally off the hook—and then pray (sincerely) that God will bless them! "That's hard," you say. Yes. It is hard. But it is required of you and me to do. Why should we do it? We do it because we take Jesus' word seriously, because we want to inherit the Kingdom and because we want to be conscious of His manifest presence as much as possible. And also we forgive because we don't want to be "outsmarted by Satan" (2 Corinthians 2:10–11, NLT). For when we hold a grudge, although we didn't mean to, we allow the devil to walk right in. Do not give him that opportunity!

There are basically two kinds of hurts: (1) when people do not intend to hurt us—they don't know they have done it; and (2) when people are deliberately unkind—they surely know they have hurt us. And yet—strange as it may seem—most people you will have to forgive don't even think they have done anything wrong! That hurts even more. What do you do then? You still forgive them.

As I advised in an earlier chapter, don't go to them and say, "You might like to know I have forgiven you." I can safely guarantee you will start World War III in a split second. Furthermore, when we tell people we have forgiven them, chances are we haven't! We only want to make sure they know how hurt we have been. We can't bear the thought that they don't know what they have done to us. But Jesus said, "Father, forgive them, for they do not know what they are doing" (Luke 23:34). Make Jesus your model!

Our Salvation Is Not the Issue

It must be repeated, as I stated in Chapter 8, forgiving others is not a condition for salvation, neither is the issue whether we will or will not go to heaven even implied. When Jesus warns that we will not be forgiven unless we forgive, it might be thought by some sincere people that He was making our forgiving others a condition of our salvation. No. Thank God this is not the case. If

it were, nobody would be saved. And yet to assert, as some do, that not forgiving others means we either cannot be saved—or, which is equally sad, that we could lose our salvation—is to miss the entire point of Jesus' teaching on the Kingdom of God. I say it again: If my forgiving others, as God requires, is a condition of my being righteous before God and therefore knowing whether I will go to heaven when I die, I would have no hope whatever of being a Christian.

I am ashamed to admit it, but I myself did not come into this teaching of total forgiveness until several years after I became the minister of Westminster Chapel. I was converted when I was six years old, called to preach when I was nineteen, pastor of a church when I was twenty and later went to university and seminary. I had been in the ministry for over 25 years when I began to forgive people who hurt me. If forgiveness was a condition of my salvation, it means I was not saved until years after I became the minister of Westminster Chapel! I do not believe that for a second.

It would also mean that if I slipped (which I have done) and momentarily judged another or felt angry toward someone who hurt me, then—for a moment—I was lost, but got saved again when I came to myself and forgave my enemy and stopped judging. What kind of Christianity is that? A person who lives like that would be a nervous wreck day and night! That also would mean that salvation is earned by sheer good works. But that is not New Testament teaching.

Forgiving others is not only a good work, it is probably the most noble, admirable and satisfying work one can achieve on this earth! And if such a work is what prepares us for heaven, then Jesus' teaching flies in the face of what Paul taught. He said, "For it is by grace you have been saved, through faith—and this not from yourselves, it is the gift of God—*not by works, so that no one can boast*" (Ephesians 2:8–9, emphasis mine). Paul went on to say that "we are God's workmanship, created in Christ Jesus to do good works" (v. 10). It is being saved that *enables* us to do good works, such as totally forgiving our enemies. But what God enables us to do—forgiving our enemies—is not what He stipulates in order to be saved.

Furthermore, believe me, total forgiveness is a life sentence—a life commitment—and something we must work on as long as we live.

Why Should We Totally Forgive?

What, then, is the reason for Jesus' teaching on forgiveness? It is to inherit His conscious and enabling presence—which is what He means by "the kingdom" in the Sermon on the Mount. Those who are offered the Kingdom are those who are already followers of Jesus. When Jesus said, "Ask and it will be given to you; seek and you will find; knock and the door will be opened to you" (Matthew 7:7), it was directed to those who had not only heard all He taught regarding the Kingdom, but who wanted all of God they could have. Jesus' teaching makes us hungry for God! When we read what He has to say in the Sermon on the Mount, our hearts should burn within us that we could experience such a relationship with the Father.

What is required for such a relationship? I answer: total forgiveness. All that Jesus taught about being merciful and blessing our enemies was not idle talk, neither was it merely putting forth lofty principles that we admire. No. His teaching is to be applied by those who have already been saved, whose justification is by faith alone; it is they—not the lost—who are called to total forgiveness.

So what does it mean that our heavenly Father will also forgive us if we forgive those who sin against us? I reply: It means we can enjoy intimacy with Him here below—His immediate, direct and conscious manifest presence. Total forgiveness, ridding us of poisonous bitterness, opens the door to knowing the Father, so that God is as real to us as the air we breathe and as real as seeing the world He has made. Real. Yes, God is real. It is what the disciples experienced on the Day of Pentecost. The person of Jesus was as real to them by the Spirit as He had been previously to them when they saw Him in the flesh. John talked about what he had "seen with our eyes, which we have looked at and our hands have touched"—namely, Jesus. The very fellowship with the Father that John was describing makes Jesus as real as if He were there before our eyes (1 John 1:1).

In a word: Total forgiveness brings the anointing of the Holy Spirit; bitterness keeps Him away. Therefore, the way we know we have forgiven is the immediate sense of God's presence. You are given this when you forgive; you lose this when you do not. You do not lose your salvation, but you do indeed forfeit—even if only temporarily—the anointing of the Spirit and the sense of His presence.

The Holy Spirit Depicted as a Dove

Paul talked about grieving the Holy Spirit, which we do chiefly by bitterness. But when we grieve the Spirit we do not lose our salvation; after all, he said, "Do not grieve the Holy Spirit of God, with whom you were sealed for the day of redemption" (Ephesians 4:30). Nothing can be clearer than that! But when we grieve the Spirit by not totally forgiving our enemies, the anointing lifts from us; He does not "remain"; He does not stay. The Dove came down on Jesus and remained on Him (John 1:32–33). I wish He would remain on me! But I admit to grieving Him, which causes the Dove to lift and fly away for a while. Total forgiveness attracts the Dove so that He comes down on us; bitterness chases Him away.

This is the meaning of Jesus' words, "For if you forgive men when they sin against you, your heavenly Father will also forgive you. But if you do not forgive men their sins, your Father will not forgive your sins"—that is, as long as you are in a state of not forgiving others. But once you confess your sins (1 John 1:9), and turn from them so as to reject all "bitterness, rage and anger," and begin "forgiving each other, just as in Christ God forgave you" (Ephesians 4:31–32), the Dove comes down and you have the witness of the Father's forgiveness. And, by the way, He won't bend the rules for any of us—for you, the high-profile Christian leader, the aged saint, the most talented minister or me.

The dove is a very sensitive, shy bird. This is apparently why the Holy Spirit is depicted as a dove in the New Testament. And yet the Holy Spirit is far more sensitive than a dove! We must learn to know God's ways, which Israel failed to do (Hebrews 3:7–11), so that we can sense when the Dove lifts from us. Bitterness chases the Dove away; total forgiveness—and nothing less—brings Him back. I'm sorry, but that is the way it is.

Refusing to Punish

Forgiving your enemy—or whoever has hurt you—means *refusing to punish them.* Perfect love casts out fear, and fear has to do with punishment (1 John 4:18). When we don't forgive, fear creeps in; we want those people we haven't forgiven to be afraid of us! We want to punish them by making them afraid. When the brothers of Joseph discovered that the prime minister of Egypt was actually Joseph (whom they had hoped never to see again), they were "terrified." But Joseph said to them, "Come close to me." The last thing he wanted was for his brothers to fear him (Genesis 45:3–4).

You must refuse to punish those who have been unjust and have sinned against you, by not damaging their credibility. We must resist damaging their reputation because of what they did to us. That is what I wanted to do—to damage the influence of those who had been unfair toward me. But God said, "No! Stop it!" I had to keep quiet about it and tell nobody.

It was hard. So hard. But a major part of total forgiveness is never telling anyone how you have been hurt. Yes, you may need to tell one other person for therapeutic reasons. But only one. And then, of course, you must tell God. He knows. Let the knowledge that Jesus knows be your peace and joy. And when you slip, and forfeit God's presence for a while, return to Him; He will return to you. The Dove will come down and reside with you. I promise it.

I suppose the hardest thing of all is to pray that God will bless them. One day I found myself saying, "Lord, bless them," but only because I knew it was the right thing to do. And then, as if the Lord intervened and had a conversation with me: "And what if I really do bless them, R. T.?" I said, "Lord, You wouldn't do *that,* would You?"

But that is the point! When you pray for your enemies, you don't merely say, "Lord, I commit them to You." That's not good enough. That's a cop-out. You are probably still hoping that God will punish them! It isn't easy, but when you really do pray for God to bless your enemy—and truly mean it—you begin to cross over into the supernatural and experience how real God is.

But how can you be motivated to do this? The way forward for wanting to experience God's forgiveness in this way is when you prize fellowship with the Father, desire pleasing Him and cherish the anointing of the Spirit above all else.

The Consequence of Unforgiveness

And yet it is most sobering to read, "But if you do not forgive men their sins, your Father will not forgive your sins" (Matthew 6:15). This is scary. Although Jesus does not mean I will go to hell, there is a danger of crossing over a line so that I forfeit such intimacy for a long time—perhaps forever.

It is serious, serious business not to forgive. I have watched lives torn to shreds because of bitterness. I have not only seen marriages irretrievably broken down and destroyed, I have watched those who once knew the joy of the Lord in their lives fall into bitterness from which they were never to be extricated. I have watched them grow old and cold. I have seen them spend the rest of their lives preoccupied with their hurt and injustice, sometimes talking about nothing else. I have watched those I have admired go to their graves with this bondage.

What does it mean at the Judgment Seat of Christ for those Christians who have not forgiven those who have sinned against them? I reply: They will "suffer loss"—which means loss of reward, or rejection for the prize they could have had. Yet they will "be saved, but only as one escaping through the flames" ("saved . . . so as by fire," 1 Corinthians 3:15, KJV).

A reward at the Judgment Seat of Christ was very important to Paul. He said he made his body his slave in order that he not be rejected for the prize (1 Corinthians 9:27). Needlessly forfeiting your reward—is that what you want? Do you want to forfeit God's "well done"? It is promised only to those who have made every effort to add to their faith, goodness; to goodness, knowledge; to knowledge, self-control; to self-control, perseverance; to perseverance, godliness; to godliness, brotherly kindness; and to brotherly kindness, love. Those who possess these qualities will be productive in the knowledge of our Lord Jesus Christ *and* will receive "a rich welcome into the eternal kingdom" (2 Peter 1:5–11).

Why does God hate an unforgiving spirit? It shows indifference to the greatest thing God ever did—namely, sending His Son to die on a cross for our sins. To be forgiven of all our sins is the most wonderful thing that can happen to us between the date of our birth and the time of our departure from this life. God forgiving us all our sins is what we most certainly don't deserve. But when we are forgiven, God wants us to be truly thankful and pass this knowledge to others—by our verbal witness and by our transparent love. When I have been forgiven but then point the finger at you, God says, "Stop! This will not do." It is a sober word, "Do not judge, or you too will be judged" (Matthew 7:1).

And yet total forgiveness is not necessarily reconciliation. It takes two to reconcile; it takes only one to forgive. The person you forgive may not want to be reconciled to you. What is more, you may not want to be reconciled to the person you forgive! It is not always good for a relationship to continue. If someone sleeps with your spouse, you forgive him or her; but you would not go on vacation with that person. If a man has been a child molester, you forgive him; but you don't let him teach young children in your church. The main thing is not reconciliation but total forgiveness in your heart.

Inheriting the Blessing

The greater the suffering, the greater the anointing. The greater their injustice to you, the greater blessing that is promised to you. So if you have suffered more than others—or, let us say, more than anyone—instead of feeling sorry for yourself, feel congratulated! You have a promise of blessing, anointing, the conscious presence of God that will be greater than what is given to those around you who have not had to suffer what you have had to suffer, and have not had to forgive what you have had to forgive. All things work together for good to those who love God (Romans 8:28), but you will postpone seeing things work together for good until you show you truly love God. You show you love Him by refusing to punish those who have hurt you but by forgiving them—totally.

Unforgiveness shows ingratitude to God for what He has done for you. God loves gratitude; He hates ingratitude. When you don't forgive after God has forgiven you, it shows ingratitude. God doesn't like that—not one bit. Show your gratitude to God by forgiving others as He has forgiven you!

I had a minister in Northern Ireland ask me a question I had not heard before: "Can your enemy be your wife?" I smiled, looked at him and said, "Yes." He looked at me and said, "Thank you." Yes, your spouse can be like an enemy. The message of total forgiveness can save most marriages. But it takes two to reconcile. The main thing is that you yourself totally forgive what your spouse has done, that there is no pointing of the finger, no keeping a record of wrongs (1 Corinthians 13:5). Your own marriage could be saved by sundown today if both of you will stop pointing the finger. And if your spouse continues to point the finger at you, you be the magnanimous one and stop it at once. The blessing of the Holy Spirit should be too important to you that you get your way in everything. After all, love "does not insist on its own way" (1 Corinthians 13:5, ESV).

The characteristics of an unforgiving spirit are resentment, keeping a record of wrongs, telling people what "they" did to you and living for revenge. Resentment chases the Dove away. Keeping a record of wrongs forfeits the immediate sense of God's presence. Living for revenge forces God to hide His face from us until we make the choice to forgive them—totally.

An Act of the Will

Total forgiveness is a choice. Yes, you have to make a choice. It is an act of the will. Caution: Don't wait until you feel "led." I meet few people who ever feel "led" to forgive. They feel "led" to hold a grudge, because holding a grudge is the natural thing to do; it always seems so right at the time. The only time you will probably feel led to forgive is when God stops you and speaks to you. Possibly like right now. If God is dealing with you as you read these lines, put this book down, ask Him to forgive you for your unforgiveness—and forgive them. Make the choice—now.

Here is a prayer I recommend you pray. If you could pray this from your heart, you will be on your way toward enjoying more of the Kingdom Jesus preached about and fulfilling God's will for your life regarding forgiveness:

Lord Jesus Christ, I need You. I want You. I am sorry for my sins. I am sorry for my unforgiveness. Wash away my sins by Your blood. I welcome Your Holy Spirit. I forgive them. You forgive them. I will not tell what they did. I will not let them be afraid of me. I will not make them feel guilty. I will let them save face. I accept that I will have to do this again and again, that this is a life sentence. I bless them. You bless them. I set them free. Thank You for Your patience with me. Amen.

If you truly meant that, you will never be the same again—unless you go back on what you have prayed. Yes, pray it again and again. God knows you struggle with this. God knows this could be major in your life. It was so major that Jesus returned to this issue after giving us the Lord's Prayer. But you will be so glad He did. This is what sets you free.

As total forgiveness is a choice, so, too, is an unforgiving spirit. When you hold a grudge you are making a choice; you choose not to let them off the hook. I'm afraid it also shows you are not sufficiently grateful that God has forgiven you. Show that you are grateful to God by totally forgiving them. You will also demonstrate you are the very kind of "workmanship" God has created for His glory (Ephesians 2:10).

God Does Not Cease to Be Our Father

And did you notice the words, "your Father"? Twice in these verses are the words, "your heavenly Father," and, "your Father." "Your Father will not

forgive your sins." Why? It is because God does not cease to be your Father. Nothing changes that relationship. He never ceases to be our Father—even when we don't forgive people who have sinned against us. It grieves Him; it disappoints Him; it hurts Him. But He is still our Father. He may chasten us. After all, whom the Lord loves He disciplines, chastens (Hebrews 12:6). He will do what He must to get our attention.

Finally, what is the real reason that Jesus adds this P.S. to the Lord's Prayer? I believe it is to motivate us to forgive; to keep us from unnecessary chastening and not inheriting the Kingdom. This verse is a warning. We all need it. It is because we are loved *so much* that God speaks as He does.

My loving counsel as I bring this section on the Lord's Prayer to a close: Forgive them. It is the greatest freedom on earth. Where the Spirit of the Lord is—and works in us un-grieved—there is liberty (2 Corinthians 3:17). Don't come short of that liberty. Set them free and you will be free. Bless them and you will be blessed. Forgive them and you will be forgiven. The anointing, freedom, joy and blessing upon your life as a consequence is infinitely greater than the fleshly wish for vengeance.

Conclusion

You may not have expected that this section on the Lord's Prayer should end with a caution about totally forgiving those who have sinned against you. But this is the way Jesus Himself, who introduced this extraordinary prayer, chose to wrap it up. I do so, too.

54. Fasting

When you fast, do not look somber as the hypocrites do, for they disfigure their
faces to show men they are fasting. I tell you the truth, they have received their
reward in full. But when you fast, put oil on your head and wash your face, so that
it will not be obvious to men that you are fasting, but only to your Father, who
is unseen; and your Father, who sees what is done in secret, will reward you.

MATTHEW 6:16–18

Jesus might have chosen to treat the subject of fasting before giving us the Lord's Prayer—since it so naturally follows giving and praying. But the Lord's Prayer was part of His example "how to pray." So He waited to treat the matter of fasting and does so now.

As I prepared this chapter, it crossed my mind that God may be speaking to a certain reader that fasting is what you should do. If you are in a situation that is extremely difficult—in which you are needing a lot of wisdom or a breakthrough of some sort—could it be that fasting is the next step forward for you?

The principles that Jesus stressed in His teaching on giving and praying are centered on the truth of John 5:44 ("How can you believe if you accept praise from one another, and yet make no effort to obtain the praise that comes from the only God?"). Those same principles are repeated in this matter of fasting. Jesus not only endorses fasting but stresses that it is to be done in secret.

Fasting means total abstinence from food but not necessarily water. To go without water is dangerous. To go without food can be healthy. Indeed, some fast purely for health reasons. But when the reason is spiritual, it is a godly inconvenience we impose voluntarily on ourselves. We perhaps do this mainly to get the leadership of the Holy Spirit.

The principle is the same as when we give and pray: He gets the glory if He is the only one who knows about it. I refer to private fasting. Corporate fasting is different. At Westminster Chapel we had occasional days of fasting, certainly at the

beginning of each year. When one meets at the end of the day for prayer (as we did), there was an implicit acknowledgment that most of the people fasted (especially those with bad breath!). But it was not anything required of any member, only recommended. God always honored us for this—no doubt about it.

Fasting is not an end in itself—it is the means to the end. The purpose is to get God's attention. This is seen in the language of ancient Israel: "Why have we fasted . . . and you have not seen it? Why have we humbled ourselves, and you have not noticed?" (Isaiah 58:3). I cannot pass over one of the most important verses in all the Bible, although it does not necessarily imply fasting: "If my people, who are called by my name, will humble themselves and pray and seek my face and turn from their wicked ways, then will I hear from heaven and will forgive their sin and will heal their land" (2 Chronicles 7:14). The principle is that when we are earnest and desperate and seek God's face in repentance, God will step in. Fasting is certainly a way of showing your desperation.

Fasting is a way of showing how earnest you are about hearing from God. It contains an implicit hope—never a guarantee—that if we fast, just maybe God will step in. When you fast, you do so fully knowing that it is no guarantee it will work. And yet Jesus attaches a condition: that we fast for His honor, not ours, and that we will keep quiet about it. We therefore have our Lord's instructions in Matthew 6:16–18, which we now examine more carefully.

A History of Fasting in the Old Testament

When Jesus says "when you fast," He assumes that His followers will fast. He also acknowledges the preexistence of fasting—it is not something new that He introduces.

He assumes His followers will fast, but they apparently didn't when Jesus was around. John the Baptist's disciples fasted. They asked Jesus, "How is it that we and the Pharisees fast, but your disciples do not fast?" He replied, "How can the guests of the bridegroom mourn while he is with them? The time will come when the bridegroom will be taken from them; then they will fast" (Matthew 9:14–15). I am intrigued by Jesus' patience with what might have been an impertinent question to Him. He might have said, "None of your business," but He graciously answered them.

In a word: Fasting is a time when God hides His face. As long as Jesus was right there with them, why fast? But after His ascension to heaven, they would fast. There is another implicit assumption: Fasting is done when you are mourning. "How can the guests of the bridegroom mourn?" That would not be the only time you fast, but it suggests that fasting is not something you do every day. As for His disciples, they did indeed fast after He went to heaven. "While they were worshiping the Lord and fasting, the Holy Spirit said, 'Set apart for me Barnabas and Saul for the work to which I have called them.' So after they had fasted and prayed, they placed their hands on them and sent them off" (Acts 13:2–3). This is seen again: "Paul and Barnabas appointed elders for them in each church and, with prayer and fasting, committed them to the Lord, in whom they had put their trust" (Acts 14:23).

Long before Jesus came on the scene, fasting was practiced. Moses fasted for forty days (Exodus 24:18). Fasting was commanded on the Day of Atonement—the only time it was mandatory. It came, however, to be practiced voluntarily. It was done out of anguish and desperation (Joshua 20:26). It was done out of grief or respect (2 Samuel 1:12). It was done when there was an urgent need for divine protection and wisdom (2 Chronicles 20:3; Ezra 8:23). It was done alongside confessing sin (Jonah 3:5). There were times when fasts were regularly instituted (Zechariah 7:3, 5; 8:19).

Sadly, fasting became an outward basis of show and piety. The Pharisees fasted twice a week (Luke 18:12). And yet Jesus, rather than discontinue the practice, assumed His disciples would fast.

Hypocritical Fasting

The practice of fasting during Jesus' time was to treat it like play-acting, this being (as you will recall, the meaning of the Greek word *hypocrites*). "They disfigure their faces to show men they are fasting." What a bold thing for Jesus to say about these people! Those esteemed men like the Pharisees and teachers of the Law were never questioned until now. Then Jesus virtually poked fun at them!

These men managed to look somber, whether they felt somber or not. They would—think about it—disfigure their faces in order to appear they were in agony. They probably sprinkled ashes on their heads. But it was all for show. All they did, said Jesus, was done for people to see (Matthew 23:5). The origin of fasting emerged in a time of deep sorrow, to seek God's face. But with these men it was a sham. "To show men they are fasting," said Jesus. If there was no one to watch, their motivation was gone—no fasting was done at all. The thought of God Himself was a million miles away. But never mind. They weren't doing it for God anyway—they were doing it to be seen by people.

What they got out of it was not a spiritual benefit—such as being given wisdom or protection—but was *knowing that people saw them*. As a consequence of this, said Jesus, they have received their reward in full. Admiration of people is what they wanted; it is what they got. But it is all they got. They were not complaining, mind you! That's exactly the "payback" they wanted in the first place! It is why they gave alms and why they prayed. Having people admire them for their piety is what they lived for. It meant everything to them.

Jesus comes along and says, "Yes, do fast, but do it for God alone to see." "I'm not against fasting," says Jesus, "I am only showing there is a wrong way and a right way to do it."

Hidden Fasting

Washing and anointing with oil were merely normal steps regarding hygiene in those days. This is not the same use of oil as in James 5:14. The oil in Matthew 6:17 was not an agent through which God promised to work. The point was merely to camouflage the fact that you were fasting so nobody would know. In other words, you washed and combed your hair and proceeded through the day like any other day.

These two important things are implicit: Nobody would ever know (you removed any hint that you were fasting), and you kept quiet about it. It is a hidden fasting—that is, hidden from people. This is the kind of fasting Jesus approves of. It is when you go to pains to be sure no one has the slightest idea you are fasting. Nothing in our way of life should be altered. You may have to go to work like anybody else. It could mean you don't get to pray as much as you may like.

Holy Fasting

There is a fasting that is holy. It is sacred. It is hidden from people and is before God alone, being done before One who is "unseen." It is done in faith. What, exactly, makes a fast "holy"? First, it is unusual or exceptional. Regular fasting is never biblical. Do it if you like, but don't claim you have the Bible backing you up. Mechanical fasting, as on certain days, is not done in faith.

Second, it is holy when you are led by the Holy Spirit to fast. This is a holy fast because it is done in obedience. When you know in your heart that God is saying, "Fast," you will not have peace unless you obey. To be honest, I have had this happen and I always hate it at first. I think, "Oh no, do I have to go without food today?" But one is never sorry if it is done in obedience.

Third, it is a holy fast when you do it without knowing—or even necessarily expecting—that God will answer as you hope. All you do is to ask meekly for mercy and appeal to His sovereign will.

Fourth, it is a holy fast when the sacrifice is not confined to food or drink. Dr. Lloyd-Jones said that fasting from anything that requires self-discipline is legitimate. For example, those who for medical reasons cannot go without eating should choose some other means. It could be sleep or forgoing legitimate pleasures—such as television or reading what you enjoy.

There is, then, a fasting that is not particularly holy but is still good for you! Fasting for physical reasons can be a good thing. Just don't put it under the category of fasting to seek God's face. Fasting from food can be good for you to do now and then. Caution: A feeling of euphoria comes (they say) on the fifth day of fasting. Those who fast for spiritual reasons need to keep this in mind; otherwise they might think it is the presence of God. It could be that, of course, but there is also a natural explanation.

There can be unholy fasting. It is when you fast for pleasure (Isaiah 58:1–5). King Saul once commanded his soldiers to go without food—a most unfortunate occasion (1 Samuel 14:24–26). Queen Jezebel proclaimed a fast for her own wicked purposes (1 Kings 21:9). In any case, hypocritical fasting is positively unholy.

The Honor of Fasting

I regard it as an honor to fast when being directed by the Holy Spirit. It is a privilege, even though (speaking personally) I react negatively to it almost every time! Frankly, I hate it. I love my food. But there are times when God apparently steps in and says, "Today you are to fast." As I look back on occasions like these, I consider it an honor that He would tap me on the shoulder to get my attention in this way. When you know you are obeying God—who would not lead you to do this without reason—it is an honor to fast.

When might one feel led to fast? First, when the burden is so great that you don't want food anyway. "My heart is blighted and withered like grass; I forget to eat my food" (Psalm 102:4). Second, when God hides His face (Psalm 42:3). Third, in a time of emergency, as when Esther knew what she had to do (Esther 4:16). Fourth, when you need clarification of God's will. Fifth, when a major change is at hand. Sixth, when the church leadership calls for fasting, you should cooperate. Seventh, when there is a need for special power. Eighth, when there is a national concern, as in praying for the nation. It has been a long, long time since this has happened in any nation. Never (in my opinion) has the time become more urgent for this sort of thing than right now.

When one is truly led to fast for the honor of God, you can expect one way or the other, sooner or later, that God will reward you. Caution: Do not expect an immediate answer—either during the time of fasting or soon afterward. I have known God to meet with me powerfully during a fast, yes. But that is not the usual case; the blessing comes down the road. It is possible that when you fast, you one want particular thing—and God has something else in mind!

Any obedience to the Spirit will be rewarded, although it may not be the kind of reward or answer to prayer you had in mind. But God will not let any work for His glory to go unrewarded.

"God is not unjust; he will not forget your work and the love you have shown him . . ." (Hebrews 6:10). He may reward with His special presence, greater wisdom or the reward may exceed your greatest dream!

What matters is His honor. If you cave in to wanting the admiration of people (whoever they are), you will forfeit the honor and praise that comes from God (John 5:44). But when only He knows—and recognizes that nobody else knows—He is pleased. "Your Father, who sees what is done in secret, will reward you." Let Him determine what that reward will be.

55. Treasure in Heaven

Do not store up for yourselves treasures on earth, where moth and rust destroy, and where thieves break in and steal. But store up for yourselves treasures in heaven, where moth and rust do not destroy, and where thieves do not break in and steal. For where your treasure is, there your heart will be also.

MATTHEW 6:19–21

Jesus slightly changes the subject, although not departing from the concept of reward in heaven. In doing so, He brings us back to the underlying theme of the Sermon on the Mount—namely, the Kingdom of heaven.

The Kingdom of heaven is the realm of the un-grieved Spirit. This means that the Holy Spirit is utterly Himself in us without being quenched, thwarted or grieved. The extent to which we inherit the Kingdom will be the degree to which we are detached from the things of the earth. Moreover, the degree to which we build up treasure in heaven on the other side will be the degree to which we inherit the Kingdom.

Matthew 6:19–21 serves as a reminder that all Christians need again and again: *We are going to heaven.* In the words of the old spiritual, "This world is not my home, I'm just a-passing through." As for the disciples of Jesus (with the exception of Judas), there was not a question whether they would be there one day. As John Stott put it, Jesus is addressing disciples who have already received the salvation of God. The same is true of the whole of the New Testament; all of the epistles are addressed to Christians. For example, "I write to you, dear children, because your sins have been forgiven on account of his name" (1 John 2:12).

The issue, then, is not whether they are saved but whether they will enjoy that realm of the un-grieved Spirit here below—and whether they will receive a reward in heaven above. The word Jesus used was, "Great is your reward in heaven" (Matthew 5:12). But He now uses a different word: *treasures.* "Store up for yourselves treasures in heaven."

Behind this teaching is a concept called "scroll of remembrance." "Then those who feared the LORD talked with each other, and the LORD listened and heard. A scroll of remembrance was written in his presence concerning those who feared the LORD and honored his name" (Malachi 3:16). This means that nothing we do below is overlooked or forgotten, except our sins that have been washed away by the blood of Jesus Christ. So what is remembered? Paul said, "Not that I am looking for a gift [from the Philippians], but I am looking for what may be credited to your account" (Philippians 4:17). This was a reference to the Judgment Seat of Christ, which will unveil what has been credited to our account.

It is like having two bank accounts: one below, like ours in First Tennessee Bank, and one above—call it the Bank of Heaven. Some live for what they possess below, as in the parable of the rich fool. He said, "I will tear down my barns and build bigger ones. . . . And I'll say to myself, 'You have plenty of good things laid up for many years. Take life easy; eat, drink and be merry.' But God said to him, 'You fool! This very night your life will be demanded from you. Then who will get what you have prepared for yourself?' This is how it will be with anyone who stores up things for himself but is not rich toward God" (Luke 12:18–21). Such a person has no treasure in heaven.

In a word: Some live for what they possess below; some live for what they put on deposit in the Bank of Heaven. The issue is what is more important to you? "For where your treasure is, there your heart will be also" (Matthew 6:21). Jesus is interested in the heart. Some people's hearts are set on earthly things. "Their destiny is destruction, their god is their stomach, and their glory is in their shame. Their mind is on earthly things." But by contrast Paul said, "Our citizenship is in heaven" (Philippians 3:19–20).

Earthly Treasure

"Do not store up for yourselves treasures on earth, where moth and rust destroy, and where thieves break in and steal," said Jesus. There are four descriptions that fit what Jesus means by "treasures on earth."

First, possessions. "For we brought nothing into the world, and we can take nothing out of it. But if we have food and clothing, we will be content with that. People who want to get rich fall into temptation and a trap and into many foolish and harmful desires that plunge men into ruin and destruction. For the love of money is a root of all kinds of evil. Some people, eager for money, have wandered from the faith and pierced themselves with many griefs" (1 Timothy 6:7–10).

When it comes to property, nothing can last—whether furniture, your computer, your television. Moths eat into clothes. The accumulation of wealth is a temptation, but what will it mean when it is time to die?

My old pastor told a story about a wealthy dying man who requested all his gold possessions be brought to his bed. They brought all his gold nuggets, gold bracelets and gold watches. He held all he could in his hands. But when he died, they all fell to the floor.

Second, treasures on earth refer to power. Power is only earthly treasure. By power I mean control. This includes control of wealth, control of people's opinions, power to influence or manipulating others' future. Two of the most powerful men in the world are Bill Gates and Rupert Murdoch. Bill Gates is the world's wealthiest man. He has probably earned millions literally since I began writing this chapter! I do know he has been conscientious in giving money away to needed causes throughout the world. Rupert Murdoch owns the London *Times* and other major newspapers. He influences not only the public but prime ministers and presidents. I don't know what God means to these men. I only know that there will come a day when all of us who lived *for this life only* will be told, "You fool! This very night your life will be demanded from you."

Third, pleasure. "Do not love the world or anything in the world. If anyone loves the world, the love of the Father is not in him. For everything in the world—the cravings of sinful man, the lust of his eyes and the boasting of what he has and does—comes not from the Father but from the world. The world and its desires pass away, but the man who does the will of God lives forever" (1 John 2:15–17). Such worldly pleasure could be in sexual gratification outside of marriage, the wrong kind of entertainment, or excess in what goes into the body. This becomes idolatry. The last word in 1 John reads: "Dear children, keep yourselves from idols" (1 John 5:21).

Fourth, praise. This includes living for the approval of people—those who know you well and those you hardly know. When a bit of prestige means a little bit too much to you, beware! Living for the praise of people rather than the praise of God will abort the process toward an inheritance in the Kingdom of heaven.

In Jesus' day things were different. Houses were made of mud stone, and people could dig beneath them. That is the way thieves would break in and steal. The Greek literally reads, "where thieves dig under." In those days there were no banks or insurance policies; people could lose everything at once.

But it can still happen, as we have seen in recent years. Wealthy people sometimes lose everything overnight. People lose their jobs, which had been so secure. We are learning that nothing is certain, no job is secure and no possessions are guaranteed to be yours tomorrow. As for those who are addicted to the approval of people, people's opinions change overnight. The people you are trying to impress today may mean little or nothing to you tomorrow.

Jesus is calling for you and me to have a spiritual detachment from earthly treasure and is giving us pragmatic advice. Summed up: All things here below are temporary. All these material things that mean so much to us will come to nothing—not to mention the sorrow we will feel at the Judgment Seat of Christ after we put our eggs in one basket: earthly pleasure.

Eternal Treasures

Jesus makes this personal. "Store up for *yourselves* treasures in heaven." You will be doing it for yourself. You won't be able to share in another's reward. I envisage a day when Jesus' parable will be fulfilled before our very eyes, when foolish people—to whom the Holy Spirit meant very little—will be saying to the wise, "Give us some of your oil; our lamps are going out" (Matthew 25:8). But this was impossible. We may be able to share our goods and possessions with our friends and loved ones here below, but when it comes to eternal treasures, "each one" will receive what is due for the things done while in the body, "whether good or bad" (2 Corinthians 5:10). Paul said it again: "Each of us will give an account of himself to God" (Romans 14:12).

There is an underlying assumption in the Gospel but which needs to be applied and brought home to every man and woman: Each person is responsible for his or her own destiny—whether he or she spends eternity in heaven or hell. For what shall it profit a man if he gains "the whole world" and loses his own soul (Mark 8:36)?

Also, each Christian is responsible for the quality of his or her reward. You can cause one to lose his or her reward (2 John 8), but you cannot share in another's reward. I can, however (God helping me), teach in a manner that will lead you to a reward. I myself want a reward in heaven. Paul did (1 Corinthians 9:25–27). You will discover then whether I have been a true man of God, and I will also learn about you. Nothing would give me greater joy than to think my teaching has led someone to receive a reward in heaven because they took seriously what I write and preach.

Laying up eternal treasure in heaven is possible for you and me at the moment, but on certain conditions. If you haven't begun already, I urge you to begin *now*. You won't always be able to do this. These are precious moments, precious days. Jonathan Edwards once made a New Year's resolution to live each day as if it would be his last. What if all of us did that! What you do on earth in this regard cannot be done in heaven. There will be no praying in heaven. There will be no soul-winning in heaven. There will be no need for obedience in heaven. There will be no tithing in heaven. No need for faith in heaven. No

dignifying the trial in heaven. No total forgiveness in heaven. No leaving God to vindicate in heaven. The old cliché is worth repeating here:

> Only one life—t'will soon be past;
> Only what's done for Christ will last.
>
> Anonymous

You cannot lose your salvation between now and the Judgment Seat of Christ—a comforting thought! God saves us forever, as I have written in my book *Once Saved, Always Saved*. But you can lose your *reward* between now and the Judgment Seat of Christ. You can start out building up treasure in heaven and then end up becoming enamored with this world, like Demas (2 Timothy 4:10), and lose that treasure.

Existing Treasure

According to Jesus, this treasure exists now. "Where your treasure *is,* there your heart will be also." "Is" means where your treasure is *now,* as we will see in more detail in the next chapter. Your treasure is either above or below! That will also reveal where your heart is.

Your heart is the seat of personality, seat of emotions. It is the "real you"—what you truly think and feel. You either have a heart set on earthly treasures that you are still counting on, or treasures in heaven. If your treasure is in heaven, then your heart will motivate you to send what you treasure ahead of you. You build on earthly treasure by loving the world and the things of this world, leaving God out. You build up treasure in heaven by walking in the light God gives you (1 John 1:7).

However, Jesus is mainly talking about money and the love of money in this section of the Sermon on the Mount. What you give to God is what is put to your account in the Bank of Heaven. The man I was named after, R. T. Williams, told of a layman in his denomination who made a million dollars and gave $100,000 to the church. He had receipts to prove it. Afterward, however, the man went bankrupt. His friends cynically said to him, "We bet you wish you had not given that money to the church." "Oh no," he replied. "It is the only money I *kept*."

Treasure in heaven. What you give to God is sent on to heaven in advance of your arrival there. What you give to God is deposited in the Bank of Heaven.

All we do is governed by the location of our treasure. For where our treasure is, there will our heart be also. Jesus implies that those who do not take His advice are fools. "You fool!" God will say to the person whose treasure was not in heaven. Don't be a fool. Be wise. Seek first God's Kingdom and—I guarantee it—you will never be sorry.

56. The Heart of the Matter

For where your treasure is, there your heart will be also.

MATTHEW 6:21

Jesus has mentioned the heart twice in the Sermon on the Mount. The first was in the Beatitudes: "Blessed are the pure in heart, for they will see God" (Matthew 5:8). The second use of "heart" was a key word in His application of the Mosaic Law: The one who lusts after a woman has "already committed adultery with her in his heart" (Matthew 5:28).

You will recall that being pure in heart has a lot to do with sexual purity. If you combine this with Jesus' treatment of adultery, it shows how sexual purity and the heart can be closely connected. Indeed, the book of Proverbs, largely about wisdom, stresses the danger of adultery in connection with the heart (Proverbs 6:21–25; 7:25). Sexual sin militates against wisdom. Indeed, the wisdom that comes from above is "first of all pure" (James 3:17).

This third use of the heart in Matthew 6:21 is in the context of the love of money, but Jesus' statement is nonetheless a truism all by itself. It is an obvious fact: Where your treasure is—that is, what you esteem as treasure—is where your heart will be. This would be true of money, sex and power. Your heart will not only follow after its treasure but simultaneously reveals itself for what it is. What you esteem as treasure unveils the present condition of your heart.

Jesus' point is to show whether our treasure—our hearts—is in heaven or on earth. The fact that He mentions heaven also demonstrates we will be there one day. Whatever would having treasure in heaven mean if we weren't going to cash in on it one day? He does not bother to elaborate on this truth; He merely assumes it. But it is a reminder: We are on our way to heaven!

God wants us to focus on it now. Because if we focus on heaven now, we will be glad we did

"then." It is a clever saying that "some people are so heavenly minded that they are of no earthly use." But I am not honestly sure there are many like that. I would suggest there is an irony: that those who focus most on heaven are those God uses most on earth. Church history shows that those who emphasized heaven and hell in their preaching and in their beliefs are the ones who have accomplished most for the Kingdom of God on Planet Earth.

Behind our verse in this chapter is an important and relevant proverb: "Above all else, guard your heart, for it is the wellspring of life" (Proverbs 4:23; "Keep thy heart with all diligence; for out of it are the issues of life," KJV). Part of my studies at Oxford required that I read a lot about Oliver Cromwell (1599–1658). Cromwell often talked about the "heart of the matter," wanting to cut across nonsense and get to what was essential.

Jesus had much to say about the heart. "Out of the overflow of the heart the mouth speaks" (Matthew 12:34). "The mouth speaks what the heart is full of" (GNT). When I ask people (as I frequently do), "If you were to stand before God and He were to ask you why He should let you into His heaven, what would you say?" their answer reveals their heart. They may say, "Because I am a Christian." I then say, "But are you a Christian because Jesus died for you?" They sometimes reply, "Of course I believe that." But I come back, "Then why didn't you say that?" If they really are trusting Jesus' death to get them to heaven, that will easily come out when asked a question like this. The mouth speaks what the heart is full of. When men shouted at Jesus for Him to come down from the cross "that we may see and believe" (Mark 15:32), they revealed both unbelief and hatred in their hearts.

What our hearts are full of will be determined by what we esteem as treasure. Treasure, like a magnet, will pull our hearts to it. Jesus also said, "The good man brings good things out of the good stored up in him, and the evil man brings evil things out of the evil stored up in him. But I tell you that men will have to give account on that day of judgment for every careless word they have spoken. For by your words you will be acquitted, and by your words you will be condemned" (Matthew 12:35–37). Why will we be acquitted or condemned by our words? It is because our words reveal the heart.

The Heart: An Index of Our True Thinking

The heart is the seat of personality. Jesus also said, "These people honor me with their lips, but their hearts are far from me," quoting Isaiah (Matthew 15:8; Isaiah 29:13). God saw that in Noah's day the thoughts of people's hearts were "evil all the time" (Genesis 6:5). God commanded that we love Him with all our hearts (Deuteronomy 6:5).

The heart is equally the seat of our faculties: *Mind* and *heart* are sometimes used interchangeably. God can write His law on our minds or our hearts (Hebrews 8:10; 10:16). The heart is also the seat of faith: "If you confess with your mouth, 'Jesus is Lord,' and believe *in your heart* that God raised him from the dead, you will be saved" (Romans 10:9, emphasis mine). Jesus said to the two men on the road to Emmaus, "How foolish you are, and how slow of heart to believe all that the prophets have spoken!" (Luke 24:25). The heart is the seat of our being filled. God "fills your hearts with joy" (Acts 14:17).

The heart can be filled with grief, too (John 16:6). Not only that, Satan can fill the heart (Acts 5:3).

The heart is the seat of feeling. What we feel in our "heart of hearts" is a fairly good indication of what we truly think. Said Paul, "I have great sorrow and unceasing anguish in my heart" (Romans 9:2). Our hearts can also condemn us (1 John 3:20). Paul urged that the peace of Christ dwell in our "hearts" (Colossians 3:15). Sometimes you feel something in your "gut." When you feel this, I think of Shakespeare's word, "To thine own self be true." But the heart can also be the seat of fear.

Jesus therefore said, "Do not let your hearts be troubled" (John 14:1). One can be filled with fear. But also in a good sense, as when the fear of God came upon every soul (Acts 2:43).

In a word: What we feel in the heart is evidence of what we truly think and believe.

The Conscience

Why guard your heart? It is the instrument of hearing God. "Today, if you hear his voice, do not harden your hearts" (Hebrews 3:15). God said of ancient Israel, "Their hearts are always going astray" (Hebrews 3:10).

If we want to hear God speak, we must guard the heart. The worst thing that can happen to us is to become stone deaf to the Holy Spirit. The Hebrew Christians already became hard of hearing (Hebrews 5:11). The worst scenario is to become stone deaf so that one cannot be renewed again to repentance (Hebrews 6:4–6). That "still small voice," or "gentle whisper" (1 Kings 19:12; cf. KJV), must be coveted by us above all other communications, and guarded, that we miss nothing God might want to say to us.

The heart, therefore, is a precious, delicate instrument. The heart is also closely connected to the conscience. When Paul referred to "great sorrow and unceasing anguish in my heart," it followed his saying, "I am not lying, my conscience confirms it in the Holy Spirit" (Romans 9:1–2). The conscience is the reflective part of the mind—and yet it comes down to feeling in your "heart of hearts."

One guards his or heart, but also we must guard the conscience. The last thing in the world we want is a conscience "seared as with a hot iron" (1 Timothy 4:2)—the same thing as not hearing God speak anymore, as I said above. When we first moved to London from Oxford, we lived in Ealing, right next to a railroad track. Trains went from London's Paddington Station to Wales at 125 mph. When we first lived there, we heard every train as it roared past our house. But weeks later we seldom heard it! We learned to "tune it out." You can do this as well with the conscience or the heart when it comes to hearing God's voice. Don't do that! Guard your heart; guard your conscience.

Your heart will follow what it treasures as a dog goes after a bone. For the treasure is what has value to you—what you think about, what gets your attention, what you dwell on, what you dream about. It is the motivation that turns you on. Paul urged, "Set your heart on things above," where Christ is seated at the right hand of God (Colossians 3:1).

What We Focus on Makes a Difference

We therefore can direct our hearts. Whereas it is in a sense true that you cannot help what you feel, what Jesus does is to show you what you feel—and what you ought to feel. He uses a technique to reveal the heart. It is sometimes said, "God offends the mind to reveal the heart." Jesus puts before us two locations to reveal the heart: heaven and earth. If your treasure is in heaven, then your heart is to do what will please God. If your treasure is on earth, you do what will gratify the flesh.

If you focus on earthly treasure, it means entanglement. You will be the big loser. And you lose both ways. You end up as a fool here below, plus the melancholy fact that you lose everything at the Final Judgment. But if you focus on eternal treasure, you will be the big winner. You will be edified and blessed—having a *good* conscience, plus the glorious fact you will receive God's "Well done" in heaven. Focusing on things eternal is the best way to live and the best way to die.

Although there is a sense in which you cannot help what you feel, you can help how you continue to feel. You can change. You set your affections on things above. When the Holy Spirit convicts you of an aimless way of living, He will point you to your heavenly treasure—what you will be so glad you focused on one day. Do it now. Don't wait. If you are in the middle of something that is wrong, stop it! If the devil puts thoughts before you, refuse to listen—and resist him!

Once you make a choice to do the right thing, it will also change what you feel. What you feel will seem so natural. You will develop such an appetite for spiritual things that it will be as though it is not hard anymore—like eating. Not that you won't be tempted. But guard the heart, beware of what grips you.

Jesus' Statement Is a Heart Exam

The location of our treasure reveals where we are in our walk with Christ. It is a test, an examination, but more important than an echocardiogram (of which I have had several). It is a good feeling to get a good report after an echocardiogram. God's echocardiogram is seeing for yourself where your treasure is. You can see for yourself where you are.

This can be a turning point at which a decisive change takes place. If I see I have passed the examination, it is thrilling. Frankly, there is no greater joy than knowing you please God. I would rather have this witness than any testimony or pleasure of the world. It is an earnest of our inheritance.

But if I see I have failed the exam—that my treasure is here on earth—this, too, can indeed be a crucial turning point. I can repent or I can draw back. To repent means not merely to say, "I am sorry," or, "I was wrong," but also to make a 180-degree turn—and start walking in a manner that is "worthy of God" (1 Thessalonians 2:12). The opposite of repentance is to draw back and be destroyed (Hebrews 10:19). The word *destroyed* means to come to "ruin." It means a ruined life. Is that what you want?

I pray with all my heart for you, dear reader, that your treasure—right now—is in heaven. If it has not been in heaven, turn now—set your affections on things above, not on things of the earth. This way you ensure that you will not become stone deaf to the Spirit.

Where your heart is at the time of the Second Coming—or your death—will determine whether you have a reward in heaven. How do we know that? God will then "bring to light what is hidden in darkness and will expose the motives of men's hearts. At that time each will receive his praise from God" (1 Corinthians 4:5).

It is the heart that will be judged. The basis of the Final Judgment will be the location of your treasure at the time you are called to give an account. "This will take place on the day when God will judge men's secrets through Jesus Christ, as my gospel declares" (Romans 2:16).

The heart of the matter is the matter of the heart. Jesus the Son of God, "whose eyes are like blazing fire," says, "I am he who searches hearts and minds, and I will repay each of you according to your deeds" (Revelation 2:18, 23).

57. Thinking Clearly

The eye is the lamp of the body. If your eyes are good, your whole body will be
full of light. But if your eyes are bad, your whole body will be full of darkness.
If then the light within you is darkness, how great is that darkness!

MATTHEW 6:22–23

Jesus moves from the heart to the whole body. He focuses on the eye, but says that the eye determines whether the whole body is full of light or darkness. Then comes a most sobering conclusion: "If then the light within you is darkness, how great is that darkness!"

I have wondered: Why this order—from heart to the eye? It would seem that Jesus would move from the eye to the heart. Why did He mention the heart first? After all, Jesus wants to show the importance of thinking clearly. I would have thought that would mean beginning with the mind first—which He does not do. I have always taught that the right order is mind, heart, will. So, by treating the heart first, is He giving credence to the idea of a "head bypass operation," as some have put it?

You will recall that heart and mind are used interchangeably (Hebrews 8:10; 10:16). The heart is the seat of faith (Romans 10:10). Both Saint Augustine and Calvin stressed *faith seeking understanding* (not the other way around). That parallels the idea of the *heart preceding the mind* when it comes to knowing you have got it right theologically.

You could say it is like experience trying to catch up with sound doctrine. My old friend Rolfe Barnard used to stress the importance of going from experience to doctrine, not doctrine to experience. What he meant was this: Those who have only an intellectual understanding of biblical teaching seldom manage to arrive at the level of heart experience. They put all their eggs into one basket: the intellect. But those who have the experience first are those who will more likely have a deep, firm and balanced grasp of truth— and believe it more firmly.

There is something, therefore, to be said for having a "brain bypass operation." As long as the brain is in control, we will forever be trying to figure things out. But if the Holy Spirit seizes the heart first, and you are able to experience what God did, you then test it by Scripture. If you begin with the brain having to figure out things first, you will never be satisfied—always wanting more "proof."

This fits perfectly with John Calvin's important teaching about the internal testimony of the Holy Spirit. That, he argued, is how you know the Bible is the Word of God. When I was ordained to the Gospel ministry in November 1964, the preacher for the occasion was the late N. Burnett Magruder. A graduate of Yale and a student of Jonathan Edwards, Dr. Magruder became one of my most respected mentors. I was not prepared, however, for his public interrogation of my understanding of theology. It was totally unrehearsed and with no hint of what was coming. He asked me which witness to Scripture was more important—the external or internal?

I had never been confronted with that issue in my life and was terrified before the congregation. I answered: internal witness. He commended my answer. I have since thought about that a lot and see how right this answer was. The external witness pertains to things like archeological evidence, testimonies from great people, and other claims that cause some people to embrace the Bible as the Word of God. The trouble with the external witness is that people often want more and more proof—and never get fully convinced about the authenticity or infallibility of Scripture. But when the Holy Spirit witnesses with Scripture being the infallible Word of God, you are set for life—fully convinced in the heart. Those who will only think "cerebrally" are always trying to figure things out and wanting just a "little bit more" evidence. Their teaching seldom manages to reach the heart. This is one reason we have so many cold and smug Christians.

What Jesus is saying in these verses is to restate verses 19–21 in a different way. And yet the order must not be dismissed. When one's treasure is in heaven, the heart will follow after that treasure—and, lo and behold, be more able to think clearly. Jesus said if we do the will of God, we shall know the doctrine (John 7:17)—and be sound. Our verses for this chapter—verses 22–23—show that one is thinking clearly by having treasure in heaven. And that is where one's heart is. Jesus thus begins with the heart—you could call it experience—and then comes to the mind.

Jesus is thinking hebraically (like a Hebrew). The eye enables the body to function. Almost everything the body does depends on our ability to see. If you have good eyes, you will walk straight and avoid an accident. If you have bad eyes, you may stumble and knock things over. So Jesus begins with a simple illustration (treasure and heart), but almost immediately it turns out to be a spiritual illustration (the eye being the light of the body). He then concludes with that dreadful observation about the light in us becoming darkness.

In one stroke, then, Jesus shows the importance of thinking clearly by the heart being put right—and demonstrates the fatality of not thinking clearly, namely, the horror of the light in us becoming darkness.

These verses (Matthew 6:22–23) therefore serve as a way to verify what Jesus had just said about the heart in verse 21. There is a way to verify the affections of the heart. Dr. Lloyd-Jones used to say again and again that the Bible was not given to us to replace immediate and direct revelation, but to correct abuses. This means that any "word of knowledge," prophecy, impression or vision must always come under the supreme judgment and scrutiny of Holy Scripture. So if one's prophecy, word of knowledge or vision does not cohere with the Word, it is to be rejected.

Anybody in his or her right mind wants to think clearly, above anything else. Billy Graham said that his greatest fear was that God might take His hand off him and thus remove his presence of mind. I could not agree more. Not only that, one of my own greatest fears is not to think clearly. I pray that God will remove me from writing, teaching or preaching if I begin not to think clearly. The worst scenario in this connection is to be given a strong delusion and believe a lie because one did not receive the love of the truth (2 Thessalonians 2:11). Paul talks about God giving some people over to a reprobate mind, a mind devoid of sound judgment (Romans 1:28).

The Cause of Clear Thinking

The cause of clear thinking can be summed up: having good eyes. Good eyes at the natural level are a gift of God. Do you thank God for your sight? There will be people who will have these lines read to them because they are blind. Never take good eyes for granted.

However, Jesus is talking about our spiritual eyes—discernment and ability to see what the Spirit shows. There are many translations of the Greek word *aplous*—single, uncompounded, pure, undivided loyalty. It is translated "single" (KJV), "pure" (TLB), "sound" (PHILLIPS), "clear" (NJB) and "good" (NIV). David said, "I know, my God, that you test the heart and are pleased with integrity" (1 Chronicles 29:17). He also said, "One thing I ask of the LORD, this is what I seek: that I may dwell in the house of the LORD all the days of my life, to gaze upon the beauty of the LORD and to seek him in his temple" (Psalm 27:4). This is pure devotion, when you have narrowed all your desires down to one: to seek the Lord. You could say that David had "good eyes"—sound, clear and pure.

You maintain good eyesight by walking in the light (1 John 1:7). This means you will watch what you read and guard your eyes. The effect of good eyes will be thinking clearly. This includes sound thinking regarding doctrine (John 7:17) and discernment—the ability to recognize the Holy Spirit and the counterfeit (1 Corinthians 12:10).

Some people are enamored with being able to detect the demonic. It is more important to recognize the genuine Holy Spirit, which will also help you to recognize the counterfeit. You will have a good sense of direction (Proverbs 3:5) and a sense of duty—knowing what you ought to do (James 4:17) with good eyesight.

The Cause of Confused Thinking

When Jesus refers to "bad eyes," the Greek word is *ponerous*—"evil." We get the word *pornography* from this word. It is the opposite of being undivided—it is when loyalty is divided. It is like double-mindedness, where one is unstable in all their ways (James 1:8).

What causes bad eyesight, spiritually speaking? It is by reading what does not edify, spending time with the wrong company, loving the things of the world (1 John 2:15), lusting or causing one to lust (Matthew 5:28). The ultimate scenario can be having "eyes full of adultery, they never stop sinning" (2 Peter 2:14).

The effect of bad eyes is being "tossed back and forth . . . and blown here and there by every wind of teaching" (Ephesians 4:14). It is what makes a person easily deceived, "swayed by all kinds of evil desires, always learning but never able to acknowledge the truth" "deceiving and being deceived" (2 Timothy 3:6–7, 13). People like this are full of dread, filled with anguishing fear. They have no sense of dignity or self-worth. They have nothing to live for and no sense of God's approval.

"If"

But Jesus has more to say, bringing in a significant "if." "If your eyes are bad, your whole body will be full of darkness." It is a scary possibility.

It is better to have bad eyes at the natural level than to have bad eyes at the spiritual level. You are better off to be blind with your natural eyes than to be spiritually blind. A blind person can have dignity and joy. But when you are spiritually blind, you may be able to see the lights around you, yes—but you will be pathetic as a person. Your "whole body" refers to you as a person. Bad eyes will lead you to where you should not go. They will direct your affections to things you should not consider. You as a person will be headed for ruin, decay, defeat and failure.

"Darkness" refers partly to conscience, a sense of "oughtness." But if that conscience is seared, you will have no sense of duty. You will not be able to see what God has made plain. You will end up rejecting the Bible and all that God has said. It means you are blind inside—"full of darkness." A person born blind would not know what he or she is missing. A person who once had vision must have the greatest pain of all: What was once visible is now invisible, what was once light is now darkness. How much worse when this happens at the spiritual level!

The Bleakest Possible Outlook

"If then the light within you is darkness, how great is that darkness!" The darkness is "doubly dark" (NEB). It means that one has now degenerated to such a low level that he or she is the aforementioned reprobate mind, a mind that cannot think clearly. One who believes a lie, having succumbed to a strong delusion that Satan administered. For once your eyes drift toward the things of the world, the devil steps in, rides on top of that disobedience and, if the process is not stopped, will bring you to utter ruin and shame. What is left is despair—no hope left. Disgrace, when nobody believes in you. Debauchery, when you are given over to what is totally shameful.

You say, "That will never happen to me." I certainly pray that it doesn't. I don't especially enjoy exegeting this passage of Scripture. I can only tell you what it means. These are Jesus' words, not mine. I pray that these lines will come as a wake-up call, that you will come to yourself and repent. If God grants you repentance, thank Him with all your heart. It means you are not stone deaf to the Holy Spirit. The ability to heed these words shows there is hope! The mind devoid of judgment can no longer repent (Hebrews 6:4–6).

There is such joy in clear thinking. "The path of the righteous is like the first gleam of dawn, shining ever brighter till the full light of day. But the way of the wicked is like deep darkness; they do not know what makes them stumble" (Proverbs 4:18–19).

I will tell you something interesting. Only an hour ago I finished my Bible reading for the day (I follow a plan), and the verses today included these: "If you had responded to my rebuke, I would have poured out my heart to you and made my thoughts known to you. But since you rejected me when I called and no one gave heed when

I stretched out my hand since you ignored all my advice and would not accept my rebuke, I in turn will laugh at your disaster; I will mock when calamity overtakes you—when calamity overtakes you like a storm, when disaster sweeps over you like a whirlwind, when distress and trouble overwhelm you" (Proverbs 1:23–27). The fact that I read these words in my own private quiet time—words in my notes I would have used anyway in bringing this chapter to a conclusion—it makes me think that someone down the road will read these words, someone who needs them desperately. Is it you?

The warning from the Holy Spirit means there is still time. The last thing you want is double darkness.

58. God and Money

No one can serve two masters. Either he will hate the one and love the other, or he will be devoted to the one and despise the other. You cannot serve both God and Money.

MATTHEW 6:24

It could be justly argued that the New Testament has more to say about money than any other subject. You may be surprised to hear that there are 500 verses on the subject of faith and about that number regarding prayer. There are 2,350 verses on money. Arguably Jesus talked about money more than anything else, and the apostle Paul had a lot to say about money. "For the love of money is a root of all kinds of evil. Some people, eager for money, have wandered from the faith and pierced themselves with many griefs" (1 Timothy 6:10).

Why did Jesus give us these words in the Sermon on the Mount about God and money? Money and possessions are likely to be a major competitor with the Kingdom of heaven. Our faith and finances, like it or not, are often closely linked together. The less we have of finances, it is predictable we will need and have more faith. The more money we have in the bank, the less faith we seem to need or have. This being true, which is more important: more faith or more money in the bank?

I have observed from my days as a young boy how money changes people—so often for the worse. I remember when my closest friend moved to another town nearby because his parents thought they could make more money. I watched the marriage split, and my friend began to distance himself from me. Nothing was ever the same again. I recall a lady in my old church in Ashland, Kentucky—"Sister Nellie," regarded as a saintly, godly and praying woman. There were always a smile and glow on her face when she sang. You felt she would be one to share a prayer request with. She was very poor, had little or nothing of this world's goods. But one day her husband died and left her with a large financial legacy from his insurance policy at work. Sister Nellie was never

to be the same again. For some reason, the smile and glow were not there, although she now wore the finest of clothes. It made me feel so sad. She had not wandered from the faith, but I always felt in my heart that she was not the same saintly woman I had grown to admire.

If you want to know what is really important to people, look at what they spend their money on. Money affects a very large part of our lives. Jesus' parables alone refer to a wide variety of money issues: investments (Matthew 13:44–45), savings (Matthew 13:52), debt (Matthew 18:23–35), earning wages (Matthew 20:1–16), capital and interest (Matthew 25:14–30), money lending (Luke 7:41–43), inheritance (Luke 15:11–32) and contrast between the rich and poor (Luke 16:19–31).

John Wesley said that the last part of a person to get converted is his wallet! Voltaire, the French atheist, observed that when it came to money, all religions are much the same. I think the issue is this: not what I would do with a million dollars were that my lot, but what I do with the hundred dollars I have. Jesus said he that is faithful in that which is least will be faithful in much—and he who is unjust in that which is least will be unjust in much (Luke 16:10).

So why is this verse put here in the Sermon on the Mount? It is the context. The issue has been one's treasure, one's heart and clear thinking. So now Jesus gives what is almost a truism—that no one can serve two masters. You have to make a choice: Which means more, God or money? The Greek word *mammona* is a Semitic word for "money" or "possessions."

Comparison between God and Money

There are striking comparisons between God and money. First, both can grip the heart. The heart

291

is the seat of faith—but also the seat of our affections. This comes out in Jesus' parable about the hidden treasure. "The kingdom of heaven is like treasure hidden in a field. When a man found it, he hid it again, and then in his joy went and sold all he had and bought that field" (Matthew 13:44).

Jesus compared money and owning property to one's devotion to Christ and His Kingdom. I elaborate on this in *The Parables of Jesus*. It describes what happens when one falls head over heels in love with the Lord. He will do anything for more of God! David wanted to build the temple because he couldn't do enough for God (2 Chronicles 6:7).

Paul said, "People who want to get rich fall into temptation and a trap and into many foolish and harmful desires that plunge men into ruin and destruction" (1 Timothy 6:9). When I think about these words, "People who want to get rich," I feel I must send out a warning to every reader. Beware of this wish. This world is not all there is. We are on this planet as a testing ground. Where we live and what we do for a living is not terminal, only an examination. Those who "want to be rich" are in grave danger of failing this exam. Beware! This could be a natural desire. Some can be trusted with wealth. But it could also be a desire that the devil will seize upon. So I am saying to you as lovingly as I know how: Be careful. Be very careful.

Ananias and Sapphira were among those converted on the Day of Pentecost. But somehow pleasing people and the love of money crept in. They had property that they purportedly sold for the purpose of handing over all the funds to the apostles. They did not have to sell the property at all, but they chose to. They wanted to be a part of what was happening. But they kept part of the money for themselves while feigning they had turned all the money over to the church. Big mistake.

Peter said, "How is it that Satan has so filled your heart that you have lied to the Holy Spirit and have kept for yourself some of the money you received for the land? Didn't it belong to you before it was sold? And after it was sold, wasn't the money at your disposal? What made you think of doing such a thing? You have not lied to men but to God." Ananias was struck dead

on the spot, and a similar scenario followed with his wife, Sapphira (Acts 5:1–10). The light in them became very dark indeed. It is hard to say which motivation in them was greater: the love of money or wanting to be a part of the crowd. But one thing is for sure: We love money partly to impress those around us.

In a word, money and God have this in common: Either can grip your heart. I pray you will determine it will be God!

God and Money Demand to Be Served

Another comparison is that both demand to be served. When Jesus talked about two masters, He used the word *douleuein*, which means "slave." If you were a *doulos* you were not your own. If you are God's slave—as Paul was (Philippians 1:1)—you are not your own.

If you were a slave in ancient times, you were owned by your master. God demands allegiance. Jesus demands it: "Anyone who loves his father or mother more than me is not worthy of me; anyone who loves his son or daughter more than me is not worthy of me; and anyone who does not take his cross and follow me is not worthy of me" (Matthew 10:37–38).

Money makes the same demands as God. You can be poor and be a slave to money. You can also be poor and outgive the rich. Jesus observed a poor widow putting in two very small copper coins in the Temple treasury and said, "I tell you the truth, this poor widow has put in more than all the others." All the others, said Jesus, gave their gifts out of their wealth, but this widow gave "out of her poverty" and put in the treasury all she had to live on (Luke 21:1–4).

This shows, too, how a poor person can be set free internally. It also goes to show that the amount of money you give to the Lord is not the important thing; it is the spirit in which you give it. Let us say that you tithe your income of $20,000 a year, which would be $2,000, while a millionaire tithes $100,000 of his million dollars. In God's sight you gave the same amount. If he only tithed $90,000 it means you gave more with your $2,000 than he did with his $90,000! That is the way God keeps records.

It reminds me when I did something (perhaps I shouldn't have) when I was a Southern Baptist pastor in Fort Lauderdale. The treasurer had to run an errand and asked me to guard the money to be deposited. Coincidentally, the records of who gave and how much were right there in the open. Oh dear, I took a look. I was stunned. Those I thought were the big givers (who had good incomes) weren't. The best givers were women—the poor, the divorcees and widows. It taught me a lesson—and I have often wondered if that is the pattern in most churches.

I don't mean to be unfair, but I think that one objective index as to how spiritual a Christian is can be traced to his or her giving—the consistency and faithfulness to tithe in the spirit of cheerfulness. For God loves a cheerful giver (2 Corinthians 9:7).

Jesus says that we will hate the one master and love the other, or be devoted to the one and despise the other. Don Carson says that the contrast between love and hate is based upon a common Semitic idiom, and neither may be legitimately taken absolutely. To hate one of the alternatives and love the other simply means that what is loved is what is preferred; what is hated means to love less. This helps to explain Luke 14:26: "If anyone comes to me and does not hate his father and mother, his wife and children, his brothers and sisters—yes, even his own life—he cannot be my disciple." It is not that you hate your parents—we are told to honor our parents—but merely you love God more. The same is true of those difficult words, "Jacob I loved, Esau I hated" (Romans 9:13). God loved Esau less.

God isn't against money or wealth. Paul said, "Command those who are rich in this present world not to be arrogant nor to put their hope in wealth, which is so uncertain, but to put their hope in God, who richly provides us with everything for our enjoyment. Command them to do good, to be rich in good deeds, and to be generous and willing to share. In this way they will lay up treasure for themselves as a firm foundation for the coming age, so that they may take hold of the life that is truly life" (1 Timothy 6:17–19).

This shows not only can a Christian sometimes be trusted with wealth, he or she can store up treasures in heaven, as Jesus had taught. Abraham was a very rich man (Genesis 13:2). All the patriarchs were wealthy men. God can make a person wealthy or poor. "The LORD sends poverty and wealth; he humbles and he exalts" (1 Samuel 2:7). It is He who gives the ability to produce wealth (Deuteronomy 8:18). Joseph of Arimathea, who looked after the burial of Jesus, was a rich man (Matthew 27:57). Lydia, whose heart the Lord opened, was a dealer in purple cloth (Acts 26:14).

Why Is This Teaching So Important?

We learn in this chapter that God is not against Christians making money, but at the same time we are to be warned lest we think we can rub shoulders with the world and not cave into worldliness. "Friendship with the world is hatred toward God" (James 4:4). Everyone must be extremely careful when dealing with unscrupulous people who are out there.

The big lesson, however, is the danger of greed. As seen above, the love of money is a root of all kinds of evil. Some people, "eager for money, have wandered from the faith and pierced themselves with many griefs" (1 Timothy 6:10). God is a jealous God and can only be served with exclusive devotion. The jealousy of God lies behind Jesus' words that you cannot serve God and money. As we saw above, we are not our own! We are bought with a price (1 Corinthians 6:19–20). Money is so deceptive (Matthew 13:22). Not only that, anyone who divides allegiance between God and money has already given in to money.

This chapter is important for another reason. It should help us to learn how to handle money. In my book *Tithing* I suggest one of the best ways for a Christian to learn how to handle money is to be a consistent tither. Learning how to handle money—which, sadly, some Christians have not learned—will help keep you out of debt. I made the decision a long, long time ago not to go into debt for anything (unless it is for a mortgage). I urge all to pay the credit cards bills in full as soon as they arrive. Debt is emotionally paralyzing and soul-destroying. The love of money is at bottom what is so wrong about people and the shape the world is in: people loving the things of this world. One of the foremost causes of marriage breakdown is money.

Make a Choice

You must make a choice. If you haven't already, read on—carefully. You must make a choice between God and money. How do you know you have made the right choice? First, esteem your place or calling above all else. Let Moses be your model. "He regarded disgrace for the sake of Christ as of greater value than the treasures of Egypt, because he was looking ahead to his reward" (Hebrews 11:26). Make treasure in heaven your reward, not things of the earth. Set your affection on things above (Colossians 3:2).

Second, ask yourself what motivates you when it comes to a choice of job. Suppose two jobs or opportunities are available. Which do you choose? If you put money ahead of your devotion to your family or church—because of the time involved—you will live to regret that decision. Time with family and availability to your church will mean a lot, lot more on your deathbed than the job that could make you more money.

Third, be a tither. This means that 10 percent of your income should be given to the Lord. Consider that one-tenth "hot money"; give it to God first, then watch God make it possible to pay your bills with the 90 percent that is left. "Whoever sows sparingly will also reap sparingly, and whoever sows generously will also reap generously" (2 Corinthians 9:6). By the way, remember that he or she who gives to the poor gives to the Lord (Proverbs 19:17).

Fourth, be generous, not stingy. This not only means giving money to God but also to others: the poor, the waitresses, the taxi drivers. I have a friend who refuses to tip a waitress or a taxi driver. It embarrasses me! A mean spirit is not a good testimony. The spirit of cheerful giving should, therefore, extend to the whole of life.

As for giving God what is His, it reminds me of a story told by the late W. A. Criswell. One asked a pastor, "How many members in your church?" Answer: 150. "How many tithe?" Answer: 150. "What? 150 members and 150 tithers?" Answer: "Absolutely. About a third of them give to God, and God takes it from the rest." God puts us on our honor to be generous—or we could be losers indeed.

Fifth, imagine that what you are spending today will have to be accounted for at the Judgment Seat of Christ. Be aware that God is watching. It is true that although the tithe is the Lord's (Leviticus 27:30), so is *all* your money! It all belongs to Him, so what you spend should be done with the view of pleasing the Lord.

The Pharisees "loved money" (Luke 16:14). John Bunyan, author of the famed *Pilgrim's Progress* wrote a poem:

> There was a man, some called him mad.
> The more he gave, the more he had.

59. Afraid Not to Worry?

Therefore, I tell you, do not worry about your life, what you will eat or drink; or about your body, what you will wear. Is not life more important than food, and the body more important than clothes?

MATTHEW 6:25

Jesus slightly changes the subject. Having dealt with money, He turns to worry. But as I said above, faith and finances often go together. Possibly our chief worry in life relates to money. This subject of worry carries right through to the end of Matthew 6.

What the King James Version refers to as "take no thought" the NIV says is "do not worry." It comes from a Greek word that means "to have anxiety or care." For example: "Casting all your care upon him; for he careth for you" (1 Peter 5:7, KJV), is in the NIV, "Cast all your anxiety on him because he cares for you." We have it in Philippians 4:6 (one of my favorite verses) this way: "Do not be anxious about anything, but in everything, by prayer and petition, with thanksgiving, present your requests to God."

Ten verses are devoted to this matter of worry in the Sermon on the Mount. Why do you suppose Jesus gives so much attention to this? We have an equivalent passage in Luke 12:22–34. This concept of anxiety is used somewhat differently in Matthew 10:19–20 ("do not worry about what to say"), a verse I always leaned on in the days I visited the late Yasser Arafat. In the Parable of the Sower, Jesus talked about the "worries of this life" (Matthew 13:22).

When I first preached these original sermons on the Sermon on the Mount, a church member mailed several of them to some Christians living in Dubai. A couple years later, I was privileged to speak to these people there, most of them being English-speaking Christians from India. I discovered that they had listened to a vast variety of my sermons. But at the top of the list of those subjects they hoped I might preach on in Dubai were these from Matthew 6:25–34. It made me

see more than ever how many Christians worry about finances.

This is why Jesus spent so much time on this matter. He knows where we are coming from. Never forget that He, too, was tried, or tested, at all points like us—including financial temptation and anxiety—but without sin. Though He is at the right hand of God at the moment, Jesus never forgot what it was like to be tried at this level. For this reason, He is "touched" with the feeling of our weaknesses (Hebrews 4:15, KJV). This encourages me. He will not moralize us when we are worried about these things.

God Does Not Want Us to Worry

So Jesus addresses this matter now. Why? There is one good, solid, truthful and encouraging answer: *God does not want us to worry.*

I will never forget something Joseph Tson said when he preached for us at Westminster Chapel. He said there are 366 verses in the Bible that say (one way or another), "do no fear" or "do not worry." Joseph concluded: "We have one for every day of the year and one for Leap Year!"

I reckon that when we get to heaven, one of the things we will blush the most about will be how we worried! Perhaps Jesus will say much the same thing to us as He did to Peter: "Why did you doubt?" (Matthew 14:31). I confess to you that there have been so many trials in my life that, when they were over, I said to myself, "I wish I hadn't worried so much."

So don't think I am on a pedestal looking down at you as I write these lines. Believe me, I have been the world's worst worrier—and I am not proud of it! So, I (hopefully) will not allow you to feel guilty; I want you to feel the sympathizing love of Jesus coming through these words. The reason for our worry, however, is simply lack of faith. But I am thankful that not only is the Son of God touched with the feeling of our weaknesses, but His Father remembers that "we are dust" (Psalm 103:14).

Jesus says, "Do not worry about your life." You may say: "Why shouldn't I? It's the only one I've got." James answers: "What is your life? You are a mist that appears for a little while and then vanishes" (James 4:14). The less we are filled with the Holy Spirit, the more seriously we will take ourselves. The more we are filled with the Spirit—and the closer to God we are—the less seriously we will take ourselves. One evidence of this is how those who overcame the devil by the blood of the Lamb "did not love their lives so much as to shrink from death" (Revelation 12:11). Jesus said, "The man who loves his life will lose it, while the man who hates his life in this world will keep it for eternal life" (John 12:25).

King Saul became yesterday's man partly because he took himself too seriously (1 Samuel 13:8–14). Equally pitiful was Absalom's making a monument to himself (2 Samuel 18:18). Paul said in his farewell to the elders of the church at Ephesus, "I consider my life worth nothing to me" (Acts 20:24). Consider those who are mentioned in Hebrews 11. What a privilege to be mentioned in that famous "faith" chapter! Whether they conquered kingdoms, shut the mouths of lions, were tortured, stoned or mistreated, they had in common that they did not take themselves so seriously. "The world was not worthy of them" (Hebrews 11:38).

So, when Jesus tells us not to worry about our life, we need to keep the bigger picture in perspective. We are all going to die. So we must answer the question: In what does life consist? For some it is their job. Possessions. Their children. Their hobby. Their goal in life. Their health. For Paul, "To live is Christ" (Philippians 1:21).

Jesus' Purpose: To Set Us Free from Worry

The purpose of this section in the Sermon on the Mount is to set us free from worry. That is Jesus' aim in these lines. He wants to set us free from having to worry—and by showing us why we don't need to worry. It is not a rebuke as much as at is an encouragement. He does not moralize or make us feel guilty.

The interesting thing is, God takes the responsibility for everything we worry about! For example, "Look at the birds of the air; they do not sow or reap or store away in barns, and yet your heavenly Father feeds them. Are you not much more valuable than they?" (Matthew 6:26). "If that is how God clothes the grass of the field, which is here today and tomorrow is thrown into the fire, will he not much more clothe you, O you of little faith" (Matthew 6:30). What Jesus wants of us is that we transfer our anxiety to God (1 Peter 5:7).

Why, then, should we not worry about our life? Why does God not want us to worry? The answer is partly this: that worry militates against faith—and it is "impossible to please God" without faith (Hebrews 11:6). God sets us free from worrying by showing us that our worrying is His problem. It is also His prerogative—except that God never worries! "You will keep in perfect peace him whose mind is steadfast, because he trusts in you" (Isaiah 26:3). "Do not be anxious about anything, but in everything, by prayer and petition, with thanksgiving, present your requests to God. And the peace of God, which transcends all understanding, will guard your hearts and your minds in Christ Jesus" (Philippians 4:6–7).

Some people are afraid not to worry. They feel they are abandoning their responsibility if they aren't worrying! They would feel guilty in not worrying. Take worry away and they will quickly find something to worry about to replace the worry that just left! It is like people who have been in prison for years. When they come out, they feel so strange that they soon commit a crime so they'll be put back in prison! Some people never know that there is such a thing as life without worrying.

Why, then, should we not worry?

The Providence of Life

"Do not worry about your life." Who do you suppose takes the responsibility for our having life in the first place? "This is what the Lord says—he who created you, O Jacob, he who formed you, O Israel" (Isaiah 43:1).

God made you and shaped you. He chose your parents. He allowed all circumstances that surrounded you as you were growing up: peer relationships, unjust treatment, abuse, situations that caused ambition to develop in you, jealousies, school influences. All these shaped your interests. God determined the time and place of your birth in the first place, plus where you live (Acts 17:26). In a word: God takes the responsibility for your being here!

Not only that, God has done a saving work in you. "Fear not, I have redeemed you; I have summoned you by name; you are mine" (Isaiah 43:1). God takes the responsibility for your being effectually called by the Holy Spirit. He "summoned" us. The bottom line: God says to you, "I love you—you are Mine." As Saint Augustine put it, God loves every person as if there were no one else to love.

Do you ever feel guilty about these things? Do you feel guilty over the way you were brought up? Are you ashamed of your parents and how they reared you? Do you feel guilty about your particular interests and ability? Do you feel guilty that you are not exceptionally bright? Do you feel guilty because you are highly intelligent? God says to you: "I take full responsibility for these things." Jesus then comes along and says, "Do not worry about your life"; after all, our heavenly Father brought you here and will nurture you as long as you live. The providence of life is out of our hands. It is in God's hands.

The Purpose of Your Life

What's it all for? Why are we here? Do you have certain goals? Certain aims? Certain wishes? What are we made for? What do we hope to accomplish in a lifetime? Is there something you feel you must achieve before you die? Or are you just waiting to die? Do you fear that life is passing you by? Are you missing out on something? Do you watch your friends succeed? Are they happily married, but you are not? Do you have unfulfilled dreams? Do you have a sense of destiny? Do you worry that you *don't* have a sense of destiny?

God says to you, right now: "Leave that with Me." He has a plan for your life. The purpose of your life is God's problem. What He has in mind for you is not what He has in mind for someone else. And what He plans for other people around you—whether friends or enemies—is not what He has in mind for you. Jesus told Peter how he would die, but Peter could only think of what would happen to his friend John! Jesus said to Peter, in so many words, "None of your business; you follow Me" (John 21:18–21).

The purpose of your life is God's business. He has a plan for your life. It is not your responsibility to map out your own life. The same God who created you, shaped you, called you by name and redeemed you wants the responsibility for you—and takes it! It is not your responsibility. It is His. And He will show you His will—if you will listen and not elbow in on His territory by taking over the controls.

His plan for you has been drawn up. What is more, His plan for your future has been determined according to your gifts and talents (which He gave you), your education and training (which He enabled) and influences that shaped you (owing to His watchful care). His idea what you should do with your life is a far, far better one than your own wishes and aspirations for it—I guarantee it. You may feel cheated, but God will not cheat you. Be careful that your wishes do not go beyond what He has already determined. Don't try to upstage what God has already planned. You could not better it if you tried with all your mind and strength.

So Jesus says to you, "Do not worry about your life." If this were a friend or foe, a minister or physician, a lawyer or accountant giving this advice, you could understandably be perplexed. But this is counsel from the Lord Jesus Christ. In fact, God says to you, "I am the One who should be worried. I am the One who made you and saved you, and I am now looking after you!" So God's word to you can be summed up: Stop putting yourself under pressure that God didn't put there.

Provisions for Life

These provisions relate to what we eat or drink or what we will wear. Question: Who made you? Answer: God. Who brought you into this world? God. He therefore takes the responsibility for your needs. He knows you need to eat and be clothed. The Lord who gave us this life will not fail to support us!

It is noteworthy that these provisions reflect the Fall of humankind in the Garden of Eden. Eating comes from our having to work (Genesis 3:19). Jesus, however, isn't telling us to be lazy. Paul said, "If a man will not work, he shall not eat" (2 Thessalonians 3:10). Clothing comes from the shame of the Fall (Genesis 3:7). People didn't need clothes before the Fall, but now they do. One thing that apparently doesn't go back to the pre-fallen state in heaven is that we are clothed. One thing that was permanent because of the Fall is clothing.

Jesus is simply telling us: Do not worry. God will give us a job or income that is equal to what we need regarding food and clothing. "I was young and now I am old, yet I have never seen the righteous forsaken or their children begging bread," said David (Psalm 37:25). "My God will meet all your [financial] needs according to his glorious riches in Christ Jesus" (Philippians 4:19).

Preservation of Life

Notice these words, "about your body." Don't forget these are Jesus' words. Don't worry about your body. You are His; you are not your own (1 Corinthians 6:20). The body being preserved means that staying alive is God's problem. It is also God's business where you live, having a place in which to live and having a livelihood. Longevity also lies within God's prerogative. "Who of you by worrying can add a single hour to his life?" (Matthew 6:27).

The same God who gave us life—and our bodies—is the One who sent His Son to tell us that He will look after us. I find this sweet and thrilling. God didn't have to tell us that. But He did. In these words of the Sermon on the Mount, our Lord Jesus—who is God—is saying to us, "Let Me worry about these things. I am taking worry out of your hands."

Are you afraid not to worry? Are you fearful that if you don't worry you will not be looked after?

Stop it! Jesus is saying to you as you read these lines: Why worry when God already takes the responsibility for preserving your life?

Productivity of Life

I refer now to the degree of success or results that flow from your life—your goals, wishes, plans and ambitions. The explanation of any success is summed up in one word: God.

"But remember the LORD your God, for it is he who gives you the ability to produce wealth, and so confirms his covenant, which he swore to your forefathers, as it is today" (Deuteronomy 8:18). God warned about Israel, who had "not acknowledged that I was the one who gave her the grain, the new wine and oil" (Hosea 2:8). "In his heart a man plans his course, but the LORD determines his steps" (Proverbs 16:9). "Many are the plans in a man's heart, but it is the LORD's purpose that prevails" (Proverbs 19:21). "No king is saved by the size of his army; no warrior escapes by his great strength. A horse is a vain hope for deliverance; despite all its great strength it cannot save. But the eyes of the LORD are on those who fear him, on those whose hope is in his unfailing love, to deliver them from death and keep them alive in famine" (Psalm 33:16–19).

No one should question whether it is true that those who are gifted produce more, or that those who work harder often succeed more. The issue is whether those who are gifted and work hard do so under the Holy Spirit's power. "'Not by might nor by power, but by my Spirit,' says the LORD Almighty" (Zechariah 4:6).

God does not want us to worry. He sets us free from it. Are you afraid not to worry? Get over it! God wants us to take Him seriously by offering to do all the worrying for us.

60. The Privilege of Not Worrying

*Look at the birds of the air; they do not sow or reap or store away in barns,
and yet your heavenly Father feeds them. Are you not much more valuable
than they? Who of you by worrying can add a single hour to his life?*

MATTHEW 6:26–27

I remind you that Jesus is not rebuking us in this section. He is not moralizing. He is using simple, common sense to encourage us not to worry. He is not angry with us because we worry about money. He is not looking around that He might find someone who is worrying so He can say, "Gotcha!" No. All He does in the Sermon on the Mount is being orchestrated in heaven by the Father (John 5:19). And the Father remembers that we are dust (Psalm 103:14). In a word: He sympathizes with us.

The point is: God does not want us to worry. It is counterproductive to worry. Jesus gives us these words to help us along—not so we'll feel guilty, but to motivate us not to worry. He is on our side, not against us! If a secular writer like Dale Carnegie can write a book on "How to Stop Worrying" in order to help people generally, how much more does the God-man who sympathizes with our weaknesses want to help us in this area? The word Jesus wants to convey to us is that the Father says, "Leave it to Me," when it comes to the necessities of life: food, shelter and clothing. "Let Me do the worrying for you."

In this chapter, I want to unpack more from this section of Jesus' sermon. There is a parallel between God's vindicating us and His supplying our need. Never forget, vindication is what God does best; He doesn't want our help. So, too, when it comes to the way He supplies our financial needs: He does not want us to worry. We are to cast all our care, or anxiety, upon Him. "Let nothing move you," said Paul (1 Corinthians 15:58).

Consider these words: God "acts on behalf of those who wait for him" (Isaiah 64:4). This means that when we wait, He works. But if we work, He waits. When we don't fret but wait for Him to

act, He gets on our case and starts working for us. But when we fret and do what He wants to do for us, He waits! That is the principle of vindication.

So, too, with His taking care of our financial problems. It does not mean for us to be lazy or not do what we can. It has to do with fretting and our not relying on Him to do what He promised to do. Some say, "If I don't do the worrying, things won't get done." The irony is: The less we worry, the more we get done.

I know that Oswald Chambers said, "Some people are so heavenly minded that they are of no earthly use." But that is more of a clever quip than reality. The truth is those who set their affections on things above end up leaving the greatest mark on earth. They get the most done and change society most. The degree to which we let God run things will be the degree to which we will be responsible and get more done. "Let nothing move you" and watch Him work.

Two Ways This May Happen

There are two ways by which we might carry out Matthew 6:26–27. First, when God simply steps in and takes over. If He chooses, He can enable us to enter His rest.

I am talking about a spiritual experience—one most profound. He might say to you, "How would you like to enter into My rest?" He can do that. It is when He overwhelms us with His peace—bypassing our brains and fleshly reasoning and giving us that peace that transcends understanding. It is incredible. So wonderful. It may last a while. It lasted the whole life of Jesus.

However, there is a second way. If entering into His rest doesn't happen, we are to exercise faith and do all we can do in order to enter into that rest. That is what is meant by these words: "Make every effort to enter that rest" (Hebrews 4:11). In this case, you reject worry as soon as it comes before you. When you find yourself worrying, or fretting, STOP IT!

You may say: "That's not always easy to do." I agree. No one said it would be easy. But it is the same with any temptation, whether sex, pride, false ambition, fear or fretting. This is why we must make every effort. Reject worry as you would sexual temptation. Just say, "No!" John Wesley actually once said, "I would as leave curse as to worry."

To summarize what I have just said: There are two ways one can stop worrying: (1) God steps in and gives you supernatural peace, or (2) you have to make an effort. You may say God stepping in is your Plan A. But if you have to go to Plan B and make an effort, it shows the latter was actually God's Plan A. Speaking personally, I have experienced this rest, a supernatural peace. But I have to admit that I eventually lost it. I then faced two choices: to require God to "do it again" and let me experience His rest, or to please Him by making every effort to resist any degree of worry. I had to do just that. This pleases Him.

A Privilege

It is such a privilege not to worry. Why call it a privilege not to worry? *Privilege* means a special right or advantage granted to a person or group. There are those "born to privilege," a phrase heard often in England—mainly meaning those born to the upper classes of society, especially aristocracy. People like this have a head start regarding a good education and getting the better jobs.

So why is it a "privilege" not to worry? Consider what is on offer in these verses in Matthew 6:26–27! It is something that the "privileged" of the world—whether aristocracy, royalty or the super-rich—would give almost anything to have: peace of mind. Jesus is offering a lifestyle, comparing it to the "birds of the air." The greatest English poets would write odes to birds—like a skylark—as if coveting their carefree freedom. That is what Jesus is talking about. He wants precisely that for us. It is on offer because we are children of God.

One of the greatest benefits of being a Christian—but perhaps the least enjoyed—is that we are offered the privilege of not worrying. It is because God Himself tells us we shouldn't! "Look at the birds of the air; they do not sow or reap or store away in barns, and yet your heavenly Father feeds them. Are you not much more valuable than they?" We are offered this "fringe benefit"—not worrying—about our essential needs. We know we are in the hands of a loving, sovereign Creator God and Father. When we get to heaven there will be no care, no anxiety, no death, no tears. But on offer to every child of God is a little bit of heaven to go to heaven in.

We are therefore called not to worry. We are to be untroubled because we trust God to take charge of our essential needs. In doing this, we have therefore transferred our anxiety to God. Whereas *saving* faith is transferring our trust in good works to what Jesus did for us on the cross, *achieving* faith is transferring our anxiety to God. We let God do the worrying. Why worry, then, when God says to us, "Leave it with Me"?

The Possibility of Not Worrying

Jesus would not put this before us if it were not a reachable goal. He does not dangle a carrot in front of us, leading us on with no hope. He therefore puts forth this incredible opportunity of not worrying because it is a real possibility. The question is, how is it achieved?

I return to the two aforementioned ways. First, entering God's rest (Hebrews 4:9–10), which is a reference neither to heaven nor conversion but to a blissful state of inner peace. It comes from casting all your care upon God (1 Peter 5:7). I referred above to my own experience of peace that lasted for a while—several months, in fact. Throughout the first day when this happened, I kept asking, "Is this in the Bible—this wonderful peace?" Then I read Matthew 6:25–27. It is precisely what Jesus described.

Some take the "rest" of Hebrews 4:9 to be heaven. Wrong. We do not have to make an effort to get to heaven! It is by sheer grace through faith (Ephesians 2:8–9). The same is true of conversion. We do not have to work to be saved. We transfer our hope in good works to the promise offered by Jesus' cross. God's rest is an inner state of peace that comes to the Christian who transfers their anxiety to God. Jesus referred to this when He said, "Take my yoke upon you and learn from me, for I am gentle and humble in heart, and you will find rest for your souls" (Matthew 11:29).

Second, if we do not enter God's rest, we exercise our faith. It means not giving up. It means fierce perseverance in faithfulness to God's Word and refusing not to worry. It is believing God so much that you take Him at His Word. You refuse to give in when tempted to fret. What often follows is the very rest you wanted to enter all along!

God will honor the faith of those who persevere and make every effort to adhere to Jesus' teachings. Speaking personally, I did not enter this rest because I expected it. It came by making every effort to please the Lord. God will do that for you, too. This is what Jesus is wanting us to experience: a life that is carefree like the birds of the air. In the great hymn "Like a River Glorious" there is that wonderful phrase, "not a blast of hurry touch the spirit there." It is like Job saying, "Though he slay me, yet will I hope in him" (Job 13:15). It is echoing the acclamation of the three Hebrews—Shadrach, Meshach and Abednego—who said, "The God we serve is able to save us from it [the burning fiery furnace]. . . . But even if he does not, we want you to know, O king, that we will not serve your gods or worship the image of gold you have set up" (Daniel 3:17–18).

The Premise of Not Worrying

Premise by definition means a statement on which reasoning is based. The premise is: God takes the responsibility of worrying for us. Jesus reasoned, "Is not life more important than food, and the body more important than clothes?" (Matthew 25).

This is Jesus' reminder that God made us; He gave us life and wants to keep us alive. He did not bring us into this world to be kept unfed and unclothed. So when He tells us that "life" and our "bodies" are more important than food and clothing, we are to conclude that God takes the responsibility for our having these things. We have to eat in order to live; He will provide food. Clothes give us warmth and dignity; God will provide clothes for us to wear.

God is not responsible for the Fall in the Garden of Eden, and yet He graciously steps in and says, "I will see you are clothed as well as fed." Remember that God provided Adam and Eve with their first clothes after their Fall—"garments of skin" (Genesis 3:21).

The Promise of Not Worrying

In these words Jesus implicitly promises us this privilege of not worrying. It is a great privilege, one no one would dispute. Are we truly promised this? Yes. It comes, however, in proportion to two things: (1) the degree to which we believe God—not merely believe *in* God but believe God; and (2) the degree to which we live within the realm of need.

Faith is believing God. The question is: How much do we believe in Him? If we believe in our head only, our hearts will still be troubled. But once the "penny drops," the heart believes. When that happens, worrying diminishes, God's Spirit increases. The Holy Spirit floods our soul with peace in proportion to our faith.

The Promise Pertains to Our Needs

This chapter now takes a slight turn. All I have been saying about not worrying assumes we live in the realm of need. Like it or not, the issue is our need. God promises to supply the need (Philippians 4:19).

There are some elementary lessons in economics that we might be reminded of. In an ascending order: There are needs, comforts and luxuries. Jesus, therefore, is not talking about your having Caribbean holidays in five star hotels. Neither is He talking about your driving an expensive car or living in the wealthiest part of town. (I'm sorry, but I have to say this.) When it comes to needs, we are talking about food, shelter and clothing. What Jesus is referring to in this section of the Sermon on the Mount pertains to our needs. There is, therefore, no promise of plush carpeting in your house, black caviar with prime beef every day or driving a Rolls Royce.

If you say, "This is no comfort to me," I reply: This is very likely why you have no peace. Worry is the result of treasures on earth, not heaven. Those who are content with God supplying the need are those who can claim this promise. You have to make a distinction between two things: what is important and what is essential—and it is the latter Jesus speaks to. What is important is food, but what is essential is your life. So God promises that we will have food to eat and live, clothes to protect us from the cold and indignity.

This is the way Jesus reasons in these lines. We might wish He had elevated the discussion to our comforts and luxuries. But what is essential are food, shelter and clothing. At the physical level, we will survive with enough food to eat. At the emotional level, we are given dignity so that we won't be naked. God always provides the "fig leaves" to cover our shame.

Our problem is, we want more. We want more than what is essential. And that is precisely where worry comes in. How many of us would overcome worry in one stroke if we were content with the essentials and with what we need? It is when greed and ambition move in that faith diminishes and worry emerges. Many Christians could overcome worry in one stroke—not merely by an increase of faith but by a decrease of greed and ambition.

The promise of not worrying, then, is not extended beyond the realm of need. Many say they are concerned about material things, but when push comes to shove we don't want to give up our fairly comfortable lifestyle. We therefore have a superabundance of worry, because we simply will not settle for the bare necessities of life that Jesus is talking about in these lines. The promise of not worrying is to those of us who are content with His supplying our needs—not our comforts and luxuries.

61. How to Overcome Worry

Therefore I tell you, do not worry about your life, what you will eat or drink; or about your body, what you will wear. Is not life more important than food, and the body more important than clothes? Look at the birds of the air; they do not sow or reap or store away in barns, and yet your heavenly Father feeds them. Are you not much more valuable than they? Who of you by worrying can add a single hour to his life?

MATTHEW 6:25–27

This is a well-known part of the Sermon on the Mount that is arguably the least explored—and, almost certainly, the least experienced. In writing this chapter on "how to overcome worry," I feel manifestly unqualified to do so. In some ways it is like Elizabeth Taylor writing on "how to stay married." But when I recall that Dale Carnegie, best known perhaps for his book *How to Win Friends and Influence People*, wrote a book on overcoming worry, why shouldn't I—a child of God and interpreter of His Word?

It should be recalled from time to time that the Kingdom of heaven is the realm of the ungrieved Spirit. We have also seen that the chief way we grieve the Spirit is by bitterness and unforgiveness, as well as lusting and doing your righteousness before men. But worrying also grieves the Spirit—and worrying does not seem to bother us. But it should. It, too, grieves the Holy Spirit because it is a product of unbelief. And yet Jesus' words are to encourage us rather than rebuke us. We should in a sense worry about worry, because worry grieves the Holy Spirit—which we must avoid doing at all costs.

In these verses we continue to explore, we find indications how to overcome worry. We saw in the previous chapter how two things help us: (1) the increase of faith—believing God—and (2) the decrease of greed and ambition. In a word: We worry largely because we bite off more than we can chew. For the promise of not worrying is not extended beyond the realm of need. If we were content with our need being supplied, worry might well diminish in many of us. Worry emerges because we choose a lifestyle far beyond

what we need. We worry over things God never promised to get involved in. It is like going outside our anointing because we want the praise of people. Our stress and fretting are brought on by a decision to have treasures on earth, not heaven. The origin is almost always pride.

The promise of our being free from worry is a promise—but a conditional promise. The condition is that we are content with what we need. Someone might say, "But that is not what I had in mind. I am going to trust God to give me a Mercedes-Benz." If you do that, you are on your own. These lines in the Sermon on the Mount—preached originally to an agrarian society where they were dependent on their food day by day—are not to be applied by those who want an extravagant lifestyle.

You may not like this chapter. You may well be interested in learning how to overcome worry. But you may not like the way forward to achieve this.

Adjustment of a Lifestyle to the Level of Need

The first thing we must do to overcome worry is to reassess our lifestyle. This is how we know that the promise of not worrying is based upon a condition—namely, that we are willing to live according to need, not wants.

How do you determine need? I answer: knowing what is important and what is essential—then stick to the latter. As we have seen, life is essential. Living. Staying alive. Having food to eat. Having clothes to give us warmth and dignity. If we see what is essential, we can be sure God will step in and give us faith to overcome worry. For God takes the responsibility for life (food) and the body (clothes). This, then, is our Lord's hint how to know what God takes the responsibility for. It is how we determine the need.

Can a Comfort Become a Need?

We have seen the ascending order: needs, comforts, luxuries. God promises to supply the need, not comforts and luxuries. The question is: Is what may be seen as comforts or luxuries for some a need for others? Yes. For example, for some people having a car is a luxury. For others it is a need. For some, having a bodyguard would be a luxury. But for others—if they are princes or prime ministers—it is a need. For some, having a chauffeur is a luxury, but for a head of state it is a need. For some, a university education is a luxury, but for others it is a need—or there would be no doctors or engineers.

We may be jealous of another's lifestyle, especially their privileges and apparent comforts. But in many cases these are needs. Remember these words: "Do not judge, or you too will be judged" (Matthew 7:1). The issue you and I must face is not the other person but whether the lifestyle to which we are called is one that we are adjusting to. In a word: What may be wants or wishes for you and me could be absolutely essential to another person. Do not judge them.

Three Basic Needs

We all have three basic needs to do the work to which we are called, whether you are a nurse, taxi driver, pastor or physician: confidence, competence and credibility.

Confidence. This means believing you can do what you are called to do, that you are up to it. Confidence is essential to survival. This is why God gives clothes. As we have seen, after the Fall God gave Adam and Eve clothes. God promises to clothe us, giving us dignity. Therefore, dignity is a need, not a luxury, in the sight of God. This is because confidence is essential for survival.

If I were asked to sit in for a doctor, lawyer or engineer for ten minutes, I would panic! I would be a nervous wreck. Why? I would have no confidence that I could do the job. But God has called me to do a job I *can* do. I am not asked to be a physician or lawyer. My calling is to preach or teach. I have confidence I can finish this book. God supplies the need of confidence; it means no fatigue, no worry. I do not need extraordinary faith to write this book. I am not worried. This is my calling.

So if you do not have confidence that you can do your job, you have been promoted to the level of your incompetence. You should not be there. God never promotes us to the level of our incompetence. The world will do that. Not God. When you worry day and night that you are not able to do your job, it may be you have taken on a responsibility God did not call you to do. The thing you should do is, simply, step down—however it may challenge your pride. But if you take a less prestigious job, one that pays less, too, you will have less worry. Perhaps no worry.

You would overcome worry in this case by swallowing your pride and living on a tighter budget. You, therefore, make a choice: to live light and lofty—and worry all the time—or climb down and stop worrying. Many people worry because they have moved beyond what they are easily able to do—and lose confidence.

The same God who promises to clothe you, to keep you from starving or being ashamed, will give you confidence to do what He has called you to do so you won't be ashamed.

Competence. This is essential to survival, too. This means ability to do your job. This is like food on your table. The God who gives life gives food. The God who gives life gives you a job. You have to eat to live; you need a job for income to buy food. God has promised you will have the competence to do the job to which you are called to do.

To have confidence requires training. Education. Qualifying by taking a course. This costs money. Is this a luxury? No. It is a need. Some have more ability than others. You need ability to do a job. A high-powered job requires a person with great ability. This is essential. When it comes to travel transportation, by jet seems like a luxury; for some it is a need. Flying business class for some would be a luxury; for others it is a need. Someone noticed Spurgeon getting in a first-class coach and said to him, "I travel third class and save the Lord's money." (In those days they had first, second, and third class.) Spurgeon replied: "You do that; I travel first class and save the Lord's servant."

Credibility. This, too, is essential for survival. The reason people believe in you is that you had some good references; you maintain a good standard; you make sure that those who employed you trust you. You want to look good. To be presentable. Nice clothes are essential, not a luxury.

God will give you faith to overcome people doubting you (unless you are not where you should be). People will be jealous of you. People will want your job. But if God has put you there, He will give you a good reputation, credibility, respect and acceptance. God will give you a good name in the sight of those who matter. "A good name is more desirable than great riches; to be esteemed is better than silver or gold" (Proverbs 22:1).

So, how do you overcome worry? First, adjust your lifestyle so that confidence, competence and credibility are maintained without effort. Second, remember that God has promised you will have strength equal to your days (Deuteronomy 33:25). Third, remember that God will not promote you to the level of your incompetence—whether it is lack of confidence, competence or credibility. If greed and ambition have landed you where you are and all you do is worry, something is wrong. These teachings of Jesus in this part of the Sermon on the Mount require an adjustment in our lifestyle to the level of need. Chances are that burnout would not happen to many if they observed this teaching.

Analogy of Lifestyle from the Level of Nature

"Look at the birds of the air; they do not sow or reap or store away in barns, and yet your heavenly Father feeds them" (verse 26). Why does Jesus refer to birds? It is because birds don't worry. Have you ever heard someone called "birdbrain"? Birds' brains are the size of a pea. Jesus put it: "Your heavenly Father feeds them." Note: not *their* heavenly Father, but *yours*. Birds are not made in God's image. They are animals.

Jesus' analogy is about birds and *worry*. Worry is what birds don't do. They are busy, yes. And what do you suppose they are doing all the time? Eating. Always eating. It is basically what they do: fly and eat. They eat what is there. It does not cross their little minds to

worry about whether there will be food. Birds don't worry.

The analogy is also regarding birds and *work*. They are always working. There are three things they don't do, says Jesus: Unlike a farmer, they don't sow. They don't reap what they sow. They don't store food. They don't worry about tomorrow. They don't think to themselves, *I should save this grain or berry for a rainy day.* They eat everything they want *now*. Yet they work for what they eat. God doesn't drop food into their mouths. This shows that faith isn't lazy. We must work by the sweat of the brow, and yet we acknowledge that God pays the bills.

The analogy is between birds and *worth*. "Are you not much more valuable than they?" (verse 26). Jesus applies a Hebraic way of thinking: by asking a question when the answer is yes. Why are we more valuable? It is because man—men and women—and not birds are made in God's image. When God sent His Son, He became flesh as we are, bone of our bone. And yet God takes the responsibility for feeding the birds!

How do we overcome worry? Remember who you are. You were created in God's image (Genesis 1:26). We are different from animals. God made the human race after His likeness. He affirmed the human race by sending His Son to be like one of us. He feeds the birds, but we are much more valuable. He takes the responsibility for feeding and clothing us.

If you are a believer and have not overcome worry, chances are you are imposing desires on yourself that faith never promised to meet. You are probably putting yourself under pressure God didn't put there. You have moved outside your calling or anointing. You cannot have a worry-free existence like a bird's because you want more than food, shelter, clothing.

You must make a decision. What do you want? Stress and worry that come from going beyond your need? Or faith that comes from being content with the anointing, calling and lifestyle God intended for you?

Question: How does one know he or she has the faith that pleases God? It is when you are content with what you have and live without stress or jealousy. It is when you keep greed and ambition under control in order that faith is constant and not interrupted. You may know you please God when your lifestyle is altered so that you don't have to work up faith to get what you want.

God doesn't want us to worry. But if we do, it is probably because we have brought it on ourselves.

I do not say this to make you feel guilty. I say it to encourage you to know there is a better way to live.

62. The Folly of Worry

Who of you by worrying can add a single hour to his life?

MATTHEW **6:27**

The purpose of Jesus' words in Matthew 6:27 is not so much to convince us of the folly of worrying but to help us to stop worrying. We all need all the help we can get. As I have observed a number of times already, His purpose is not to send us on a guilt trip for worrying—which would worry us all the more—but to show us the way forward. Speaking personally, these studies from this part of the Sermon on the Mount have helped me immensely. I hope you will find the same. God wants to set us free from worry.

Neither is Jesus encouraging laziness or ir-responsibility. If we look at the previous verses in a wrong way, we could tell ourselves to be so carefree—to worry about nothing and become passive and lazy. The birds of the air are anything but lazy; they are flying and working and looking for food all the time. And yet it is our heavenly Father who feeds them—but in proportion to their work.

Productive Anxiety

There is such a thing as creative anxiety. There is an anxiety that is productive and not draining on our spirits. It is what makes you get to work on time. It is how we meet deadlines. It is how we plan to get things done. If I have six months to plan a sermon—as when I get an invitation way in advance—chances are I will not work on it until a day or two before the time! I do best when I am under a little bit of pressure. When I was studying at Oxford, and I heard of those students around me who were failing right, left and center, it made me take nothing for granted—to read more, prepare harder and not miss the goal I had come to England for.

Even God gets our attention by producing anxiety in us. It ought to make us anxious when we are confronted with the question, "What good

is it for a man to gain the whole world, yet forfeit his soul?" (Mark 8:36). When the writer of Hebrews warns of being dull of hearing—with the possibility of falling and not being able to be renewed unto repentance (Hebrews 5:11; 6:4–6)—it is God trying to get our attention by a wake-up call.

But the anxiety Jesus is wanting us to be free from is worrying over what God has already taken the responsibility for: namely, life and death—two huge things. God determines the time of our birth and our death. He knows exactly when—to the day, hour, minute and second—we will die. In a word: These two things are out of our hands. "Who of you by worrying can add a single hour to his life?"

In the verse on which this chapter centers, then, Jesus is trying to reason with us graciously. He knows the pain of worry. God knows our frame, remembering we are dust (Psalm 103:14). He wants to spare us of worry. He gives a pragmatic reason for not worrying: namely, *worrying doesn't work!*

What Is Certain versus What Is Up to Us

The issue implicit in Jesus' words in Matthew 6:27 are two things: what is certain and what is up to us. What is certain is that our need—not unnecessary luxuries—will be supplied by our heavenly Father.

Jesus also affirms that other things are out of our hands—e.g., our height or length of life. Nobody knows whether the Greek is referring to how tall we are or how long we live. The words are used in different ways and can be translated either way. The English Standard Version translates it, Who "can add a single hour to his span of life?" and adds a footnote: "Or a single cubit to his stature; a cubit was about 18 inches." This means you can't make yourself any taller, neither can you extend your life by worry. For it is certain: Worrying doesn't work; it is counterproductive.

What is up to us, then, is whether we will take Jesus' words seriously. We cannot make ourselves taller or add an hour to the length of our life, but we can determine whether we will listen to Jesus. Taking Him seriously will increase our faith. So we can do something about our level of faith. We can determine whether we grow spiritually. In a word: We can stop worrying if we will apply Jesus' words.

Worry and Responsibility

Is it not fantastic that God takes the responsibility for our lives and our length of days on earth? I find this so very settling, agreeable and peace-giving. Since He takes the responsibility of these things, why not let Him have it? Why worry when He says, "This is My problem"? God says to you and me, "Why ever would you choose to worry when this is My responsibility?" I say: Let Him have it!

In Matthew 11:28 Jesus asks us to give Him the burden of our sin ("Come to me, all you who are weary and burdened, and I will give you rest"). In Matthew 11:29 He asks us to give Him our cares ("Take my yoke upon you and learn from me . . . and you will find rest for your souls"). Indeed, we are invited to cast our anxiety upon Him because He cares for us (1 Peter 5:7).

Why, then, does He take this responsibility? It is because His own purposes are at stake. "Who of you by worrying can add a single hour to his life?" Behind Jesus' words is what Job learned after his long ordeal: "I know that you can do all things; no plan of yours can be thwarted" (Job 42:2). This word thrills me to my fingertips. Or, to quote the prophet Isaiah, "I make known the end from the beginning, from ancient times, what is still to come. I say: My purpose will stand, and I will do all that I please" (Isaiah 46:10).

Some might find these words too good to be true. We are afraid not to worry lest He forget us! We are afraid He won't take care of us unless we worry day and night. Wrong. He gently and graciously invites us to turn all these things over to Him and watch Him work.

God's provision is straightforward. He takes care even of animals and creatures that are not made in His own image: birds, ravens, giraffes, kangaroos, monkeys. So, how much more will He take care of us who are created after His own image (Genesis 1:26)? Not only that, His province is sacred. What is His province? The whole world. The entire universe, every square inch of it. Almost every day scientists have a further discovery how huge and vast the universe is. God owns and controls it all. Always has, always will. All of it is sacred to Him. Sin got into the picture, yes. But this did not take God by surprise. Jesus Christ was the Lamb slain from the foundation of the world (1 Peter 1:19–20).

Do you want to hear the safest prediction I could ever make? Here it is: When we get to heaven, we will see how unnecessary worry was. Worrying was the last thing we needed to do. Fortunately, Job learned it before he went to heaven. Why not be like Job? Learn this lesson now: No plan of God can be thwarted. No purpose aborted. No goal frustrated. We need not be put through the ordeal Job was put through in order to learn this. Our privilege: Learn it now by taking Jesus seriously. The silliest thing on earth is to worry about what has been taken out of our hands: God's care for us. He says to you and me: "This is My province, My responsibility."

Worry and Reality

Question: What does worry do? We know what it can't do. It can't make you taller than you are— although it might make you shorter! Worry can cause arthritis, which can make you shorter. Worry can't extend your life. It might shorten it! Jesus did not say that worry would not shorten it! After all, worry can cause ailments in the body that could shorten one's life.

So, what does worry do? I reply: *nothing positive and everything negative.* It is counterproductive; it achieves the opposite of what you wanted. Worrying is crippling, both emotionally and physically. If it gets out of hand, it will turn us into neurotics.

Worrying can control you. It will keep you from being yourself. You can become a slave to worry. I will come clean with you: I worried the whole time I was at Oxford. I found it painful. Apart from the snobbish atmosphere, there was absolutely no security or assurance that I would pass and secure the D.Phil. degree I went to Britain for. I used to say to my supervisor, Barrie White, "Can't you tell me whether I will pass?" He would say, "Sorry, no." I replied: "There surely ought to be some way of knowing I will pass." His reply: "It's a wicked world, Robert" (that's what he always called me).

I was so filled with worry that I can recall driving from Geneva to Interlaken, Switzerland—possibly the most gorgeous view of nature in the entire world—and I didn't see a thing. I was too worried about my Oxford thesis, whether I would pass. I wish God had given me oath-level assurance on September 1, 1973, when we arrived at Heathrow: "R. T., don't worry—you will get your D.Phil." But He didn't. He could have. He has given me assurance regarding other things. But for some reason, not that. As a result, I was unable to enjoy those years. Worry is controlling. I regret and am ashamed and sorry to admit that I did not have more faith in those days.

Worry is costly. It is expensive. It costs you time, money, friends. When we worry all the time—and talk about it—people don't want to be around us. They say, "Look who's coming." They tiptoe away as if they didn't see us. Worry is also competitive. It competes with God, His presence and His peace. "Worry belongs to Me," says God. "Stop elbowing in on My territory."

Worry and Reason

"Who of you by worrying can add a single hour to his life?" Jesus is appealing to our natural sense of reason. He appeals to our common sense. He is saying: Use common sense. Since worrying doesn't achieve its aim, why worry? Since worrying is crippling, counterproductive, controlling, costly and competitive, why do it?

What we are to learn here is this: Worry is a choice. It is a choice we make. We can choose to worry or not to worry. You can become in bondage to the thought, *What if this happens?* and lose time and energy and sleep. Or, you can let God do the worrying for you. Here is my advice for you and me, to say: "God, I know You know the future and how things will turn out. I choose to leave this with You—from this moment. Amen."

Worry is to be rejected as resisting the devil. See the face of Satan when worry seizes you. Worry is the devil's opportunity to move in and control. Learn to recognize this when worry becomes a preoccupation. It gives the devil entrance into our minds and spirits he doesn't deserve. Again, we do well to remember the 3 R's of spiritual warfare: recognize, refuse, resist. Recognize the devil when worry overcomes you. Refuse to think about what the devil wants you to worry about. Don't give him this pleasure. Resist him, resist him, resist him. Claim the Scripture: Resist the devil and he will flee from you (James 4:7). He will.

It is an opportunity to let God be God. Time is His domain. Learn to enjoy not knowing what the turnout will be by knowing that He knows! Trust Him, rely on Him. Don't miss the reward that is promised: "Without faith it is impossible to please God, because anyone who comes to him must believe that he exists and that he rewards those who earnestly seek him" (Hebrews 11:6). Don't forfeit that reward by giving up and giving in . . . to worry. Worry must therefore be resisted the way you resist the devil. Faith must be pursued because you want to please God.

Replace worry with worship. Sing hymns and choruses. When you get to heaven and watch a DVD of yourself singing like that, you will see (I guarantee it) the angels gathered around you.

Worry is what the devil does best. He knows that his time is short (Revelation 12:12). The next time the devil reminds you of your past, remind him of his future! He has a lot to worry about. He wants to make you worry. I repeat: Don't give him this pleasure.

Release your worry to God. Take Him seriously. Say to Him: "Heavenly Father, I can't handle this anxiety. You said for me to cast it on You. I do it right now as best as I know how. I give it to You. Take it, it's Yours. In Jesus' name. Amen."

May God grant you the grace to do this. And keep doing it. It honors Him. He will give you that rest of soul (Matthew 11:29). He is never too late, never too early, but always just on time.

63. Worry and Appearances

And why do you worry about clothes? See how the lilies of the field grow. They do not labor or spin. Yet I tell you that not even Solomon in all his splendor was dressed like one of these. If that is how God clothes the grass of the field, which is here today and tomorrow is thrown into the fire, will he not much more clothe you, O you of little faith?

MATTHEW 6:28–30

We have seen that clothing basically serves two purposes: a covering for warmth but also for our dignity—to protect from nakedness. However, Jesus introduces a thought that may surprise you. He brings in the matter of appearance. He might have left the issue with the bare need of warmth and covering for our dignity. But no. He refers to the beauty of the lilies of the field and brings in Solomon in all his splendor. This shows that sometimes the matter of need may be extended to comfort.

Then, does comfort sometimes also mean need? Yes. This is because, believe it or not, God wants us to feel good about ourselves. He does not want us to be ashamed in front of others when it comes to clothing. If all that matters is a covering for your nakedness, Jesus would have said so. But it is more than that—which is why Jesus brings in lilies and Solomon's glory.

Two Extremes

The devil would want us to go from one extreme to the other. One extreme is that the devil would not want you to care about your appearance at all. This is why some mentally ill people (or those who are demon-possessed) don't care about their appearances. Take a tramp who has lost hope for living a better life. He becomes content with a lack of concern for hygiene and a sense of dignity. A child of God should never look like that.

But the other extreme is that one's pride motivates him or her to live entirely for appearance—to get people to take notice of his or her clothes. People like this sometimes dress to make others jealous. This is not glorifying to God. Jesus made light of the Pharisees, who did everything for

people to notice, including flamboyantly making their phylacteries "wide and the tassels on their garments long" (Matthew 23:5). So if the devil will bring you to where you don't care about your appearance at all, he's happy. If you live to make people admire you because of your clothes, this, too, pleases Satan.

Having lived in Britain for a good number of years, Louise and I were shocked at the way so many Christians live in America. We were invited to attend a huge convention. I was a speaker. But Louise was cautioned that she would need a different outfit to wear for each service! Those who were with us were utterly consumed with appearance. They put on their makeup every five minutes (it seemed) and rushed back to the hotel to change clothes for the next service. We did not realize how British we had become! But we were at the same time saddened to see good, sincere Christians become so preoccupied with their clothes and appearance.

When you think of "lilies of the field," you may have a beautiful Easter lily in mind. But almost certainly Jesus was referring to a wildflower that does not stand out, but nonetheless beautifully blends in with the grass of the fields. Beautiful in its own way, but not ostentatious—even surpassing Solomon in his glory!

And yet I will never forget seeing people in East Germany, Poland and the old Soviet Union in the days before the Iron Curtain fell. They all looked the same. Their clothes were a dismal gray, brown or black. They had no choice of color or style in their clothes. They only had the essentials to keep warm. It suggested to me that the satanic regime that kept everybody in check made sure they all looked alike. There was no personal dignity or sense of freedom.

God loves color and beauty. Jesus would not have mentioned the lilies of the field or Solomon's splendor had He not intended to send a signal that God wants His people to look nice and maintain a sense of self-respect and dignity. It therefore shows that need may sometimes imply comfort. God does care how we look! Communism kills not only national identity but a personal sense of worth. Every country has its culture and favorite colors. A totalitarian regime kills things like that. What is lovelier than the distinctions and individuality of any culture—Swiss, Norwegian, Brazilian, Nigerian, Spanish?

It is my view we should avoid the extremes between a slavish preoccupation with appearance on the one hand and loss of personal dignity on the other. I think of God's word to Samuel: "Do not consider his appearance or his height, for I have rejected him. The LORD does not look at the things man looks at. Man looks at the outward appearance, but the LORD looks at the heart" (1 Samuel 16:7).

And yet God does not want us to feel uncomfortable about our appearance. Like it or not, people do notice what we wear. I recall a traumatic experience when I was about fourteen years old, playing basketball with my team before hundreds of people. I forgot to bring socks to wear with my basketball shoes. My girlfriend was in the audience. There I was playing the game with no socks! I don't know whether we won or lost, but I remember how embarrassed I felt. Whereas the word *stigma* ("offense") is something we bear for the Gospel—and it largely means embarrassment—being self-conscious because of our appearance is not an embarrassment God has in mind for us.

If we worry about our appearance because we look shabby or uncaring, it detracts from what we are called to do. God is able to dress us to any standard of measurement He is pleased to do. He is the one who made flowers. He put Solomon on the throne. God can make you and me as attractive as anything He created—or as glorious as any king or queen. God will dress us as we need to be dressed. He doesn't want any to feel ashamed. That is the way Adam and Eve felt (Genesis 3:7).

Being confident (or unembarrassed) in our appearance is a need He will supply. Confidence is not a luxury. Confidence is a need He will supply.

Why Does Jesus Stay on This Subject?

These verses are, in fact, an elaboration of what Jesus has said already. He keeps on emphasizing that we should not worry. In a sense He says nothing new. So why does He continue along the same line? Because it is so important that we are set free from worry.

The answer is also that we will see His comments about not worrying were not an offhand, throwaway remark—but that the issue of worry is important to us and to God. Jesus actually spends more time on the matter of worry than He does the issues of lust, adultery, divorce and remarriage. He gives more space to worry than He does to oaths and the name of God. We may quickly conclude, therefore, that when He says, "Do not worry about your life, what you will eat or drink; or about your body, what you will wear," it was not a passing thought. Jesus knows our frame, our need, our concerns, our heart. The Father knows this. Jesus is echoing all that the Father told Him to say (John 5:19).

Jesus thus gives ten verses in the Sermon on the Mount to the subject of worry, that we might see the importance of trust in God when it comes to our financial security. He concludes: "If that is how God clothes the grass of the field, which is here today and tomorrow is thrown into the fire, will he not much more clothe you, O you of little faith?" If we become fully convinced how much God assumes the responsibility for supplying our needs, I think we would get to the place where we really do turn these matters over to Him! It is what He wants us to do.

The lilies of the field do not "labor or spin." These words are intended to encourage us. Lilies don't worry or fret. Neither should we. This may be new teaching for some. It might well have been new teaching for Jesus' hearers in Galilee. It may be partly what contributed to their amazement and astonishment (see Matthew 7:28–29). And yet although His teaching is so encouraging—and worrying is so counterproductive—it still isn't easy to stop worrying. Jesus knows that. He therefore spends a lot of time on this subject.

Think, too, about this: Our clothes tell a lot about us. They are not merely a covering from coldness or nakedness. They reveal more than we perhaps imagined—our class, for example. We indicate our status, our culture, even our background. Some people in Britain try to hide this. They "dress down," especially the gentry, looking as ordinary as they possibly can.

I recall sitting with an Arab guide in Jericho a few years ago. He said to me, "Look at all those Brits getting off that bus." He was right—they were British. Then he said, "Look at all those Swedes getting off that other bus." I said, "How do you know they are Swedes?" He could only say, "Well, look at them—it's obvious." So I walked over to the bus and asked where they are from. "We are from Sweden," they said proudly. So I said to this Arab, "Tell me where I am from." He replied: "From England." Oh well—I was wearing a British mac!

Your job may require that you dress in a certain way. If you don't, you could lose credibility. Clothes reveal your confidence. Essential to faith is confidence—and if your clothes make you feel awkward or strange, you might lose a bit of confidence. David could not fight Goliath in Saul's armor. And all of us must be at ease and at home with our dress. David had to be comfortable in fighting God's battles, and God wants us to be like that, too.

Jesus' Examples

He mentions lilies. Lilies were not beautiful like a rose, a tulip or an iris (my favorite flower). He is talking about the plainest flower imaginable. The lilies of the field were probably never used for bouquets. The lilies that Jesus refers to had no problem of trying to keep up appearances! They "do not labor or spin." You don't use these lilies to create fabric.

Consider a little flower like this—its texture, petals, form, design and color. In comparison with other flowers, these lilies were so lackluster. And Jesus said that even Solomon in all his glory was not dressed like one of these. "If that is how God clothes the grass of the field, which is here today and tomorrow is thrown into the fire, will he not much more clothe you, O you of little faith?" Grass and lilies of the field were used for fuel. They were cut down, dried out and thrown into fire.

Here is Jesus' point: Lilies of the field are largely unnoticed and temporary. They are certainly not made in the image of God. And yet God takes care of them. This means that all you see in nature—birds, flowers, trees, animals, beautiful lakes and streams, mountains and the sea—are looked after by our heavenly Father. God is behind all creation, "sustaining all things by his powerful word" (Hebrews 1:3). He nourishes and upholds creation and its beauty day and night, while you and I are asleep. Keep in mind that nothing in all God's creation was made in His image—only man. And yet God looks after birds, flowers and trees, etc.

Jesus then mentions Solomon. First came an example from nature—now comes an example of fame and wealth. Solomon is an example of pomp, glory and money. Jesus extols His heavenly Father's creative ability. The wildflower that clothes the field is probably one of the plainest examples of all flowers. But nature at its plainest is lovelier than man at his best (insofar as wealth and pomp go). See 1 Kings 4:20–34 and 2 Chronicles 1:7–17 for a description of Solomon's wealth.

And so we have it: Nature at its plainest is greater than man at his finest. And that is how God will keep you and me from being embarrassed or shamed. All this is to say nothing about Solomon's Temple. And have you ever considered Ezekiel's Temple (Ezekiel 41–43)? It is an example of what God was willing to do for Israel—amazing plans He had for them! He takes the same care for us, too. We also could miss what God would do for us, if we take our lives into our hands and ignore this invitation from Jesus to let His Father do the worrying for us.

Jesus' further point is to explain to us how this wild lily of the field is looked after. "If God clothes the grass of the field, which is here today and tomorrow is thrown into the fire, will he not much more clothe you, O you of little faith?" Here is what Dr. Martyn Lloyd-Jones says about these lines: "The flower that is never perhaps seen during the whole of its brief existence in this world, and which seemingly wastes its sweetness to the desert air, is nevertheless perfectly clothed by God."

So, if God does this for the most insignificant flower, how foolish are you and I to worry! That is Jesus' ultimate point. We are foolish because of our lack of faith.

He ends with this exhortation: "O you of little faith?"

> Said the robin to the sparrow, "I should
>   really like to know
> Why these anxious human beings rush
>   about to worry so."
> Said the sparrow to the robin, "Friend,
>   I think that it must be
> That they have no heavenly Father,
>   such as care for you and me."

The truth is, the birds have no heavenly Father. Nor do flowers. Jesus doesn't say that *their* heavenly Father feeds them. It is *your* Father, says Jesus. Birds are not self-conscious. Flowers are not self-conscious. They are not self-conscious regarding their appearance, as you and I are. And yet we are prone to worry about things like that, and God knows it. When we get to heaven, we will find out that the things that concerned us concerned Him as well—when we are embarrassed, when we are hurt, when someone says something cutting about us. He feels it, too.

Therefore, what is essential to our self-esteem and ability to function, God calls *need*. And that is precisely what He promises to supply! When these things get on top of us, our heavenly Father steps in and gently seeks our attention, to tell us, "Leave it to Me."

64. Faith and Weakness

> If that is how God clothes the grass of the field, which is here today and tomorrow is thrown into the fire, will he not much more clothe you, O you of little faith? So do not worry, saying, "What shall we eat?" or "What shall we drink?" or "What shall we wear?" For the pagans run after all these things, and your heavenly Father knows that you need them.

MATTHEW 6:30–32

I want to focus on the famous phrase of Jesus, "O you of little faith?" It comes from the Greek word *oligopistos*. It is a word He uses only here in the Sermon on the Mount, but it is found three other times in Matthew (8:26; 14:31; 16:8) and in Luke 12:28.

Pistis is the Greek word for "faith"; *oligo* means "small" or "little." Having shown the unreasonableness of worry, Jesus now hurls a gentle, loving slap on the wrist. He addresses His hearers and implies they have little faith! And yet how does He know to say this? It is a sermon preached to thousands. Had He received feedback from His hearers that prompted Him to say this? No. He knows what we all are like! It is so comforting.

What is Jesus' aim and purpose by using this phrase? What is He trying to do? The answer is, not to judge us or moralize, but to help us to overcome worry and increase our faith. Worry is rooted in unbelief. "Without faith it is impossible to please God, because anyone who comes to him must believe that he exists and that he rewards those who earnestly seek him" (Hebrews 11:6). Worry is a sin and therefore grieves the Holy Spirit. Jesus wants to spare us of doing this. And yet He is amazingly gentle, knowing our frame and remembering that we are dust (Psalm 103:14).

Faith and weakness. Do you feel weak? Do you feel that your faith is weak? If so, I have good news for you: God never condemns the person who is weak in faith. Paul said, "Accept him whose faith is weak, without passing judgment on disputable matters" (Romans 14:1). Indeed, "We who are strong ought to bear with the failings of the weak and not to please ourselves" (Romans 15:1).

God does, however, commend those who are strong in faith. "I tell you the truth, I have not found anyone in Israel with such great faith" (Matthew 8:10). Jesus said to the woman who persevered to get His attention, "You have great faith! Your request is granted" (Matthew 15:28). But He never condemns the weak. "A bruised reed he will not break, and a smoldering wick he will not snuff out, till he leads justice to victory" (Matthew 12:20).

This gentle, nonthreatening spirit of Jesus lies behind the admonition to come to the throne of grace to request "mercy" before anything else. When you ask for mercy, it is because you have no bargaining power—you have nothing to give in exchange. The sinner's prayer is, "God, have mercy on me" (Luke 18:13). We never outgrow the need for mercy. When we are conscious of our weaknesses and proneness to sin, we are therefore directed to come to the throne of grace—because mercy is our primary need (Hebrews 4:16). Indeed, a requirement of a high priest was that he would be able "to deal gently" with those who are ignorant and are going astray, since he himself is subject to weakness (Hebrews 5:2).

Assumption of Weakness

Keep in mind that there has been neither a dialogue nor any apparent activity by Jesus' hearers. And when these verses come up in Matthew later on, people's weakness was plain!

When Jesus was asleep on a boat during a violent storm, the disciples cried out, "Lord, save us!

We're going to drown." Jesus then replied, "You of little faith, why are you so afraid?" (Matthew 8:25–26). When Peter was walking on water but starting to sink, he cried out, "Lord, save me!" Immediately, Jesus reached out His hand and caught him. He did not say, "You scoundrel, you weak, pitiful man." No. I think there was a smile on Jesus' face when He lovingly said, "You of little faith, why did you doubt?" (Matthew 14:30–32).

Jesus said "You of little faith" to His disciples when they did not discern the point He was making regarding the "yeast of the Pharisees and Sadducees" (Matthew 16:6–8). There was one other time Jesus comes close to using this word. It is when the disciples asked why they could not cast out a demon. He answered, "Because you have so little faith" (Matthew 17:19–20).

But in the Sermon on the Mount, His hearers had not said a single word. And yet Jesus says, "O you of little faith." It lets us know that God assumes all of us are weak in faith. As Gerald Coates used to say: God never gets disillusioned with us; He never had any illusions about us in the first place!

This is why the common people heard Jesus gladly. It is why "all the people hung on his words" (Luke 19:48). I have prayed that I could be like that. To preach without moralizing, to accept people as they are without adding to the guilt they already have. Jesus knew what was in man (John 2:25). We all need to see those around us as bruised reeds, not towers of strength. It was Jesus' tenderness that attracted people to Him.

Jesus not only assumes His hearers are weak but accommodates His language to this. Why? Jesus accepts us as we are—to lead us to a greater faith. Rather than moralize or send us on a guilt trip, He takes us as we are. All that Jesus is saying in these ten verses pertaining to worry is aimed to help us to overcome it. So He accommodates us with tender instruction. He wants to increase our faith.

Jesus' Approach

So, how does Jesus approach us who have a weak faith with the view to increasing it? He uses reason! If God looks after nature—birds and flowers,

which are not created after God's image—how much more will God look after us human beings, who were indeed created in His image (Genesis 1:26)?

He appeals to our common sense from the beginning of this section. His reasoning runs along these lines. God takes responsibility for what is essential: life, the body (verse 25). We are not plants and animals, but human beings that are far more valuable than the rest of creation (verse 26). Not only that, worry does not even help us at the end of the day (verse 30). Jesus reasons rather than moralizes. He was that way with the Twelve and with Peter.

We may feel that His words are rebuking us, as if He is upset with us. But no. He fully understands. His words are aimed to affirm us, to lift us up and uphold us! It is like Jonah's chastening. Jonah felt the love of God in it all, including when Jonah was angry. God merely said, "Have you any right to be angry?" (Jonah 4:4). So, too, in the Sermon on the Mount, He discloses His aim: "Do not worry" (verse 31).

We are given a command not to worry. God does not ask us to do what cannot be done. He always supplies the grace to keep His word. "Command what Thou wilt," said Saint Augustine, "and give what Thou commandest." We are therefore charged with the responsibility not to worry. God begins where we are. But He doesn't leave us there. He brings us to the place where we can carry out our responsibility.

I am told that I started walking when I was twelve months old. My parents tied a towel around my waist and walked behind me. Then they stopped walking and let me continue, since I thought they were right there because I could feel the towel. Jesus wants to teach us all to walk. What begins as seemingly insurmountable is in fact doable.

This is true with all Jesus puts to us—including forgiving our enemies. It seems impossible at first—but once we take a step, God gives grace. So, too, with worry. Little by little we grow up. We mature. Believing Jesus' words, then, becomes our responsibility. "Then we will no longer be infants, tossed back and forth by the waves, and blown here and there by every wind of teaching" (Ephesians 4:14).

What Is a Weak Faith?

It is worth noting that Jesus did not say, "O you of *no* faith." He said "little faith." Big difference! What is "little" faith? It is saving faith without achieving faith.

It is good to be reminded, too, that there are basically two kinds of faith: saving faith and achieving faith. *Saving faith* is a positive response to the Gospel—when we accept the Good News that Jesus paid our debt on the cross. It does not take great faith to be saved—it takes faith in a great Savior! *Achieving faith* is what follows saving faith. It is believing God after you have become a Christian. Between the time of our conversion and the moment of our glorification (when we see Jesus face-to-face), we continue to believe God in all that He has commanded and promised. Hebrews 11 is not a description of saving faith. It provides a list of those who achieved things through faith.

Those who have "little" faith are saved. John Calvin used the term "implicit" faith to describe those who were saved but who had not developed very much. I would say "little" faith is believing God as Savior but not sufficiently in God as Provider. It is believing God as Redeemer but not God as Vindicator. Saving faith is trusting what God did for you 2,000 years ago. Achieving faith is trusting God to supply your need *today.*

In a word: Saving faith gets you to heaven; achieving faith takes care of you on earth. When you worry, saying, "What shall we eat?" or "What shall we drink?" or "What shall we wear?" your faith is hardly beyond the thinking of the pagans!

Pagans worry about things like that, says Jesus. We—His followers—ought to be a cut above the pagans! They worry, yes. But so do you, says Jesus. They panic. But we do, too, says our Lord.

We should be different from pagans. We are of incalculable value. We are made in God's image—and God therefore takes the responsibility for our need. He even takes care of birds and flowers! Worry, then, is right against common sense. God will look after us—providing us with food, a job, a place to live and whatever else is essential to our confidence and self-esteem.

Antidote to a Weak Faith

What do we do when we are conscious of our weak faith? I answer: Focus on God. "Your heavenly Father knows that you need them"—that is, food, shelter and clothing. God will take care of you. Focus on God your Father; He belongs to you. He not only made you but bought you with the price of the blood of His Son (1 Corinthians 6:20). You are adopted into His family (Ephesians 1:4–5). You are as secure in Him as He is in the Godhead.

Focus on His omniscience. "Your heavenly Father knows you that you need them." He knows. He knows everything. He who looks after lilies, birds, grass and trees—and knows every blade of grass and every leaf on every tree—knows you. He knows you backward and forward. He knows your need exactly. And He promises to look after you to the hilt. "My God will meet all your needs according to his glorious riches in Christ Jesus" (Philippians 4:19). It was true for Paul. It is true for you. It was true then. It is true now.

65. First Things First

But seek first his kingdom and his righteousness, and all
these things will be given to you as well.

MATTHEW 6:33

This was my dad's favorite verse. I virtually grew up on it. He quoted it all the time. He lived by it. He truly believed that if you put God first, you would not have to worry about anything else.

My father was never a wealthy man. He worked as a rate clerk for the Chesapeake and Ohio Railway Company. I can recall that his salary was $8 a day, $40 a week, for many years. He always tithed—he literally gave $4 weekly to his church in Ashland, Kentucky. He reckoned that the 90 percent we keep for ourselves after giving God His 10 percent goes as far as the 100 percent we started with. He sometimes wondered if it went even further than the 100 percent!

In my hometown of Ashland, we were what might be called lower middle class. All I know is, we had all we needed. I do not recall wanting for a single thing. My father was also a preacher's dream: He loved preachers and respected them with an awe that is possibly rare. He supported his pastor to the fullest degree possible. He was always in church, three times a week—Sunday morning and evening and Wednesday prayer meeting. He taught a Sunday school class, never felt called to preach. He prayed thirty minutes every morning before going to work. He lived by Matthew 6:33. He was really a very pragmatic sort of man. He believed that Christianity works!

This verse summed up means: Put God first, and you will have all you need.

I suppose there is more than one way of being motivated to come to the Christian faith. Some would testify it is the best thing that ever happened to them—that they have never been sorry and that they highly recommend that others come to the Lord—mainly because of what it does for you. I know what they mean by that. But the most moving statement I ever heard along this line came from Joni Eareckson Tada, the woman who became a quadriplegic through a swimming accident. She said, "I am not a Christian because of what it does for me. I am a Christian because it is true."

Matthew 6:33 is truly one of the great promises of Scripture. It ranks alongside Romans 8:28, Philippians 4:6 and John 3:16 (which Martin Luther called the Bible in a nutshell). This is one of those verses that can be understood in its context or out of it. Some verses must be understood only in their context, or they will not be truly understood. But Matthew 6:33, which we will look at in its context, reads by itself and stands by itself. Believe it!

The context, as we know by now, is the matter of worry. Do not worry, says Jesus. Food, shelter and clothing are items God has on His prayer list for us. He has obligated Himself to look after us in the essentials. Even out of context, the verse covers all we need, ever. Get your priorities right, says Jesus, and all else falls into place. Those who place a priority on material things—prestige, earthly honors and a huge savings account at the bank—won't like this verse very much. But to the person who already wants to put God in his or her life, this verse is an almost unexpected bonus. If you had not sought for material things but God in the first place, here comes a wonderful surprise: God is going to look after your physical, material needs as well!

Solomon's Request

God came to Solomon and asked him what he wanted. This was Solomon's moment—he could have had anything. Solomon's reply was: "Give your servant a discerning heart to govern your people and to distinguish between right and wrong. For who is able to govern this great people of yours?" (1 Kings 3:9).

God was pleased with this request. Lo and behold, God responded to Solomon in a wonderful and extraordinary manner. "Since you have asked for this and not for long life or wealth for yourself, nor have asked for the death of your enemies but for discernment in administering justice, I will do what you have asked. I will give you a wise and discerning heart, so that there will never have been anyone like you, nor will there ever be. Moreover, I will give you what you have not asked for—both riches and honor—so that in your lifetime you will have no equal among kings" (1 Kings 3:11–13).

We learn from this account that it is prudent and shrewd to please God by your requests to Him. Jesus reveals some very valuable information to us—we are foolish to ignore it. It is a very simple formula: Seek God and His righteousness, and you will have everything you want. That's it.

A Pursuit

"Seek," says Jesus. The word *seek* means to make a search for, to try to find or obtain. Two things are implied: time and effort. It may take time.

This is not a "quick fix" verse—it refers to a lifestyle. It is not a verse that says, "Try seeking God today if you want material things." No. It is a lifetime pursuit. It is a way of living. What makes a search a search is that it may not result in immediate success, if at all. In the ancient Hellenistic world, this Greek word (*zeeteo*) referred to a philosophical investigation that could mean a lifelong pursuit. It means making an effort. This means energy is needed. What you want to find isn't going to come to you—you must go to it.

Had Jesus said, "Receive the Kingdom of God" instead of "seek first his kingdom," that would have meant we do nothing. We just take it and say, "Thank You very much." Thus, by accepting what is offered, the promise of getting our material needs would be ours—no need to worry. But no. Jesus said, "*Seek* first his kingdom." It is a pursuit.

This Greek word *zeeteo* (used 119 times in the New Testament) was often used in terms of God seeking man. For example, "The Son of man came to *seek* and to save what was lost" (Luke 19:10, emphasis mine). As to philosophical investigation,

"Greeks *look for* wisdom" (1 Corinthians 1:22, emphasis mine). It is used in Hebrews 11:6: "Without faith it is impossible to please God, because anyone who comes to him must believe that he exists and that he rewards those who earnestly *seek* him" (emphasis mine). And if Matthew 6:33 was my dad's favorite verse, the one that I have sought more than any other to be governed by over the past fifty years is John 6:44: "How can you believe, which receive honour one of another, and seek not the honour that cometh from God only?" (John 5:44, KJV).

What is fascinating is that nothing is said about finding the Kingdom! Jesus does not mention finding the Kingdom before you get the benefit of this promise. All we are asked to do is to pursue it! Pursue, not find, the Kingdom of God first—seek the Kingdom and these things will be added. Our task is to seek. God's task is to add those things such as food, shelter and clothing.

Priority

But notice that Jesus said, "Seek *first* his kingdom." Had Jesus not added this word "first," one could regard the Kingdom of God as you would a shopping list. One could pursue the Kingdom of God while pursuing your job, trying to get a raise in pay; pursuing a hobby, recreation, entertainment; pursuing friendships or seeking after a bit of prestige. This would mean that seeking the Kingdom of God is on your list of things you hope eventually to get done: redecorate your home, read more, get more exercise, get more education, work in your garden.

The word *first* is used two other times in the Sermon on the Mount. It means no postponing. When you remember that your brother has something against you, "First go and be reconciled to your brother" (Matthew 5:24). When you see the speck of sawdust in your brother's eye, "first take the plank out of your own eye" (Matthew 7:5). Don't postpone what is clearly your duty. So, "Seek the LORD while he may he found; call on him while he is near" (Isaiah 55:6).

David said, "One thing I ask of the LORD, this is what I seek: that I may dwell in the house of the LORD all the days of my life, to gaze upon the beauty of the LORD and to seek him in his temple" (Psalm 27:4). Priority means what you regard as having precedence over in the whole of your life—24 hours a day.

Privilege

You will recall that the Kingdom of God is the realm of the un-grieved Spirit. It means the anointing. We are talking about the very presence of God. It is not a place, like a church or something political. It is the immediate and direct presence of the Holy Spirit.

It also means the power of the Spirit. Power and the Holy Spirit are sometimes used interchangeably. "You will receive power when the Holy Spirit comes on you" (Acts 1:8). "The kingdom of God is not a matter of talk but of power" (1 Corinthians 4:20). There is a legitimate seeking of power. Jacob said to God, "I will not let you go unless you bless me," and God replied, "You have struggled with God . . . and have overcome" ("You have power with God"—Genesis 32:28).

What Jesus is saying is this: Your relationship with God is more important than anything else. Spending time with God is more important than anything else. The will of God is more important than anything else. The glory of God and seeking God's honor are more important than anything else.

Seeking His face is your most important pursuit. Finding out what pleases Him is your most important discovery. The esteem you place on your relationship with God is your most important sense of value. Most of all, it is such a privilege to get to do this!

Purity

"And his righteousness," adds Jesus. Notice it says "his" righteousness, not "its." It is not righteousness of the Kingdom—it is His, God's, righteousness.

This means a relationship with God Himself. "And" is put there to emphasize that it is God Himself you are seeking. It is not a vain search, moreover. "But if from there you seek the LORD your God, you will find him if you look for him with all your heart and with all your soul" (Deuteronomy 4:29). "You will seek me and find me when you seek me with all your heart" (Jeremiah 29:13).

Righteousness is to be defined here as *keeping His commands*. It is not (in this case) "imputed" righteousness. You don't need to seek that. Imputed, or credited, righteousness is instantaneously put to your credit the moment you rely on Jesus' death on the cross for your salvation and forgiveness. The righteousness of Matthew 6:33 is getting to know God so well that you know what pleases Him. This knowledge comes from three things: (1) spending time with Him in prayer, (2) reading His Word—the Bible—faithfully every day and (3) walking in the light God gives you as you listen to His voice. This righteousness, when summed up, means *purity*. Blessed are the pure in heart, said Jesus, for they will see God (Matthew 5:8).

Promise

"All these things will be given to you as well." That is what comes to you when you seek God's Kingdom and His righteousness first. You receive the very things you worried about. By asking God for more of Himself rather than material things, although essential, God will give you more of Himself—plus the very things you put to one side because God meant more to you than anything else.

There are two kinds of promises: conditional and unconditional. Conditional is usually preceded by the word *if*. It will be implied even if there is no word *if*. But unconditional promise has no conditions. Like the Second Coming of Jesus, He will come one day, ready or not.

Matthew 6:33 is conditional promise. "If," though not explicitly inserted in this verse, is nonetheless implied. The assumption is that you have sought the Kingdom of God and His righteousness. If you haven't, then sadly the promise does not apply to you. God puts His integrity on the line. If you put God first, you will be taken care of. Put God first, and your needs will be supplied.

I had an uncle who developed a brain tumor. He asked the church to pray for him to be healed. He vowed to give $10,000 to the church if he was healed. I don't say he was right to do that, I am only reporting what he decided to. As it happened, he was miraculously healed. But he never gave the $10,000. He should have kept his word.

Years later, he developed a mental condition and went to his death in total insanity. The Bible says it is better not to make a vow than make it and not pay it (Ecclesiastes 5:4).

Provisions

"All these things will be given to you as well." You will recall the context of this verse: worrying about the essentials of life—food, shelter and clothing. What Jesus is saying is this: Don't worry about food, shelter and clothing—these are God's problem. What you should worry about is whether your priority in life is to know God better and to perfect your relationship with Him. When that is in order, you have a promise you can claim as yours because you met the condition. The provision is: God will take care of you.

Principle

There is a subtle principle here: Forget about "all these things" and you will receive them. Seek these things and they will elude you. Seek success and you will not find it. Seek God and forget about success, and He will bless you more than you dreamed. Seek vindication and you will not find it. Seek God and forget about vindication, and it will come to you in an hour when you were not thinking about it. That's the way it is!

Jesus later said, "For whoever wants to save his life will lose it, but whoever loses his life for me will find it" (Matthew 16:25). "The man who loves his life will lose it, while the man who hates his life [that is, loves his life less] in this world will keep it for eternal life" (John 12:25).

The principle is exactly the same as we saw with Solomon. Solomon could have asked for fame and fortune, but he didn't. He sought God's favor by asking for wisdom. God gave him wisdom—but He added fame and fortune to exceed all Solomon could have ever imagined.

You might find this hard to do. But it really isn't. If you commit—today, right now—to seek God's face and think of what pleases Him, God

will work behind the scenes in your behalf. But you must not keep looking over your shoulder with the view of "what's in it for me?" That would betray that you are seeking "these things" first. I ask you now to commit to these three things: spending time with God daily, reading the Bible daily and walking in all the light He gives you. Make this a priority. Forget about everything else. Seek His face with all your heart. And you will find out what my dad always said was true: It works!

However, if you try it for a day or two—or a week or two, or month or two—just to see if it works, you disqualify yourself. It betrays that your heart is not bent on seeking God's face but His hand (i.e., what He can do for you).

I regularly recommended to the members of Westminster Chapel that they pray for thirty minutes (including both prayer and Bible reading). Seek first His Kingdom—spend time with Him. You will not regret one minute you spent alone with God when you face Him at the Judgment Seat of Christ. Seeking His Kingdom and righteousness means time with Him. It also means obeying Him when He puts His finger on something in your life—what you might have to give up and what you may have to start doing.

A pivotal moment for me was practicing total forgiveness—that is, forgiving every single person who had done me wrong. Another pivotal moment for me was when I knew I had to start the Pilot Light ministry at Westminster Chapel. I have sought to do everything and anything God required of me. I walked in the light. That means taking with both hands anything God shows you. By the way, His commands are not burdensome (1 John 5:3). Take His yoke upon you and learn of Him, and you will find rest to your soul (Matthew 11:29). Then you discover along the way—surprise, surprise!—all your needs were met as well.

I think my dad picked a pretty good verse to live by. The Christian faith works.

66. Afraid of the Future?

Therefore do not worry about tomorrow, for tomorrow will worry about itself. Each day has enough trouble of its own.

MATTHEW 6:34

This is our Lord's final comment on worry in this part of the Sermon on the Mount. We have been looking at His analysis of worry that began with Matthew 6:25. Dr. Martyn Lloyd-Jones observed, "You will not find anywhere in any textbook a more thorough analysis of worry, anxiety and the anxious care that tends to kill man in this world."

Does it surprise you that so much attention is given to this subject? Why does Jesus spend so much time on the issue? First, God knows we worry and wants to help us to overcome it. Second, to worry is to sin, being the result of a lack of faith. Third, worry doesn't help—it is unnecessary to worry. The things we tend to worry about, God takes the responsibility for.

In this chapter, we see some further reasons we should not worry. You might have thought that Matthew 6:33 ended the discussion on worry. But Jesus is not finished. What we have in verse 34 is like a "P.S." at the end of a letter. But it is a most important statement. However, after saying what He does in this verse, Jesus closes down this section and changes the subject.

Matthew 6:34 contains three short sentences: (1) Do not worry about tomorrow. (2) Tomorrow will worry about itself. (3) Each day has enough trouble of its own. We learn from this verse that we should live one day at a time. There is no need to add to the troubles each day brings. One day's trouble is enough for one day.

What This Verse Does Not Mean

Before we pursue this verse, there are three things it does not mean. First, it does not mean we shouldn't make plans. Jesus implied the importance of planning ahead in one of His parables: "Suppose one of you wants to build a tower. Will he not first sit down and estimate the cost

to see if he has enough money to complete it?" Otherwise one could be ridiculed: "This fellow began to build and was not able to finish" (Luke 14:28–30). Second, Matthew 6:34 does not mean we shouldn't take precautions. We ought to say, "If it is the Lord's will, we will live and do this or that" (James 4:15). Third, this verse does not mean we shouldn't think about tomorrow.

When I first prepared this chapter as a sermon, Louise asked me, "What are you preaching on tomorrow?" I replied: "Take no thought for tomorrow." She answered: "Then why are you preparing the sermon?" I had quoted "take no thought for the morrow" from the King James Version! But the word *thought* is a translation of the Greek word meaning "anxious." The point is, we all have to think about tomorrow. But Jesus is telling us not to be anxious—that is, nervous or fearful—about tomorrow.

Jesus has given mainly theological reasons up to now for not worrying: (1) God takes the responsibility to supply our need, (2) God's love and compassion for us, (3) worry stems from unbelief and (4) worrying should be brought under the role of God's Kingdom in our lives. In addition to this, Jesus has given pragmatic reasons not to worry: Worrying doesn't help! Worrying is even counterproductive. Not only that, worrying about food, shelter and clothing puts you in the class of pagans—which is beneath a child of God!

But in this chapter we are to see the P.S. that shows yet another powerful reason we should not worry.

Fear of the Future

We have seen that the root of worry is unbelief, generally. But in particular, it is derived from fear—the fear of the future. We worry about what might yet happen—or not happen.

We are in the "not yet" of our lives. All worry is in a sense to be understood as concern about the future. We worry about the essentials—food, shelter, clothing—and whether we will be provided for. We worry about finances; will we have enough to live on? Even our worry about the past is largely worry over the future; how will past mistakes affect our future? Even guilt has a way of making us worry as to what hasn't yet happened.

This is why Jesus says "tomorrow" in verse 34. He is referring to the "not yet"—five minutes from now, five hours from now, or tomorrow. We worry over the outcome of things. It isn't what is happening now—it is what we anticipate, what might happen, what could happen. This is the root of worry: fear of the future.

Fear of Failure

One of the most powerful fears in the world is this: "Will I make it? Will things turn out all right?" I recall hearing Ron Dunn tell of his anticipation of preaching to a group of pastors. He asked the man who invited him: "What should I speak on to these pastors?" The man's reply to Ron: "They only need to know that they are going to make it through their present trial." Many of them were in severe ordeals, having all kinds of problems personally and difficulties in their churches.

Fear of the future: Will I make it? Will I succeed? As I said earlier, my whole time at Oxford was eclipsed by the fear that I could come across the Atlantic with my wife and children, spend three years working day and night on my thesis, then fail entirely. Could that have happened? Yes. It did with many of my friends around me. And all of them seemed brighter than I. One of them had a first-class honors degree from Edinburgh University. He failed. One of them had a Ph.D. already from an American seminary. He failed. Here I was from the hills of Kentucky, feeling vastly inferior to everybody! But I had a wife who kept encouraging me. She was convinced that God would not have led us to live in England for three years simply for me to fail.

One thing we can always remember: God never promotes us to the level of our incompetence. Ambition may do that; pride, too, may promote you to the level of your incompetence. But God doesn't. It may mean coming to terms with less prestige or less pay in order to take something you can do with ease. To dream the impossible dream is not the usual way God works. It is true that eye has not seen nor ear heard, neither has it entered into the heart of man what God has prepared for them that love Him (1 Corinthians 2:9). But we should never attempt to achieve beyond what is realistically possible.

Foreboding Fear

This is a feeling of evil ahead, that trouble is coming. The text refers to "trouble" (Gr. *kakia*—evil, malice). It brings in the idea of misfortune. As Dr. Martyn Lloyd-Jones put it, worry is a definite entity. It is a force, a power. We have not begun to understand it until we realize what a tremendous power worry is. The thing is, Satan seizes upon this. When he sees our anxiety, he exploits it to the hilt. Dr. Lloyd-Jones went so far as to say that "there are cases where worry is the work of evil spirits."

In a word: Satan takes advantage of our worry. He takes advantage of certain people. They may be in a low state physically. They may already be in a low state emotionally. The devil is ruthless and accepts no concept of fair play. He will exploit to no end one who is ill, handicapped, hurting or mentally stressed.

The fear of tomorrow, then—the fear of the "not yet"—is a vehicle Satan will ride in order to bring a person down. This is why worry is so serious. We should do all we can by the help of the Holy Spirit to overcome worry. There are three stages: (1) obsession—when you are consumed with the fear of tomorrow; (2) oppression—when the devil torments you by exploiting your fears; and (3) possession—when you have completely lost control and the devil has taken charge. The moment you feel oppressed, mark it down: That is not God, it is the devil.

Caution: Foreboding fear is a way Satan enters into our lives. There are a number of ways the devil can get into our lives. He can use lust that leads to sexual sin (Matthew 6:28). He can come in through unforgiveness (2 Corinthians 2:11). He can also intrude our lives when we are obsessed with a foreboding fear, by a preoccupation with misfortune coming upon us. This is why worry must be rejected at once. The moment worry intrudes, treat it as you would a poisonous snake: Run from it, refuse to think about it and resist it completely. Learn to recognize, refuse and resist the moment a negative anticipation enters your mind. It often begins with anticipation—namely, what could happen but hasn't, yet you imagine the worst scenario.

The Relentlessness of Worry

"Tomorrow will worry about itself. Each day has enough trouble of its own." Worry won't give up. It is not going away by itself. Why? There will always be something to worry about. Jesus says precisely this: "Each day has enough trouble of its own." Don't let tomorrow intrude. Today has enough to occupy our attention. Jesus is saying that life isn't perfect. Start adding tomorrow's possibilities to what you have on your plate today and you are asking for more trouble.

Michael Eaton has made the observation that Jesus talks about "tomorrow" as if it were a person. Let that person called Tomorrow do its own worrying, Jesus is saying. Tomorrow comes to us as a kind of demon wanting to seize and harass us. Worry, said Dr. Lloyd-Jones, always gives the impression that it does not really want to be relieved. Our Lord personifies worry when He talks about "tomorrow" taking thought for the things of itself. Worry is a power, almost a person who takes hold of you. In spite of yourself, it keeps arguing with you. It says one thing, then another. Worry has an active imagination. It can envisage all sorts of possibilities. It thinks of strange eventualities. It is a very convenient vehicle for Satan to ride.

The Rejection of Worry

"Take no thought" (Matthew 6:24, KJV). At the end of the day, the only way forward is to treat worry as you are commanded to treat the devil. Recognize it as being the vehicle of Satan. Often worry and the devil are the same. Refuse to think about what worries you. That is, don't let your mind even dignify the thought of worry. Resist it. Keep on resisting. Once the devil sees you are not going to listen to him, he will make his exodus. He will flee from you (James 4:7).

Treat worry as you would sexual temptation. Refuse to go there. Treat worry as you would an astrology chart. Refuse to look at it. Treat worry as you would a wild animal coming at you. Run from it. Treat it as you would an approaching violent storm. Stay away from it. The moment a worrisome thought emerges in your head, do whatever it takes not to entertain the thought. Don't give the devil the pleasure of seeing you cast down. And if the devil reminds you of what happens to be true? Again I quote William Perkins: "Don't believe the devil even when he tells the truth."

Remember that not to worry is our Lord's command. It is not a polite suggestion from Jesus that this is merely a rather better way to live. It is a command to set you free from a vicious habit. He wants to set you free from the need to worry. Furthermore, not to obey His command is to give place to the devil. You surely do not want to do that.

Worry is a spirit of fear. God has not given us a spirit of fear (2 Timothy 1:7). The devil comes as angel of light (2 Corinthians.11:14) and will make you think the worry that comes to you is from God. Wrong. Recognize any spirit that breeds fear: It is the devil at work. The devil can counterfeit the Holy Spirit. The fruit of the Holy Spirit is love, joy and peace (Galatians 5:22). The counterfeit will divert you from God's Word, prayer, goodness, peace, pleasantness and all those things that come from God (Philippians 4:8).

The devil will make you think worry is your friend, that it is there to protect you. Satan will make you think you are being irresponsible not to worry. The devil is a liar (John 8:44). Read and follow this carefully: Refuse and resist worry, because you are refusing and resisting your enemy the devil.

Fall on your knees in prayer. Read your Bible. Seek His face. Worrying is a bondage that must be broken, like any addiction. The worst thing you can do is to dignify what is the very breath of Satan.

Jesus closes this section by appealing to our common sense. Why worry over what might happen when you have enough to do today? Worrying about tomorrow only cripples you today—which is proof that the devil is behind your worrying.

In a word: Worrying doesn't even help. It is counterproductive.

God says to us as He did in ancient times: As your days, so will your strength be (Deuteronomy 33:25). Today's grace is sufficient for today only. Don't waste it on tomorrow! If tomorrow does bring new trouble, you will have grace for that, too.

Finally, nothing can happen without God's permission. "No temptation [or trial] has seized you except what is common to man. And God is faithful; he will not let you be tempted beyond what you can bear. But when you are tempted [or tried], he will also provide a way out so that you can stand up under it" (1 Corinthians 10:13). What God allows comes by His wisdom. "I am letting this happen because I have a purpose in mind," He says. As for the future, He is already there. He can report back to say: Don't worry.

67. Avoiding Criticism

Do not judge, or you too will be judged.

MATTHEW 7:1

Although Jesus now changes the subject as we enter Matthew 7, do not forget Matthew 5:48—"Be perfect, therefore, as your heavenly Father is perfect." This verse no doubt concluded what Jesus had been saying about the way the Law should be applied. But it nonetheless set the stage for maintaining a very high level of Christian maturity indeed, as we have seen in Matthew 6. Matthew 7:1 restates Matthew 5:7, "Blessed are the merciful, for they will be shown mercy." Being merciful is showing graciousness. Judging another person is the opposite of graciousness.

Never to judge another person is arguably the most difficult thing in the world to accomplish. I only know how hard it is for me! To put it another way, judging another is the easiest thing in the world to do. This is because we are all self-righteous and tend automatically to see the fault in others but not in ourselves. I am possibly dealing with my own greatest weakness. Again, I feel like a fraud in writing this chapter. Several years ago, I became so convicted of my tendency to judge people that I began reading Luke 6:37 every morning at the beginning of the day, with the hope that it would stem this tendency: "Do not judge, and you will not be judged. Do not condemn, and you will not be condemned. Forgive, and you will be forgiven." This verse (almost certainly) is taken from Luke's account of the same sermon that Matthew records.

Definition of Judging

I define judging as *uncalled-for criticism*. It is criticism that is either unfair or unjustified. The criticism may be true, but that does not make it right. If William Perkins can say, "Don't believe the devil even if he tells the truth," it is equally true that we should not mete out uncalled-for criticism—even if what we say is true. We could

even be the devil's instrument to another person. After all, he is called the "accuser of our brothers" (Revelation 12:10). Accusing is what he does! We should want to avoid being like the devil in every possible way.

N–E–E–D

I came up with an acrostic that apparently helped a number of people. It is based upon the premise that what we say should be designed to meet other people's need. If we do not meet their need, we should withhold our comments. But if we truly meet their need by what we are about to say, carry on.

There is a fairly good way to determine whether we are meeting other people's needs. You put these questions to yourself before uttering a comment:

Necessary? Is it truly necessary to say this?

Encourage? Will it uplift their heart?

Energize? Will it empower their spirit?

Dignify? Will it increase their self-esteem?

Alan Bell once said to me there are basically two types of people: those who drain you and those who energize you. I know what it is to spend time with a person and feel drained of any motivation when it is over. But there are also those who energize. I want to be an energizer. A good way to know which you will be the next time you spend time with a person is to put the acrostic N-E-E-D before you as you talk to them. Your goal: to build them up, not tear them down.

Remember that Satan's accusations are sometimes true. They are designed to bring us down and to discourage us. Let us pray that we will never be instruments of the devil. The devil never wants to meet a need in us—he wants to impoverish us, strip our self-esteem and makes us all the needier.

Why Did Jesus Give Us This Teaching?

The Greek word that is translated "judge" in Matthew 7:1 is *krino*. It means "to make a distinction." Being discriminate can, of course, be a wise thing to do. "The spiritual man makes judgments about all things," said Paul (1 Corinthians 2:15). But that is not what Jesus means in Matthew 7:1. He is talking about our judging people. Pointing the finger is man's way of playing God.

Why does Jesus give us this teaching? It is partly because judging grieves the Holy Spirit. The Kingdom of heaven is the realm of the Spirit. The degree to which the Holy Spirit is in us un-grieved and unquenched will be the degree to which we inherit and enjoy the realm of the Spirit. You might disagree, but I respectfully ask you to trace the cause and effect: Pointing of the finger tends to spring from bitterness. We forfeit our inheritance as long as we are being judgmental. Bitterness is the number-one way we tend to grieve the Spirit (Ephesians 4:30ff.).

Jesus also gave us this teaching for a practical reason: because judging is almost always counter-productive. It achieves the opposite aim it wanted. Judging, sooner or later, backfires. You begin by telling yourself, "I want to straighten this person out. This person needs to change, and I will change them." But in practice it usually offends the other person rather than helps them.

Moreover, the degree to which we resist the temptation to judge will be the degree to which we ourselves are largely spared of being judged. Do you like being judged? Do you enjoy receiving unfair criticism? Then don't judge! Being judged is painful, whether it is totally untrue or if it is true (in which case it adds to guilt).

Jesus, therefore, begins this section by appealing to our self-interest. The Greek word in Matthew 7:1 is *hina*, which means "in order that." Do not judge *in order that* you are not judged, says our Lord. You can protect yourself from being judged by stopping your pointing of the finger. It is a pragmatic reason for not judging others.

It is harder to say which is more painful: to be falsely accused or to be judged truthfully. Either way, we don't like it! So Jesus gives an aid

to how to win friends and influence people. Try it! Jesus' word not only keeps us from grieving the Holy Spirit, but helps us in all our relationships—our marriage, in the office, in the home, at church. One of the best ways to win friends is to stop keeping a record of wrongs (1 Corinthians 13:5).

In a word: Jesus is showing how we can spare ourselves from being judged. This is because we get it back if we judge others, whether friend or foe. Like it or not, it shows we are equally guilty when we judge—equal to the people we judge! We automatically put their backs up. Judging puts their backs up. They are going to be defensive and, probably, go on the offense.

God knows the true truth about each of us. He could throw the book at us anytime He chose to do it. When He sees us judging one another, He takes note of it Himself—and ensures we get it back one way or the other.

We should note other versions: "Don't criticize, and then you won't be criticized" (TLB). "Do not judge others, so that God will not judge you" (GNT). "Pass no judgment, and you will not be judged" (NEB). To quote Somerset Maugham, "When people ask for criticism, they really want praise."

A Practical Command

This is such a timely word. It is a word that applies to us at any given moment during a 24-hour span. Whenever I read this word, it is relevant. It is why I began reading Luke 6:37 every day. It is so easy to criticize. Finding fault does not require a university education. Those with the highest IQ, who have the most experience in research, who claim to be the most spiritual and who are well along in years find it easy to criticize—and hard not to.

Why? Because dishing out unfair criticism flows from our sinful, depraved and deceived hearts (Jeremiah 17:9). You might bristle at this, but it is what the Bible says about all of us. Jesus' word is practical because it invariably relates to the tongue. Read James 3 and see what He says about tongue control. None of us likes to be criticized. The practicality of this verse is that it shows how to avoid being criticized. Avoid doing it and you will avoid getting it!

Preventable Criticism

You may say, "I can't stop criticizing." But you can. You can stop yourself from pointing the finger all the time. How do you manage this? Here are three suggestions.

First, consider the blessing that is promised from not pointing the finger. If we do away with the "yoke of oppression, with the pointing finger and malicious talk," and if we spend ourselves in behalf of the hungry and satisfy the needs of the oppressed, "then your light will rise in the darkness, and your night will become like the noonday" (Isaiah 58:9–10). Second, consider the pleasant atmosphere you live in when it is devoid of criticism. "How good and pleasant it is when brothers live together in unity!" (Psalm 133:1). Third, if all else fails, consider the pain you get for criticizing. Do not judge and you will not be judged!

In a word: If you don't like criticism, don't criticize. I do not say you will never be criticized. I do say we can be spared of a lot of grief by tongue control. All our conversations should have a two-fold purpose: (1) to avoid criticizing and (2) to speak blessings. "Let your conversation be always full of grace, seasoned with salt, so that you may know how to answer everyone" (Colossians 4:6). "Do not repay evil with evil or insult with insult, but with blessing, because to this you were called so that you may inherit a blessing" (1 Peter 3:9).

Painful Consequence

There is, sadly, a painful consequence if we do not take Jesus' counsel: We will be judged. We will get it back. The Greek is in the subjunctive mood: "you should or might be judged." You *could* get away with it once in a while. But don't count on it. Uncalled-for criticism does two things: (1) It calls for a defensive reaction that usually leads to a counter charge, and (2) it gets God's attention— He gets into the act to ensure we are judged.

Luke 6:37 is actually a promise: "Do not judge, and you will not be judged. Do not condemn, and you will not be condemned. Forgive, and you will be forgiven." By the way, it works! Live this way and you will be spared unnecessary forest fires caused by lack of tongue control (James 3:5). And yet, according to Jesus, the painful consequence of pointing the finger is just. You asked for it!

There are, then, two levels of motivation for applying Matthew 7:1. First, the lower level: Spare yourself unnecessary warfare. This is not the highest sort of pursuit, but it is still suggested by our Lord as a way of staying out of trouble. The second level—the higher level—is that you avoid grieving the Holy Spirit because you place such a high value on your relationship with Him. Aim for this. Let not grieving the Spirit be what lies behind your conversations from this day forward.

68. Playing God

For in the same way you judge others, you will be judged, and
with the measure you use, it will be measured to you.

MATTHEW 7:2

These words are but a filling out or unpacking of Matthew 7:1: "Do not judge, or you too will be judged." Whereas Matthew 7:1 warns you will be judged if you offer uncalled-for criticism, verse 2 shows on what basis we will be judged. In a word: God gets involved and is behind the whole matter. "Because the judgments you give are the judgments you will get, and the standard you use will be the standard used for you" (NJB). "For God will judge you in the same way you judge others, and he will apply to you the same rules you apply to others" (GNT).

In the previous chapter, we saw two levels of motivation for not judging others: (1) the lower level, to keep from being judged by people; and (2) the higher level, to keep from grieving the Holy Spirit. The latter means we will be judged by God. That is what happens: When the Holy Spirit is grieved, God steps in and will, somehow, judge me. The moment I point the finger, I grieve the Spirit. Something also happens inside, even if I don't feel it for a day or two. Something closes down within—and it is only a matter of time before I realize I am operating under my own strength. I don't lose my salvation—having been sealed for the day of redemption (Ephesians 4:30). But I lose the presence of the mind of the Spirit. That means I don't think clearly and am therefore unable to see what is there. Furthermore, God does not bend the rules for any of us.

What This Verse Does Not Mean

This does not mean we are unable to see another's error or unfairness. We are not blind to their faults. We don't pretend not to see what is there. Neither do we live in denial, as if injustice did not take place. We certainly see what is wrong,

but we choose to keep no "record of wrongs" (1 Corinthians 13:5).

Neither does Matthew 7:2 mean that we never offer criticism, for there is a place after all for lovingly giving criticism. Faithful are the wounds of a friend (Proverbs 27:6), and we may be showing friendship by offering a critical but timely word. We must discern between truth and error, between goodness and evil. We are not required to contradict the way God made us—namely, having the ability to make value judgments. This very Sermon on the Mount assumes we will use our critical powers. For example, one cannot avoid seeing the silly façade of the righteousness of the Pharisees, neither are we blind to false prophets (as we will see later in Matthew 7). In Matthew 7:6, Jesus will say, "Do not give dogs what is sacred; do not throw your pearls to pigs"—which shows we must have discernment and keep our heads screwed on. Not only that, sometimes church discipline is necessary, when a person must be excommunicated from the local church (1 Corinthians 5:5).

What we are not allowed to do is offer uncalled-for criticism, or unjust criticism. John Stott says it comes down to the word *censoriousness*—that is, harsh criticism and extremely critical faultfinding. Jesus is opposing actively hurting other people's feelings. Calvin calls it inquiring curiously into people's affairs. It is claiming to know why people make certain choices. It is claiming to know why people make certain decisions—why they spend their money as they do, claiming to know why they don't go to church or get involved, why they don't attend prayer meetings, why they dress as they do or why they are upset.

In a word: Jesus condemns trying to read people's minds. You think you know why they are depressed. You judge why they are in their present situation. The Lord said to Samuel, "Do not consider his appearance or his height. . . . The LORD does not look at the things man looks at. Man looks at the outward appearance, but the LORD looks at the heart" (1 Samuel 16:7). Only God can do this.

What Jesus warns of is playing God. This simply is not allowed. Elbowing in on His territory is a precarious venture.

Motivation for Judging: Jealousy

Why do we judge others? We want to put them in their place. We do this partly because we resent that these people aren't seen as they should be seen by others. Perhaps they are too popular. We resent it that they are liked when they shouldn't be (in our opinion). We don't want them to be appreciated. It gets our "goat" that they would get away with something and not be punished. The whole time we tend to forget our own malady. It is almost always true: *The truth is worse than what they know.* But we act as though we are the most worthy people with no skeletons in our closets.

Do you want God to get involved in your life? Like it or not, here is a sure way to achieve this: Start judging another person. You will see! God will see that you get judged.

What is at the bottom of this? It is usually jealousy. It is resentment over others getting away with something, fearing they are admired too much and will never get their comeuppance. We suddenly feel qualified to do God's job. We step in and make sure these people are found out. It doesn't seem to bother us that this is God's sole prerogative. We may recognize that vengeance belongs to Him (Romans 12:19), yes, but we say, "Lord, You are so slow."

Jealousy often springs from the fear someone won't get justice. Whereas we want mercy for ourselves, we require justice for others! It may not necessarily be a personal grudge that motivates us. It can be based on a solid, objective principle—as in the parable Nathan gave to David. When King David could see that injustice was being perpetrated somewhere, he became furious—asserting that such a person "deserves to die!" (2 Samuel 12:1–6). Nathan then had to tell David, "You

are the man"—that is, you are guilty of the very injustice you have just condemned (verse 7). It took Nathan's parable (which David did not see coming) to convict David of one of the most heinous sins in the whole Old Testament. David committed adultery with Bathsheba, then had her husband killed. It didn't seem to bother David. But he was angry when he saw the equivalent injustice in another!

In Jesus' parable of the unmerciful servant is an illustration of a person being totally forgiven of his debt but who would not totally forgive another for their debt. "I canceled all that debt of yours because you begged me to. Shouldn't you have had mercy on your fellow servant just as I had on you?" The result was that God stepped in (Matthew 18:32–35). We want injustice judged because we would be jealous if they got mercy.

The Eternal Judge

Jesus warns us that God Himself will judge us and apply to us the same rules by which we ourselves judged another. In other words, we actually set the standard of fairness and justice which we demand of others. Funnily enough, God lets us set the standard of justice. He says, "Fair enough. You do that—set the standard. But do remember, that is the same standard by which you yourself will be judged."

One of the differences between God and us in this connection is that God admits to being a jealous God (Exodus 20:5; Deuteronomy 4:24). You should know it is the one aspect of God's character you and I are not allowed to imitate—unless it is a jealousy for God's glory. We must imitate His integrity and holiness, but not jealousy. Jealousy is the motivation we ourselves rarely admit to. We may take a long time to admit that jealousy lay at the bottom of our motivation. But at the end of the day, we will be forced to reckon with it. Judging others is crossing over a line—entering God's territory. He won't stand for it. "It is mine to avenge" (Deuteronomy 32:35). This is why Jesus tells us plainly, "Do not judge, or you too will be judged"—then lets us know the standard we set for others will be the exact standard by which we will be judged (Matthew 7:1–2).

Three Things to Remember When We Judge Another

If you and I are foolish enough to persist in meting out uncalled-for criticism, remember these three things. First, God is listening. "The LORD listened and heard" those who feared the Lord, and a "scroll of remembrance was written in his presence" (Malachi 3:16). The same, however, is true of those who don't fear the Lord. "I tell you," says Jesus, "that men will have to give account on the day of judgment for every careless word they have spoken" (Matthew 12:36). (I have said it before: Matthew 12:36 is my most "un-favorite" verse in the Bible!)

Second, remember that God knows the whole truth about us. "Nothing in all creation is hidden from God's sight. Everything is uncovered and laid bare before the eyes of him to whom we must give account" (Hebrews 4:13). Here is a practical word of wisdom: "Do not pay attention to every word people say, or you may hear your servant cursing you—for you know in your heart that many times you yourself have cursed others" (Ecclesiastes 7:21–22). God also knows perfectly and totally what we have thought, what we have done and what we have said. He knows our backgrounds completely and past actions clearly, as though they happened a second before—including all the sins for which we have been forgiven. Never think that our sins being buried in the "sea of God's forgetfulness" (as a hymn put it) means He can't recall them. If only. He knows full well what He has forgiven us of—and is very upset indeed when He sees us pointing the finger at another for the same or equivalent sin we have committed—and been forgiven of.

Third, remember that God is ruthlessly fair. He is not on "their" side or "your" side. This is what took Joshua by surprise. When he saw the angel with a drawn sword, having just crossed over into Canaan, Joshua asked, "Are you for us or for our enemies?" The sobering reply: "Neither." It may have been God's way of saying, "I have not come to take sides, but to take over." Instead of being angry, Joshua worshiped (Joshua 5:13–15). Ruthlessly fair—yes. He is on the side of truth. He knows whether you and I chose to be merciful, or whether we chose to withhold mercy and play God.

If you want to be like God, here is where such Godlikeness is welcomed: "Blessed are the merciful, for they will be shown mercy" (Matthew 5:7). You must make a decision whether to throw the book at them or let them off the hook. As James put it, "Speak and act as those who are going to be judged by the law that gives freedom"—that is, since we are free from the penalty our sins. But "judgment without mercy will be shown to anyone who has not been merciful" (James 2:12–13). When we have been set free but do not extend that freedom to others, God steps in to judge us. He is ruthlessly fair.

Equal Justice

Equal justice is guaranteed the moment I open my mouth. "For in the same way you judge others, you will be judged, and with the measure you use, it will be measured to you" (Matthew 7:2). This is precisely what you and I must keep in mind when we make the unhappy choice to dish out uncalled-for criticism. We are being watched. We are being listened to. Every word will be accounted for.

Question: Are you prepared to be judged in the exact way you pass judgment on another? Are you really? After all, I must ask: When I judge you, have I been perfect? If I judge you for what you have said, have I always spoken in a way I would be happy for the world to hear?

Two things show equal justice. First, you will be judged by the very way you judge. Second, the standard of measure you choose will be applied to you. For example, you could decide to withhold judgment and choose mercy. This means you will receive mercy! If you opted for graciousness as opposed to throwing the book at them, you will be graciously treated. God is listening, the angels are watching! Choose to show mercy, and you will get mercy shown back. Choose to require rigidity with the truth and doctrine, God will be rigid with you.

Which standard of measure will you choose? A standard of mercy? Or a high standard of justice? Or will you show a little bit of both? God says, "Okay, so, too, with you and Me." He is ruthlessly fair.

When Does God Judge?

Note the future tense: "It *will* be measured to you" (Matthew 7:2, emphasis mine). Count on it: This judgment will take place—sooner or later. It can come almost immediately—an hour later or on the same day! And yet God may wait a while. I have long upheld the view that the angrier God is, the longer He waits. It is a good thing if He steps in instantly. This way, you are judged quickly and you can confess quickly (1 John 1:9). If you seem to get away with pointing the finger over and over again, it is not a good sign. It ominously suggests that God will turn up in judgment further down the road, and it will not be a happy moment. This is why one wants to be convicted quickly of a fault—in order that we can have as much unbroken fellowship with the Father as possible.

John Chrysostom (d. 407), ancient bishop of Constantinople, believed that the judgment takes place in the life to come. That suggests the Judgment Seat of Christ (2 Corinthians 5:10; Romans 14:10). I can only say that if God does not step in during our present existence, it certainly would be at the Final Judgment.

And yet God can step in before then. This is what happened in Corinth. The Christians there had abused the Lord's Supper by treating certain fellow believers with contempt. As a consequence of this, some of them were afflicted with weakness, some with sickness, some died. Paul makes it clear it was God stepping in with judgment (1 Corinthians 27–32). Jesus, from the right hand of God, warned the church of Ephesus that if they did not return to their first love and repent, He Himself would come and remove their lampstand from its place (Revelation 2:4–5). Sometimes God rolls up His sleeves and steps in before the Final Judgment.

Whether this comes now or later, you can count on it. It will be equitable judgment. And the amazing thing is, we set the rules by how we will be judged! But when we violate the very standard we set up, it is playing God. Don't even think about doing that.

69. God's Sense of Fair Play

With the measure you use, it will be measured to you.

Matthew 7:2

There is in Britain a broad sense of "fair play" that is generally never far from the thinking of British people. If a situation rises that seems unfair, one often hears this expressed by the remark: "It's just not cricket." More specifically, in legal and procedural matters in the U.K., there is a strong application of a related legal philosophy called *natural justice*. I had not come across this concept before, for some reason. However, like the wider concept of "fair play," the application of "natural justice" requires just and fair process in legal and procedural matters. This is not defined in any legislation, but is rather based upon the concept that certain basic legal principles are so obvious that they should be applied without needing to be set out in legislation.

That is British fairness. I was always amazed by it and how I myself was helped by it. But I am continually amazed at God's fairness. As I said in the previous chapter, He is ruthlessly just and fair. I marvel at the way He administers justice, how I myself get found out and yet how kind He is. And when you and I stand before the Judgment Seat of Christ one day—and we certainly will—we will see unprecedented brilliance in the manner in which the Supreme Judge of the Universe will administer justice. This will include how He clears His own name. After all, the most maligned person in the universe is God Himself.

I think of King Solomon's wisdom when two prostitutes, each of whom had babies, came to him after one of the babies died in the middle of the night. Each woman claimed to be the true mother. Solomon gave the order: "Bring me a sword," then "divide the living child in two, and give half to the one and half to the other." The woman who was the true mother immediately pleaded with King Solomon to give the baby

to the other woman. It was Solomon's shrewd way of finding out who the true mother was. It worked. Solomon saw it clearly: The true mother would never let her own baby be killed. "She is his mother," declared Solomon (1 Kings 3:27). All Israel stood in awe of the king "because they perceived that the wisdom of God was in him to do justice" (verse 28).

This is true in God's sense of fair play. God demonstrates this in everything He ever does. "Will not the Judge of all the earth do right?" asked Abraham (Genesis 18:25). Nobody can buy God off. He is no one's debtor. God's justice is always equitable justice, that is, always absolutely fair.

The Promise of Equitable Justice

"In the same way you judge others, you will be judged, and with the measure you use, it will be measured to you." Note again the future tense: "*will* be judged," "*will* be measured." Jesus is not merely passing along practical commonsense wisdom, as if to say, "You should know this about people," or, "This is the best way to make friends and influence people." It is much more than that.

Jesus is here guaranteeing God's sense of fair play down the road sooner or later. It is God Himself who is the One who will do the judging. So if we elbow in on His territory without His getting to do what He does best, He immediately notices it! Keep in mind, too, that God's essential nature is that He is a God of justice. "Do not be afraid of any man, for judgment belongs to God" (Deuteronomy 1:17). "Many seek an audience with a ruler, but it is from the Lord that man gets justice" (Proverbs 29:26). "God will bring every deed into judgment, including every hidden thing, whether it is good or evil" (Ecclesiastes 12:14). When Jesus promises equitable justice, then, it is like introducing the A-B-Cs of God's ways.

The Place of Equitable Justice

Where is this justice administered—here in the present life or at the Final Judgment? It can be either. We must all stand before the Judgment Seat of Christ to give an account of the things done in the body, "whether good or bad" (2 Corinthians 5:10). "You, then, why do you judge your brother? Or why do you look down on your brother? For we will all stand before God's judgment seat" and "each of us will give an account of himself to God" (Romans 14:10, 12). If, for example, we have not been judged for our injustices in the present life—and quite soon—it is a bad sign, namely, that we will have to face it later, at the Judgment Seat of Christ. The angrier God is, the longer He waits.

It is important to remember that no one will escape this judgment. Even "the sea gave up the dead that were in it" (Revelation 20:13). Evil men like Adolf Hitler and Joseph Stalin—indeed, all evil people in human history—will stand trial. There is no evidence that these were personally judged below. Their day of judgment will come.

The place of judgment, then, can be in the present life, as when God stepped in at Corinth (1 Corinthians 11:30). And if we are tempted to point the finger or be swift to clear our own names, remember Paul's loving caution: "Judge nothing before the appointed time; wait till the Lord comes. He will bring to light what is hidden in darkness and will expose the motives of men's hearts. At that time each will receive his praise from God" (1 Corinthians 4:5).

The Day of Judgment, therefore, may be any day that God chooses. God can intervene any moment He pleases to make us give an account for idle words, hasty comments or uncalled-for faultfinding (Matthew 12:36). God has a way of making today or tomorrow a day of judgment. It is when He rolls up His sleeves and exposes us—letting us get embarrassed before others. As revival is heaven brought forward and healing is heaven brought forward, so, too, can God bring judgment forward and put us in our place—or even make us undergo premature death. He did this with Ananias and Sapphira (Acts 5:1–10).

Imagine you are holding a 12-inch ruler. Consider a scale of 1 to 12. Let 1 be when you show mercy, let 12 be your pointing of the finger. In much the same way—on a scale of 1 to 12—God can step in and bring justice. If it is a little misdemeanor, like a 4 or 5, He may merely give a slap on the wrist. He has a way of doing that. He has a way of making you see you can't get away with it. It can hurt. And yet when you are found out, you should say, "Thank You, Lord." When Jonah was found out for running from God by the sailors on the ship, you can be sure he was a grateful man that God went to such pains to correct him (Jonah 1).

Therefore, don't despise it if you get caught! Being judged in this life is proof you won't be condemned with the world (1 Corinthians 11:32). To be condemned with the world means eternal punishment—going to hell. You surely don't want that! Be thankful for judgment from Him in the here and now. To be judged in this life means that God is sparing you the ultimate punishment but nonetheless making you face your sin here below and giving you loving correction. For whom God loves He disciplines (Hebrews 12:6).

Four Principles of Equitable Judgment

We can sum up these principles we have been examining. First, consider that of sowing and reaping. "Do not be deceived: God cannot be mocked. A man reaps what he sows. The one who sows to please his sinful nature, from that nature will reap destruction; the one who sows to please the Spirit, from the Spirit will reap eternal life" (Galatians 6:7–8). This is seen also in the matter of generosity in giving of our finances. "Remember this: Whoever sows sparingly will also reap sparingly, and whoever sows generously will also reap generously" (2 Corinthians 9:6).

Also, you may be sure that the greater the challenge, the greater the potential reward. The greater our suffering now, the greater the anointing later. For example, when it comes to a severe hurt: The greater the injustice you have to forgive, the greater the blessing that will be yours if indeed you let them off the hook. When you show mercy as opposed to throwing the book at them, your reward "will be great" (Luke 6:35). The same is true when you refuse to judge although you are tempted to point the finger. The refusal to show mercy, when God knows full well how He has protected you, is what lies behind Jesus' words: "The same way you judge others, you will be judged, and with the measure you use, it will be measured to you" (Matthew 7:2). That is God's sense of fair play.

So, when you have been landed with great abuse, severe hurt, the most painful injustice but show mercy, *God notices.* When you don't throw the book at them but forgive them, *God remembers.*

Second, consider the seriousness of moving in on His territory. He is the eternal, absolute and Supreme Judge. Vindicating and bringing vengeance is what God does best. Don't deprive Him of this prerogative, which is His alone. As we have seen, He is not happy when you try to do His job! He longs to bring justice, which will be absolutely fair.

There is a question often asked: Are some sins worse than others? Answer: Yes. The Mosaic Law makes this clear, that some sins deserve greater punishment than others. Some sins also get God's attention quicker than others, although He may not unveil His opinion to you and me immediately. If you should be interested to know how to annoy Him the quickest, here is how to do it: Try trespassing where no trespassing is allowed—namely, moving in on His territory. It is God who avenges (Psalm 94:1), and He does not want your help or mine.

One of the principles that lie behind God's sense of fair play is what happens below when we compete with Him on His prerogative to vindicate. When you make Him step aside and not let Him do what He does best—as when you roll up your sleeves and do His job for Him—He will stand back and say nothing. He will let you proceed. But in due course, your foot will slip and you will regret that you ever moved ahead of Him. With the measure you use—either by exercising patience or running ahead of the Lord—it will be measured to you.

Third, consider the "only a matter of time" principle. This relates to the aforementioned issue of when and where God judges. If God steps in now, it is a fairly good indication He won't return later to judge you for the same thing twice. It is

this matter of being judged in the here and now, as opposed to having to receive the condemnation that is coming to the world (eternal punishment in hell). But it also follows, if one is not judged in the present life—say, in the cases of people like Hitler and Stalin, it will be worse for them later on. Would you like to be in Adolf Hitler's shoes? Did you think that Stalin got away with all those murders? Not at all. God only appeared to do nothing with these evil men.

There are millions of others who have been so wicked and horrendous and who appear to get away with unbridled evil. But God's sense of fair play will be seen one day. To quote Yogi Berra, "It ain't over 'til it's over." In a word: The final judgment hasn't come yet.

If, then, one is not judged in the present life, he or she will be judged later—but far worse. The same is true with the Christian at the Final Judgment. Some will receive a reward; some will be saved by fire (1 Corinthians 3:15). The latter means they will still go to heaven—but without a reward at the Judgment. I myself will do anything to avoid being saved by fire. I want God to deal with me *now*—not then—if and when there is something in my personal life that displeases Him. I prefer the present discipline of God, my loving Father—however painful it may be—than to have Him deal with me later on. The sooner God steps in, the better. "For there is nothing hidden that will not be disclosed, and nothing concealed that will not be known or brought out into the open" (Luke 8:17).

Fourth, you and I determine how it will be. Here again is God's sense of fair play. He says to us: "Would you like to determine how your punishment or reward will be meted out?" "With the measure you use, it will be measured to you." Take my example above of the 12-inch ruler. God's sense of fair play consists in His letting us determine how we will be judged. If I judge you severely—a 12—God will do the same with me. If I let you off the hook—a 1—God will let me off the hook. If I show partly restraint and partly indignation—a 4 or 5—God will mete out the disciplinary action He thinks best. He is a gracious God and very, very fair. If I withhold mercy and mete out what I think is justice, God will see that I get equitable justice accordingly.

Matthew 7:2 connects to Matthew 6:14–15: "If you forgive men when they sin against you, your heavenly Father will also forgive you. But if you do not forgive men their sins, your Father will not forgive your sins." The truth is, when you judge them—that is, you point the finger at them—it is because you have not totally forgiven them. When you have totally forgiven them, you don't judge them.

The Purpose of Equitable Judgment

Why does God step in and judge? What's it all for? First, it is partly to show that God is for the underdog. He also blesses those who are for the underdog. "Whatever you did for one of the least of these brothers of mine [who were hungry, needing hospitality and clothing], you did for me," said Jesus. And God blesses them accordingly, giving them their inheritance (Matthew 25:34–40). He equally judges those who neglect the poor, needy and hungry (Matthew 25:41–46). So God says to us and to those who judge us, "Why do you judge your brother? Why do you look down on your brother? . . . So then, each of us will give an account of himself to God" (Romans 14:10, 12).

Second, God steps in to show Himself for what He is. He wants the world to know that He knew everything that went on. His glory will be revealed in the manifestation of His justice. He will demonstrate clearly and unmistakably that He is worthy of our utter admiration.

Third, God will judge to show that no stone is unturned. "Every valley shall be raised up, every mountain and hill made low; the rough ground shall become level, the rugged places a plain. And the glory of the LORD will be revealed, and all mankind together will see it. For the mouth of the LORD has spoken" (Isaiah 40:4–5). As Mordecai's recognition was delayed but eventually rewarded (Esther 6:1–14), so will God give to every single person who ever lived the justice that was due. No human being who ever lived—whatever the matter and whatever their status—will sidestep God's awesome scrutiny. All those who abused people will get their consequence.

Prevention of Equitable Judgment

How can judgment be avoided? In a word: Don't play God. Don't judge! Once, however, you realize you have done so, don't be defensive or excuse yourself. Fall on your knees and beg for mercy. "If we confess our sins, he is faithful and just and will forgive us our sins and purify us from all un-righteousness" (1 John 1:9). Don't sweep anything under the carpet. God would prefer to bring us to repentance than to bring us to judgment. If we judge ourselves—that is, if we repent, says Paul, we will not come under judgment (1 Corinthians 11:31). Simply put: Judge yourself. That doesn't mean acquit yourself or excuse yourself. It means to mirror God's sense of fair play and come down on yourself with ruthless fairness and objectivity. When you see you have sinned, admit it. When you realize you have been pointing the finger, confess it—and stop it.

The total picture will come out on the Final Day. That is when all will see God's fairness clearly.

But we have an invitation to settle "out of court"—that is, to judge ourselves now and avoid what is coming otherwise. "Search me, O God, and know my heart; test me and know my anxious thoughts. See if there is any offensive way in me, and lead me in the way everlasting" (Psalm 139:23–24).

If God should choose to judge you in the here and now—however He chooses to do it—take it with both hands.

70. Faultfinding: Its Cause and Cure

Why do you look at the speck of sawdust in your brother's eye
and pay no attention to the plank in your own eye?

MATTHEW 7:3

Why do you suppose Jesus puts this question forth? Is He addressing people He knows? If so, is He not violating His own teaching? Is it not judging when He asks, "Why do you look at the speck of sawdust in your brother's eye and pay no attention to the plank in your own eye?" How does He know they do this?

The answer is, He knows people. "He did not need man's testimony about man, for he knew what was in a man" (John 2:25). Jesus was more than an observer of people. Jesus was the God-man—and He knows all of us. So, never has there been a human being born in the world that is not described in these lines. We all do this. We all see the speck in our brother's eye and sister's eye but remain unaware of the plank in our own eye. We are all judgmental and self-righteous by nature and prone to point the finger yet never see our own malady.

Why the "Eye"?

Why does Jesus focus on the eye in the first place? Why not the ear? Why not the nose? Why not the face generally? Or, why not refer to the heart rather than the eye? Is it not the heart that makes judging such a sin? After all, we judge people's hearts. So why does He choose to talk about the eye?

I think there may be three reasons. First, it refers to appearance. The eye is probably what we focus on first when we look at a person—and a person's appearance is inseparably connected to his or her eyes. Second, Jesus possibly focuses on the eye because it refers to the way people see us. We can often surmise what a person thinks of us by how he or she looks at us. Most of us smile if someone smiles at us. We can often tell whether a person likes us or dislikes us by his or her eyes.

Most of us like others, if we think they like us. It is reflected in the eyes. Third, the eye may refer to one's perception of things—his or her viewpoint. How we see or perceive things is, after all, at the heart of this discussion. As the old saying goes, "Beauty is in the eye of the beholder." Or, to quote Alexander Pope, "All is yellow to the jaundiced eye."

Why Is This Verse So Important?

First, it helps us see and understand ourselves by Jesus' infallible understanding of people. This way we need not feel embarrassed or singled out. We are the way we are because (like it or not) we are like everybody else: fallen men and women.

Second, this verse helps us not to be surprised that most of our quarrels are within the family of God. That is why Jesus said, "How can you say to your *brother*?"

Third, Jesus wants to help us avoid being judged. How so? For one thing, if we will spend time judging ourselves, we won't get around to pointing the finger at others! This verse can therefore help to keep us from offending our brother or sister by uncalled-for criticism.

Fourth, this verse shows so candidly how we tend to let small things in the other person upset us. It is that "speck of sawdust" that we build out of proportion that gets us annoyed. At the same time, it is astonishing how we overlook the big negative things in our own lives—which should upset us more!

Fifth, a verse like Matthew 7:3 demonstrates so vividly how all of us are filled with self-love. It is a perfect illustration of how sinful we all are, with particular reference to self-righteousness.

This verse is about faultfinding: *meddling in what seems wrong in the other person.* The fault is what Jesus calls a speck of dust. The King James

Version translates it as "mote." It is a splinter, something very small in comparison to what is wrong with us. We are so quick to gaze at the speck of dust in our brother's eye. Small though it is, it grabs our attention. Jesus asks: Why do we pay no attention to the plank—board, or log—in our own eye?

Cause of Faultfinding: The Plank in Our Eye

What exactly is this plank, board or beam that is in our own eye? It should be pointed out, as Don Carson reminds us, that this is a hyperbole—a figure of speech, an exaggeration. Jesus loved to do this, like His expression of straining a gnat and swallowing a camel (Matthew 23:24). There might be a speck of sawdust in one's eye but not a board!

The plank is Jesus' word for what is wrong with us. It is sin in us—evidence of our fallen nature. If we say we have no sin in us, we deceive ourselves and the truth is not in us (1 John 1:8). In a word: The plank in our own eye is precisely what makes us want to point the finger.

What the Plank in Our Eye Does

First, our plank magnifies the specks of dust in others. It magnifies their fault or defect. And it has blinding power when it comes to having objectivity about ourselves. It enables the eye to focus on what we think is wrong in others. So the plank in our eye focuses on and magnifies the faults in others, making the faults in others appear worse than they are.

The plank in our own eye will pick up on what gets our goat. We may also be reminded of some personal hurt, even if this happens unconsciously. It is really our own weakness, but we think it is theirs. For example, we may accuse another person of social climbing or being jealous. The weakness in me is what I project onto you and claim it's your problem when in fact it is my problem. "You, therefore, have no excuse, you who pass judgment on someone else, for at whatever point you judge the other, you are condemning yourself, because you who pass judgment do the same things" (Romans 2:1).

The plank in my eye, then, is self-blinding. It blinds me to my own sin but illuminates yours! I lose all objectivity about myself but think I have true objectivity about you. If I am not careful, I will actually tell you that "the Lord told me this about you"! What I can't admit is that your problem is really my own problem. But I refuse to see it. I don't want to see it.

Second, the plank in my eye is a defense mechanism. It is a way of protecting myself from pain—what I am really like. I ease the pain by showing you what is wrong with you. Misery loves company. If I am in pain, I will ease that pain by making you feel as miserable as I do. So I point the finger at you. The plank in me results in my inability to think clearly. The plank is my prejudice. I make a judgment based upon appearance.

Third, the plank in my own eye is my self-righteousness. It is self-elevating. It makes me feel qualified to judge you, to play God for a moment. It keeps me from judging myself. What Jesus wants us to see is that we have a worse problem than they do when we point the finger. Faultfinding is worse than the fault we think we see in the other. That is why Jesus calls their problem a "speck of dust" and our problem the "plank."

The Cure for Faultfinding

There are major steps we must take here if we are going to overcome this defect. The first is agreement. We must agree with what Jesus is saying. In a word: The problem is not with you but with me. The moment I find fault, I become the guilty party. Question: Do you agree with Jesus? Our faultfinding is worse than their fault. That is what we are being taught here. How does this make you feel? The truth is, my own fault blinds me to what I am truly like. It keeps me from seeing my self-righteousness. The heart is deceitful above all things and "desperately wicked" (Jeremiah 17:9, KJV).

Second, we must pay attention to the plank. Jesus asks a question: "Why do you look at the speck of sawdust in your brother's eye and pay no attention to the plank in your own eye?" That's the question: *Why?* The answer is painful. We do it because we are guilty sinners, we are wickedly self-righteous and we are blind to our fault. We want the other person to look worse than we do, so we are determined to expose him or her. We want to punish him or her in order to keep our gaze away from our own sin.

Paying attention to the plank in our eye—if indeed we will do it—can result in three things: (1) We can begin to judge ourselves—a full-time job that will keep us occupied and busy and restrain us from trying to straighten others out. (2) We should begin to feel ashamed of ourselves. It makes us realize we have no right to meddle in another's affairs. (3) We will be granted repentance. Our being sorry for the way we have been results in change. We see that faultfinding is wrong, so we agree to stop it. Thank God if He grants true repentance—in our case, admitting we were wrong—and gives grace to change our ways.

Third, we overcome faultfinding by correcting our gaze. "Why do you look at the speck of sawdust in your brother's eye?" Jesus says to us here: "Stop looking!" He refers to nonverbal communication. It is not what we *say*—it is *looking* at the speck of dust. Sometimes a person can see you looking without your uttering a word. You may defensively say, "I didn't say anything, did I?" But in your heart you thought it and conveyed it without opening your mouth.

Judging, therefore, begins in the heart. It is what we think that gets us into trouble—and this comes by gazing at another's speck of dust. Jesus is telling us to "stop looking" at this speck because it leads to what you will say—and regret. You will regret it because you will be judged for it. "Everyone should be quick to listen, slow to speak and slow to become angry" (James 1:19).

We may not be in trouble for what we don't say—true. But if we think it, we are probably going to say something sooner or later. The more we focus on another's fault, the more we build up thoughts inside, thoughts that will almost certainly explode and leave us blushing that we said what we did. As lusting is committing adultery, so looking at the speck of dust is inwardly judging others rather than judging ourselves. It is to pass judgment without speaking. It gets fixed in our minds and keeps us from judging ourselves.

The cure: Stop focusing on the speck of dust in your brother's eye. You only get churned up inside. You become vulnerable to saying something you will regret. The truth is, you don't have an objective picture anyway. Again, "All is yellow to the jaundiced eye." The plank magnifies his fault out of portion and blinds us to ourselves.

Our Lord Jesus not only wants to show us our sin but help us see the folly of faultfinding. When we engage in pointing the finger, we manifest a defect worse than theirs. Self-righteousness is a horrendous sin. If we become conscious of the plank in our eye, it should keep us from gazing at the speck of dust in theirs. We should know so much of what is wrong with us that we would be too embarrassed to judge another! The skeleton in our closet should close down our gaze of another's faults, not to mention shut our mouths.

I don't meant to be unfair, but do you ever stop to think how much God knows about you—your past sins and present weaknesses? Do you think about how much has been wrong with you—and how this wrong is perpetuated by pointing the finger at another person? What if—immediately after you pointed the finger—God let that other person see what is absolutely true about you? What if God were suddenly to spill the beans about you?

Consider what you have been forgiven of. You know, too, don't you, that the whole truth is worse than what they know? But God knows.

71. Mind Your Own Business!

How can you say to your brother, "Let me take the speck out of your
eye," when all the time there is a plank in your own eye?

MATTHEW 7:4

In this section, Jesus asks two questions: (1) "Why do you look at the speck of sawdust in your brother's eye and pay no attention to the plank in your own eye?" and (2) "How can you say to your brother, 'Let me take the speck out of your eye,' when all the time there is a plank in your own eye?" The latter verse, which I deal with now, implies meddling—interfering in people's affairs.

Sometimes judging is secondhand, that is, we pass judgment about people. The other word for it: gossip. The text, however, refers to firsthand judging, sometimes called "confrontation." Jesus asks: How do you do it? He assumes we are rational, fair-minded people. He is showing the absurdity of it.

The purpose in these lines is basically twofold: (1) to wake us up and bring us to our senses. It is as if Jesus says, "How can you do this?"—meaning, "It's not appropriate, surely, for you to confront another. You haven't thought things through, or you would not speak like this!" (2) To show we are disqualified to judge when our own house isn't in order. Thus, "How can you say to your brother . . . ?" Imagine Hitler speaking against racism, or *Playboy* magazine speaking against sexual promiscuity, or a corrupt TV evangelist speaking against inappropriate behavior.

So, Jesus asks, "How can you?" And yet we do! It shows how hypocritical the human heart is. Yes, yours and mine.

You will recall that the cause of faultfinding is that plank in our eye. It magnifies their fault and blinds us to our own. The issue in the verse we look at here is the unreasonableness of meddling. You have not only located a fault in the other person (so you think), but you even feel qualified to straighten that person out! Another assumption, however, is that if you had no plank in your eye it would not be unreasonable to offer help. That comes up in the next chapter. But when you do have the plank—which you do—you are the guiltier and more ridiculous by meddling in another's business.

Why Do People Meddle?

We meddle in another's affairs, and yet it does not bother us! Why? It is because the plank in our eye becomes a comfort zone. The plank—which blinds us to ourselves—enables us to live in a dream world. We stay blind to our faults. We therefore meddle in other people's affairs before we know we are doing it.

For example, let us say I misunderstand the little bit of grace given to me (and fancy that I possess a lot of grace). I tell myself I must sort this person out who (I am convinced) doesn't have much grace. So I make myself a committee of one to straighten them out. Make no mistake, the grace given to me (I fancy) is very real. I have insight, renewed strength and feel God's presence. But before I know it, I begin to take myself very seriously indeed. I reckon I don't have the old problem anymore! I think this qualifies me to sort another out. I forget that this grace given to me is only God being gracious and not because I am a cut above others. Therefore, I feel no conscience at all in moving in on another's privacy and sorting them out.

This is how it often happens. And a frequent ingredient in this scenario is that I may not have had a problem with my own weakness lately. So, unconsciously I tell myself that I don't have this problem anymore! It may have to do with pointing the finger, losing my temper or controlling my tongue. I see that you have the problem I used to have—so I feel qualified to sort you out.

Jesus says, "How can you do this?" I have shown how I can do it!

But only to get my hands burnt. Perhaps I did not have their particular problem—never have, possibly never will—but I tell myself that I am the one to help them. The truth is, I don't have a clue what it is like to be them or to have their particular weakness. Nothing could be more insensitive than my trying to help them. But I carry on.

I was with someone a few years ago immediately after he had been on a diet and lost sixty pounds. He was really pleased with himself—and rightly so. Except for one problem: He was feeling self-righteous and became judgmental as he watched fat people in the restaurant where we met. He assumed he had the right to look down on these people. (Sadly, this man gained all that weight back in a few months.)

My blindness to my own plank, then, leads me to judge your lack of vision, spirituality, involvement or sound theology. My plank blinds me also to the fact that you have graces I don't have, gifts I don't have and virtues I don't have. You actually excel in areas where I fail!

Again we are reminded by Clyde Narramore: "Every person is worth understanding." If only we knew their background, their parents or childhood traumas. Almost certainly we would be no different. Joseph's way of forgiving his brothers—and letting them save face—included his implied word to them that he would have done what they did had he been in their shoes (Genesis 45—see also my book *Total Forgiveness*).

Therefore, when you and I attempt to take the speck out of our brother's eye, we show grossest impertinence. When I say to you that I am qualified to take the speck out of your eye, I am saying you are inferior to me in some way and that I am a cut above you.

Being on the Receiving End of Meddling

What is it like when we are on the receiving end of meddling? You surely know. Have people tried to meddle in your life? Can you say you love it when someone—uninvited—intrudes in your life?

This is exactly what Job's "friends" did! They were complete and perfect meddlers! (See Job 2:11–13 and the following chapters.) The meddler always takes the initiative and is almost always uninvited. They feel qualified to meddle, things are so clear to them. But Peter says that if we are going to suffer, be sure it is not because you are a "meddler" (1 Peter 4:15).

How many of us could tell stories of "if only." If only we had minded our own business! For a meddler is uninvited, but also unwelcome. There is such a thing as an uninvited guest who is most welcome. But not the meddler. Would you want to go where you are not wanted? Remember this when you are tempted to say, "Let me take the speck out of your eye." You are an uninvited and unwelcome guest. You might like to know, too, that the first major onslaught to the Christian faith was by the Gnostics—they were meddlers! (See Jude 4, 12).

Meddlers are not only uninvited and unwelcome, but also their opinion is unwarranted. That is, the meddler has no right to speak. Jesus has a right to judge. Why? He was sinless. There is no speck or plank in His eye. He died for us—His blood gives Him entry to do what He pleases with us. We are bought with a price (1 Corinthians 6:20). Our Lord Jesus sees clearly. His eyes are like "blazing fire" and He "searches hearts and minds" (Revelation 2:18, 23). As Christians, we follow that which is warranted, whenever God wishes to speak. He has a right to enter, to intrude, to confront. He loves us totally. He has nothing to prove. All He does is for our good.

But you and I do not have a warrant from the Holy Spirit to meddle in another's affairs. Why? There is a plank in my eye. That plank disqualifies me from meddling. This is true of each of us. We forfeit the right to straighten another out as long as we have a plank.

But what about when I write a book? Or when I preach a sermon? Am I not meddling? I could indeed be guilty of meddling when I write or preach. I hopefully will not be a meddler. Some of us preach "at" the people (which is cowardice), some preach "for" the people (that is entertainment), some preach "up" to the people (that is fear), some preach "down" to the people (that is patronizing). My duty is to preach "to" the people. And so, too, in writing a book—I want to speak "to" you. If you feel patronized or "got at," I have failed. "We have this treasure in jars of clay to show that this all-surpassing power is from God and not from us" (2 Corinthians 4:7). If God uses any of us, it is His sheer grace.

Meddling is unwholesome. It is harmful to your well-being. It is not good for you. It oppresses. It demoralizes. It gives so many of the negative effects that Satan can put on a person. Why is this? It is because meddling almost always emanates from a spirit of fear (which gives Satan an entry point). The person who meddles is probably governed by fear and by a need that is rooted in unresolved conflict. The person who meddles often is covering his or her own sense of guilt. Pointing the finger is copping out.

So, what does meddling do to the person on the receiving end? It hurts, possibly makes him or her feel guilty, probably lowers his or her self-esteem and discourages. In a word: It is counterproductive. It achieves the opposite effect of what you intended. Why so? Because it is not God's way of edifying one another.

Our Response to Meddling

What are we to do when someone comes uninvited and points the finger at us? First, agree with them. "Settle matters quickly with your adversary" (Matthew 5:25). We have already seen: Soft words—a "gentle answer"—turns wrath away (Proverbs 15:1). After all, there is usually a bit of truth to what they are saying. So a good reply is: "I see what you mean." "Quite right you are, how foolish I have been."

By agreeing with them you defuse them. You even learn from them. Paul admitted he was a debtor both to the wise and the foolish (Romans 14:1).

You can also thank them for what they said to you. This will achieve one of two things. If it annoys them, it shows they were up to no good. If it pleases them, you have avoided an unhappy confrontation—you even let them save face. You may ask: "Will I not be abetting them, encouraging them to keep meddling?" I reply: You are not their judge. You are not the one to straighten them out—or you might become a meddler!

Always maintain a sweet spirit. After all, you must not grieve the Holy Spirit by the way you react. Their meddling—almost certainly of the devil—is aimed to throw you. If you grieve the Spirit by the way you react, the devil has achieved his aim. Again, remember: Soft words turn away wrath.

What you must not do is to defend yourself. "If someone strikes you on the right cheek, turn to him the other also" (Matthew 5:39). Always maintain a sweet spirit. Agree with them. Thank them. Job's big mistake was defending himself. Don't try to impress them or show them how good or right you think you are. Never, ever try to make yourself look good. You never have a warrant to do this. Never punish them. Perfect love casts out fear which has to do with punishment (1 John 4:18). Never get even—or try. Never make them look bad.

There are two more things you can do: (1) Ask them to pray for you. This is when you can voice something that is most valid. Say to them, "I need all the help and prayer I can get." (2) Pray for them. But don't tell *them* you are doing that! But by all means, pray for them.

Meddling is of the devil. Like it or not, you and I are the devil's instrument when we meddle in others' affairs. It hurts them and backfires on you—and that is Satan's aim in all of this. But the devil always overreaches himself. If you will be like Jesus, turn the cheek and not defend yourself, God will turn evil into good. Job's situation changed when he prayed for those "friends" who made his life so miserable (Job 42:10). When you meddle, confess it to God (1 John 1:9). When they meddle, pray for them.

72. Qualified to Judge?

You hypocrite, first take the plank out of your own eye, and then you will see clearly to remove the speck from your brother's eye.

Matthew 7:5

We have seen that we are not allowed to play God by judging others. This is His sole prerogative. We have also understood that judging is best defined as uncalled-for criticism. If you dish out uncalled-for criticism, you will get it back. God Himself will even turn on you for the moment. So it is in our best interest to practice Jesus' teaching—that if we judge we will get it back, and if we don't judge, we won't be judged (Matthew 7:1; Luke 6:37).

In this chapter, we notice that Jesus calls us hypocrites if we engage in judging. There is this blatant inconsistency Jesus picks up on: "Why do you look at the speck of sawdust in your brother's eye and pay no attention to the plank in your own eye? How can you say to your brother, 'Let me take the speck out of your eye,' when all the time there is a plank in your own eye?" The plank in us magnifies and blinds: It magnifies the other person's fault and blinds us to our own malady.

But Jesus adds a very interesting P.S. onto this section. "First take the plank out of your own eye, and then you will see clearly to remove the speck from your brother's eye." This raises a difficult question. Is He telling us that we are qualified to judge after all? Or that some people are qualified to judge? We have seen that the plank in our eye disqualifies us from judging. But should we succeed in obliterating this plank, are we then set free in some sense to judge another—that is, to remove the speck in their eye?

To put it another way: Does Jesus start out this section by saying "Do not judge" (verse 1) but end it by saying that we can judge after all (verse 5)—on the condition that there is no plank in our eye? The obvious question follows: Who can say they have no plank in their eye? Furthermore, will there not be those who take advantage of this,

claiming they have no plank and are therefore qualified to judge? If this is a scenario that Jesus is allowing, all you have to do to qualify to judge is to say, "I no longer have a plank, therefore I am qualified to sort you out." Are we therefore to believe that this is what our Lord is teaching? If so, we are back to square one. We all go back to pointing the finger—because we have removed the plank!

But wait a minute. We defined judging as *uncalled-for criticism*. In this case, no one ever is qualified to do this! Uncalled-for criticism can never be a right thing to do.

Why Is This Verse So Important?

This is a delicate teaching we have to sort out. It is important, first, because we all face unjust situations every day. How long do you tolerate a wrong? How long do you let people take unfair advantage of you? There comes a time when we feel we must speak out! But we are told not to judge. Yet Matthew 7:5 hints that we can apparently judge if we have no plank in our eye. Who is bold enough to say they have no plank? Therefore, who can step in and speak out?

Second, this verse is surely saying at least one of two things: (1) No one ever gets rid of the plank; therefore, no one can ever judge. (2) One can get rid of the plank. Then, and only then, can you judge another person. But uncalled-for criticism is never a valid option—that's for sure. Is there a little flexibility here that, maybe, somewhere in between these two principles is room for judging?

Obvious Purpose

The clear motive of Jesus in this teaching is to help us in a difficult situation. Our Lord's purpose is to promote honesty. We must admit we are unqualified to judge as long as there is a plank in our eye. We must admit to the plank! His further purpose is to promote humility in us. We must realize it would be arrogant to claim we have gotten rid of the plank in our eye. This would be tantamount to claiming to be without sin, which—if we do this—we are deceived and without the truth (1 John 1:8).

What Jesus wants to do by giving us this statement is to show a way forward. This comes as a little surprise. Jesus never says we should not help one another or deny whatever is in the person that is clearly wrong. The very next verse assumes that we must discriminate: "Do not give dogs what is sacred; do not throw your pearls to pigs" (Matthew 7:6). Moreover, in the same gospel of Matthew, Jesus tells us what to do if our brother sins against us. Go and show him his fault, just between the two of you. If he listens to you, you have won your brother over. But if he will not listen, take one or two others along, so that every "matter must be established by the testimony of two or three witnesses" (Deuteronomy 19:15). "If he refuses to listen to them, tell it to the church; and if he refuses to listen even to the church, treat him as you would a pagan or a tax collector" (Matthew 18:17).

There is another verse we have to consider. "Brothers, if someone is caught in a sin, you who are spiritual should restore him gently. But watch yourself, or you also may be tempted" (Galatians 6:1). In Matthew 7:5, Jesus is promoting honesty and humility, but nonetheless is offering help in situations where things are wrong, where something needs to be said. There comes a time when someone must speak out. Jesus is aware that there are times when someone must step in, that it would be irresponsible not to. There is a way forward. This verse is intended to help in this kind of situation.

Order of Priority

What do you do *first*, before anything else? Jesus used this word "first" before this: "If you are offering your gift at the altar and there remember that your brother has something against you, leave your gift there in front of the altar. *First* go and be reconciled to your brother; then come and offer your gift" (Matthew 5:23–24, emphasis mine). This verse actually coheres with Matthew 7:5. Having the right spirit toward another is paramount. And do not forget Matthew 6:33: "Seek *first* his kingdom and his righteousness, and all these things will be given to you as well" (emphasis mine).

So with our present verse: "*First* take the plank out of your own eye, and then you will see clearly to remove the speck from your brother's eye." If, therefore, we want to help where there is a need, and to speak up against injustice or step in where someone is needed, remember that it is more important to get it right in ourselves than to sort out others. It is more important to judge ourselves—to recognize the plank in our eye—before we proceed. We've all sinned. Also keep in mind Paul's words to Timothy: "Christ Jesus came into the world to save sinners—of whom I am the worst" (1 Timothy 1:15).

The Heart of the Matter

There is an ostensible paradox here. How do we obliterate the plank? Is this Jesus' tongue-in-cheek way of saying you can never help sort out a person with a fault because you can never remove that plank in your eye? Or is Jesus teaching a sinless perfectionism? Surely not! This would mean that only the alleged "perfect" (which some no doubt claim) could restore another.

I believe the answer is that this verse must be applied not absolutely but in two ways: *approximately* and *accommodatingly*. If you were to apply Jesus' teaching absolutely, then nobody would ever be qualified to judge, for we all have planks in our eyes. Jesus is not saying here that the removal of the plank is possible. That would be to teach sinless perfection, allowing a self-righteous person to point the finger.

But I believe we can apply His teaching *approximately*. This means "almost exact but not completely so." This is the way the Greek *teleioi* ("be perfect") is to be understood in Matthew 5:48. It means maturity, not absolute perfection. Matthew 7:5 can likewise be interpreted not absolutely but approximately. This would not require the obliteration of the plank in order to correct another, but of the refusal to dish out uncalled-for criticism. A rule of thumb is that the one who is hardest on himself can often be the hardest on others—but the one who is humbly aware of his own weakness, and is not dishing out uncalled-for criticism, is more likely to help another. He won't moralize but encourage. He will engage in a ministry of reconciliation and restoration. When he finds another brother or sister overtaken in a weakness, he will attempt to restore that person in a spirit of meekness and gentleness, knowing his own vulnerabilities.

I conclude that Matthew 7:5 cannot be fulfilled absolutely but approximately. For the person who comes lovingly to restore another (1) knows all too well he or she has a plank; (2) is painfully aware of his or her weakness; (3) is likely to succeed whereas a meddler would fail, and (4) is likely to be welcomed whereas the meddler would be rejected.

The following things will likely describe our efforts if we follow Galatians 6:1 when approaching another who needs help. First, one must never be emotionally involved in the person's life you are trying to help. If there is a danger of emotional involvement, mark it down—you are not the person to engage in this delicate ministry of restoration. But if you are not personally involved and won't get churned up, just maybe you can help. In a word: If your own self-esteem, ego and pride are not ingredients, you may do some good.

This means that one must be sympathetically detached. This is true of any professional counselor. You care about the person you are trying to help, but you cannot be fixated on the person who needs correction. One must never moralize, punish or give a guilt trip—that is always uncalled for. Furthermore, if there is the slightest hint of your being involved in a vendetta regarding the person who needs correction, your efforts will explode in your face.

Finally, the only consideration is the honor of God's name. This is the ultimate reason why one must step in.

Delicate Surgery

How, then, does one help accommodatingly? This means you are willing to accommodate because you are invited—they have come to you. Far from being a meddler, you are brought into the situation. A meddler is always unwelcome. But if you are brought into the situation and show compassion, you are far more likely to be welcomed. When you did not initiate the encounter but are brought in, chances are you also will be impartial, show objectivity, aren't personally involved and will not be churned up.

You may ask: "Can I approach a person without being asked to do so?" Perhaps. But only if there has been a relationship of mutual trust. In this case, you might, just maybe (but with fear and trembling) seek to correct a person.

Let's face it, this interpretation of Matthew 7:5 can be abused. If one doesn't follow Jesus (in the light of other New Testament passages), he or she will get into deep trouble. Fools rush in where angels fear to tread. Self-righteous people (who have no sense of sin) will be pointing the finger right and left. In that case, Jesus will be seen by some people as if He began Matthew 7:5 by condemning judgmentalism and then condoning it in the end. In short: Jesus does not rule out correcting another person as long as we don't do it self-righteously.

This is why I believe the verse must be understood as a paradox. No one can judge absolutely, but one can be accommodating. This means a delicate operation equal to a surgeon operating on someone's eye: You approach the person with extreme caution. When you apply Matthew 7:5 in this approximate sense, it will require that you have a sense of sin (knowing you still have a plank) as you seek to remove the speck. But judging at this stage could not be called uncalled-for criticism but rather a gentle suggestion. One must be loving and caring. It must show in your eyes.

Jesus never tells us how to remove the plank. This is because in the absolute sense, it is not possible. The full removal of the plank comes only when we are glorified in heaven (Romans 8:30; 1 John 3:2–3). But if we pay attention to our own plank the whole time we are trying to help another person, we will not likely be meddling or pointing the finger. We would be fulfilling Galatians 6:1—restoring a person gently, considering ourselves lest the same situation befall us. I believe, therefore, we would be able to help another person with their "speck" without violating Matthew 7:1.

Objective Principles

When do you rule yourself out as being the one who performs this delicate surgery? This requires painful honesty on our part. First, when your nose is out of joint you must back off quickly. If something or someone gets your "goat" and you are churned up, stay out! Second, when you are personally involved, even if there is an injustice, you are disqualified to help. Third, when your desire is to see the other person punished and you want to get even, you must stay away—miles away. Fourth, when there is the slightest tinge of envy or jealousy, keep out of the situation. Fifth, when your self-esteem is related, you must graciously disqualify yourself from being the restorer.

How do you know you are qualified to judge in the sense I have outlined above? I reply: If you are meeting an undoubted need, and have embraced the principles I've outlined, proceed. If you would be irresponsible not to speak, get involved if you are in a position to relieve suffering. When you have been asked to help because there is no personal interest on your part, you should seek to restore. When you are at total peace and have no inward churning or agitation, carry on. When the unquestioned honor of God is at stake, you have a duty to do what you can.

73. Godly Shrewdness

Do not give dogs what is sacred; do not throw your pearls to pigs. If you do, they may trample them under their feet, and then turn and tear you to pieces.

MATTHEW 7:6

Although Jesus changes the subject, one cannot help but notice that these words follow the section about being judgmental. Using a figure of speech (referring to dogs, pearls), Jesus shows we do need to discriminate. So why is this unusual verse placed here? Michael Eaton reckons that this is "the most searching, challenging and humbling part" of the Sermon on the Mount.

Why did Jesus say this here? He says it, first, lest we take the previous section to extremes and never offer any judgment. The assumption here is that we can and must make judgments. It is not a case of pointing the finger but knowing when not to speak, when to speak and to whom. This verse shows, moreover, that there is a place for Church discipline and also a time when false teaching must be exposed.

Second, it teaches us that we may be right in our judgment about a person but wrong as to when and how we apply it. For example, we may see clearly that a person is dead wrong in what he or she does, says or in his or her attitude. But if we don't act with great judiciousness, all we say will backfire on us. It would mean we violated this verse. This verse is primarily a call for wisdom.

Third, as we proceed through the Sermon on the Mount, we all need to be reminded of the teaching how not to grieve the Holy Spirit. How many of us have grieved the Spirit unwittingly, because we did not exercise the kind of wisdom implied in this most unusual verse?

Matthew 7:6 is given to us, then, that we will not misjudge the previous section on judging—and that we don't misjudge people in our relationships. Although all people have sinned, not all people are the same. Indeed, every single person we meet is in a sense unique.

What are the issues raised by this verse? It teaches us that we often must make a quick but silent judgment of the people we are with. It calls for shrewd, godly discernment. Our Lord assumes we should be able to do this. It also means we must exercise control regarding our words and deeds. This verse is about controlling the tongue. As in the previous verses, it means we must be swift to hear, slow to speak (James 1:19).

Examples of Casting Pearls

This verse relates to what we reveal about ourselves in a testing situation—but don't realize at first we are being tested. Take Hezekiah, a godly king, one of the undoubted best in the Old Testament. But he did something foolish. Hezekiah received envoys from Babylon and showed them what was in his storehouses—the silver, gold, spices, fine oil, indeed, "his entire armory and everything found among his treasures. There was nothing in his palace or in all his kingdom that Hezekiah did not show them" (Isaiah 39:2).

This was a classic case of casting one's pearls before swine. Solomon made a similar mistake, giving the queen of Sheba "all she desired and asked for" (1 Kings 10:13). Keep in mind that Solomon's greatest gift was his wisdom. It shows how the wisest people on earth have weak and blind spots, that they can be trapped and do stupid things. Samson, too, revealed the secret of his strength to Delilah, resulting in his temporary forfeiture of his great anointing (Judges 16:17–20).

Why This Verse Is So Important

This verse is given primarily to save us from unnecessary offense. The Gospel of Christ, as well as life in the Holy Spirit, already has sufficient stigma built in. Our Lord does not want us to add to it unnecessarily! This is why Paul could say, "To the weak I became weak, to win the weak. I have become all things to all men so that by all possible means I might save some" (1 Corinthians 9:22).

We must never forget that people have feelings. Some have tender consciences. We don't want to hurt them unnecessarily. Not all can cope with what is new and different to the same degree. We must reach people where they are and not assume they should be stronger or more experienced than they are. "Accept him whose faith is weak, without passing judgment on disputable matters. One man's faith allows him to eat everything, but another man, whose faith is weak, eats only vegetables" (Romans 14:1–2). There is no good reason to lead a weaker Christian to anger, not to mention disillusionment.

This verse also relates to the gospel of liberty. Paul cautioned, "Be careful, however, that the exercise of your freedom does not become a stumbling block to the weak" (1 Corinthians 8:9). Never assume that all those Christians around you have the same maturity, background, knowledge or culture. Matthew 7:6 relates precisely to this sort of issue. We must not only accept people as they are but avoid trying to change them by casting our pearls. They may not be "pigs" tomorrow, but they could well be today! The last thing we want to do is destroy them while they are unseasoned in doctrine or practice.

This verse is also important with regard to whom you confide in. Many a deep hurt has taken place because we confided in someone who couldn't cope with the information given to them. You must be sure that this person not only can be trusted with what you share, but also able to cope with it. Remember, too, that we have all been swine or dogs at one time or another.

Jesus is not giving a permanent label to certain people. The truth is, we've all been weak and immature at one stage. There was a time when I could not cope with things I know now. There was a time, looking back, I would wish people would have treated me as Jesus counsels here. Jesus exercised this exact principle to the Twelve: "I have much more to say to you, more than you can now bear" (John 16:12). So He withheld certain things from them.

Therefore, a verse such as Matthew 7:6 should help us not to judge people around us who are yet unable to bear what we can cope with. We need to be patient with them, watching carefully our words and actions. I myself have violated this verse more often than I care to think about. It comes under the category of Matthew 12:36, my most "un-favorite" verse: "I tell you that men will have to give account on the day of judgment for every careless word they have spoken."

The Principle

This verse is about making your life and teaching count. It means not to waste words, time or energy. It means that we should shrewdly anticipate another's reaction, then act accordingly.

This verse does not mean we should not preach the Gospel to the lost. This verse is not a basis for not allowing people to observe believers partaking of the Lord's Supper, as some in the early Church thought. Indeed, as Calvin said, observing the Lord's Supper being carried out can be an evangelistic setting to make people hungry for Christ. Neither does this verse mean that we should never offend people by what we teach. That there is a violent reaction to preaching or teaching does not necessarily mean you have violated this verse. This verse means that we should not persist when people are unteachable. It means we should not offend by being too persistent.

The principle is this: Do not waste what is valuable and precious. Pearls are precious. Don't waste what is holy. Don't waste truth. Don't give out what will be unappreciated. Don't share what is beyond one's ability to take in. It means we should not try to change people by a challenge too great for them. We should not overestimate their maturity or ability to cope.

This Verse Is about People

This verse is not about animals. As I said at the beginning, Jesus uses a figure of speech here. He is not talking literally about pigs, or dogs. Dogs in Jesus' day were not pets that sit on your lap or that you take for a walk. They were wild dogs, dangerous and living only to eat. The idea of feeding a pearl to a pig means not only is this wasting what is precious, but that the pig would swallow it, realize it is not food and possibly turn on you for giving what is inedible. The picture is: As a pig or dog could turn on you, so can certain people react negatively to what you offer—and "turn and tear you to pieces."

Jesus has two types of people in mind—wicked people and weak people. The wicked are the lost who don't want to know. They remain unteachable. There comes a time you may have to give up on certain people. This category could also refer to apostates—those who were a part of the Church but never converted. Some apostates hang around to disturb, to draw attention to themselves and cause division (see Jude 4,12–13). We had people like this who would come to Westminster Chapel, those who once professed faith but were never converted by the Holy Spirit. They would take your time, sap your strength.

Weak Christians are those who must be treated like children. Perhaps they are like those in Corinth who never move beyond a diet of milk. But among the weak are those who are hypersensitive—easily hurt and unable to cope with needful criticism or suggestions. The weak can include those who are jealous—they can't cope with your success or financial status. The weak could even include those who are not highly intelligent. They include those who are immature in their understanding. If you aren't careful, they will turn on you.

Do not be angry with people like this. We will always have them. Some of us were once like that! We may still be like that in some ways. The irony of Matthew 7:6 is that Jesus is talking about all of us.

What Is Precious

Jesus talks about what is holy. What is sacred should not be given to dogs. He talks about pearls, meaning truth, deeper truths. He is talking about truth that can only be revealed by the Holy Spirit. Take the teaching of predestination. There are insensitive people who ram this doctrine down people's throats. Foolish mistake! The same is true regarding the manifestations of the Holy Spirit. We should not demand that all our fellow believers see eye to eye on what is more precious to some than others. We must take people where they are.

Let us say God has given you a special insight. Call it a pearl. It is a precious breakthrough regarding truth. Perhaps you were given a word of knowledge. Or a vision. The Lord confides in those who fear Him (Psalm 25:14). The "secret of the LORD" is with those who fear Him (KJV). If it is a secret, then keep it a secret! Keep it to yourself. The fact that the Lord shows you something—or possibly confides in you—does not mean you should blab it to the world. The opposite is true! Joseph's big mistake was telling his dreams to his brothers (Genesis 37:5–11). His error was casting pearls (his dreams) to swine (in this case, his brothers). They could not cope with what was in fact revelation from God. They would later see the full truth, but not then.

This verse is about prevention. The best way to deal with a crisis is to avoid it. Jesus wants to keep our words from being counterproductive. He appeals to our self-interest. Do you want people to turn on you and tear you into pieces? Then don't give what is holy to dogs, don't give your precious pearls to pigs. "Do not rebuke a mocker or he will hate you" (Proverbs 9:8). As Dr. Martyn Lloyd-Jones put it, "Don't be the cause of antagonism."

Consider the peace you forfeit if you neglect this verse. The early verses of Matthew 7 show us how we forfeit peace by what we say. Matthew 7:6 shows how we can maintain peace by what we don't say.

74. Asking God

Ask and it will be given to you.

MATTHEW 7:7

Jesus now reintroduces the subject of prayer. This first came up in Matthew 6:5, followed by the Lord's Prayer with its six petitions (Matthew 6:9–13). This time He does not suggest any specific petitions in our praying, He only tells us to "ask." Whereas the Lord's Prayer gave us specific things to pray for, this section on prayer is by comparison vague and open-ended.

Or is it? We have a parallel passage in Luke 11:9–13, which comes shortly after Luke's account of the Lord's Prayer (Luke 11:2–4). The passage in Luke is a clear indication of how to interpret Matthew 7:7–11.

Two questions must be asked: (1) Why are these verses—which begin with "Ask and it will be given to you"—put precisely here in the Sermon on the Mount? (2) What kind of asking does Jesus have in mind? Are we to believe that "the sky is the limit"—that we are to just ask and we will receive? Is this the place to ask for a Rolls Royce, a raise in pay, winning the lottery or obtaining the things of the world?

When I graduated from high school in 1953, I recall the main speaker quoting Matthew 7:7 as the foundation of his talk. He managed pretty much to keep God out but used the idea of "ask and you will receive" as an optimistic way of looking at life. In other words, he gave the impression you could apply this verse any way you like. I'm afraid some television preachers apply this verse in much the same way today, appealing to people's ambition and greed rather than their desire to know God.

Keep in mind that Jesus is directing our prayer to the same Father as in Matthew 6:9 (see also Luke 11:13). It is, therefore, the Most Holy God to whom we are praying. Do not forget also that our Lord's concern is the Kingdom of heaven

and that His Father has a will of His own that we should preeminently desire.

This means Jesus is not changing the subject of the Kingdom to something material. Some people, however, hastily seize upon this verse "ask and you will receive" as if Jesus is enticing us to ask for selfish, carnal things. As a matter of fact, Matthew 7:7 is not referring to material things at all. The issue of food, shelter and clothing has already been dealt with in the Lord's Prayer. Not only that, Jesus told us to "seek first his kingdom and his righteousness and all these things will be given to you as well" (Matthew 6:33). There would be no need to start praying all over again about material things. The nearest hint as to the content of this further praying is in Matthew 7:11: "good gifts" ("good things," ESV) but is rendered as "Holy Spirit" in Luke 11:13.

This is very important if we want to understand Jesus' teaching. Matthew's account tells us that our Father is eager to grant good gifts—or, good things—to those who ask Him. But when you put Luke 11:9–13 side by side with Matthew 7:7–1,1 you find that it is virtually verbatim until you get to Luke 11:13, which says "Holy Spirit" instead of "good gifts" or "good things." Why? It is because Jesus is still talking about the Kingdom of heaven!

A Most Important Assumption

Here is a key. Jesus assumes certain things when He gets to Matthew 7:7. First, He knows that what He has been teaching from the beginning of this Sermon has amazed and gripped His hearers (Matthew 7:28–29). Those who listened also know that Jesus has not changed the subject, but realize He wants His Word to change their lives and for them to experience all He has been talking about. He also assumes that we have taken on board His command to "seek first" God's Kingdom (Matthew 6:33). His word should also create a hunger and thirst for righteousness (Matthew 5:6). I can never forget the effect that John Sutherland Logan's preaching at Trevecca Nazarene College had on me in the autumn of 1954. Not only was it the greatest preaching I had ever heard, it created in me an intense hunger for more of God. Never before had I experienced anything like this.

I say, then, that if we had carefully and sympathetically followed Jesus up to now, His application "ask and you will receive" is directed to our hungry hearts. That means we want more of the Holy Spirit! Luke 11:13 proves this is what Jesus means. I love something I heard Rodney Howard-Browne say about preaching to a church where he has never been before: "I preach them hungry." I know what he means by this. Jesus has preached His hearers hungry thus far in the Sermon on the Mount. And if I have done my job in faithfully interpreting the Sermon on the Mount up to now, it has made you hungry and thirsty for the very essence of God and godliness that Jesus has put before us.

The assumption, then, in Matthew 7:7 is that we are hungry for more of God and craving a greater intimacy with Him. Indeed, a hunger for a greater anointing. The Kingdom of heaven is the realm of the un-grieved Spirit. Therefore, we are convicted not to worry but rather to trust God, are convicted to stop pointing the finger but judge ourselves instead and are shown our need for godly shrewdness—from all of which should come the cry, "O God, I want to experience all Jesus is preaching!" Then comes Jesus' encouraging word: "Ask and it will be given to you." That is the context of Matthew 7:7 and what Jesus has in mind for us when He tells us to "ask."

A Good Definition of Prayer

A good definition of prayer is *asking God to act.* Three things—asking, seeking, knocking—come to the same thing but are nonetheless slightly different. You ask because you want to receive; you seek because you want to find; you knock because you feel you need to get God's attention when He could be hiding His face or testing your earnestness and sincerity in wanting more of Him.

This triad or set of triplets is in two parts: a plea and a promise. The plea is when we go on bended knee. The promise is God's response to that plea, namely, that we will receive. This also shows that the Lord's Prayer—though the perfect pattern for praying in the will of God—is not the only prayer a Christian should pray. Some may be more comfortable with a prayer already provided and wish to keep repeating it. We can certainly do that. But this section on asking, seeking and knocking tests our earnestness and encourages us to pour out our hearts to God if we have been touched by Jesus' teaching. The question is: Do you want to have more of God? If so, in this section Jesus tells us how to have more of God.

The Plea: Ask

The word *ask* is found 71 times in the New Testament alone. Our Lord explicitly invites us to ask. "Ask of me," said the psalmist, "and I will make the nations your inheritance, the ends of the earth your possession" (Psalm 2:8). "Call to me and I will answer you and tell you great and unsearchable things you do not know" (Jeremiah 33:3). It is as though God is saying, "I won't act until you ask—but I'm asking you now to ask!" John Wesley would say that God "does nothing but in answer to prayer." But God invites us to act—by our asking. The invitation is from God to ask Him.

Paul said, "Do not be anxious about anything, but in everything, by prayer and petition, with thanksgiving, present your requests to God" (Philippians 4:6). It is gracious invitation—undeserved, coming from a sovereign God—which is greater than an invitation from Buckingham Palace. But it also comes with a guarantee that we will receive. "It will be given to you." It is guaranteed from the lips of the Son of God Himself. It will be given to you. You will find the door will be opened to you.

Who takes the initiative here? God does; we do. The Lord takes the initiative by giving us this gracious invitation. "Call on me," "Ask of me." "If my people, who are called by my name, will humble themselves and pray and seek my face and turn from their wicked ways, then will I hear from heaven and will forgive their sin and will heal their land" (2 Chronicles 7:14). God takes the initiative by inviting us and motivating us to pray. As the hymn put it,

> What more can He say than to you He
> hath said,
> To you unto Jesus for refuge hath fled?
>
> Anonymous

And yet we take the initiative! Prayer is something we do in response to the invitation. But accepting the invitation requires an act of the will on our part—as if in our own strength. This is why Paul said for us not to give up when we may not feel very motivated. For example, one is to preach the word in all conditions, to be "prepared" (KJV, "instant") in season and out of season (2 Timothy 4:2). "In season" refers to the ease of praying, when God comes down and enables you to soar without effort. Those times are lovely. But they do not come as often as we may like. "Out of season" refers to feeling nothing when you pray—but you pray anyway! This, therefore, means we must take the initiative. In other words, don't wait until you feel "led." Do you feel led to go to work each day? Do you feel led to get up every morning? Do you feel led to brush your teeth? Do you feel led to fill out your income tax form?

No. You just do it, don't you? So it is with seeking God. Speaking personally, I would have to say that 99 percent of all I do—preaching, preparing, praying, tithing, witnessing and worshiping—is by my own initiative as far as my feelings go. I don't wait until I feel "led."

"Ask," says Jesus. And yet it is not only His invitation—it is an imperative. "Ask" is in the imperative mood. It is a command. Jesus is simply saying: Do it.

The implications, however, are vast. When you answer the invitation you are now going outside yourself—you are on bended knee, seeking the One who has power to act. And yet nothing is promised to happen until you ask. It is true that God already knows your need and desire (Matthew 6:8). But He will not likely answer you until you ask. Like it or not, that is the way it is. If you challenge Him without asking, you probably never get a response. The wrath of man does not achieve the favor of God (James 1:20).

But the tender, sweet and reliable news is: He is waiting to be asked!

It is humbling because it is begging. Yes. You may say, "I'll never beg." I reply: You certainly will if you expect to get God's attention. The rich man to whom Jesus refers in Luke 16:19–31 would never beg. That is, until he was in hell—then he pleaded with God to send Lazarus to his brothers. The thing is, those in hell become beggars. But those who avoid hell are those who become beggars in this life. The leper went on bended knee to Jesus and said, "Lord, if you are willing (you can heal me)" (Matthew 8:2). There was no snapping of the finger. There was no feeling of "entitlement"—one of the great curses and sins of our generation. The leper was already a beggar. So we, too, must become beggars. The first thing we are to ask of God when we come boldly to the throne of grace is for "mercy" (Hebrews 4:16). You don't command God to give you mercy. You ask. Humbly. On bended knee.

The Promise: It Will Be Given to You

It is a calculated promise—that is, given deliberately to get an intended result: to motivate you and me to pray. It is calculated to move us to seek intimacy with God and to want a greater anointing. If the teaching of Jesus in the Sermon on the Mount has produced in you a hunger, it is because that was the intended purpose. This hunger is an entry point by which God has pressed the right button. You respond because you see how much you matter to Him and how much He matters to you. In a word: The promise is calculated to get your attention.

We all tend to ask for things too often that may not be in God's perfect will. But the only way to be heard is to pray in His will (1 John 5:14). We saw earlier that praying the Lord's Prayer is one time for sure you may know you are praying in God's will. So here, too. When you are asking for more of God's presence, anointing, intimacy and knowledge of His ways, you may be absolutely assured you have asked in His will. You are not asking for a Mercedes-Benz—you are asking for more of God. You are responding to the Word of the Son of God. So, then, all that Jesus has been doing in the Sermon on the Mount is to preach you hungry. You took the bait! And whenever you ask for more of the Holy Spirit, you can be sure it is in God's will (Ephesians 3:14–16; 5:18; Philippians 1:9; James 4:8).

But it is a conditional promise, namely, that you did indeed ask. There is, of course, an anointing in us already (1 John 2:20, 27). That is in the grace package (1 Corinthians 1:7). You received the Holy Spirit at conversion (Romans 8:9; 1 Corinthians 12:13). And yet Paul could say to the Ephesians, "I keep asking that the God of our Lord Jesus Christ, the glorious Father, may give you the Spirit of wisdom and revelation, so that you may know him better" (Ephesians 1:17). You should covet earnestly the best gifts of the Holy Spirit (1 Corinthians 12:31). So, too, with all there is on offer from the throne of grace. If you desire more of God, ask Him! Tell Him your heart. Don't reason in your mind by saying, "He already knows what I want." Become like a child and ask Him as if He were being informed.

James said that we have not because we ask not. The trouble is we ask so often for the wrong things (James 4:2–3). What Jesus means by asking God in Matthew 7:7 is an invitation presented to you on a golden platter. You are invited to ask for the most noble and glorious gift you can possibly put to your heavenly Father. You are asking Him to give you what He wants for you: more of Him. What is more, He wants this more than you want it yourself.

75. Seeking God

Seek and you will find.

MATTHEW 7:7

It is our Lord's wish that our spiritual appetite has been whetted through the Sermon on the Mount—indeed, that our keenest desire after experiencing His Word is to enjoy more of God. God wants us to hunger and thirst for righteousness, a righteousness that outclasses the Law, that carries out total forgiveness, that longs to trust God to the hilt and seek first His Kingdom. He wants us to live a lifestyle of not pointing the finger and to have wisdom to discern—such as knowing when not to cast your pearls before pigs. Do you want this wisdom? If so, these words of Jesus in this section are for you. His return to the subject of prayer is that we might ask God for such wisdom and to experience a deeper, closer relationship with the Father. This comes by our receiving more of the Holy Spirit.

Jesus now moves from asking to seeking. Why? It is because the first time you ask may not result in an immediate answer. There have been those, sadly, who perfunctorily say, "Okay, Lord, I ask to be closer to You," and stop. They say, "I asked, nothing happened." Some think they are doing God a favor if they pray this once or twice or begin to read their Bibles. But God is looking for those who want Him so much that they not only ask but seek!

How Important Is God to You?

Seeking is aimed to test our earnestness. For those who say, "I asked, nothing happened," I say: How important is knowing God to you? How interested are you in having a greater anointing of the Spirit? This section of the Sermon on the Mount is about prayer, yes. But it is all about God—and wanting more of Him. Seeking is a relentless pursuing of God. As A. W. Tozer has said, we can have as much of God as we want.

So Jesus' added word *seek* is given to test our earnestness, our sincerity. We discover for ourselves whether we are still interested in pursuing God with all our hearts. "You will seek me and find me when you seek me with all your heart," says the Lord (Jeremiah 29:13). God is looking for those who wish to enter the Big Leagues, the arena of the great saints of history. He has qualified us to "share in the inheritance of the saints in the kingdom of light" (Colossians 1:12). So what are we waiting for?

How would you like to follow in the steps of Abraham, Sarah, Isaac, Jacob, Joseph, Moses, Deborah, Joshua, Samuel and the prophets? Frankly, this interests me—a lot. What about you? Why not you? Why shouldn't you be in their league? All that is required of us is to do in our day the equivalent of what these great men and women of God did in theirs. Enoch walked with God and was given the witness that he pleased God (Hebrews 11:5). This grips me to my fingertips. Abraham by faith "when called to go to a place he would later receive as his inheritance, obeyed and went, even though he did not know where he was going" (Hebrews 11:8). How would you like to be a companion of the great saints of all time? "I, John, your brother and companion in the suffering and kingdom and patient endurance that are ours in Jesus" (Revelation 1:9). These are our true friends. I want to be in their company.

How? "Ask. Seek." We must see the benefit of pursuing and waiting, as they did. A lot can happen on the journey in pursuing God. While we wait, we can worship. While we wait—and enjoy Him working in our behalf (Isaiah 64:4)—we will be notified of things to do on the way. So if you asked once, good. Ask again. A third time. Ask a hundred times (see Luke 18:1–8). The asking becomes seeking. The longer the wait, the more glorious is the finding! When God seems to delay coming to our rescue, know, too, that this has a purpose. God put Pharaoh through the ten plagues that He might receive even greater glory—yes, "gain glory" (Exodus 14:4, 17). In the same way, when God delays answering our prayers but we keep seeking, He is pleased. The longer the delay, the greater the reward; the greater the suffering, the greater the anointing.

Why do we seek? Seeking, you could say, is Plan B. Had you received immediately after you first asked, you would not bother to seek. What makes seeking *seeking* is when you are prompted by the awareness that what you asked for wasn't granted—but don't stop asking. So you seek—you engage in a relentless pursuit. God's Plan B actually turns out to be His Plan A. It is what God wanted for us all along. He lures us to ask in order that He might teach us to seek.

Why Are These Words Important?

Jesus brings in the matter of seeking because there is a reason for every unanswered prayer. Whenever God apparently says no, it is because He has a better idea than ours. Jesus said no to healing Lazarus, then showed up four days after his funeral to unveil the true reason for the delay: Raising Lazarus from the dead gave God more glory than keeping him from dying (John 11). There is a reason for hope deferred. Seeking God means effort on our part. This is what we must experience to enter the Big Leagues. It is when we break the betrayal barrier. It was an amazing achievement in the twentieth century for aeronautics to break the sound barrier. But when God hides His face and seems to betray us, He looks for those who—instead of quarreling with Him—break the betrayal barrier and discover how real God is.

Finding also can refer to what had been lost. Could it be that someone reading these lines has lost what he or she once experienced—e.g., joy and the sense of God's presence? Do you want this back? This word is for you. God wants us to see for ourselves what He means to us. It is not that He learns anything about us—we learn about ourselves. When God said to Abraham, "Now I know that you fear God" (Genesis 22:12), it was for Abraham's benefit. It is always encouraging for

God to share with us that we are pleasing Him. I can think of no greater satisfaction.

We saw earlier that God initiated the invitation to us that we might ask Him. So, too, with seeking. God is behind it all. "You have said, 'Seek my face.' My heart says to you, 'Your face, LORD, do I seek' " (Psalm 27:8, ESV). Seeking God goes through stages: (1) duty—when you know in your heart what you should do; (2) desire—when there is a yearning to seek Him; (3) decision—when you stop any delay, only act; (4) determination—you will not let things hinder you; (5) discipline—when you overcome any diversion that would turn you in the wrong direction; (6) discovery—when you find out how real God can be. "I love those who love me, and those who seek me find me" (Proverbs 8:17). "Whoever finds me finds life and receives favor from the LORD" (Proverbs 8:35); (7) delight—the joy of His presence. "You will fill me with joy in your presence, with eternal pleasures at your right hand" (Psalm 16:11). It is worth waiting for, worth seeking.

What Exactly Are We Looking For?

The object of seeking God can be put several ways. First, we seek His face. We should primarily seek His "face, not His hand," as one put it. To seek His hand is to appeal to your own personal needs, asking Him to do this or that for you. To seek His face means you want to reach through to His heart, just to get to know Him. This is the same thing as seeking first the Kingdom, knowing all we need will be added (Matthew 6:33). The face of the Lord symbolizes His approval (Psalm 17:15). It also indicates a breakthrough—i.e., when you have found Him!

Seeking His face is the goal. You keep on seeking. Refuse to come short of all God has in mind. "Since ancient times no one has heard, no ear has perceived, no eye has seen any God besides you, who acts on behalf of those who wait for him" (Isaiah 64:4). Paul wanted for the Ephesians that they grasp "how wide and long and high and deep is the love of Christ, and to know this love that surpasses knowledge—that you may be filled to the measure of all the fullness of God" (Ephesians 3:18–19).

As you seek, there will emerge a focus—namely, narrowing in on what God has in store.

This includes knowing His will (Ephesians 5:17). We also discover sin in our hearts we hadn't seen before, which is followed by the next step forward we had not been ready for until now. All this is summed up: fellowship with the Father (1 John 1:7). It is when you get to know God's "ways" (see Exodus 33:13). What is more, He may begin to confide in you, sharing His secrets (Psalm 25:14). It is when He trusts you not to blab to everybody the latest thing He has shown you. God gave Joseph dreams, but the mistake Joseph made was in telling them (Genesis 37:5–11). It may be God would show us more if we could keep quiet about it. He will treat us as His friends (John 15:15). This fellowship results in the fruits of the Spirit (Galatians 5:22–23). Such brings great glory to God (Matthew 5:16).

This, then, is what we are looking for: getting truly to know God. We likewise become His instruments in the church and the world.

Obedience

All our seeking is, after all, following His command. It is not a luxurious option. It is not going beyond the call of duty—it *is* our duty. But, as we saw above, that duty issues in delight as long as we keep seeking. "God cannot be mocked. A man reaps what he sows. The one who sows to please his sinful nature, from that nature will reap destruction; the one who sows to please the Spirit, from the Spirit will reap eternal life. Let us not become weary in doing good, for at the proper time we will reap a harvest if we do not give up" (Galatians 6:7–9).

This means obedience to the Word. The Word of God is His revealed will. If you want to know God's will, seek Him in His Word. We live in a time when so many people only want a so-called *rhema* word—a quick word that is direct, specific and to the point. God can do that. But I can promise you, if it is a *rhema* word that you want, it will likely come by seeking Him in the Bible—over the long haul. Do not become preoccupied with the prophetic word, or the word of knowledge—often shortcuts to knowing the Divine will (and sometimes with little or no regard for God Himself). Therefore, do not begin with wanting that quick word—but rather seek God daily in the Bible, to know and follow His revealed will.

Our obedience also means walking in the Spirit and developing a sensitivity to the Holy Spirit. You learn not only to know God's ways but find what grieves the Spirit. My advice to you, reader: Find out what grieves the Holy Spirit and *don't do that*—then you will discover a life of joy and peace. Walking in the Spirit means walking in the light God gives you. God will show you things, including new levels of obedience. Failure to walk in the light means forfeiting fellowship with the Father and gaining further insight. If God shows you something He wants you to do, take it with both hands.

The matter of obedience in waiting is crucial. Wait for the Lord (Psalm 27:14; Isaiah 40:31). Don't run ahead of Him, don't lag behind. And don't give up. He is never too late, never too early, but always just on time. To be walking in the light is to be in a good, good position. It means no condemnation but rather a sense of God's approval. All we need to do is to walk in the light and wait.

God's integrity is on the line. He has made a promise: You will find what you are seeking for, if indeed it is God Himself you are seeking.

76. Getting God's Attention

Knock and the door will be opened to you.

MATTHEW 7:7

An "ascending scale of urgency" is what Matthew 7:7 has been called: ask, seek, knock. You go from Plan A (asking) to Plan B (seeking), then to Plan C (knocking) when you still are waiting for God to act. But, as we saw in the previous chapter, Plan B becomes God's Plan A. So, too, again: Plan C becomes God's Plan A! Why? Because God likes our company. He also wants to get our attention. His method is to drive us to prayer in such a manner that our motive is to get His attention. The truth is, He wants our attention as much as we want His attention.

If prayer isn't answered after asking, then, make seeking God's face a life's pursuit. There is always a reason for unanswered prayer—you can count on that; but it often has to do with God trying to get our attention. Had God answered as soon as we asked, we could miss the beauty of waiting and seeking His face.

And now we see that Jesus isn't finished. He moves from seeking to knocking. He now implies not only that asking might not result in an immediate answer—so, too, seeking. Isn't seeking enough? What is God trying to do with us? Surely my seeking God shows my earnestness. Is it not unfair for Him to keep luring me to do more? But here is what He says: "Ask and it will be given to you; seek and you will find; knock and the door will be opened to you." In Revelation 3:20 Jesus does the knocking: "I stand at the door and knock. If anyone hears my voice and opens the door, I will come in and eat with him, and he with me." But in Matthew 7:7 we do the knocking.

I remind you that primary object of our seeking is that we might find God's face. This means awareness of His approval. "The LORD bless you and keep you; the LORD make his face shine upon you and be gracious to you; the LORD turn his face toward you and give you peace" (Numbers 6:24–26). His disapproval can be reflected in the position of His face as well: "Do not hide your face from me, do not turn your servant away in anger" (Psalm 27:9). Furthermore, "the face of the Lord is against those who do evil, to cut off the memory of them from the earth" (Psalm 34:16). But the preponderant usage of God's face is with reference to getting His attention. "How long will you hide your face from me?" (Psalm 13:1). "Restore us, O God; make your face shine upon us, that we may be saved" (Psalm 80:3). We therefore seek God's face because we want His attention—that He will take notice of us.

Finding the face of God means gaining immediate access into His presence. But did we not have this already when we first came to God in faith through Jesus Christ? Yes, we have been justified by faith through God's Son "through whom we have gained access" into this grace (Romans 5:1–2). Since we already have access, then, why do we need to keep knocking? It is that our Lord wants us to gain our full inheritance—fellowship with the Father and a reward at the Judgment Seat of Christ.

Being justified by faith qualifies us for heaven, yes. But Jesus invites us to enjoy a little bit of heaven to go to heaven in. The Puritan Thomas Brooks wrote a treatise called *Heaven on Earth*. Sadly, not all who are saved seem to take advantage of this privilege. Matthew 7:7 is about inheriting the Kingdom of heaven to the full. This means not only assurance of heaven when we die, but the knowledge that we please God by the care to please God on earth. This comes by asking, seeking and knocking.

The Purpose of Knocking

We knock to get the attention of one on the other side of the door. Why do we knock on the door to get God's attention? It is because God requires it. We must never underestimate what a privilege prayer is. We must never take for granted the inestimable joy that is on the other side of the door—when it opens. When something is given with ease or granted by a mere press of a button, we tend not to appreciate this. I took a friend of mine bonefishing—his first time to do this—and, would you believe, he hooked a large bonefish within two minutes of his first cast. He said, "I thought bonefishing was hard. This is a piece of cake." As it happened, that fish got away. Not only that, we fished for two more days—and he never hooked another bonefish. He then appreciated what an accomplishment it is to catch a bonefish.

When a person asks God and gets an immediate answer, they think praying is a piece of cake. But after asking and then seeking, one realizes that prayer is not an enterprise by which you snap your finger at God and expect Him to salute you. God wants us to appreciate prayer itself, not to mention what prayer will do for us. That is, if we seek—and then knock.

While you are knocking, you begin to know something of God's ways. Most people do not care about God's ways. It is not on their radar screen, not something they ever knew about much less wanted. God lamented of ancient Israel, "They have not known my ways" (Hebrews 3:10). God wants to be appreciated not for what He can do for you but for what He is in Himself. He has certain "ways." The more you get to know a person, the more you see their "ways"—their personality, their likes and dislikes, their mannerisms and habits. God has ways, likes and dislikes, and a certain way of doing things. He wants you to get to know them. It comes through knocking. Effort. Persistence. Not giving up.

Chances are, you do not discover God's ways in a flash or instantaneous moment of revelation. Knowing His ways comes gradually. By continually knocking, you begin to perceive something about the God of the Bible. The interesting thing is, the more you know God's ways the more you want to know Him. Nobody—*nobody*—knew God as Moses did. And yet when Moses was given a blank check to fill out one day—when he could have asked for anything—his choice was: "If you are pleased with me, teach me your ways" (Exodus 33:13). There is no grander invitation than the opportunity to know the ways of our heavenly Father. And yet one of God's ways (which you might not like) was discovered by the prophet Isaiah: "Truly you are a God who hides himself, O God and Savior of Israel" (Isaiah 45:15). This is one of His characteristics.

You might say: "I don't think I like God's ways very much if He is going to hide Himself." I reply: God wants to see if, as you get to know His ways, you will keep knocking. Jesus keeps knocking on our door because He loves us and knows our truest need. We must keep knocking in order to get God's attention, even when He chooses to hide His face.

When God Sets You Up

God sometimes plays hard to get. He may tease us, not revealing for a while that it is He who's on your case or what He really feels. Be on the lookout, therefore, for God's strategic setup. It is the Divine tease. When Jacob wrestled with the man who appeared as an enemy, he had no idea the man was actually an angel. But once Jacob perceived what was going on, he said, "I will not let you go unless you bless me" (Genesis 32:26). It was a setup to see if he would persevere.

Martin Luther said that you must know God as an enemy before you can know Him as a friend. Jesus appeared to two men on the road to Emmaus, but they were "kept from recognizing him" (Luke 24:16). When Jesus "acted as if he were going further," it was a setup to see whether these two men wanted Him to remain. They passed the test: "They urged him strongly, 'Stay with us' . . . so he went in to stay with them" (Luke 24:28–29). Then they found out it was Jesus. "Knock and the door will be opened to you."

The opportunity to knock and keep knocking can therefore come in disguises. It is a setup to see how much we really want more of God. It is like breaking the betrayal barrier, as I said earlier. It is said of Hezekiah, "God left him to test him to know everything that was in his heart" (2 Chronicles 32:31). While we are knocking, God is testing. Those who keep knocking get

God's attention. Those who give up along the way forfeit the incalculable joy that could have been theirs.

What Knocking Does

Knocking wakes one up. One knocks for one reason: *to be heard.* Sometimes God appears to be asleep. "Awake, and rise to my defense!" cried David (Psalm 35:23). "Awake, O Lord! Why do you sleep? Rouse yourself!" (Psalm 44:23). And yet the truth is, "He who watches over Israel will neither slumber nor sleep" (Psalm 121:4). "Even the darkness will not be dark to you; the night will shine like the day, for darkness is as light to you" (Psalm 139:12).

A sure way to be heard is to pray in God's will, as we have seen already (1 John 5:14). And yet God said to Hezekiah, "I have heard your prayer and seen your tears" (2 Kings 20:5). Sometimes tears get God's attention. "Those who sow in tears will reap with songs of joy" (Psalm 126:5). I do not say this is necessarily required, but sometimes tears become a form of knocking and getting God's attention.

Ancient Israel were frustrated because they were not getting God's attention. "Why have we humbled ourselves, and you have not noticed?" The prophet responded to that, telling them what to do: Try a different kind of fasting, "to loose the chains of injustice, and untie the cords of the yoke, to set the oppressed free and break every yoke . . . to share your food with the hungry" (Isaiah 58:3–7). Indeed, while we wait for God to show up, we can learn things that God wants us to do. This is why God does not immediately answer when we first ask or even seek. So we knock. We keep knocking. Why? Because until God answers, we don't know we are being heard! In the meantime, we not only get to know God's ways but, may it be so, we develop character. "We also rejoice in our sufferings, because we know that suffering produces perseverance; perseverance, character" (Romans 5:3–4).

In other words, knocking—while we are waiting to be heard—carries many fringe benefits. What is required, then, is persistence in knocking. Persistence means to keep at it, even stubbornly.

The throne of grace (Hebrews 4:16) is the door to the throne room. But we know that a person may not be right inside a door to hear. So we keep knocking. The assumption in knocking is that the person you want to reach is at home, on the other side of the door. They won't know you are there until you knock. Jesus tells us to knock. For God is there.

A Further Assumption: Praying Isn't Easy

Praying isn't necessarily fun. It can be work. Sometimes it is hard work. John Wesley reckoned we should spend two hours in prayer for every one hour in conversation with each other. I have written of meeting Richard Wurmbrand many years ago, when he said to me, "Young man, spend more time talking to God about men than talking to men about God." It is easier to talk to people and with each other. Prayer, as Jacob discovered, can be a wrestling match. If only it were simple, like pushing a button or snapping your finger.

Jesus therefore implies in these words of Matthew 7:7 that you won't only be seeking but also knocking before it is over with. Knocking shows greater effort and can reflect greater anxiety. We wonder: Is the person there? Are we being heard? But we are told by Paul never to be anxious, but merely put our prayer and petitions to God with thanksgiving (Philippians 4:6). And yet God promises to answer the door! On one occasion, the place shook when God showed up and the Spirit of God fell (Acts 4:31). God opened the door and stepped in when the Church prayed earnestly for Peter (Acts 12:5–7).

Knocking would appear to be the last resort. Jesus does not add any further instruction once He mentions knocking. Ask. Seek. Knock. When you have ascended this scale of urgency to knocking, the answer is not far away. After all, God's own integrity is at stake. The persistence and patience are not for nothing. The greater the suffering, the greater the anointing; the longer we wait, the greater the reward; the harder we knock, the greater the answer. Getting God's attention is worth all the effort it took. He will come. The opening of the door is worth waiting for.

77. Answered Prayer

*For everyone who asks receives; he who seeks finds; and
to him who knocks, the door will be opened.*

MATTHEW 7:8

It might be said that this verse is redundant—that Jesus already said the same thing in Matthew 7:7. But Jesus emphasizes this truth by summarizing it. The only thing that is different is that He switches from second person plural in verse 7 ("you") to third person singular in verse 8: "For everyone who asks receives, he who seeks finds; and to him who knocks, the door will be opened." By beginning with "For" He is emphasizing what He just said, appealing to a general principle—namely, that our heavenly Father is a God who answers prayer.

This is an encouragement and a warning. It is an encouragement to let us know how strongly this should be believed. But there is an implicit warning: The full benefit of answered prayer is promised only to those who keep praying and are found knocking when God steps in to answer prayer.

What, then, is Jesus' emphasis in Matthew 7:8 telling us? First, that God answers prayer. This verse is about answered prayer. Second, we should never stop praying; those who keep praying are the ones who will be rewarded. Third, the promise of answered prayer is extended to those who faithfully and continually ask, seek and knock. But do be reminded: The asking, seeking and knocking relates to wanting more of God. That is why these lines are put precisely here in the Sermon on the Mount. God is not against our praying for healing, prosperity or material benefits. After all, the Bible is full of encouragements along these lines. But the context of Matthew 7:7–8 is what Jesus has been teaching regarding the Kingdom of heaven.

This verse is primarily for people who hear Jesus' teaching and yearn for an anointing of being merciful, having a righteousness that outclasses the Law and a faith that eclipses all worry about material things. This verse appeals to that person who is saying, "If only I could be like that! If only I had grace to bless my enemies! If only I could overcome worry!" It is to this concern that Jesus says, *Ask for it.* "For everyone who asks receives; he who seeks finds; and to him who knocks, the door will be opened." Jesus is, therefore, telling us that the lifestyle He portrays in the Sermon on the Mount is possible. Being merciful is possible. Rejoicing in persecution is possible. Blessing your enemy is possible. Not committing adultery in your heart is possible. Not having to prove yourself by using God's name is possible. Not worrying about your daily needs is possible. Living a life of not pointing the finger is possible. And if you and I desire to live this way, Jesus simply says: *Ask for it.* Our heavenly Father answers prayer.

The Promise of Answered Prayer

Jesus restates verse 7 as an encouragement. If anything, it is stronger. "For everyone who asks receives." He would not say this if you were praying to be a millionaire. But because you are praying for this righteousness that Jesus envisages for the people of God, "Everyone who asks receives." So if you have taken on board the teaching of the Sermon on the Mount and want to be the living example of this, "Ask," says Jesus. If there is a delay, "Seek." And if you feel God is hiding Himself, "Knock."

I remind you, God has put His integrity on the line. If our heart-cry is for more of Him, it touches His heart. You are on safe territory. You are not asking "amiss" to consume it on your lusts (James 4:1–4, KJV).

You need not fear you will be persevering in the wrong request, as did those when God granted their request but sent a wasting disease on them (Psalm 106:15). No worries about that! When you are asking for more of God and true godliness, you are safe, safe, safe. You have captured God's heart. For Matthew 7:8 is a promise to those who want what Jesus is talking about. As Don Carson put it, no spiritual progress is made apart from God's grace, but nothing is more crucial than to ask for that grace.

The Paradox of Answered Prayer

There are two principles that will bear our examination. First, *any prayer prayed in the will of God will be answered.* The proof of this: "This is the confidence we have in approaching God: that if we ask anything according to his will, he hears us" (1 John 5:14). It is not Jesus who tells us this here in the Sermon on the Mount. John tells us. And so does Paul. He says we don't always know what to pray for, but the Holy Spirit in us intercedes for us "in accordance with God's will" (Romans 8:26–27). It is gratifying to know that the very Holy Spirit in us is continually praying for us—always in God's will! We have also Jesus at God's right hand interceding for us (Romans 8:34).

If this presents a dilemma—namely, that we don't always know what the will of God is—I ask: Are we always better off to know God's will? God *could* reveal His will by the Spirit—and sometimes does: "If we *know that he hears* us . . . we know that we have what we asked of him" (1 John 5:15, emphasis mine). That is a big "if," and sometimes God lets us know as we pray that we are being heard.

I ask also: Would it slow down or speed up our praying if we knew in advance our prayer was heard? I suggest it would slow down our praying, if not stop it. We would relax and be grateful God has heard us. But if we don't know for sure, we pray harder. That is almost certainly the reason God does not let everybody know that they are being heard. It is not that some are more spiritual than others, or that some have more faith. It is God's sovereign, gracious overruling in order to keep us near the throne of grace. Jesus appeals to us in Matthew 7:7–8 as if we knew little or nothing about the sovereign will of God in prayer. Jesus' point is that answered prayer comes to the persistent. But there is an exception to this. It

is a sobering truth: If we pray in the will of God but don't know we have prayed in His will, only to stop praying, the fallout of answered prayer can be negative as well as positive. Zechariah obviously prayed in the will of God when asking for a son. The proof: "Your prayer has been heard," said the angel Gabriel to Zechariah—many years later (Luke 1:13). But when Zechariah was notified that his prayer was going to be answered, he foolishly wanted to argue with Gabriel! This was an unwise thing to do. In any case, it did not abort the answered prayer. That prayer would absolutely be answered.

But there is a second principle. Although any prayer prayed in the will of God will be answered, *the shape an answered prayer takes is determined by our readiness at the time.* Zechariah was not ready. He and Elizabeth apparently asked for a son, but did not seek or knock. They gave up a long time before. Zechariah concluded that with the aging of Elizabeth and himself (Luke 1:18), it was a prayer that was going to remain unanswered. He was wrong. It was answered, but he would be struck dumb in the meantime: "silent and not able to speak" (Luke 1:20). His prayer was answered, but Zechariah was left with an embarrassing affliction.

The paradox of answered prayer is that God will ensure that any prayer prayed in His will *will* be answered. But if we have given up in the meantime, the shape it takes is determined by our readiness at the time it is answered. Zechariah was not ready. He stopped seeking and knocking. He gave up too soon.

In Luke 12, Jesus presents the happy scenario of those who stayed near the door, having been commanded to be dressed and "ready for service." "Like men waiting for their master to return from a wedding banquet, so that when he comes and knocks they can immediately open the door for him" (Luke 12:35–36). The way we can open the door immediately is to be near the door—to hear the knocking! This shows expectancy. So when one keeps knocking he or she will be heard. If we have prayed and are waiting for God to show up, we need to be near the door so we don't miss His coming.

This is the same thing put to us in Jesus' parable about the persistent widow. He gave the parable that we should always pray and never give up. He described a judge who finally yielded to the request of a persevering widow. Jesus used this example to show how much more our Father will bring about justice to those who "cry out to him day and night." But there is more: "When the Son of man comes, will he find faith on the earth?" (Luke 18:1–8). Though this ultimately may well refer to the Second Coming, it is put in the context of being ready for answered prayer. The question is: When God answers, will we be found believing at the time?

The Preconditions of Answered Prayer

To be sure that our prayer will be answered, two conditions must precede. First is that what we want is what God wants. This is what is meant by *the will of God*. It is also what is meant by wanting *more of God*. This is when the teaching of Jesus so grips us that we long for this above all else. The second thing, says Jesus, is that we don't give up praying. Many fail at this point. They ask once, maybe twice. But they give up—and don't even seek, much less knock. But the precondition of the answered prayer Jesus puts to us in the Sermon on the Mount is that we are *found praying*—right to the moment God steps in.

We come now to the main reason Jesus repeats verse 8 as He does. Because these words are present participle in the Greek, it means that prayer is answered to those who are still asking, seeking, knocking. It is not to those who asked, sought, knocked. It is to those who were found asking, seeking and knocking right up to the time God showed up. This is merely another way of showing that the promise is to those who keep at it.

Postponement of Answered Prayer

The very fact that Jesus moves from asking to seeking—and then knocking—shows that answered prayer is very often delayed. Why? Because unanswered prayer is God's will as much as answered prayer. This is partly because God often has something more in mind than what we envisage at first. But it is mainly because we get to know His ways while He waits. While we wait, we can worship. The postponement means time for us to discover God's ways and become refined in our own grasp of His will. We may see

our desires modify. Our desires become sanctified. However, if indeed all we asked was for more of God, it is hard to figure out how a request like that needs refinement. "Surely wanting more of God is complete in itself," we might say.

I will explain. We must be sure that our desire for a greater anointing is entirely for God's glory. I wanted a greater anointing on my preaching at Westminster Chapel. But was that necessarily a holy wish? Could it not have been partly my pride in wanting to be a greater preacher? You will say: "Surely that is a good motive." Perhaps. But the heart is deceitful and desperately wicked (Jeremiah 17:9). I have learned to have a healthy mistrust in my own motives. And it could well be that we all need to reassess our motives in our praying. If we delight ourselves in the Lord, He will give us the desires of our hearts, yes (Psalm 37:4). But the more our delight is in the Lord, our desires and motives under God's searchlight could likely bear with some more refinement.

The postponement means time to get to know God better and to learn what exactly He wants to do with us. Postponement of answered prayer means we are given more time to change. God doesn't change, we do. When God delays in answering prayer, it means we are given time to move out of our comfort zone. To learn God's ways. To forgive—totally. To discover what grieves the Spirit.

The Process of Answered Prayer

Answered prayer may come in stages. God could zap us instantaneously. But could we cope with that? We might take ourselves too seriously. Never forget this: A greater anointing can lead to pride. But if God answers our requests for more of Him in stages—even in very small increments—it keeps us on our knees and on our toes! We might be less vulnerable to pride.

It often happens, then, that answered prayer for more of God and godliness comes in imperceptible stages. We may not be conscious of any dramatic change. Therefore, we keep on praying, hoping, too, that nothing will go to our heads. We may find ourselves discovering evils in our makeup we hadn't seen before. Instead of making progress, we may feel we are going backward. The truth, however, is frequently this: We are making very substantial progress indeed. One of the greatest evidences of seeing the glory of God is to see our sin (Isaiah 6:1–5).

Do not be surprised, therefore, if you discover that it is after a period of time—and looking back—that you notice a change in yourself. Others will see it, too. "You're not like you used to be," they may say to you—meaning that the change is positive. This is a frequent way God answers prayer. It is not a good sign when you never change. I recall having a deacon boast to me, "I haven't changed in thirty years," referring to his perspective on certain matters. I felt sad.

I'd rather identify with John Newton, who once said to his friend William Cowper: "I'm not what I ought to be, I'm not what I want to be, I'm not what I hope to be, but thank God I'm not what I used to be."

We must not lose heart. Any new exposure of sin in our hearts should be taken as a good sign that God isn't finished with us yet. To those who persist in asking, seeking and knocking, it is a guarantee: "Everyone who asks receives; he who seeks finds; and to him who knocks, the door will be opened." So with you: Your prayer is being answered.

78. The God Who Answers Prayer

Which of you, if his son asks for bread, will give him a stone? Or if he
asks for a fish, will give him a snake? If you, then, though you are evil,
know how to give good gifts to your children, how much more will
your Father in heaven give good gifts to those who ask him!

MATTHEW 7:9–11

Our Lord now brings in an illustration—by way of a question—to apply what He has been teaching about prayer. So far we have seen five things:

(1) *God wants us to pray.* The devil doesn't want us to pray. As William Cowper put it, "Satan trembles when he sees the weakest saint upon his knees." Martin Luther noted that Satan is well aware of what prayer achieves and can do. That is why the devil creates so many obstacles and disturbances, to keep us from getting around to prayer.

(2) *God does not promise to answer prayer until we ask.* Rule number one: Ask. "You do not have, because you do not ask God" (James 4:2). As John Wesley taught, God does nothing but in answer to prayer. So it was when it came to Pentecost. Though the falling of the Holy Spirit was planned and predestined, it was preceded by ten days of intercessory prayer by Jesus' followers (Acts 1:12–14).

> Oh what peace we often forfeit, oh
>   what needless pain we bear,
> All because we do not carry everything
>   to God in prayer.
>   Joseph M. Scriven (1819–1886)

(3) *God answers prayer.* "How much more will your Father in heaven give good gifts to those who ask him!" (Matthew 7:11).

(4) *The process of prayer is often delayed.* This is why Jesus turns from asking to seeking and, after that, when seeking doesn't come through for us, we are to knock. For some reason, answered prayer rarely occurs the first time we approach God. In this chapter we will see why this is.

It is why we have the illustration in Matthew 7:9–11.

(5) *It is the anointing of the Holy Spirit,* not material things, that God primarily has in mind in this passage on prayer. There is nothing wrong in praying for physical and material needs. We have plenty of verses in the New Testament for this, not to mention the Lord's Prayer. But the immediate context in the Sermon on the Mount is mainly regarding our spiritual need, and that it is a greater relationship with God we should want. It is assumed that our spiritual appetite has been whetted by what Jesus has taught up to now. And if you need further proof of this, I remind you to examine the parallel passage in Luke, ending with these words: "How much more will your Father in heaven give the Holy Spirit to those who ask him!" (Luke 11:13).

Jesus now turns to what you might wish to call a ridiculous illustration: "Which of you, if his son asks for bread, will give him a stone? Or if he asks for a fish, will give him a snake?" But Jesus gets our attention and makes the point: If a child asks for something wholesome to eat (bread or fish), will one's earthly father grant something unwholesome or inedible (a stone) or something harmful (a snake)? Jesus does this that we might focus now on the kind of God who answers prayer. Keep in mind it is the same God who also may withhold an answer to our prayers. There is a reason for answered prayer, a reason for prayer delayed, and a reason for unanswered prayer. It is that the God who hears and sees—namely, our heavenly Father—controls the results of our praying.

Dr. Martyn Lloyd-Jones said that if he were asked to state in one phrase what he regards as the greatest defect in most Christian lives, he would say it is "our failure to know God as our Father as we should know Him." It is my own opinion that the reason for this is partly psychological as well as spiritual. None of has have had perfect parents. Many have very imperfect parents indeed. Our only frame of reference for what we call "father" conjures up an image utterly unlike what Jesus wants us to have of His Father.

Take, for example, the perfectionist father whose child never fully comes "up to standard." I relate to this. I had a wonderful dad, but I never felt I ever came up to his standard. He wanted A's instead of B's, A plusses instead of A minuses. However, I don't relate to the absentee father, who is never around when you need him. Or the cruel father, who abuses his child. But people with imperfect fathers therefore struggle in varying degrees to make the switch from the natural to the heavenly. We have to cross over into the supernatural to see and embrace a Father who is perfect in every way. It is beyond our natural comprehension, but that is the God Jesus puts before us. And dare I say it: Jesus proudly puts His Father before us. Jesus is proud of His Father.

We need to make an important clarification, as seen earlier in this book. This teaching does not cohere well with the popular idea of "fatherhood of God and brotherhood of man"—which, generally speaking, is theological liberalism and not New Testament teaching. God is our Father only through His Son (John 1:12). He is Father not because of Creation but only regeneration (John 3:3) and our being adopted into the family (Ephesians 1:4).

The question is: *Who is this God who answers prayer?* What is He like? Why does He wait and withhold giving what we ask for? I answer: He is the totally just God, indeed, the perfect Father. He does everything right. He makes no mistakes. He is not demanding an impossible perfectionism of us. He is there when we need Him and He is never cruel.

Comparison between Our Human Father and Our Heavenly Father

What we—or our parents—would never do is intentionally harm or hurt. If a son asks for bread,

would the father give him a stone? If he asks for fish, would the father give him a snake? Of course not. The perfectionist or absentee parent would not do that sort of thing. Bad parenting comes from bad teaching. Where did our parents get their training? From their parents, who were also imperfect. They pass on the only way they know to be. It is usually not intentional cruelty they manifest—it is repeating old habits that eventually seem harmless to them.

This is why we have these amazing words, that God punishes sin by punishing "the children and their children for the sin of the fathers to the third and fourth generation" (Exodus 34:7). What our parents do is to give bread if we ask for bread, and fish if we ask for fish. Jesus concluded: "How much more will your Father in heaven give good gifts to those who ask him!"

Contrast between Human Fathers and Our Heavenly Father

First, they are not the same in nature. We—and our parents—are "evil," says Jesus. We are all evil. All of us have sinned (Romans 3:23). In Adam, "all die" (1 Corinthians 15:22). God alone is totally good and without sin. How does this make you feel?

In what might appear to be a throwaway comment, Jesus gives His assessment of humankind. No philosopher, psychologist or theologian has come up with a better explanation for why the human race is the way it is. The truth is, we are all depraved. Jesus thus unveils His doctrine of original sin: It is the condition of the entire human race, of every human being, man or woman, without exception. He calls all of us "evil." This does not mean that all of us are as bad as we could be. After all, we give "good gifts" to our children, which is hardly evil. Wicked people may want to give their children good things. The godfather of the Mafia can order to have someone's knee caps cut off but be nice to his own children. The worst want what is best for their kids. Our parents are "evil," and we as parents are "evil," says Jesus.

The contrast between our parents and our heavenly Father is they are not the same in nature—or nearness. We as parents, being human, can only be in one place at a time. But our Father in heaven can be with you and me simultaneously even though we are separated by distance. Our Father in heaven is not only devoid of evil, He is able to get things done. He is incapable of making a mistake. He is omnipresent. "Where can I go from your Spirit? Where can I flee from your presence? If I go up to the heavens, you are there; if I make my bed in the depths, you are there" (Psalm 139:7–8). God is closer than our hands or our feet, closer than the air we breathe.

Our parents and our heavenly Father differ also in that they are not the same in knowing, supplying or assessing our need. For one thing, our parents may not have the ability to give us the gifts we want. When I was growing up in Ashland, Kentucky, my friends in the neighborhood would get better presents than I at Christmas. I got one new pair of shoes a year (no matter how much my feet had grown in the meantime). My dad would only say, "Son, I work for wages, I have done my best for you." But God is able to give us anything. However, because God alone is good and wise, He knows the difference between good and evil as nobody does. Because our parents are "evil," they make mistakes. Our Father in heaven is the perfect parent—never making a mistake even when disciplining us (Hebrews 12:10–11). God our Father therefore knows what the need truly is. Our parents—and we as parents—can only give an estimate and a good, educated and loving guess. But our heavenly Father is all wise and knows exactly what is a "good gift." No good thing will He withhold from us (Psalm 84:11).

The Character of Our Heavenly Father

We have seen that God can delay in answering our prayer. But since it is a spiritual need that Matthew 7:7–11 is primarily about, why does He wait? Surely God wants what is spiritually right for us as soon as possible—immediately. So why does He not supply our spiritual need all at once? I think the answer is, first, that we will truly appreciate it. He wants us to esteem His "good gifts"—indeed, the Holy Spirit (Luke 11:13)—beyond all else.

Second, the seeking we are called to do is to *find* in this case; we are wrestling with God. Doing that is to get to know Him and thus find our anointing increasing—by stages. We may be unconscious of any progress. Moses did not know that his face was radiant with God's glory (Exodus 34:29).

Third, God does not give us everything that is spiritual all at once in order that success in answered prayer comes when we are ready for it. As Dr. Lloyd-Jones used to say to me, "The worst thing that can happen to a man is to succeed before he is ready." This can happen if your prayer is answered too soon! You might begin to take yourself too seriously and become self-righteous.

Fourth, God withholds from us things until the time is exactly right. He not only gives good gifts, He withholds—in two ways: (1) until we are ready and (2) what was never right or good for us in any case. It is only a matter of time that all of us see that God does everything right, whether by answering prayer or the withholding of answered prayer. What He has in mind is infinitely better for us than what we wanted at first. To quote Shakespeare, "All's well that ends well." God is unimprovably wise.

Why did Jesus refer to "bread" and "fish"? Why not money? It is because Jesus is talking about what is essential to our spiritual lives—namely, the anointing. The anointing is as essential to our spiritual life as food is to our living. He thus emphasizes what our prudent, omniscient Father in heaven can do in comparison to what our natural parents can do.

What Jesus does is to use an argument by way of comparison: "how much more." We see this in the book of Hebrews: "*How much more,* then, will the blood of Christ . . . cleanse our consciences" compared to Old Testament sacrifices (Hebrews 9:14, emphasis mine)? "*How much more* severely do you think a man deserves to be punished" who has treated Christ's blood an unholy thing when compared to disobeying Moses (Hebrews 10:29, emphasis mine)? So here: *How much more* will your Father in heaven give good gifts when compared to our human parents?

If only we could make the switch—and cross over—from the perception we have regarding our natural father to our all-powerful heavenly Father, we would see how secure we are with Him. This is true not merely with reference to our eternal security but in having all that is right and good for us.

79. Spiritual Gifts

If you, then, though you are evil, know how to give good gifts to your children,
how much more will your Father in heaven give good gifts to those who ask him!

MATTHEW 7:11

What are the "good gifts" that are promised to us? Is it possible that they could include various spiritual gifts? Yes. Paul talks about gifts such as having wisdom, knowledge, faith, healing, miracles and prophecy in 1 Corinthians 12:8–10. Could Jesus' reference to "good gifts" mean these spiritual gifts? Yes.

The parallel passage in Luke, as we have seen, substitutes "Holy Spirit" for "good gifts" (Luke 11:13). This is not the only meaning, but these gifts would be included. After all, Paul said we should earnestly desire the greater gifts (1 Corinthians 12:31). And what we are urged by the Holy Spirit to covet would most certainly be included in Matthew 7:11. We have seen that Matthew 7:7 and following does not refer to material or financial needs, but rather desiring more of God and a greater anointing of the Holy Spirit. The context is seeking more of God, not material things. As we observed, there are plenty of New Testament passages that cover our daily physical needs, but Matthew 7:7–11 is not one of them.

Eagerly Desire the Spiritual Gifts

Do you desire the spiritual gifts? I'm afraid that if you and I have a "take it or leave it" attitude regarding spiritual gifts, it suggests we don't have a healthy desire for more of God.

Earlier, I discussed the silent divorce in the Church, speaking generally, between the Word and the Spirit. Those on the "Word side" stress the fruits of the Spirit. Those on the "Spirit side" emphasize the gifts of the Spirit. Most of the Sermon on the Mount deals with fruits more than gifts. But the truth is, we should want both the fruits and the gifts—all we can have—if we are asking, seeking and knocking because we want more of God. An earnest desire is a prerequisite

to receiving more of God and godliness. David narrowed his desires down to one: "One thing I ask of the LORD, this is what I seek: that I may dwell in the house of the LORD all the days of my life, to gaze upon the beauty of the LORD and to seek him in his temple" (Psalm 27:4). "Delight yourself in the LORD and he will give you the desires of your heart" (Psalm 37:4). "My soul waits for the Lord more than watchmen wait for the morning, more than watchmen wait for the morning" (Psalm 130:6). "I have treasured the words of his mouth more than my daily bread," said Job (Job 23:12).

When Jesus compares bread and fish to "good gifts," He does so because food is essential to physical life—and the good gifts Jesus mentions are essential to our spiritual life. As bread is to the body, so is the anointing of the Spirit to your soul. If you are in medicine, you need knowledge and clear thinking to help your patients. If you are in law, you need the same thing for your clients. Whatever your job or occupation, you need certain essentials to do what you are paid to do. So with your spiritual life: You need all the help you can get to inherit the Kingdom of God. The purpose of spiritual gifts is for edification. These gifts edify you and also the Body of Christ generally. "Now to each one the manifestation of the Spirit is given for the common good" of the Church (1 Corinthians 12:7). This means that everybody is better off if you flourish in the gifts of the Spirit as well as exhibit the fruits of the Spirit.

Testing Your Gift

A key as to whether you truly have a gift of the Spirit is whether it manifests without effort on your part. In other words, do you have to "work it up," or does it come effortlessly? One of the greatest proofs of the anointing is that you function with ease and without effort. When you go outside your anointing or gifting you will struggle—an indication that something has gone wrong. To the spiritual, the supernatural seems natural. The greatest freedom is having nothing to prove.

A true gift of the Spirit ought to convey excellence. The "most excellent way"—namely, that of love (1 Corinthians 12:31–1 Corinthians 13)—should be the backdrop of all spiritual gifts. This means the simultaneous combination of the Word and Spirit—of both fruits and gifts of the Spirit. Nothing is sadder than the gifts manifesting without the fruits. They tend to fall flat, show pride and sometimes draw more attention to the person's gifting. One does not need to be spiritual to have the gifts functioning (Romans 11:22).

My family and I had the privilege of spending an hour with Corrie ten Boom in Holland in 1975. I had heard she was a strong believer in the gifts of the Spirit, and so I asked her to confirm this. "Yes," she replied. "First Corinthians 12 and 14, but don't forget 1 Corinthians 13," she added. How wise. The folly of the Corinthian church was partly that they were preoccupied with the gift of tongues but lacked the excellence of love.

The Quest for Spiritual Gifts

We should be asking, seeking and knocking for good gifts. What do they have to do with the Holy Spirit? Everything. Take away the Holy Spirit from Matthew 7:11, and what is left? Would you want any gift if God was not behind your having it? What makes the gift "good" is that it is what God wants for you. Speaking personally, I have prayed for all the gifts of the Holy Spirit—along with the fruits of the Spirit—for years and years. I will not give up praying for these. As for you, would you insist on having what God doesn't want you to have? But you are safe in praying for both the gifts and the fruits of the Holy Spirit.

Let us briefly look at the gifts of the Spirit as they emerge in 1 Corinthians 12:8–10. These gifts may be said to be functions of the Holy Spirit, that is, His special activities or purposes. We must not press the distinctiveness of these gifts too far, for they often overlap with each other. There is (1) *wisdom*: the presence of the mind of the Spirit,

having 20/20 foresight vision as to what is the next step forward in knowing God's will; (2) *knowledge*: spiritual or theological knowledge generally, or a specific prophetic word for someone particularly; (3) *faith*: not saving faith but *faith beyond faith*—a special grace to know and apply what God will do next; (4) *healing*: faith to cure a sick person, sometimes through the laying on of hands; (5) *miraculous powers*: extraordinary healings such as removing blindness, creative miracles, seeing arms outstretched or deliverance from the demonic; (6) *prophecy*: ability to see God's will for the present or future; (7) *discerning of spirits*: to know the difference between the Holy Spirit and the demonic; (8) *different kinds of tongues*: which, though it might include linguistic ability, is more likely a private prayer language but also a public utterance that would require an interpretation (1 Corinthians 14:1–5); (9) *interpretation of tongues*: to explain the meaning if one publicly prophesies in a tongue no one understands.

There are further gifts described later in 1 Corinthians 12:28: (10) *helping others*: possibly the lowest in profile but wonderfully relevant for those who need support and encouragement; (11) *gifts of administration*: the ability to keep things in order, to delegate authority and ensure that some in the church are not overloaded with responsibilities. These gifts may be put alongside those listed in Romans 12:6–8: *prophesying*: possibly a higher level of anointing than in 1 Corinthians 12:10, perhaps more like that of Agabus (Acts 11:18); *serving*: being a deacon (Acts 6:1–3); *teaching*: interpreting Scripture and handling apostolic doctrine; *encouraging*: possibly the same as "helping others," as in 1 Corinthians 12:28; *contributing to the needs of others*: possibly referring to those who are wealthy, since Paul says, "Let him give generously"; *leadership*: which could refer to having the aforementioned "gifts of administration" or to a pastor; *showing mercy*: which, though all of us are required to manifest this gift, may refer to those doubly endowed with this grace—but even this person is admonished to "do it cheerfully."

There is yet another set of giftings in Ephesians 4:11. Some would call these offices. I prefer to call them "functions": *apostles*: those sovereignly "sent," mainly to found churches; *prophets* (like Agabus); *evangelists*: those whose paramount gifting is to preach the Gospel to the unsaved; *pastors*: those who oversee congregations or churches; *teachers*: as seen above, those who interpret Scripture and handle apostolic doctrine.

There is a point of view called "cessationism," the belief that the miraculous gifts "ceased" with the closing of the canon of Scripture. I have good friends who uphold this view. I do not. The case for this perspective is very weak indeed. I regard the gifts of the Spirit referred to above as available to the Church today. The fact that these gifts are not seen very much or too often abused—or that too many who allegedly have them "overclaim" (meaning, they claim miracles that did not really happen)—does not warrant throwing out the baby with the bathwater. I have already quoted Dr. Martyn Lloyd-Jones: "The Bible was not given to replace the supernatural, or miraculous. It was given to correct abuses."

The Gift of Friends

There is one more gift in the Body of Christ I must mention: friends. Do you thank God for friends? Do you thank God for Christian fellowship? Chances are that your best friends are Christians. You found them in church. It is commonly said that "blood is thicker than water," that your relatives mean more to you than any friend. But I doubt that—unless your relatives are also a part of the Body of Christ. I know one thing: I need friends and thank God for them.

Not only that, I need friends to whom I will be accountable. We all need to be accountable to one another (Ephesians 5:21). The famous last words of a fallen Christian leader: "I am accountable to God." Sorry, but that's not good enough, even though it sounds pious. We need

friends who will call a spade a spade in us and, if necessary, be lovingly ruthless with what is wrong in our lives. The common thread that is found in every fallen leader: They were in isolation and not accountable to anybody.

Qualifications for Receiving "Good Gifts": Ask, Seek, Knock

Regarding the gifts described in 1 Corinthians 12, Paul says that we should "eagerly desire the greater gifts" (verse 31). What a pity that this exhortation would be rendered irrelevant by those who say it is not possible to have these gifts today. Have you ever wondered how much of the Bible would be deleted if we went through the New Testament and cut out those passages about the supernatural?

But what are the greater gifts? That is a hard call. Probably wisdom, knowledge and prophecy. But I would love to have the gift of healing and miracles, too! Paul primarily urges not speaking or praying in tongues but that prophecy should be mostly sought for (1 Corinthians 14:5). To those, however, who dismiss "tongues" out of hand, pointing out they are the "least" of the gifts, I reply: If you want the greater gifts, be willing to start at the bottom. I don't mean to be unfair, but I have wondered if it is mostly pride that puts people off tongues. Speaking or praying in tongues is the only gift that challenges your pride.

Some desire the gifts but not the fruits. Some desire the fruits of the Spirit but not the gifts of the Spirit. Both approaches are lacking in balance. We need both—equally and simultaneously—and as soon as possible. And if you say, "I asked, but I have not received," I reply: Keep asking. Seek. Knock. God will answer. His Word—His integrity put on the line—is at stake. He will show up.

80. The Gift of the Holy Spirit

How much more will your Father in heaven gift good gifts to those who ask him!

MATTHEW 7:11

How much more will your Father in heaven give the Holy Spirit to those who ask him!

LUKE 11:13

The greatest possible "good gift" to which Jesus refers in Matthew 7:11 is none other than the Holy Spirit Himself, as Luke's account indicates. When Peter said to his hearers on the Day of Pentecost, "Repent and be baptized . . . And you will receive the gift of the Holy Spirit" (Acts 2:38), he knew this is what these amazed Jews were interested in.

It began with the commotion caused by the falling of the Holy Spirit earlier in the day (Acts 2:1–4). This resulted at first in people scoffing and accusing the disciples of drinking "too much wine" (verse 13). That in turn led to Peter's sermon (verses 14–36). Though people scoffed, the truth is they were gripped and fascinated. Many of those who looked on wanted what those 120 disciples had. Peter knew this. He therefore used the platform to explain Joel's prophecy and to preach the cross and Jesus' resurrection from the dead. They were smitten, "cut to the heart" (Acts 2:37). They pleaded, "What shall we do?" Peter told them to repent and be baptized, then assured them that they, too, would receive the "gift of the Holy Spirit." And this is exactly what happened to 3,000 people that day.

The gift of the Holy Spirit is the Spirit Himself. It is more than having the Spirit convict us and lead us *to* Christ. It is the immediate and direct witness of the Spirit, to quote Dr. Martyn Lloyd-Jones. The first time I heard him use that expression was when I was pastor of a Baptist church in Lower Heyford, Oxfordshire, while I was a student at Oxford. I had come up with a catechism for all my members, and Dr. Lloyd-Jones's only correction was that I include that

phrase when I spoke of the inner testimony of the Holy Spirit.

Those who received Peter's message were not only saved but received this immediate and direct witness on the same day. But that was then. Since that time, for some reason, all who are Christians experience this immediate and direct witness. There are two ways to understand the witness of the Holy Spirit. There is (1) the soteriological work of the Spirit—which means salvation—but there is also (2) the Holy Spirit's immediate and direct witness—which is the highest form of assurance. This full assurance is sometimes given at conversion, as at Pentecost and also in the case of Cornelius (Acts 10:44). The evidence that not all believers receive this highest form of assurance is seen in Acts 8:14–17. This shows that some believers await such a receiving of the Spirit. Indeed, after the dazzling conversion of Saul of Tarsus, he, too, would receive the Spirit. Ananias went to Saul's house, placing his hands on him that he might be "filled with the Holy Spirit" which, for some reason, had not taken place until then (Acts 9:17). Paul's epistles show that his readers needed more than assurance of salvation but rather a full, or infallible, assurance.

In any case, Jesus refers to this immediate and direct witness of the Spirit in Luke 11:13. That we are to ask, seek and knock shows that not all who are followers of Jesus have necessarily received this. I myself was converted on April 5, 1942, at the age of six. But my sense of assurance went up and down like a graph on a chart. Then, on October 31, 1955, I was unexpectedly blessed with an immediate and direct filling of the Holy

370 — The Sermon on the Mount

Spirit that made Jesus real, salvation mine and the Bible a new book—not to mention gave me the undoubted assurance of my eternal security. I was never to be the same again. Ever. The person of Jesus was more real than anybody around me. My salvation was so sure to me that I knew I could never be lost. I could see that the Bible teaches predestination; I had never been taught it. My theology changed in hours. I have never looked back.

All Christians have the Holy Spirit in some measure. This comes at conversion by being born again, born of the Spirit (John 3:3). We cannot come to Christ unless we are drawn by the Spirit (John 6:44). We cannot say Jesus is Lord but by the Holy Spirit (1 Corinthians 12:3). Paul affirms that all Christians have the Holy Spirit (Romans 8:9), and yet not all have received the full measure of the Spirit that is mentioned by Peter and the writers of the New Testament. So the Sermon on the Mount creates in us a hunger for more of God, and this hunger will be met by our receiving the Holy Spirit Himself—not merely having the Spirit point us to Christ.

Why Is This Subject So Relevant?

There is so much confusion in the Church today about the Holy Spirit. This is due in part to the sad fact that some Christians are threatened by the idea of "more" when it comes to the Christian faith. Some Christians, sadly, are very content indeed with the knowledge they have believed that Jesus died for them and know that by faith in His death they are going to heaven. And they *will* go to heaven! Their being threatened by more of God does not mean they are not truly converted. But for some reason there are Christians who will have no more talk about this issue and dismiss out of hand what I am writing about in this chapter. They are as saved as I am. More of the Holy Spirit does not make you more saved! But more of the Holy Spirit will give you a taste of heaven below and a blissful life in Christ on the way to heaven that too many know nothing about.

I myself knew nothing about this. Although I was brought up in a church that emphasized being "sanctified" subsequent to conversion—which they also called the "baptism with the Holy Spirit"—I knew nothing about the immediate

and direct witness of the Spirit until October 31, 1955. I wondered at first if I had received a "third" work of grace, only to realize eventually that it was the immediate witness of the Spirit that made me know I was truly saved—and which also made the Cross, the Resurrection and the Second Coming of Jesus indescribably real.

I will put it this way. If what I have described so far is foreign to you—that it is something you yourself have not experienced but you would like to receive it—then Matthew 7:7–11 is absolutely relevant to you. Jesus appeals not to people's greed for material things but their hunger for more of God. And if you have that, I say to you, dear reader: Ask, seek, knock. God will show up. That is His promise, not mine.

Various Terms to Describe This

It would be a mistake to be sidetracked by terms. Whether we talk about the "baptism" (Acts 1:5) or "filling" (Acts 2:4) of the Holy Spirit, or the "earnest" (KJV) or "seal" (2 Corinthians 1:22; Ephesians 1:13), a "rose by any other name would smell as sweet," as Shakespeare put it. In Hebrews, it is God's "rest" (Hebrews 4:10), inheriting what is promised (Hebrews 6:12; 10:36), having God swear an oath to you (Hebrews 6:13–20).

Neither should one be unnecessarily dogmatic about the issue of speaking in tongues. There is a case to be made that tongues comes with the immediate and direct witness, but also a case to be made that it does not always happen that way. I myself speak in tongues, but this did *not* come to me on October 31, 1955. It is my pastoral observation, too, that some speak in tongues and know little or nothing about the immediate and direct witness of the Spirit. The main thing is that we experience what Paul envisaged, that we are filled "to the measure of all the fullness of God" (Ephesians 3:19)—indeed, "filled with the Spirit" (Ephesians 5:18). It is not a particular gift or manifestation one should seek for but for the Holy Spirit Himself. This is what the Sermon on the Mount should make us hungry for.

Full Assurance

What comes with the gift of the Holy Spirit Himself? It brings the highest form of assurance of salvation, the clarification of truth from error, a witness that the Bible is the infallible Word of God. It is contrasted with "syllogistic reasoning," as the Puritans sometimes called it: a major premise followed by a minor premise, then a conclusion. The major premise: Those who trust Christ's death, and not their own works, are saved. The minor premise: But I trust Christ's death on the cross, not my works. The conclusion: Therefore, I am saved. That kind of reasoning—also called the "practical syllogism"—is fair enough. This is good to do. But it does require reasoning.

The immediate and direct coming of the Spirit, however, bypasses the need to reason this way. His own witness conveys with infallible assurance that you are saved. The Greek word *plerophoria*— "full assurance"—sometimes applies to theological understanding (Colossians 2:2–3).

In my own case, the Gospel was made clear, and I would not be where I am today without having had this gift of the Holy Spirit. The Holy Spirit wrote the Bible (2 Timothy 3:16; 2 Peter 2:29–21) and is therefore the best interpreter of Scripture. When He graciously comes in, He makes the Bible clear and is the reason we can affirm the infallibility of Holy Scripture.

Power for Service

But there is more: The Holy Spirit gives power for service. This was D. L. Moody's view. Moody tells how he was walking in Brooklyn when suddenly the Holy Spirit came on him, although he had already been converted for a good while. The power of the Spirit was so great that Moody said that he asked God to "stay His hand" because he could not take it anymore. This power is what enabled the disciples to preach as they did (Acts 1:8), and it is what will enable you and me to witness for Jesus Christ to our friends, even strangers. Before he was filled with the Spirit, Peter was a coward, denying he even knew Jesus (Luke 22:57). But after he was filled, he was bold as a lion and had his fellow Jews begging him to help them (Acts 2:37). "We cannot help speaking about what we have seen and heard," said Peter and John (Acts 4:20). "We must obey God rather than men!" said Peter. "We are witnesses of these things, and so is the Holy Spirit, whom God has given to those who obey him" (Acts 5:29, 32).

When I consider how Peter and John rejoiced after being flogged and warned, I am deeply moved. This account often brings me to tears. They left the Sanhedrin "rejoicing because they had been counted worthy of suffering disgrace for the Name" (Acts 5:41). Think about that for a moment. Suffering disgrace. Embarrassment. Being seen as fools. It is what all of us by nature run a thousand miles to avoid. But not Peter and John. Why? The gift of the Holy Spirit gave them comfort that made their suffering seem as nothing. The Holy Spirit made the difference.

Not all the Puritans (whom I studied at Oxford) believed what I have taught in this chapter, teaching the practical syllogism as a way of coming to assurance. But there were two exceptions that I know of: John Cotton and Thomas Goodwin. Thomas Goodwin's exposition of Ephesians 1:13 brings this out. Dr. Martyn Lloyd-Jones once asked me to read the fifty pages of Goodwin's treatment of Ephesians 1:13, which takes the view that the sealing of the Spirit is over and above what regenerate people normally receive at conversion. When I met with Dr. Lloyd-Jones the following week, he asked, "Well, what did you think?" I merely answered, "It is exactly what I believe." He looked at me with tears in his eyes. "That is the greatest thing I ever heard you say," he said.

The world longs to see that which is real. Fervent. Lively. On fire. Our arid orthodoxy won't do it. Dr. Lloyd-Jones used to speak of those who were "perfectly orthodox, perfectly useless." I don't want to be like that.

The answer is the Holy Spirit—His immediate and direct witness. Does this interest you? Does it grip you? If this is something you do not have, how much do you want this? Thomas Goodwin's words to such people were, "Sue Him for the promise." Yes, sue Him! You have it coming; it is in His Word. Quote His Word back to Him. Ask. Seek. Knock. Everyone who asks receives; he who seeks finds; and to him who knocks, the door will be opened. Don't give up. God will test you to see how important this is to you. Say to the Lord, "I will keep asking, I will keep seeking and I will keep knocking. I won't give up." That is exactly what the Lord wants to hear from you.

81. The Golden Rule

So in everything, do to others what you would have them do
to you, for this sums up the Law and the Prophets.

MATTHEW 7:12

Do to others as you would have them do to you.

LUKE 6:31

This verse, known as the Golden Rule, is without doubt one of the best-known verses of Jesus' teaching. If everybody lived this way, we would have the perfect world! But we don't live this way, sadly—yet you and I are commanded to do so.

The Golden Rule is the bottom line of Jesus' teaching on the Kingdom of heaven. And yet it may be a little hard to understand why Jesus' words were put precisely here in the Sermon on the Mount. The Greek word *ouv*—"therefore"—suggests that the command to live this way follows what Jesus had just said. "So" (the same as "therefore") do to others as you would have them do to you.

What has Jesus said in Matthew 7:7–11 that would lead to this "therefore"? There are at least three possibilities. The first is that our heavenly Father loves us much more than our earthly parents do, and would therefore grant "good gifts" indeed to us. We should do precisely this for others, including being merciful. Second, Jesus had been telling us not to judge in the section preceding these verses on prayer (see Matthew 7:1–5). The "therefore," then, could apply to refusing to judge, since not pointing the finger would be doing to others as we wish they would do to us. But third, it is not unlikely that Matthew 7:12 was Jesus' own conclusion of the whole of His teaching about being merciful (Matthew 5:3), being the salt of the earth (5:13), all He has taught regarding the Law, and how we are to fulfill it (5:20–48; 7:1–5). If so, Matthew 7:12 could have begun a new paragraph (as in the ESV) rather than making it a part of Matthew 7:7–11.

In any case, following the Golden Rule in our lives day and night will be the best way not to grieve the Holy Spirit, to be spared of more grief, and to be loved and respected, not to mention find healing in marriage and other kinds of relationships. No wonder this verse is called the Golden Rule! It is a way to defuse any tension in relationships.

And yet Jesus may not have been the first to say this. The equivalent saying is found in the Apocrypha (Tobit 4:15): "Do not do to anyone what you yourself would hate." It is said that in A.D. 20, when asked to teach the whole Law while standing on one leg (which means you had to think of something very quickly), Rabbi Hillel said: "What is hateful to you, do not do to anyone else; this is the whole law; all the rest is only commentary." Confucius allegedly said, "Do not do to anyone what you yourself would hate." But these quotes are put negatively. It was Jesus who made it positive: "Do to others as you would have them do to you" (Luke 6:31). As Martin Luther said, "Jesus wraps it up in a little package where it can all be found. You are your own Bible" if you live this way. To quote Michael Eaton, "It is a one-sentence rule of thumb that will give us what to do in a thousand complicated situations."

The Opposite of Self-Love

What we have in this verse is the self-love principle put in reverse. It is when selfish love should become absolutely unselfish. You impose the opposite of self-love. You already know full well what you want for yourself, and yet you hope that the other person might do it for you. But, says Jesus, you do it for him or her instead! You should do this without waiting for him or her to do it and get it right. It means you must take the initiative. All you do is begin with yourself, since you know what you would want. We are to love our neighbor as we love ourselves (Leviticus 19:18). We by nature love ourselves. No one has ever hated his own flesh, but feeds and cares for it, says Paul (Ephesians 5:29). "So in everything, do to others what you would have them do to you."

As we will see further below, carrying this out may also be your response to what they have first said to you. It therefore can mean becoming vulnerable, when you show no defensiveness; it can mean turning the other cheek (Matthew 5:19).

Luke's account of the Golden Rule is in the context of loving our enemies, doing good to those who hate us and praying for those who mistreat us (Luke 6:27–31). Matthew's account, as we saw above, is in the context of what a father would do for a son—giving "good gifts." And as our Father's love is so much "more," so we should be to that person what you wish your heavenly Father would be to you. And if you doubt what that is, "Do to others as you would have them do to you." In Luke's account, Jesus added, "Be merciful, just as your Father is merciful" (Luke 6:36). You will recall that Jesus promised to fulfill the Law (Matthew 5:17), which meant He would live this way Himself—which He did. Nobody but Jesus lived this way every day of His life. And yet it is the way you and I are instructed to live as well.

Genuineness

You and I have a fairly shrewd idea how we want others around us to live. First, we want them to be *genuine*. That means we hope they will be true, unfeigned, not hypocritical. We want to be able to trust them. Often, relationships go through three phases: lyrical (when we think we have met the perfect friend), disillusionment (when we feel deceived if not devastated), then reality (when we see things in balance). It takes a little time to find out what the other person is like. Most people do not end up on the pedestal we initially put them on. In fact, I would have to say that every person I have ever admired a little bit too much

sooner or later disappointed me. But that is not his or her fault—it is mine. I should never, ever admire anybody too much! He or she is bound to disappoint—as I would disappoint others, too.

When you are disillusioned with a relationship, you have two choices: (1) to be bitter, if not also to give up your faith. Some people's faith is overthrown when their hero falls. In any case, it shows confidence misplaced. Your other choice is (2) to be the genuine person you thought that person was. I know what it is to be let down—hugely—by one I trusted too much. I have sought to vow (when this happens) to be the kind of person I thought he or she was! My responsibility is to be genuine myself. Trustworthy. To keep my word. That I will be no hypocrite, putting on a "front." I want to be the kind of person who will not let my admirer or follower down. That is what we want from another—and we must be that way ourselves . We want this trust in others, whether we buy from them, listen to them or invest time, money or energy with them. We all want to believe in what is absolutely true. Genuine. Real. Reliable. We want that in others. Let us be that way ourselves—whether or not they are that.

Gentleness

Second, we want others to be *gentle*. That they will be pleasant. Easy. Not severe. Not strict. Not legalistic. We therefore want them to be approachable. We all fear rejection more than almost anything. We never go where we fear we will be rejected. It is an awful feeling to be rejected or to feel rejected. We will avoid this like the plague. An unkind look will put us off. A person who is officious—who takes himself or herself seriously—will put us off. The pretentious person puts us off. The smug person puts us off. The person who wants to create an aura of mystique puts us off. I have had people ask me about this or that person, "Is he or she real? Are they the real deal?" I want to be the real deal.

Jesus was the most unpretentious person that ever was. It is, in a sense, the essence of His glory. He was transparently unpretentious. He made Himself "nothing" (Philippians 2:7). He was meek and lowly in heart (Matthew 11:29). He accepted the underdog. Whereas the devil hits people when they are down, a "bruised reed he will not break," it is said of Jesus (Matthew 12:20).

Are you a bruised reed? Jesus calls for you—*you*—just as you are. It was not only His words but His spirit that enticed the most godless person to flee to Him. He took people as they were. The first person to approach Jesus after the conclusion of the Sermon on the Mount was the leper who knew in his heart that, though rejected by others, he would not be rejected by Jesus—and he was not rejected but accepted (Matthew 8:1). Jesus was popular with sinners. They knew they could trust Him. I want to be Jesus to everybody—never (if possible) to let them down.

Ask yourself this question: Can people approach you? Do people find you unapproachable? We want people to be approachable. Gentle. Jesus is saying that to all of us: to be gentle. "Let your gentleness be evident to all," said Paul (Philippians 4:5).

Graciousness

Third, we want them to be *gracious*. As a matter of fact, the word translated "gentleness" in Philippians 4:5 comes from the Greek word *epieikes*. In Hellenistic literature, this word was used to show that if you had a chance to throw the book at somebody because you had the goods on them, you set them free instead. That is the meaning of this word—which actually comes to the English word *graciousness*. The opposite of graciousness is throwing the book at them—making them pay, rubbing their noses in it because you have found them out, remembering every fault, making them feel guilty through fear of punishment, making them suffer, keeping a record of wrongs. But love keeps no record of wrongs (1 Corinthians 13:5). Why do we keep records? To prove we paid. So when you say to someone who made an inappropriate comment, "I will remember that," and throw it up later, it shows you kept a record of that wrong. But love will tear up that record.

Do you have the "goods" on somebody? Do you have the power to "spill the beans" on him or her? Do you have a record of wrongs that would hurt, embarrass or ruin this person? I answer: *Tear that record up.* Do it—do it now—and you will be set free. It is letting him or her save face. This way you win a friend for life. You overlook what

this person is already aware of. He or she already feels guilty. He or she is already conscious of that skeleton in the closet (we all have them). Why add to his or her guilt? Jesus wouldn't.

Graciousness is overlooking their fault. "He who covers over an offense promotes love" (Proverbs 17:9). "A man's wisdom gives him patience; it is to his glory to overlook an offense" (Proverbs 19:11). "It is the glory of God to conceal a matter" (Proverbs 25:2). Be gracious in private—set the person at ease. Be gracious in public—not telling the wrong he or she did, indeed, telling nobody. And you must be gracious in prayer—praying that he or she will be dealt with by God as you want God to deal with you. I hope you will smile when I give three principles here: (1) It is never wrong to be gracious. (2) It is never wrong to be gracious. (3) It is never wrong to be gracious.

Goodness

Fourth, we want people we encounter to be *good*. The Law is "good" if a person uses it properly (1 Timothy 1:8). The proper use is to apply its righteousness by the Golden Rule. This way you will, for example, honor your parents. That is an Old Testament command but affirmed by Paul (Ephesians 6:2). The point is, we should be *good* by honoring our father and mother. People who are not kind and gracious to their parents are not very nice people.

The sixth Commandment—"You shall not murder"—was applied by Jesus to the heart. If we follow through with Jesus' interpretation, we will not hate, let our enemy fear us, speak evil of anybody or gossip. Do you like it if a person gossips about you? Of course not. Therefore, return this goodness—do not gossip about anybody. There is an Arabic proverb: Those who gossip to you will gossip of you. The Golden Rule would therefore eliminate gossip. The seventh Commandment—"Do not commit adultery"—is applied by Jesus to lusting or causing one to lust: i.e., adultery in the heart. How do you want someone to treat your wife or husband? The eighth Commandment—"Do not steal"—would be carried out without knowing it existed if you lived by the Golden Rule. The Golden Rule virtually writes some of the Ten Commandments. If there were, for example, no fifth, sixth, seventh, eighth or ninth

Commandment, the Golden Rule would produce the same lifestyle without knowing about these commands. They are all for our good.

We want people to be good. This is why He says that the Golden Rule sums up the Law and Prophets. The Commandments, "Do not commit adultery," "Do not murder," "Do not steal," "Do not covet," and whatever other Commandments there may be, are summed up in this one rule: "Love your neighbor as yourself." Love does not do harm to its neighbor. Therefore, love is the fulfillment of the law (Romans 13:9–10).

Gratitude

Fifth, we want people to be *grateful.* God loves gratitude. God hates ingratitude. Gratitude must be taught. But those people who have not been taught to show thankfulness still notice it when one isn't thankful to them! If you do not show appreciation for what they did for you, they will make note of you from that day forward. We all want to be appreciated—and told that we are appreciated. We may say to the person who says, "Thank you," "Don't mention it"—but woe unto that person if he or she doesn't mention it!

The truth is, we love it when people are grateful and when they say, "Thank you." I lovingly ask you, therefore, how often do you say, "Thank you"—and mean it? How often do you make sure that you show genuine gratitude when people do things for you? Rule of thumb: Always remember to show sincere gratitude. And then watch their responses. You make them feel good. Say "thank you" to your parents for what they have done for you. Show appreciation to your husband, wife, children, boss. You like it when they are that way to you. Do it to them. I am not talking about feigned, silly, over-the-top bowing and scraping, but sincere words that let people know you are grateful to them for the things, large or small, they have done for you.

Our Warrant

We have received written authorization to live this way. Although we all fail and come short all the time, the truth is, living this way is a possibility. It is not unachievable. We should do it actively (taking the initiative) and passively (by how we respond).

This means graciousness in responsibility. It means not murmuring when we take the initiative.

We may say, "Let them take the initiative." This is where the problem often emerges. The husband will say of his wife, "When she submits to me, I will love her." She will say of her husband, "When I feel he loves me, I will submit." The Golden Rule is *never* to wait for the other person to do the right thing first. I say, beat him or her to the draw! Go first. Become vulnerable.

Carrying out the Golden Rule, therefore, not only means not to complain when you take the initiative, but never to be defensive when responding. Do not be defensive, whether or not the other person is genuine, gentle, gracious, good or grateful to you. We have a duty to respond with magnanimity whether or not he or she is magnanimous. Become vulnerable, whatever he or she does or says to you. Doing that is the essence of meekness.

Remember: God is always for the underdog. The underdog is in an inferior position. He has been discriminated against, avoided by people, a failure. He has low self-esteem, has been rejected by society, has not had the educational opportunities of others. The list goes on and on. You can afford to be gracious to people who are like this. There is a principle of love that is the fulfillment of the Law. I will share an acrostic I have sought (not always consistently) to follow for years—L-O-V-E:

> Let be. Don't panic, judge or try to change things.
> Overlook. It is your glory to overlook an offense.
> Vulnerable. We must become vulnerable and not be defensive.
> Effort. We make an effort because it is our duty.

Not to live by the Golden Rule shows our sin and selfishness. Doing this carries out the bottom line of the Sermon on the Mount. The guaranteed result: "A good measure, pressed down, shaken together and running over, will be poured into your lap. For with the measure you use, it will be measured to you" (Luke 6:38). God did not have to promise a blessing to us because we carry out our duty. But He does.

82. The Narrow Way

Enter through the narrow gate. For wide is the gate and broad is the road
that leads to destruction, and many enter through it. But small is the
gate and narrow the road that leads to life, and only a few find it.

MATTHEW 7:13–14

Jesus' preaching of the Sermon on the Mount is virtually over. When He gave us the Golden Rule, it was a summary of His main teachings—the exposition of the Law and its relationship to the Kingdom of heaven. What follows is *application,* which refers to how His hearers—and those of us who read His sermon—should respond and live in the light of the teaching.

Any sermon worth its salt has at least two things: (1) exposition—the explanation and teaching of the Scriptures—and (2) application—the practical part when the preacher exhorts the hearer to put that teaching into effect. You have this in Peter's sermon on the Day of Pentecost. He quotes three Old Testament passages and then applies them. But after his hearers cried out, "What shall we do?" Peter even further applied his teaching by calling for their repentance and public decision (Acts 2:37–40).

Beginning with Matthew 7:13, then, we have Jesus' application of His amazing teaching. And yet the application is, if anything, even more astonishing. Whereas Peter's hearers needed to be converted on the Day of Pentecost, the Sermon on the Mount was, as we would say today, "preaching to the choir." Jesus' disciples were affirmed by Him as true believers throughout the sermon. Peter's hearers, however, needed to come to Jesus Christ in faith and repentance. Jesus' disciples needed instructions further how to inherit fully the Kingdom of heaven.

And what is the first thing Jesus says when He begins His application? "Enter through the narrow gate." By saying this, He implies they have not done it yet. But is not one's initial conversion to Christ entering the narrow gate? Yes. Surely, then, His hearers had already entered a narrow

gate. Coming to Christ always means a narrow way. Not only that, relatively few Jews—and Gentiles—came to Christ 2,000 years ago. It was a narrow gate then. It is still true today: Few they are who come to salvation by acknowledging that Jesus is the way, the truth and the life (John 14:6). Make no mistake: To be saved is to be among a small minority of people. Salvation implies a narrow way.

An Exhortation to True Believers

But here Jesus poses a narrow gate with regard to believers and their relationship to the Kingdom of heaven. Think about this. He is teaching His own disciples—believers. And yet He tells them they have more to do—namely, to "enter through the narrow gate." How would this make you feel when you are told, "Though you are saved, you will still need to enter the narrow gate"?

In Luke's account, Jesus said, "Make every effort to enter through the narrow door, because many, I tell you, will try to enter and will not be able to" (Luke 13:24). The words "make every effort" translate the Greek word *agonizesthe*—from which we get the word *agonize.* It is translated "strive" in the KJV. We have similar language in Hebrews 4:11, addressed to Christians: "Make every effort [Gr. *Spoudasomen*—"earnestly," "with haste"] to enter that rest," namely God's rest.

God's rest is not a reference to heaven but to our inheritance. This coheres with the disciples' exhortation, "We must go through many hardships to enter the kingdom of God" (Acts 14:22). These men (Paul and Barnabas) were surely saved and in the Kingdom, in the sense they were born of the Spirit (John 3:3). And yet they said they enter the Kingdom through suffering. What does this tell us? First, we are not born again through hardships but by a sovereign work of the Holy Spirit. But, second, to inherit fully God's Kingdom, we go through tribulation. I conclude: These verses (Luke 13:24; Hebrews 4:11; Acts 14:22) all refer to the same thing: our fully inheriting the Kingdom of heaven.

What does Matthew 7:13 therefore tell us when put alongside these connecting verses? Answer: *Believers need to persist in faith even though they have saving faith.* Moreover, this persistent faith will not be easy—it means overcoming obstacles. Although the faith that justifies us before God ensures we will go to heaven when we die, that is not all the New Testament teaches about the Kingdom of heaven. We who know we are going to heaven need to persist in the same faith not in order to be saved but to come fully into our inheritance—in His Kingdom here below. And that is what Jesus is telling us at this point in the Sermon on the Mount.

Five Reasons for Jesus' Application

Why would Jesus begin His application with words like these: "Enter through the narrow gate"? First, He wants His disciples to experience what He has been talking about—and what they have not yet fully experienced. Jesus has explained His view of hate; it equals murder (Matthew 5:21–22). He has explained His view of lusting; it means adultery (Matthew 5:27–30). He explained that using God's name by making a vow is taking His name in vain (Matthew 5:33–37). He has told us how to pray (Matthew 6:5–13). He has described the life of faith (Matthew 6:25–34). He has told us not to point the finger (Matthew 7:1–5). He has told us that we enter the Kingdom by asking, seeking, knocking (Matthew 7:7–11). The bottom line of all He has taught is what is universally called the Golden Rule (Matthew 7:12). He wants His followers to inherit fully the Kingdom of heaven. But it means entering a narrow door and "only a few find it."

Second, He predicts that not all His disciples, sadly, will experience this. Even though they have heard Jesus preach—even if they understand what He taught and are truly followers (they are called disciples in Matthew 5:1–2)—"only a few" will fully inherit the Kingdom. That is why He applies

what He said. It is not enough to hear or even understand. There is more: They must "enter" through a narrow gate.

May I ask you, dear reader: Would it bless you or disturb you to learn that there is more down the road—this side of going to heaven—that Jesus wants you to inherit? I say this because I have observed that some do get annoyed. But most I have encountered are thrilled. Whereas some are content with a salvation that says, "God, I will see You in heaven," and want no further responsibility between conversion and glorification, others are prepared to "make every effort" to come to their full inheritance.

Third, prayer (Matthew 7:7–11) must be authenticated by further effort. The reason Jesus taught that we must ask, seek and knock is we do not usually get what we are asking for the first time we ask or turn to God. Like it or not, God plays hard to get. He tests our earnestness by seeing if we will persevere, persist and make every effort. Parallel with praying, therefore, will be taking on board all else Jesus has said, beginning with this application of Matthew 7:13–14.

Fourth, this further effort is put in terms of entering a gate. A gate means an entrance through which is otherwise a fence or wall. A wall is to keep people out. A gate is to let people in. Jesus said, "I tell you the truth, the man who does not enter the sheep pen by the gate but climbs in by some other way, is a thief and a robber. . . . I am the gate for the sheep" (John 10:1–3, 7).

Behind the walls and through the gate is what we desire: a beautiful inheritance. But we get it by going through the gate—by a persistent faith in the same Jesus who saves us.

Fifth, the gate through which we are urged to enter is a narrow gate. Any baggage must be left behind—the gate is too narrow to bring anything with you. It is so narrow that only you can come through it. You cannot bring anybody with you; you cannot carry with you any extra clothes, suitcase or belongings. You make a choice between a narrow gate and a wide gate. The narrow gate leads to "life"—your inheritance, knowing God, finding Him real. The wide gate leads to destruction, blowing away your inheritance.

Question: Why "narrow gate"? Why is the way, or road, described as a "narrow road"? The answer is partly that one makes a choice between two gates: a narrow gate and a wide gate. The narrow gate leads to life; the wide gate leads to disaster and ruin. What about you? What choice are you making? According to Luke, entering the narrow gate is far from an easy matter. It can be easily missed. "Make every effort to enter through the narrow door, because many, I tell you, will try to enter and will not be able to" (Luke 13:24).

As we saw above, the Greek word means to agonize, as an athlete working for an award. The Greek *agon* means stadium. The word *agonizomai* means winning in a stadium. One thinks of the exhortation, "Since we are surrounded by such a great cloud of witnesses, let us throw off everything that hinders and the sin that so easily entangles, and let us run with perseverance the race marked out for us" (Hebrews 12:1). A narrow gate is easily rejected for a wider gate. You don't need to agonize to enter a wide gate, but it was required if you entered a narrow gate.

Difficult Theological Questions

This leads to some fairly obvious but difficult theological questions. For example, is this verse about the narrow gate and "few" finding it relevant for a non-Christian? Or is it mainly for the believer? In other words, do the concepts of "narrow gate" and "only a few find it" refer to those who go to heaven, and do those who enter the wide gate go to hell? Or do they refer to believers who fully inherit the Kingdom of heaven and those who blow away their inheritance?

Matthew's account says nothing about *striving* to enter in. If we did not have Luke's account, which talks about striving, we could say that Matthew 7:13–14 could be applied to whether a person is saved or lost. But if you assume that Luke's account about making "every effort" echoes what Jesus actually meant in Matthew 7:13–14, it should not be applied to the non-Christian. Here is why: A person does not need to agonize, make every effort or strive in order to be saved. Salvation is by grace through faith, not by works. It is God's free gift (Ephesians 2:8–9). Saving faith is believing the Gospel. It is relying on Christ, not our works. The idea that we must "strive" to be saved implies works. Effort. Agonizing to get to heaven. This would

go right against the whole of the New Testament, particularly Paul's teaching.

As for Paul, he was not worried whether he himself would make it to heaven. That was not an issue for him. He was concerned whether he would get the "prize," "crown" or "reward"—referring not to heaven but to a reward at the Judgment Seat of Christ. This is why he said, "I beat my body and make it my slave so that after I have preached to others, I myself will not be disqualified for the prize" (1 Corinthians 9:27). In other words, in order to get this prize or reward, it meant effort, persistent if not agonizing. That is not how we are saved—it is how we come fully into our inheritance.

I therefore interpret Matthew 7:13–14 to refer to the Christian's inheritance. It comes by entering the narrow gate and "only a few find it." This means only a few believers find it.

So, what are the consequences of those who enter the "wide" gate? Does it mean they are lost? No. Does it mean the Christian loses his or her salvation? No. The Greek word for "destruction" is *apoleian*. It is translated "ruined" in Matthew 9:17. It is translated "waste" in Matthew 26:8. The "wide" gate that leads to destruction means these people have blown away their inheritance, they have ruined their lives despite the fact they are saved.

Michael Eaton observed that the appeal to enter the Kingdom of heaven through the narrow gate is not an appeal to experience the first stage of salvation, new birth, repentance or saving faith; it is an appeal that His disciples will press on into a rich experience of the power of God's Kingdom in their lives. Entering the Kingdom of God is like traveling on a pathway and coming to a junction where you have to pass through one of two gates. The person who is already a disciple is faced with two pathways through life. The fact that he or she is already a disciple does not mean they automatically follow the right way. The way ahead might bring you to life, finding for yourself how real God can be (John 17:3). Or, the way ahead might bring you to ruination—you forfeit your inheritance below and lose your reward at the Judgment Seat of Christ, to be saved by fire (1 Corinthians 3:15). As Michael Eaton also pointed out, one is saved forever the moment he or she truly believes—but that does not mean a Christian cannot make a wrong decision.

What Is It Like to Follow the Narrow Way?

What is the narrow way? It is a way of conflict. It means a fight, a struggle. It means to overcome the world, flesh and the devil. It means overcoming temptation. It means to forgive rather than hold a grudge. It means to be sexually pure as opposed to falling into sexual sin. It means to respect God's name and not use His name to increase your own credibility. It means to live a life of not judging and pointing the finger. It also means not looking over your shoulder to be seen of men, to be in fear of what people think. It means to put personal integrity above the approval of people, to be willing to face persecution, however fierce. In a word: The narrow way is a way of conflict.

Entering the narrow gate is a way of choice. You make a choice between two gates. You can choose the wider gate, a road that most, sadly, choose. The narrow gate, however, may lead to loneliness. The choice to enter the narrow gate must be a deliberate choice. It is what is done on purpose—carefully, thoughtfully. It is a disciplined choice where you have trained yourself to be obedient. Even Christ learned obedience through suffering (Hebrews 5:8). It means self-control, manifesting the fruits of the Holy Spirit (Galatians 5:22). It is a daily choice; it is not an on-off matter. "If anyone would come after me, he must deny himself and take up his cross *daily* and follow me" (Luke 9:23, emphasis mine).

We are talking about the way of the cross, a subject I shall go into more in the following chapter. This will mean the way of shame. The disciples rejoiced that they were counted worthy to suffer the shame of His name (Acts 5:41). It is the way of silence. As a lamb before its shearers is silent, "so he did not open his mouth" (Isaiah 53:7). It is the way of solitude. All Jesus' disciples forsook Him and fled (Matthew 26:56).

"Enter through the narrow gate," then, is the way Jesus began His application of the Sermon on the Mount. He puts before us a choice between two gates: the narrow and the wide. The right choice is the narrow gate. It is costly when it comes to pride and what God may require us to give up. But it is the best way to live. Which gate have you chosen?

83. The Road Less Traveled

Enter through the narrow gate. For wide is the gate and broad is the road
that leads to destruction, and many enter through it. But small is the
gate and narrow the road that leads to life, and only a few find it.

MATTHEW 7:13–14

Although these words are often applied to the issue whether one goes to heaven or hell, we saw in the previous chapter that they actually are addressed to believers—not unsaved people—who need Jesus' application of what He has taught. They are being asked to "enter through the narrow gate . . . the narrow road." If you are a believer, you, too, are being asked to do this. I am being asked to do this. It is a word you and I must apply every day.

These words are often used to show the folly of missing heaven by taking the wide gate that leads to destruction. But when you put Jesus' words in Matthew 7:13–14 alongside the account in Luke 13:24, where we are told to strive—"make every effort to enter through the narrow door"—one realizes this is not referring to salvation or a person's initial conversion to Christ. Why not? Because salvation is a free gift of God, by His sheer grace (Romans 6:23; Ephesians 2:8–9). Having to make an effort smacks of getting to heaven by our good works. Never!

Jesus instructs those who are regenerate. We are on a road after our conversion and eventually we have to make decisions—hard decisions. Which way do we go? Just because you are saved does not mean you cannot make a bad choice. Jesus warns us. The right choice is the narrow gate—the bad choice is the wide gate. A gate is what gets you through a wall or fence. What we want is behind that wall: our inheritance. You and I as true believers are called to an inheritance. Some get it; some don't. Some come into their inheritance; some blow it away. I don't want to blow away mine! Do you?

Five Questions

A further look at Matthew 7:13–14 raises questions. First, what is "life"? Jesus tells us that the narrow road leads to life. And yet if Christians are regenerate (born again), surely they already have life. A second question is, why—since Christians already are regenerate—do only a few find this life? A third question is, what exactly is the narrow way that leads to life? Fourth, what is the wider gate that leads to destruction? Fifth, what is this destruction?

The purpose of this chapter is to show how to enter the narrow gate and therefore how to be among those who find "life." You and I must accept responsibility to choose the narrow way. As I said in the previous chapter, it is the way of the cross.

The Narrow Way: The Way of the Cross

The way of the cross means *submission.* "During the days of Jesus' life on earth, he offered up prayers and petitions with loud cries and tears to the one who could save him from death, and he was heard because of his reverent submission" (Hebrews 5:7). To submit means to yield yourself to the authority and control of another—God our Father. Jesus did this in Gethsemane. He fell with His face to the ground and prayed, "My Father, if it is possible, may this cup be taken from me. Yet not as I will, but as you will" (Matthew 26:39). The first step of submission is to accept the responsibility to yield to God's sovereign authority. Question: What might be your Gethsemane?

The way of the cross is *sacrifice.* This is when you give up something in order to achieve something else. Jesus gave up His life to achieve our salvation. He appeared "once for all at the end of the ages to do away with sin by the sacrifice of himself" (Hebrews 9:26). God has a way of putting His finger on something and to say, "That's Mine—that belongs to Me. You cannot have it." "All the vain things that charm me most, I sacrifice them to His blood," wrote Isaac Watts. Or to quote another hymn: "My ambitions, plans and wishes at His feet in ashes lay." Said Paul: "In view of God's mercy . . . offer your bodies as living sacrifices, holy and pleasing to God—this is your spiritual act of worship" (Romans 12:1).

The way of the cross is *suffering*. As we saw above, Jesus learned obedience through suffering (Hebrews 2:10; 5:8). How much more do we need suffering to produce obedience? To suffer means to undergo pain, grief, loss. There is more than one kind of pain. Pain is often found in the responsibility regarding choosing the narrow way. There may be physical suffering, which Jesus endured. The day has already come for some—it may come to us in the West, when we must endure physical suffering to uphold our faith. Even if our suffering is not directly owing to our faith, we must still dignify every trial. The same is true with emotional or mental suffering. There is also spiritual suffering—when God hides His face.

Emotional and mental suffering include bearing the shame. It can mean embarrassment. Our friends may think we have lost our heads. We may have to endure the shame of damaged reputation, all because of our efforts to follow Jesus Christ. But the good news is that this gets God's attention, too—quickly! He is moved when He sees His children willing to bear the shame of Jesus' name.

Part of this pain is sometimes having to suffer in a manner that does not allow us to explain our reasons. Jesus' suffering included having to watch Mary Magdalene sob her heart out, since He was not allowed to explain to her that it was what He came to the earth to do. The way of the cross, therefore, can mean solitude. It means suffering alone. Jesus' "inner circle" (Peter, James, John) fell asleep in Gethsemane when Jesus had asked them to watch with him. He realized that He would have to go through His ordeal utterly alone. "Sleep on, now," He said to them as He came to terms with this solitude (Matthew 26:45, KJV). The way of the cross is the way of loneliness.

Why "Only a Few"?

There are Christians who, sadly, opt for the wider gate. "They have not been truly converted," some sincere pastors or theologians sometimes say. It is no doubt true that some people who claim to be saved and who choose the wide gate have not been converted. But to say they could not possibly be converted is unfair.

I believe there are those true believers who let things come into their lives that cause their affection for spiritual things to wane. Who among us has not had low moments when we made bad choices? I know I have. But God was patient with me. He turned me around. We must therefore not conceive that a bad decision means that these people have opted for the broad road. But those who are not granted repentance in due course will suffer the consequence—though they may well have been truly converted.

But why does Jesus say "only a few" enter the narrow gate? The easy answer is that people don't want hardship—and they do want an easier way. But as a pastor (I have been the pastor of five churches) it is my observation that 25 percent of a typical membership do 75 percent of the work. Sometimes, I honestly wonder if the figure is more like 10 percent doing 90 percent of the work. Am I to believe that only 10 percent of the congregation has been converted? No. As a pastor, I have listened to thousands of the 90 percent. I am sure some of them were not truly converted. But a responsible pastor develops a sense of discernment, and can often tell whether the person is serious about their coming to Christ and their reason for assurance of salvation.

I have watched this "90 percent"—many of whom come and go from Sunday to Sunday—go up and down in their zeal. But they still show up now and then. You just can't get them to be heavily involved in church. In my own experience, I would say many of these have been converted—that, yes, they are saved and will go to heaven. But to get them to witness for Christ in public daily, to tithe consistently, to help with menial tasks when there is a need, to persuade them to pray thirty minutes a day, to go out of their way to take people to church, to take their turn in the nursery, to have a burden for the lost, to have a deep concern for the poor, to welcome persecution when the going is tough, to forgive their enemies totally, to respond positively to God's chastening, not to murmur but to dignify the trial when things collapse all around them and bear the cross—as I have written above, it is often an unsuccessful venture. That is what Jesus means by the "few" who choose the narrow way. It is the road less traveled.

The Wide Gate

The alternate route to the narrow way is to enter the wide gate and broad road. But Jesus tells us straightaway: It leads to ruin. Destruction. Defeat. Loss of inheritance.

For some reason, most people enter the wide gate. It is easier, convenient. For one thing, the broad way is easier to find and to stay on. It is the way of least resistance. You can even take others with you—and also cause them to miss the narrow gate, sadly. You can take your baggage with you, stuff you should have left behind long ago. Your worldly bent will be accepted. You do not need to leave anything behind that militates against your love for the things of the world, pride of life and lust of the flesh. You may hang on to the vain things that charm you most, and you certainly do not have to pour contempt on your pride.

To choose the wide gate may mean more opportunities. You might make more money this way and mix with the "beautiful people"—the rich, famous and prestigious. The world beckons for people like this. The idea of finding friends from this category is enticing. You may have more fun. After all, the Church is often filled with odd people. I'm sorry, but it's true. "The flakes you have with you always," I once heard Rodney Howard-Browne say. I believe it. It can be so embarrassing.

It is easier to give in to natural urges. The wider gate beckons with sexual temptation. The broad way will let you look at pornography (the chief sin of preachers). One of the most respected evangelical philosophers of the twentieth century was said to be addicted to pornographic magazines. This was discovered after he died. The broad road will affirm your lusting, holding grudges and giving in to what makes you feel "good." The wide gate is also the way forward if you crave quick appreciation and cannot wait for the honor that would have come from God (John 5:44). For one thing, people at church may not appreciate you or give you accolades. Perhaps your intellect is not appreciated—or your talent. So the broad way beckons you toward a crowd of people who will give you the respect you wanted. The broad road is a deceitful alternative route to the narrow way.

What Is the Destruction to Which the Broad Road Leads?

Jesus said that the broad road "leads to destruction." As we noted in the previous chapter, it means *waste*. Ruin. Therefore, those who think they are wasting their time and talent trying to serve God will truly come to waste if they choose the wide gate. It is only a matter of time. In the words of Robert G. Lee's famous sermon: "Payday Someday." As King Saul put it, when it was too late: "I have acted like a fool and have erred greatly" (1 Samuel 26:21). Among his last words were these: "God has turned away from me. He no longer answers me, either by prophets or by dreams" (1 Samuel 28:15).

For years I took the view that King Saul was never truly converted in the first place. It was Dr. Martyn Lloyd-Jones who convinced me otherwise—that Saul was indeed a saved man. The same was true of Eli the priest, who failed in many ways but was a man who truly feared God (1 Samuel 4:12–18). A believer whose name was Demas was right in the middle of God's activity in the early Church, was associated with Paul and Luke (Colossians 4:14; Philemon 24). But later he chose the broad way. Among Paul's last words were these: "Demas, because he loved this world, has deserted me" (2 Timothy 4:10). Ananias and Sapphira were a part of the earliest Church, but they let the love of money take over. They were found out, even lied to the Holy Spirit, and were struck dead (Acts 5:1–10). "When we are judged by the Lord," said Paul, who noted people in Corinth who were sick or dying prematurely, "we are being disciplined so that we will not be condemned with the world" (1 Corinthians 11:32).

When I was a student at Trevecca Nazarene College, I had a close friend whose name was

Paul. He had the most brilliant intellect I had ever come across. His devotion to Christ was possibly deeper than anybody I had met. He greatly impressed all the members of the faculty. He influenced me greatly, and I still think of him all the time. Whether it was languages, physics, mathematics, science, literature or the Bible, this man excelled. One day he drove with me to my church in Palmer, Tennessee, and began to cry. "I'm afraid my gift won't be discovered," he lamented to me. He later became impatient and turned to the world. He ended up in shame and ruin and died a premature death.

On the other hand, consider the story of a young Canadian who was gifted with one of the most extraordinary bass-baritone voices ever—a voice that comes around perhaps once in a century. He was given offers to move to New York, where his voice could be heard around the world. His mother was convinced this would be a wrong move, but hardly knew how to say this to her son. She placed a poem on the piano, where she knew he would see it. It read:

> I'd rather have Jesus than silver or gold;
> I'd rather be His than have riches
>   untold.
> I'd rather have Jesus than houses or
>   lands;
> I'd rather be led by His nail-pierced
>   hand.
> I'd rather have Jesus than men's
>   applause;
> I'd rather be faithful to His dear cause.
> I'd rather have Jesus than world-wide
>   fame;
> I'd rather be true to His holy name.
> Than to be the king of a vast domain
> Or be held in sin's dread sway.
> I'd rather have Jesus than anything
> This world affords today.
>
>   Rhea F. Miller (1894–1966)

The young man sat at the piano and read the poem. He was smitten. He even composed the music that fit the words. He turned down the chance to go to New York. That young Canadian was George Beverly Shea, who later became Billy Graham's soloist for over fifty years. Beverly Shea became a household name in the Christian world, and has been given more fame and accolades than he would have received, almost certainly, had he gone to New York. Jesus said, "The man who loves his life will lose it, while the man who hates life [i.e., loves less] in this world will keep it for eternal life" (John 12:25).

The destruction that Jesus forecast is partly understood as having to live—and die—with the folly of a bad choice. One sees too late that "it wasn't worth it." Even if one ascends to heights for a while—gaining fame and money—it is only a matter of time until one will see the tragedy of a wasted life. This life could even last a long time, but in many cases it ends in a premature death.

Life after Life

Jesus says the narrow road leads to "life." Life in this case does not mean regeneration, or salvation. The person who makes this choice is already converted. But why does Jesus use the term *life* as if this is the reward for the right choice? It means *life after life*. One already has life through being born again. But a regenerate person needs to discover afresh how real and how true Christianity really is. Jesus put it like this: "I have come that they may have life, and have it to the full" (John 10:10). The KJV says life "more abundantly." The Living Bible says "life in all its fullness."

Life after life is what all of us are called to experience. It is one thing to be saved and know by faith you are going to heaven. It is regeneration—life—that makes this inevitable. But there comes a time when we all need to discover for ourselves how real and how true the Christian faith is.

Take, for example, those who were converted at an early age, as I was. It was such a consolation to me to find Christ anew as I drove in my car on that Monday morning, October 31, 1955—when the person of Jesus was more real to me than anybody around me. I think, too, of both of our children. They made professions at a fairly early age. Each of them would need to discover "life"— abundant life—which they happily have done.

And yet life after life also needs to be repeated. Paul calls it being changed from "glory to glory" (2 Corinthians 3:18, KJV). When that ceases to happen, it is not a good sign. But as long as we are being changed "from one degree of glory to another" (ESV), it shows we are not opting for the broad way, but for the narrow road that leads to life—which few find. Regeneration—life—is an unconscious work of the Holy Spirit that needs to become a conscious experience. This comes by saying no to ungodliness and worldly passions and living "self-controlled, upright and godly lives in this present age" (Titus 2:12).

When one comes into this life, a first reaction often is, "The Christian faith is so *real.*" Whether one was converted at a young age or as an adult, the same is true. We all must grow and recommit our lives to the Lord Jesus Christ by showing our love for Him. This is manifest by rejecting the broad road that leads to destruction.

You and I are called to an inheritance. It is what accompanies salvation, or belongs to it (Hebrews 6:9). The Hebrew Christians were in danger of losing theirs, even becoming stone deaf to the Holy Spirit that would forfeit ongoing repentance (Hebrews 6:4–6). God chose our inheritance for us (Psalm 47:4). What He has for me may not be what He has in mind for you. Joseph's inheritance was being prime minister of Egypt. It came by overcoming sexual temptation (Genesis 39:6–12) and totally forgiving his brothers (Genesis 45:1–15).

God has an inheritance for you. If you choose the narrow way, you will absolutely come into it—not to mention to receive a reward at the Judgment Seat of Christ. Look at George Beverly Shea's inheritance. Consider Billy Graham's. All of us should be able to say with David, "The boundary lines have fallen for me in pleasant places; surely I have a delightful inheritance" (Psalm 16:6). As for me, I could have blown away my inheritance—being a Bible teacher—many times across the years. I am certain, for example, that had I rejected Arthur Blessitt in all he did and taught us at Westminster Chapel in 1982, I would have forfeited my ministry in London. I had challenges after that, too, when I had to decide whether to please people or God only. I am now 75. God isn't finished with me (or you) yet. I want to end well.

But we must make every effort to enter the narrow door. Don't forget that it means to agonize. It means praying hard—asking, seeking, knocking. It means accepting all that God puts before us—walking in all the light He gives us. It means refusing to vindicate yourself. Resisting the temptation to make yourself look better can be agonizing. Resisting sexual temptation can be agonizing. The narrow way is the way of discipline. Others may fall to one side, but you don't. Why? Because you choose to keep your eyes on Jesus, not people (Hebrews 12:2). Others seem to get away with a certain lifestyle—but you can't. Why? Because they chose the broad road, and you have chosen the narrow road.

Why is it that "few find it"? It is because few want it. Few persevere. Few overcome the obstacles. God puts obstacles in your way to see how badly you want this. To find means to discover by search or effort. Finding life after life is a wonderful rediscovery. For a few? No, it is for all. But, sadly, not all want the narrow way.

84. False Prophets

Watch out for false prophets. They come to you in sheep's
clothing, but inwardly they are ferocious wolves.

MATTHEW 7:15

Midway in my ministry at Westminster Chapel, we became interested in the prophetic in a manner that, for some reason, I had never really thought about. When I used to think of prophecy I thought only of eschatology—but an entirely new perspective emerged. In 1990, a group of men came to London, later called the "Kansas City prophets." I dismissed them all out of hand at first, but later came to look at them more carefully. To be honest, I eventually got burnt pretty badly by some of these men (since our retirement), and yet I also profited from them. Looking back, I would say their influence on Westminster Chapel was good. The question I have asked: Does a questionable lifestyle, or a person ever getting it wrong, necessarily mean they are false prophets?

The Rise of the Prophetic

According to Jesus, Abel was the first prophet (Luke 11:50). Abraham was called a prophet (Genesis 20:7). Moses was a prophet (Deuteronomy 18:15). An unknown man of God prophesied to Eli (1 Samuel 2:27–36). Samuel was the first of a new era of great prophets (1 Samuel 3:19). There were the canonical prophets (their words becoming Scripture), such as Isaiah, Jeremiah, Ezekiel, Daniel. There were non-canonical prophets, such as Nathan, Gad, Elijah and Elisha.

But false prophets eventually emerged, too. There were the prophets of Baal whom Elijah encountered and had destroyed (1 Kings 18:18–40). During the time of Jeremiah, there was Hananiah, whose prophecies proved false (Jeremiah 28). The devil will try to overturn the truth of God by false prophets.

Jesus' Second Application

Jesus virtually finished the Sermon on the Mount with His teaching of the Golden Rule. He then began to apply what He taught. His first application had to do with entering the narrow gate (Matthew 7:13–14). We now look at His second application, His warning against false prophets.

False prophets have been around for a long time—and they exist now. False prophets come in "sheep's clothing," said Jesus, meaning you cannot go by their outward appearance, which at first may appear so benign. The Lord said to Samuel that one should not go by outward appearance, for God looks at the heart. Even Samuel got it wrong when he hastily inferred that Eliab would be the next king (1 Samuel 16:7). This alone should caution us not to jump to conclusions. That includes hastily assuming a person is a false prophet because he gets it wrong once in a while. Even Nathan got it wrong once (2 Samuel 7:3, 5). And yet the interesting thing about Samuel and Nathan is that both corrected themselves and did not stick to their guns. A false prophet will not admit to a mistake.

Jesus is not referring to the gift of the prophecy as outlined in 1 Corinthians 12:9, which is elaborated on in 1 Corinthians 14. Jesus was not saying that unless one is an Isaiah or Daniel they are false prophets. Paul assumed that Christians in the early Church might get it wrong. This is why he said to test prophecies (1 Thessalonians 5:20–21). Those sincere believers who get it wrong in their prophetic utterances or words of knowledge are not necessarily to be regarded as false prophets.

False prophets are not true Christians. They were never saved. Jude talks about them. Certain men whose condemnation was foreordained got into the church through the back door (Jude 4). False prophets, said Peter, "secretly introduce destructive heresies, even denying the sovereign Lord who bought them—bringing swift destruction on themselves" (2 Peter 2:1).

The Purpose of Jesus' Second Application

Why did Jesus apply His teaching as He did at this stage? First, it shows the need for discernment. Jesus later (in the Mount Olivet discourse) talked about false prophets who would "deceive even the elect—if that were possible" (Matthew 24:24). He implied it is not possible for the elect to be ultimately deceived, but perhaps they could be temporarily shaken. It is the false prophet—the utterly fraudulent person who has never been given saving faith in the first place—that Jesus warns about.

Second, Jesus applies His teaching as He does because the devil will try to divert or deceive the believer who wants to put God first. Paul said to the elders of the church of Ephesus, "I know that after I leave, savage wolves will come in among you and will not spare the flock" (Acts 20:29). Satan moves in quickly, even appealing to one's sincere desire to hear directly from God. Satan's chief method: to deceive. "Such men are false apostles, deceitful workmen, masquerading as apostles of Christ. And no wonder, for Satan himself masquerades as an angel of light" (2 Corinthians 11:13–14).

Third, sometimes the godly are the most gullible of people. Some Christians can be surprisingly naïve—almost too open, especially when they so ardently want not to miss what God has in mind for us.

Fourth, it is a reminder that there will always be false prophets. In the earliest Church there were zealots, antinomians, scribes, Gnostics and Judaizers who twisted people's faith. Their equivalent will always be around.

Finally, false prophets are recognizable. If they were not recognizable, Jesus' words would be in vain. They are indeed recognizable and must be rejected. But it requires discernment. Caution: Don't become preoccupied or enamored with what is false; get to know the true and genuine so well that the false is immediately recognizable. In my pastoral experience, those who loved mostly to read books on the occultic or demon possession never seemed very spiritual to me.

Jesus assumed that false prophets would come along, or He would not have said, "Watch out for false prophets." They are always around. The Greek word is *pseudopropheton*—pseudo-prophets. In a word: They were counterfeit. They claim to speak for God, to have a word directly from God.

There is something very appealing about the idea of a word directly from God. Some people turn to the occult for a quick word that will give them a good feeling. A Christian should never consult an astrology chart, a medium, a fortune-teller, a witch or anybody who practices in the occult. Don't even wear a good-luck charm. Stay away from such—you never know how strong you will be. Anyone who seems to speak with authority is very appealing. It is the way Hitler ascended to the top: He spoke with uncanny authority. A false prophet seems so real. But, as Jonathan Edwards said, when the Church is revived, so also is the devil. When the Holy Spirit falls on the Church in great power, you can expect the counterfeit to surface in a very short period of time.

The one thing you can count on from a false prophet: Their prophecies don't ultimately pan out. Hananiah prophesied the end of the Babylonian captivity in two years. Jeremiah said it would be seventy years. Hananiah died shortly thereafter; Jeremiah was vindicated (Jeremiah 28). There is a reason a false prophet's long-term forecasting cannot come true: They don't hear from God. Only God knows the future perfectly, and He may sometimes choose to reveal some of that future to a true servant of His. But a false prophet has only the devil to hear from. The devil does not know the future—whether it be what is at hand or the distant future, as Hananiah showed.

The Warning: "Watch Out"

Jesus' admonition: Be on your guard. Expect false prophets to show up. Why beware of them? First, false prophecy may take time before it is clearly seen as being utterly false. When Hananiah prophesied the end of the Babylonian captivity within two years, everybody cheered. Jeremiah stood alone. But when the two years passed by and Hananiah died, as Jeremiah said he would, the people came to their senses. But in the meantime, they were deceived.

False prophets give people what they want to hear. I don't mean to be unfair, but I am reminded of some people on Christian television today who seem to play into people's greed, fears and self-love, claiming to uphold the Bible. They fulfill Paul's own prophecy that in the last days people will flock to those teachers who say "what their itching ears want to hear. They will turn their ears away from the truth" (2 Timothy 4:1–4).

Second, false prophets do great damage to the cause of Christ. They discourage Christians who sincerely want to be open to what the Spirit is saying to the Church. Some become disillusioned and even give up their faith entirely because of a false prophecy. There is, however, a difference between a false prophet and a prophecy that is false. A good person who is not a phony could get it wrong. But they, too, do damage. And yet what Jesus is warning against is a person who is not a true man or woman of God at all. A prophetic person who truly loves God but gets it wrong did not want to hurt God's Church. But the false prophet wants to destroy the work of God, the Church of God and all who earnestly contend for the faith.

The problem becomes more complicated because a false prophet can get it right once in a while. If he gets it right, it is always remembered by the gullible. The thousand times the false prophet gets it wrong is often brushed aside. People so want to hear a word that makes them feel better. This is why people turn to a fortune-teller. A slave girl in Paul's day had the ability by a "spirit" to predict the future (Acts 16:16). She made money doing this. A false prophet, therefore, could get demonic help. It is my view that a false prophet may forecast what could happen in a day or two—not because they can see the future but because they guess correctly. The slave girl, by being demon-possessed, had access to a demonic network that knows the past and present perfectly. She could therefore sometimes accurately predict what would happen shortly—but not in the distant future. The future—even one hour from now—is known infallibly only to God.

The false prophet can give a sense of expectancy. But it is based upon lies. I repeat: The devil knows the past and present—not future. He can guess what will happen because he has access to past and present. The problem is, when the false prophet's word of knowledge or prediction turns out right, some are mesmerized and will never be

persuaded this prophet is false. The devil knows your date of birth, past friends and experiences, phone number and address.

The Arena of False Prophets

False prophets hang around the Church, the people of God. After all, who is Jesus addressing in Matthew 7:15? The Church! And you can be sure that nowadays it will be the evangelical wing of the Church that the false prophet will pursue. He will largely stay away from those who deny the infallibility of Scripture, because they are not a serious threat to his interests. The devil fears those who enter the narrow gate and who would go to the stake for their theological views. And so the false prophet will center on where the interests of Satan are most threatened. Jesus would not warn the Pharisees to beware of false prophets. He did not warn Sadducees to watch out for false prophets. He warns those who are born again, who want to keep the Golden Rule and follow the narrow way.

It is the "sheep" that the false prophet is after. False prophets come in "sheep's clothing" in order to get an entry to the faithful. They will have the appearance of being docile and gentle. They will appear to be harmless. They will look credible. They may even have credentials. They might suggest the appearance of class. Some might think at first they are conscientious. This is why they come close in deceiving the elect (Matthew 24:24). The Judaizers, said Paul, were so cunning and persuasive that "even Barnabas was led astray" (Galatians 2:13), although this deception was temporary.

False prophets have a predictable approach. First, "they come to you." They don't wait for you to go to them—they come to you. They take the initiative. I think of the cults, such as Jehovah's Witnesses and Mormons. They don't wait for you to come to them. They are aggressive in knocking on doors and passing out literature on the streets. (It is a pity that we who have the truth are often so passive.) Jude speaks of how false prophets intrude into the fellowship of God's people—they are "blemishes at your love feasts, eating with you without the slightest qualm" (Jude 12). They worm their way into churches.

Their aim? To destroy the sheep. They are "ferocious wolves." They kill sheep. Devour them. They set out to ruin God's people. They often come out of the blue to deceive, divide and destroy the Church. And partly because of their appearance—sheep's clothing—they often succeed.

I wish it weren't so. So, if we choose the narrow gate and stay on the narrow way, we need discernment.

85. Recognizing the False Prophet

By their fruit you will recognize them. Do people pick grapes from thornbushes, or figs from thistles? Likewise every good tree bears good fruit, but a bad tree bears bad fruit. A good tree cannot bear bad fruit, and a bad tree cannot bear good fruit. Every tree that does not bear good fruit is cut down and thrown into the fire. Thus, by their fruit you will recognize them.

MATTHEW 7:16–20

You might think Jesus is contradicting Himself. First He says that false prophets are hard to recognize—because they come in "sheep's clothing" (verse 15). But He goes on to say that they are easy to recognize—"by their fruit." But what Jesus means is that if you know what you are looking for, as we often hear when looking for an address, "It's easy when you know the way!"

Matthew 7:16—"Ye shall know them by their fruits" (KJV)—is frequently applied to the question, "Is so-and-so a Christian?" I don't think it is necessarily wrong to do this. After all, it follows a valid principle. Jesus said, "Wisdom is proved right by her actions" (Matthew 11:19). Paul affirmed the Philippians as being eternally saved: "He who began a good work in you will carry it on to completion until the day of Christ Jesus" (Philippians 1:6). Paul knew these people intimately. After all, truth produces certain results. It sets one free and changes lives.

But Matthew 7:16 is not really referring to whether a person is truly a Christian. Jesus is talking about the fruit of a false prophet or religious leader. So, how do you tell a false prophet? Because a false prophet comes in sheep's clothing—which means he mixes with the sheep—he is hard to identify. But Matthew 7:16 tells us that if you know what you are looking for, you will spot the false prophet—and avoid a heap of trouble down the road.

Why does Jesus single out prophets rather than false teachers or apostles? He surely would include these, but a prophet seemed to carry a lot of authority and weight in those days. The prophetic had a long tradition, going back to Samuel,

Elijah, Elisha, Jeremiah, Daniel. There was a certain aura—mystique—to being a prophet. People were fascinated by a prophet. "I can see you are a prophet," said the Samaritan woman to Jesus (John 4:19). There is nothing greater than a true prophet, nothing worse than a false one.

An Illustration of the False Prophet's "Fruit"

Jesus chose to use the word *fruit*. He might have said, "You will know them by their failure." Moses said, "If what a prophet proclaims in the name of the LORD does not take place or come true, that is a message the LORD has not spoken. That prophet has spoken presumptuously. Do not be afraid of him" (Deuteronomy 18:22).

Jesus might have said, "You will know them by their folly." Peter said, "They have left the straight way and wandered off to follow the way of Balaam son of Beor . . . he was rebuked for his wrongdoing by a donkey—a beast without speech—who spoke with a man's voice and restrained the prophet's madness" (2 Peter 2:15–16). "Their folly will be clear to everyone," Paul said about people like this (2 Timothy 3:9).

It comes to this: You will recognize false prophets by whom they want you to follow. Moses said that if a prophet or one who foretells by dreams says, "Let us follow other gods," you must not listen to that prophet. He must be "put to death, because he preached rebellion against the LORD your God" (Deuteronomy 13:1–5).

Jesus tells us that we are to look for certain fruits that will let us know whether this person is false or true. We might have expected Jesus

389

to say, "Wait for a true prophet who will speak God's Word to you, to edify and bless you." But instead of being directed to the fruit of the true prophet, we are told to look for the fruit of the false prophet. Jesus gives this illustration: "Do people pick grapes from thornbushes, or figs from thistles?" You don't pick grapes from thornbushes or figs from thistles. Grapes grow on vines; figs grow on trees.

The Ironies of Jesus' Warning

Having said it is hard to tell if one is a false prophet, Jesus changes metaphors from sheep and wolves to trees and their fruits. He moves from nonrecognition to recognition. Although we may mistake a wolf in sheep's clothing for a true prophet, this would hardly be so with a tree. The irony is, then, that a false prophet is both hard to recognize and easy to recognize. If you keep looking for a wolf in sheep's clothing, it is hard. So Jesus says to stop looking at the flock of sheep. The key is to look at trees and their fruits.

A second irony is that fruit is normally used in the New Testament in a positive way. I think of the "fruit of the Spirit" (Galatians 5:22) but also "fruit of the light" (Ephesians 5:9) and "fruit of righteousness" (Philippians 1:11). However, Jesus here refers to fruit in a negative way. We are told to look for negative signs, evidence that indicts the false prophet.

A third irony is that the fruit we look for in the false prophet is, in fact, no fruit. By their "fruit," Jesus really means *fruitlessness*. This is because fruit cannot be found in thornbushes or thistles. Everyone then knew that thornbushes had little black inedible berries that could be mistaken for grapes. If you got close to them, your hands could get stuck with thorns. Thistles had a flower that from a distance might be mistaken for a fig. Jesus appeals to one's common sense. You should no more listen to a prophet like this than you should look for a grape in a thornbush. This is also Jesus' sense of humor coming through.

I should add a fourth irony: A false prophet may get it right once in a while. A true prophet can get it wrong once in a while. Balaam, a false prophet, got it right when he was forced to prophesy blessing on Israel (see Numbers 24:5, 17). As we saw in the previous chapter, Nathan jumped the gun regarding David's building of the Temple (2 Samuel 7:3, 5), and Samuel jumped the gun when he assumed Eliab would be the next king (1 Samuel 16:7). Each of them climbed down in a very short period of time, however. As for Balaam, he would not need to climb down regarding his actual prophecy, but he never repented for his efforts to curse Israel.

Identifying the False Prophet

We saw above that the "fruit" of the false prophet is fruitlessness. This simply means that the false prophet cannot deliver the goods. What he promises doesn't come to pass. His message will not change your life for good. Any idea of following a narrow road is foreign to his message. He is incapable of telling you how to live a godly life. Neither can he tell you how to die.

The true prophet is a man of God. His predictions are true. His message will affirm the narrow way. This means you can expect persecution by following him. The true prophet can also tell you how to die. After all, the true Gospel focuses on where you will spend eternity. John Wesley used to say of the early Methodists, "Our people die well." That is a beautiful testimony to the early Methodists. And yet Wesley himself held to certain teachings I would not agree with. Does that make Wesley a false prophet? No. We therefore would not demand that a true prophet must dot every "i" and cross every "t" according to our cherished convictions. But, in the main, a true prophet will uphold the Gospel and tell you how to live and how to die.

The false prophet lives for the here and now. He is motivated by greed. He never speaks for God in the first place. I remind you of the intriguing comment from the *Didache,* the early Christian document dated to around A.D. 150, on how to tell a false prophet: "If he asks money, he is a false prophet." Oh dear. If that document was inspired by the Holy Spirit, where would that leave many today? In any case, it had a profound effect on me fifty years ago when I first came across it.

Jesus, therefore, implies that not only is fruitlessness an ironic evidence of a false prophet, He demonstrates the impossibility of the fruit of a false prophet. "Likewise every good tree bears good fruit, but a bad tree bears bad fruit. A good tree cannot bear bad fruit, and a bad tree cannot bear good fruit." This is Hebraic style of speaking, to say something a second time in reverse to make sure you understood it correctly the first time. So we conclude: A good tree is going to bear good fruit; a bad true will bear bad fruit.

What would that good fruit be? First, the preaching of the true Gospel. A true prophet of God will faithfully represent the God of the Bible—a God who punishes sin. From this message true godliness will flow. The influence of a true prophet would be producing a love for the Bible in his followers—and making them want to read it. A true prophet would also encourage a believer to be open to the Holy Spirit. In other words, good fruit means a positive effect on their followers. Elijah utterly opposed the prophets of Baal—who turned people from the true God—to glorify the God of Israel. Good tree, good fruit.

The bad tree produces bad fruit. This would mean either the perverting of the Gospel—or never mentioning the Gospel at all. The emphasis would not be on being ready to face God at the Judgment Seat of Christ, but would focus on, "What's in it for me?" in the here and now. One would use God's name for his or her own ends. There would be no interest in God for His sake. Whereas the true prophet would focus on "What's in it for God?" the false prophet would focus on, "What's in it for me?"

But with a good tree there would be no bad fruit. The biblical preaching of the Gospel would not result in fruitlessness. A correct view of God would result in a fear of God. The false prophet's ministry would not bring about a fear of God. A wrong view of the Gospel would not result in a person having assurance of salvation.

The Inglorious Consequence of the False Prophet

"Every tree that does not bear good fruit is cut down and thrown into the fire." This is what happens with thornbushes and thistles. They are good for nothing and destroyed. One does not trim them or fertilize them. They are simply removed, put out of the way. They are like weeds—put to the fire. Does this mean false prophets will be sent to hell in the end? I answer, they most certainly will be sent to hell. These are unsaved people. But

the reference to the fire may be referring to the result of their prophecies—that they will come to nothing in the end.

Jesus' main point is that it is only a matter of time before the false prophet will be exposed. And yet a person who does not know better may think one of those tiny black berries from a thornbush is real fruit. They are inedible.

Think about Balaam's prophecies. They looked good. But never once are they quoted in the New Testament. They are seen as divination—occultic—in the Old Testament (Joshua 13:22). The sobering truth about Balaam's prophecies is that they were quite true—that is, they forecast Israel's brilliant future. And yet no writer of the New Testament quoted any of them—not even once. (Again I think of William Perkins's statement: "Don't believe the devil even when he tells the truth.") It was Balak, Israel's enemy, who asked Balaam for a prophetic word, thinking Balaam would curse Israel. God overruled and turned Balaam's prophetic utterances into what in fact infuriated Balak (Numbers 22–24).

False prophets may also draw away some of God's people. Balaam actually taught Balak to "entice the Israelites to sin" (Revelation 2:14). But false prophecies like those of Balaam will eventually be exposed and finally "thrown into the fire." Balaam's name, never forgotten in ancient Israel, would live in infamy (Deuteronomy 23:4–6; Joshua 13:22; 24:9–10; Micah 6:5; Nehemiah 13:2; 2 Peter 2:15; Jude 11; Revelation 2:14).

Conclusion

What is the difference between a false prophet and a false prophecy by a sincere person? Paul anticipated that good people would get it wrong, as we saw earlier (1 Thessalonians 5:19). I repeat therefore: Do not judge a sincere Christian—or call him or her a false prophet—merely because their prophecy does not come true. It does not mean they are frauds. We all make mistakes. The true Christian who makes a prophetic statement that does not come true has good motives. He or she never intends to hurt anybody, much less to destroy the work of God.

But the false prophets Jesus warns against are as follows: (1) They are not Christians, (2) they may even use the name of the Lord—often introducing their prophecy with "Thus says the Lord," (3) they actually hate the God of the Bible, (4) they want to destroy the Church, (5) they will be exposed in a due time, (6) they are to be recognized and avoided and (7) they will come to a dreadful end. Balaam was killed shortly after his notorious efforts to curse Israel (Numbers 31:8). Bad tree, bad fruit.

When a person who comes along with a prophetic word and simultaneously extols the Gospel of Jesus Christ, makes you want to pray and read the Bible more and encourages you to pursue the narrow way, he is a "good tree" bearing "good fruit."

86. Why Prophecies Go Wrong

A good tree cannot bear bad fruit.

MATTHEW 7:18

Jesus' words in Matthew 7:18 raise the question why a sincere Christian would give a prophetic word that was obviously not from God. We have seen that a bad tree—i.e., a false prophet—cannot bear good fruit. But why is it that a good tree—i.e., a true servant of God—can get it wrong when it comes to prophesying?

Why is this chapter important? First, I would want to encourage anyone who may have a prophetic gift to exercise it and develop it. After all, Paul did this. "Follow the way of love and eagerly desire spiritual gifts, *especially the gift of prophecy.*" Not only that, "he who prophesies edifies the church" (1 Corinthians 14:1, 4, emphasis mine). Not all have this gift, but those who do have it should not be discouraged or kept from developing it. Second, this is an important word for those who have been on the receiving end of a prophetic word that went wrong and may have been badly bruised. There are countless stories. You may be one of those who was given false hope because of a word given to you. Or maybe you lived in fear for years because of a word from someone you trusted—and time proved it was not from God. Why do prophecies given by reasonably good people go wrong?

Of course, one might dismiss this matter by merely saying, "Prophecies go wrong because they were given by a false prophet." But it is unfair to paint all misguided words with the same brush. The fact that Paul tells us to test what is good (1 Thessalonians 5:19) suggests that good people can make mistakes—both in giving a word and the way a person receives it. When Paul says, "Do not treat prophecies with contempt," he shows how our first reaction to a prophetic word might be to dismiss it out of hand because we would only accept a word if it were from Samuel raised

from the dead. I have learned to be open to the most insignificant person who comes to me with a "word." Some of them have been very timely indeed. It is the same principle as being helpful to strangers lest we have had an angel before our eyes without knowing it (Hebrews 13:2).

Paul Was Warned by Prophecies He Rejected

Paul himself rejected prophetic words from some unknown disciples who urged him *through the Spirit* (Luke says) "not to go on to Jerusalem" (Acts 21:4). Had Luke not added the words "through the Spirit," I, too, would dismiss those who pleaded with him. But Luke, under divine inspiration, says they spoke to Paul as they did through the Spirit. Luke certainly thought Paul should not have gone on to Jerusalem. Paul went anyway. And a good case can be made it was the worst mistake of his Christian life! Little if any good came of it. All things work together for good, yes (Romans 8:28). Paul could later say of this scenario, "What has happened to me has really served to advance the gospel" (Philippians 1:12). True. God will always see to this. But it is also true that Paul suffered unnecessarily by rejecting those prophetic words.

A man called Agabus got it right when he prophesied that a severe famine would spread over the entire Roman world—which was fulfilled (Acts 11:28). But the same Agabus got it wrong later on. He joined the aforementioned disciples who warned Paul about going to Jerusalem. Agabus prophesied certain things that would happen to Paul if he went to Jerusalem (Acts 21:10–11). Wayne Grudem has shown that a careful study of Agabus's words, matched by the actual events in Jerusalem, shows how his prophecy missed it on several counts (see Acts 22–26). Agabus's general thrust was right, but the details of the subsequent events show his word was not infallible. And yet Agabus was not a false prophet. I do not believe Paul would have labeled Agabus or those who warned him as false prophets.

Analogy of Faith

What Paul further taught concerning the prophetic gift will bear our examination. He said, "If a man's gift is prophesying, let him use it in proportion to his faith" (Romans 12:6). This is an extremely important verse. It means one has a proportion (share, amount, limit) of faith. It shows how we must test doctrine, prophecy and, indeed, all gifts. The Greek word translated "proportion" is *analogian*—from which we get the word *analogy*. Theologians refer to the "analogy of faith," which means that we arrive at sound doctrine by comparing Scripture with Scripture. If a teaching cannot be supported solidly from Scripture by all relevant passages echoing the same truth—it is suspect. We must not go outside Scripture if we want our theology to be sound.

In Romans 12:3, Paul spoke of living within the "measure of faith God has given you." This means our faith is given to us, but with a certain limit. Only the Lord Jesus Christ had the Holy Spirit without limit (John 4:34). Jesus had all the Holy Spirit there is! You and I have but a "measure," or limit, of the Spirit. This means a measure of faith. When we go outside that limit or measure, we get into trouble. If we live within that measure, we are safe. The Holy Spirit will never lead us outside the measure of our faith. But if we go outside it anyway, we will mess up theologically—and if we prophesy, we will do so with words that are of the flesh, not the Spirit.

Perhaps the best example I can give here is how I prepare a sermon and then preach it. If I prepare a sermon, it must first be sound. Theologically correct. Second, I must know how much to say about a verse. I ask for the Holy Spirit's guidance. If the Holy Spirit in me is un-grieved, I can usually tell when to wrap up a point so that I have been fair to the text—but also simple. If I speak in a way that the people in the congregation will not understand, I am foolish to proceed. Then, when I preach it, I must be willing to depart from my notes but never go outside the measure

of faith I have been given. I may be tempted to go on a tangent, perhaps, or apply my word to someone I see in the audience I think needs a special consideration. If that person has been known to oppose my ministry, I may be tempted to "get at" them. I'm sorry, but I have done that. But I simultaneously went outside my measure of faith. I grieved the Spirit, but it was too late. It is a case of starting out in the Spirit and ending up in the flesh. Does this make me a false prophet?

Here is how prophecies often go wrong. A sincere person may indeed start out in the Spirit but at some point end up in the flesh (not unlike what is described in Galatians 3:3). So when Paul says that any prophesying must be carried out in proportion to one's faith, he means that he or she should not go outside one's clear conviction, gifting or anointing. When one does this, he or she gets it wrong—and will regret it. Hopefully, he or she will admit the error. As we saw earlier, Samuel erred for a moment, then retracted (1 Samuel 16:6–8). Nathan made the same mistake (2 Samuel 7:3–5). Both of them showed the humility to climb down. It is foolish pride that makes people stick to their guns even though they know they got it wrong.

I once asked a well-known prophetic person if he ever got it wrong. His reply: "No, I never have." Those were his exact words. I knew of cases where, in fact, he got it wrong. But people with a reputation of being an awesome prophet don't like to admit their fallibility. The problem is, one's sanctification does determine one's gift. The gifts are irrevocable, not tied to one's repentance (Romans 11:29). King Saul was backslidden but not a false prophet. On his way to kill David, he prophesied—and it was said yet again, "Is Saul also among the prophets?" (1 Samuel 19:23–24; 10:6–11). But if a prophet is backslidden, it is difficult to know whether such is a false prophet. A curious story of a backslidden prophet who badly influenced a true man of God is told in 1 Kings 13. Neither, however, was said to be a false prophet.

And yet when one goes outside his or her anointing or gifting, it is tantamount to becoming a bad tree. He or she crosses over a line and becomes like a thistle. The "fruit" is fruitlessness. Such a person gets in the flesh, the devil gets in, people are discouraged, and the cause of God— as well as the prophetic—is hurt. In a word: A

Christian can for a time become a bad tree and produce bad fruit when his or her prophetic word does not edify or come true. It means this person is not hearing from God, or that he or she started out well but ended up in the flesh. This is why Paul said that words need to be tested (1 Thessalonians 5:19). But this does not mean those who make mistakes like these are Balaams who want to destroy the people of God.

How to Prevent a Prophecy from Going Wrong

There is a cure for the person who might prophesy off the mark. First, be sure you've got good theology. I fear that so many today who seem to flourish in this area are not what I myself would regard as sound. It is my view that if a person is reformed in his or her doctrines, providing they are not cessationists (those who believe that the prophetic ceased with the closing of the canon of Scripture), they would be less apt to make bad prophecies.

Second, be sure you are a godly person who wants to glorify God. This means you will adhere to the teaching of Jesus as in the Sermon on the Mount, including forgiving all your enemies and ensuring that the Holy Spirit in you is not grieved. To put it another way, even though sanctification does not determine a person's gift, it would be of inestimable value if you make sure that you *are* a holy man, a holy woman—without any bitterness in your heart.

Third, live within your anointing. Stay within your measure of faith. Prophesy according to the clear word that you know is right. If you have a prophetic gift, you should know what is right already—and know better than to utter a word that has not been clearly given to you. It may mean you have no word at all. The problem with many prophetic people, especially if they are asked to "give a word," they give it whether or not they have one. They don't want to let people down—and, consequently, they transgress. Be humble enough to say, "Sorry, I don't have a word."

Fourth, do not trust your personal feelings when you are prophesying to those you know. You may want to please a friend or "get at" an enemy. A prophetic gift can be abused. Your whole gift system could break down and prove unreliable when your feelings intrude. The heart is deceitful and desperately wicked with the best of men (Jeremiah 17:9). If you lose objectivity, you will have egg on your face and lose credibility. You may think your feelings are what God put there and then speak thinking it is God's Word—when it may be sheer flesh.

Fifth, do not use God's name when you give a word. The worst mistake prophetic people make is to say, "God told me to say this," or, "Thus saith the Lord." This violates the third Commandment about taking God's name in vain. The main reason you would bring in God's name is not to make Him look better but to make your prophecy seem more credible. Don't do this. It displeases God. If it is a word from God you have to share, it will have the ring of authenticity without using His name. The truth, in any case, will become apparent in due course. You don't have to bring God's name in to make it more credible. What is more, should your word turn out wrong, it disgraces God's name all the more.

When You Are on the Receiving End

Have you had a prophetic word given to you? How did it make you feel? Do you believe God spoke to you? How can you know it is God speaking when someone speaks prophetically to you?

You never need to be controlled by a prophetic word. You need only to be controlled by the Bible. God does not hold you responsible for a word given to you as if it were the same as Scripture. This is why Paul says to "test everything. Hold on to the good" (1 Thessalonians 5:21).

Put any prophetic word to you on the back burner. If it comes true, good. You are not responsible for it. The only way you can know for sure a prophetic word is from God—unless Gabriel personally appears to you—is to wait and see if it comes to pass. I have prophetic words that good people have given me that I have been sitting on for years!

My best counsel to you is this: Know the Bible so well that God speaks to you all the time through His Word. This way you will be less likely to queue up to those prophetic people asking (which always annoys them), "Do you have a word for me?"

Infallibility is not required for those who have the gift of prophecy. But if they imply to you that they are infallible, walk away from them. I will listen to the person who fearfully and humbly says, "I think I might have a word for you." I am obliged to treat such a word with respect and courtesy. But neither do I have to believe it. Therefore, "Do not treat prophecies with contempt" (1 Thessalonians 5:20). "Despise not prophesyings" (KJV). "Do not scoff at those who prophesy" (TLB).

Don't be gullible. Don't be controlled or governed by words given to you. Test everything. Wait and see. When you are given a word, give it to God and leave it with Him. Only the Bible is infallible.

87. Doing the Father's Will

Not everyone who says to me, "Lord, Lord," will enter the kingdom of
heaven, but only he who does the will of my Father who is in heaven.

MATTHEW 7:21

Jesus continues to apply what He has preached and now brings back "Kingdom of heaven," a major theme of the Sermon on the Mount. We saw the Kingdom mentioned last in Matthew 6:33—"seek first his kingdom"—and before that in the Lord's Prayer (Matthew 6:10). He brings up this subject now partly to show what a great privilege it is to enter the Kingdom of heaven. "Not everyone who says to me, 'Lord, Lord,' will enter the kingdom of heaven."

It is striking that Jesus is referring to Himself: "Not everyone who says to me, 'Lord, Lord.'" He is stating a fact about Himself—that He is the Lord God. But calling Jesus "Lord" is in itself not sufficient to inherit the Kingdom. To say "Jesus is Lord" shows the sovereign operation of the Holy Spirit (1 Corinthians 12:3), indicating that such a person is born of the Spirit (John 3:3). Likewise, the Kingdom of heaven in the Sermon on the Mount is addressed to those who are already believers but who need to pursue their full inheritance—which Jesus calls entering the Kingdom. In a word: These people are born again but have a further responsibility. To say to Jesus, "Lord, Lord," is simply not sufficient to qualify one for his or her inheritance. It is only the beginning.

The issue He puts to us now is: Who will fully inherit the Kingdom and who won't? Who will: those who do His Father's will. Who won't: those who don't do the Father's will.

What is doing the Father's will? First, what this isn't. Jesus is not here referring to God's general will for your life—your vocation, career, whom you marry, what job to find for yourself or where you live. Not that God does not care or have an opinion about these matters, because He does. Neither is Jesus referring to what the Father's will

may be in your immediate situation or crisis, although He has an opinion on it.

Jesus brings in the Father's will and assumes two things. First, He refers to those who are believers. The hearers of the Sermon on the Mount would have much to learn. They had what John Calvin calls "implicit faith." Any true believer will embrace the Gospel. He or she would embrace the truth that he or she is justified not by his or her works. Such people learn they could not "plea bargain" with Jesus at the Final Judgment.

Second, it is the Father's will that all believers discover and experience the Holy Spirit. The Kingdom of heaven can be called the anointing—the realm of the Spirit experienced to the degree that the Spirit is *un-grieved* in us. The Holy Spirit is a very sensitive person. He is likened to a dove (John 1:32) and can be grieved (Ephesians 4:30). We grieve Him chiefly by bitterness, pointing the finger and holding grudges. When He is not grieved, it means we sense the anointing, which leads to closeness to God, clear thinking and self-control. It leads to our inheritance. Those, therefore, who do the Father's will are those for whom the anointing is not merely the important thing but the only thing.

A Warning on Two Levels

The warning that not everyone who calls Jesus "Lord" will enter the Kingdom is issued on two levels. First is the danger of presumption, assuming that religious knowledge is enough for getting into the Kingdom. If the Bible says "Jesus is Lord" and you therefore call Him "Lord," the question follows: Where did you get this information? Is this secondhand religion? Did you learn it in school? At church? Or from your parents or friends? In other words, perhaps you have amassed certain facts—though absolutely true—which you assumed gave you access to the Kingdom.

Perhaps you have had a religious experience. You pray. You have sought God in a time of need. I have quoted General Douglas MacArthur, who said, "There are no atheists in foxholes or trenches." In recent wars—beginning with the Falklands in 1982, then the first Gulf War of 1989, and more recently the war in Iraq—there have been hundreds of soldiers who cried out to God and claim now to be saved. But so many of these have no time for God when the war is over and they come home. You say you believe in God? Good. The devil also believes—and trembles (James 2:19).

In a word: It is not enough to talk about Jesus, to refer to Him as Lord, to believe in God, to have a good start by making a profession, to be baptized or to admire Jesus or His teaching. General William Booth, founder of the Salvation Army, once predicted that the day would come there would be a Christianity without Christ, salvation without the blood and religion without the Holy Spirit. Those described above, at this first level of warning, almost certainly have never been converted.

The second level of warning, however, is to believers. I refer to those who are truly converted. And yet you could be in danger of presuming you have all that God has in mind for you. Why? Because you have confessed Jesus as Lord, and you do believe in your heart that Jesus was raised from the dead (Romans 10:9–10). It is quite true that you have done the Father's will insofar as being saved goes. But do you not want to enter the Kingdom that Jesus is talking about?

This warning, then, is double-edged. Jesus' concern is not only that you know the way of salvation, but that you enter the Kingdom as He has taught it. It means abiding in the realm of the un-grieved Spirit. You may recall that there is a twofold use of the word "entering." It refers (1) to being born again, thus entering the Kingdom of God (John 3:3), but also to (2) entering the Kingdom of God by suffering or tribulation (Acts 14:22).

An Illustration: Two Circles

Imagine a circle within a circle. These circles are surrounded by darkness. Inside the circles is light.

When you were born of the Spirit, you crossed over from the kingdom of darkness into the Kingdom of light (Acts 26:18). That's entering the first circle. But now envisage the smaller circle inside that larger circle. The smaller circle is even brighter—with brilliant brightness. Entering the smaller circle comes, however, through hardships (Acts 14:22).

To summarize: Entering into the larger circle puts you in the Kingdom of God because you have been born again. But entering the smaller circle is what Jesus means by entering the Kingdom in Matthew 7:21.

Entering the Kingdom of heaven, then, does not refer to one's initial coming to salvation or being born again. Jesus assumes these disciples were born again. But the Kingdom referred to in Matthew 7:21 is that inner circle of brilliant brightness and glory—which is to be experienced here below. Jesus therefore addresses this sobering statement to all believers. This could mean you. He wants you to enter the Kingdom of heaven in this deeper sense. And He tells us now, whether we like it or not, that calling Jesus "Lord," valid though it is, is not sufficient warrant for entering into the realm and rule of the un-grieved Spirit of God.

The Withholding of the Kingdom

Jesus' teaching is more sobering and stunning than most people have considered very much. He warns that the Kingdom of heaven will be withheld from those who do not honor Jesus' interpretation of the Law by their lifestyle. Read again Matthew 5:21–48. For example, to those who glibly assume they do not break the sixth Commandment, "You shall not murder," because they have not killed anybody but have nonetheless murdered by name-calling, gossip, anger or destroying another's credibility—these people are now told in Matthew 7:21 that the Kingdom of heaven will be withheld from them. For this is what Jesus means by "doing the will of my Father in heaven." To those who hastily assume they have not broken the seventh Commandment, "You shall not commit adultery," merely because they have not slept with a woman other than their wife, yet have lusted, devoured pornography and deliberately caused another to lust—these are now told the Kingdom of heaven will be withheld from them.

The list goes on. The Kingdom of heaven will be withheld from those who abuse God's name, who live for vengeance as opposed to praying for their enemies. I'm sorry, but Jesus is demanding a higher level of righteous living than that which the Pharisees lived. Their righteousness was entirely external, all for people to admire (Matthew 23:5). Entrance into the Kingdom requires an inner righteousness that never came on the radar screen of the Pharisees.

Therefore, not "everyone" who calls Jesus "Lord" will enter the Kingdom of heaven. *But some of them will.* Who are they? They are those who press on and value this Kingdom more than anything in the world.

The Kingdom of heaven is thus withheld from those who would not be gracious, would not show mercy, were not pure in heart, fled from persecution rather than suffering disgrace for the name. Those who continue to judge one another, keep a record of wrongs and point the finger are those who, sadly, will be withheld from the Kingdom of heaven.

The Kingdom of heaven is withheld from those who lived for the honor and praise of people. It was their motivation for giving, praying, fasting. Their priority: that people would notice. They did not even attempt to receive the honor that comes from the only God, but opted for the praise and glory of people (John 5:44).

These same people are saved and in the Kingdom in that they are born again. But the way Jesus uses the phrase "Kingdom of heaven" in the Sermon on the Mount is the way it is used in Acts 14:22: "We must go through many hardships to enter the kingdom of God." Paul and Barnabas are referring to the Kingdom in the precise way Jesus explains it in the Sermon on the Mount.

Because of this high standard of living, there are those who say Jesus is referring to a future time, not the here and now. Others simply say Jesus' teaching is unachievable. It is true that we all fall short. This is why we need the Lord's Prayer and should pray it often. But doing the Father's will is nonetheless the way we are to strive for, agonize for, yearn for, ask for, seek for and knock—until the door is opened. To those who refuse this pursuit, the Kingdom is to be withheld.

Warrant for Entering the Kingdom

Only those who do the Father's will have a warrant to enter. What authorizes you and me to enter the Kingdom of heaven? It is perhaps best put in the following order: (1) Desiring God's will. We begin here. Do you desire to do the will of the Father? Said David, "One thing I ask of the LORD, this is what I seek: that I may dwell in the house of the LORD all the days of my life, to gaze upon the beauty of the LORD and to seek him in his temple" (Psalm 27:4). (2) Discovering God's will, namely His Word as disclosed in the Sermon on the Mount. Do you want to know the will of God? Read the Sermon on the Mount! *The Sermon on the Mount is the will of God.* (3) Doing the Father's will—that is, carrying out this very teaching. (4) Delighting in the will of God. As opposed to resenting the teaching of this Sermon, you are described this way: "Blessed is the man who fears the LORD, who finds great delight in his commands" (Psalm 112:1). (5) Displaying the will of God. Stephen displayed it when he said, "Lord, do not hold this sin against them," referring to those who stoned him to death (Acts 7:60). It is what Paul meant by graciousness, gentleness (Philippians 4:5).

What assurance is there that you will indeed enter the Kingdom of heaven? Two things: that you (1) are on the foundation, and that you (2) build a superstructure of gold, silver, precious gems.

You begin with the true foundation. This means you have received the Gospel. You do call Jesus Lord. "No one can lay any foundation other than the one already laid, which is Jesus Christ" (1 Corinthians 3:11). You trust Christ's blood for salvation, not your works. That is the foundation. But the Kingdom of heaven—the realm of the un-grieved Spirit—is inherited by building a superstructure on the foundation that will last. Indeed, it will survive the fire that will be revealed at the Judgment. The possible ingredients for this superstructure are put metaphorically by Paul: wood, hay, straw, gold, silver, precious stones (1 Corinthians 3:12). Pour kerosene on these six items, strike a match, watch the flames arise—and what is left afterward? Only the gold, silver, precious gems. The wood, hay and straw (faulty superstructure) are burned up.

When you and I point the finger, cause one to lust, abuse God's name, live for vengeance and disdain Christ's commands, we build a superstructure of wood, hay and straw. They will burn up. Saying to Jesus, "Lord, Lord," is not enough. But if you and I lead lives of love and total forgiveness, of sexual purity, of wanting only God's honor and of praying for our enemies, we build a superstructure of gold, silver and precious stones. The content of our superstructure "will be revealed with fire, and the fire will test the quality of each man's work. If what he has built survives, he will receive his reward. If it is burned up, he will suffer loss; he himself will be saved, but only as one escaping through the flames" (1 Corinthians 3:13–15).

The good news: All who are on the foundation will be saved, regardless of the superstructure they erect. The bad news: They will receive no reward at the Judgment Seat of Christ, because they did not pursue their inheritance in the Kingdom of heaven here below. Those who build their superstructure with gold, silver and precious stones will not only be saved, but will receive a "rich welcome into the eternal kingdom of our Lord and Savior Jesus Christ" (2 Peter 1:11).

Those who do the Father's will are those whose lives are dedicated to building a superstructure that will last. What kind of superstructure are you building? Nothing would give me greater joy than to learn that some reader will receive a reward in heaven through this book. That is why I wrote it. We may have come to the most important part here. Not everyone who calls Jesus "Lord" will enter the Kingdom of heaven. But some will. Are you one of them?

88. The Surprising Judgment

Many will say to me on that day, "Lord, Lord, did we not prophesy in your
name, and in your name drive out demons and perform many miracles?" Then
I will tell them plainly, "I never knew you. Away from me, you evildoers!"

MATTHEW 7:22–23

Our Lord now moves from the Kingdom of heaven to the Final Judgment. The first implicit reference to the Final Judgment was in Matthew 5:12: "Rejoice and be glad, because great is your reward in heaven, for in the same way they persecuted the prophets who were before you." The second reference is slightly more explicit: "But I tell you that anyone who is angry with his brother will be subject to judgment. Again, anyone who says to his brother, 'Raca,' is answerable to the Sanhedrin. But anyone who says, 'You fool!' will be in danger of the fire of hell" (Matthew 5:22). There is also Jesus' admonition, "Do not judge, or you too will be judged" (Matthew 7:1)—but it may not necessarily refer to the Final Judgment.

What is obvious, however, in Matthew 7:22 is an explicit reference to the Final Judgment. This idea is something never far from Jesus' mind or His hearers. John the Baptist said to Pharisees and Sadducees: "You brood of vipers! Who warned you to flee from the coming wrath?" (Matthew 3:7). But when Jesus referred to "that day," it was enough. Everybody knew what He meant by it.

There was a long pre-history in Judaism regarding the idea of God stepping in to judge. "The LORD Almighty has a day in store for all the proud and lofty, for all that is exalted (and they will be humbled)" (Isaiah 2:12). "Wail, for the day of the LORD is near; it will come like destruction from the Almighty" (Isaiah 13:6). "Alas for that day! The day of the LORD is near; it will come like destruction from the Almighty" (Joel 1:15). "The day of the LORD is great; it is dreadful. Who can endure it?" (Joel 2:11). "The sun will be turned to darkness and the moon to blood before the coming of the great and dreadful day of the LORD" (Joel 2:31).

The Final Judgment

Although God has stepped in many times to judge His people, the Bible teaches that there will be a Final Judgment—when all people who ever lived from the first day of Creation will be present. The saved and the lost will be raised from the dead—whether they had burials, cremation or were buried at sea. John described it:

> I saw a great white throne and him who was seated on it. Earth and sky fled from his presence, and there was no place for them. And I saw the dead, great and small, standing before the throne, and books were opened. Another book was opened, which is the book of life. The dead were judged according to what they had done as recorded in the books. The sea gave up the dead that were in it, and death and Hades gave up the dead that were in them, and each person was judged according to what he had done. Then death and Hades were thrown into the lake of fire. The lake of fire is the second death. If anyone's name was not found written in the book of life, he was thrown into the lake of fire.

REVELATION 20:11–15

Jesus Is the Judge

And who do you suppose will be the Judge? It is none other than the Lord Jesus Christ Himself. "Many will say to *me* on that day," says Jesus. This shows that Jesus knew then—at the beginning of His ministry—He would be coming a second time after His death on the cross.

There is an inseparable connection between the Second Coming and the Final Judgment. "Just as man is destined to die once, and after that to face judgment, so Christ was sacrificed once to take away the sins of many people; and he will appear a second time, not to bear sin, but to bring salvation to those who are waiting for him" (Hebrews 9:27–28). Jesus also calls Himself the Son of Man. "At that time the sign of the Son of Man will appear in the sky, and all the nations of the earth will mourn. They will see the Son of Man coming on the clouds of the sky, with power and great glory" (Matthew 24:30). He also said, "There is a judge for the one who rejects me and does not accept my words; that very word which I spoke will condemn him at the last day" (John 12:48). This coheres with Paul's sermon in Athens: God has "set a day when he will judge the world with justice by the man he has appointed. He has given proof of this to all men by raising him from the dead" (Acts 17:31). Paul also said, "In the presence of God and of Christ Jesus, who will judge the living and the dead, and in view of his appearing and his kingdom" (2 Timothy 4:1).

Matthew 7:22 therefore shows: (1) Jesus Himself will be the judge at the Final Judgment, and (2) many will be surprised at the Judgment—namely, those who trusted in their works and exploits.

General Summary

When it comes to eschatology, things are not as clear to us as we might like. We will know a lot more about heaven five minutes after we have been there than all the guesswork done in advance. So, too, it is with the details of the Second Coming and the Final Judgment. I can only assert my own grasp of this grave teaching with fear and trembling. Apart from the exact chronological order of events, this much we can be sure of:

1. There will be a Final Judgment following the Second Coming (Hebrews 9:27).

2. Jesus Himself will be the Judge (Acts 17:31; 2 Timothy 4:1).

3. All the dead throughout the ages—saved and lost—will be raised to be judged: "Some will rise to live, and those who have done evil will rise to be condemned" (John 5:29).

   a. The "dead in Christ will rise first." Those alive at that moment will be caught up to join the sainted dead (1 Thessalonians 4:16–17).

   b. All the unsaved will stand trial before the Judge (Revelation 20:11–15).

4. Every single person, saved or lost, who ever lived on this planet—from Adam and Eve to Pharaoh to Balaam to Nebuchadnezzar to the Caesars to Hitler and Saddam Hussein to the last person to be born—will bend the knee and confess that Jesus Christ is Lord. Not necessarily because they believed it on earth, but "to the glory of God the Father" (Philippians 2:9–11; Romans 14:10–11).

5. Two classes of people, therefore, will be judged (2 Timothy 4:1).

   a. Those who are unsaved.

   b. Those who are saved.

      i. Some will be given a reward (1 Corinthians 3:14).

      ii. Others will suffer loss of reward (1 Corinthians 3:15).

Therefore, when Jesus said, "Many will say to me on that day, 'Lord, Lord, did we not prophesy in your name'" (Matthew 7:22), He was referring to the Final Judgment. But what is the purpose of these verses? Why are they put precisely here? First, they further show the seriousness of the words of Jesus in the Sermon on the Mount. As we just saw, His teaching will condemn people at the last day (John 12:48). You and I will face Jesus' very words at the Final Judgment. Second, they show how surprised some people will be on that Day. They thought their good works, their gifts, their fame and all their accomplishments on earth would determine whether they were in or out.

But there remains an obvious question: Does this passage refer only to the lost—those not in but out with regard to going to heaven or hell? Yes. Whereas Matthew 7:21 refers to believers who may or may not gain their inheritance in the Kingdom of heaven, Matthew 7:22–23 refers to heaven itself—and why these people will miss it.

Lost People Will Plead with Jesus at the Judgment

Three things show that Matthew 7:22–23 describes the unsaved at the Judgment. First, the context. Jesus had just been speaking of false prophets (Matthew 7:15–20). These people were never saved. They were those who somehow got into the Church and wielded vast influence. This no doubt included people like the Gnostics—described in Jude 4; 1 John 2:19; 2 Peter 2:1–22 and possibly in Colossians. It would also include legalistic people like the Judaizers, those Jews who followed Paul everywhere with the view to discredit the Gospel. They are described in 2 Corinthians 3:1; 11:13–15 and Galatians 1:7; 2:4; 4:17; 6:12.

Apart from these two groups, there have always been enemies of the Gospel—both in the Old Testament era as well as in the Church throughout the ages—who have dazzling gifts and appear to be a part of the community of believers. They are able, charismatic, oratorical and highly gifted with spiritual powers. Some are endued with at least three gifts: prophecy, miracles and the ability to drive out demons.

People with gifts such as these do at least two things: (1) They influence vast numbers of people. Who wouldn't be fascinated by people like this? Sheer curiosity would cause people to drive distances to see them, watch them on television and even contribute to their ministries. (2) These gifted people took their own abilities as proofs and signs they would go to heaven. This is why they used their gifts to plead with the Supreme Judge, "Lord, Lord, did we not prophesy in your name, and in your name drive out demons and perform many miracles?"

Second, we know these are unsaved people because Jesus will plainly say to them, "I never knew you. Away from me, you evildoers!" This is strong language: *I never knew you. Evildoers.* Jesus does not say, "I knew you for a while, but you fell away." He says, "I *never* knew you." The language cannot be stronger than that.

Third, consider the reason these lost people thought they were saved. In a word: They trusted their good works, their illustrious exploits, their extraordinary gifts and accomplishments. I once put this question to a head of state: "If you were to stand before God—and you will—and He were to ask you—and He might—'Why should I let you into My heaven?' What would you say?" He replied that he felt his accomplishments would let him in. This is what so many important people—inside or outside the Church—truly believe. They think their position, reputation, faithfulness,

responsible job, strategic decisions or hard work count for righteousness. Sadly, it shows they are blind to and unaware of the Gospel.

If you wonder why high-profile preachers and faith healers never preach the Gospel—but refer to the cross only in terms of health and wealth—it is because the true Gospel is not theirs. It is a "different gospel" (Galatians 1:6), "a Jesus other than the Jesus we preached" (2 Corinthians 11:4), that they have embraced. When a preacher and worker of miracles can appear on live television (shown all over the world) night after night and month after month, but never once preach the Gospel, it shows he does not know the Gospel. I do not say that every television preacher who boasts of a ministry of healing automatically falls into the category of Matthew 7:22–23. But if I were one of them I would be scared to death.

By the way, what is your hope of going to heaven? What exactly would you say to the Lord Jesus Christ if He were to ask you why He should let you into His heaven? I will tell you plainly: If you are trusting your good works, you will go to hell. I must also say: Our only hope of heaven is the sinless life and shed blood of Jesus Christ—and trusting Him alone. We have no other hope.

I must add that even if you are not a high-profile person and have no gift of healing or miracles, but inwardly you think you will get to heaven by your best efforts—your prayer life, your good works, the money you have given to the Church or other ministries, your sacrifices, helping people, your "Christian" example—you reveal that you have no more hope of heaven than those described in Matthew 7:22–23. I'm sorry, but He would say that He never knew you.

The Difference between Matthew 7:21 and Matthew 7:22

Because these verses—one referring to the Kingdom of heaven, the other to heaven itself—are placed side by side, one might assume at first they describe the same lot of people. But they are not the same. In Matthew 7:21, Jesus in a sense summarizes His teaching—and how one could be a believer and not enter the Kingdom. Matthew 7:22, however, describes those who were in the Church but never regenerate.

Whereas Matthew 7:21 refers to the Christian who by faith professes that Jesus is "Lord," verse 22 describes lost people who cannot enter heaven but will go to hell. Verse 21 describes the true believer who may not necessarily gain his or her inheritance in the Kingdom; verse 22 refers to those who cannot enter heaven itself. In verse 21, these people affirmed the deity of Jesus in saving faith, but verse 22 says they call Him Lord by being forced to. Verse 21 shows that a profession of faith alone is not sufficient to bring one into his or her inheritance; verse 22 shows that these people lose everything. Verse 21 refers to the Kingdom of heaven, an inheritance below; verse 22 refers to the Final Judgment that shows why people go to hell.

Not "everyone" who calls Jesus "Lord," then, will enter the Kingdom of heaven, but some will—because they pursued their inheritance. Yet those described in verse 22 were never saved; in the end they confessed Jesus to be "Lord" because they *had* to do it. One day "every knee shall bow and every tongue shall confess that Jesus Christ is Lord" (Philippians 2:10)—whether they like it or not. These are the ones who will try to plea bargain with the Supreme Judge. They will fail in their plea and be sent to hell.

Verse 21 describes those who may not have pursued meekness, shown mercy or prayed for their enemies, but verse 22 shows those who were never converted in the first place. "I never knew you," says Jesus. In short: Verse 21 refers to the Christian: verse 22 refers to the lost. Verse 21 shows the Christian who could forfeit his or her inheritance; verse 22 shows the lost person who loses his or her own soul forever. Verse 21 shows the possibility of a true believer not persisting in faith; verse 22 shows the counterfeit who got in the church through the back door but will be kept from entering heaven.

Question: Can a case be made that Matthew 7:22 refers to the Christian who loses his or her inheritance—but will be saved by fire? I answer: It is a very thin case. Jesus' words "I never knew you" are too strong to suggest He is addressing believers who would be saved but by fire. There will be a judgment among the saved at the Judgment Seat of Christ (1 Corinthians 3:13–15; 2 Corinthians 5:10). But Matthew 7:22–23 is not it.

Martin Luther's saying about heaven bears repeating. He said he expected to have three surprises there: First, there would be those present he thought would not be there. Second, there would be those missing he thought would be there. Third, the greatest surprise of all—that he is there himself!

None of us deserves to go to heaven. We all deserve to go to hell. But if we go to heaven, it will be solely by the sheer grace of God—through faith, not works (Ephesians 2:8–9). Dr. Martyn Lloyd-Jones used to say that a Christian is one who is surprised that he or she is a Christian.

Do you know for certain that if you were to die today you would go to heaven?

89. Faith on Trial

Therefore everyone who hears these words of mine and puts them into
practice is like a wise man who built his house on the rock. The rain
came down, the streams rose, and the winds blew and beat against that
house; yet it did not fall, because it had its foundation on the rock.

MATTHEW 7:24–25

We have now reached the conclusion of this magnificent sermon—the greatest sermon ever preached. You may recall that Jesus' original teaching on the Mount might have taken several days—that Matthew gives us a summary of it. In any case, we now examine the final application of this sermon. He is drawing all He said to a conclusion.

The phrase "these words of mine" refer not merely to the previous verse but to the whole of the sermon, beginning with Matthew 5:3. Jesus ends the sermon by showing the pragmatic benefit of living the way He has outlined—and the grave tragedy that will come if we don't. We may conclude that living the way Jesus has proposed not only is the way to gain an inheritance in the Kingdom of heaven—it is also the best way to live on earth!

Jesus applies His teaching to life and the storms of life. He shows how life can be for us when a trial comes—a severe trial. The Christian faith does not exempt one from trial. It equips one for trial. As Chuck Colson put it, God does not promise to take us out of the fire but promises to get into the fire with us.

Jesus puts His own teaching on trial. No wonder He is said to have spoken with such authority (Matthew 7:28–29). He shows how strongly He believes in His own preaching! "Everyone who hears these words of mine and puts them into practice is like a wise man who built his house on the rock. The rain came down, the streams rose, and the winds blew and beat against that house; yet it did not fall, because it had its foundation on the rock."

Why is this part of the Sermon on the Mount so important? What are the lessons to be learned

here? First, it shows that *hearing* the truth is not enough. Jesus is about to describe those who hear His words *and put them into practice*. "Do not merely listen to the word, and so deceive yourselves," says James, but "do what it says" (James 1:22).

Second, these words of Jesus demonstrate that trials will come. "In this world you will have trouble," Jesus said elsewhere (John 16:33). In fact, "Time and chance happen to them all" (Ecclesiastes 9:11). If you are not a Christian, you will have trials. If you are a Christian, you will have trials. If you are an obedient Christian, you will have trials. The rains will come down, streams will rise and the winds will blow and beat against us.

Third, the principles of the Sermon on the Mount ensure not only a reward in heaven but a greater faith and anointing here below. What is good enough to die with is good enough to live by. You are not ready to live until you are ready to die—but if you are ready to die, you have the greatest way forward to living here below.

The Practice of Truth

Jesus now refers to what He has preached: "everyone who hears these words of mine." We don't know how many heard it, but it was a lot of people—"crowds" (Matthew 5:1). And yet what a privilege to have been there! Can you imagine getting to talk with someone who was actually present when Jesus preached this historic sermon? Would they not have to pinch themselves years later to believe they were there? And yet what an honor to hear this now—even to have someone read this sermon to you. Therefore, when Jesus says, "Everyone who hears these words," it includes those who hear it read today—or hear it interpreted (as I have sought to do in this book). In a word: He speaks to you if you have read this book.

So hearing the words of Jesus is an essential beginning to living the Christian life—but not enough. Jesus wants His preaching to be put into practice. The Hebrew *shamar* means both "to hear" and "to obey." So if we truly have heard what Jesus has said to us in the Hebraic sense, we will put them into practice. And yet the fact that He says *and*—"and puts them into practice"— shows it is possible to hear His teaching and not obey it. This means it was not enough merely to have been present in Galilee on that mountain (or to have read this book!).

I trust that what I have written is a faithful filling out of all Jesus taught in the Sermon on the Mount. I hope one day to hear from the lips of Jesus Himself, "Well done," for the way I have interpreted Him. But even if I have got it right, the onus is on all who read this book to carry out what Jesus has taught.

Wisdom

The focus is on "a wise man." If you practice what Jesus has preached, you will be a wise man or woman. You are foolish if you don't practice it. A brief look at the Greek word used here—*phronimos,* meaning "wise"—will be helpful. It comes from a root word that means "mind," "consciousness," "understanding." The verb *phroneo* means "to think." In a modern vernacular, we might say, "Use your head," meaning, "Don't be stupid." If a person does not apply Jesus' words, he is just plain stupid.

Phronimos is also used in Matthew 24:45, where Jesus refers to a man being responsible in governing his household—and being ready when the master shows up. If a man is truly "wise," he will plan, prepare and be found watching for the return of his master. It is also used in the Parable of the Ten Virgins—five of whom were wise, five foolish. The wise virgins took oil in their vessels in anticipation of the coming bridegroom, but the foolish took no oil. The word *phronimos* means "preparedness." It means thinking ahead. So if you apply Jesus' teaching you will be wise—prepared, shrewd, thinking ahead. In the present life there

will be troubles—storms. How will you weather the storm? Those who practice Jesus' teaching will be wise, or ready for a storm.

When I was at Westminster Chapel there were a lot of people who came to "hear." They were "sermon tasters." I used to wonder how many actually came to apply what they heard. So many wanted to hear me, check out my theology and compare me to other preachers. Again I quote F. F. Bruce, who said there are two types of Scotsmen: those who come to church to hear the Gospel preached, and those who come to see if the Gospel is preached! Sadly, people like this feel no need to apply what they hear. They fancy themselves the experts on what good preaching or good theology is. I worry about those who would even say to me, being complimentary, "That is good preaching on total forgiveness." But I wonder in my heart: Do these people themselves actually forgive their enemies? Paul put it similarly: "You who preach against stealing, do you steal? You who say that people should not commit adultery, do you commit adultery? You who abhor idols, do you rob temples?" (Romans 2:21–22).

There was a man who began coming to Westminster Chapel from the first week I arrived. He was somewhat cerebral, intellectual. But he never had assurance of salvation, it seemed. He would come to the vestry week after week for me to help him. I tried. He always left feeling better by what he "heard." But he never applied it. It was all in his head. He never asked for membership, feeling that he wasn't ready to do this until he was assured of his salvation. He eventually went to another church, and I didn't see him for years. He did not join the other church, either. He showed up in the congregation during my last year at Westminster—25 years later. He came to see me in the vestry with the same old problem. He was a hearer only. Too many people do not want their problems solved; they only want them understood.

"Everyone who hears these words of mine and puts them into practice is like a wise man." Wisdom comes when two things coalesce: hearing and heeding. This means that you and I must show graciousness, are truly peacemakers and are determined to be pure in heart (Matthew 5:7–9). It means we will not lust or cause lusting, we will not hate our enemies but will truly bless and pray for them, give our money to God for God alone to notice, pray not merely to be seen by others and seek first the Kingdom of God. Hearing plus heeding equals wisdom. If you have theology in your head only, that means an arid, dry intellect. You will be like those Dr. Martyn Lloyd-Jones used to describe: "perfectly orthodox, perfectly useless."

The wise man, says Jesus, builds his house on a rock. He knows that the foundation is extremely important. If there would be no wind or rain, then the foundation would not be so important. But only a fool would neglect a proper foundation when building a house. Whether you build on a rock or sand, each house looks secure in good weather. But Palestine is known for torrential rains that can turn dry wadis into raging torrents. Only storms reveal the quality of the work of a builder. The foundation needed was a rock—not sand.

Jesus knows that His teaching is absolutely true. Yet what makes the foundation a rock is not only the content of His message but its application by the hearer. It was not good teaching alone one needed, but heart theology. "Guard your heart, for it is the wellspring of life" (Proverbs 4:23). A house built on a rock will mean a foundation of solid, biblical theology—and also anointing by the Holy Spirit. It brings us back to the beginning of this book. The Sermon on the Mount is Jesus' doctrine of the Holy Spirit. When you not only accept the theology but also "ask, seek, knock" in order to be blessed by the Holy Spirit, you are on the rock. You are a wise man or woman.

The Promise of Trial

Are you in a trial right now? If you are not, you will be. It is only a matter of time before the rains will come. Jesus said, "The rain came down, the streams rose, and the winds blew and beat against that house." What Jesus describes is a storm. "Storm" is often used poetically to describe a severe time of testing.

Trials are predestined. Does this surprise you? Paul hoped that his converts would not be "unsettled by these trials. You know quite well that we were destined for them" (1 Thessalonians 3:3). This encourages me no end. When I know that "every joy or trial cometh from above," as they hymn writer put it, I know that every trial—every

storm—is to be welcomed, not rejected. "Consider it pure joy, my brothers, whenever you face trials of many kinds, because you know that the testing of your faith develops perseverance" (James 1:2–3). Some people also forget that trial is a part of the package when we become Christians. "For it has been granted to you on behalf of Christ not only to believe on him, but also to suffer for him" (Philippians 1:29).

Every trial is predestined and planned for us—according to our grace, calling and temperament. God deals with each of us individually and personally. "No temptation [or trial—Gr. *perasmos* means either] has seized you except what is common to man. And God is faithful; he will not let you be tempted beyond what you can bear. But when you are tempted, he will also provide a way out so that you can stand up under it" (1 Corinthians 10:13).

We can therefore conclude that every trial is personalized. Possibly my favorite verse in all the Psalms is this: "He knows how we are formed, he remembers that we are dust" (Psalm 103:14). "Do not be surprised at the painful trial you are suffering, as though something strange were happening to you" (1 Peter 4:12). It is true that we can bring some trials on ourselves unnecessarily (see 1 Peter 4:15)—but even these are within the scope of God's purpose for us. Do not despise the rains that come down in any case.

The storms of life may be medical. In my old age, I have had open heart surgery. Arthritis is in my hands. I always took health for granted. We never know when our health will fail—or when that last illness will bring on the grave. The storms of life might be mental, when the pressure seems almost too great. My dad developed Alzheimer's—a fear I suppose I will always have. The storms of life could be marital. I thank God for Louise, who has stood by me for 52 years. The storms of life could pertain to a misunderstanding with someone. They could be money problems. Satan will exploit any weakness in our frame. These trials show how strong we are.

Jesus said the "winds blew and beat against that house; yet it did not fall, because it had its foundation on the rock." He did not promise any great "plus" from the trial, only that the house did not fall. He did not say the house got a new paint job or that it doubled in size. Therefore, those who get tried by the storms do not jump up and down with excitement. Their illnesses are not miraculously healed. Our finances are not increased. But the one thing promised: The house will not fall. It survived.

This means *you* will not fall. The promise is to all who hear Jesus' words and apply them. Such people will not crack up in the storms of life. They will not go to pieces. They will not give up their faith. They will not panic and shake their fists at God for allowing the trial.

When Satan tries us, we are to stand, says Paul. Four times he uses the word *stand* in his classic paragraph on spiritual warfare (Ephesians 6:10–18). "Stand your ground" (verse 13). When you stand, you don't fall. You don't trip. You don't go backward. You don't run. You don't even walk. When Satan buffets and trials come, it is huge progress merely to stand.

The promise Jesus gives us is that the house—meaning, you and me—will not fall. It will remain because it was built upon a rock. The rock—hearing and applying Jesus' word—was the foundation. It promised to keep us from falling. The promise is true. "On Christ the solid rock I stand, all other ground is sinking sand."

90. Folk Religion

But everyone who hears these words of mine and does not put them into practice
is like a foolish man who built his house on sand. The rain came down, the streams
rose, and the winds blew and beat against that house, and it fell with a great crash.

MATTHEW 7:26–27

Folk religion is a little bit of religion that makes us feel comfortable and spiritual—but it does not change our lives or show us how to die. It keeps us in our comfort zones. Every generation has its own brand of folk religion. The main ingredients are smugness, self-satisfaction and superiority. It is whatever helps us avoid pain or inconvenience in the here and now. It is having a form of godliness but denying its power (2 Timothy 3:5). The teaching may sometimes be fairly sound, but it will not disturb our lifestyle. Perhaps you have heard of a product called Brylcreem—a hair cream. "A little dab will do you," was their slogan. Folk religion is "Brylcreem religion."

This is what Jesus describes in His closing sentence of the Sermon on the Mount. "Everyone who hears these words of mine and does not put them into practice is like a foolish man who built his house on sand." We saw that wisdom is thinking ahead—building a house on a rock. A fool builds his house on sand. Such a person does not think ahead and anticipate the possibility of a violent storm.

The folly is having heard the preaching of Jesus—the greatest teaching in the whole world—but not putting that information into practice. It is *not applying* what you heard. "Anyone who listens to the word but does not do what it says is like a man who looks at his face in a mirror and, after looking at himself, goes away and immediately forgets what he looks like" (James 1:23–24). The person who hears may agree with what was said. He may even *love* what was taught. But he never applies it. People like this get a pious feeling from strong, "close to the bone" preaching. But they still don't apply it!

A member of my old congregation in Westminster happened to be in Los Angeles when Arthur Blessitt addressed the Southern Baptist Convention, which was taking place by coincidence. My friend returned to London absolutely lyrical about Arthur's sermon. He quoted from it line after line. The bottom line: These Southern Baptists need to be evangelizing the world. "Will Los Angeles be any different after 25,000 Southern Baptists leave?" Arthur said to them. "It was absolutely fantastic to hear Arthur," said my friend. I myself was gripped by what he told me.

In fact, I was so gripped by what he told me that I eventually managed to get Arthur to come to Westminster Chapel. Arthur turned us upside down. My best decision in 25 years there was bringing him to Westminster Chapel! I was not, however, prepared for the way he would shake us up. He got us out on the streets to give out tracts and evangelize passersby. I was never to be the same again. It absolutely changed my own life forever.

Not so for my friend whose report of Arthur's ministry in Los Angeles caused me to invite Arthur. This friend totally deserted me in a very short period of time. It was tremendous that Arthur preached as he did to Southern Baptists in Los Angeles. But when Arthur came to London and urged us to do this, my friend disappeared for all time. It is as Ed Stetzer stated: "People like everything about evangelism but doing it."

Foolishness

What Jesus does in His concluding remarks is to pose the ominous possibility of *only hearing, never applying*. It is like those who are always agreeing with what they hear but never obeying it. "The fear of the LORD is the beginning of knowledge, but fools despise wisdom and discipline" (Proverbs

1:7). "The wise inherit honor, but fools he holds up to shame" (Proverbs 3:35). "The lips of the righteous nourish many, but fools die for lack of judgment" (Proverbs 10:21). "The way of a fool seems right to him, but a wise man listens to advice" (Proverbs 12:15). A fool is a person who does not apply the good wisdom they have heard. He is arrogant, doesn't take advice, won't ask for advice and suffers unnecessarily in life. All he needed to do was to listen and obey. In the words of the hymn:

> Trust and obey for there's no other way
> To be happy in Jesus than to trust and
> obey.
> John Henry Sammis (1846–1919)

Jesus says three things regarding a fool:

(1) He doesn't plan ahead. He is like the foolish virgin who took no oil. There was no preparedness (Matthew 25:3).

(2) He lives for the present only. Jesus elsewhere described a prosperous man who said, "I will tear down my barns and build bigger ones, and there I will store all my grain and my goods. And I'll say to myself, 'You have plenty of good things laid up for many years. Take life easy; eat, drink and be merry.' But God said to him, 'You fool! This very night your life will be demanded from you. Then who will get what you have prepared yourself?' This is how it will be with anyone who stores up things for himself but is not rich toward God" (Luke 12:18–21).

(3) The fool does not apply the truth he heard. He heard the same exact teaching the wise man heard. The wise man applied what he heard. The fool did not apply the same teaching.

The wise man and the foolish man also endured the same storms. "The rain came down, the streams rose, and the winds blew and beat against that house." They both had heard the same message, they both built houses, they both weathered the same storms. The difference: The wise man had applied Jesus' teachings, the foolish man had not. You could say that the foolish man was only interested in appearance. By looking at the house, you would not know whether the house was on sand or a solid foundation. The fool wanted an immediate dwelling place, whereas digging the foundation took time. Luke's account says the wise man "dug down deep and laid the foundation on rock" (Luke 6:48). The foolish man was too lazy to do that and also did not want to wait.

Surviving the Storm

The wise man's house did not fall. When the storm came, it stood, survived. The foolish man built on sand. When the same storm came, his house fell and collapsed with a "great crash."

Folk religion is comfortable. It lures one into a comfort zone. It keeps him there. One's life remains unchanged. That is, until the violent storm appears. Then his life would change. The inconvenience of moving outside one's comfort zone does not compare with the inconvenience that comes with the storm that results in losing everything.

We all have to make a choice between inconveniencing our lives now by applying Jesus' teaching, or letting the storm inconvenience our lives later with unspeakable discomfort.

The storm exposed the foundation. Nobody knew the foundation was sand until the storm came. Without the storm, the wise man's house and the foolish man's house looked the same.

Those who are all out for God and His will in their lives will be sneered at by those who hear the same teaching but choose not to apply it. They want only a "little dab" of religion. A little dab does them—for a while. But not for long. Those who hear Jesus' word and apply it can never seem to have enough of God. They want more, more. But those who don't apply His teaching only want a dab—folk religion. What will one do when the violent storm comes? Folk religion doesn't teach a person how to live, neither does it teach a person how to die. A "little dab" won't be enough for that moment.

The wise man dug down deep. How deep? He hit the rock. Those who dig deep want to pray more than ever, read their Bibles more than ever, learn more than ever, walk in all the light they can get—and find out how real God is. What is more, it brings confidence in the day of the Final Judgment (1 John 4:18).

The Crash

The man who paid my tuition at Oxford University was James H. Milby (whom I called "Harlan"). I preached his funeral since we moved to Tennessee. I can never forget an occasion many years ago when the two of us were bonefishing in the Florida Keys. He began to tell me about Kenneth (name changed), with whom I had attended college. He had set Kenneth up in business. Kenneth had become a multimillionaire in a short period of time. He told me about Kenneth's fancy cars and huge homes, how he would fly to London to buy a suit.

I was always a little envious of Kenneth. I asked: "Harlan, why didn't you set me up in business like you did Kenneth?" He replied that he never felt like doing it! Two years later, Harlan wrote me a letter out of the blue. He asked, "Have you heard about Kenneth?" He described Kenneth during the past two years. Everything had changed. "Kenneth and his wife are divorced. He has lost everything. The Mafia are looking for him." He ended his letter with these words: "R. T., you chose the rock, Kenneth chose the sand."

King Saul became "yesterday's man" largely by putting himself above the Word of God (1 Samuel 13:9–12), as I show in my book *The Anointing*. Saul assumed that Scripture should apply to everybody else but himself. He became consumed with jealousy, could no longer keep his word and refused to be accountable to anybody. His life ended in suicide (1 Samuel 31). It all began because he would not apply Scripture to himself. The worst mistake a human being can make on this planet is to underestimate the Word of God, its importance and relevance for our lives.

The Eschatological Crash

"The greatest storm is eschatological," says Don Carson. As the ancient prophet put it, "When a flimsy wall is built, they cover it with whitewash, therefore tell those who cover it with whitewash that it is going to fall. Rain will come in torrents, and I will send hailstones hurtling down, and violent winds will burst forth. When the wall collapses, will people not ask you, 'Where is the whitewash you covered it with?' . . . When it falls, you will be destroyed in it; and you will know that I am the Lord" (Ezekiel 13:10–12, 14).

You and I will face God one day. One of two things will come next: the Second Coming of Jesus or our death. If it is the Second Coming (a blessed thought), Jesus will come with clouds and "every eye will see him, even those who pierced him; and all the peoples of the earth will mourn because of him. So shall it be! Amen" (Revelation 1:7). John said, however, that we need not be among those who weep and wail and gnash our teeth; we can have boldness in that day (1 John 4:17). The same is true when it comes our time to die. The greatest test of all will reveal our foundation. Are you ready for that moment?

> Hold Thou Thy cross before my closing eyes;
> Shine through the gloom, and point me to the skies;
> Heaven's morning breaks, and earth's vain shadows flee:
> In life, in death, O Lord, abide with me.
> Henry Francis Lyte (1793–1847)

91. Awesome Authority

When Jesus had finished saying these things, the crowds were amazed at his teaching,
because he taught as one who had authority, and not as their teachers of the law.

MATTHEW 7:28–29

The Sermon on the Mount is over. Jesus has brought this verbally inspired message to a close. And I could well end the book with the end of the sermon, as in the previous chapter. But I have always been intrigued by the response Jesus got. He didn't give an altar call. Apparently, the people just left, returning to their homes. The only person to come forward was the leper—a man who knew his place in that culture, but knew Jesus would accept him (Matthew 8:1). But it is the reaction of the people that fascinates me, and I feel I must not end the book just yet.

Two words stand out: The crowds were *amazed* because He spoke with *authority*. Amazement. Authority. Two ingredients missing in the modern Church.

The word *authority* means different things to different people. To some it may mean leadership. For some it might refer to the police—or to government, as we speak of the "authorities" (as in Romans 13:1). Or, it could refer to parental authority. Or ecclesiastical authority. The Oxford Dictionary defines *authority* as the power or right to give orders and make others obey.

The Greek word used by Matthew is *exousia*—which is used 103 times in the New Testament. It means the ability to perform an action without any hindrances in the way. *Exousia* could refer to action by a king or government, or to one's salvation (John 1:12). In Mathew 7:29 it meant power or freedom given to Jesus. In His high priestly prayer, Jesus said of Himself to His Father, "You granted him authority over all people that he might give eternal life to all those you have given him" (John 17:2). "All authority in heaven and on earth has been given to me," said Jesus after His resurrection from the dead (Matthew 28:18).

Anointed Preaching

In Matthew 7:29, *exousia*—authority that embraces power as well—is used to describe the impact and impression Jesus made on the people as a result of His teaching. They were "amazed" (Gr. *ekpleso*)—astonished—at two things: (1) the content of His sermon and (2) His style.

This authority is actually a synonym of what used to be called "unction" on preaching, that is, anointing. But as Jesus had the Holy Spirit without any limit (John 4:34), imagine what it must have been like had you the privilege of being right there to witness it! This anointing is what Peter had in great measure on the Day of Pentecost. Another Greek synonym is *parresia*—boldness, confidence (Acts 2:29). It is similar to what Paul requested prayer for, that he be given "words" and the ability to speak without any fear (Ephesians 6:19). It is what every preacher wants when he addresses a congregation. Peter even said that we should speak "as one speaking the very words of God" (1 Peter 4:11). In any case, Jesus is our model.

It is my view that if these two things—amazement and authority—were restored to the ministry, it would make all the difference. It is rare to hear a preacher speak with undoubted authority nowadays. It is even rarer when people are amazed or astonished when they hear preaching. From what I can learn about the preaching of George Whitefield in the eighteenth century, his ministry carried an unusual authority and produced a sense of amazement.

Reaction of the Crowds

The people were "amazed at his teaching." We might have expected Matthew to say they were amazed at *Him*. And no doubt they were amazed at Jesus Himself. But that is not what Matthew picks up on. He says it again after Jesus' confrontation with the Sadducees: "They were astonished at this teaching" (Matthew 22:33).

Mark says the same thing. "What is this? A new teaching—and with authority!" (Mark 1:27; 11:18). This suggests that Jesus did not focus on Himself but on the objective truth—the doctrine, the teaching.

Consider three types of windows in a church: those which are clear, opaque or stained with color. When the window is clear, it does not cross your mind to say, "What a beautiful window," but, rather, you see what is out there. The opaque window won't let you see past it. The colored, stained window is designed to draw attention to itself. Good teaching will be like a clear window, causing one to focus on what is said rather than who said it. Nothing was said about Jesus' delivery or oratory, although He no doubt had that, too. "No one ever spoke the way this man does" (John 7:46).

Jesus' teaching touched their feelings. The Greek word *ekpleso* evokes an emotional reaction. It is the word used to describe onlookers who witnessed Jesus casting out an evil spirit from a child (Luke 9:43). Mark 7:37 says the people were "overwhelmed with amazement" when they saw a man who was deaf and mute healed. It was the way people reacted to the healing of the man at the gate Beautiful (Acts 3:11). The interesting thing is that Jesus could astonish with His teaching as easily as He could do by performing a miracle. It shows in any case that Jesus reached their hearts.

Aristotle said every speech should include *ethos, logos* and *pathos. Ethos* referred to a speaker's reputation that preceded him. When people come with great expectancy, it only enhances the atmosphere in which he or she speaks. *Logos* referred to the verbal content of the talk. *Pathos* referred to the emotional impact the speaker made. Some sermons are short on *logos,* long on *pathos.* Some are long on *logos,* short on *pathos*—which (without the anointing of the Spirit) would probably be very dry if not boring. It seems to me that when the Word and the Spirit coalesce, the crowds will be "amazed." Jesus was the embodiment of Word and Spirit in one: He was the eternal *Logos* and was given the Holy Spirit without any measure or limit (John 4:34). There is one thing for certain: The crowds could feel that Jesus knew what He was talking about.

The Secret to His Authority

The crowds were fascinated. What impressed them? Jesus' fearlessness.

As we saw earlier, Paul requested prayer that he would be given utterance when he spoke and that he might do so without any fear. Fearlessness means just that: no fear. Courage is not needed when you have no fear. Courage is needed when you are filled with fear but proceed anyway. Jesus was fearless because He was filled with perfect love. Perfect love drives out fear, and fear has to do with punishment (1 John 4:18). Jesus did not need to punish anybody, neither was He worried that His Father might be displeased with Him. He was at total peace when He spoke. To be fearless, then, means to have no fear at all—to be as calm as when a lake is like a mirror: no ripples at all.

That was Jesus when He spoke. He was not afraid of man, the crowds, the devil. He wasn't worried that He might get a word wrong here or there. When He would finish a sermon, He would not need to turn to a close friend to get reassurance that He did okay. Can you imagine Jesus turning to Peter following the Sermon on the Mount, "Peter, how did I do? Did you like that point I made about asking, seeking, knocking? Do you think the people enjoyed Me? Will I probably be invited back again?"

Authority springs from pure freedom from within. Where the Spirit of the Lord is, there is freedom (2 Corinthians 3:17). The greatest freedom is having nothing to prove. Jesus had no ax to grind, no need to set the record straight, no desire to impress anybody in the crowd, no strategy to prove Himself. He knew no bondage. He was not intimidated by who in the crowd might be spying on Him. He did not need to copy anybody's mannerisms or turns of phrase. He was utterly and totally Himself. His only role model was His Father. "The Son can do nothing by himself; he can do only what he sees his Father doing, because whatever the Father does the Son also does" (John 5:19). "I seek not to please myself but him who sent me" (John 5:30). "I always do what pleases him" (John 8:29).

His authority sprang also from His unpretentiousness. As I said in this book, Jesus' unpretentiousness was closely akin to His glory. I have long thought it was His most attractive feature. He was the polar opposite of smugness, arrogance or superiority. He was, simply, Himself. Nobody on this planet had been like that before. The people were dazzled.

There was a freshness in Jesus' words. What He said was not repeating what He had heard before. He was not "learned" in the sense that the rabbis, the Pharisees, the scribes and Sadducees were. Part of the people's amazement was precisely this. "The Jews were amazed and asked, 'How did this man get such learning without having studied?'" (John 7:15). The nearest He came to quoting any authority was when He said, "You have heard that it was said . . . " referring either to the Mosaic Law or traditions surrounding it. This would be followed by, "But I say unto you."

His authority therefore sprang partly from His not quoting anyone else. The scribes and teachers of the Law would never imagine speaking without quoting the commentaries or rabbinic authorities for their "authority." Not Jesus. This is one of the main reasons why they were amazed—"because he taught as one who had authority, and not as their teachers of the law" (Matthew 7:29). He could even almost laugh at the Pharisees. I would not be surprised if the crowds laughed, too, when He said that the hypocrites "announce their giving with trumpets."

I don't know how this made the teachers of the Law feel. Actually, I do know. "By what authority are you doing these things?" they asked Jesus on another occasion. "And who gave you authority to do this?" (Mark 11:28). The truth is, the teachers of the Law had nothing new to say. All their talks would be predictable. There would be no spontaneity. Old stuff rehashed. It would not have blessed the Temple authorities or the synagogue rabbis. But Jesus was not running for political office. He was mirroring the heart of the Father.

When Matthew said that the crowds were amazed because Jesus spoke with authority, he revealed in one stroke what people want when they go to church. I will never forget a talk I heard by Jack Deere, "Why Go to Church?" It was an eye-opener for me. Most people go to church out of duty, expecting little when they get there. Wouldn't it be marvelous if all of us in the ministry could have the kind of unpretentious freedom, power and freshness that Jesus had—at least in some measure? Remember that Jesus could dazzle with His words as easily as He could by performing a miracle. The people were awestruck, as if they had seen a miracle before their eyes. And yet it was *teaching* that did it.

Remember that Jesus' unpretentious style sent a signal to that leper who knew, somehow, he would get away with it if he fell at Jesus' feet. He would not have approached a rabbi, priest, scribe, Pharisee, Sadducee or teacher of the Law—never in a thousand years. But he discerned in Jesus' spirit a welcoming voice that made him say to himself, "There's a man who would accept me as I am."

It is what the anointing does. It communicates not merely truth, but *God*—a point Alex Buchannan made to me one day. Jesus communicated not merely doctrine, sound theology, accurate exposition, but *God Himself.*

Let us pray that God will hasten the day when a touch of what Jesus had will be given to all of us ministers. We need all the help we can get. We are all learning. What we need most is this authority that will leave the people with amazement. Pray for your minister. Pray for your spiritual leaders. Pray for the Church of Jesus Christ throughout the world. Pray for the manifestation of the glory of God, that the "earth will be filled with the knowledge of the glory of the LORD, as the waters cover the sea" (Habakkuk 2:14).

May the blessing of God Almighty—Father, Son and Holy Spirit—be upon you from this moment. Now and forever. Amen.

Index

Dr. R. T. Kendall was born in Ashland, Kentucky, on July 13, 1935. He has been married to Louise for more than fifty years. They have two children, a son (Robert Tillman II, married to Annette) and a daughter (Melissa), and one grandson (Tobias Robert Stephen).

R. T. is a graduate of Trevecca Nazarene University (A.B.), Southern Baptist Theological Seminary (M.Div.), the University of Louisville (M.A.) and Oxford University (D.Phil.*Oxon.*). His doctoral thesis was published by Oxford University Press under the title *Calvin and English Calvinism to 1647.* He was awarded the D.D. by Trevecca Nazarene University in 2008.

Before he and his family went to England, R. T. pastored churches in Palmer, Tennessee; Carlisle, Ohio; Fort Lauderdale, Florida and Salem, Indiana. He was pastor of Calvary Baptist Church in Lower Heyford, Oxfordshire, England (paralleling his three years at Oxford). He became the minister of Westminster Chapel on February 1, 1977, and was there for exactly 25 years, succeeding G. Campbell Morgan and D. Martyn Lloyd-Jones. He retired on February 1, 2002. His 25 years at Westminster Chapel have been written up in his book *In Pursuit of His Glory.*

Shortly after Dr. Kendall's "retirement," he became involved in the Alexandria Peace Process, founded by Lord Carey, former Archbishop of Canterbury, and Canon Andrew White, the archbishop's envoy to the Middle East. From this came a special relationship with the late Yasser Arafat, president of the Palestinian National Authority, and Rabbi David Rosen, Israel's most distinguished orthodox Jewish rabbi. R. T. and David wrote a book together, *The Christian and the Pharisee.*

Dr. Kendall is the author of more than fifty books, including *Total Forgiveness, The Anointing, Sensitivity of the Spirit, The Parables of Jesus, God Meant It for Good* and *Did You Think to Pray?* He has an international ministry and spends his time preaching and writing. He and Louise currently live on Hickory Lake in Hendersonville, Tennessee, where he fishes occasionally.